P9-DEP-685

SADE

A Biography

Farrar, Straus and Giroux

New York

A BIOGRAPHY

by Maurice Lever

Translated by Arthur Goldhammer

Translation copyright © 1993 by Arthur Goldhammer
Originally published in French as Donatien Alphonse François, marquis de Sade
© 1991 by Librairie Arthème Fayard
Published simultaneously in Canada by HarperCollinsCanadaLtd
All rights reserved
Printed in the United States of America
First printing, 1993
Second printing, 1993

Library of Congress Cataloging-in-Publication Data
Lever, Maurice.
[Donatien Alphonse François, marquis de Sade. English]
Sade : a biography / Maurice Lever ; translated by Arthur Goldhammer.
p.   cm.
1. Sade, marquis de, 1740–1814—Biography. 2. Authors,
French—18th century—Biography. I. Title.
PQ2063.S3L48   1993   843'.6—dc20   [B]   92-36993   CIP

FRONTISPIECE : Portrait du marquis de Sade vers l'âge de
vingt ans, by Charles Amédée Philippe Van Loo; courtesy Jean-
Jacques Lebel Collection, Paris

To Evelyne

Contents

A Note
on the Translation
and Abridgment

This English edition is an abridgment of the original French. In making cuts I first eliminated materials primarily of interest to scholars, much of it in the extensive appendices and footnotes. Second, I shortened some of the many letters that Maurice Lever reproduced in full in the body of the text. The flavor of eighteenth-century correspondence is an important element in achieving the balance for which the author aimed, and I hope I have kept enough of that essential spice. Third, I eliminated some episodes that seemed less pertinent than others to the main sweep of the narrative. Occasionally it was necessary to interpolate a sentence or two to smooth a transition or fill a gap where part of the text had been deleted. Maurice Lever was kind enough to read the entire translation and approve the changes. I also wish to thank him for his help in translating problematic passages. It has been a pleasure to work with him. Titles of Sade's works are given in French. Some English translations are cited in the Bibliography.

—*Arthur Goldhammer*

Preface

This book belongs, first of all, to the comte de Sade and his son Thibault de Sade, without whose help it could never have been written. "Sadologists" are well aware of their immense debt to the descendants of the "divine marquis." We owe it to the comte de Sade that a major part of his ancestor's work was retrieved from oblivion some time ago. With his cooperation Gilbert Lely was able to put together his well-known biographical corpus. And thanks to his confidence and generosity we are today able to rediscover the author of *Justine*. Xavier and Thibault de Sade placed at my disposal the entirety of their family archives, which contain a considerable number of unpublished letters and documents that open up wholly new perspectives on the life of the marquis de Sade. I should like to take this opportunity to express my deep gratitude and abiding friendship.

Au comble de la solitude,
Un accent inconnu de grâce et de fureur.

—GILBERT LELY, *Ma Civilisation*

SADE

A Biography

Prologue
The Star with Eight
Golden Rays

The origins of the house of Sade bristle with legend. Its very inception is said to have been miraculous: the line is supposed to have originated with one of the three magi. In his *Histoire de Provence* César de Nostredame claims to have read somewhere that the family issued from the princes of Les Baux, who prided themselves on being directly descended from the Balts—not the inhabitants of Baltic shores but the Bolds, priestly offspring of a redoubtable family of Visigoths. The arms of these princes featured a star with sixteen rays, a mysterious comet whose origins the heraldists cannot trace. By a surprising coincidence the same star served as the emblem of the gypsies of Saintes-Maries-de-la-Mer, who brought it with them from the east. For the people of Provence there was not the shadow of a doubt: Balthasar had visited Les Baux. When? How? No one can say.

Also according to Nostredame, this luminous star was stripped of half its rays and "differently emblazoned" to distinguish the elder and cadet branches of the family. This, we are told, is the origin of the arms of the house of Sade: a star with eight golden rays on a field of gules. Of course no one ever took this fabulous explanation seriously: Nostredame had a weakness for legends. Nevertheless, the three magi remained fixed in the family's memory, and in the genealogy of the Sades we find several Gaspars and a few Balthasars but not a single Melchior.

Bénézet, the Little Shepherd

Another legend attaches to Louis de Sade, the first of the line. In the year of grace 1177, a child named Bénézet (little Benedict) was tending his mother's sheep when a voice spoke to him from heaven. Greatly agitated, the shepherd lad raised his head: "I am Jesus Christ," said the voice, "and I command you to leave your flock and build me a bridge across the Rhône."

The child protested that he knew nothing of rivers or construction, but the voice insisted and promised to provide a guide and someone to tend the shepherd's sheep while he worked. So Bénézet started on his way, and soon he met an angel disguised as a pilgrim, who took him to the banks of the Rhône. "Take this bark," the stranger told him, "and cross the river. Then go to Avignon and show yourself to the bishop and his people." Upon reaching the other bank of the river, the boy set off in search of the prelate and found him preaching to his flock. The bishop, after mocking the lad's tale, sent him to see the dreaded provost of the city, who also greeted the boy's story with laughter. "At my palace there is a stone," he said. "If you can move it, I will believe that you are capable of building a bridge." Pleased with this turn of events, Bénézet returned to the bishop and told him he was ready to meet the test the provost had set him. "We shall see," said the bishop, who brought his people with him.

Whereupon Bénézet, laying hold of a stone so large that thirty men could not have moved it, raised it up and set it down on the river's bank where the first arch of the bridge was to be placed. Dumbfounded, those who witnessed the event gave the child the money to begin work at once. It took no fewer than ten years to complete the famous *pont d'Avignon*.

Behind the legendary figure of the little shepherd is the first known representative of the Sade family: Louis de Sade, *viguier* (provost) of Avignon in 1177, who financed the construction of the bridge. His descendants took a keen interest in maintaining and restoring the work. In 1355 Hugues de Sade left a bequest of 2,000 gold florins for its repair, and that is why the Sade coat of arms can still be seen today on the bridge's first arch.[1]

Hemp and Salt

The house of Sade, referred to in ancient documents as *Sado, Sadone,* and sometimes *Saze* or *Sauze,* was one of the oldest in Provence and the Comtat Venaissin. According to sieur de Remerville, historian of the city of Apt and well versed in family origins, the house took its name from a small town in Languedoc called Saze, located on the banks of the Rhône two leagues from Avignon.[2]

Hugues de Sade, first mentioned in the documents in 1298, was in the business of making textiles from hemp, a prosperous industry at the time in the Avignon region. The Sade family also had interests in lumber, brewing, fulling, ropemaking, and probably other aspects of the textile industry, including the silk business, not to mention a brisk trade in salt and collection of tolls on the Rhône. Bourgeois originally, the family soon acquired nobility, thanks in part to its wealth but also to the influence of the Italian model, which was strong in fourteenth-century Avignon. Merchants, shippers, and bankers obtained noble status by papal bull declaring that the profession of merchant no longer constituted a derogation from nobility. Thus the feudal prejudice against ennobled bourgeois that Donatien de Sade would exhibit throughout his life was a pose that had survived many generations. Although the nobility of the Sades predated that of the Montreuils (the family of the marquis's wife) by three centuries, its origins were the same. Unlike the Montreuils, however, the Sades had over the years acquired the honors associated with the *noblesse d'épée* and had intermarried with the most illustrious families in Provence: the Forbins, the Cambis, the Barbentanes, the Simianes, the Causans, the Grimaldis, the d'Astouauds, and the Crillons—to say nothing of the Medicis and the Dorias. Its ancient roots, its prestigious marriages, its services to the papal court and the counts of Provence, and its military exploits guaranteed the house of Sade an unassailable position among the nobility of the Comtat. Traces of its grandeur survive throughout the region. In Avignon itself, besides the *"pont Bénézet,"* there used to be a Sade Tower, known by corruption as the *tour des Sauzes,* and a rue de Sade, where the hôtel de Sade once stood.

Laura

Such were the origins of the Sade clan. But its truest nobility, that of genius and love combined, it owes to poetry: "Illustrious by reason of her virtues and sung of at length in my verse, Laura appeared to me for the first time, in the flower of my youth, in the year of Our Lord 1327, on the morning of April 6, in the Church of Santa Clara at Avignon. And it was in the same city, on the same day in the same month of April of the year 1348 that she was taken from the light of day while I, alas, was in Verona, ignorant of this stroke of fate . . . Her most chaste and very beautiful body was laid to rest on the day of her death, at vespers."

These words of Francesco Petrarca were inscribed on the back of a flyleaf of his edition of Virgil, which is today preserved in Milan's Ambrosiana Library. How often he recalled that sixth day of April, 1327, the Monday of Holy Week, when he first caught sight of beautiful Laura in the pale early-morning light at Santa Clara chapel. His was a vision of the most immaterial, idealized, diaphanous kind. It marked the inception of a passion that would find its sole consummation in poetry.

Laura symbolizes spiritual perfection: a guileless soul, a pure body, a face aureoled by grace. But now and again the young madonna stepped down from her pedestal, trod on grass and flowers, stripped off her clothing, and dove into the clear waters of the Sorgue. Shedding her matchless pallor of pearl, her beauty took on precise color and form: a deepened gaze, cheeks aglow with a gentle flame, a beautiful young bosom. Yet she seems to have lacked some vital spark, to the point where some have wondered whether she really loved the poet while others ask if her "respectability" was not perhaps a sign of frigidity, conjugal duty, prudence, or flirtatiousness. Because the appearances are so contradictory, Laura has often been taken for a mere allegory of the muse.

Petrarch's love itself has little to do with human passion. Better to call it an "amorous meditation," baptized by sweet tears: "I am one of those for whom crying is a joy," he confessed. But Petrarch was familiar with more searing pains, with pangs that turned savory dishes into bitter poisons, nights into torments, and his bed into a cruel battlefield. His estrangement from his beloved became confounded with his anguish; Laura's image was effaced by his own torn self, and it was then that his music achieved its most distinctive note.

Strangely, the poet who composed so many lines in praise of the beauty that kindled so bright a flame in his heart, who spoke so often of Laura in his letters and works, has left us in ignorance not only of the details of her private life but even of her last name. All he tells us is that she was of roughly his own age and was born to an ancient house. Which one? The historians disagree. On the strength of Alessandro Velutello's testimony most of the Italians maintain that Laura was the daughter of Henri de Chabaud, lord of Cabrières.[3] In France, however, and particularly in the region of Avignon, tradition has it that she belonged by marriage to the Sade family. The abbé de Sade, who patiently researched the family archives in the eighteenth century, is categorical: Laura, the daughter of Audibert de Noves and Dame Ermessende, was the wife of Hugues de Sade, the second to bear the name.

The house of Noves, distinguished for its ancient nobility and for the high offices it had held, outranked all others in the town of Noves, two leagues from Avignon. According, once again, to the abbé, the city of Avignon cannot be denied the honor of being beautiful Laura's birthplace: "Petrarch makes this point a thousand times in his poetry," he says. Audibert de Noves, syndic of Avignon, died around 1320, leaving his wife as guardian of his three children: Jean, his elder daughter Laura, and Marguerite. In his will he named his son Jean as his heir and bequeathed 6,000 *livres tournois*,* the money of France, for Laura's dowry. A young woman who was well-born, pretty, and provided with such a fine dowry was not apt to want for suitors. Ermessende had any number to choose among but finally settled on Hugues de Sade, known as *"le Vieux,"* and the son of Paul de Sade. The marriage contract was signed on January 16, 1325, when Laura was little more than seventeen or eighteen.

Little is known about her apart from her having been the inspiration of Petrarch's finest verse, as if the poet's passion were enough to fill her existence. The memoir writers note, however, that under the auspices of her aunt, Etiennette Gantelmi, dame de Romanil, who had "raised her in good literature," Laura belonged to the circle of learned ladies who made up the *Cour d'Amour*, the "Love Court" of Avignon. "They eagerly wrote romances in Provençal poetry of all sorts, in the manner of Etiennette, comtesse de Provence, and Alasie, vicomtesse d'Avignon, and other Provençal ladies noted for their learning . . . They held an open tribunal in which they judged works of the mind

---

* The basic unit of currency in eighteenth-century France was the livre (or franc); the écu was worth three livres, and the gold louis was equivalent to twenty francs. In the 1760s, an unskilled laborer might earn around one livre per day. According to Jacques-Louis Ménétra, the king's master locksmith at Versailles earned 5–6 louis per month, or less than 1,500 livres per year, and this was a wage that other skilled workmen envied (see *Journal of My Life*, trans. Arthur Goldhammer [New York: Columbia University Press, 1986], p. 38). —Trans.

and all that pertained to manners of decent lovemaking and politeness."[4] Thus Petrarch's fair Egeria ostensibly dallied with the muse in her own right and sat alongside other *"femmes savantes"* in this academy of poetry and courtesy, the *Cour d'Amour.* Was the poet's nymph somehow transformed into a Molièresque Bélise?

She died, a victim of the plague, on April 6, 1348, having made her will three days earlier.[5] She chose to be buried in the church of the Friars Minim of Avignon, in the family vault in the Sainte-Croix chapel.

Two centuries later her tomb would be twice profaned. First, the poet Maurice Scève, a man of broad culture and leading light of the "School of Lyons," had the vault opened in 1529.[6] There he allegedly found among the bones a small leaden box containing a bronze medal and a parchment. The medal featured the profile of a woman chastely hiding her breasts. The parchment contained a sonnet in the manner of Petrarch. Then, in 1533 King François I, returning from Marseilles where he had arranged the marriage of his second son, Henri, duc d'Orléans (the future Henri II), to Catherine de Médicis, learned of the "marvelous story of Laura" and conceived a desire to contemplate "what remained of an unprecedented love." Upon viewing the object that Maurice Scève had unearthed four years earlier, along with the sonnet, the king himself composed an epitaph in verse, placed both poems in the leaden box, and ordered the tomb sealed. Although the king's quatrains have survived, they add little to the memory of a prince renowned as the "restorer of belles lettres."

It is scarcely necessary to add that the facts reported here belong to the realm of the imagination. But when the imagination impels first a poet and then a prince to meditate on the most divine allegory of love and beauty the world has ever known, when their alacrity to claim the secret of a woman's tomb attests to astonishment at the impermanence of human passion, then the fantasy has more to teach us than the most learned tomes.

Was Laura de Noves, the wife of Hugues de Sade, really Petrarch's beloved Laura? The question has been the subject of long and fruitless controversy. Lely, for one, had no doubt that she was (it would have been astonishing had he reached any other conclusion). The abbé de Sade was sure of it (which is even less surprising). Yet the debate has been endless. Scholars have marshaled endless arguments, citations, documents, genealogies, eyewitness accounts, and other "evidence," none of which is truly convincing. Even today nothing is certain, although the latest research tends to deprive the house of Sade of its finest ornament.[7]

In any case Laura's true identity scarcely matters. She has long been part of the Sade legend, as much as if not more than the star of Balthasar and the bridge of Bénézet. She cannot be easily dislodged. Since the fourteenth century she has been the guardian angel of the house of Sade. Her ghost has watched over generation after generation of its offspring, and the ancestral cult continues undiminished to this day. Laura is the Sades' White Lady, the very one who haunted Donatien's sleep when he was a prisoner in the dungeon of Vincennes on the night of February 16, 1779: "It was around midnight. I had just fallen asleep . . . Suddenly she appeared . . . I saw her! The horror of the grave had not diminished the splendor of her charms, and her eyes still burned as brightly as when Petrarch celebrated them. She was completely wrapped in black crepe, and her beautiful blond hair floated negligently above. It seemed that love, seeking to make her beautiful again, had attempted to alleviate the mournfulness of the manner in which she appeared before me. 'Why do you moan on earth?' she asked. 'Come be with me. In the vastness I inhabit there are no more woes, no more suffering, no more troubles. Have the courage to follow me.' Upon hearing these words I threw myself prostrate at her feet and said, 'O! My Mother! . . . Sobs stifled my voice. She held out a hand to me, which I covered with my tears. She, too, shed tears. 'I liked to look into the future,' she added, 'when I lived in this world that you detest. I looked upon the multitude of my posterity down to you, and *you did not seem so unhappy.*' Then, absorbed in despair and tenderness, I threw my arms around her neck to hold on to her, or to follow her, and to moisten her with my tears, but the phantom disappeared, leaving only my pain."[8]

The Two-Headed Eagle

Laura's much-celebrated chastity did not prevent her from giving her husband eleven children. Only seven months after her death, on November 19, 1348, Hugues de Sade married Verdaine de Trentelivres, by whom he would have six more children. The eldest son of Hugues and Laura, also named Hugues (the third to bear that name) and nicknamed Hugonin or *"le Jeune,"* would carry on the line. His marriage to Giraude de Ledenon, the daughter of Jean de Ledenon, lord of Aramon, produced three sons and four daughters.

The second of these sons, Elzéar de Sade, first equerry and later cupbearer to Pope Benedict XIII and co-lord of Essarts, obtained from the emperor Sigismund of Luxemburg, in reward for services rendered to the Empire by him and his ancestors, the privilege of adding the two-headed imperial eagle to his family's coat of arms.[9] Henceforth the Sades' arms would conform to this sonorous heraldic description: On a field gules, a star with eight golden rays, bearing an eagle, with spread wings of sable, membered, beaked, unguled, and crowned with gules.[10]

•

The house of Sade distinguished itself over the ages through important service to church and state. Between the inception of the lineage and the birth of Donatien Alphonse François, marquis de Sade, there stood an uninterrupted line of prelates, captains, magistrates, syndics, *viguiers*, *conseillers* of *parlement*, priors, governors, papal chamberlains, diplomats, and knights of Malta, men who helped to make the France of the Ancien Régime what it was and whose feudal pride our hero would cherish throughout his life. And one other fact is not to be forgotten: the family also produced abbesses and nuns, dozens of whom populated the convents of the Comtat.

I

THE NOBLE

LIBERTINE

1

A Don Juan

The "blood of our fathers," the "breast of the female"

What stood in the way of my success was that I was always too much the libertine to bide my time in an antechamber, too poor to bribe my servants to serve my interests, and too proud to flatter the favorites, the ministers, and the mistress. I've said it a hundred times: let those who hope or desire to secure their aid pay them court. I am a free man. It was not always so, because at one time I was ruled by my passions, but the passion of ambition was never mine.

For a long time I lived in a whirlwind of lies and slander. Only today do I enjoy something that kings cannot bestow because they do not possess it, namely, liberty.[1]

Such were the thoughts, late in life, of Jean-Baptiste Joseph François, comte de Sade, seigneur of Saumane and La Coste, coseigneur of Mazan, and father of the marquis de Sade, at the end of a long and pleasure-filled career. The man is worth lingering over, for Donatien de Sade's previous biographers have too often neglected, misunderstood, or even ignored him. Today, thanks to family archives, we can not only gain a glimpse of the private life of one of the most illustrious libertines of Louis XV's reign but, more importantly, appreciate the significance of the role he played in the life of the future author of *Justine*. So deep were the bonds between the count and the marquis de Sade that it is impossible to paint a portrait of the one without conjuring up an image of the other. Through childhood and adolescence Donatien lived in close symbiosis with his father. This symbiosis was undeniably emotional, a product of reciprocal affection and shared confidences, but it was also literary and intellectual. The count was hardly the distant, cold, unkind father he has sometimes been accused of being. Documents recently brought to light have some fascinating things to tell us on this score.

The close relationship between father and son stands out all the more because the mother was virtually nonexistent. Neglected by her unfaithful husband until she chose finally to bury herself in a convent until the end of her days, she had little importance in Donatien's life. Some may say that the void was more apparent than real, for the child did not want for surrogates: Mme de Saint-Germain, for one, or Mme de Raimond (whose existence I am the first biographer to uncover). But these women, former mistresses of the father (at least in the case of Mme de Raimond), never filled the void left by the marquis's real mother. As "fallen" women, they even represented the opposite of the original "virgin mother" first idolized and then repudiated by the son.

In a departure from the normal course of development the shape of Sade's initial psychological conflict was determined not by hatred of the father but by hatred of the mother (who was remote, absent, and indifferent, whereas the father's fond affections were constant). Pierre Klossowski was right when he suggested some time ago that this complex of mother-hatred, far rarer and generally less blatant than its paternal counterpart, surely contributed to the distinctive nature of the Sadeian ideology. What we are dealing with, then, is a negative Oedipus complex. Rather than kill the father the son forges an alliance with him and turns his powerful hostility against his mother. Later, when Donatien was forced to confront the redoubtable maternity of his mother-in-law, *la présidente* de Montreuil, his murderous and pro-fanatory impulses would rise to the level of consciousness. He then developed an all-consuming hatred of all matriarchal values—com-passion, tenderness, consolation, sacrifice, fidelity—and devoted con-siderable energy to laying bare the self-interest and fear from which he believed those values stem.[2] His desire to punish maternal power would also find satisfaction in his treatment of his wife, Renée-Pélagie, especially when maternal supplanted conjugal love soon after their marriage. Her boundless devotion, self-denial, and solicitude in the face of all adversity were, in Donatien's eyes, maternal stigmata to be punished pitilessly with contempt and sarcasm. His work offers an extraordinary kaleidoscope of all the tortures, physical as well as moral, that a son (or daughter) is capable of inflicting on his (or her) mother. Maternity is gleefully berated, debased, humiliated, and reduced to its primary condition as a byproduct of pleasure. "I love my father to distraction," Eugénie says in *La Philosophie dans le boudoir*, "and I feel that I hate my mother." To which Dolmancé responds: "There is nothing astonishing about such a predilection: I have had the very same thought. I have not yet gotten over my father's death, but when I lost my mother I made a bonfire . . . I cordially detested her. Do not be afraid to feel this way, Eugénie: such feelings are part of nature. Formed solely from the blood of our fathers, we owe absolutely nothing to our mothers. They did nothing but submit to the act, whereas our fathers instigated it. Our fathers therefore willed our births, whereas our mothers merely acquiesced. What a difference of feeling!"[3] The matricide Bressac, hero and symbol of the antimaternal complex in *Les Infortunes de la vertu*, illuminates this crucial component of Sade's thought in a single passage: "Was she thinking of me, this mother, when her lubricity caused her to conceive the fetus from which I came? Do I owe her a debt of gratitude for pursuing her own pleasure? It is not the mother's blood that forms the child, but the father's alone. The breast of the female nurtures, preserves, elaborates, but supplies nothing: such a thought would dissuade me from any attempt on my father's life, whereas I regard it as a simple thing to cut short my mother's days."[4]

In fact, Sade saw the mother as the principal obstacle to direct relations between father and son. This in itself was a good reason to hate her.

Group Portrait (Sketches)

Let us return, however, to the marquis's beloved—perhaps too beloved—father. Born in Mazan on March 12, 1702, the son of Gaspard François de Sade and Louise Aldonse d'Astouaud,[5] he was the eldest of the three boys (out of five) who survived the rampant child mortality of the period. The twelfth day of October 1703 witnessed the birth of his younger brother Richard-Jean-Louis, who soon entered the Order of Malta and would end his life as grand prior of the province of Toulouse. He was the family's moral conscience: pedantic, solemn, tedious, wreathed in pieties and steeped in rhetoric, he spoke like a judge, lectured everyone, and made a great impression on Mme de Montreuil. On September 21, 1705, Louise d'Astouaud gave birth to Jacques-François Paul Aldonse, the future abbé de Sade, "the priest of Epicurus." Absentminded in company, witty in his letters, learned in his study, and most attentive to the ladies, this friend of Voltaire and Mme du Châtelet was the very type of the libertine priest.

As for Gaspard's five daughters, only one found a husband: Henriette Victoire de Sade, born in 1715, who would marry (for a few years only) the absurd Joseph Ignace de Villeneuve-Martignan. Gifted with rare energy, pragmatic to the point of cynicism, selfish, and without illusions, her only known weakness was her unflinching indulgence of her mischievous nephew. Her four sisters for their part entered convents never to leave them. Gabrielle-Laure became abbess of Saint-Laurent of Avignon and Anne-Marie Lucrèce was a nun in the same establishment, while Gabrielle Eléonore became abbess of Saint-Benoît of Cavaillon and Marguerite-Félicité, known as Mme de La Coste, was an ordinary nun at Saint-Bernard in the same city. Immured in the silence of their cloisters, the marquis's religious aunts would remain all their lives nameless silhouettes. They looked so similar beneath their veils that it was difficult to tell them apart. Wild rumors about Donatien reached them in their convents, distant echoes of the outside world replete with words seldom heard in the cloister: "sodomy," "prostitutes," "flagellation," "pillory," "prison." Compassion taking precedence over outrage, occasional letters to the lost child would be dispatched through the cloister gates. Their large, shaky script and rustic spelling identifies the origin of these epistles at a glance. What did the humble nuns have to say to their nephew? Sweet and simple things, reminiscent of another time, words plucked from childhood, as stubborn and naïve as the women who wrote them, as well-worn as holy medallions and redolent of the sacristy. "I hope," wrote one of them, "that you will give your family as much consolation in the future as you have given it sorrow in the past. As for myself, I shall pray constantly to the Lord to obtain for you all the temporal and spiritual forgiveness you may need, and I shall always be your affectionately devoted *bonne tante*."[6] Indefatigably Donatien answered these missives with letters full of solicitude and piety in which it is hard to distinguish truth from artful deception.

Brilliant Beginnings

As was often the case in the old provincial nobility, the house of Sade never left its fief. Its members occupied the highest positions, as we have seen, but always within provincial limits: Avignon, Provence, Comtat. There they were born, there they lived, there they made their careers, and there they were buried in the family vault. The distant

court always struck them as a place thick with illusions, rife with cov-
etousness, and of course full of danger. They viewed it with a mixture
of envy and revulsion. Never before had a Sade dared to try his luck
there. Jean-Baptiste would be the first to do so.

Impetuous, picaresque, fond of adventure, he decided one day to
quit the land of his ancestors and try his hand at court, about which
so many harsh words had been said, especially since the regency of
Philippe d'Orléans, but whose splendor had not ceased to dazzle. We
may wager that the marquis de Mazan (as Gaspard de Sade was known)
pulled out all the stops to hold on to his eldest son, in whom he had
invested so many hopes, but Jean-Baptiste remained deaf to his father's
pleas. What future did his native region hold? Inheriting his father's
title? Becoming, as his father had been, lord of a village? Perhaps, if
all went well, *viguier* of Avignon? To tell the truth, it was a rather
dreary prospect for a young man full of fire, aspiring to the highest
offices, and of course dreaming of a brilliant life, of pleasures, spectacles, glittering balls, and pretty women. When the moment came to
bid his son farewell, Gaspard de Sade gave him, as was customary,
letters of recommendation addressed to distant relatives living at court,
that they might guide the young novice's first steps in a world fraught
with danger.

The exact date of Jean-Baptiste's arrival in Paris is not known.
We do not pick up his trace again until September 1721, when the
marriage of the eleven-year-old Louis XV to the Spanish infanta was
announced. "Mme de Ventadour is to go to the border to meet her,"
Jean-Baptiste wrote his father. "The young princess will live in the old
Louvre. She will not yet have a house. The king cried the day his
marriage was announced to him, but he now seems quite happy about
it. I went yesterday to pay him my respects. No one spoke of the
marriage, but after much banter he asked young Conflans to compliment him on it."[7]

At age nineteen Jean-Baptiste was already well versed in the secrets of the court and not loath to parade his knowledge. All his life
he would take pleasure in reporting petty gossip as well as great events,
all spiced with comments of his own devising that make his letters
living chronicles, tossed off by a quick and mordant pen. From the
time his cousins the Simianes introduced him to Versailles he made
rapid progress. Received in the best houses of the faubourg Saint-
Germain—at Mme de La Rochefoucauld's, Mlle de La Roche-
Guyon's, and M. de Chavigny's—he quickly acquired a reputation as
a man of wit. At the hôtel de Sassenage he fell in love with the mistress

of the house, who did not scold him for it. He had the rare gift of pleasing women without incurring the hatred of men. Hence he enjoyed a large number of friends, at least as large as the number of his mistresses. To be sure, he lacked none of the gifts needed for success in society: good looks, a quick and nimble wit, sprightly conversation, ambition, nonchalance, and a great reserve of philosophy beneath an apparently frivolous exterior. Above all he had an astonishing talent for composing short pieces in prose and verse, most of which were preserved thanks to the piety of his son. The collection contains a little of everything: compliments, epistles, couplets, songs, impromptus, *bouquets à Chloris* and *madrigaux* (witty amorous verse), compositions of every sort. The slightest pretext was enough. Was a woman cruel? A couplet of complaint was her immediate reward. Or was she conquered, reduced to helplessness? In that case a sweet epithalamium. A journey, a rendezvous, a ball, a dream—all were pretexts for verse. To be sure he often slipped into affected delicacy in the manner of Dorat. But such was the fashion, and women like fashion. His letters especially delighted those to whom they were addressed. This was the genre in which he excelled: high spirits, humor, and grace were never lacking. What is more, the young comte de Sade loved theater with a passion and never refused to appear in society comedies. In short, within the space of a few months he became one of the gentlemen whom one encountered everywhere. There is a word for him in French that has no English equivalent: *petit-maître*, meaning a young man of talent, shrewdness, and charm but perhaps a bit affected and quite the libertine.

Henchman of the Condés

What was the good of so many qualities, however, without an influential protector? The duchesse de La Roche-Guyon, a distant relation of the count's, exerted herself on his behalf and introduced him to Louis-Henri Bourbon, prince de Condé, usually referred to as Monsieur le Duc. Great-grandson of the so-called Grand Condé, head of the Regency Council, and superintendent of the king's education, the prince was the most illustrious personage in the kingdom.

Profiting from his high position, the prince de Condé had been helping himself to money from the public treasury and had made enormous profits in John Law's financial manipulations. Devoid of common sense, a man of limited views, lacking self-confidence, knowing nothing and loving nothing other than his pleasure and hunting, and without practical experience, he nevertheless became Principal

Minister in 1723 on the death of the Regent. Thereafter he continued with his financial manipulations, granted exorbitant privileges to the Compagnie des Indes in which he had an interest, and in all circumstances showed that greed for cash which, along with depravity of morals, was characteristic of the house of Condé. What is more, he was under the thumb of his mistress, the marquise de Prie, who was herself, albeit unwittingly, a tool of the brothers Pâris, rapacious and short-sighted financiers. As if that were not enough, he was also said to have "unnatural tastes."

Starting out as a captain of dragoons in the prince's regiment, the young comte de Sade soon became the prince's favorite and later his confidant. The prospect of a career of favor and high employment opened up before him. Before long he had also become an intimate of Monsieur le Duc's brothers and sisters, the comte de Charolais, the comte de Clermont, and above all Mlle de Charolais, all notorious for, in the words of d'Argenson, "debauchery, dissolution, and extravagance." Not one to spend endless months with his regiment, the young officer divided his time between Paris, where he occupied the hôtel de Bretagne, rue de Seine, and Chantilly, where he followed his protector.

To hitch one's destiny to that of the great of this world always involves a certain risk, and that risk is all the greater when the benefactor's reputation fails to rise to the level of his power. In attaching himself to the house of Condé, Jean-Baptiste did his career a great deal of good but himself an enormous disservice. Whatever he attempted thereafter, he would remain the Condés' liegeman, as much hated as he was feared. His position made him one of the most brilliant and envied of courtiers but also one of the most secretly despised. As long as he enjoyed the favor of Louis XV, no one dared attack him openly. But once the sovereign's confidence was lost and all efforts to regain it had failed, Jean-Baptiste found himself condemned to solitude and bitterness.

All that still lay in the future, however. For the moment, the young count, not yet twenty-five, was enormously successful at one of the roles for which he seemed best suited, that of libertine. For if ambition filled half his life, the other half was devoted to romance, which in the absence of passion settled on no one object. Already Jean-Baptiste's mistresses were beyond counting, and their rank was perhaps even more impressive than their number. M. de Sade did not content himself with easy conquests. Women of the bourgeoisie left him indifferent. Those whom he sought—and usually conquered—were women of the court, women endowed not just with wit and beauty but also with illustrious names, credit, influence, or fortunes, in a word women capable of serving his interests and of consolidating his position at court. Reconciling romance with ambition, he more than once used the former to serve the needs of the latter. His amorous aspirations knew no limits: after burning for Mme de Sassenage and Mlle de Charolais, the latter a royal mistress, he sighed at the feet of the duchesse de La Trémoïlle and the duchesse de Clermont, the young princesse de Condé, and, somewhat later, Mme de Pompadour. In general these ladies were loath to make him suffer, though a slight doubt remains as to Mme de Pompadour. I tarry over these names only because they represent the highest rungs of favor. To arrive at a full accounting of the conquests of this young Provençal Don Juan one would have to add dozens of others.

His amorous ambitions accorded well, moreover, with his taste for luxury in all things, for if he loved women in high places, he adored coaches, festivals, balls—a free and easy life, in short, filled with pleasures of all kinds, not excluding the most costly. Since, moreover, he frequented the most select houses in Paris, he was also obliged to fit himself out, both in society and in his private quarters, in a manner befitting his rank. As one can well imagine, the money his father sent him turned to water in his hands, and debts mounted. But having gotten off to such an impressive start, he was not about to stop in midcourse. His wild spending and constant need for cash caused him to commit certain indiscretions for which he would be severely reproached later on, as we shall see. Within a few years Jean-Baptiste de Sade had squandered the family fortune and brought his house to the brink of ruin. It would be left to the son to complete the father's work.

"Friar Angel"

The prince of Condé's sister, Louise-Anne de Bourbon, known as Mlle de Charolais and more succinctly as Mademoiselle, was reputedly the most beautiful of the Bourbon princesses. By nature lively, intelligent, and curious, her amorous education was complete by the age of fifteen. From that time on she engaged in an endless series of romantic escapades. "Among the thousand perfections that nature had bestowed on her," notes the baron de Besenval, "she had eyes of such great beauty that at balls they shone through her mask and always gave her away." By the age of twenty she was able to boast of several conquests, including the duc de Richelieu, the Regency's most notorious rake.

Their affair became so flagrant that one way or another it had to end, in marriage or otherwise. Marriage was not in the cards. Mlle de Charolais succumbed to neither sorrow nor anger. A few days later she gave herself to the duc de Melun, whose reign was brief, and then to the chevalier de Bavière. It was said of her that she had traveled from Richelieu to Melun and from Melun to Bavaria (Bavière). The itinerary might have been enlarged to include the province of Dombes, because the prince of that name, the second son of the duc du Maine, was the next to enjoy her favors. It would be tedious to list all her lovers. Among them were the son of the duc d'Aumont (who died in 1723 of his debauches with the princess) and M. de Vauréal, the bishop of Rennes, who hoped that through her he might gain a cardinal's hat. Later she apparently had no difficulty winning the heart of Louis XV, whom she lured to romantic dinners at her château de Madrid, a hotbed of intrigue and licentiousness. She was without rival when it came to organizing intimate dinners and encounters, as passionate as they were ephemeral, and the talk of the town as well as the court. She regularly selected pretty young students and introduced them to the king, playing the role of procuress with skill, not to say cynicism. "She began early to practice the pimp's trade and derived her consideration exclusively from that profession," observed d'Argenson, who detested her. "Mademoiselle would have been a receiver of stolen goods, a thief, or a shopgirl if she had been born among the people," he added.

Among her excesses, it has been said, were religious crises, but the evidence is thin. Although she liked to have herself painted wearing a Franciscan habit, it was not religious feeling that motivated her but a desire to excite the imagination of the lovers to whom she offered these portraits as gifts. They usually portrayed her either holding the cord of Saint Francis in her hand or tying a knot in it. The erotic allusion is clear (and it may have had a *sadistic* component, since the rope conjures up the idea of a whip).[8] This disguise inspired the following quatrain of Voltaire's:

> *Frère Ange de Charolais*
> *Dis-nous par quelle aventure,*
> *Le cordon de saint François*
> *Sert à Vénus de ceinture.*

[*Friar Angel de Charolais, tell us how Saint Francis's cord came to serve as Venus' sash.*]

•

Though older than the comte de Sade by seven years, Mademoiselle could not fail to attract a man of his sort. She was the kind of woman men despise yet seek out. Close to the king and his ministers, sharing her alcove with men in high places, informed of every intrigue, she was in a position to grant all sorts of favors, pensions, commissions, and embassies among them. Jean-Baptiste therefore set out to conquer her, which for him was no great feat. As an intimate of her brother, Monsieur le Duc, he could see her whenever he pleased at either the hôtel de Condé or Chantilly, and he lost no time winning her love, a victory as flattering to his pride as it was to his senses. Soon he was received at the château du Petit-Madrid, a gift from Louis XV to *la belle cordelière* (the beautiful "Franciscan"), in whose honor he wrote a mediocre poem.

If we had only his poems to go on, it might seem that all that took place between the count and the princess was a sort of abstract idyll. But there are also letters, especially Mademoiselle's to Jean-Baptiste. Donatien piously preserved them among his father's papers, and thanks to him we can read them today. They attest to a genuine affair in which the senses occupied their rightful place, an affair that began, oddly enough, when a sprain obliged the comte de Sade to take to his bed. Here are two excerpts:

. . . The twenty-fourth of November is the happiest day of my life if, by the rights of the bed in which I swore to you an oath of loyalty, I have regained possession of my kingdom and my sovereignty. I trust that I received your oath as well, and I live now for the handsomest king in the world . . .[9]

. . . I forbid you to stay alone, or I shall quarrel with you, because you fall into the blackest of moods. Come, then, my angel, or I shall come and break down your doors if you don't come to me of your own free will. If you absolutely refuse to come to me, say if you want me to spend two hours consoling you, and tell me how long it will be before I see you.[10]

But fickle Jean-Baptiste soon met the duchesse de La Trémoïlle, who set his blood racing. Her husband, Charles-Armand-René, duc de La Trémoïlle, at the age of sixteen had had homosexual relations with young Louis XV, then fourteen. Although the two never went beyond mutual masturbation, the episode cost the young nobleman a brief period of exile. "I will tell you why M. de La Trémoïlle is exiled from court," Voltaire wrote to the marquise de Bernières. "It is for having very frequently placed his hand inside His Very Christian Majesty's fly. He hatched a little conspiracy with M. le comte de Clermont [Mlle de Charolais's brother] designed to make the two of them masters of Louis XV's breeches and not to permit any other courtier to share their good fortune . . . All of which makes me expect very great things of M. de La Trémoïlle, and I cannot withhold my esteem from someone who, at the age of sixteen, sets out to master and discipline his king. I am virtually certain that he will make a very fine subject."[11] A few years later Louis XV and the duke had forgotten their youthful mischief to the point where they had eyes and feelings for the fair sex only. As for the duchess, née Bouillon, her chief passion was for Jansenism, and she surrounded herself with men and women of the sect, who became her exclusive agents. The duke and his wife idolized each other, so much so that they agreed to separate if either of them contracted smallpox, which was widespread at the time. Mme de La Trémoïlle was the first to fall victim. But her husband could not bring himself to allow anyone but himself to care for her and remained at her bedside day and night. She recovered, but her unfortunate spouse died, a victim of his conjugal devotion.[12]

This was the woman who, early in her marriage, pretty, and mildly flirtatious, set our Provençal's heart beating. Annoyed at the time by the attentions of Mlle de Charolais, of whom he had begun to tire, he wrote a letter breaking off their affair. Rarely has a mistress who has ceased to please been dismissed with such cynicism or shrewdness:

I considered your advances, Madame, as overtures of your mind and not your heart. I had not the honor of knowing you, I owed you nothing, a sprain forced me to take to my room, I was at loose ends, your letters were pretty, they amused me, I am flattered if I truly conquered you, you cured me of an unhappy passion that occupies me exclusively.

Yes, Madame, I am in love. And today I have too much evidence of your friendship to hide from you what is happening in my heart. I have the honor of belonging most intimately to Mme la duchessse de Bouillon. Mlle de Bouillon offered me her friendship. She has married her niece to M. de La Trémoïlle, she lodges them and feeds them, and this has given me the opportunity to see Mme de La Trémoïlle quite often. Her figure pleased me, her character attracted me. She is fond of her husband, and the more often he is unfaithful to her, the more she would be flattered to please him: his indifference stimulates her, and I sometimes feel that I owe to the desire for vengeance what I should like to owe only to love.[13]

Mademoiselle was not a woman to tolerate a rival. She refused to allow her lovers the luxury of divided loyalties that she so easily allowed herself. Her answer is couched in a bantering tone that scarcely disguised her wounded pride, much less her desire to injure her unfaithful lover. A scratch administered by such an enemy could easily prove fatal. But if there was cruelty in the response, there was still more cruelty in having earned it. Still, Mlle de Charolais aimed well: "courtier" and "*petit-maître*" are the insults she hurls in Jean-Baptiste's face, and, harsh as they are, they are fully as justified as the accusations of ambition and self-regard. Jean-Baptiste must have found it difficult to defend himself, because everything about him betrayed his desire to obtain the highest positions without worrying too much about the means.

A brief excerpt from her letter will suffice:

It is true, Monsieur, that I have received three of your letters without responding, because you ask me for orders, and I refuse to give them to one who would receive them as would the regiment of Champagne[14] . . . Do you not know that he who quits the game loses? As for me, when someone goes a month without caring to see me, I go four. In all sincerity, I thought I loved someone quite sensible in whom intelligence took the place of feeling, someone who would know how to make a friend of his mistress. But I recognize you as a perfect *petit-maître*, who turns the heads of princesses and amuses them with his stories.[15]

The Way of Sodom

Versatile as to the object of his loves, the count was no less versatile as to the object of his desires. On both counts he liked to allow his senses free rein, imposing no rule even at the risk of being lured beyond the bounds of what was permissible. The savor of the unknown was in any case an essential ingredient of what was then called *le vice italien*. If the fair sex attracted Jean-Baptiste and if illustrious names flattered his ego, his inclinations drew him with equal zest to young men of his own age. In these affairs it did not matter that his partners were of inferior social rank. Social position was completely unimportant. Though fiercely proud of the names of his mistresses, he appears to have been totally indifferent to the names of his catamites. He even preferred boys of common birth and generally chose them among the male prostitutes who walked the streets of the capital. Calculation gave way to pleasure, coupled inevitably with a wish to provoke, with the allure of danger, and with the intoxication of feeling above the common law. The same pleasure *de s'encanailler*, of mingling with the common herd, drew him to female prostitutes as well. With them as with his Corydons of the street, there were no fine words, no high-flown wit, no verses, only carnal pleasure in its pure form. These secret desires constitute the comte de Sade's hidden face, his dark mask, his mystery.

The suspect pleasure of hunting for boys frequently led him to stroll in the vicinity of the Tuileries Garden, one of the most popular places for those referred to as *infâmes* (reprobates) or *chevaliers de la manchette* (homosexuals). There was constant traffic among individuals of the most diverse sort, from the great lord to the messenger boy, from the chimney sweep to the prince of the Church. By a gesture, look, or sign they recognized one another and engaged in a dialogue, generally brief, that went straight to the point in the crudest terms. The police, using informers, kept the area around the garden under surveillance night and day and stopped many individuals for questioning. *Mouches* (literally, flies) was the term used for youths sent out to get themselves picked up by "clients" only to turn them in at once to an officer of the watch hiding in the bushes.

One fine autumn evening young Jean-Baptiste, eyes aglow and a smile on his lips, was seated in the garden, obviously on the lookout for a good time, when he spotted a young man he had approached a few days earlier. He engaged the youth in conversation and then invited him to join him behind a clump of trees. Unfortunately for the count, the boy turned out to be a *mouche*. When the prearranged signal was given, the officer of the watch moved in with a squad of deputies and placed the imprudent young noble under arrest.

The police report on the incident is composed in the frank manner of such documents, a style in some ways reminiscent of that which Donatien de Sade would adopt some fifty years later:

At around eight-thirty in the evening, the aforementioned sieur de Sade, after taking several turns around the wooded area, sat on a nearby bench. When the young man passed by, he allegedly greeted him and asked him to sit down, which he did. He then made various lewd propositions, saying that although a man had already shaken his rod, he would put it to him if he wished; that if he was not afraid if people noticed his inclination for these pleasures, he would take him to dine and go to bed with him. And he would have taken him immediately behind the trees, but the young man was unwilling to go along and proposed instead that they go to his room, which was not far away, where they would be free. Sieur de Sade allegedly agreed to this. As the two got up and started on their way, sieur Haymier [the officer of the watch], who had observed them and who knew from the young man's signal that he was with a reprobate who was actively soliciting him, attempted to arrest the man but in view of his quality did not but rather released him after taking his name and address as above and receiving his assurance that he would appear before the magistrate.

Note: The young man stated that this was the second time he had been solicited by the aforementioned sieur de Sade; that he had approached him some days previously and had made similar propositions, which, since no one was observing, he had been unwilling to entertain, and that on this day they recognized each other quite well.[16]

Jean-Baptiste boasted of his kinship with the duchesse de La Roche-Guyon and named other illustrious relations, and that was the end of it. He was issued a reprimand and asked to sign an *acte de soumission* (a pledge to behave in the future). The *police des mœurs*, or vice squad, very rarely took severe action against nobles. And no one was surprised to find a client of the Condés involved in debauch. The Condés themselves were reputed, with good reason, to be the worst of reprobates.

At the time of this incident the comte de Sade was twenty-two. No doubt there were others like it, and his correspondence suggests that he also enjoyed some very tender relations with some of his male friends, such as the young Anne-Théodore de Chavigny, who had already embarked on a diplomatic career and who would later succeed Amelot de Chaillou as minister of foreign affairs.

If Jean-Baptiste practiced Greek love, it was not out of an irrepressible taste for boys but as a way of escaping the monotony of his usual erotic activities. In this form of love he experienced more unusual, more powerful sensations than in his other adventures, and these feelings were further enhanced by fantasies of punishment. For him as for many young lords the "philosophical sin" was nothing more than an aristocratic caprice, a sort of game made more exciting by being forbidden, in which one could amuse oneself by courting fear without incurring any real danger. What was the risk when one possessed a great name and powerful patrons? Surely there was no danger of being sent to Bicêtre or the Châtelet. At most one risked forty-eight hours in the Bastille and a paternal sermon from the *lieutenant général de police.*[17]

Between affairs with women the comte de Sade appears never to have given up his Socratic encounters, at least not until old age approached and he underwent a conversion that caused him to look back in horror on the "follies" of his youth. Two poems found in his notebooks tell us all we need to know about the ambiguity of his desires. The first even suggests that he did not limit the practice of sodomy to his male partners. If so, then Donatien, who preferred sodomy to all other forms of intercourse, might claim to have inherited the taste.

> *J'ai tous les goûts quand je vous rends hommage,*
> *J'y trouve en même temps la femme et le garçon,*
> *J'adore en vous une femme volage,*
> *Un ami sage, un aimable giton.*

[*When I pay you my respects I savor all tastes. With you I find both the woman and the boy. I adore in you a fickle female, a wise friend, a delightful catamite.*]

> *Comme un habitant de Sodome*
> *Je fais la femme avec un homme,*
> *C'est ce qui vous met en fureur.*
> *Mais pourquoi vous fâcher, Mesdames?*
> *Vous seules faites mon bonheur:*
> *Je suis très homme avec les femmes.*[18]

[*Like a resident of Sodom, I play the woman with a man: that is what puts you in a rage. But why get angry, Ladies? You alone make me happy: with women I am all man.*]

The "charming trio"

Along with love and ambition literature occupied an important place in the life of the comte de Sade. In addition to poems and countless letters he was the author of comedies, tragedies, heroic verse, novellas, tales, philosophical and ethical treatises, and anthologies of anecdotes—twenty-some works in all, none of them published to this day.[19] His son collected and preserved these works with extreme care. He read and reread them constantly, annotating them in his own hand, reworking a sentence here, adding a title there, copying or commissioning copies of letters in poor condition, ordering pages bound and sewn. He did not like to be separated from his father's works. When he was away from La Coste, he asked his agent Gaufridy to send them to him. In prison he piously kept an untitled pamphlet by Jean-Baptiste on his person and added his own title on the flyleaf: *Morality and Religion: My Thoughts*. When he died at Charenton, his father's manuscripts were found carefully arranged on the shelves of his library along with other family papers. Nothing tells us more about Donatien than the pages of his father's manuscripts in which his own handwriting is inserted between the lines of his father's, replacing one adjective with another, adding a word in the margin, deleting a passage with a bold vertical stroke, the two hands at times mingling, joining together, intertwining, at other times clashing or contradicting each other—just as their souls did, at once so close and so remote, so complicitous and so contrary.

The comte de Sade wrote a great deal, but for amusement, as a dilettante, and above all without boasting about it, for to have done so would have been to forfeit prestige. The old prejudice was not yet dead that required the nobility to take an interest in the arts but forbade the practice on pain of derogation. Montesquieu had found a diplomatic career closed to him on account of his writings. Bernis, an ambassador and minister, was greatly embarrassed by his literary reputation. Choiseul would accuse Saint-Lambert, captain of the Gardes-Lorraines and author of *Les Saisons*, of having derogated twice, once as a "man of quality" and a second time as a "soldier." Jean-Baptiste de Sade was both, and since he aspired to high position, prudence required that he publish nothing.

His attitude toward men of letters was that of the *grands seigneurs*, men of fashion, and women of the world who lionized Voltaire for his literary talent and reputation but who did not forget themselves to the extent of treating him as an equal. Indeed, Voltaire was among the men of letters whom the count saw often, although the *philosophe* was closer to Jean-Baptiste's brother, the abbé de Sade. Both parties were flattered by the connection: Voltaire to know the descendants of Laura, the Sades to correspond with the most illustrious author of the day. The friendship among Voltaire, the comte de Sade, his brother the abbé, and their cousin Joseph-David de Sade d'Eyguières, whom Voltaire in one poem apostrophized as "charming trio," did not go much further than an exchange of witty compliments and the expression, in elegantly turned phrases, of good intentions on both sides.

•

The comte de Sade's unpublished correspondence reveals a lively curiosity about everything to do with the theater and literature. However far he might be from Paris, whether on campaign in Flanders or on diplomatic mission to Bonn, he regularly inquired about the latest books, plays, and operas, elections to the Academy, literary gossip, and behind-the-scenes tattle. His interests soon led him to seek out the company of writers and poets. Apart from Montesquieu, with whom he exchanged several letters after the two met in England, and Voltaire, whose path he crossed at the hôtel de Sassenage and again at the see of Philippsburg, Jean-Baptiste enjoyed continuing relations with a number of men of letters. His penchants inclined him toward licentious authors and writers of risqué songs. He shared his table with Crébillon *fils*, Collé, Piron, and Gentil-Bernard, all assiduous members of the celebrated *Caveau*, which met at the *cabaret de Landel* on the rue de Buci, where their ribald verses were sung.

There is no better picture of these dinners, from which women were excluded and whose tone could hardly have been more unfettered, than that provided some years later by a friend of the comte de Sade:

The all-male suppers that you made such pleasant occasions are no more. Prior to my departure we still had them with Crébillon, Collé, du Tertre, and several others. We went at it with a natural zest, especially as there was nothing to stand in our way. It must be allowed that women, pleasant as they are, interfere with such fun. They have to occupy the center of attention and want to be the life of every party, and with most of them you have to be afraid of showing any wit. The attention they demand and the romantic banter they require dampen the fires of wit and narrow the circle of ideas. A woman without pretensions always has some that she hides from herself but allows us to see. With the ladies, moreover, there is an obligation of decency that constrains and hobbles the imagination. Among men, our conversation was free, without filth or impiety, high-spirited but not slanderous or frivolous. We sometimes said nasty things about women but never about any particular woman. I have noticed that attacks on them came generally from their most zealous admirers, and often only the coldest or feeblest man of the company rose in their defense. I dare not say where this reflection leads. Finally, to make a success at one of our suppers, or merely to be invited, one had to exhibit qualities of intelligence and courage. We would not accept a fool or a coward or a scoundrel.[20]

The writer Baculard d'Arnaud, inventor of the maudlin horror novel, was often a guest at these occasions. His relations with the comte de Sade were those of a recipient of favors with his benefactor. To be sure, the count held him in high esteem and treated him as a friend. It was thanks to the good offices of Jean-Baptiste (and not Voltaire) that Baculard became Frederick II's literary correspondent. It should come as no surprise, then, that his *Epreuves du sentiment* bear such an uncanny resemblance to Donatien de Sade's *Les Infortunes de la vertu*. Baculard's novels occupied a place of honor in Jean-Baptiste's library, along with other contemporary works whose authors were no doubt also the count's friends.

Much of what Jean-Baptiste read became part of his son's cultural heritage. And who knows how many stories, souvenirs, encounters, anecdotes, and confidences surreptitiously made their way from the father's memory to the son's? Such things cannot be inventoried or counted or classified, and their influence is difficult to measure. The myriad circumstances of daily life, the thousands of subjects that may have come up in conversations between father and son, will forever remain a mystery. Yet these things *too* nourished the imagination of the marquis de Sade.

A Libertine's Wedding

Left a widower at age twenty-eight when Marie-Anne de Conti died in 1720, the prince de Condé bore his loss stolidly, all the more so because he never loved his wife and Mme de Prie occupied his heart. Upon her death the prince replaced her with the comtesse d'Egmont. A few years later, he gave in to pressure from his family, primarily from his mother, the dowager princess, and agreed to marry again. For his bride he chose a ravishing German princess, Caroline Charlotte of Hesse-Rheinfeld, who was only fifteen years old.[21] The prince was by this time nearly forty. Such a disparity of age made it likely that the prince would play the cuckold, and so it came to pass. The old man's marital misadventures, compounded by his inability to satisfy his young wife, were on everyone's lips. "M. le Duc has made so much use of men and women," Mathieu Marais observed, "that he has fallen into the void. His wife, who was born the princess of Hesse-Rheinfeld, is quite delightful and extremely pretty. Nevertheless, people say that her marriage has not been consummated. They say she makes no secret of it, and claim it is because she does not know how to arouse him." This did not prevent her from giving birth to a boy, Louis-Joseph de Condé, born in 1736, who would become the supreme commander of the émigré armies after the Revolution and whose grandson, the duc d'Enghien, would end up in a grave at Vincennes on orders of Napoleon.

During the summer or at the latest the autumn of 1733, the comte de Sade, stirred by the beauty of the young princess, began to court her. The undertaking was not easy, because Monsieur le Duc was extremely jealous and kept the young lady under close guard. If Jean-Baptiste's hopes were to be realized, he would have to find some way to live in her vicinity. An opportunity presented itself. The daughter of the princess's lady-in-waiting, Mlle de Maillé de Carman, a fairly pretty girl but without a fortune, had reached the age of marriage. The count asked for her hand, and the prince granted it. Once inside the fortress, there was no difficulty in gaining access to the woman he loved, whom he saw daily, and ultimately he succeeded in winning her favors. And so it was that the comte de Sade became the lover of the princesse de Condé and the husband of Mlle de Maillé.

But let him tell his own story in an autobiographical fragment found in the family archives. The scene of the wedding night, in which the princess excites his ardor by holding his young wife's hand, might have been taken straight from one of Crébillon's tales:

... The princess was placed in the hands of reliable people who were required to report her every step, word, and glance. Three or four years of her life passed in innocence. But the women who composed her court were at pains to spoil her mind. They continually held up the example of her mother-in-law, her sisters-in-law, and her husband's carrying on. They made her feel how offensive it was for her to have a jealous husband who did not love her. The young princess swallowed deep draughts of the poison they poured into her heart. Those who were out to ruin her seemed the most likable, and she preferred them to all the rest. When M. le Duc was asked why he left his wife surrounded by such evil-minded women, he answered that since he forbade her the company of men, he believed it was unjust to forbid her that of women.

Mme la duchesse was high-spirited, and her heart asked only to be loved ... I had been going to Chantilly for three or four years, and M. le Duc seemed fond of me ... After I broke off with Mme d'Autry, I found myself free again and looked for something to occupy my time. From things that had been reported to me I sensed that I lacked only the opportunity to become the possessor of the most charming woman in the world. Since Mlle de Carman was available to marry, it occurred to me that Mme la duchesse would be grateful if I offered myself as a husband, and that once I was lodged in the house as the husband of a person for whom she felt the warmest friendship, it would be easy for me to worm my way into her heart.

So I went and offered to marry Mlle de Carman. The princess seemed to doubt the sincerity of my proposal. So energetically did I assure her that it cost me nothing to please her that she appeared to believe me and to be touched by what I was doing. She ordered me to speak to her husband and not to say that I had spoken to her about it. Which I did. M. le Duc also seemed quite pleased by what I told him, that I was making this marriage for the sole purpose of attaching myself to him. He assured me that he would take care of my future, a promise that had little effect. Mme la duchesse, when informed of my proposal by her husband, urged our marriage in the strongest possible terms. She bought the clothes and made all the wedding preparations.

Finally the day arrived. M. le Duc returned from Chantilly to perform the wedding, which took place at the hôtel de Condé. I was already in bed but Mme de Sade still held on to the hand of Mme la duchesse and begged her not to leave. The presence of the princess heightened my rapture and made me keener and more eager than ever not to be without her, although my wife was a woman of pleasing figure. In the end everyone seemed pleased. My wife at having found a husband, although she had no property. M. le Duc at having made his wife happy by placing her in the company of a woman of good reputation who had always behaved well. Mme la duchesse at having with her a person on whom she could rely and to whom she could say whatever was on her mind. And I—I had a pleasant wife, the prospect of a regiment that M. le Duc had promised me, and the hope of being loved by a charming young princess. I pointed out to her the sacrifice I had made in marrying a girl without property for the sole purpose of being closer to her and obtaining permission to see her at all hours.

My marriage afforded me considerable familiarity. I could enter her quarters at any time. The princess's heart was unoccupied. No doubt she could have found men who would have pleased her more than I, but she was not at liberty to see them. Everything persuaded her that I loved her, and if she hesitated to surrender, it was only to make me savor her defeat all the more. I had won over her wardrobe maid, who let me in through a door at the bottom of my staircase. No one else was in on the secret of our relations. Thus they were secret and would have remained so but for the jealousy of my wife. But what will a jealous woman not find out? She had me followed, and one day that ill-fated door opened and I walked out while her lackey stood sentinel at the bottom of the staircase awaiting my return. I did not see him, but from the state my wife was in I knew that something unusual had happened . . . Nothing satisfied her. Mme la duchesse was the first to suspect that she was the object of [my wife's] jealousy. We took precautions to talk less in front of her, but even our precautions helped give us away . . .

One day, when I thought I had satisfied [the princess]—and what woman would not have been!—she began to cry and told me that she was very unhappy and that she was risking her life by yielding to me, because if her husband discovered our relations he would not fail to sacrifice her to his rage and that I did not love her enough to compensate for such fears. I burst out laughing in response:

"What, Madame, you still doubt the ardor of my love for you? What must I do to convince you?"

She was somewhat disconcerted.

"I would have reason to be content," she said, "if I did not know that you can do better when you want to, and Madame de S[ade] has told me details of your wedding night that make me worry you like her better."

"Madame de Sade was such a novice," I said, "that it was easy for me to deceive her. Besides, there is so little difference that it is not worth bothering about."

"But you are still sleeping with her," she said, "and if you loved me, you would be less diligent. I love that you love me, and I worry about the proof only because the evidence is reassuring."

It did no good to tell her that I slept with my wife only to put her off the scent. She made me promise that I would sleep in a separate bed, and I kept my word.[22]

•

So Jean-Baptiste de Sade married for the sole purpose of possessing the delightful princesse de Condé, on a whim of the passions or, more precisely, in a fever of the senses, without the slightest feeling for the woman who would become his wife and without regard for her dowry, which was in any case rather meager. But he certainly did not marry without calculation or premeditation. For what he does not say in his story is that the marriage was an excellent move. Marie-Eléonore de Maillé de Carman was, in the fifth generation, a cousin of Claire-Clémence de Maillé de Brézé, the niece of cardinal de Richelieu, who had married the Grand Condé. With this marriage, more illustrious than profitable, our Rastignac allied himself with the cadet branch of the house of Bourbon-Condé, thereby scoring several victories at once: he had the princess, the prestige, and the resources to satisfy the highest ambitions. He played the game quite well.

The marriage was celebrated in great pomp in the chapel of the hôtel de Condé on November 13, 1733, in the presence of the duke and duchess. The next day the *Mercure de France* in reporting on the ceremony made a point of rehearsing the genealogy of the couple without omitting a single one of their titles and without failing to recall that among the count's illustrious ancestors was the beautiful Laura, "known for the praise the famous Petrarch . . . bestowed on her in verses he wrote in her honor." It was reported, for example, that the father of the bride was named Donatien, *chevalier*, marquis de Carman and comte de Maillé, and that he was baron de Lesquelen, seigneur of the estates of Dameny and Villeromain, and second baron de Bretagne, and that his mother was named Louise Binet de Marcognet. Jean-Baptiste was almost thirty-two and Marie-Eléonore almost twenty-two. As a wedding present the duc de Condé appointed the young comtesse de Sade lady-in-waiting to the duchess, and the couple moved into an apartment set aside for them in the hôtel de Condé.

Only three months after his wedding the comte de Sade received orders to rejoin his regiment in Germany as aide-de-camp to maréchal de Villars. Upon learning simultaneously of the count's marriage and his departure for the army, Voltaire sent him this "worthless tidbit":

> *Vous suivez donc les étendards*
> *De Bellone et de l'Hyménée?*
> *Vous vous enrôlez cette année*
> *Et sous Carman et sous Villars.*
> *Le doyen des héros, une beauté novice,*
> *Vont vous occuper tour à tour:*
> *Et vous nous apprendrez un jour*
> *Quel est le plus rude service*
> *Ou de Villars ou de l'Amour.*

[*So you march behind the standards of both Bellona and the Hymenaea? You are enlisting this year under both Carman and Villars. The dean of heroes and a novice beauty will occupy you by turns. And one day you will teach us whether the harsher service is that of Villars or that of Love.*]

Jean-Baptiste responded in the same vein:

> *Ami, je suis les étendards*
> *De Bellone et de l'Hyménée.*
> *Si je quitte une épouse aimée,*
> *C'est pour voir triompher Villars.*
> *Mars et l'Amour me trouveront novice,*
> *Mais je m'instruirai tour à tour,*

Avec Villars, des rigueurs de service,
Avec Carman, des douceurs de l'Amour.[23]

[*Friend, I march behind the standards of Bellona and the Hymenaea. If I leave a beloved wife, it is to see Villars triumph. Mars and Love will find me a novice, but I shall educate myself first with Villars in the rigors of service, then with Carman in the pleasures of Love.*]

2

A Broken Career

The Comte de Sade, Secret Agent

Like many officers of his age, the young captain of dragoons had conceived the ambition of serving in embassies and making a career in politics. He had the prerequisites for the job: a fine presence, adequate wealth, charm, wit, cultivation, a liking for luxury. In short, he seemed born to cut a fine figure in foreign courts, in addition to which he had acquired experience in negotiation that augured well for his future.

At the age of twenty he was entrusted with a mission to The Hague, about whose purpose we know nothing but for which he received a letter of recommendation from Prince Henri of Auvergne, the archbishop of Vienne.

Four years later he set out for the duchy of Saxe-Gotha with instructions from Chauvelin, the minister of foreign affairs, and a recommendation from Baron von Bernstorff, the Danish minister to the court of France, who also served as a spy for the king of England. Bernstorff commended him to the duke's chaplain, a man named Huhn, who would show him "all there is to see," including the "library, collection of medals, and so on. This Huhn is a man of letters with a fairly good library, and since I know you admire genius in letters, I take the liberty of recommending you to him and hope you will be pleased."[1] During his stay in Gotha the comte de Sade made the acquaintance of Prince von Anhalt, brother of the future empress Catherine II, with whom he would maintain a regular and friendly correspondence.

In 1730 he was named French ambassador to the court of Russia, but the death of the young Czar Peter II and the policy of the new empress, Anna Ivanovna, formerly duchess of Kurland, a German first and last and keen to govern exclusively with the aid of other Germans, thwarted the purpose of his embassy. The king's principal minister, Cardinal de Fleury, then entrusted the comte de Sade with entering into confidential negotiations with the court of London.

In the course of this mission our secret agent established close ties with Sir Henry Pelham, the treasurer of the Whig Party and a man thoroughly familiar with the secrets of the English court, who had just been named paymaster of the army. He also savored the charms of the beautiful Mme de Vaucluse, his first cousin and mistress of the duc d'Ormond, over whom she reportedly enjoyed absolute power. One of the count's tasks was to gather information on the activities of the English Jacobites, supporters of the House of Stuart and fierce opponents of the Hanover dynasty. Knowing that many Jacobites belonged to Masonic lodges, he decided to join the order himself so as to keep an eye on the dissidents.

The initiation ceremony took place on May 12, 1730, at the Horn Lodge, which met at a tavern of the same name in Westminster. Another initiate presented himself that night at the temple gate, ready to "receive the light": Charles-Louis de Secondat, baron de Montesquieu. Thus the comte de Sade and the author of *The Spirit of the Laws* became "brothers" in masonry. Among those in attendance were illustrious members of the British aristocracy, such as the duke of Norfolk, Nathanael Blackerby, marquess of Quesne, and Lord Mordaunt, marquess of Beaumont. Presiding over the ceremony was a senior member of the lodge, the duke of Richmond.[2]

A Good Investment

Following his marriage and the campaigns of 1734–1735 as aide-de-camp to maréchal de Villars, the comte de Sade obtained from the king the post of *lieutenant général* for the provinces of Bresse, Bugey, Valromey, and Gex, which he purchased in 1739 for 135,000 livres from the marquis de Lassay. The price may seem exorbitant, but really it was not considering the advantages that such a post conferred. Offices of this kind were in fact much sought after, because each province paid its lieutenant general a lifetime income. The occupant of the post was not even required to take up residence in the province and was free to spend most of his time at court. A better investment could not be found.

But such offices were expensive, and the king awarded them only to a lucky few. The comte de Sade owed his good fortune entirely to the intervention of Cardinal de Fleury, who was probably keen to reward him for various diplomatic missions in which he had acquitted himself with distinction. All told, the count's revenue from the provinces of Bresse, Bugey, and Gex came to 10,200 livres per year, or slightly less than an eight percent return on his investment.

The royal letters-patent officially bestowing the post of lieutenant general were dated May 29, 1739. A month later the comte de Sade delivered his acceptance speech to the *parlement* of Dijon.

On November 24 of the same year Gaspard François de Sade died in Avignon. "I was greatly affected by my father's death," the count told Monseigneur de Crillon, the archbishop of Narbonne and a friend of the deceased.

A Whirl of Names

It was four years before a first child was born to the comte and comtesse de Sade. In 1737 Marie-Eléonore gave birth to a little girl, who received the name Caroline-Laure (Caroline being the first name of her god-mother, the princesse de Condé, and Laure a sort of fetish with the family, there being a Laure de Sade in practically every generation). But the child died just two years later, in 1739.

On June 2, 1740, a year after Caroline-Laure's death, Mme de Sade gave birth to a boy, who was baptized the following day at the church of Saint-Sulpice (in the parish where the hôtel de Condé was located). The child's maternal godfather, Donatien de Maillé, marquis de Carman, served as godfather and his paternal grandmother, Louise Aldonse d'Astouaud de Murs, as godmother. Both were unable to be present at the ceremony and sent proxies instead. The child's mother was still recovering from the delivery. Thus none of the child's relatives were present, and the fact that all were represented by servants accounts for the errors committed by the priest who officiated at the ceremony.

The newborn was given the names Donatien Alphonse François, but only the first of these corresponded to the family's wishes. Donatien had been the name of the child's maternal grandfather, so called in honor of the martyred Breton saint who had been tortured along with his brother Rogatien for spreading the Christian faith in Armorica. As for the second name, the count had wanted to name the boy after his own mother, *Aldonse*, an old Provençal name given to both boys and girls but unknown in Paris. The priest of Saint-Sulpice misunderstood his instructions and wrote *Alphonse* on the birth certificate. And the name *Louis*, which the father had wanted in honor of his protector Louis-Henri de Bourbon, was simply forgotten and replaced by *François*.

And so it was that the marquis de Sade was named Donatien Alphonse François instead of Donatien Aldonse Louis. Yet he never renounced the name he had been meant to receive and took care to sign most official documents with the latter signature. In his marriage contract, for example, he is called *Louis Aldonse Donatien* de Sade. Often he preferred the spelling *Aldonze*, which reflected the Provençal pronunciation. During the Revolution he abandoned all his first names but *Louis*. These onomastic fantasies would scarcely be worth recalling but for the fact that they had some rather unfortunate consequences, as we shall see.

Monsieur l'Ambassadeur

Only seven months after the birth of his son on January 20, 1741, the comte de Sade learned of his appointment as minister plenipotentiary to the Elector of Cologne, the archbishop Clement Augustus. Cardinal de Fleury, who appreciated the count's talents as a negotiator, had suggested his name to Louis XV, and the king had accepted the recommendation. Admittedly this was not a post of the first importance on the European chessboard. The courts of the Rhineland were dependencies of the Holy Roman Empire and as such did not enjoy full sovereignty. Young men fresh from the ranks of the army but of high birth and good company were generally sent there to be initiated into the art of diplomacy. The honor was by no means comparable with one of the great embassies: London, Vienna, or Madrid. Still, it was not a bad beginning. The comte de Sade finally had his wish: he had his embassy, and a life of honor, fortune, ease, and luxury lay in prospect.

Since the court of France was the most brilliant in Europe, it was essential to make an impressive demonstration of the king's prestige before the representatives of other powers. Royal ambassadors therefore received generous stipends, so that they might live in a manner worthy of their master. Did the comte de Sade possess the "subtle competences" so essential for success in the Rhenish courts? He commanded, in any case, a budget that made the task easier: 24,000 livres annually, plus 12,000 livres to defray the costs of "initial settlement" and an additional six to ten thousand livres for "extraordinary" expenses. This was enough to overcome many obstacles, even at an ecclesiastical court like that of Cologne, where money was "the golden key that opens all locks."

Jean-Baptiste therefore left for Bonn, the seat of his embassy, in the final days of January 1741, leaving his wife and son at the hôtel de Condé. As for his mistress, the "little princess," she had replaced him in 1739 with M. de Bissy, the commissioner-general of cavalry. Annoyed at finding himself displaced by such a lady's man and even more worried that this new affair might lead to discovery of his own earlier one with the princess, Jean-Baptiste allegedly took it upon himself to advise the prince de Condé of his misfortune. That, at least, is the imputation of d'Argenson: "They say that M. de Sade, feeling threatened, did nothing to hinder this most awkward discovery." In a jealous rage Monsieur le Duc ordered his wife's windows barred and her doors locked, dismissed most of the women who had waited on her (but kept the comtesse de Sade, surely the least suspect of the lot), and had M. de Bissy summoned to his regiment. "It is to be feared that for so unforgivable a crime this pretty princess may find herself locked up in some dreadful castle," d'Argenson concluded.

On February 10, Jean-Baptiste de Sade settled in Bonn, while the news of his appointment met with a mixed reception in Paris. D'Argenson was severely critical of the king's choice: "M. de Sade has just been appointed our envoy to Cologne and the chevalier Desalleurs France's minister in Dresden. These two are fops with some intelligence but no substance, and it is always astonishing to see such men appointed to foreign posts. This is the mark of our current attention to German affairs and shows that we have by no means been surrendered to the interests of the queen of Bohemia as we were to those of her father."[3]

D'Argenson's worries are more easily understood if we recall the delicate situation in which France found herself vis-à-vis the German states. After the death of Charles VI (October 19, 1740), his daughter Maria Theresa was to succeed him as head of the Empire under the terms of the Pragmatic Sanction, which had been accepted by nearly all European states. On November 10 Louis XV recognized her as heiress of the Austrian domains but decided to support Charles Albert, Elector of Bavaria, in his candidacy for the imperial crown.[4] The French policy was to drive a wedge between the German princes and the house of Hapsburg and induce them to give their votes to Charles Albert, the brother of the Elector of Cologne. Allied to France under the terms of an agreement signed in 1734 and renewed in May 1740, the latter was urged by Louis XV to honor his commitment and declare his opposition to Maria Theresa. This was the mission of the comte de Sade.

From his very first audience, which took place on March 4, 1741, with the usual pomp, the count realized that the common opinion of the Elector was not inaccurate. A man of mediocre intelligence, indecisive, inclined to melancholy and above all to the most extreme dissimulation, Clement Augustus enjoyed frivolous amusements, gala celebrations, hunting, architecture, and little else. He liked, moreover, to be flattered about his tastes and magnificence. Amorously inclined, he had had several favorites whom he had kept under jealous scrutiny, but apart from these enthusiasms the prince-archbishop seemed, according to the abbé Aunillon, "scrupulously attached to the essential duties and even the most insignificant practices of religion. Not a day goes by without time set aside for mass, prayer, and the rosary." But, the abbé goes on to say, "these pious exercises were often interrupted by banquets, hunts, games, rather mournful little suppers, operas, comedies, and balls." What is more, "it is fairly common to see the elector pontificate in the morning in cloak and miter and dance in the evening *en domino*."[5]

The comte de Sade was soon frustrated by the Elector's reluctance to choose between Vienna and Versailles. He needed Austrian support to protect his bishoprics, which were located in Lutheran territory, yet he felt bound by his pledges to the king of France and the Elector of Bavaria. With powerful help from the French armies that had just invaded Prague, our ambassador finally persuaded the Elector to subscribe to the treaty of Nymphenburg (March 28, 1741), which he had had drawn up. Under the terms of this treaty France, Spain, the Kingdom of the Two Sicilies, the Elector Palatine, and the Elector of Cologne pledged to support Charles Albert of Bavaria, and on January 24, 1742, he was duly elected emperor. Clement Augustus personally attended the coronation of his brother as Charles VII. This triumph of French policy was also a diplomatic victory for its representative.

A Somber Affair

The count's triumph was short-lived, however, for relations between him and the Elector soon deteriorated. Stiff in his episcopal and princely dignity, Clement Augustus had little liking for this free-spirited French libertine, who spoke lightly of serious things and allowed himself an "excessive familiarity." Initially the Elector had tolerated and even encouraged this familiarity, but something offended him and he abruptly changed his mind. For his part Jean-Baptiste took an ironic attitude toward the vain prelate, who wallowed guiltily in pleasure yet devoted himself to religion with the punctiliousness of a spinster. The count, moreover, had little patience with the Elector's doubts, caprices, and sudden changes of humor.

This mutual irritation worsened over the course of the year 1742. Inevitably it had to end in an explosion, which finally came in August 1743. What caused it? No one knows. There was talk of an amorous rivalry, but according to the Elector's principal minister, Count von Hohenzollern, the comte de Sade had hit on the secret of winning the Elector's confidence but had lost it "by attempting to make changes in his household and ministry."[6] Others speak of a gambling dispute. The prince was a passionate gambler but hated to lose, which put anyone imprudent enough to win against him in a delicate position.[7]

An anonymous letter, sent to the count after his dismissal, reveals that the Elector had other reasons for his displeasure with the king's envoy:

Here are the three crimes of lèse-majesté with which you are charged so as to frustrate you of your present:

The first is: your attachment to the emperor and your complaints to him against the person of the master. Add to this the knowledge you must have had of the intrigues in which the imperial court and the court of France are involved with the king of Prussia.

Second: your undue attachment to Duke Theodore, in preference to the master, which was revealed by your alacrity to find him the money needed to leave here and negotiate for the election to the principality of Liège to the detriment of the Elector.

Third: your unwillingness to induce the court of France to pay what it owes the Elector.

These are the three serious crimes that you will find it difficult to justify in your court. Be careful, Sir, with this, because if it were to be known that this information comes from here, you would compromise a worthy person, and another would be lost with him.[8]

If the precise reasons for the dispute elude us, we know at least that the consequences for the count were serious. Here are the facts as generally reported. After asking for and receiving permission from the French court to return temporarily to Paris, M. de Sade led the Elector to believe that he was being recalled permanently and officially took leave of his court. Contrary to what the anonymous letter says, there was a farewell ceremony, during which the count received the customary present, probably a handsome cash bonus, from Clement Augustus personally, after which he returned to France. A few days after his arrival, the prince-archbishop sent him his letter of recall, dated December 31, 1743.[9]

Thus Jean-Baptiste apparently deserted his post without orders from the king and returned to Paris without saying a word about his quarrel with the Elector. As for the letter of recall, which he should have remanded to Louis XV, he presumably pocketed it so that he might continue to enjoy the rank and emoluments of his post for another year. The abbé Aunillon, who is the source of this information, indicates that these facts were not discovered until March 1745.[10] D'Argenson is even more critical, accusing the count of having sold his influence and of having employed the services of a venal scoundrel by the name of Baumez.[11]

Jean-Baptiste naturally tried to defend himself against these grave charges. He wrote a memorandum to d'Argenson, for example, in which he spoke of himself in the third person:

. . . He is accused of having taken a letter of recall from the Elector. It is true that he received one, which he did not regard as such and which he sent back to his secretary to be returned to the prince. He is also accused of not having revealed that he had quarreled with the Elector. If he said nothing, it was because he knew nothing . . . He is in a position to prove what he asserts.[12]

Suffice it to say that the evidence in the matter remains contradictory. But the public believed that the ambassador's guilt had been sufficiently demonstrated. No one doubted that he had deserted his post without orders from the king and that he had continued to collect his stipend. As for d'Argenson's other charges, concerning traffic in influence and "unscrupulous, self-interested" dealings, we know that the minister, to put it mildly, felt little sympathy for the plenipotentiary.

The Citadel of Antwerp

None of these charges were known at the court of Louis XV prior to March 1745. D'Argenson himself was surely unaware of them when he succeeded Amelot de Chaillou as secretary of state for foreign affairs on November 19, 1744, for otherwise he would never have sent the comte de Sade back to Cologne in February 1745. In the meantime the death of Emperor Charles VII on January 20, 1745, had plunged France's foreign policy into disarray. D'Argenson stubbornly refused to support the candidacy of Maria Theresa's husband Francis of Lorraine and threw his backing instead to the Bavarian heir-apparent, Maximilian Joseph, despite his notorious incompetence. The comte de Sade departed once more with the mission of bringing the Elector of Cologne round to the fairly absurd French position. The instructions he received in January 1745 throw a cruel light on the astonishing naïveté of the French government. He was told, in effect, to appeal to "the Elector's good heart and affection for the late emperor's children and to his human obligations." Such an absence of political realism is breathtaking.

In any case the king's envoy set out on February 2, 1745. But no sooner had he left Paris than Clement Augustus indicated to the French authorities that "for private reasons" he did not wish to accept this ambassador and asked for another. This step proved unnecessary, because the count, upon entering the Elector's states and passing through the tiny village of Sinzing between Andernach and Bonn was caught in an ambush by irregular troops loyal to Maria Theresa and taken as a prisoner to the citadel of Antwerp.[13] Naturally Clement Augustus refused to demand his release. Meanwhile, the French court had just learned of its envoy's earlier misconduct and seemed in no great hurry to secure his freedom. D'Argenson triumphed: his dear friend the abbé Aunillon, who was already in Bonn, was named chargé d'affaires: "He works wonders," the minister rejoiced.

Though treated with all the respect due his rank, Jean-Baptiste attempted to forget his captivity by writing poems, stories, and memoirs. Informed of his misadventure, his friends sent him news of the court and the city, along with songs, jokes, and a thousand other bagatelles designed to amuse: Maupertuis was moving to Berlin, Mme d'Etiolles had become the "official mistress," the king had just won a victory at Fontenoy, the dauphin had married, Gresset had produced his play *Sidney*, a "mixture of the lugubrious and the clownish," the Opera was doing *Amadis de Grèce*, and so on. Voltaire sent him a charming letter together with his latest play, *La Princesse de Navarre*: "It is a work done on commission, which is supposed to be forgotten once the party is over," he warned. "But you want it, and to a prisoner everything is good." He concludes with a "thousand compliments" from Mme du Châtelet.[14]

The minute the comtesse de Sade learned of her husband's arrest, she called upon the good offices of her most influential acquaintances.

The duchess of Aremberg and the countess of Trotti promised their support. D'Argenson, whom she tirelessly assailed, sent her to the duc de Choiseul, who assured her that he would do everything in his power. But the king's consent was needed, and that depended on the minister. She went back to d'Argenson, but to no avail. She tried again, only to fail once more. She then wrote to Prince von Kaunitz, the Austrian ambassador in Paris, begging him to intervene; she literally bombarded him with letters.

Finally, after ten months in prison, the countess's zealous campaign not only to win his release but to reclaim the count's withheld stipend met with success. On November 16, 1745, d'Argenson wrote the following letter, whose venom is only partially concealed by its amiably commanding tone:

You know, Madame, what caused M. le comte de Sade's stipend to be suspended, and you also know that if he had not held on to the Elector of Cologne's letter of recall he would have continued to be paid and it would not have been necessary to seek the king's orders on the matter. Nevertheless, upon receiving the report that I had the honor to make concerning the sad situation in which [the count] finds himself and your own need for consolation given the misfortune that befell M. de Sade in the course of a journey he made in the king's service and on his express orders, His Majesty has commissioned me to tell you that he is awarding your husband the sum of 6,000 livres, money of France, as his stipend for six months, and I have issued an order to that effect. I have also dispatched letters to various places asking that the queen of Hungary be urged to release M. le comte de Sade, and I hope that these letters will produce the effect you anticipate.

I have the honor, Madame, with respect, to be your most humble and obedient servant.

d'Argenson

P.S. I have just received M. de Stainville's response with a copy of a letter from M. von Kaunitz that gives me some reason to hope.[15]

On November 23 the comte de Sade learned from Prince von Kaunitz himself that he would be released the next day, November 24, 1745.

•

From the moment he returned to Paris the comte de Sade sought by every means available to defend his honor and reestablish his situation. His most pressing need was to find a new post and regain at least some of his emoluments, since he stood on the brink of ruin. In Cologne he had lived in high style. His house was reputed to have been among the most splendid in the principality, admired as much for the sumptuousness of the furnishings as for the delicacy of its table and the quality of its wines, all ordered direct from Burgundy. The ostentation required by the count's mission accorded all too well with his passion for grandeur. He sacrificed everything to his love of show. Now, without credit or income, he offered himself for every vacant embassy. D'Argenson assured him of his "affectionate devotion" but refrained from proposing his name to Louis XV. Impatient, Sade wrote this letter:

No, truly, I am not complaining that you have not proposed me for an embassy. When you do me that honor, when you report to the king on my zeal to serve him, I shall be grateful to you for the favor. And were you to do nothing of the kind, I should not complain of your severity. What I call severe is to send me off with a promised stipend of twenty-four thousand francs and to tell me upon my return that the king is giving me only twelve.

I do not know if the king has many ministers employed at the rate of twelve thousand francs. But if he has, they are not of my sort, and I am not worried about being confused with them. The two thousand écus that you have granted me as a favor were partly [due] me because when I left I already had five weeks on the quarter. I believe that when His Majesty severs the stipend of his ministers or others employed in his service, he is good enough to inform them of the fact, for one adjusts one's expenditures to what one has. What is more, the two thousand écus in question barely sufficed to cover the costs of my travel. Is it right that I have been ten months out of pocket?

To be in slavery, far from one's family and country, unable to attend to one's affairs, and, what is more, deprived of the glory of being useful to one's master—is this not misfortune enough? If I have done something wrong, the loss of your good graces is a sufficiently harsh punishment. You need not ruin me as well.[16]

But d'Argenson was a man to bear a grudge. For him the comte de Sade remained the creature of the Condés, one of the "race of the Condés" as he contemptuously expressed it. Not daring to attack that powerful family head on, he went after its clients, and most of all after the man he considered his enemy's factotum: Jean-Baptiste de Sade.

Henceforth the count was used almost exclusively for inconsequential if not unillustrious missions. A man of society to the tips of his fingernails, he served as a figurehead in foreign courts, in roles more symbolic than they were substantial. In particular he was dispatched to find marriage prospects for royal princes. But never again would he be offered an embassy he considered worthy of his abilities.

The Gaffe

At the court of France his name remained shrouded in suspicion, which his enemies worked hard to perpetuate. All who saw themselves as adversaries of the Condés would be hostile to him, and their number was legion. Among the most notable of his enemies were the cliques of d'Argenson and Choiseul. All he needed was to incur the wrath of the king, and when that happened his disgrace became inevitable.

The count had the misfortune of displeasing His Majesty in circumstances that the abbé de Sade reported to his brother on December 15, 1744:

I spent several days in Montpellier with M. le maréchal de Richelieu, who was more friendly to me than ever.[17] For some time now I have been bothered by something he let slip concerning you. I asked him for details. He told me that you had railed against him and Madame de Châteauroux in the presence of friends of that lady, who had reported the incident to him, and that she was especially irritated because she had resolved to help you and your wife, who was her friend; she has spoken to the king about the incident, and since then he has been highly annoyed with you. I assured him that you were not capable of any such thing, that it was pure calumny, that you had always seemed to me highly devoted to Mme de Châteauroux and incapable of ingratitude. That is all I was able to get out of him.[18]

The count received this letter shortly after the duchesse de Châteauroux, the king's mistress, died, on December 8, 1744, at the age of twenty-seven, of a disease as mysterious as it was sudden. Panicked by his brother's revelations, he immediately asked for further explanations. The abbé responded on January 26, 1745, in veiled terms:

I cannot tell you anything about what you wish to know. I know no details. The man who is going to England [Richelieu] told me only that his master [Louis XV] was very annoyed with you owing to certain things you had said about the dead woman [Mme de Châteauroux]. When I tried to defend you, he laughed in my face and assured me that the story was true, and it seemed to me that he was quite stung by it. That is all I know . . .[19]

Connected with the Noailles and powerfully supported by the duc de Richelieu's clan, which had plotted two years earlier to attract Louis XV's favor to her, the duchesse de Châteauroux had enjoyed considerable credit at court. In attacking her the comte de Sade committed an act of imprudence for which he would repent the rest of his life. This offense to the royal mistress earned him the lasting enmity not only of the sovereign but of all those who would henceforth be afraid to be counted among his friends.

•

I have spent a considerable amount of time on the career of Jean-Baptiste de Sade, in part because it will help us to understand the change in attitude, born of bitterness, that would gradually lead him into more substantial occupations and more serious forms of thought, ending ultimately in his religious conversion, but even more because the social ostracism of which he was the victim would also affect his son. Donatien's start in life was certainly hampered by the count's bad reputation, and his later misfortunes may be blamed in part on his father's disgrace.

3

Uprooting

During the comte de Sade's long absences, little Donatien lived in the hôtel de Condé with his mother, the princess's lady-in-waiting, who, owing to her position, occupied a large apartment on the second floor of the building situated between the so-called Court of the Archives and the second courtyard.[1] Located at numbers 9–15 of the present rue de Condé, the hôtel's gardens extended almost to the rues de Vaugirard and Monsieur-le-Prince. It was one of the most magnificent residences in the capital. "As for the furniture," Germain Brice marveled, "it is difficult to find any other palace with a richer or more numerous selection. There are also paintings by masters of the first rank, among them a *Baptism of Our Lord* by Albano, which for a long time belonged to the duc de Lesdiguières, extraordinary tapestries, which come from the illustrious house of Montmorency, and more gems than anywhere else. The palace also houses a large library of curiosa and the rarest of playing cards. The garden must be seen: in a limited space it shows that art and nature when joined together always yield very considerable pleasures. There are trellised nooks in the Dutch manner, very meticulously done. At the end of each path there is a small victory arch of similar workmanship. In summertime the garden is filled with orange trees and bushes that make it a very pleasant place to stroll."[2]

At his death on January 27, 1740, the very year in which the marquis de Sade was born, Louis-Henri de Condé left a son, aged four, Louis-Joseph de Bourbon, who would become Donatien's playmate. The late duke's brother, the comte de Charolais, became guardian of the young prince. Charolais did not reside in the hôtel but made frequent visits to his nephew. And since the two children were raised together under the supervision of Mme de Roussillon, Louis-Joseph's governess, the guardian could not avoid seeing Donatien as well. Thus from earliest childhood the future marquis de Sade would have constantly before his eyes a man who embodied, to a rare degree of perfection, the concept to which the marquis would give his name.

Indeed, the comte de Charolais was reputed to be one of the most truly "sadistic" men of his time. Never had anyone taken such pleasure in crime. He killed his fellow human beings for sport, as other men went hunting. One day he shot a man in the town of Anet to prove his skill with a gun: "Watch, I'll shoot that body there!" His favorite amusement was to fire a musket at workmen repairing nearby roofs. When he hit one, he jumped for joy. To avoid prosecution he then went to the king and begged forgiveness. One day, tired of his petitions, Louis XV is supposed to have answered: "Monsieur, the pardon you ask of me is due your rank and quality as prince of the blood, but I shall be even more pleased to pardon the man who does the same to you." ("Sublime reply!" the marquis de Sade would later comment.) Charolais had a son by a woman named Delisle, a prostitute who was a favorite of the Condés. When the child fell ill some time between its sixth and eighth month, Charolais caused him to swallow a glassful of spirits that killed him instantly. "That child certainly was not mine," the prince exclaimed, "if that drink made him die!"[3] Mathieu Marais tells another story about the count's insane behavior. In a fit of jealousy he went looking for Delisle one day in a café below her apartment between the rue de Richelieu and the Palais-Royal. He had the establishment surrounded by the watch and bludgeoned the unfortunate patrons. Afterward, while returning via rue Traversière, he spotted the woman he was after, seized her, slapped her twice and kicked her in the behind, ordered her up to her room, removed her clothes, rained blows on her servants, ordered supper to be served, and ended by spending the night with her.[4]

A thousand other examples of his ferocity could easily be cited. "All the vices were part of his character, except those that aristocrats of the day still called *bassesses* (low, contemptible actions) . . . Charolais had genius and talent, but his heart was cruel and his actions were bloody . . . Debauches of all kinds were to his taste, at first singly, then all together. He was energetic and particularly bold, but because his upbringing was flawed, he abused these fine qualities."[5]

How could the future author of *Justine* forget such a wicked *grand seigneur*? As for his playmate, little Prince Louis-Joseph de Condé, four years older than the marquis, the duc de Luynes described him as big for his age and well-built but quarrelsome. "He is prodigiously serious," the duke adds. "He does not look like either his father or his mother, but he is very blond." Furthermore, "people are already saying that he is strong-willed. M. de Charolais occasionally has him punished for that reason."[6]

The School for Scorn

Donatien's character was no better. Raised in the conviction that he belonged to a superior species, he was soon schooled in that aristocratic haughtiness of demeanor known as *morgue*. From a very early age he believed himself to be above others and entitled to use them as he saw fit, to speak and act as a master without censure of conscience or humanity. At the age of four his despotic nature was already formed. The years to come would only harden it. Blind to the world around him, he soon shut himself up behind a wall of incommunicability and incomprehension, cutting himself off from others in his vicinity, even those he loved—especially those he loved. From earliest childhood his actions reflected a tragic inability to speak.

His violent nature outweighed all considerations of prudence or self-interest, even with his playmate Louis-Joseph de Bourbon, who was also his master. Donatien would always reject all principles of moderation. But let him describe his own games and rages as a child. His lucidity renders any commentary superfluous:

Connected, through my mother, to all that was greatest in the kingdom; attached, through my father, to all that was most distinguished in the province of Languedoc; born in Paris in the bosom of luxury and plenty, I believed, from the time I could reason, that nature and fortune had joined together to heap their gifts upon me; I believed it because people were foolish enough to tell me so, and this ridiculous prejudice made me haughty, despotic, and angry. It seemed that everything must give in to me, that the whole world must flatter my whims, and that it was up to me alone to conceive and satisfy them. I shall recall for you only one feature of my childhood to convince you of the dangerous principles that others so ineptly allowed to germinate in me.

Since I was born and raised in the palace of the illustrious prince to which my mother had the honor of belonging, and who was of roughly my age, people hastened to forge a bond between him and me, so that by being known to him from childhood I might count on his support throughout my life. But my vanity of the moment, which still understood nothing of such calculations, being offended one day in our childish games that he coveted something in my possession, and still more that with his most illustrious titles he no doubt thought he was entitled to it by virtue of his rank, I avenged myself for his resistance with repeated blows, which no consideration could stop, and nothing short of force and violence could separate me from my adversary.[7]

It was no doubt following this incident or one like it that the comte de Sade, worried by the course that things were taking, decided to send the boy to Provence. Donatien had just begun his fifth year; it was time to humble his pride by introducing him to the harsh realities of life. On August 16, 1744, the community of Saumane dispatched its consuls and secretary to Avignon "to compliment M. le marquis de Sade, son of M. le comte, lord of this place, on his happy arrival in Avignon, and to wish him long and happy years as his presumptive heir."[8] The thought of these eminent citizens bowing to a child of four is rather amusing. But the budding nobleman did not smile: he took his role quite seriously.

Saumane–Silling

Grandmother d'Astouaud was quietly growing old in the shadow of the papal legate's modest ecclesiastical court and in the practice of a worldly religion, while the marquis's religious aunts wore out their eyes on pious works and psalms. They welcomed the child as a veritable Jesus, plied him with candy and caresses, and immediately created a kind of cult around him. Was he not the sole inheritor of the family name, the only male descendant? His birth in a princely household, his upbringing in the company of a Bourbon, and his father's high position at Versailles enhanced Donatien's prestige in this devout provincial milieu, a fact of which he was only too well aware. He was a marvel, a miracle, an idol whose every whim was indulged. Knowing this, the apprentice tyrant asked for everything and got it, only to become more unbearable than ever. "I was sent to a grandmother in Languedoc, whose hopelessly blind affection fostered all the faults I have just confessed," he would later admit.[9]

Seeing that these women, with all their coddling, were only en-

couraging the boy's mischief, the count begged his brother the abbé
to take him into his home in Saumane. Only a masculine authority
could control the lad, his father believed. The request came at an
inopportune moment, because Paul Aldonse de Sade had just been
named commendatory abbot of the Cistercian abbey Saint-Léger
d'Ebreuil in Auvergne, an appointment that required him to spend
part of the year there.[10] But never mind, Donatien would follow him
in his travels. And since it was also time to find the boy a tutor, the
count was advised to hire a young Savoyard, a tonsured cleric from
the diocese of Geneva, a twenty-nine-year-old native of Annecy by the
name of Jacques François Amblet. Although he had made substantial
theological studies, he was not ordained and held no ecclesiastical
charge, hence he was perfectly free. The abbé was delighted with the
choice:

M. Amblet has arrived, my dear brother. His journey was most pleasant. I
cannot yet make a judgment; I do not know him. All that I can tell you is that
he is intelligent and kind. Unless I miss my guess, you have made a find for
your son. I shall soon send you a more definite assessment. In the meantime
I am quite pleased to have him with me. He is learning to tutor from a woman
friend of mine to whom he is teaching Italian. He seems to be going about it
quite skillfully.[11]

•

Donatien had heard a great deal about the château de Saumane. He
knew that it had always belonged to his family and that his father had
rented it for life to the abbé, but he certainly was not prepared for what
he was going to find. No doubt he imagined something like the hôtel
de Condé transported to the countryside, a palace bulging with tapestries, works of art, and fine furniture and endowed with sumptuously
painted ceilings, marble staircases, and brocaded walls. What a disappointment!

Perched on a rocky crag overlooking the village, halfway between
L'Isle-sur-la-Sorgue and Vaucluse, and squeezed between two narrow
depressions, the château dominated the whole valley. The view from
its terrace embraced some thirty towns and villages from the mountain
of Vaucluse to the Alpilles, from the Luberon to the Cévennes. The
twelfth-century *castrum*, altered in the fourteenth and fifteenth centuries, has miraculously escaped destruction, and one can still see it
today much as Donatien, then almost five, discovered it for the first
time. From the outside it has the somber, graceless look of a fortress:
uniformly gray walls six feet thick, a walkway, loopholes, cannon. To

the north and west there are bastions and casemates with large openings for artillery pieces. The façade is tall and smooth, and the eye searches in vain for the slightest ornament. The one entryway, sealed by a portcullis, is reached by a drawbridge spanning a deep moat hollowed out in the rock. The interior, less austere, has the appearance of a handsome aristocratic residence, with great vaulted halls and a majestic Renaissance staircase with panels. Upon taking up residence the abbé de Sade added new windows and enlarged others, decorated several apartments, and constructed an *orangerie*. He also installed a studio for the pursuit of natural history and a medal room. The coat of arms of the old lords can still be seen engraved in the stone ceilings: the star with eight rays of gold bearing an eagle with wings unfurled.

This was Donatien's new home—and his first prison. In visiting Saumane one cannot help thinking of the other fortresses—Pierre-Encize, Miolans, Vincennes, the Bastille—that would loom so large in the marquis's imagination. Nor can one help conjuring up the walls of the château de Silling and the voluptuous rituals they concealed, because with Sade the world of pleasure always coincided with the world of prisons. But the visitor to Saumane is most struck by the deep cellars, the secret, subterranean galleries that date back to the thirteenth century, in which windowless, airless cells were hollowed out. The ground is still littered with the chains of the unfortunates who were incarcerated here and forgotten, without hope of returning to the world. It is an ideal torture chamber, since from here no cry can reach the outside world. The thought of endless confinement, solitude, and anguish is dizzying. These dark tombs made a profound impression on young Donatien.[12] Their memory would haunt the author of *Cent Vingt Journées de Sodome* as he described the "entrails" of the château de Durcet: "A fatal rock was lifted mechanically from underneath the steps of the altar of the little Christian temple we pointed out in the gallery. There one found a very narrow, very steep spiral staircase with three hundred steps, which descended into the entrails of the earth and a kind of vaulted dungeon sealed by three iron gates and containing all that the cruelest art and most refined barbarity could invent in the way of atrocity, as much to terrify the senses as to perform the most horrifying acts . . . Woe, a thousand woes, unto the unfortunate creature who in her distress found herself at the mercy of a lawless, godless scoundrel, who was amused by crime and had no interest there other than his passions and nothing to restrain him other than the imperious laws of his perfidious desires."[13]

The Licentious Abbé de Sade

Born on September 21, 1705, Jacques François Paul Aldonse, abbé de Sade, had just turned forty when he welcomed his nephew to Saumane. Vicar-general of Toulouse in 1733, then of Narbonne in 1735, he was sent by the Estates of Languedoc on a mission to the court and resided for several years in Paris, where he lived on intimate terms with Mme de La Popelinière, a charming woman twenty years his senior and the established mistress of the maréchal de Richelieu. Richelieu, though not unaware of the situation, made no attempt to find out if the abbé consoled the lady during his frequent absences and saw to it that she continued to receive her regular allowance.

Ardent in love, the abbé gave free rein to his instinct for gallantry and love of letters. Close to Voltaire and Mme du Châtelet, who held him in high esteem, he and the couple exchanged splendid letters full of wit and civilities. When Jacques François was named grand vicar of Toulouse, the *philosophe* commented ironically on his double ministry as priest and libertine:

They say you are going to be priest and grand vicar. That's quite a few sacraments for one family. No wonder you tell me you're going to renounce love . . . Your verse and your prose are surely the work of a man who knows how to please. I am so sick that I won't say any more about it. And in any case what better could I find to say than that I love you with all my heart? . . . Farewell, I shall be devoted to you throughout my brief life. Volt.[14]

Mme du Châtelet was also won over by the sprightly priest, whose witty prose was better than his verse. "M. l'abbé de Sade owes it to me to be my friend," wrote the *divine Emilie*, "because he is one of the men I like best. I am sure that his wit and character will have pleased you, unless four or five years of priestifying have terribly spoiled him."[15] The purity of his style, his vast knowledge, and his way of mixing irony with the most serious observations gave his letters a lively and powerful elegance.

A Gentleman's Library

At Saumane the abbé spent long hours with books he had assembled with love and discernment. In addition to Greek and Latin authors, theological treatises, books of history and geography, works of erudition, and travel accounts, his shelves groaned with all that was fit to grace a gentleman's library: Locke's *Essay Concerning Human Understanding*, Bayle's *Pensées diverses*, the marquis d'Argens's *Lettres chinoises*, Montesquieu's *Oeuvres*, and Hobbes's *De Cive*, along with the major classical authors of the previous century: Malherbe, Boileau, La Fontaine, Mme de Sévigné, Racine, Molière, Regnard, and such novels and novellas as *Don Quixote*, the abbé Prévost's *Mémoires et aventures d'un homme de qualité*, Le Sage's *Le Diable boiteux*, Mme de Pringy's *L'Amour à la mode*, and Mlle de Lubert's *La Princesse Sensible et le prince Typhon*.

New works joined these as they were published: *La Nouvelle Héloïse, Emile, The Social Contract, Letters Written from the Mountain* and other works by Rousseau, Voltaire's *Ingénu* and his plays, Diderot's plays, the works of Gresset and Destouches, and Cardinal de Bernis's *Poésies diverses*. There were also works that had been condemned or were highly controversial such as Jean-Frédéric Bernard's *Le Monde, son origine et son antiquité*, Charles de Brosses's *Culte des dieux fétiches*, Beccaria's *Treatise on Crimes and Punishments*, and Ange Goudar's *L'Espion chinois*.

Other, lighter works were intended to distract the abbé from his learned labors: the (apocryphal) *Memoirs* of Mme de Pompadour, for example, or Pidansat de Mairobert's *Anecdotes sur Mme du Barry*. The comte de Sade's friend Crébillon was the best represented of contemporary authors: *La Nuit et le Moment, Ah quel Conte!, Le Hasard du coin du feu, Dialogue moral, Lettres de la duchesse de *** au duc de ***, Les Heureux Orphelins, Les Egarements du coeur et de l'esprit, Tanzaï et Néadarné, Le Sopha*, and *Lettres athéniennes*, among other works.[16]

Here, in silence and solitude, bent over his desk, the abbé de Sade labored on his great work, the *Memoirs for the Life of Francesco Petrarca*, to which he devoted twenty years of research. This was not only a homage to his ancestor Laure de Sade but a monument of erudition concerning the political and literary history of fourteenth-century Italy. Not a single notable personage of the period went unmentioned nor a single remarkable event unreported or unilluminated. The abbé de Sade cited all of Petrarch's biographers and commentators, discussed their opinions, and corrected a large number of errors. But even this labor did not occupy him fully. He also worked on a book (never published) about the French poets and troubadours of the Middle Ages and in his spare time wrote a history of the village of Saumane, about which he possessed voluminous documentation. For relaxation he engaged in research into his family's genealogy. Genealogy was in fact his passion; he spent days deciphering old parchments and transcribing them from Latin to French in his beautiful, unhurried hand.

It was in the abbé's *cabinet* that Donatien began his study of the humanities under the guidance of his tutor. He knew its arrangement so well that he could locate almost any book with his eyes closed. His hand found its way unerringly to the six huge ledgers of the Sade cartulary, which contained, in chronological order, step by step, the entire history of his ancestors from the thirteenth century down to himself, together with a host of legal documents: wills, marriage contracts, receipts, honorific titles, and diplomas on huge, finely calligraphed sheets of yellowing vellum.[17] Among other things that Donatien acquired from the abbé was surely his feeling for archives.

He knew all the nooks and crannies of the library, even the most secret ones, where the abbé hid his small collection of licentious literature. As he approached adolescence he surely must have explored these works without the knowledge of his uncle and the abbé Amblet. The collection included the works of Aretino, the *Lauriers ecclésiastiques*, published in "Luxuropolis," *Les Jésuites en belle humeur*, and *Le Philotanus moderne*. His eyes certainly came to rest on this alluring title: *Le Bordel ou le Jean-Foutre débauché* (The Bordello, or Everyman Debauched), with its enigmatic publisher's address: "A Anconne, chez la veuve Grosse-Motte" (Incunt, at Widow Big Mound's).

A small calf-bound duodecimo volume on a nearby shelf would also have attracted his attention. Its title page reads: *History of the Flagellants, in which the good and bad uses of flagellation among the Christians are pointed out. Translated from the Latin by Abbé B****, Amsterdam, 1701. The initial *B* concealed the identity of the abbé Jacques Boileau, a doctor of theology and distinguished controversialist, who reexamined a question raised a half-century earlier by the German physician Meibomius in his *Epistola de flagrorum usu in re venerea*, to wit, whether there was a "bad use" of flagellation.[18] The dauntless abbé Boileau dwelt at length on the ways in which flagellation could excite the senses and discoursed learnedly on the grave question of whether it was better to discipline oneself on the back or on the buttocks. He also mentions numerous cases in which the whip stimulated *furia amorosa*. Pleasure through suffering: there was a precept Donatien would not soon forget.

The library's "forbidden" shelves were not his only source of initiation into the mysteries of sex, however. He had only to observe his good uncle. The abbé did not spend day and night with his parchments, and those who believed he had settled down were sadly mistaken. What is more, he lived not alone but in the company of two women, a mother and daughter, of whom he made free use, to the great scandal of the village busybodies. There was also a great deal of gossip about the proprietress of a tavern, a notorious prostitute, whom the abbé protected, as well as about a maid by the name of Marie Curt for whom he hastily arranged a marriage with a local youth named Pépin. "Priest though he is, he still has a pair of trollops in his house," Donatien would write a few years later. "Is his château a seraglio? No, better still, it's a bordello." In the same letter, written when he was twenty-five and in justification of his own escapades, he adds: "Forgive my mischief. I am taking up the family spirit, and if I have anything to reproach myself for, it is to have had the misfortune of being born into it. God keep me from all the foolishness and vice with which it is rife. I should think myself almost virtuous if by the grace of God I were to take up only a portion of the family's evils."[19]

To conclude this section on the libertine life of the abbé de Sade, I should mention that on May 25, 1762, during a stay in Paris, he was caught in the act at a select house of prostitution in the rue du Chantre kept by a woman named Moisson, also known as Piron. He was found there in the company of a prostitute known as Léonore but whose real name was Marie-Françoise Thérèse Dieu (God). Thus, in the words of the police report, the abbé "knew carnally to the point of complete copulation" a woman who bore the name of his Maker!

The Happy Days

Meanwhile, the months and the years passed without incident. Saumane was seven leagues from Avignon. This was a considerable distance, too far for daily contact, and news of the "city" reached the castle only after a delay and as if muffled by distance. News of Paris was rarer still. Mail arrived only once a week. In the village and surrounding countryside the paths were too steep and narrow to permit the use of a carriage. Travel was by muleback, and one has to imagine the abbé de Sade and his nephew riding down the mountainside on their mules and wearing straw hats to protect them from the sun. As crickets chirped the two men would have made their way at a gentle trot down pebble-strewn trails cut into the wall of rock, followed the roiling waters of the Sorgue to the town of L'Isle, where the river divided into several branches, and entered the maze of narrow, poorly paved streets. Sometimes, at a spot a quarter of a league from the castle, they stopped to pay homage to the memory of Laura and Petrarch where a small house surrounded by gardens once had stood. There the poet had sought refuge far from the vexations of Avignon. "Not a trace of it remains," the abbé noted. "The residents of Vaucluse have carried off all the stones." A short distance away, at a place called Fontaine, the Sorgue gushes in a torrent from the foot of a cliff and crashes thunderously onto enormous moss-covered rocks.

There being no prince of the blood in the vicinity, Donatien found his playmates among the peasants of the village and nearby farms and occasionally among the sons of the *bourgeois*, the doctors, merchants, and lawyers of the town. From them he learned the Provençal dialect whose flavor he loved and never forgot. He probably adopted their accent and something of their way of life as well. In the company of these provincial children the young Parisian not only discovered the rural soul but measured the prerogatives that he would one day enjoy as their lord. In other words, he played a role with these local children analogous to that which the young Condé had played with him. Did he make them aware of his superiority? Undoubtedly, for caste prejudice would remain one of the most constant traits of his personality.

Among Donatien's playmates was a boy of about his own age with whom he soon became friends: Gaspard François Xavier Gaufridy. He was the son of a businessman from Apt who managed the comte de Sade's properties. Gaspard and Donatien got on wonderfully. They took long hikes together and stayed at La Coste with Donatien's grandmother d'Astouaud. Often Donatien's little cousin, Pauline, the daughter of Mme de Villeneuve, played with the boys in the château's lower great hall. Memories of these childhood games were among the rare souvenirs that the marquis would later share with his erstwhile companion.

Back in Saumane life resumed its monotonous course, interrupted by sojourns at the abbey in Ebreuil on the banks of the Sioule, whose well-cultivated estates afforded their commendatory abbot a comfortable income. The fact of the matter is that Paul Aldonse de Sade took little interest in his monks and mismanaged their property so badly that he soon brought the abbey to the brink of ruin.[20] In the meantime his dissolute life sowed scandal in the heart of the community.

•

Donatien thus spent all his childhood years with his uncle and tutor and without any female presence other than that of the abbé's "companions." Taken from his mother at the age of four, transported to a princely palace on a rocky summit, imprisoned in a fortress with a libertine priest, and surrounded by debauched women: all the ingredients of a Sade novel are present in this early traumatic experience. The abbé de Sade's château served the same dual and paradoxical function as the château de Silling: to inflict torture and protect from punishment, to imprison evil and liberate crime.

"Cherished" Studies

In the fall of 1750 (as Donatien began his eleventh year), the comte de Sade decided to recall his son from Saumane and enroll him in a large Parisian *collège* (grammar school). He nursed high ambitions for the boy, ambitions that could never be realized if he left him in a hole in Provence. Donatien, accompanied by the abbé d'Amblet, therefore set out for Paris by postal coach, an episode that he would later recount in the autobiographical passages of *Aline et Valcour*, where he has warm praise for his tutor: "I returned to Paris for my studies, accompanied by a steadfast and highly intelligent man, well suited to mold my youth, I am certain, but whom, to my misfortune, I did not keep long enough."[21]

After arriving in the capital Donatien entered the Collège Louis-le-Grand, a school kept by the Jesuits on the rue Saint-Jacques in the heart of the school district. He lived either with abbé Amblet in the rue des Fossés-Monsieur-le-Prince, "opposite the cartwright," or with his mother at the hôtel de Condé, a short distance from the rue Saint-Jacques.

Louis-le-Grand at the time was the school where all nobles sent their children and reputedly one of the most expensive in Paris. In choosing to send his son there the comte de Sade imposed a sacrifice on himself, all the more so in that his financial situation had continued to deteriorate over the past few years. In 1752 he considered sending Donatien to Lyons, where schools were less costly. There was even talk of selling Saumane or his land at Glatigny to continue paying the boy's tuition. Short of that, he reduced his expenditures as much as possible and accepted the invitation of his former mistress, Mlle de Charolais, to join her at her château d'Athis-Mons. In November 1752 he again found himself short of funds and asked for help from one of his uncles, the provost of the church of L'Isle-sur-la-Sorgue: "Today I ask only for your advice. Consult with my brother,[22] who is in the area. Figure out together what my son should be spending, and see to it that the stipend is sent directly to M. Amblet. If there is not enough to leave him in school in Paris, I will send him to one in Lyons. If I must retire to a monastery to spend less, I will go. It will not cost me anything. At last, my dear uncle, the moment has come when I need your friendship. Advise me, and rest assured that I am prepared to do all I can to prove my affection and respect."[23]

The Theater of Good Fathers

Declared a royal foundation by Louis XIV, with all the rights attached to that title, Louis-le-Grand was one of the most illustrious schools in the kingdom. It served nearly five hundred pupils, including all the jeunesse dorée: the Contis, the Bouillons, the Soubises, the Villars, the Montmorencys. The teachers were also among the best. Some even acquired a measure of notoriety, such as Father Buffier; Father Porée, the celebrated abbé d'Olivet, who became Voltaire's colleague in the Académie; the abbé de Châteauneuf, a distinguished musicologist, who introduced young Arouet (Voltaire), then aged thirteen, to [the illustrious courtesan] Ninon de Lenclos; and Father Tournemine, who also taught young Arouet and later became a friend of his friend as well as of the comte de Sade.

More "literary" than the Oratorians, the Jesuits excelled in the teaching of Latin, Greek, and rhetoric. But they also had another specialty, one to which Donatien certainly was not indifferent. Striving above all to educate men of the world, the good fathers initiated their disciples in the arts, especially theater, which occupied a central role in the life of the school. They organized dramatic presentations and staged tragedies, comedies, pastorals, and even oratorios and operas, which the good fathers generally wrote themselves on edifying subjects and assigned their students to interpret with the aid of professional dancers from the Opera. They acquired such a reputation, in fact, that they drew audiences from outside the school, as enthusiastic as they were select, consisting not only of parents of students but also of great lords and ladies from the court. The school's productions were notable for their sumptuous scenery and complex machinery, which served to evoke splendid palaces, grand perspectives, colonnades, and fantastic landscapes.[24] Formal performances were held every year in August, when school prizes were given out in the main courtyard. A vast canvas tent covered spectators ranged in three amphitheaters, and all the windows of the school's buildings served as loges. There was also an indoor theater for winter performances and rehearsals in preparation for the August ceremonies.

The Jesuits put on no fewer than seventeen plays and ballets during Donatien's time at Louis-le-Grand (August 1750 to the end of the school year 1753). Since he did not become a student until the autumn of 1750, he was present for only fifteen of these. Did he make his début as an actor on any of these occasions? The honor of appearing on stage was reserved for the best students. Some of the programs describe the performers in tragedies as *selecti rhetores*. But Donatien never once figured on the end-of-the-year list of prizewinners.

Even if he did not enjoy the privilege of performing on the stage of Louis-le-Grand, he took away from these plays in which he participated if only as a spectator a passion for the theater that would stay with him for the rest of his life. His taste for the machinery of the theater, as revealed in a fantasy like *La Tour enchantée*, surely came from these marvelous school spectacles. And all the theatricality of Sadeian eroticism, with its sexual choreography, its tableaux vivants and ballets of postures, drew on the same reservoir of memories but subverted them, diverted them from their original function. There is theater, too, in the pleasure machines that Sade was forever inventing in works like *Justine* and *Juliette*: the whipping machine, the raping machine, the impregnating machine, and the orgasm machine (the Prince of Francaville's automatic dildo).

Loyola's Rods

The entertainments produced by the Jesuits should not be allowed to obscure their essential vocation, which was the education of children. The regime at Louis-le-Grand does not seem to have been particularly severe compared with that of other *collèges*. Its schedule demanded neither extraordinarily hard work nor extremes of piety. The school day as such was nine hours long, beginning at 5:30 in the morning and interrupted for lunch, dinner, snack, and supper, each meal being followed by a recess. Religious exercises consumed no more than an hour a day: a half-hour for mass and two quarter-hour prayers. Clearly the good fathers had no intention of inspiring a distaste for religion in the young gentlemen entrusted to their care.

By contrast, they maintained the tradition of corporal punishment in all its rigor. In the eighteenth century the whip was an essential adjunct of the educational system. An *Instruction for Christian School Masters* published in 1708 recommended that they not spare the rod: "The rod is necessary. It produces good behavior, and it must be used when fear and kindness require its aid. Slaps, kicks, and punches are to be avoided, as are ruler blows to the head and stomach. The ears should not be pulled violently, and anger and rage are to be avoided.

All these things are dangerous in their consequences for the children. They serve only to foster rebellion and to reveal the passion of the master."[25] The Princess Palatine adhered to the same principles in raising her son. In her diary for February 15, 1710, she noted: "When my son was little, I never slapped him, but I whipped him so hard that he still remembers it. Slaps are dangerous." To judge from his behavior, the Regent derived little benefit from his mother's whippings.

Thus slaps were deemed humiliating, whereas the whip was seen as a noble punishment. No one escaped whipping, and the most illustrious posteriors in France submitted to the canes of the Molinists. But to confine our attention to Louis-le-Grand, consider this "burning" memory reported by d'Argenson, who was seventeen at the time of the incident: "I had the whip, or something very like, in my next to last year in rhetoric, in 1711. My friend the duc de Boufflers, then acting governor of Flanders and colonel of his regiment, who was in the same class, had the whip for the same reason. We had together hatched a kind of rebellion against Father Le Jay, our regent. We shot peas at him with a peashooter." The episode caused quite a stir. The maréchal de Boufflers complained to the king about it and withdrew his son from the school. "The poor boy was terribly upset. A few months later he came down with smallpox and died."[26] For laudable reasons of delicacy fathers were not supposed to whip their children themselves. The task was entrusted to a servant, whose job it was to inflict the *ultima ratio patrum* on the unfortunate child.

Although the importance of corporal punishment in religious schools has often been exaggerated, its practice nevertheless maintained a climate of violence in these establishments that could not fail to make an impression on newcomers. The students of course did not submit to these punishments passively, and Mercier recounts that in the Collège Mazarin one student turned on the preceptor who was whipping him and stabbed him to death. Similar incidents occurred at other schools in Paris and the provinces.

Another danger, doubtless more insidious but no less common, was that corporal punishment could arouse the victim sexually. As everyone knows, Rousseau felt erotic pleasure when he received his first spanking from Mlle Lambercier. It may be that Donatien discovered at Louis-le-Grand a form of pleasure that he would later cultivate enthusiastically. Anal-erotic sexuality often originates in this type of experience, and Sade's work is of course full of it. If the Sadeian myth has focused essentially on the inflicting of pain ("sadism"), it must be kept in mind that pleasure in suffering ("masochism") was no less important an element in the marquis's sexual behavior. He took as much pleasure in the blows he received as in those he inflicted.

Sodomy, moreover, was known to be widespread in the *collèges*, and if public opinion is to be believed the good fathers made a specialty of it. They were accused not only of running hotbeds of pederasty and of encouraging, indeed fomenting, "special friendships" but also of attacking their own students. Although these charges were wildly exaggerated by pamphleteers and songwriters of the time, they were not entirely without foundation. My earlier research in the police archives turned up some interesting revelations in this regard.[27]

Did the Jesuits introduce Donatien to the *vice italien*, of which he became such a fervent adept? Did the fact that he always assumed the passive role in homosexual relations stem from punitive flagellation? There is a close connection between passivity and masochism and even a desire for persecution. Did Donatien find in suffering and even shame the "mélange of sensuality" that threw Rousseau into a panic? Would he say, as did the author of the *Confessions*: "This child's punishment . . . determined my tastes, my desires, my passions, my self, for the rest of my life"? For Donatien as for Rousseau "normal" sex never yielded more than incomplete satisfaction, and his sexuality became fixed very early at an infantile stage. In both men passive pleasure and happy humiliation defined an erogenous zone beyond the limits of normality. Yet Sade's masochism, unlike ordinary masochism (such as Rousseau's), was devoid of all imaginative content. It did not give rise to any scenario of humiliation, narrative fantasy, or other form of literary expression but was wholly circumscribed within a point-by-point inversion of sadism. The distinction generally drawn between the two forms of behavior, the one (sadism) transitive, the other (masochism) intransitive, vanishes in favor of an absolute complementarity of the two poles. Sade's primary figure of pleasure was the coincidence of heterosexual sodomy with passive penetration (or the endurance of pain), wherein a single body became the locus of contrary perversions.

Theatricality, flagellation, sodomy, passivity: all the themes that make up Sadeian eroticism were thus potentially combined in his actual or fantasized experience at Louis-le-Grand. Add to these the crimes of the comte de Charolais, the dungeons of Saumane, the abbé's whores, the father's mistresses, and the mother's abandonment: the structures are in place, the scene is set, the characters are cast. Let the show begin! But was the outcome determined in advance? Sade thought so, when in a dazzling moment of insight he wrote, a century before Freud, that "it is in the mother's breast that the organs are fashioned which make us susceptible to this or that fantasy. The first objects presented, the first utterances heard, complete the construction of the mechanism. The tastes form, and from then on nothing in the world can destroy them."

4

"A most unusual child"

The Lady of Longeville

Specialists on Sade often deplore the absence of all information on their hero's adolescence. "No family correspondence from this period has survived," Gilbert Lely lamented. Yet in working on the same family archives that Lely used I had the good fortune to discover an important exchange of letters between the comte de Sade and a mysterious lady of Longeville. These unpublished letters help to fill the gap in the marquis's life between his eleventh and eighteenth years. Little by little an image emerges of an adolescent with delicate features and a sensitive, secretive soul. For the first time we glimpse the marquis de Sade in the unspoiled nudity of childhood.

Every year when school ended (that is, in late August or early September), Donatien left Paris to spend his vacations at the château de Longeville near Fismes in Champagne with one of his father's former mistresses, the comtesse de Raimond, widow of Roger, comte de Raimond and governor of Ingolstadt. This aristocrat from Saintonge lived an extraordinary life. Sentenced to death in 1698 for having murdered a man in a dispute, he was exiled to Germany, where he entered the service of the duke of Bavaria. Twenty-four years later, after winning annulment of his sentence and restoration of his fortune, he returned to France. It was probably around this time that he married Jeanne-Marie de Bède de Blaye de Montrozier, the daughter of an army commissary in Charleville and thirty-three years his junior (she was born in 1705). A short while later she met the comte de Sade and fell passionately in love with him. Years passed; the comte de Raimond died around 1750, and his wife retired to the château de Longeville.

The capricious Jean-Baptiste had the knack of moving from one woman to another without incurring the hatred of the one he left. He possessed a kind of gift (perhaps one ought to call it genius) for turning his former conquests into trustworthy friends and loyal confidantes, all the more zealous to serve him because they cherished, in memory of past transgressions, mixed feelings of gratitude and tenderness. Long after the end of their affair Mme de Raimond felt warm affection for the man she lovingly called "my Sade." But her passion now focused primarily on his son, the charming Donatien, to whom she always referred in her letters as "my son," "our son," or "our child."

The château de Longeville was located below the commune of Dravegny in a narrow valley roughly opposite the hamlet of Montaon on the banks of a small river, the Orillon. Apart from a barn and the ruins of a grain mill, virtually nothing remains of the old castle, but on the ground one can still see distinct traces of the moats that surrounded this once imposing fortress, burned during the Fronde but reconstructed around 1650. According to Mme de Raimond it was already fairly dilapidated a century later. When the comte de Sade proposed a visit, she sent this warning: "Expect to find an old house. My bridge is brand new, or at any rate rebuilt, but my beautiful moats are as green as meadows and full of reeds and my gardens are neglected. It's a great pity. We haven't so much as a handful of parsley or a head of lettuce or a piece of fruit, but we have heart, and that makes everything tolerable, everything seem good." On another occasion she wrote: "We have no walking path. The only one I have is condemned: the little garden bridge frightens me. They are working on it, but it won't be done before next week . . . I crossed it once, shaking with fear, and swore never to go back. My little Marie-Louise fell there yesterday and was lucky not to fall into the moat. The moats are the one ornament and only beauty of this place, and they are full of reeds. You must live in these houses or come here some time. It's frightening. Everything is wretched here, but you will brighten things up."[1]

Apart from brief stays in Paris or Saint-Germain, Mme de Raimond lived in Longeville year-round, along with her mother and her daughter, Mme de Preysing, wife of a minister serving the Elector of Bavaria. She frequented the best society this part of France had to offer: M. de Burigny, her neighbor from Arcis-le-Ponsard, who often came to dine with his nephew and niece; that gentleman's brother, M.

de Pouilly, "a most amiable man who never displays his knowledge except with modesty and pretends to remind you of what he teaches you";[2] the provost of the church of Rheims; the chevalier de Fontenay; the chevalier de Mézières; and the chevalier Brisconnet. And Crébillon *fils*, when he was traveling in the region, never failed to pay a visit to his old friend the comtesse de Raimond.

A host of charming women also graced the company: a *demoiselle* from Tournai, "beautiful, shapely, and witty"; Mlle de Champeaux, who, "along with a strikingly pretty face, is most agreeably witty, charming, and gracious, without being obscure as provincial wits sometimes are"; her cousin, "who is also quite nice"; and a friend "who has the ingenuity of youth without the foolishness or the figure," Mme de Lagrange, "who sings like an angel, plays the harpsichord as Marchand did, and dances like a *painting*." In the good season these women enjoyed themselves in the countryside, visited nearby farms, and participated in village festivals. During long winter nights a select society gathered around the fire to listen to music, discuss the latest works of Helvétius or Rousseau, recite the poetry of Saint-Lambert, or play *cavagnole* (a game like lotto) or faro. Mme de Saint-Germain and Mme de Vernouillet were among the regulars. The former, of whom we shall hear more in a moment, felt the same maternal sentiments for Donatien as did Mme de Raimond, and the latter was his father's mistress.

"Non so più cosa son, cosa faccio . . . "

Indeed, our young marquis reminds us of Cherubino, surrounded by flirtatious women who waited on him, cajoled him, caressed him, mocked his innocence, and toyed with his heart as Countess Almaviva did with Cherubino's. Sighs, touches, stolen kisses, tender glances, teasing, sweet promises: these games of love, innocent as they may have been, excited the imagination and stirred the senses. "I no longer know who I am," Beaumarchais's hero exclaimed, "but my chest has been pounding now awhile. My heart flutters at the mere sight of a woman. The words *love* and *desire* cause it to skip and ache. The need to say 'I love you' has become so urgent that I say it when I am all alone, running in the park, to your mistress, to you, to the trees, to the clouds, to the wind that carries off my wasted words . . . A girl! A woman! O! how sweet those names sound! How interesting!"

Mme de Vernouillet delighted in turning the child's head. After being courted first by the duc de Richelieu and then by the comte de

Sade, she was now the center of the Longeville scene.[3] Mme de Raimond adored her and could not do without her: "Pleasure gains a new
lease on life when Mme de Vernouillet is around," she wrote the count.
"She has a loveliness all her own. A priest, a Premonstratensian who
reads us the mass, a hunchback who acts like Aesop, a bourgeois, a
semi-noble—all provide her with images that she embellishes in the
liveliest and most hilarious colors. When I looked at the same things,
I came away only with a disagreeable impression. She portrays them
so strikingly and by making them ridiculous renders them bearable."[4]

At the age of thirteen Donatien felt his heart flutter for the first
time over this delightful woman, who threw herself into the game with
a touch of perversity, much to the amusement of Mme de Raimond:

He is truly in love with her. It made me laugh so hard I cried. Nothing is so
amusing as to see him express his affection, and one guessed that *he felt things
he could not say, which astonished him and drove him wild.*[5] His confusion was
charming. He was mad, then he stood still, and later he gave way to fits of
jealousy and other signs of the tenderest, warmest love. And his 'mistress' was
indeed touched and moved. She said, 'This is a most unusual child.' She thinks
he looks like you. Do you know that he has gotten much handsomer? I cleaned
him up with almond oil, because I like him to look good. It does no harm.

I was so afraid for him. He went horseback riding twice. M. Amblet was
not too happy about my fears. He was afraid I might pass them on to the boy.
But he is fearless. He will be as courageous as he is witty. Take good care of
him.[6]

What this letter reveals—to my mind of the utmost importance—
is what Simone de Beauvoir once called Sade's "autism," the key to
which, as she intuitively recognized, must lie in his childhood. "The
curse that lay on Sade, which only his childhood can explain, was the
autism that prevented him from ever forgetting himself and recognizing
the presence of others. Had he been a man of cold temperament, no
problem would have arisen. But his instincts sent him rushing toward
external objects that he was incapable of embracing. He had to invent
extraordinary ways to lay hold of them."[7]

Although de Beauvoir had no knowledge of these letters, which
are published here for the first time, no one ever understood better or
expressed more aptly the nature of a difficulty from which Sade would
suffer all his life, despite his innate demonstrativeness. Although his
temperament was as ardent as burning lava, the only means it found

to express itself were symbolic: theater, oaths, "signals," ciphers, eroticism, money.

A torrent suddenly arrested in full flood: that is what young Donatien's emotional outbursts, immediately repressed by implacable censure, remind one of. We see the same mechanism at work at the end of the school vacation, when the time comes to bid farewell to his dear *"maman"* and suppressed despair suddenly finds resolution in a burst of sobs. Listen once more to Mme de Raimond: "Alas, our child has departed and left us in sadness. He has a heart, this charming boy. I learned that when he left me, he burst into tears, though he hid them from me. Mlle Adélaïde tells me that he told her, 'I've run away from mama.' If she had said one more word, I would have dissolved in tears. But tell him how much I love him and am touched by his thoughtfulness. Adélaïde was moved as well. He also told her: 'I am afraid she won't have me to Longeville any more and perhaps not much in Paris either.' He will have many other affairs. I am not even sure he will love his *mistress* as much."[8]

A few days later, Mme de Raimond returned to the subject of her "son's" loves: "Are you aware that what he felt for Mme de Vernouillet was a genuine passion? It has all the characteristics of one: jealousy, worry, all the outward signs of love. Do not be afraid of his indiscretion. He still has nothing to say. He will sense the value of mystery when the time comes. He wrote a very amusing letter to his good friend. For my part, he treats me more seriously and like a real mama. I love him too as if he were my child. I hope he loves me as a mother, because I like to be loved."[9]

The young marquis, now thirteen, definitely awakened the maternal instinct in women, because Mme de Saint-Germain, another habituée of Longeville, also claimed him as her son. Yet there was no rivalry between the two surrogate mothers.[10] She too invited Donatien to her country home and ultimately became so attached to him that she refused to send him back to his father and begged the count to leave the boy with her longer: "Yes, Monsieur," wrote this second "mother" in another previously unpublished letter to the comte de Sade,

yes, I take pleasure in loving your child. Time, which consumes all things, only increases my passion for him. You will know the full extent of my weakness, for in my present situation I have nothing more to hide. Your brother has been trying to take him from me for the past two weeks. I am driven to the point of distraction. He tells me that you keep insisting on having the boy back. Could you be so cruel as to deprive me of my child, to deny me the only pleasure I ask of you on bended knee? Leave him with me a while longer. If I had the honor of being known to Madame de Sade, I would write to beg the same favor of her. Do it for me. The court and the city provide you with so many amusements and distractions that you can easily sacrifice to me the bourgeois pleasure of having your child with you. I shall bring him back to you myself this summer. He will lose nothing as to his education: on that you may count. He will have M. Amblet here just as he does in Paris, and I, in my lonely leisure, can attend to him in ways that your occupations in Paris and Versailles do not allow. All vanity aside, may I say that I have taught him quite a lot in the time I have had him with me. The nephew's stay will in no way disrupt the uncle's travels . . . I have not the strength to thank you for your attention. My head is so full of my child that I cannot think of anything else.

Adieu, Monsieur, I am in a state of mortal anxiety. I await your answer as the warrant of my fate. You may respond at your convenience, but I declare that I will not let my child leave before I have your answer, for I cannot believe that you could be so inhuman as to refuse.[11]

Mme de Raimond and Mme de Saint-Germain, the two women who served Donatien as surrogate mothers, remained in his memory. In homage to the former he wrote the short novella entitled *La Châtelaine de Longeville ou la Femme vengée* (The Lady of Longeville, or Woman Avenged).[12] The action is set in the Middle Ages, and the heroine in no way resembles Donatien's good *maman*, but the location and description of the place are accurate: "In the days when lords lived despotically on their domains . . . the lord of Longeville lived on his, a fairly large fief near Fismes in Champagne . . . The town, or, rather, the hamlet of Longeville had little to offer in the way of resources." The text also mentions the "moats filled with water that surround the castle" as well as the park, court, halls, and a certain "study alongside the chapel." In a note at the bottom of the page Sade remarks that "all these places still exist at the château de Longeville."[13]

As for Mme de Saint-Germain, Donatien would honor her all his life with feelings bordering on veneration. Thirty years later, while imprisoned in the dungeon of Vincennes, he recounted a "dreadful" dream to his wife: "Dreams are foolish things. In any case I dreamed that M. le duc de La Vallière, whom I never saw or met, had died. Three days later, you sent me the almanac containing the news. I had the same dream about Mme de Saint-Germain, but if she has died, do not tell me, because I love her, I have always prodigiously loved her, and I would never get over it."[14] In 1784, still in Vincennes, he again told his wife of his abiding affection for Mme de Saint-Germain: "I beg you to make my excuses to Mme de Saint-Germain if I do not write her . . . You will permit me to except from your scenes of buffoonery, as ridiculous as they are insipid, the one woman in the world I love most after you, to whom I surely owe as much as a son can owe his mother. When she knows my reasons, I am certain she will forgive me. I beg you, in the meantime, to give her a sense of them and to assure her of my deepest affection. You may tell her, with a great deal of truth, that not a day has passed since I have been here when I did not think of her."[15]

•

Rather than disapprove of his son's amorous amusements with the ladies of Longeville, the comte de Sade seems to have been enchanted by them. The little fellow showed a decided taste for the libertine life! So much the better. At least he would have nothing to teach him on that score. And in order to encourage the precocious child he rented for him, not far from the hôtel de Condé, a *garconnière* where the comte de Clermont had formerly lodged his mistress. At the age of thirteen the young marquis was free to receive his *petites conquêtes*. A promising beginning!

"My son spent the autumn with Mme de Raimond," the count wrote to one of his friends. "She arrived the day before yesterday and came to supper. I have rented a house in the neighborhood where *la Carmago* lived when M. le comte de Clermont lodged where Prince von Grimberghen lodges now.[16] I've set my son up in it. There he goes about his little business, and the ladies have been kind enough to come try the place out. The child is in love with Mme de Vernouillet, and she amuses herself with him while waiting for him to grow up."[17]

Entirely devoted to his son's career, the comte de Sade not only made financial sacrifices on his behalf but also subjected himself to carnivals and balls and other such amusements that, past the age of fifty, he could well have done without had the little tyrant not forced him to come along. Grumble though he did, the marquis's father chaperoned him everywhere in the secret hope that his pretty face would attract the attention of some wealthy heiress: "Here we are at the end of carnival," he wrote his friend, the marquis de Surgères. "My son fears it and I desire it. The obligation he has placed me under to go to the ball seems a little hard. I even gave one to please him. Only thirty people were invited, but well chosen for their figures and their love of dance, and they danced long and happily. There was no finer ball at any time during the carnival."[18] A year later he was still complaining to the same correspondent: "Let us speak of pleasure. I am on my third ball, but it is not what I find most amusing. It is something I do for my son."[19]

Cherubino Goes to War

Toward the end of the school year in 1754 the comte de Sade took his son out of Louis-le-Grand to serve in the army. He was just fourteen years old and had completed his sophomore year. He had the rudiments of Latin and was an above-average speller. At the time it was not unusual to join a regiment at the age of twelve or to become a colonel by twenty. These youthful officers were known as "bib colonels." Some were so young that their tutors accompanied them to the battlefield, but this was not the case with Donatien, who was forced to separate from his beloved abbé Amblet sooner than he would have liked.[20]

Later he would vigorously denounce this early recruitment, which allowed his father to take him from his studies and cast him among soldiers:

War broke out. Eager to see me serve, [my father] left my education unfinished, and I departed for my regiment, where I was employed at an age when it would have been more natural to enter the academy.[21]

Could we reflect on the dominant vice of our modern principles, we might see that the crucial thing is not to have very young soldiers but to have good ones. If current prejudice is adhered to, this most useful class of citizens will never be perfect so long as the sole criterion is to join the ranks at an early age without knowing if one has the necessary prerequisites and without understanding that it is impossible to acquire those virtues unless young aspirants are given the opportunity to do so through proper and lengthy education.[22]

Through his connections the comte de Sade obtained for his son a place in the *Ecole préparatoire de cavalerie* (Cavalry Officers Training School), which was founded in 1741 by M. de Bongars and annexed in 1751 to the light cavalry regiment of the king's guard, garrisoned on the avenue des Sceaux in Versailles. The tuition was 3,000 livres annually. It was one of the most aristocratic units in the army and consequently one of the most highly sought after.[23] In 1754 it comprised nineteen officers and two hundred guardsmen under the command of the duc de Chaulnes. To join its ranks one needed a certificate attesting to at least four quarters of nobility, duly established by M. de Clairambault, "genealogist of the king's orders." Donatien obtained such a certificate on May 24, 1754. As proof of the ancient roots of the lineage he had to submit documents from the family archives, which his uncle the abbé, the family "memory," lent him in trepidation that he might never see them again: "I have sent your son all the papers he requested for his genealogy," the abbé wrote the comte de Sade. "Since these are originals, I confess that it was not easy for me to remove them from the huge books in which they were bound and subject them to the hazard of being lost. But what else could I do? Could I refuse? M. de Baujon is asking for still more so as to follow the line all the way back to the source. There are some that cannot be submitted because my father made corrections that are glaringly obvious. This has caused me some embarrassment. I have sent all that I could. I beg you to see to it that they are properly returned to me when they are no longer needed."[24]

During his service with the light horse, Donatien was often obliged to participate in the parade of arms, a ceremony that almost always took place in the king's presence. It is easy to imagine him cutting a fine figure in his scarlet uniform with sword loops and white silk trousers with silver buttons and wearing a three-cornered hat with gold braid and plume while banners decorated with lightning bolts and bearing the proud motto *Sensere gigantes* flapped in the wind.

On December 14, 1755, after twenty months of training and thanks to the favor his father still enjoyed, Donatien was named sublieutenant without allowances in the king's infantry regiment—a tribute, of course, to his ancient nobility rather than his military exploits. He thus traded in his handsome red coat for a white one with "nine rose decorations and an equal number of yellow buttons and blue facings with three ornaments." But this time it would not be just for parade.

The rattle of arms could be heard throughout Europe. Russia, Austria, and France joined in a coalition against Frederick II and England. Major troop levies were expected soon. From her remote country seat in Longeville Mme de Raimond worried about "her son" even as she attempted to reassure his father: "I cannot think of the war without fear for him and anguish for you. Let us not agonize over the uncertainty we face. This is still the least unhappy time. If we were certain of war, we would have reason to agonize but not to despair. I have a nephew whom I love as you love your son, and I must bear his parents' pain as well as my own. Yet not everyone who goes to war is killed. People die everywhere, and one can grow old in [the military] profession as in any other if one's hour has not struck."[25]

Fighting erupted the following year. No one knew that it would last seven years. As an opening maneuver French troops took Port-Mahon, the most impregnable fortress in Europe after Gibraltar. The operation unfolded under the command of old maréchal de Richelieu on the night of June 27, 1756. There our Cherubino underwent his baptism by fire. As a first experience of battle it could not have been better chosen. Without excessive pride he might have exclaimed with Rodrigue:

> *Je suis jeune, il est vrai, mais aux âmes bien nées,*
> *La valeur n'attend pas le nombre des années.*

[*I am young, 'tis true, but valor in well-born souls does not wait on the number of years.*]

Prancing at the head of four companies of grenadiers from Hainault, the Soissonais, and Cambis, Lieutenant de Sade performed some dashing feats in the especially dangerous assault on the Queen's Redoubt. The *Gazette* reported on his exploit: "At ten o'clock at night, all batteries having ceased their fire, the marquis de Monti, upon signal from a cannon and four bombs fired from the signal tower, attacked the fortifications at Strughen and Argyile, while the marquis de Briqueville and sieur de Sade energetically assaulted the Queen's Redoubt, and after a heated and rather deadly exchange of fire, managed by frontal assault and scaling to lay hold of the objective and establish a position there, after the besieged defenders had touched off four blast holes."[26] The two days of battle cost the French forces 424 dead: twenty-four officers and four hundred soldiers.

In describing these armed exploits in the autobiographical passages of *Aline et Valcour*, Sade credited not his courage but his natural aggressiveness, which found an outlet on the battlefield: "The campaigns began, and I dare say I acquitted myself well. The natural impetuosity of my character, the fiery soul I received from nature, lent all the more strength and energy to that fierce virtue we call courage, which is seen, no doubt incorrectly, as the only one necessary to our estate."[27]

A Father's Fears

The comte de Sade's anxiety was not that which a father usually feels for a son in the front lines. What he feared most was not musketfire but bad company, gambling, prostitutes, and worse: the habits inherent in a society of young men living together in close comradeship. Apparently the count had forgotten his escapades of old. In any case, the father, who has so often been portrayed as an old fogey, watched his son with the nervous eye of a mother hen. The figure is apt, moreover, because the count played both mother and father to Donatien.

His worries were increased by the report he received from his friend, the marquis de Poyanne: "I had previously learned, Monsieur, from an officer who saw your son at camp and had a great deal of good to say about him, of his colonel's peculiar fantasy. Should he not wish he might fill his regiment with subjects educated in this school? The libertinage and gambling there are frightening. What a misfortune! You are a worthy father to preserve your child from this as best you can."[28] And the father was indeed frightened by the perils that beset his son, especially gambling, which was so fashionable among the young and had ruined so many families. He broached the subject directly with his old friend Mme de Raimond and asked her advice: What should he do to save his boy from such nefarious influences? "If our child does not acquire all the virtues you wish to inspire in him," the lady of Longeville replied,

it will not be your fault, and perhaps it will not be entirely his either. The tastes of his age play a part, and the example of his comrades. So many battles to fight! I think you are right not to abandon him. At least you are delaying his defeat. Surely with age your teaching will reassert itself, but one learns good behavior only at one's own expense, unless one is born wise. I have faith only in the virtues of temperament. Education corrects, or, rather, mollifies or disguises the passions but does not extinguish them. Everything takes time. Alas, it happens more quickly than one wants.

As for the gambling passion, hold firm. Let him have money so that he need not desire it. Let him learn to defend what he gambles, and if possible let it be only for amusement and not to make a fortune. I confess to you that I still tremble for those who succumb to this passion.

As for love, it is not dangerous when it is invested honestly. Prostitutes are expensive and dangerous to health, but such misfortune is a stronger corrective than any oath. I say nothing of other kinds of errors. I do not think that nature teaches them, and I cannot believe that corruption is as common as people say. It takes superior merit to erase the horror and scorn inspired by those who have this vice and indulge in it shamelessly. Except for two or three I have known, the rest are an abomination to everyone. Our child, it seems to me, is not inclined toward such horrors. He had a passion. The sight of a pretty woman turned his head, I think. So what are you afraid of? He may have some disease. Well, then he will have himself cured. Just tell him not to let it go unattended. If you are too hard on him, you could easily turn his taste away from women. But they say there is no more security with the others.[29]

The Cornet and the Chaperon

When Donatien turned fifteen, his father's ambition began to focus on the Carabineers, one of the most prestigious units in the army. A century earlier Louis XIV had prided himself on being their colonel, as a token of the high esteem in which he held them. Later he designated his own son, the duc du Maine, as their commander. In 1758 they were again commanded by a member of the royal family, the comte de Provence (the future Louis XVIII). The unit's standard featured a golden sun at its center, and Louis XIV had granted the Carabineers the privilege of decorating their banner with his own glorious motto: *Nec pluribus impar.*

Only tall, well-built men were admitted into this elite unit: an order of March 20, 1751, prescribed that members must be at least five foot four inches tall. Donatien, however, was only five foot two. But his father decided to make use of his connections. He learned that his old friend the marquis de Poyanne, brigadier, had just been named commander-in-chief of the Carabineers. Poyanne was reputedly a part of Mme de Pompadour's faction at court, and she was indebted to the comte de Sade for certain small favors he had done in the past for her father, M. Poisson. Thus the royal favorite could not refuse to intervene in his behalf. M. de Poyanne was said to be a "mediocre man and insolent as a lackey" (d'Argenson), but he could be useful. In September 1756 the count recommended his son for a commission. On October 4 he received this response:

. . . You would be very unjust if you doubted my friendship for you and yours. Like you I find the profession of guardian very hard. I offer you a cornet's commission in the Carabineers for your son. This is a distinguished unit in which it is pleasant to have served. Furthermore, I shall be pleased to have him as my aide-de-camp, although I am assigned the number I have already. But no rule will ever stand in the way of what you desire of me. I cannot offer you anything else, but you may definitely count on my willing devotion.

If you choose to follow one of the courses I propose, you haven't a moment to lose in bringing your son to Paris.[30]

On January 14, 1757, Donatien officially received his cornet's commission in the Saint-André Brigade of the Carabineers. The cornet was the standard-bearer of a cavalry company. The rank had been abolished for some time, but Louis XV had just revived it in early January. Donatien was thus among the first to receive the new rank. He now wore a blue uniform "in the French style, with red facings, cuffs, collar, and lining." His horse was also decked out in blue cloth "edged with white piping in the Burgundian manner."

•

Nevertheless, the comte de Sade continued to worry about his son. In order to keep an eye on him he followed him from garrison to garrison like a duenna. He visited his son's superiors and begged them to keep an eye on the morals of their troops. In April 1757 he escorted Donatien to Abbeville, where he dispatched this report to Mme de Raimond:

You would laugh, my dear countess, if you saw me in Abbeville: [at] all the coquetry, all the art that I employ to win the good will of all the king's regiments. I should like to make the old officers mentors of the young. My polite entreaties are supposed to say: 'Gentlemen, do not seduce this child! What good would it do you to turn him into a libertine? Aren't there enough of you already? Respect his naïveté.' I am perfectly well aware that it will all prove pointless. The old ones will let him do foolish things, and the young ones will make him. Nevertheless, I am trying to gain time and slow them down. This is to save him.[31]

Has a father ever taken more of an interest in the virtue of his son? Mme de Raimond complimented the count on his efforts:

I am moved by your sentiments, and yesterday I could not stop myself from exclaiming that no one is more virtuous than you. Who can deny that no one is more loving, and in reading your letters I feel that no father is more affectionate or more concerned with making his son virtuous. A libertine would not take such care. Where can one find a father who follows his son to his regiment, who subjects himself to the boredom of courting all the officers, old and young, who finds associates for him, who is sensitive enough to fear that the passions may speak more loudly than reason, and who sets such an example of good behavior in so pleasant a manner. Good God, what a guardian! Live, my dear Sade, to pluck the fruits of your labors. Is it possible that the child is not moved by the deepest gratitude and is not aware of all your trouble? Do not be alarmed, even if he proves less appreciative than you wish. There will come a time when what the love of pleasure obscures at present will reappear in his memory. Sometimes we must sin in order to find our way back to virtue. The age of passion is terrible to get through. I am very pleased that he does not suffer from the passion of gambling. This is the most dangerous of all, not only because it ruins [fortunes] but because it leads to dishonesty. But no woman in her right mind will take up with a child, and among garrison women it is hard to find any with principles.[32]

At times, however, the count was too busy to dog his young son's steps. The marquis de Poyanne then took responsibility for keeping an eye on him, a task in which he proved zealous. After the first escapade he dispatched a report to the count:

Your son did some foolish things in Strasbourg, the worst of which was to run through his money far too quickly. I scolded him somewhat, especially for his failure to visit the intendant and the senior officers of the unit. He accepted my remonstrances with such equanimity that he disarmed me. M. de Saint-André, who commands the brigade with which he came from Strasbourg to Metz, was delighted with him. I have given M. de Liverne the twenty-four livres you sent me for him. He will pay for his inn and his servant's food and will give him one louis per month, unless you order him to do otherwise. I accepted his commission as cornet and had him drill his company for me, which he did quite well. He will go with his unit to join the army, as this will cost less, and as soon as I rejoin [the unit] he will come live with me.[33]

"I am departing in search of freedom . . ."

In 1758 Donatien embarked on his nineteenth year. His father began to relax his surveillance because Poyanne seemed so satisfied with the boy. Everyone was pleased by his "extreme gentleness," according to the brigadier. Such a characterization of the man who a few years later would be taken to be the very incarnation of evil may seem surprising, but it only confirms Mme de Raimond's estimation of his unusual sensitivity.

I have nothing but good to say about your son. He is even better than last year. He has an extreme gentleness in his character that makes everyone like him. Since he has nothing at all to do, I am going to assign him the job of excerpting M. de Feuquières, which is the best book I know on war.[34] You should not leave without obtaining a definite promise from the Maréchal that he will give him a cavalry company. His chances of obtaining favor are mediocre at present; he falls under the provisions of the new order, since he is in his second year as cornet. I had Major Dorléans give the 400 livres to his servant. With what you are giving him he is certainly in good shape.[35]

Now confident in the future of his son, who had been promised that he would soon command a cavalry regiment, the comte de Sade felt compelled to retire to his estate in Provence. Disappointed in his ambitions, ruined, and disillusioned, he suddenly became aware of his uselessness. Even the pleasures of the court had lost all attraction for him. He saw nothing but artifice, lies, and betrayal. Moreover, only a short while before, the woman who had meant the most to him, and with whom he had been living for several years, had died: on Friday, April 7, 1758, at five in the morning, Mlle de Charolais expired in Paris after an illness of three months. At the age of fifty-six Jean-Baptiste found himself alone, homeless, aimless, and helpless. His wife had retired to the Carmelite convent on the rue d'Enfer, and his son no longer needed him. He therefore decided to leave for Avignon. His affairs would have to be put in order if he hoped to make an advantageous marriage for Donatien. He had been thinking seriously about this for some time. On the way he planned to make a detour through Auvergne to take the waters there and to visit his brother in Ebreuil. Before taking to the road he bade farewell to Mme de Raimond:

27 April 1758

At last, my dear countess, I am leaving, I am abandoning Paris. I do not say forever. It would be imprudent to announce so violent a decision, in view of how changeable men are by nature. What is more, I have a son who can recall me at any time. But for now I think that pleasure will not bring me back. I have lost all that attached me to it . . . One mustn't be old in Paris. To live in a manner appropriate to one's age is to be sad and virtually alone. To act young when one no longer is young is indecent and ridiculous . . . I went to see the queen. She said, "M. de Sade, it has been a long time since I last saw you." I thought of telling her, "Alas, you will see me no more." I was moved, but I said nothing. What a difference, my dear countess, to see the court as one who is leaving rather than as one who clings to it! What madness to have gone there in search of happiness! Slavery is all that is to be found. I am departing in search of freedom, independence, and tranquillity, as well as to care for a mother whom I love and to forget all that I have seen and remember only you.[36]

In her response Mme de Raimond would try in vain to dissuade him from going through with his plan by inviting him to come live with her in Longeville. I cannot resist the pleasure of quoting at length from this charming woman's letter for what it reveals of emotional perceptiveness and sensitivity to the people she loved:

Think about it carefully, my dear Sade, before making such a violent decision. Pain, when we surrender to it, prevents us from seeing into the future. The first effects are violent, and the more violent they are, the briefer their duration, for the soul is not made to endure sadness for long. I appreciate all that you are losing: an essential friend for whom you also felt more tender feelings. We convince ourselves that we will never get over it, but experience teaches us every day that we do, and I hope you will put your reason to work toward that end . . .

Your son, whatever you may say, is not old enough to be left on his own. You succeeded, but you had what he still only promises: all the talents, all the graces—you had them. Although I am highly prejudiced in his favor, I still do not see him as resembling you. But one can be very good and still not come close to you . . .

You say some very lovely things, my dear Sade, but they don't seem very plausible . . . If you go to Avignon, won't people also think that your affairs are in disorder? And won't that harm your son's future? For you know the malice of men. And though it is painful to think of, your wonderful mother is eighty-three years old. It is to be feared, is it not? that you would have to watch her die. That would be to heal one ill with an even greater one. Think carefully, my dear Sade. Arrange for your housing and wait awhile . . . You will [then] not be a hundred leagues from your affairs and from me, and I should like very much to count for something. But in truth I know what I am worth and count myself for nothing, although I love you tenderly.[37]

After returning to his estate, the comte de Sade did not forget his dear Mme de Longeville. If he had not yet found his way back to God, as his friend so devoutly wished he would, he nevertheless took her advice and wrote, for his son's benefit, treatises on philosophy and morality that eventually began to show signs of the converted libertine's religious fervor. For the time being he gave his imagination free rein to savor the delights of rebellious thought unfettered by moral concerns and absorbed in the idea of pleasure. Far from the capital the count's thoughts of libertinage sometimes seem a bit nostalgic, though never repentant. Indeed, he presents his ideas with a zest spurred by frustration. The eulogy of inconstancy he wrote for Mme de Raimond admirably exemplifies a febrile jubilation that one is tempted to call Sadeian because of the way it anticipates the son's immoralist teach-ings. Note, moreover, that the count enthusiastically invites his son to follow his lead in the matter of infidelity:

Would to God that I had never loved anyone but you! But how is it possible, my queen, not to be unfaithful? Only fools never change. We should never stop loving what we truly loved, but we must surrender when the opportunity arises: we are then more worthy of being loved. M. de Richelieu would be but a mediocre man had he had but a single woman. When someone pays him court, do you suppose it is he they are courting—that shriveled apple? No, not he but the lover of a hundred women! Women think to make themselves prettier by adding their names to the list of those he has had. They labor not for pleasure but for their reputations. When a woman preaches constancy, it is not because she wants the same lover always but because she would rather leave him than be left. I have seen faithful lovers on occasion: their sadness, their gloominess, is enough to make one tremble. If my son were to be constant, I would be offended. I'd just as soon he became a member of the Academy . . . The company is good for the provinces, but still it is the provinces, and if I remember Paris, I suppose the tone there is different. Here to be comfortable I must play the imbecile. If I were to show any wit, people would make fun of me and not listen to what I say. But when I talk about the house, about food, about repairs, people listen, admire, and think me a great genius for having learned so much about such things already. In the provinces, I think, one cannot be a libertine. The girls are pretty but so gloomy that you must first subject yourself to boredom with them. In the most natural actions art is still necessary. One can't be devout either. They talk so poorly about God, they give me such a trivial idea of Him, that I lose my appetite. Despite all this, I am quite comfortable. I vegetate quietly. I am calm. I feel loved. I do good for my peasants, which convinces me that I am reigning.[38] This illusion flatters me. That is all we live on. Without the illusion that you love me, do you think I would be so happy? Adieu, my dear countess.[39]

A Young Hero

Meanwhile, the Seven Years War was raging, and Donatien did his duty with a zeal that won him the esteem of his superiors. On June 23, 1758, he found himself with his regiment at the battle of Krefeld, not far from the left bank of the Rhine about thirteen miles from Düsseldorf. The French army was under the command of the comte de Clermont, brother of the late Monsieur le Duc, whose nullity equaled his birth and who knew infinitely more about back rooms and bedrooms than he did about battlefields. Out of incompetence and

laziness he permitted Brunswick to launch a surprise attack. Rocham-
beau and Saint-Germain withstood the shock and defended their positions inch by inch while awaiting reinforcements, which could have
been sent in plenty of time. But Clermont believed that the attack was
a feint and stood fast. Overwhelmed by superior forces, the two generals
fell back, and Clermont was soon obliged to sound the retreat. While
the French forces withdrew to Cologne, leaving 7,000 dead on the
battlefield, the cities of Neuss and Ruremonde fell to the Hanoverians
and Prussians. Thus what little prestige still attached to the house of
Condé after the ignominies of Monsieur le Duc and the crimes of the
comte de Charolais finally evaporated on the battlefield of Krefeld.

A short while later Mme de Raimond wrote the comte de Sade:

> I was in quite a state of alarm, my dear Sade, for our child and my nephew.
> I had no news of your son until a few days ago, for there was not a word about
> him in the *Gazette*. But this was a "sign of a good mark," to speak in the
> manner of the locals . . . The Carabineers were not spared. I had your pain,
> my own, and that of my brother and sister-in-law, as I imagined what I felt
> and was unable to learn any news. I did not write you then, because I did not
> know what to say . . . Come back to establish our child's position. Will you
> leave him in the Carabineers? It appears to be a distinguished unit, and reg-
> iments now will not be so easy to get. M. de Poyanne is your friend: your son
> cannot be at a better school.[40]

The Lost Regiment

Four months later, in October 1758, Donatien was promoted to the
rank of captain of cavalry. Did he owe his promotion to his conduct
during the battle of Krefeld or to the recommendation of M. de Poyanne? We do not know. In any case, since there was no vacant company,
the promotion had no effect. Nevertheless it earned his father a letter
of congratulations from the comte de Sonning.

The comte de Sade repeatedly petitioned the maréchal de Belle-
Isle, who was secretary of state for war, to grant his son command of
the first available company. At long last a company was left free by
the departure of the marquis de Tocqueville for the Lusignan regiment.
The comte de Sade purchased it for 13,000 livres, and on April 21,
1759, Louis XV signed a commission appointing Donatien de Sade a
company captain in the Burgundy Cavalry Regiment. Our young officer
could now strut about in a gleaming uniform "in the Polish style, of
blue fabric, with crimson linings, cuffs, and collar and white piping."

The good news reached him in the principality of Cleve, where he was bivouacked. On Sunday, April 22, he celebrated the event with a display of fireworks. A rocket unfortunately landed on a private home but luckily caused no damage. Donatien nevertheless offered his excuses to the "gentlemen of the regency of Cleve," citing not his own good fortune but that of the maréchal de Broglie, who had just beaten the combined Hessian, Hanoverian, English, and Prussian forces, some forty thousand men in all under the command of the prince of Brunswick, near the small village of Berghen, between Frankfurt and Hanau:

Gentlemen,

On the agreeable news we had just received that Mgr le duc de Broglie had utterly defeated your Hanoverian and Hessian troops, and being a good patriot with a passionate interest in the success of my nation, I last Sunday, the twenty-second of this month, set off fireworks in celebration of this agreeable news, and a rocket unfortunately fell on the home of Mr. Streil. It caused, sirs, no harm or damage. I enclose a certificate from the owner of the house. If, gentlemen, circumstances cause me to remain here for some time, and seeing that occasions for celebration may become more frequent, I shall choose, sirs, an area more remote from the city and safe from all danger for my fireworks.

I am, meanwhile, gentlemen, with the consideration you deserve, your respectable assembly's most humble servant.[41]

Nonchalant, ironic, and insolent: that is how he portrays himself in this letter, the earliest we have in his hand.

This stay near Cleve also left him with another memory, which he would recall twenty years later:

In Germany, where I engaged in six campaigns before I was married, I was told that to learn a language well it was necessary to sleep regularly and habitually with a woman of the country. Convinced of the truth of this maxim, I equipped myself, in my winter quarters near Cleve, with a nice fat baroness three or four times my age, who educated me very nicely. After six months I spoke German like Cicero![42]

5

A Fine Marriage

The Apprentice Libertine

For a young officer garrison life was a dream come true, and particularly for a man who was good-looking, blessed with several quarters of nobility, and equipped with an elegant horse and a blue-and-red uniform that tucked in snugly at the waist. Donatien had all of these things along with blue eyes, a pouty smile that pleased the ladies, enough money to lose at gambling, and a heart that blazed up at a glance. He frequented salons, marched in parades, never missed a show, was dazzling at balls and parties, acted in plays, wrote poetry, ran up debts, collected mistresses, and got himself in trouble—in short, he proved himself a worthy son of his father. "Surely," he would later concede, "there are few worse schools than garrisons, few places where a young man can more quickly corrupt his manners and morals."

Among his regimental comrades was a boy of his own age by the name of Castéja (and not Castéra, as other biographies state), the son of the governor of Toul and Saint-Dizier, a highly responsible young man with whom Donatien nevertheless struck up a friendship. In May or June of 1759 Castéja sent news of his friend to the comte de Sade: "Your dear son is doing marvelously. He is friendly, easygoing, and amusing . . . Travel is putting back weight and color that the pleasures of Paris had rather taken away. We are taking good care of him . . . His little heart or, rather, *body* is furiously combustible. German girls, look out! I will do my utmost to keep him from doing anything stupid. He has given me his word not to gamble more than a louis a day with the army."

Furious, the count sent a copy of this letter to his brother the abbé with this note: "As if that scoundrel had a louis a day to lose! He promised me not to risk an écu. But what he said amounts to nothing. Nevertheless, we mustn't fret. This M. de Castéja is only twenty years old and has never done anything stupid. He is so surprised that anyone can be a libertine that he can't get over it."[1]

In the same dispatch he included a "confession" that Donatien had sent to abbé Amblet but written expressly so that Amblet would show it to his father. No doubt he hoped by means of this naïve subterfuge to win a pardon for his escapades. We may admire him in the role of repentant son:

The number of mistakes I made during my stay in Paris, my dear abbé, and the manner in which I behaved toward the most affectionate father in the world make him regret that he ever brought me there. But I am amply punished by remorse at having displeased him and fear of losing his friendship forever. Nothing remains of pleasures that I believed so real but the bitterest pain at having irritated the most affectionate of fathers and the best of friends.

I woke up every morning looking for pleasure. This idea made me forget everything else, [and] I thought I was happy the minute I found what I was looking for. But this supposed happiness vanished as quickly as my desires turned to regrets. At night I was desperate. I saw that I was wrong, but only at night, and the next day my desires returned and sent me out again in pursuit of pleasure. I no longer remembered my reflections of the evening before. Someone made a proposition, I accepted it, I thought I was enjoying myself, and then I saw that I had been a fool and had amused myself at my own expense. The more I reflect on my behavior now, the stranger it seems. I see that my father was right when he told me that three-quarters of the things I did, I did for show. Oh, if only I had done only what really gave me pleasure, I would have spared myself so much suffering, and I would have offended my father far less often. Could I have thought that the girls I was seeing really could give me pleasure? Alas, does one ever really enjoy a happiness that one buys, and can love without decency ever be very affectionate? My self-esteem suffers now at the thought that I might have been loved only because I paid less badly than some others . . .

Farewell, my dear abbé, and I beg you to send me your news. But I won't receive your letter for some time, because I'm not to stop anywhere and won't receive mail until I rejoin the army. So don't be surprised if you don't hear from me until I arrive.[2]

Clearly Donatien had not forgotten the lessons he had learned from the Jesuits. But the comte de Sade was not taken in and wondered whether he ought to have his son recalled to Paris and return there himself in order to keep a closer eye on him. He consulted his friend M. de Prie on the matter and received this advice:

Apart from praise for your decision, your heart, your paternal affection, and your courage, I admire still more your resolve to spend the winter [in Paris] and to supervise [your son's] education. This would be without precedent . . .

At your son's age, good examples make no impression. The young are heedlessly drawn to the bad. No one is more aware than I of the dangers of this regiment . . . It would not be practical to recall your son to Paris in order to supervise his conduct. Every day, every moment, he would elude you and soon learn not to fear you. Do you want my advice? Here it is. I would not hesitate to do everything possible to have him sent back to the light horse. Despite his unwarranted aversion, you can tell him that some twenty of his comrades returned to that unit after serving as he has done as lieutenants and captains in regiments of infantry, cavalry, and dragoons.[3]

Donatien's Dower

But this advice would not do. Donatien would never agree to return to the light horse. He would see it as a demotion, and his pride would be offended. The ideal thing would be to find a good match for him, a wealthy young lady of noble birth. But for that he would need a suitable endowment. The comte de Sade therefore petitioned His Majesty to be allowed to resign his post as lieutenant general of Bresse, Bugey, Valromey, and Gex in favor of his son. The king granted his wish on March 4, 1760, but reduced his *brevet de retenue* (stipend) from 80,000 to 60,000 livres.[4] The count protested this decision and urged the chancellor to ask the king to grant his son the same stipend he had received, but to no avail: the king of France was not one to haggle.

Daughters to Marry

Meanwhile, the count had already begun looking for a match. He had been thinking about it for some time, ever since Donatien turned twelve! It was never too early to begin on such an arduous task. To find a woman who met the requirements of both birth and fortune was all but impossible in the best of circumstances and even more difficult in the present case because of the father's libertinage, his reversals of fortune, his alleged misdeeds, his contempt for the court and for people in high places, and his retirement to Provence, to say nothing of the rumors that were already circulating about Donatien. The number of obstacles was thus considerable. But far from losing heart, the count put his head down and charged full speed ahead into a veritable hunt for an heiress. On this point too the family archives yield an abundant harvest of hitherto unpublished information.

To aid in his choice the comte de Sade kept a list of marriageable daughters, all from noble families, ranging in age "from fifteen to forty-five." The first column in this list gave the parents' name and the second the number of daughters, while the third mentioned any marriages contracted since the compilation of the list:

Demoiselles Choiseul	2	
La Villeneuve	1	
La Bourdonnais	1	Married M. d'Annonville
Caroline de Vaudreuil		
et cetera		

The count also called upon the services of marriage brokers in the provinces, who sent him the names of potentially interesting matches and put him in contact with the families. A certain M. de Montmorillon, a choirmaster in the cathedral of Lyons who also served as an intermediary in these matters, turned up a Mademoiselle de Rochechouart. Although she appeared suitable in all respects, M. de Sade judged the dowry inadequate: "I am deeply saddened," the amiable choirmaster wrote,

by Madame de Rochechouart's inflexibility and unwillingness to change or add anything to the conditions I had the honor of submitting to you for her daughter's marriage. In her most recent letter, dated August 29, she assures me that she is fully cognizant of the value attaching to her daughter's union with your son by virtue of both birth and property, but that she had established the highest possible dowry at the outset and can add nothing to it. You have no doubt kept her conditions. Would you therefore be so kind as to review them to see if they might suit you? The assurance you asked for of fifty thousand livres income from her property to be remitted to her daughter seemed to her to indicate some distrust on your part, and I was unable to change her mind by telling her that these kinds of assurances are normally included in marriage contracts without difficulty or hesitation on either part. She persists in wanting full discretion to give her daughter a greater or lesser amount from her own property depending on whether or not she continues to be happy with her . . .

I leave you, Sir, entirely free in this respect, because, being unable to foresee the future, I wish in any event to avoid even the slightest reproach, especially from you, whom I honor infinitely and of whom I shall always be pleased, Sir, to call myself the most humble and obedient servant.[5]

The count responded:

I find Mme de Rochechouart charming, Sir. I am mad about her character, and if I thought that her daughter resembled her, I would take her without dowry. Most women are tender, either out of weakness or out of the goodness of their hearts. When it is a question of a suitable establishment, one wrests from them what they do not wish to give. Mme la marquise de Rochechouart is firm. She has said since the first day what she wished to give. She cannot be forced to give a hundred additional écus for her daughter's trousseau, and for that I revere her. But here are two items that cause me difficulty.

The first is that you represented her to me as having an income of twenty-five thousand livres. Yet she says that she is not wealthy, and I take her at her word. It seems to be true. Furthermore, she states that she is sacrificing a property that she needs, a property in land yielding a thousand écus in rent, against which there are charges and reparations. What land is free of such things? Her daughter costs her at least a hundred pistoles for food and necessities. Thus her sacrifice amounts to fifteen or sixteen hundred francs in rent . . .

If Mme la marquise de Rochechouart had consented to what I first asked for, namely, the guarantee of the fifty thousand francs and the trousseau, the deal would have been done. I follow Mme de Rochechouart's example of firmness and stay with my original offer. If this marriage were to bring me closer to her, if I might be allowed the hope of spending time with her, whether at my home or hers, I think I would subscribe to all the conditions. But I imagine that once her daughter is married, she will not trouble herself very much about us.

I am returning her letters to you. I offer you a thousand thanks for the trouble you have taken to arrange an agreeable situation for my son. I have not lost hope that he may some day be married through your efforts. I have the honor of being, Sir, with infinite devotion, your most humble and obedient servant.[6]

•

A few weeks later another possible match turned up in Burgundy. This time the young lady was a canoness of the abbaye de Remiremont by the name of Damas de Fuligny de Rochoir, about whom another agent, M. Auban de La Feuillée, had gathered the following information:

The Rochoirs are not Rochechouarts but are their equals. The brother of the young lady's father is presently count of Lyons, and the young lady herself is canoness of Remiremont: this proves that all the mothers are good. The name is Damas de Fuligny; the mother is named Pons-Rennepont; the land on which she lives is called Agey and is charming and worth at least a thousand livres in rent. She owns, in addition, the Sandaucourt estate, which is worth at least a thousand écus in rent and which would sell for more than fifteen thousand francs, because in Burgundy one pays nothing to the suzerain and always asks more than the *denier trente* [that is, a selling price more than thirty times income].

Mme de Rochoir has a son with whom she is not happy. He was in prison for a long time. I do not know if he is presently free. He is an only son; she has only one daughter.

This, my dear count, is all that I have been able to find out thus far. If I am able to learn more, I will keep you informed, and my information is above suspicion since I have never seen anyone belonging to this house, because Mme de Rochoir is a woman of great intelligence, even learned and, I believe, an author, but so private that she sees very few people . . . There may be other properties of which I am unaware, because they are thirty leagues from here. In two or three months I should be able to learn more, because I am spending the winter in Frôlois.

In a postscript, as if it were a trivial detail, the agent added: "As to the appearance and character of the young lady, who is known as Mme de Fuligny, I can say nothing, other than that one of my friends, who was in Agey some months ago and saw her there, tells me that she spoke very little, that she was not bad looking, and that it seemed to him that her mother spoke to her in a friendly manner but in the most imperious tone, which might have contributed to the polite silence he observed."[7]

The deal did not go through. What a pity! A canoness for a wife and a brother-in-law in the Bastille: what a harbinger of things to come!

•

A third prospect presented itself in the person of Mlle de Bassompierre, a lady of the highest nobility (her mother was a Beauvau and lady-in-waiting to Mesdames, the king's daughters) and a kin of Choiseul, who received the proposal rather coolly.

I have just received, Sir, the letter you did me the honor of writing on the eighteenth of this month, in which you are kind enough to inform me of the marriage you propose to make between your son and Mlle de Bassompierre. Since I have the honor to be related to her, I can only be pleased at the prospect of this union, and I beg you to believe that I shall look with pleasure for opportunities to be useful to your son.[8]

Anyone but the comte de Sade would have left things there, only too happy at the unexpected opportunity that presented itself to his son. But the blundering count took it into his head to ask at once for a colonel's commission for Donatien. It is not difficult to imagine the unfortunate impression that this request made at a time when discussions concerning the marriage were entering their final stages. The response was quick. It was a polite but definitive refusal. A dramatic development followed three weeks later: the marriage negotiations were broken off. M. de Bassompierre awarded his daughter's hand to another man. The miserable count witnessed the collapse of all his hopes and had to make an enormous effort to force himself to congratulate the young lady's mother, who seemed as distressed as the count by her husband's sudden change of heart: "I very much hope, Sir," she wrote in reply, "that your son finds a party worthy of him and of you. I shall always take the warmest and most affectionate interest in matters regarding both of you."[9]

What had happened? In all likelihood it was Choiseul who turned the family against the two Sades and did everything he could to prevent the marriage. As secretary of state for war since January 27, 1761, he probably ordered an investigation of Donatien and received deplorable reports. If the young man's conduct in battle merited only praise, the same could not be said of his everyday conduct. His superiors saw him as a wild youth who uninhibitedly indulged his whims as a gambler, spendthrift, and sensualist. "The major of his regiment dined here the other night with M. de Saint-Germain, who questioned him," the comte de Sade remarked. "Everything he says about him is horrible."

Another incident may have helped to turn the minister against Donatien. In April 1761 the count had obtained for his son an appointment as an ensign, or company standard-bearer, in the gendarmerie, a signal favor but very expensive.[10] Unable to pay the price, the count was forced to decline the honor in Choiseul's presence. What is more, he waited until the last minute to make his intentions known, so that the incident came while negotiations for the marriage to Mlle de Bassompierre were still going on. The minister must have been quite irritated, to judge by this letter from his secretary: "The company's impending departure is probably the reason why M. le duc de Choiseul spoke to you as he did during his audience, fearing with good reason that the man who will replace your son, on whom he was counting, will not have the time to make the arrangements necessary to begin the campaign at the appointed time. Rest assured, in any case, about your son's fate. The minister is too just to hold him responsible for something over which he had no control and which cannot and should not hinder his advancement."[11]

A Standard for Sale

The count's efforts to arrange a marriage for his son required his presence in Paris. In late March or early April 1761 he returned to the capital with the intention of raising the money necessary to purchase the standard-bearer's post and to find Donatien a worthy match. He took up residence in the Seminary of Foreign Missions on the rue du Bac and wrote to Mme de Raimond to inform her of his return:

My dear countess, you are in Champagne and I am in Paris. You have not answered my last letter from Avignon, which makes me wonder if I should recall myself to your memory. But the heart always silences reason. I love you, I forget your wrongs, and I do not want you to forget my existence, insignificant though it may be.

I find Paris greatly changed yet still the same. Frivolity still reins, appearances still rule, pleasure is still what people seek and boredom is still what they find, luxury is what they display and misery what they feel. The mood in families has never been blacker, yet never have theaters and walking paths been so crowded, and dances and public places. People are looking to forget their misfortunes. Yet still it is better to be miserable in Paris than happy in the provinces, and they are right who say that Paris will not make you happy but will prevent you from being happy anywhere else.[12]

Following his return to Paris the count assailed Choiseul with petitions. Whatever it took, his son must have a colonelcy. His obstinacy was close to being in bad taste, but he did not care. He would not leave the minister in peace until he had obtained what he wanted. But Choiseul hid behind administrative difficulties while taking a perverse pleasure in twisting the knife. He had been offered an ensignship? Why hadn't he taken it?

I have received, Sir, the letter that you did me the honor of writing on the sixth of this month, in which you renew your request for a colonel's commission for your son, a captain in the Burgundy Cavalry.

The distinction of his birth and his diligence are considerations of which I have not lost sight and which will dispose me to contribute to his advancement the moment I have the opportunity, and my position in this regard is the same as I told you last June. But the king is more reluctant than ever to award commissions contrary to what His Majesty himself prescribed in the regulation of April 29, 1758. This is an obstacle that seems to me quite difficult to surmount, and I must not conceal it from you, even in offering you my assurance that I am as eager as you are to see your ends achieved. It is unfortunate that you were unable to help [your son] take advantage of His Majesty's offer of an ensignship in the gendarmerie. In that unit he might have found promotion sooner.[13]

A month later the count renewed his requests in two more letters, dispatched in quick succession. This time Choiseul had had enough: "I have received, Sir, the two letters that you did me the honor of writing on the fourth and sixth of this month on behalf of your son. I can offer him only an ensignship in the gendarmerie. Notify me if you intend to purchase this post for him, so that I may make the necessary arrangements before proposing this award to the king when the opportunity arises."[14] In plain language: You can't afford an ensignship? Then don't expect anything else!

The comte de Sade next called on Louis-Joseph de Condé, with whom Donatien had played as a child. He asked for a room for his former playmate in the hôtel de Condé and a recommendation for a colonelcy. Perhaps the young prince would take him on as aide-de-camp. The answer was no:

I am convinced that there is nothing but good of all kinds to be said about your son, but I am not in a position to speak of him, and in any case it is to the generals under whom he has served that M. de Choiseul will turn for recommendations in his behalf. I will, however, speak of him to the minister as someone whose advancement I desire, and I hope that my recommendation may be of some use.

If the Burgundy Regiment does not serve in the next campaign, I would be happy to have your son accompany me, but having already made commitments to more aides-de-camp than I can take with me, I am afraid that I cannot do as you wish on that. I hope, Sir, that you will be persuaded nonetheless of the high esteem I have for you.[15]

There is no room for doubt: it was as difficult to win a promotion for Donatien as it was to find him a wife, and the reason was that there were serious prejudices against him. His father's past played a large part, as we have seen. But there was more to it than that. The young marquis de Sade already suffered from an execrable reputation, though still uncorroborated by any public scandal. What was this reputation based on? For the time being on slander, rumors, and barracks gossip. The charges must have been fairly serious, because they remained shrouded in a prudent silence.

"My confession, in full"

What had become of the dear child? He was still in the field with the army, except for periods of leave during which he tried his best to fall in love in each new city. On August 12, 1760, we find him in camp at Obertestein, not far from Korbach, where the maréchal de Broglie had just won (on July 10) a stunning victory over the Hanoverian army. From this village he wrote his father a long letter in which he explained the movements of the troops in detail before coming to a more important matter, namely, himself. He responded to the count's criticism of his behavior with a "confession" that I will quote in full because it is the best evidence we have of the man he was and the way he thought at age twenty. The writer is already clearly in evidence, with all his ruses and ambiguities:

You ask me for an account of my life and occupations. I will give you, in all sincerity, a detailed report. People reproach my fondness for sleep. It is true that I suffer somewhat from this fault. I go to bed early and get up very late. I frequently ride out to examine the enemy's positions and our own. Once we've been in a camp for three days, I know it down to the last ravine as well as the maréchal himself. I act in accordance with my thoughts, good or bad.

I tell people what I think and am praised or blamed in proportion to the little if any common sense there is in my ideas. Sometimes I make visits but only to M. de Poyanne or to my former comrades in the Carabineers or the king's regiment. I don't make a big ceremony of it, because I don't like ceremony. If it weren't for M. de Poyanne I would not set foot in headquarters during the campaign. I know I'm not doing myself any good. One has to pay court to succeed, but I don't like doing it. I suffer when I hear one person flatter another, often by saying a thousand things he does not believe. It is more than I can do to play the fool to such a degree. To be polite, honest, noble but not proud, obliging but not tepid; to do the little things we like when they do no harm to ourselves or others; to live well and have a good time without ruining ourselves or losing our wits; few friends, perhaps none, because there is no one who is truly sincere and who would not sacrifice you twenty times for the slightest advantage; equanimity of character that enables you to live with everybody without surrendering to anyone, for the moment you do you have reason to regret it; to say the greatest good about, to heap the greatest praise on people who, often without cause, have said the worst about you without your knowledge (for it is almost always those who are outwardly most attractive and who seem most to want your friendship who deceive you most fully). Those are my virtues, those are the virtues to which I aspire. If I can claim to have a friend, I think I have one in the regiment, but I'm not really sure. He is M***, son of M. de *** and is even, I believe, somewhat related to me through our kin, the Simianes. He is a boy of many merits, extremely friendly, the author of very fine verse, a very good writer, diligent and respected in his work. I am truly his friend; I have reason to believe he is mine. What can we believe anyway? Friends are like women: when put to the test the merchandise often proves defective.[16] That is my confession, in full. I open my heart to you not as to a father whom one fears but does not love but as to the most sincere of friends, the most affectionate friend I think I have in the world. Give up your reasons for pretending to hate me, give me back your affection and never deprive me of it again, and believe that I will do everything in my power to try to keep it.[17]

We recognize in this text themes that Sade would go on to develop until they became the hallmark of his style: the pleasure principle, confinement, and what he would come to call "isolism," his word for the radical impossibility of communication between human beings. One could of course say much more about this "confession," which in my view constitutes the first *literary* act of Donatien de Sade.

A "very tender heart"

Summer 1762. In garrison at Hesdin, a small town in the Pas-de-Calais, Donatien was bored to death. One day he met a woman ten years older than himself and not at all pretty but of good family. He fell in love at once. Overnight the town's upper crust learned of the association. The handsome captain's love for Mlle de *** was soon the only topic of conversation. But the girl's parents were keeping a close eye on the situation: it would be marriage or nothing. Donatien refused to let such an obstacle stand in his way: he would go to the altar if necessary. To make sure of the young man's intentions the girl's father took her away for several days. Caught up in the game, Donatien immediately wrote his own father for permission to marry.

This request put the comte de Sade in a foul mood. A self-important provincial, well-born though she might be, was not to his liking. He dreamed of a more illustrious match. But Donatien insisted that he wanted no other. In any case he had already flatly stated to his father that he would marry only "in accordance with his heart." The count bemoaned this turn of events to his sister Gabrielle-Laure:

He still has this marriage in his head. He wrote me about the event, and his letter ends thus: "As for marriage, I am still very determined to make none other than the one I had the honor to speak to you about. You are my father, and the affection I have reason to hope for from you ought to dispose you to be good enough to appreciate my feelings . . . What reassures me most is your kind promise that you will never dictate what I must feel. I have the honor, etc."

Monsieur l'abbé will judge what decision should be taken. I will take no more part in the discussions and will not answer. He did not fool me. I knew that it was essential to marry him off quickly. No one believed me. Everyone said "no hurry."[18]

Fortunately the duc de Cossé, the colonel of Donatien's regiment, had a nose for trouble. He succeeded without too much difficulty in calming his hotheaded captain, and Donatien dropped the young lady as easily as he had become infatuated with her. The duke dispatched a report on the outcome to the count.

Your son, Sir, has a very tender heart, or at any rate he persuades himself easily that he is in love and that the feeling is reciprocated. That is why he asked your permission for an unwarranted marriage, which I have persuaded him to renounce with hearty laughter on both sides . . . So, Sir, you may feel secure about your son, whose only desire is to please you and be agreeable to you. He is doing well and acts marvelously well in the theater, which amuses him and keeps him busy, and certainly he is most fortunate not to be bored in this city, which is an unbearable place to live.[19]

Reassured, the count continued his investigations, passing up good prospects in the hope of finding better ones, waiting, like the heron in La Fontaine's fable, for something better to turn up.

Discharged

On February 10, 1763, the Treaty of Paris was signed, ending the Seven Years War. The entire city erupted in celebration. But despite the fireworks and torchlights, the restoration of peace left a bitter aftertaste. France had made a poor showing in the conflict. Now it found itself with its fleet destroyed, its treasury depleted, and its colonies lost. Louis XV was forced to surrender to England his possessions in North America as well as his empire in India, with the exception of some trading posts such as Chandernagor and Pondichery. Only the Antilles escaped the debacle. France's defeat sealed England's maritime and commercial superiority and consolidated Prussia's military power. In the provinces as well as in Paris people saw the stain on France's honor and were sarcastic about the Treaty of Paris, which shrank the empire to a shadow of its former self. Poets and songsters lampooned the ineptitude of France's generals, but the jokes could scarcely hide a deep sense of humiliation.

On February 2, shortly before the treaty was signed, Choiseul, then minister of war, ordered a reduction of the cavalry, infantry, and dragoons, much to the dismay of the officers who were brusquely dismissed from the service and obliged to return home with a pension of six hundred livres in return for their years of service—a pittance. In fact there was nothing unusual about such a measure: similar steps had been taken after other peace treaties, affecting large numbers of soldiers and officers. Those discharged did not lose their rank and were eligible to return to their original units or other branches of the service.[20] For the comte de Sade it meant catastrophe, as he explained to Choiseul:

My son's situation, his pain at not having been assigned a place, the prospect of a reduction in force indispensable to the king but dispiriting for the officers—all these things have occasioned a mortal illness that has spared you my importunities for the past three months. Now, at last, my son has been discharged. I am losing the company, more than ten thousand écus that I spent for him and for his gear, which he lost twice. I had no regrets as long as he was serving the king. But now I find myself with forty thousand francs of debt and my son without a position and without hope of returning to the service after having participated in all the campaigns, including the last, and all the battles. What should I do? What should I tell him? What should I advise him? If you would be so kind as to attach him to some unit so that he might not lose that spirit and taste for service that I always tried to inspire in him, it would be a good deed. If not, I beg you to order him to return to Avignon. In my present state I do not wish to see anything that might upset, worry, or sadden me.[21]

The comte de Sade was scarcely exaggerating. Over the past few months his health had seriously deteriorated, and his irritation with Donatien did little to improve his condition. He had recently suffered an attack from which he thought he might not recover, as he wrote his brother: "I was so weak on Sunday that my frightened servants sent for the priest. I came to soon enough to countermand the order. I was very bad again last night. A surgeon told me the other day that I might suddenly die and suffocate [sic], but I feel strength and courage and think I shall be unfortunate enough to drag on for quite a while."[22] A few days later, on February 24, 1763, he received the last rites but again recovered. These repeated alerts, combined with a growing misanthropy and serious financial worries, estranged him from society more and more with each passing day and hastened his return to religion: "I hope to retire to some corner of the world," he wrote his sister, the abbess of Saint-Laurent, "to think only of my end and live ignored by the entire world. I shall soon bid you an eternal farewell, begging your pardon for all the sorrow and suffering I have caused you. I hope that my son does not cause you far more. *You may dispose of all the effects I left there. I take no share. I no longer need anything.*"[23] If he sought refuge in a religious community, it was not out of devoutness so much as to reduce expenses as much as possible and to avoid "having to welcome my son, with whom I am unhappy."[24] As for the state of his fortune, he summed it up this way: "I am dying of poverty, doing without necessary things, and always afraid of running short." No doubt he was exaggerating: the comte de Sade always had an annoying tendency, which his son would inherit, to paint things blacker than they really were.

A Match for Donatien

Officially Donatien was demobilized as of March 16, 1763. In fact he had been back in civilian life for more than a month and living in Paris without a care in the world. He frequented balls and parties, never missed a play or an excursion to the country, haunted the wings of theaters and houses of prostitution, and gave not a moment's thought to his future. While he dizzied himself in this whirl of pleasures, his miserable father worked desperately to find him a wife. Once married, Donatien would cease to be a burden and might settle down, or so his father hoped. But the young man's dissolute behavior made it difficult to find a match, and the comte de Sade lived in constant fear that some new escapade would forever compromise his chance of success.

At around this time the count met Jean Partyet, formerly France's commercial representative in Cadiz and Madrid and since 1758 superintendent of the Invalides (the royal veterans' home). Partyet mentioned a young niece of his whose parents were looking to find her a suitable husband. The count mentioned his son. While the girl's family studied the proposition, the count announced the news to the abbé:

My health is improving steadily, and I am in good shape to depart tomorrow. This marriage is the only thing holding me up. If it falls through, I'm leaving. My son is not yet ready to marry. He is dying to find a wife, but when something needs to be done, he doesn't do it. I begged him to call on the superintendent of the Invalides and M. de Gramont; he did not have the time. I begged him to come to dinner at my house with the superintendent to talk things over. He did not come and said that he had forgotten. I've never seen anything like it! The girl's mother admits she has heard that he is deeply in debt and wild: "What young man hasn't done foolish things?" she says. "Let us proceed." This makes me think that it will work out. All the others have fallen through on account of his very bad reputation. Did I tell you that they were prepared to offer five years' board rather than three and will keep the two of them as long as they wish? And that if they leave they will give them ten thousand francs to buy furniture, not to be counted as part of the dowry? And that they believe the *légitime* of each child will amount to five or six hundred thousand francs? I do not think we can do better. The father is *président* (presiding judge) in the Cour des Aides; he has five children.[25] He is the son of M. de Launay, who ennobled her [*sic*: he means the bride's] father.[26] So the daughter can enter Malta.[27] All this comes with good houses and people who now enjoy a certain credit and will exert themselves on my son's behalf. I can go and trust them to do what is necessary. I secure my property, substitute him, and reserve for myself only the income of ten thousand écus to revert to him after my death.[28]

Indeed the match was far from inconsiderable. Although the Cordier de Montreuils belonged to the lesser nobility of the robe and had been ennobled only since the seventeenth century, their fortune was considerably greater than the Sades'. Marriages between the *noblesse d'épée* and the *noblesse de robe* stemming from the mercantile bourgeoisie were not unusual in the eighteenth century; they are explained by the growing impoverishment of the court nobility. In a society where social success depended largely on expenditure for prestige and show, bankruptcy was a constant danger. Generally it took two or three generations for a family to fall into ruin. In the case of the Sades it had taken only one, that of Jean-Baptiste. He alone had put his house into financial peril, without help from any of his ancestors. The ambition to serve in the highest offices had led him to spend prodigiously and far beyond his means. Eventually, however, the count was forced to admit defeat and abandon the exhausting race that had led him to the edge of the abyss. He emerged from the experience crushed and bitter.

•

In 1763 Claude-René Montreuil bore the title of honorary president of the Cour des Aides of Paris.[29] He lived with his family on rue Neuve-du-Luxembourg (today rue Cambon) in the parish of the Madeleine, one of the most elegant neighborhoods of the capital, where the property once occupied by the maréchal de Luxembourg's hôtel had been subdivided into lots. On August 21, 1740, M. de Montreuil married a young woman from a family as recently ennobled as his own: Marie-Madeleine Masson de Plissay, the daughter of Antoine Masson, esquire, royal counselor, and secretary, and Marie-Pélagie Partyet.[30] Energetic and authoritarian, this woman, known to all as *la présidente de Montreuil* or just simply la Présidente, ran her household with an iron hand.

The marriage produced six children, three girls and three boys, including the twins Charles and Marie-Joseph. The eldest of the daughters was named Renée-Pélagie. Born on December 2, 1741, she was eighteen months younger than Donatien. She was to be his intended. "The future wife was rich," Maurice Heine wrote, "not because of her dowry, which was rather modest, but because of her solid prospects. More important, her parents were unusually influential and had powerful connections at court."[31] Too keen a connoisseur of reputations and too shrewd a calculator not to have guessed that if the comte de Sade was willing to condescend to a marriage so unflattering to himself, it must be because his son's behavior was enough to frighten the mothers of prospective brides, la Présidente, in the bitter negotiations that the two parties began in March, cynically speculated on her suspicions so as to reduce the Montreuils' contribution.

In the meantime another proposition of marriage arrived from Provence. This one was on behalf of Mlle de Cambis, the daughter of an old family of Florentine bankers that had settled in Avignon and was remotely related by marriage to Mme de Pompadour. But the comte de Sade preferred Renée-Pélagie de Montreuil, as he informed his brother:

If this son were a good subject, I would regard the marriage he is making as excellent and would prefer it in all respects to a marriage with Mlle de Cambis: there will be much more property and I like the connections better. I would rather see my son a cousin of M. de Prie[32] and M. de Toulongeon,[33] who has a fine post in the gendarmes, than of Messieurs de Brantès and de Presles with relatives in Tarascon. But in Paris my son will soon be lost, ruined by debt. His wife will be extremely unhappy, and he will be banished from his father-in-law's house. That is how he will end up. In Avignon he would not find it so easy to stray. That is why I have always wanted the most mediocre marriage in the provinces.[34]

In fact the count seemed entirely in accord with the marriage to Renée-Pélagie, in which he saw nothing but advantages. In another letter to his brother he wrote:

The more I think about this marriage, the better it seems. Yesterday I went to see M. de Montmartel[35] who knows everybody's property and was a close acquaintance of M. de Launay,[36] who held the same post as special treasurer for war. He told me that Mme de Launay[37] had an income of more than ten thousand livres she did not live on; that M. de Montreuil would have at least eighty thousand at her death, counting property from which he already receives income today; that since Mme d'Azy[38] has no children, her share would be divided and he would get one-third; that he would also get a great deal from his wife, and that at a rough guess he would say that M. de Montreuil's children might have incomes of twenty-five thousand livres barring accidents; that this was not a property in the air, subject to ups and downs (*révolutions*) like a businessman's; that he would rather have the five years' board than a hundred thousand additional francs; that the mother was a worthy woman of great intelligence, which he considered quite important; and that in all respects these were good people with whom my son would be quite happy. All this pleased me no end. As for me, what makes up my mind is that I'll be rid of the boy, who has not one good quality and all the bad ones.[39]

He even claimed to feel remorse at the thought of duping such good people: "I pity them for making such a bad buy, someone capable of all sorts of foolishness," he hypocritically confessed to the abbess of Saint-Laurent. Actually he found it difficult to contain his joy. From now on the in-laws could take responsibility for his no-good son. "I have done things to get rid of him that I never would have done had I loved him tenderly," he would confess to the abbé. "I do not think I can pay too much for the pleasure of never hearing about him again. Although this business is very far advanced, M. de Sade's escapades might still put an end to it. I won't be sure of anything until I see them at the altar."[40]

Mlle de Lauris

While his father arduously negotiated his marriage to Mlle de Montreuil, Donatien, who had long since forgotten the woman in Hesdin, fell madly in love with a ravishing beauty whom he had just met and who immediately became his mistress. Laure-Victoire Adeline de Lauris was twenty-two years old, had beautiful eyes, and belonged, like Donatien, to the most illustrious Provençal nobility. Her line dated from the thirteenth century. Here, he thought, was a match more worthy of a gentleman than the "daughter of tax extortionists" his father wanted him to marry. From the beginning of their affair he asked Mlle de Lauris to marry him. Her father, the marquis de Lauris, was apparently willing, but the young beauty refused, or so she said, to break up a marriage that was nearly concluded and force her way into a family. That is where things stood on the twentieth of March, when the comte de Sade, convinced that negotiations with the Montreuils had ended, suddenly decided to return to Provence and sent his son ahead to prepare for his arrival. No doubt he also hoped that the separation would calm the young man's ardor and put an end to his idyll. In a cloud of gloom Donatien started on his way. No sooner had he arrived in Avignon, however, than he invited his mistress to join him, but she cruelly spurned the offer. A few days later events took another dramatic turn: the marriage was on, the Montreuils had patched things up with the comte de Sade. Of course they had no idea that Renée-Pélagie's fiancé pined for another woman.

Donatien was now to return docilely to Paris to marry the woman his father had chosen for him. But the young man saw things in a rather different light. This time it was serious: he was quite simply smitten with Mlle de Lauris. He loved her to distraction and declared himself ready to do anything to win her hand. In any case he had already announced that he had no intention of marrying against his heart's desires. He implored his mistress to hasten to his side; she refused. He grew impatient; she resisted. He became enraged and lost first his temper, then his hope; she remained a block of marble. Had he not sworn eternal love to her? What was she doing in Paris? Deceiving him for sure. On top of all this, he was sick. A chancre had appeared. It was being treated with mercury, the only known remedy for venereal disease. His father panicked when he heard the news. What if the Montreuils found out? That would be the end of the marriage. This was to be avoided at all cost, if necessary by claiming that he was suffering from some other disease. The marriage ceremony was set for May, and it was now April. The count begged the abbé to send him a letter that he could show to his prospective in-laws: "You must write that he had not fully recovered from his fever and had a relapse on arriving, but that the attacks are sporadic and you will not send him back until he is fully cured."[41] Above all the foolish boy must get treatment, and quickly. Everyone was awaiting his return. "He must be cured, and if he carries on in Avignon as he did in Paris, he will never get better. He must be made to feel the necessity of submitting to the proper remedies to hasten his return to Paris and a marriage he desires."[42] Go back to Paris? To marry this Renée-Pélagie, whom everyone said was ugly and devoid of charm? Lord no! It was out of the question. He informed his father of his decision. The wretched count no longer knew which way to turn: "He wrote me yesterday that he was more in love than ever [and] that it was not Mlle de Lauris who made him ill. He forgets that he told me he had not been with any other women. Fortunately she no longer wants him," the count wrote to his brother.[43]

"We shall never be one without the other"

Donatien, however, refused to believe that he had been abandoned. Despite the letters he received informing him that the affair was over, he continued to believe that Mlle de Lauris would come back to him. He took up his pen and let loose the torrent of contradictory emotions that were agitating him in a long letter impressive for its verbal fury, its noisy tumult of hatred, passion, suffering, threat, and supplication. Of the eight large sheets he covered with his fine hand, I cite only the most significant passages:

Avignon, April 6, 1763

Liar! Ingrate! What became of your promise to love me as long as you lived? Who is forcing you to change your mind? Who is making you break the knots that were to marry us forever? Did you mistake my departure for running away? Did you think I could run from you and go on living? Your family no doubt influenced your judgment of my feelings . . . You were afraid of being reunited with one who adored you. These links of an eternal chain began to weigh on you, and your heart, which is charmed by inconstancy and frivolity and nothing else, was not delicate enough to appreciate all its charms. It was leaving Paris that frightened you. My love was not enough for you. I was not made to hold your heart. Go ahead, never leave the city, monster, born to make my life a misery. May the deceptions of the scoundrel who will replace me in your heart make it as odious to you as your deceptions have made it to me! . . . But what am I saying? Oh, my dear beloved! Oh, my divine friend! Mainstay of my heart, light of my life, my dear love, where is my despair taking me? Forgive the outbursts of an unhappy wretch who no longer knows himself, for whom, after the loss of the one he loves, death becomes the sole resource. Alas! I draw near that moment which is going to deliver me from the world I detest. My only wish now is to see that moment arrive . . . Oh, if you still love me, if you love me as you always loved me, as I love you, as I adore you and will adore you all my life, have pity on our woes, rail against fortune's devastating blows, write me, try to justify yourself . . . Alas! You will not suffer much. What truly tortures my heart is that I find you culpable . . .

But no matter what state you may be in, nothing will prevent me from giving you the tenderest proof of my love . . .

Beware of inconstancy; I do not deserve it. I confess that I would be furious and would stop at no horror. The story of the *c* . . .[44] should persuade you to go easy with me. I confess that I will not hide it from my rival, and it will not be the only confidence I share with him. There is, I swear, no horror from which I would shrink . . . But I blush at the thought of holding on to you by such means. I will, I must, speak to you only of your love. Your promises, your oaths, your letters that I reread constantly every day—only these things should hold you in chains: I rest my case on them alone . . .

Love me always. Be faithful to me if you do not wish to see me die of pain. Adieu, my beautiful child, I adore you and I love you a thousand times more than my own life. Though you tell me to go, I swear to you that we shall never be one without the other.[45]

Amid protestations of love Donatien does not hesitate to threaten his mistress with the most vile blackmail if she should deceive him. It seems reasonable to assume, moreover, that, contrary to what he implies, he contaminated her and not vice versa. Garrison life and diligent frequentation of brothels surely involved greater risks than the staid life of a young lady of the provinces over whom her father kept a watchful eye. One wonders if this letter was actually sent. Donatien later had it recopied by his secretary Carteron along with other juvenilia (love letters, occasional verse, entr'actes, songs, compliments, and so on) and had the whole collection bound into an anthology to which he gave the title *Oeuvres de M. de Sade*. From this it seems plausible to conclude that he regarded it more as a stylistic exercise than an authentic document. It may even have been written some years after his adventure with Mlle de Lauris. A born writer, he always liked to cover his tracks by mixing fiction with reality.

Artichokes and Thyme

Meanwhile, in Paris, something happened that flattered the Montreuils' pride: His Majesty agreed to grace the marriage contract with his approval, an honor that was accorded to only a very few, and in this case to the kinsman of the Maillés far more than to the great-granddaughter of M. Cordier. The ceremony was to take place in Versailles on May 1. In mid-April Donatien was still waiting for his love in Avignon, while his father pawed the ground in Paris. The days passed, the date drew near, and still Donatien did not arrive. The comte de Sade confessed that he understood nothing about his son. How could he still love this Lauris woman, who had given him the pox and now threatened to ruin an advantageous marriage? "Is it possible that this child has regrets about this marriage after all that he has heard about the girl and all that he has gained? Clearly he must be without feelings or honor."

Donatien did indeed demonstrate little ardor for marrying Mlle de Montreuil. She was wealthy, to be sure, and full of prospects, but totally without charm. Everyone agreed that she was unattractive. This was not stated in so many words but intimated. To his sister, for example, the comte de Sade wrote: "I did not find the young lady ugly on Sunday. She is very nicely built, with a pretty bosom and very white arms and hands. Nothing shocking, a charming character."[46] This is not enthusiasm. And the young woman's own mother, la Présidente, displayed even less indulgence—or more lucidity—in describing her daughter to the abbé de Sade: "When she has the privilege of meeting you, Monsieur, and the family of M. de Sade, I hope that she will inspire genuine interest, at least by virtue of her reason and gentleness. Figure and charm are gifts of nature, which it is not within our power to obtain for ourselves."[47] Residence certificates issued to Renée-Pélagie during the Revolution mention her physical characteristics: height, four foot ten, nose large, mouth average, jaw round, hair brown, face round and full, forehead low, eyes gray."[48]

Renée-Pélagie not only lacked good looks but had no talent for coquetry. She had masculine ways, a grenadier's demeanor, and made no attempt at elegance. She wore old clothes, had her shoes resoled, and put on heavy gloves to split wood. In addition, her education, like that of most girls of the time, was neglected. She read little and her spelling could hardly have been more fanciful, yet her judgment of others was sound and her writing lively, colorful, and often picturesque. Her letters are never boring. She described things as she saw them in vivid, direct, natural sentences without affectation or pretension and occasionally with surprising felicity of expression. Broadly speaking she was a resolute woman, active, realistic, unswervingly upright, yet not lacking in critical intelligence or thoughtfulness.

•

On the morning of May 1, the day of official introductions at court, both families went to Versailles in full complement, except for the future bridegroom, who had yet to resign himself to leave Avignon. The occasion being too important, the decision was made to forgo his presence. Louis XV affixed his august signature to the bottom of the marriage contract, along with the signatures of the dauphin and dauphine, the duc de Berry, the comte de Provence, Mesdames (the king's daughters), the prince de Condé, the prince de Conti, and Mlle de Sens. By some perverse stroke of fate Donatien's name was once again deformed, as it had been at his baptism: this time he was marked down as Donatien *Aldof* François. When the ceremony finally ended the comte de Sade returned to Paris, exhausted: "The day did me in," he confided to Gabrielle-Laure. "I returned home with my legs swollen."[49]

The Montreuils barely had time to recover from their emotion at meeting the king when they learned what had been hidden from them:

the affair with Mlle de Lauris and the true nature of their future son-in-law's illness. In a panic at the thought that the heiress might slip from his son's grasp, the former ambassador of Louis XV flattered these petty nobles, whom he secretly despised, and cajoled them in every possible way. To his sister he wrote:

I think that, having read the latest mail from Avignon, Mme de Montreuil knows everything. This and the other story [Donatien's venereal disease] have made her remarkably cool toward my son, but there is no turning back . . . No matter what blunders he makes, I help things along a little with my concern, politeness, and attention. The whole family seems happy with me. I dine and spend every day with one of them. I see no one else, and you cannot imagine how attentive they have been. I cannot help feeling pity for them on account of the acquisition they are about to make, and I reproach myself for deceiving them as to the character of the groom. The abbé in his last letter concedes that no one is less nice than [Donatien]. When I told him so, he did not want to believe me and assured me that he would make him into whatever he wished. Only his tone is gentle, but whether about the smallest thing or the most important, it is impossible to make him change his mind. I think I shall be in a great hurry to leave Paris once he is here.[50]

La Présidente, for her part, was so keen on a marriage that would join her family to one of royal blood that she closed her eyes to everything.

The signing of the marriage contract before a notary was set for May 15 and the religious ceremony for May 17. And still Donatien did not come! The marriage could not be celebrated without him. By now everyone was exasperated. To his sister Gabrielle-Laure the count wrote:

You tell me to expect the groom on the fifteenth, and the next day the abbé writes me that he won't be leaving before the fifteenth . . . Well, now it is too late for them to renege, but they are very impatient with the slow pace of things and soon the whole family is going to be asking for him. The président de Meslay, the wealthiest of the uncles, is leaving on Monday: one present lost, and I believe the others will follow. I told them to expect him on the fifteenth on the basis of your letter, and I never went to announce the second delay. You must go on talking about his attacks of fever, because that is what I am saying here. Since the disease is public, how can the marriage [to Mlle de Lauris] be hidden? For nothing was more important, or easier, than to keep the disease hidden. I do not own up to it. If people know, they can put it down to local slander. If he is sent by postal coach, it will cost a lot of money.

He should bring two or three dozen artichokes. There are none here on account of the frost, and they can serve as a wedding present. If you could send thyme, that would very welcome. This is in case he comes by postal coach.[51]

•

And so he arrived. The prodigal son returned with his artichokes and his thyme. And none too soon! On the afternoon of Sunday, May 15, the bride and groom and their families met in the hôtel of the président de Montreuil to sign the contract in the presence of the notaries Fortier and Lebrun. The terms had long been set. Renée-Pélagie's dowry amounted to 300,000 livres, a considerable sum, to be sure, but only a small part of it was to be paid in cash, the rest coming in the form of income and future inheritances. From the Sade side, Donatien was to receive, in addition to the post of lieutenant general for the provinces of Bresse, Bugey, and so on, which yielded an annual income of roughly 10,000 livres, "bare ownership" (without revenue) of the lands and seigneuries of La Coste, Mazan, Saumane, and the farm at Cabannes, and other properties present and future, out of which his father reserved the right to dispose of 30,000 livres. In addition, the count left his son 10,000 of the 34,000 livres owed him by the comte de Béthune, the buyer of his estate at Glatigny, "to clothe [his] son and his people and to buy himself a carriage and two horses." Finally, the young marquis assigned an income of 4,000 livres to his wife as dower, with the capital to pass to any children that might be born of the marriage.[52]

Maurice Heine had this to say about the terms of the contract: "As the father of a prodigal and libertine son, the comte de Sade was apparently concerned not to leave the youth in control of a large sum of capital. This concern presumably meshed well with the outright greed of the Montreuils, who were infinitely more willing to provide the young couple with an income than to give up possession of a genuine dowry."[53] But there was another clause in the contract at least as important as the ones mentioned so far and that affected Donatien's personal status: "In view of the aforementioned contract, the comte de Sade has declared that he emancipates the future husband and frees him from paternal power." Thus two years before his legal majority (set at age twenty-five under the Ancien Régime), the young marquis was able to dispose freely of his person and property. He would not wait long to make use of this right.

On the day after the signing, which was also the eve of the religious ceremony, la présidente de Montreuil could not refrain from letting the abbé de Sade know how pleased and proud she was that her daughter was about to join such an illustrious house. She did not stint on praise for her son-in-law either:

No one can be more touched than I am, Sir, by the tokens of satisfaction that you have been kind enough to show me at the marriage that it is our privilege to conclude with you. I am very flattered and content in every way. Your nephew seems as charming as can be and all the more desirable as a son-in-law thanks to an air of reason, gentleness, and good breeding that is apparently due to your efforts. My daughter is also properly grateful for all your marks of kindness. She sends you her respects and wants you to know how much she hopes to please you and win your friendship along with that of the family to which it is your privilege to belong. M. de Montreuil and I share this feeling and hope that you will convey it to the rest of your family, and we want you to know that we are particularly grateful to you . . .

I beg you, Sir, to offer my daughter your kindness and advice. She can receive none better. Our satisfaction would be complete if only you could witness it.[54]

The following day, May 17, 1763, the marriage was celebrated in the church of Sainte-Marie-Madeleine parish in Ville-l'Evêque, in the presence of numerous witnesses: for the groom, his cousin the abbé de Sade d'Eyguières, canon of the chapter of Marseilles, and his kinsman the duc d'Ancezune; and for the bride, her great-uncle Joseph-Marie Masson, former Grand Master of Waters and Forests; her maternal uncles, Antoine Masson de Meslay, président of the Chambre des Comptes, and the marquis de Villette, former trésorier-général de l'extraordinaire des guerres; and her paternal grandmother, Anne-Thérèse de Croëzer, widow of Jacques Cordier de Launay.[55]

6

"Wild as the wind"

"Oh, the rascal!"

When the ceremony was over, the young newlyweds moved into the apartment prepared for them on the second floor of the hôtel de Montreuil on rue Neuve-du-Luxembourg. Under the terms of the marriage contract, the Montreuils had pledged to provide the couple with free room and board for a period of five years from the date of the marriage, along with a valet and a chambermaid, either in Paris or in their château at Echauffour in Normandy, where they often went for extended periods.

The comte de Sade took up residence a short distance away in the rue Basse-du-Rempart, where he lived quite simply, with a manservant, a housekeeper, and a footman (but no carriage). M. de Montreuil visited every day, but Donatien refused to cross the street to see his father. The count professed not to care: "What he does now makes absolutely no difference to me, and I am doing well," he wrote the abbé. "He will come when he needs me. He wants to put on one of my plays. He will come to me for it. I'm not suffering because of him."[1] In fact, relations had never been so bad between the father and the son. The count fumed at having to pay Donatien's old debts and took offense when his son asked to see an accounting of the income on his lieutenant-generalcy for the previous three years. "I must be prepared for anything," he moaned. "As for my feelings, I've never been in any doubt: I know no one else so ill bred, and, as I wrote you, I did more for him in this marriage than I should have done simply to be rid of him and for fear that I might still have him on my hands."[2] His scoundrel of a son, he complained, had repaid all his favors with ingratitude and mean tricks. Just recently he had obtained for his son the immense favor of being allowed to ride in His Majesty's carriage and hunt with the king, but the miserable wretch had not even bothered to show up. "I have made up my mind to inflict no further pain on myself," the count declared. "Nothing my son does can cause me to lose sleep. I am upset that he is so ill bred. He will drive me out of Paris if only to put an end to hearing him talked about, but I will not suffer because of it. Whatever he does, I have made up my mind."[3]

La Présidente, far from sympathizing with the unfortunate father, literally became infatuated with Donatien; she swore by him alone. "Oh, the rascal! That is what I call my little son-in-law," she confided to the abbé de Sade. "Sometimes I take the liberty of scolding him. We quarrel, [but] we make up at once. It is never very serious or very long. In general we are happy with him. Confidence is never won overnight, any more than a lawsuit is. Yes, he's distracted, but marriage is settling him down. Unless I miss my guess, you would already notice the progress if you saw him."[4] The count was scornful: "Mme de Montreuil has fallen for all my son's fantasies. She's mad about him. Her family no longer recognizes her. And as for him, he's as wild as the wind and avid only for pleasure that he can't find anywhere he looks."[5]

In the bitter dispute that was soon to erupt between father and son, la Présidente took the son's side—not without reason. What was the quarrel about? In 1760, as we have seen, the comte de Sade resigned the post of lieutenant general in favor of his son. What no one knew, however, was that he had already collected the stipends for the next three years, 1761, 1762, and 1763, without mentioning the fact to Donatien, who incurred a substantial loss as a result. Under the terms of the marriage contract the count was manifestly in the wrong.[6] He tried to justify his action by claiming that he had had to pay for his son's upkeep up to the time of his marriage, but the argument only earned him accusations of bad faith. Mme de Montreuil pleaded her son-in-law's case to the abbé de Sade:

I admit that this time I can find no wrong on my son-in-law's part in either substance or form. When one has a grievance, can one do better than to maintain a respectful silence? This is what he has been doing for the past six weeks, yet a certain person is complaining about him to the families to which he has just been joined by marriage, to his friends, and perhaps even to the public as though he were an ungrateful and unnatural son . . . We have been in the country since early August. My son-in-law remained in Paris a few days longer to take care of registering his letters of appointment to office, and he joined me a week later with his wife, whom I entrusted to him. It seems silly to say that one "entrusts" a woman to her husband, but he is so young, so very young, that he still must pardon me for that.[7]

Outraged that a son should have been treated so badly by his father, Mme de Montreuil even tried to persuade the count that Donatien was worth more than he believed. To that end she sent him this note, which the count must have read with a smile on his lips. It is not every day that one sees a woman of sound common sense so badly miss the mark:

I am perhaps speaking to you too frankly, Monsieur, but if I ever have the honor of knowing you well, you will judge my feelings. I have absolutely no desire to estrange you from your son. He has been mine for too brief a time for me to have made any impression whatsoever on his mind. His heart is better, fundamentally, than you have been told and perhaps than you imagine. The excessive warmth of his feelings only seems to put him in the wrong. I hope with all my soul that, when it comes to your son, you heed only the feelings of nature. If so, pecuniary matters will be easy to dispose of. Judge for yourself. I vouch for his heart. To see you reunited by affection and trust would make my heart content.[8]

The Iron Lady

Mme de Montreuil had quite plainly been conquered by the young cavalryman with the sensual lips and fiery temperament. The lady carried her forty years quite easily and had not given up trying to please. She was "a charming woman, a good storyteller, still quite unspoiled, short rather than tall, with a pleasant figure, a seductive laugh and eye, a mischievous wit, the wisdom and simplicity of an angel, yet shrewd as a fox, although still likeable and in her way attractive."[9] The marquis for his part strove to enter still more deeply into his mother-in-law's good graces. Through attentiveness and flattery he soon managed to turn her head. He excelled in the role of wheedler. Of course Mme de Montreuil knew what mischief he was capable of, but she sincerely believed that his changed circumstances would settle him down. In any case his ferocity and rebelliousness did not displease her. His wildness even drew them together. She felt a secret satisfaction at the thought that they were of the same species. As dominating personalities, neither la Présidente nor Donatien troubled much about the feelings their authoritarian passions aroused, whether hatred or fascination. They felt nothing but indifference for the rights or sufferings of others. Both knew how to seduce, intimidate, corrupt, and use whatever influence was available to arrive at their ends, without regret or remorse. Both possessed, to an equal degree, the kind of energy and audacity that nothing can thwart. Woe unto those who refused to bend to their desires! Donatien would discover what this meant the day these two wild beasts squared off for a fight to the finish, from which la Présidente would emerge victorious, not because she was the stronger of the two but because she possessed qualities that would always be sorely lacking in Donatien: prudence to the point of extreme wariness and, above all, unfailing self-control. Against an adversary who was unmethodical and without discipline Mme de Montreuil mustered an iron will and an orderly mind. Rapidly and accurately calculating her moves down to the last detail, she brought to the game the instincts of a cat that knows how to stalk its victim patiently and then suddenly pounce. Her hatred proved fierce, all the more so because she felt she had been seduced and then deceived. Donatien had outfoxed her prudence, repaid her kindness with insults, defiled her favorite daughter, and alienated the affections of the other. She would pay back this son-in-law she had loved too much; she would avenge herself unremittingly.

As for Donatien, for the first and only time in his life he had met someone as brutal as he, and as unscrupulous, but infinitely more shrewd. At the end of an unrelenting struggle he would find himself dashed to pieces against this rock of good conscience, this implacable embodiment of the law. In his eyes Mme de Montreuil represented the baying pack of hounds thirsting for justice and compensation. He was *merely* guilty; she turned him into a defendant, or worse, a criminal. Little by little she would assume the mask of his sins, a vision of horror against which he would attempt to respond with insult and calumny. Through her, however, it was his own nature that he was seeking to annihilate; it was himself against whom his murderous impulses were directed. The torturer turned himself into the victim of this other torturer, who happened to be his wife's mother but who was in fact the image of *the* mother, of *his* mother, of all mothers. His enemy was indeed Mme de Montreuil, but beyond her it was *the* mother, in the figure of Mme de Mistival on whom he would inflict his most atrocious vengeance in the final pages of *La Philosophie dans le boudoir*, defiling and debasing her with the frenetic jubilation of a man who knows he is lost.

Compared to this superior woman Monsieur de Montreuil cuts a rather paltry figure. He scarcely even exists. Utterly dominated by la Présidente, basically good-natured, weak, and pusillanimous, he had long since given up all thought of making himself heard in his own home. His wife controlled everything, watched over everything, and gave orders to everyone. The président's weak character might elicit compassion or even sympathy if it did not simply relegate him to oblivion. He did play a role, however—an obscure one to be sure, but not negligible, although it has hitherto gone unnoticed. With the help of my friend and colleague François Moureau I have been able to discover what it was. M. de Montreuil was his family's memory. He regularly kept a diary in which he recorded items of interest to himself and his family: genealogies, births, deaths, souvenirs, autobiographical notes, memorabilia of his travels, what have you. The président kept an extremely faithful record of his impression of the places he visited and the people he met. His diary contains a wealth of information on a thousand different subjects, and I have made extensive use of it.[10]

A Well-Matched Couple

For now, however, our young newlyweds were still enjoying their honeymoon. The first weeks passed quickly in a whirl of plays, receptions, concerts, and visits. On June 9 Mlle de Sens presented the young Mme de Sade to the court, an honor generally reserved for the highest nobility. The summer and early fall was a time of unclouded happiness, apparently shared. Renée-Pélagie looked for opportunities to please her husband, and he, for his part, proved solicitous and affectionate. Mme de Montreuil had every reason to rejoice. If she had harbored any doubts as to her son-in-law's morals, she could now feel fully reassured. She had ample reason to believe in the virtues of matrimony.

"He is very good with his wife," his father observed. "As long as that lasts, I will overlook the rest."[11] Four months after the wedding la Présidente wrote to the abbé de Sade: "Their tender friendship seems perfectly reciprocal. There is but one affliction in the household: the inability as yet to assure you and me that it will be a *large* one. I hope that it will be, but I await the news without impatience. Neither of them comes of sterile stock."[12] On October 20 she wrote again: "As for your niece, however much she wishes to obey you, she will never scold him. She will love him all you like. That is fairly simple: he is lovable. Thus far he loves her mightily, and no one could treat her better."[13]

Mask or reality? Was Donatien truly a loving husband, or was he playing a part? For Renée-Pélagie the question did not arise. Subject to her parents' authority, she took it as a duty to love this young man whom she hardly knew. In this respect little had changed since Molière's time: younger sons were sacrificed to older ones and daughters were sacrificed to husbands, without allowing the victim any say in the matter and without regard to the heart's desire. Girls were handed over to strangers and told to behave like ladies, but really they were pawns in a game of ambition and profit, tokens in a traffic of influence, a quest for preferment and wealth. What generally became of such forced marriages is not difficult to imagine: religion sustained morose resignation, while time eased the bitterness. Some marriages ended in open rupture, but there was abundant opportunity for vengeance in the form of amorous adventures. This, however, was not the path that Renée-Pélagie would take. In her heart she never abandoned religion. If she thought occasionally of ending her marriage, she did so only long enough to dismiss the idea more out of a sense of duty than out of respect for the proprieties. Her fate cannot be compared to any other woman's because the man to whom she was bound was unique. Renée-Pélagie would never succumb to the melancholy, torpor, or other afflictions of the soul that plunged so many wives into a state of lethargy akin to death. Her singular destiny was not, as has often been said, that of pitiful victim but that of accomplice, or better yet, of a diligent and devoted partner, who, assigned a role she had not chosen and for which nothing had prepared her, would play it with all the resources of her woman's instinct.

Mme de Sade sacrificed herself to her husband serenely, naturally, almost gaily, and never demanded an explanation. She submitted to his injustice, his insults, and his blows. For his sake she was willing to perform the most vile acts. All that would normally have estranged a woman like her from a man like him only brought them closer together. Therein lies the great mystery of this couple, in which neither pity nor lassitude nor compromise nor any of what ordinarily debases conjugal love ever played a part. Renée-Pélagie accepted the violation of her conscience as someone else might accept the passing of the seasons, with meekness and simplicity. In carrying out tasks that could not have been more contrary to her nature she displayed a kind of lucid grace as remote from cynicism as it was from martyrdom—and strangely akin to love. This voluntary servitude—in which some commentators have seen, not without reason, a masochistic impulse—sprang initially from Mme de Sade's profound insight into the marquis. Instinctively she understood that behind the man of domination there lurked a helpless child, sometimes cruel and sometimes needy but always requiring unflagging support. She learned to reconcile the two contradictory personalities that coexisted within him: the slave of an imperious sensuality, carried away by his "fiery soul," unable to satisfy himself without suffering or inflicting suffering, and the anguished being pierced by an irresistible need to feel loved. To him she made a gift of herself as only a mother might do, offering absolute loyalty at the cost of her own integrity. What mistress, what wife would have braved so many dangers to defend, with such stubborn determination, a lost soul?

But for nearly thirty years Renée-Pélagie also felt herself being lifted up by Donatien, raised to inconceivable heights. For nearly thirty years she had the feeling of living above the law, both human and divine, above other women, even above herself, somewhere in that "seventh region of the sky" to which the Sade eagle transported its prey. As for the marquis, he would always consider his marriage to Mlle de Montreuil as "a mercenary and vile pact, a shameful traffic in fortunes and names, which, binding only persons, abandons their hearts to all the disorders of despair and spite."[14] What is more, he had no intention of depriving himself of any adventure for the sake of fidelity: "Woe unto the woman who takes it in mind to be jealous of her husband," he wrote. "Let her be content with what he gives her, if she loves him, but let her not try to restrain him. If she does, she will not only not succeed, but she will soon earn his hatred as well."[15] Renée-Pélagie heeded this lesson.

Mme de Sade's "Misconstruction"

One knows what the wedding night meant for most young women in this period. The prince de Ligne paints an amusing portrait: "A girl is taught never to look a man in the face, never to respond to him, never to ask how she came into the world. Two men in black [the notaries] arrive with a man wearing a robe embroidered on every seam [that is, the priest in his chasuble]. They tell her, 'Spend the night with this gentleman.' The gentleman, all aflame, brutally asserts his rights, asks nothing, but demands a great deal. She gets up in tears at the very least, and he in a lather."[16] Mme de Saint-Ange says much the same thing but in another tone in *La Philosophie dans le boudoir*: "Consider a young lady, barely out of her father's house or boarding school, knowing nothing, utterly without experience, forced to go from there suddenly to the arms of a man she has never seen, forced to swear to this man, on the altar, an obedience and fidelity all the more unjust in that she often harbors in her heart of hearts the greatest desire to break her word. Is there in all the world a more dreadful fate, Eugénie?"[17] Such was the situation of Renée-Pélagie at the time of her marriage.

It is reasonable to assume that the marquis did not spare the woman he joined for the first time in their marriage bed, and that he forced her that night to submit to the brutality he had previously reserved for prostitutes. In his fantasies, of course, he always favored sodomy (whether homosexual or heterosexual) over all other forms of pleasure. Scenes of sodomization recur with such regularity in his "libertine" novels that "normal" relations are all but forgotten. The "sodomite pleasure" surpassed all others: "This pleasure is such," Dolmancé declares, "that nothing can interfere with it, and the object that serves it cannot, in savoring it, fail to be transported to the third heaven. No other is as good, no other can satisfy as fully both of the individuals who indulge in it, and those who have experienced it can revert to other things only with difficulty."[18]

There can be no doubt that Mme de Sade put up no resistance to her husband's demands. The Church itself recommended that Christian wives bow to their husbands' wishes, and Renée-Pélagie had sworn before God to do so. A letter (dated June 1783) from Donatien to Renée-Pélagie makes it clear that the couple regularly practiced anal intercourse: "Here's to a good screw up the ass, and may the devil take me if I don't give myself a hand job in honor of your buttocks! Don't tell la Présidente, though, because she's a good Jansenist and doesn't like for women to be *molinized*. [The allusion is to Luis Molina, the sixteenth-century Spanish Jesuit whose doctrine of grace the Jansenists opposed. —Trans.] She pretends that M. Cordier never *discharged* anywhere but in the *vessel of propagation*, and that whosoever distances himself from the *vessel* must boil in hell. But I, who was raised by the Jesuits, who was taught by Father Sanchez not to *swim in a vacuum* any more than was necessary, because, as Descartes tells us, *nature abhors a vacuum*— I cannot agree with *Mama Cordier*. You, though, are a philosopher. You have a very pretty *misconstruction [contresens]*, and a manner of moving and a narrowness in that *misconstruction*, and heat in the *rectum*, that makes me get on with you quite well."[19]

Jeanne Testard

In the eighteenth century marriage was no obstacle to libertinage. How many husbands abandoned their wives immediately after the wedding night so as to continue living their fantasies! The man who had several mistresses the night before his wedding found his way back to them the night after. Such habits were so commonplace that marital fidelity and unwavering love seemed ridiculous. Married in May, the marquis de Sade rented, in June, a small house on the rue Mouffetard, which he furnished on credit. He also had the use of an apartment in Versailles and a furnished house in Arcueil, which he rented for 800 livres annually and which would soon become notorious. The young debauchee was rather well set up. He frequently changed residences to cover his tracks and escape the recriminations of the prostitutes he recruited all over town and took home with him in hired carriages with the curtains drawn. If there were complaints about his brutality, he would not prove easy to find. Meanwhile, his young wife waited for him at her parents' home, uncertain whether these lonely nights ought to frighten her more than the nights when her husband subjected her to the most humiliating experiences. Naturally Mme de Montreuil was perfectly aware of what went on under her own roof. But she knew what marriage meant and was discreet in her remarks about her son-in-law's behavior. Donatien was quick to take offense; they would quarrel for a few hours and then patch things up. La Présidente still hoped that marriage would settle the young man. And, as we saw earlier, she thought she had noticed progress: "Unless I miss my guess, you would already notice the progress if you saw him," she wrote the abbé on October 20, 1763.[20]

•

She was wrong. On October 29, exactly nine days after this letter was written, scandal erupted: the marquis de Sade was arrested on orders of the king and taken to the dungeon of Vincennes. What had happened?

Donatien had spent early autumn at the château d'Echauffour with his wife and mother-in-law. M. de Montreuil remained in Paris and was to join them later. On October 15 Donatien took the postal coach to Paris for the purpose—he said—of going later in the month to Fontainebleau to pay his respects to the king and solicit a position from the duc de Choiseul. From there he was to go to Dijon, where the *parlement* would officially install him as *lieutenant général*. In reality he left Normandy not to go to Fontainebleau but to escape his conjugal enslavement.

In Paris he stayed with his father-in-law on rue Neuve-du-Luxembourg. On Tuesday night, October 18, however, he offered a twenty-year-old woman employed as a fan maker the sum of two gold louis to go with him to his house on rue Mouffetard. The woman's name was Jeanne Testard, and according to the police report she was known to "meet men occasionally." The two had been introduced earlier that evening by a *femme du monde*, or madam, by the name of Du Rameau. After entering his building's courtyard via the carriage gate, Donatien, accompanied by his valet, a man named La Grange, led his female companion up to the second floor, showed her into his bedroom, sent his servant back downstairs, and locked and bolted the door. Left alone, he asked the woman if she had religion and believed in God, Jesus, and the Virgin Mary. She answered that she did believe and that as far as possible she abided by the practices of the Christian religion in which she had been raised. Suddenly the marquis burst out in a stream of dreadful insult and blasphemy. God does not exist, he said, and he had proved it. He then masturbated into a chalice, profaned the names of Jesus Christ and the Virgin Mary (*motherfucker* and *bugger* might be good Anglo-Saxon equivalents for the words he used), and told a story about having gone to Communion with a woman with whom he had slept: he took the two hosts, placed them in the woman's vagina, and entered her, shouting, "If thou art God, avenge thyself!"

He next told Jeanne Testard that there were extraordinary things to be seen in the next room. "I am pregnant," she replied, "and do not want to look at things that might frighten me." Pushing her into the room, he answered: "Have no fear. These things won't scare you." While he locked the door behind them, the terrified Jeanne confronted a strange sight. She first noticed, hanging from a room divider, four cane whips and five cat-o'-nine-tails, three of hemp, one of brass filaments, and another of iron filaments. On the walls hung three ivory Christs, two engravings of Christ, engravings of the crucifix and the Virgin, and several obscene prints and drawings. Sade asked her first to whip him with a cat-o'-nine-tails, the one made of iron filaments, to be heated until they glowed red hot, and then to choose the whip with which she wished to be beaten herself, but she strenuously refused. At that point he took down two ivory Christs and trampled on one while he masturbated with the other, after which he ordered her to do the same. When she resisted, he pointed to two pistols lying on a table and, placing his hand on his sword, threatened to run her through. Frightened to death, the poor girl did as she was told, trampling on the crucifix and repeating in a faint voice words that he shouted into her ear: "B..., I don't give a f... about you." Then he insisted that she submit to an enema and relieve herself on the Christ. So stubbornly did she refuse, however, that he was forced to give up.

She spent the night with her tormenter. They neither ate nor slept, but the marquis read her poetry "filled with impieties and totally contrary to religion." He then proposed that she submit to sodomy and made her promise to return the following Sunday at seven in the morning: they would go together to Saint-Médard, take Communion, make off with two hosts, burn one, and use the other in the ceremony he had described earlier. At nine in the morning Du Rameau, the madam, came looking for Mlle Testard. Before he would agree to let her go, Sade made her sign an oath that she would never reveal any of what had gone on between them.

Jeanne Testard went directly to the home of the lieutenant general of police, who was out, and from there to see Inspector Marais, who was also absent. But his clerk took her to see Sieur Mutel, commissioner of the Châtelet, who took down her deposition.[21] In the ensuing investigation other prostitutes whose services the marquis had previously enlisted told what they knew, and the result was a warrant for his arrest. The marquis was taken, under guard of Inspector Marais, to Fontainebleau, where he appeared before M. de Saint-Florentin, minister of the royal household, who submitted the file on the case to His Majesty with a recommendation that such excesses deserved severe punishment. Louis XV devoured the facts with his usual voracity (he was known to be an avid reader of reports on the debauches of his subjects) and then ordered the miscreant locked up in the dungeon of Vincennes until arrangements could be made to incarcerate him in a fortress at his family's expense. Still escorted by Marais, Sade was imprisoned on October 29.

According to police reports, highly instructive in such matters, flagellation was a common practice in the capital's bordellos. Inspector Marais, charged with keeping the marquis de Sade under surveillance, offers this interesting observation: "There is no public house today in which one does not find cane whips in large numbers ready for the 'ceremony,' as the practice of spurring the ardor of jaded debauchees is called. This passion is strangely prevalent among clergymen, moreover. In these sorts of establishments I have found many men who came looking for a good thrashing, including the librarian of the Petits-

Pères in the place des Victoires,[22] on whose body two women used up two entire brooms, after which, having run out of cane, they were forced to take straw from a doormat. When I came in, his whole body was dripping." Others, not content merely to be whipped, beat the prostitutes with a variety of scourges, including some festooned with studs, knots, or feathers.

A close reading of Jeanne Testard's deposition reveals that the marquis did her no physical harm. He is accused only of having "proposed" sodomy, and he did not insist or use physical force to satisfy his desire. To be sure, he threatened his victim with pistols and sword, but there is no evidence that he would actually have used them. In fact, the marquis would have escaped prosecution altogether if the only charge against him had been one of sexual aggression. But there were also charges of blasphemy, disrespect toward the crucifix, and incitement to sacrilege. The arrest stemmed primarily from these crimes, which, by the light of the criminal code of the time, were far more serious. A man guilty of such offenses against religion, even if purely verbal, would have risked his neck had he not been a member of the high aristocracy.

This taste for sacrilege is rather surprising and more than a little odd in a man who throughout his life denied the existence of God. Blasphemy makes sense only as transgression of a recognized value. The true atheist is not the person who combats God by denying that he exists but the one who never thinks about his existence. Such a contradiction raises doubts about the reality of Sade's atheism. The more the marquis rails against religion (and his hatred of priests was close to hysterical), the less convincing he is. Silence on this issue would have been a hundred times more convincing than all his invective. To deny that the host and crucifix are sacred and then choose them as instruments of revolt seems naïve.

In a passage in *La Philosophie dans le boudoir* published thirty-two years after the episode with Jeanne Testard, Sade would argue that for the atheist sacrilege can be justified if it is a stimulus to pleasure. His defense is admittedly shrewd, but it fails to carry conviction, for even if making a fetish of sacred objects excites the senses, it still implies recognition of the sacred as such. In regard to religion as to so many other values it seems to me that Donatien de Sade remained a "very young head," capable of spewing forth "horrible impieties" expressly to provoke the wrath of adults, which he found exciting. Religious objects were never a matter of indifference to him (cold contempt was not in his nature). His attitude toward them would continue to be one of impotent rage accompanied by immature gestures of defiance.

"On my knees, tears in my eyes"

The marquis was not so irresponsible as to ignore the risks that this episode entailed. On the very day of his imprisonment at Vincennes he wrote to the lieutenant general of police, M. de Sartine, with whom the Montreuils fortunately had connections. He would be lost for life, he moaned, and totally defenseless if his imprisonment became public; he would no longer be able to return to the service.

That day or the next he sent a tearful plea to M. Guyonnet, the governor of Vincennes, whom he asked to see to it that an accompanying letter be dispatched to Mme de Montreuil. He also begged that the marquise be allowed to visit him:

This is a favor that I dare to ask you on my knees, tears in my eyes. Do me the kindness of reconciling me with a person who is so dear to me and whom I was so weak as to grievously offend . . . I beg you, Monsieur, do not refuse to allow me to see the dearest person I have in the world. If she had the honor of being known to you, you would see that her conversation, more than anything else, is capable of restoring to the straight and narrow a wretch whose despair at having departed from it has no equal.[23]

He also asked to see his valet: "He is a man whom my parents placed in my service long ago. It would be a consolation for me to have him."[24]

On November 2 he again petitioned M. de Sartine that he be allowed to see his wife and to have his valet with him. He added an unexpected request: to see a confessor!

Unhappy as I am here, Monsieur, I do not bemoan my fate. I deserved God's vengeance, and I feel it. Crying for my sins, detesting my errors—these are my sole occupations. Alas! God may do away with me without giving me the time to recognize and feel my wrongs. How many prayers must I offer up before I am allowed to see into my self? Give me the means to do so, I beg you, Monsieur, by allowing me to see a priest. Through his good lessons and my sincere repentance, I hope before long to achieve those divine feelings whose utter neglect became the primary cause of my ruin.[25]

Tartuffe! If he could feign piety to such perfection, is there not also reason to believe that he feigned conjugal love as well? In the meantime, poor Renée-Pélagie, three months pregnant, suffered simultaneously from morning sickness, the chagrin of knowing that her husband was in prison, and her parents' consternation. But about the details of the case she probably knew nothing. To be sure, she had no illusions about Donatien's sexual appetites or strange preferences. She had already experienced them and could readily guess what had happened in the house on rue Mouffetard. But what she probably did not know, and what the marquis, aware of her piety, tried strenuously to keep her from finding out, was the charge of blasphemy and profanation.

The letter to Sartine contains a curious detail. Sade mentions the existence of an "unfortunate book, which dates only from the month of June." Was it, as Gilbert Lely suggests, a journal kept by the marquis or a pornographic anthology he had bought, perhaps the one from which he read passages to Jeanne Testard? No evidence has yet come to light that would help to answer the question. The marquis ends his letter by asking the police official to keep the true grounds of his detention hidden from his family: "I would be hopelessly lost in their minds." In any case, his "errors" lasted only a week. But, he admits, that was enough "to annoy the Supreme Being, whose just wrath I feel."

M. de Saint-Florentin was glad to assign the prisoner a confessor and asked Father Griffet, a former teacher at Louis-le-Grand, to find him one. In other respects, however, he kept him under the "ordinary regime," on the grounds that his crime was too serious to warrant special treatment. Therefore he could have no servant. If absolutely essential, it was up to M. Guyonnet to provide one. The minute the comte de Sade heard of his son's arrest, he raced to Fontainebleau to ask the king for a pardon, all the while cursing the son who dishonored his name and obliged him to waste ten louis on his journey, enough to live on for two months. Louis XV yielded to the pleadings of his former ambassador and signed an order to release the marquis on November 13. Donatien had been in his cell for fifteen days.

Supervised Liberty

Liberation did not mean liberty. The king consented to Donatien's release but confined him to the château d'Echauffour under the supervision of Inspector Marais, who was assigned to accompany him there and to keep an eye on him throughout his stay. Louis Marais, known as the "monitor of Cythera," was justly reputed to be the leading police expert on libertinage. Up to the minute on bedroom gossip and backstage tattle, he frequented suspect establishments, inspected the *hôtels garnis* used for brief assignations, followed debauched priests, spied on the affairs of gentlemen, and knew the prices of Opera prostitutes and the allowances paid by their protectors. Paris held no secrets for him. Adventures, intrigues, jealousies, rivalries, assignations, affairs, infidelities, ruptures, scandals big and small—all reached his ears. Prostitutes and their madams confided in him, and of course they were capable of describing in detail the extravagances of their clients and the daily and nightly debauches that took place in their establishments or were arranged through them. With all this information he prepared reports for M. de Sartine, and Sartine in turn took notes to be passed on to Louis XV, whom this chronicle of scandal delighted. Marais, the argus of the boudoir, had actually been on Sade's trail for some time. For years he would continue to dog his steps and report on his scabrous excesses. From now on the marquis would have to reckon with this man, whom he viewed with contempt though he feared his cunning.

•

With Donatien at Echauffour, his family could breathe a sigh of relief. Fortunately, news of his detention had not spread widely. The count advised his brother the abbé to deny everything if word of the scandal reached Provence: "This business has been going on for two weeks," he wrote on November 15. "I was afraid to tell you, and that kept me from writing. But now you must know. If word gets out, it must be denied. Nothing has yet come to light, and since he is in the provinces, it will be easy to squelch any rumors. Do not speak of this to my sisters. I am very unhappy."[26]

Mme de Montreuil took the news philosophically. Donatien's escapade did not dampen her confidence or her enthusiasm. Donatien appeared to resign himself to provisional liberty, supervised by his wife and parents-in-law. Despite bouts of nausea, Renée-Pélagie's pregnancy went fairly smoothly. Meanwhile, Mme de Montreuil cited her daughter's condition to explain why she planned to stay on at Echauffour through the winter, since no one could be told the real reason. She did not want Renée-Pélagie to give birth there, however: "She is delicate, and we are far from assistance." In fact, the child, born at full term, did not survive; it died (we do not know its sex) a few days-after it was born. "Heaven was unwilling to grant me much time to enjoy the happiness of being a father," the marquis sighed.

On April 3, 1764, M. de Saint-Florentin informed M. de Montreuil that His Majesty had decided to allow the président's son-in-law to return to Paris and to reside there for a period of three months starting on the fifteenth. He acceded to the wishes of his family, which deemed his presence in the capital necessary.[27] This was only a first step toward suspension of his sentence. On September 11, 1764, the sovereign definitively revoked the order confining him to residence at Echauffour.

As soon as he was free, Donatien devoted himself to his first love, the theater. He took charge of a playhouse at Mme de Sade's uncle's château in Evry, some twenty miles outside of Paris. There he staged performances of turn-of-the-century works such as Regnard's *Le Retour imprévu*, a prose work first performed at the Théâtre-Français in 1700, and Brueys and Palparat's *L'Avocat Patelin*, a three-act comedy first performed at the same theater in 1706, as well as more recent plays such as Rochon de Chabannes's *Heureusement*, a verse play that premiered at the Français on November 29, 1762; Gresset's five-act comedy *Le Méchant*, which had debuted in 1747 and in which Sade probably played the lead as Cléon; and Voltaire's *Nanine ou le Préjugé vaincu*, a three-act comedy in decasyllabic verse, whose first performance was on June 16, 1749. The troupe included, in addition to the marquis, other family members and friends: Mme de Sade, Mme de Montreuil, Mme d'Evry, Mme de Plissay, mother of la Présidente, Mme de Bourneville, Mme de Mondran, Mme de Montreuil's son M. de Launay, M. de Lionne, M. de Ripière, M. de Noinville, and young M. d'Evry.

For the finale of *L'Avocat Patelin* Sade, almost exactly six months after his incarceration at Vincennes, composed verses that alluded to the events. Thus Donatien (Valère) tells Renée-Pélagie (Henriette) that "it is but a step from evil to good," to which Henriette responds: "I fear no longer."[28]

•

On May 4, 1764, the minister of the royal household informed M. de Montreuil that His Majesty, "with great pain," had decided to allow M. de Sade to go to Dijon to be received by the *parlement* there as *lieutenant général* of Bresse, Bugey, Valromey, and Gex. The ceremony took place on June 26. Donatien delivered a most academic speech, one suffused with a humility hardly in keeping with his temperament: "To be worthy of you is my ambition. That one day you may judge me so is the height of my wishes."[29]

While in Dijon he took advantage of the opportunity to visit the library of the Carthusian monastery in order to do research in its archives, which suggests that he already had some historical work in mind. Contrary to common opinion, his literary vocation was not born in prison. The ambition to write and publish his work was always with him.

Mademoiselle Colet of the Théâtre-Italien

Had the marquis resigned himself to a quiet, happy family life? Had he abruptly renounced his follies to become a good husband and obedient citizen? Do not be deceived by the mask. A consummate actor, Donatien excelled in complex roles: the repentant sinner was one that he played with particular gusto.

After five months of exile and frustration in the Norman countryside he thirsted for pleasure. No sooner had he returned to Paris than he threw himself into a frenetic round of debauch. He lavished ruinous sums on one woman after another. Night followed night at a furious pace, some passed in the faubourg Saint-Marceau, others at his house in Arcueil. All the while the invisible but vigilant Inspector Marais kept the marquis under surveillance and noted his activities. The inspector's reports are our best source of information concerning the marquis's escapades.

A few of the many women he knew earned his special attention, and therefore ours. On July 15, 1764, following a performance at the Comédie-Italienne, our ladies' man was introduced to Mlle Colet, a twenty-year-old actress, tall, well-built, with a slender waist and somewhat irregular features, who granted the marquis's request that he be allowed to accompany her home. An unusually liberated lover, she apparently excelled at eliciting the rarest of pleasures. "People say she is even more amusing in conversation than on the stage," Marais notes. Lord Elgin, one of many young English gentlemen who came to savor the freedom of Paris, paid thirty gold louis for one night of her company and did not regret the expense. On the day after Donatien met her, he dispatched his servant with this ardent note:

It is difficult to see you without loving you and more difficult still to love you without saying so. I have kept my peace for a long time, but further silence is impossible. I am madly in love with you, and the only happiness that remains for me in this world is to spend my life with you and share with you my fortune.

Please send a word in answer, I beg you. If I, the sincerest of men, am fortunate enough not to have my wishes rejected, grant me a date when we might make arrangements . . . My happiness is in your hands. I can no longer live without you.[30]

Naturally Donatien did not believe a word of this, nor did the recipient of his note. Such language was mere sport, pleasantly inconsequential, its only purpose being to disguise desire as passion. The code according to which "I love you" meant "I want you" fooled no one. It licensed sensuality and demystified sentimentality, nothing more. In other words, it was a "true lie," typical of the ethos of the libertine, who was generally fond of masks and teases and apt to hide an iron fist beneath honeyed words. In this theater of lies everyone was a winner and no one a dupe. Love was feigned with impudence and nonchalance. Smiling at the corners of their mouths, the players listened to one another moan, plead, and beg. Oaths were abused, the better to denounce their fraudulence. Love was almost always an illusion. Crébillon *fils* puts it nicely: "There are very few affairs in which sentiment serves. Nearly all are born of opportunity, convenience, and idleness. People tell each other, without feeling it, that they look appealing. They come together without trust and part for fear of boredom." Donatien regarded his letters to Mlle Colet as choice specimens of the art, so much so that he did not fail to have them copied in their entirety and inserted into the collection of his miscellaneous works.

How could the lady resist such a declaration when, coupled with such promising "arrangements," Donatien mentions "sharing his fortune"? This particular lady was a sharp customer, however, and a long way from a novice: she had been a professional of romance since she was seventeen, could spot a libertine a mile away, and was not one to fall for the first man to proposition her. Kept initially by a wealthy old American, M. de Bréan, she left him for the duc de La Ferté, who gave her syphilis, then for Sieur Rozetti, who cured her of it but left her when she betrayed him with the vicomte de Sabran. In the spring of 1763 Mlle Colet left M. de Sabran for the marquis de Lignerac, who paid twenty louis per month for the privilege of sharing her favors with the comte de Rochefort, from whom she received a monthly allowance of thirty louis and a promise to pay 6,000 livres of her debts. A generous protector, Rochefort also gave her a pair of diamond earrings whose value was estimated at 4,000 livres. But the lady was not above engaging in a brief affair when it was to her advantage. Shrewd at dispensing her favors, she knew how to drive up the price before selling herself to the highest bidder. She greeted Sade's protestations of love with feigned anger and in a display of outraged virtue threw the messenger out with a warning that she was not a woman to tolerate such an insult.

An hour later Donatien sent a second letter, even more pressing than the first and quite contrite. It might even seem sincere, except that it ends by requesting a response before ten the next morning. Otherwise, he threatened, his servant would be there at noon to fetch a reply directly. This injunction is strangely at odds with the humble words of contrition that precede it.

O, God! Permit me, Mademoiselle, to throw myself at your feet to repair the insult of which you accuse me! . . . Did you think that I was offering my fortune to buy favors? Delicate and sensitive as you are, you would indeed have reason to hate me had I wished to obtain them at such a price! My tears, my sighs, my fidelity, my obedience, my repentance, and my respect: that is the price of a heart such as yours, of the only heart that can make my life happy . . . I shall expect your answer tomorrow. If I do not receive it in the morning mail by ten o'clock, I shall be forced to assume that you do not wish to give it, and my servant will be at your place tomorrow at noon to take it.[31]

With jubilation and virtuosity Sade employed a double language; he simultaneously stated a thing and its opposite and mocked the sentiments he set forth. A master of coded language, he subverts amorous discourse in this letter by parodying its tics and absurdities. Never was cynicism so skillful at assuming the colors of passion. The very expression of passion, its excesses, extravagance, tears, and naïveté, are so many barbs aimed at the "sensitive soul," so many jibes at the infatuated heart. Sade, who hated to wallow in emotion, mocks love's suffering even as he professes sincerity. With joyous ferocity he wraps in mawkishness sarcasms aimed at this venal woman, whose carrying-on was a matter of public notoriety and whose reputation for "virtue" and "decency" he celebrates with ironic insistence. His repetition of this theme comes close to bad taste, not to say cruelty. And the allusion to wealth conjures up images of the courtesan's sordid dealings.

Did the shrewd little woman detect the mockery? In any case she kept her suitor waiting several months before promising him a rendezvous, the delay serving only to fan the flames of the marquis's desire to possess this object, in which he saw a paradise of prurience: "How cruel you are thus to delay the moment of my happiness. I no longer live, I no longer exist. By your grace, let it be today at four o'clock.

What nastiness to tarry so! Yes, you want me to die, I see it clearly. You can still let me know if you can today."[32]

We do not know if Mlle Colet gave in to these desperate appeals. When did she finally surrender to her admirer's entreaties? We do not know that either. What we can say is that by December 7, 1764, she no longer had anything to refuse him. By then Donatien was paying his mistress twenty-five louis per month, although she was still living with the marquis de Lignerac, a man sufficiently forbearing to step aside in favor of a rival if his protégée found it to her advantage. He was by no means unaware of her intrigue with M. de Sade.

The latter occasionally abandoned his backstage courtesans in favor of common whores. He availed himself of the services of Mme Brissault, the most notorious madam in Paris, who was often referred to as "la Présidente Brissault" in recognition of her superiority over her colleagues. Marais noted that it was "difficult to find a woman in this line of work who is cleverer or more decent. She therefore does a very good business."[33] Donatien could no doubt allow his fantasies freer rein with "professionals" than with luxuriously kept women. But Marais, who knew what violence the marquis was capable of, advised Mme Brissault not to send girls off for assignations with him lest something dreadful occur.

On December 21 a family decision forced M. de Lignerac to leave Mlle Colet entirely to M. de Sade, but the beneficiary, not being wealthy enough to support a demanding and expensive actress by himself, was not pleased by the news. The partnership with Lignerac had offered two advantages: the marquis could share the expense and hide his intrigue behind a convenient shield. Forced into the spotlight as the actress's official lover, he risked incurring the wrath of those close to him, especially Mme de Montreuil. No fool, the lady was fully aware of her son-in-law's escapades (and possibly kept informed by Marais himself). As long as there was no scandal, Donatien's mother-in-law was willing to close her eyes, since the youth was merely leading the life that all young noblemen of his generation led. But if his affair were to become public, she was likely to come down hard. Sade confided his doubts to Mme Brissault and asked for advice. The procuress urged him to leave Mlle Colet, whose upkeep was indeed very expensive. But really she was afraid that if he attached himself to the actress he would cease to visit her establishment, and she would lose a loyal client who paid regularly for brief assignations.

Meanwhile, Lignerac continued to see Mlle Colet, but as his family had cut him off, he was reduced to the role of *guerluchon* (the lover of a woman kept by another man). He was content to visit her in her dressing room and to hide beneath the dressing table if someone knocked at the door. Donatien, meanwhile, suffered terrible pangs of jealousy since discovering in his mistress's apartments a pair of earrings worth a thousand écus and an enormous *sultan* (silk-lined dressing basket), the size of a commode, which she had received as a Christmas gift and showed to all her friends as a curiosity. These sumptuous gifts came from one of the wealthiest noblemen in the kingdom, the duc de Fronsac, son of the maréchal de Richelieu, who had inherited his father's powerful libertine inclinations. Donatien nevertheless continued to sleep with her, as if to deny her betrayal. Oddly enough, it was Mme de Montreuil who took it upon herself to open his eyes. Eight months later, on August 8, 1765, she wrote of the incident to the abbé de Sade: "I managed last year to separate him from Colette [*sic*] and make him listen to reason after persuading him that he had been deceived."³⁴ Convinced that he could never outdo this new rival in either fame or fortune, he decided to end the affair and asked his mistress to return his letters. Intoxicated by her new conquest, puffed up with pride, exalted at having one of the most illustrious names in France at her feet, she answered in a haughty and wounding manner. Donatien then bade her an eternal farewell, without concealing his spite or fury:

A woman's vengeance is never anything but contemptible, and I write only to show that I am not afraid of it. Why do you complain that I ask to have my letters back? The request is quite a simple one, and anyone but you would find nothing indecent in it. What did I do to you for you to treat me so? And why are you so uncouth as to humiliate one whose only fault was to have loved you? . . . What are you? You are making it all too clear. What am I? Your fool. Which of us plays the more humiliating role? . . .³⁵

•

Our lover was quick to console himself with a Mlle de C*** (possibly the same Mlle de Cambis whom he had almost married), with whom he had fallen madly in love at a ball. He professed to regret not having met her sooner, for she would have made an ideal wife. But this was no more than a passing fancy, the pretext for a pretty letter that plucks the string of nostalgia and that Donatien also included in his anthology. It is not even certain that he became the lady's lover.

•

While singing of romance to the ideal wife, Donatien was also carrying on with another actress from the Italien, Mlle Beaupré. After being kept by the Russian Count Bruss, she had replaced him with the chevalier de Choiseul, who lived with his mother on rue Saint-Honoré and was willing to pay twenty-five louis per night. "This is far too much for her age," Marais observed. "There is reason to fear that she may lead him on quite some way, for I have learned that she is already asking for earrings worth 5,000 livres. He would be greatly embarrassed if he had to pay cash, but he can find credit."[36] This did not prevent the lady from taking Monsieur Linguet, the theater's cashier, as her *guerluchon*. The marquis de Saint-Sulpice, who was also keen for her favors, offered twenty louis per month. "She refused him, preferring to take six louis from the comte de Sade, with whom she slept twice," Marais reported on February 8, 1765. Four days later Mlle Beaupré moved into an apartment on the rue de Richelieu furnished for her by an Englishman, Mr. Stevenson, known to be a very heavy gambler. He paid fifty louis per month and reserved the right to make gifts to his mistress "commensurate with the satisfaction he receives." The chevalier de Choiseul, upon discovering that his actress not only betrayed him but was "insatiable when it comes to money," left her. M. Linguet remained her favorite *guerluchon*, a privilege for which he reportedly paid dearly.

7
First Scandals

La Beauvoisin

In the spring of 1765 we find Donatien fully occupied with his latest conquest. This time it was a renowned courtesan, Mlle Beauvoisin, as celebrated for her beauty as for the number of her lovers. Once the servant of a surgeon, la Beauvoisin had made her début at the Opera while still very young and had been initiated into prostitution at the age of sixteen by the celebrated comte du Barry, husband of the royal favorite. She was courted by the most illustrious of men, some distinguished by birth, others by position, and contrived to make them all happy without denying herself the occasional dalliance on the side. In addition to her regular liaisons she did not disdain brief affairs if the price was right. Her rates were as high as any in the demimonde, which put her out of reach of the less well-to-do. She is generally described as a likable woman with a pretty face but "no figure, short, and thickset." This was not a dancer's body, and she soon abandoned that career, but fortunately another awaited her in the industry of love. There she succeeded brilliantly and soon outstripped her rivals.

No trace exists of a connection between this latter-day Lais and the marquis de Sade prior to April 26, 1765. On that date Inspector Marais noted that "la demoiselle Beauvoisin does all she can to deceive M. Douet de La Boulay, who lavishes gifts on her. Sieur de Pienne is still the *guerluchon* in favor, and M. le comte de Sade picks up the tab for finery and entertainment, which comes to at least twenty louis per month."[1]

For several months Mlle Beauvoisin had been servicing both the marquis de Louvois and M. Douet de La Boulaye, whom she cajoled into giving her the moon. Though not bedecked with diamonds, she was reputed to be doing "very well in business." She was also "very elegantly established. She lives on rue Courteauvillain [today rue de Montmorency], and few women can boast of a wardrobe as well stocked or of such an extensive collection of lace. At home she is always attractively tidy in her attire, the most enticing of *déshabillé*, and no one does a better job of showing her figure to advantage. People today consider her one of our prettiest women. She even enjoys a reputation for being fairly faithful to her lovers. My report, however, proves the contrary, and I am assured that, despite her reserved and humble air, she denies herself nothing that her very ardent temperament desires. The marquis de Louvois left on Wednesday to rejoin his regiment, and the same night she slept with the chevalier de La Tour, whom all these beauties take to be a real stallion."[2]

Another point worth noting is that Mlle Beauvoisin had been pregnant for about a month when Donatien became her lover.[3] This was the second time he had lusted after a pregnant woman (Jeanne Testard was the first). Ten years later he would take another pregnant mistress in Italy.

The Counterfeit Mme de Sade

On March 26, 1765, Donatien informed Maître Fage, a notary residing in Apt, of his intention to depart imminently for Provence. This unpublished letter shows us a Sade in a highly euphoric mood (something very rare for him), absolutely gleeful at the idea of escaping from Paris, that "plague-ridden place," and from his two "guardians" (probably Marais and one of his agents, who kept him under close surveillance), to return to "the azure plains of La Coste."[4] He left the capital on April 2, spent a month at the home of a sister-in-law near Fontainebleau with his wife and la Présidente, resumed his journey on May 9, stopped for four days "before Fontainebleau" (probably in Melun) for a tryst with an unidentified partner, and then finally set out for Provence. His first idea was that this was purely a pleasure trip, but Mme de Montreuil persuaded him to mix business with pleasure and ask his uncle the abbé for information about properties that would one day be his. For unknown reasons this trip annoyed the marquis's father. Perhaps he was upset by the expense, or perhaps he was afraid of being done out of his property while he was still alive. By contrast, la Présidente was delighted to see her son-in-law go, in the hope that the abbé, in whom she placed absolute confidence, would be able to use his counsel and authority to set the young man back on the proper path.

When no one heard from Donatien after his departure, she asked the abbé to inform her of his arrival and to scold his nephew appropriately:

He is in great need of advice from you to turn him from his frivolous ways. He has confidence in you. You have to go easy with a spirit like his, because his first impulses are invariably violent and hence to be feared. But he can be reasoned with through reflection. He needs only the time to make himself understood and not to be obsessed by any passion.

I am a fine one to be telling you what your nephew is like. You surely know him better than I and have no need of advice. You should be advising me. But what is written is written. As a member of the public I have nothing to complain about. As a mother-in-law with a more particular interest . . . my continuing to praise him as I did was up to him alone and his willingness to keep his promises to me. I know that his age demands indulgence, but it also requires decency of behavior. You can start with what I am telling you now, and if he is willing to be sincere with you, you will judge whether I am wrong.[5]

For the moment la Présidente refused to withdraw her indulgence of Donatien or her support. Her characterization of his behavior was fairly restrained, and she continued to hope that he would mend his ways. Clearly his escapades with actresses, dancers, and even prostitutes had failed to shock her. Such things were normal and one might even say conventional. Donatien's behavior was highly libertine, to be sure, and he spent far too much, but there was none of the sacrilege, profanation, or scandalous, Luciferian conduct that had marked his affair with Jeanne Testard.

Within a month, however, Mme de Montreuil was taking a harder line and had begun to sound more discouraged. In the meantime, to be sure, she had received information that had aroused her ire: her son-in-law was not traveling alone. Mlle Beauvoisin had followed him to Provence. He had snatched her away in the greatest secrecy, unbeknownst to anyone including that keen-scented bloodhound Marais, who believed that the lady had "buried herself" for the summer at the marquis de Louvois's residence in Longchamp to hide her pregnancy.[6] To make matters worse, it was even rumored that he had passed his companion off as his wife. There was no doubt that he had spent the months of June and July and part of August in the Lubéron with his mistress.

On the day of his arrival in La Coste, with Mlle Beauvoisin hanging on his arm, villagers dressed in their Sunday best had crowded into the vestibule of the château to welcome him. Boys and girls dressed as shepherds and shepherdesses sang two pastorals in Provençal that had been composed especially for the occasion, while their "deputy" carried a lamb bedecked with flowers and ribbons. One of the songs explicitly congratulated the marquis on his wedding.

Since "moussu lou marquis" (as he was called in Provençal) did not bother to set his servants straight, everyone in the village took Mlle Beauvoisin for Mme de Sade. The abbé, who witnessed the scene, immediately notified la Présidente. Outraged by the insult but even more wounded in her pride, humiliated at seeing her efforts nullified, abused in her affection, she took pains to conceal what had happened from her daughter and replied in a long letter that spared neither Donatien nor his uncle, whom she bitterly reproached for his negligence and weakness:

Although experience has given me the right to expect anything from M. de S[ade], I had not wished to believe him capable of such an extreme of indecency in his deranged loves, and while I have often suspected what was happening, I always dismissed the thought as insulting to him yet remained afraid to dispel my doubts by shedding light on the matter. I could not inform myself, moreover, without also alerting others, and that is something I wished to avoid for his sake. Such hidden infidelities are an offense to his wife and to me, but this public misbehavior before the entire province, insulting to his neighbors, will do him irreparable harm if it becomes known here—and how can it fail to? When I am working so hard to use my friends for his advancement and benefit, when he is indebted to his wife and to us for hushing up an affair that might have ruined him forever and earned him years in a dungeon, these are the tokens of gratitude we receive! And then in an earnest tone he will complain of his destiny and of the violence of the passions that compel him and profess regret at making those devoted to him unhappy. We are not always masters of our hearts, but we can always control our behavior, and it is on the basis of our behavior that we are judged . . . He has taken too much advantage of my forbearance, though I have not been as forbearing as he has led you to believe. The letters I wrote to him during his stay in Provence will attest to this, [but] I doubt that he will dare show them to you. I, however, should be glad for you to see them for my justification. I had thought, given the portrait I was painted of his character and what I thought I knew of it, that a little indulgence for the fires of youth and the weakness of the heart might win for me his friendship and confidence and thus preserve him from the great dangers to which he heedlessly subjects himself. His mistresses are tyrants—and what mistresses! If he gave them less pleasure and treated them with less generosity he would soon find himself abandoned, adored though he may be. Though he is a good actor, the comtesses de Saint-Pré are far better . . . All I can do is moan and hope that you still feel kindly enough toward him not to abandon him absolutely to his own devices. As for myself, I shall no longer take any part. I am all too convinced that friendship has no influence on his heart. He was less extravagant in both behavior and expenditure while on his own [during] six years of war and under his father's guardianship. Strictness was thus more successful with him than our kindness.[7]

Since the abbé de Sade had also seen fit to inform his sister, the abbess of Saint-Benoît de Cavaillon, about the scandal at La Coste, the old nun issued a sharp warning to her reprobate nephew. Far from bowing his head, Donatien vehemently denounced the rumors circulating about him and launched a counterattack, violently lashing out at his aunt Villeneuve and the abbé, whose scandalous behavior came in for particularly harsh criticism:

Your criticism is scarcely muted, my dear aunt. Frankly, I was surprised to meet with such strong words from the mouth of a holy nun. I neither permit nor suffer nor authorize anyone to look upon the person living in my house as my wife, and I have told everyone the contrary. "Do not introduce her as your wife," M. l'abbé told me, "but let those who wish say what they want, even if you tell them the exact opposite." I am following his advice. When one of your sisters [Mme de Villeneuve], married as I am, lived here publicly with her lover, did you regard La Coste as accursed? I do no more harm than she did, and neither of us will have done much. As for the person from whom you heard what you are telling me, priest though he may be, he always has a couple of trollops with him—pardon me if I use the same term as you. Is his château a seraglio? No, it's a bordello.

The rest of the letter has already been quoted: "Pardon my misdeeds. I am taking up the family spirit, and if I have anything to criticize myself for, it is for having had the misfortune to be born into it. God protect me from all the foolishness and vice with which it is rife. I would consider myself almost virtuous if God gave me the grace to adopt only some of the family vices."[8]

Donatien was quick to regret the vehemence of his language. In October of the following year he made amends to his uncle, blaming the letter on that wicked "siren," Mlle Beauvoisin:

I have only one more favor to ask of you, my dear uncle. That is to forget wrongs that I committed in the blindness of a passion over which I had no control. Please believe that the letters so wickedly and imprudently placed in your hands would never have been written but under the dictates of the siren who held me in her spell. Had I been in control of myself I would not have been capable of such blackguardry, and now that the illusion is entirely dispelled, I blush for it and find it inconceivable.[9]

Interlude

While the comedy of the counterfeit wife was being played out at the château, Donatien had one large room turned into a theater so that he might stage and act in plays he admired. Performances were followed by balls, parties, and collations to which he invited the local aristocrats. These glittering occasions drew large crowds, and Mlle Beauvoisin, playing the role of the marquise de Sade or one of her relatives, did the honors of the château. The abbé (whose presence is hard to fathom given his criticism of what was going on) did not miss a single one of the parties given during the week he spent at La Coste at Donatien's invitation. Perhaps, as Mme de Montreuil believed, he hoped by attending to spare his nephew "the humiliation of being deserted by respectable company." But in view of what we know about him, it seems more likely that he came because he enjoyed himself and because the pretty women he met there diverted him from the austerity of his fortress in Saumane. Nevertheless, Mlle Beauvoisin's imposture caused tongues to wag, and the carousing at the château was severely judged. The abbé was accused by some of having given his blessing to these revels. He strenuously denied the charges, publicly condemned the impudence of the devilish couple, and went so far as to deny any commerce with his host: "I do not see my nephew," he proclaimed to anyone who wished to listen, "and I should be outraged if anyone behaved as badly."

Renée-Pélagie knew almost nothing of what was happening at La Coste. She believed only that her husband was innocently amusing himself by performing plays with other nobles of the region and that that was the sole reason for his silence. This was the version of the story she got from her mother to assuage her anxieties, because Donatien had not written for three weeks. Meanwhile, la Présidente was thinking of ways to separate her son-in-law from Mlle Beauvoisin, and she shared her thoughts with the abbé de Sade. The task was not easy, because the courtesan held him in her spell and had plenty of ways to hold on to him, vanity and devotion among them, to say nothing of a variety of underhanded schemes. The best thing would be for the abbé to keep him in Provence, because if he returned to Echauffour he would promise, sincerely or insincerely, to behave reasonably and would persuade himself that he had convinced his mother-in-law of his good intentions. Things would go well for two or three months until he returned to Paris and his old habits. "I confess that I am very discouraged," la Présidente confided to her correspondent on August 8, 1765.

My daughter's fate depends on you, because her husband is in your hands. Neither she nor I can do anything from here except perhaps to reason incorrectly. Things will always go well in your hands, assuming that you wish to take the trouble. Philosophy does not lead to detachment; it always wills the good. In any case I have no doubt that your philosophy does. Four days ago I was in solitude. Solitude is pleasant when one has something sad to muse upon.

In postscript she added:

You will see, Monsieur, when you read my letter, that in telling you what I think, I have written in such a way that you can show the letter to my son-in-law if you think he still has enough deference for me and for his wife that it might make an impression on him . . . What can be done in these circumstances? The situation seems difficult. Here are my views, though I unhesitatingly defer to yours.

Force them to separate? On that score I am sure that I could without difficulty obtain from the minister whatever I asked, but it would cause a stir and be dangerous for [Donatien]. Therefore this method should not be used. But you must not appear to fear your nephew, much less to tolerate his follies. Never let him out of your sight: the only way to deal with him is never to leave him alone for a moment. That is how I managed last year to separate him from Colette [*sic* for Colet] and made him listen to reason after convincing him that he was making a mistake. I doubt that he loves this one more ardently than he loved the other: it was a frenzy. Everything went rather well from then on until this Lent, when he fell for this one. Invent a pretext, something about real estate, to return [to La Coste] to see how things stand and find out whether he is still as smitten as ever. Shout at him, speak firmly, and you will oblige him, out of respect for you, at the very least to behave more decently, to reduce his expenditure, to live a quieter life, to receive no visitors. That way, it will be less scandalous, less widely known. And let him think that if he causes less of a stir in the province, there will be no scandal here. Always try to arrange for private conversations during which you can talk reason to him and indicate your unhappiness at being obliged to stand by and appear to participate in his mischief by seeming to condone it. They will get bored if hindered. The nymph will find it easier to make up her mind to leave. If, as I suspect from his last letter, which I am sending to you, he is beginning to lose interest in her, you can seize the moment and take advantage of such clouds as may appear on the horizon, of such quarrels as may erupt between them, which may provide opportunities that he would never have the strength to seize himself. He is easy. If you succeed, do not allow him to follow her. Keep him with you for a time and do not let him go. Find something for him to do. And then we shall see. As long as he continues to be crazy about her, I would rather have him in Provence than here. [The scandal] will not be as widely known. And then, too, his presence here would worry me. He would want, for the sake of appearances at any rate, to live with his wife, and his creditors would persecute him. He would incur fresh debts. And if he lost interest in his mistress, he would take another. I prefer that he take one in Provence. He might be fortunate enough to attach himself to a lady: they are always less dangerous than kept prostitutes.[10]

The Clandestine Return

The date is August 20, 1765. While Renée-Pélagie and her mother were ending the summer at Echauffour, Donatien's valet Teissier arrived with his master's baggage at rue Neuve-du-Luxembourg. The servant declared that he had been sent ahead and that the marquis would not be returning for another week. In fact, traveling incognito, M. de Sade had returned the very same day with Mlle Beauvoisin, and the two were living together in her apartment. Mme de Montreuil guessed the truth: "If I were in Paris, I would go myself and snatch him from that harlot's door as I did a year ago. But I am not there. In any case, I can no longer count on wielding the same influence over his mind and heart."[11]

Donatien returned with his wallet empty, having left some 4,500 livres in debts in Provence. Since what he had left was hardly enough to live on in Paris, what happened next was akin to a miracle. Mlle Beauvoisin, known for her greed, sold her jewels for 8,600 livres, to which she added funds in cash and handed the total, some 10,000 écus, to her lover, who pledged to establish a perpetual annuity of 500 livres in her favor. The contract, signed in the presence of a royal notary by the name of Pontelier, was dated August 21, the day after their return.

Ten days later Donatien finally decided to inform his wife and mother-in-law of his departure. He would not be able to join them in Normandy, he explained, because there still was business to attend to: the 4,500 francs he owed in Provence, for which he needed cash, and the establishment of his genealogy, which he was to submit to the royal genealogist, probably for the purpose of obtaining a higher rank should he rejoin the army. Mme de Montreuil reacted angrily. She knew that her son-in-law was spending more time at Mlle Beauvoisin's than at his own home, and that only made her angrier. She promised in writing to find him the money by November—"not at my expense or your wife's," she added, for "it would be too much to pay for your pleasures"—but only on condition that he return to Echauffour without delay. As for the family papers that had to be submitted to M. Baujon, he had only to ask his uncle for them while he was in Provence rather than write inane letters to his mother-in-law. On that point Donatien protested. He had never insulted his uncle. He had kept copies of his letters. He could prove it. And so on. "I am not happy with his style," la Présidente confided, "and I was firm in my response. He wrote his wife that as soon as his business was finished, he would come. My family pressed him to leave on Wednesday the eleventh [of September] at the latest." And she added this, concerning his affair with Mlle Beauvoisin: "I know from people who have seen him that he is still quite smitten. They don't believe anything he says, and neither do I. That is most unfortunate. Despite my anger, I shall abide by your most recent advice. When I have him here, we shall see."[12]

A Miscarriage

Finally, on September 15, late at night, Donatien's coach passed through the gates of the château d'Echauffour. Renée-Pélagie, who still knew nothing of his mischief, welcomed him with joy. For several months she had led the life of a young lady residing at home with her parents, dying of boredom and solitude and afflicted by memories of her dead child. Her mother had told her nothing of what was going on. No doubt Mme de Montreuil feared adding to her daughter's distress, but more than that she had no interest in sharing her son-in-law's escapades with anyone other than the abbé. She believed that she alone was strong enough to stand up to Donatien and that she alone would prove victorious in the end. Her daughter was too sensitive.

A man like the marquis could not be restrained by tears. As for her husband, le Président, she never even gave him a thought. The good man would have difficulty enough just backing her up. In any case, she did not think it necessary to keep him informed. Who besides herself would have the energy, tenacity, and intelligence to tame a soul as rebellious as Donatien's? What is more, Mme de Montreuil was too fond of a challenge not to feel an obscure pleasure at the thought of testing herself against such an adversary. As intransigent as Donatien himself, she seemed invincible. She might tire or lose heart but never for very long. Recovery always came with surprising rapidity.

According to la Présidente, the marquis had seemed rather cheerful since his return and quite relaxed. His relations with Renée-Pélagie took an almost normal course. Indeed, it was during this visit, and more precisely during the month of October 1765, that the couple conceived the child that would be born nine months later.

Suddenly, in early November, Donatien learned that Mlle Beauvoisin had suffered an "accident" associated with her pregnancy and brought on by her trip to Provence: probably a miscarriage. He hastily left Echauffour and flew to the bedside of his unfortunate mistress. His mother-in-law did all she could to stop him, but in vain. In Paris, where no one knew of his return, he never left the bedroom of his "nymph," on whom he lavished care. "In the state she is in," Mme de Montreuil viciously commented in a letter to the abbé,

I don't imagine he has many resources for his pleasure. If he were to become bored enough that he never returned, it would be a great boon. But one would have to assume that another one would not take her place, and I don't count on that any more than you do. Someone once said, I no longer remember where,

> *Au vide de son coeur peut-on s'accoutumer,*
> *Quand on a contracté l'habitude d'aimer?*

[*Can one get used to the void in one's heart when one has contracted the habit of loving?*]

To the admittedly very harsh letters I write, he responds with a great deal of decency and even gentleness and with the trust that might come from friendship. But is he sincere or pretending? This I can learn only from experience or from those who know him more thoroughly than I. I confess that I am still distressed that he left you in so base a manner. He does not admit it, however, and has told me more than once that of all his relatives you were the one for whom he had the greatest respect, friendship, and trust.[13]

"There you are unmasked, you monster!"

On December 13, 1765, Mlle Beauvoisin, fully recovered, appeared at the Italiens in the full splendor of her beauty. "Her pregnancy has made her more beautiful," Marais noted. Now she could aspire to more illustrious conquests. From the moment she reappeared in society she found herself surrounded by a host of suitors, all young and rich and begging to be allowed to ruin themselves for her benefit. All the fashionable ladies' men vied for her favor. Young M. de Saint-Contest was the first to succumb. For his sake she dismissed M. de La Boulaye and the marquis de Louvois, in whose home she had allegedly hidden her pregnancy (no one knew that she had been in Provence with M. de Sade). The chevalier de Raconis promised her fifty louis, and even the baron de Saint-Cricq, an officer in the French Guard, offered to sacrifice his mistress of the moment, Mlle Lafond, a dancer at the Italiens. Poor Donatien had no shortage of rivals. But the most dangerous of all was the chevalier de Choiseul, whom Mlle Beaupré had previously left for Donatien. This time he found himself in a decidedly less advantageous position. For some months the chevalier had been racing from conquest to conquest. "He has a showiness and brilliance quite capable of turning the head of a little mistress," Marais remarked. When the police inspector noticed that Choiseul appeared to have his eye on Mlle Beauvoisin, he complimented him on his choice. The conceited youth turned toward him and said: "I've just caught a look on her face that convinces me that within a few days she will be mine." He was not mistaken.

Ten days later the chevalier de Choiseul was chosen over all his rivals, including Sade, and he was not even obliged to open his purse. Mlle Beauvoisin could afford this dalliance because M. de Saint-Contest, who noticed nothing, was paying her bills: this was within the rules. The victor, meanwhile, praised his prize to all who would listen, lauding her as a choice morsel preferable to all the other beauties he had known. "This enthusiasm will last until the theater season begins, and for him that is a long time," predicted the ironical Marais, laughing up his sleeve.[14]

On January 3, 1766, Mlle Beauvoisin ended all contact with the marquis. Out of spite Donatien immediately threw himself into the arms of Mlle Dorville, a "most appetizing fat girl," who had only recently escaped from the seraglio of Mme Hecquet, another celebrated madame and rival of Mme Brissault. He gave her only ten louis per month, but her expenses were paid by Lord Elgin, who visited her at least once a week and paid her four louis each time.[15]

But nothing could console Donatien. Betrayed, mocked, supplanted, mad with jealousy, and dreaming only of revenge, he loosed a violent tirade against his former mistress:

There you are unmasked, you monster! Your scurrilousness is without equal . . . You've brought me back to my senses. I shall detest you all my life, you and your ilk. I shall take no vengeance. You're not worth it . . . The dishonor and discredit that you would reap might serve as my vengeance. But do not worry, my sovereign scorn for you is the best vengeance of all. Adieu, for the last time. With what pleasure I think that at this time tomorrow I shall be fifty leagues from you! I am leaving, and I shall surely flee from you as fast as I can. But your unworthy image will vanish from my heart more quickly still.[16]

Inspection Tour

At least one of these promises would be kept. Early in May 1766 Donatien set out for Avignon. Despite what he said, the purpose of his trip was not to flee Mlle Beauvoisin but to inspect construction at La Coste that he had ordered begun during his last visit, almost exactly a year earlier. He did not arrive in the capital of the Comtat until the twenty-first, having stopped for several days in Melun, as he had done the year before, at the home of an unidentified woman, a mysterious personage "with whom he is now infatuated."[17] His uncle had ended his retreat on the fifteenth in order to meet him and bring him back to Saumane. But two days later, Donatien, burning with impatience to see how far work had progressed, mounted his horse and without a word of farewell to the abbé galloped off in the direction of La Coste.

After crossing the new bridge and passing through the two almost completed *portes flamandes*, he turned his attention to the two parts of the building that most interested him: the new apartment for Mme de Sade and the theater. The first was well on its way to completion, which was planned for early 1767. With the three new rooms to be added to the one already present, the marquise would have a winter bedroom, a summer bedroom, a boudoir, and a study. For the theater, or "salle de Comédie," he planned to use the same room as the year before, together with several additional rooms; a theater covering more than a thousand square feet with a view onto the château's terrace was to be constructed at the northern end of the second floor gallery. A stage of some 300 square feet was built along the northern wall, and the adjoining room was converted into a foyer.

Beautifying the grounds also called for a great deal of attention. Donatien added a bower and a maze of shrubbery and had a variety of fruit trees planted in the rock of the hillside alongside the existing olive and almond trees.[18]

When his inspection was done, the marquis returned to Saumane, where he spent several days with his uncle, who apparently nursed no hard feelings over the infamous letter to Mme de Saint-Benoît. Not that he had forgotten the insult, just that it seemed wiser not to talk about it. The more he reproached his nephew, the abbé reasoned, the more likely it was that the harebrained youth would do something foolish. The abbé confided as much in Mme de Montreuil, with whom he could sometimes speak frankly: "It would be dangerous to go against the grain with him, as his father did. He may be capable of the most extreme mischief. Gentleness, indulgence, and reason are the only hope of dealing with him. You have tried, Madame, as well as anyone can. He has a great deal of confidence in and respect for you. Sooner or later you will succeed in making him what you want him to be."[19] How wrong he was!

During long evenings alone with his uncle, Donatien spoke warmly of La Coste, which he was literally crazy about, and discussed the many improvements he planned to make the castle more livable. He was happy for this to be his only residence in the Comtat. The abbé seized the opportunity to say a few words about business matters, land values, the collection of rent, and so on. Donatien listened with one ear before moving on to more intimate matters. He spoke of his wife, whom he praised enthusiastically. He claimed to appreciate just how much she was worth. He considered her a friend and held her in high esteem. If he displeased her, he would be desperate, but still he found her "excessively chilly and devout." That is why he went elsewhere in search of amusement. His wife knew nothing of his follies, he added, and he would be most distressed if she were to find out. "When he has passed the ebullient age of passion," the abbé wrote to Mme de Montreuil after his visit, "he will appreciate the value of the wife you have given him. But he must get through this period, which will last longer than we might like. May it please God that he not cause you and me too much sorrow!"[20]

Making the Rounds

Upon returning to Paris Donatien threw himself more vigorously than ever into the pursuit of his pleasures. As his passions grew ever more insatiable and his drives ever more imperious, he entered into affair after affair. His reputation as a "dangerous" libertine spread like wildfire. Dancers and prostitutes followed one upon the other. We do not know all their names, not by a long shot. The police reports are quite fragmentary, and Donatien himself maintained a prudent silence about his less avowable adventures. And Mme de Montreuil, for all that she kept a close eye on her son-in-law, had no way of finding out about his secret life. There could be no scandal without a complaint to the police, and no complaint was recorded after the Jeanne Testard affair. This of course does not mean that Donatien had given up the practices that had gotten him into trouble, but he didn't inflict them on every woman who shared his bed. It goes without saying that he refrained from cruelty with Mlles Beaupré, Colet, and Beauvoisin. Highly visible, avidly sought after, and lavishly kept, such women were the aristocrats of prostitution and thus safe from the grosser forms of mistreatment. Donatien recruited his victims at the bottom of the ladder, among the girls of the "little houses" sent to him, despite Marais's warnings, by professional procuresses.

•

At around this time the marquis made the acquaintance of a certain Mlle D***, a dancer at the Opera, whose name has not been preserved. After seeing her in *Armide* he sent her a full page of mawkish compliments, of which he kept a copy. Amid the torrent of adulation we find a note concerning his present situation:

You have someone, I know, who pays dearly for the good fortune of being loved by you. How happy he is! If only I had a fortune to offer you, as he does! What am I saying, a fortune? A throne is what you need. The queen of love should be queen of the whole world. Thus I aspire only to second place. Deign to grant it to me, I beg you. I am worthy of it by the ardor of my love. I am not as wealthy as my rival, but I have more youth [initially he wrote *vigor*] and more love . . . The excess of my love will not allow me to wait any longer.[21]

In other words, being short of funds, he proposed to become the lady's *guerluchon*. At roughly the same time he also pursued another actress, Mlle M***, who was temporarily in Marseilles. But she loved another and could offer only friendship. He answered the cruel temptress's refusal with a torrent of tears and protestations, which he wasted no time in copying for his *Miscellaneous Works*. Like the other letters in the collection, this one is a pure exercise in style, this time on the theme of despair. Nothing else had changed: still the same bombast, the same excess, the same counterfeit lyricism:

I have told you and will go on telling you: nothing in the world can keep me away from you. I am prepared to do anything. I shall follow you to the grave . . . What a dreadful torture! How cruel my situation! If only you could see the state you have put me in! Then at least I would move you to pity. Are these ties indissoluble, then? O, great God! But no, I shall not try to break them. They are too dear to your heart. They will be the cause of my misfortune, but what does it matter? Be happy. I sacrifice everything to your happiness.

Since the lady in question was the mother of a young boy, moreover, the marquis carried heroism to the point of offering to take care of the boy as of his own child:

I assume full responsibility. I shall have him brought up on one of my estates. There he will be like my own son, and receive the same care and the same respect. He will want for nothing in nature. And then, whenever you wish, I personally will take you to him. His progress will be my achievement. His mother will be a little grateful to me, and in her eyes I will at least see gratitude. I will have been the cause of some feeling.[22]

A pointless parade of empty words, this missive fortunately fooled neither its author nor its recipient. As in the other letters of the collection, the apprentice writer was practicing his scales, testing himself in all the keys of passion. If the results fail to carry conviction, let us not be too harsh: this is the work of a schoolboy. It would take many more years, and many more drafts, and much suffering too, and the freedom that suffering bought, to produce the author of the *Cent Vingt Journées*.

His Father's Death

The news reached Donatien in the midst of a bacchanalia. For some time the comte de Sade had been suffering from a mysterious malady that kept him in bed for weeks at a time, his legs refusing to support him. After trying several remedies without success, he resigned himself to his suffering, alleviated by briefer and briefer intervals of remission. His quarrel with his son, his worries about the "ingrate," and the cruel disappointments he had suffered on Donatien's account contributed in no small way to the aggravation of his ills.

His only consolation was in prayer and piety. As he approached the age of fifty, the time of pleasure having passed, the count, like any number of celebrated libertines, had found his way back to God and religion. Thereafter he spent his time putting his affairs in order, writing essays, nearly all dedicated to his son, on history, morality, and philosophy, collecting his memories of the court of Louis XV, and compiling an anthology of "English anecdotes." Nor did he give up his favorite occupation, writing verse.

As for love and women, which had been the central focus of his life, he no longer thought about them except as a philosopher and sage. His essays on these subjects, based on wide reading but above all on personal experience, exhibit great lucidity. In unpublished notes composed late in life we find this thought on love:

The idea I had of love in the past is very different from the one I have today. I found it charming and was familiar only with its pleasures; its pains were unknown. I loved without sighs. If my mistress was cruel, I left her and at most regretted the time she had made me waste. When I found one who corresponded to my desires, the time I spent with her was delightful. I assured her that I loved her tenderly. I was not deceiving her. I believed it. I had never felt anything more powerful, and I developed a modest taste for the most passionate love. What happy ignorance! The vanity of women makes it easy to persuade them of the truth of anything one says on this score, and the confidence they have in their beauty makes them believe that their lovers are sincere. My mistress believed me, and she seemed to doubt my love only so that I might give her further proof of it.[23]

If his judgments of women often reflect the ambient cynicism regarding the fair sex, he never missed an opportunity to pay homage to the ladies, for he had learned to know them without ever ceasing to love them: "Only women are made to touch the heart, stir the senses, and please the mind," he wrote in one of his last letters.

His health had apparently been stable for a month. His son and the comte de Crillon, who had seen him on January 19, had found him "as usual," each day getting up and moving about his room, eating and sleeping normally. He was so weak, however, that there was little hope of recovery. Five days later, on Saturday, January 24, shortly before his sixty-fifth birthday, at about one in the afternoon, the comte de Sade breathed his last in the small house he was living in at the time in Le Grand-Montreuil, a suburb of Versailles. The burial took place forty-eight hours later, after a religious service at the parish church of Saint-Symphorien. The président de Montreuil, who accompanied Donatien, described the ceremony in his journal:

I left on Saturday, January 24, 1767, for Versailles, after learning that the comte de Sade was very ill. I arrived only to learn that he had just expired, about an hour after dinner. My son-in-law and I had his body watched for twice twenty-four hours. We followed his procession to the church of Le Grand-Montreuil, in which he was buried at ten-thirty in the morning. The procession and burial were most decorous. The church had been draped in black. Twelve paupers with torches attended the burial. In his home we found twenty-four or twenty-five pages written in [the count's] hand and full of anecdotes about the court and reflections on morality that deserve to be printed. He was buried in the church of Le Grand-Montreuil opposite the left pulpit. The abbé d'Aumasle, a friend of the comte de Sade's, was in charge of the whole ceremony.

•

In his will, which the family preserved and which has never before been reproduced, Jean-Baptiste de Sade settled his succession. After the customary introductory formulas he bequeathed to his wife, Marie-Eléonore de Maillé, his furnished apartment in the state it was in at the time of his death, the enjoyment of all his diamonds and jewels, and the carriage and horses she was using. Eventually the diamonds would pass to his daughter-in-law and after her to his son or his son's heirs. He increased the annual pension he paid to his brother Richard Jean-Louis by four hundred livres until such time as the recipient obtained a commandery and also bequeathed him six paintings stored in Avignon. He left a life pension of one hundred livres to each of his sisters "to augment the ones they already have." The abbé, for his part, was given his library, his silver service, and the use of all the furniture in the château de Saumane, to revert to Donatien after the abbé's death. As for Donatien, the count did not add to the general donation he had made at the time of his son's marriage. To his valet Barrois and his coachman François he left two hundred livres each, to be increased to four hundred if they had served more than fifteen years at the time of his death. His other servants were to receive amounts in proportion to the length of their service. For all his other movable and immovable property, "rights, names, reasons, and actions present or to come," he named and instituted as his residual legatee his son Donatien and his legitimate offspring in perpetuity and in order of primogeniture, "preferring males to females."[24]

In fact, Donatien inherited a disastrous financial situation. Buried under half-a-century's worth of debts that consumed more than half his annual income of 18,000 livres, the old man had lived meanly, often at the expense of the generous hosts and hostesses who offered him free room and board. "Every trip costs me," he had confided to his sister, the abbess of Saint-Laurent, shortly before his death, "and I haven't a sou."[25]

•

"The way his son felt this loss and was touched by it entirely reconciles me with him. Be a father to him, Monsieur. He cannot find a better one than you." These were the sentiments of la Présidente, expressed in a letter to the abbé a week after the count's death.[26] Later in the letter she informs her correspondent of her daughter's pregnancy, which was now "almost two-and-a-half months old." She had her doubts, however, that the child's birth would be as joyful an event as it ought to be: "The father does not seem all that eager either," she wrote the abbé three months later. "He is occupied with matters more interesting to his way of thinking, but I fear that the mother's suffering will overwhelm her, particularly at the end, at the time of the delivery, since she is not at all prepared for what lies in store . . . What a pity! He has everything he needs to be happy and to make the people he must live with happy. If only he cared to be reasonable and decent and did not like to forget himself with unworthy creatures!"[27]

How badly she mistook Donatien—and Renée-Pélagie! What a bizarre idea to expect that infernal couple to conform to bourgeois standards, to settle for bourgeois beatitude! Blinded by her abstract and universal conception of justice, la Présidente had absolutely no understanding of the bond between torturer and victim. Ecstasy and violence, inextricably intertwined, create a powerful, fundamentally ambiguous tie. The lover caresses his wife even as he plots the darkest of machinations against her person, and she swoons with pleasure and gratitude toward her persecutor: virtue folds itself in evil's embrace and becomes its accomplice. Far from considering Renée-Pélagie his enemy, Donatien felt for her the ambivalent affection that tyrants always feel for those who unconditionally surrender to their demands.

Homage to the Lord

On April 16, 1767, the marquis de Sade at last received his promotion to the rank of captain in the cavalry with orders to join his company immediately.[28] The good fortune was ill-timed, because Donatien had other projects in mind. The marquis therefore sought and obtained special leave from his colonel and on April 20 discreetly left Paris for Lyons, where he pretended to have a meeting with his uncle the abbé. In reality he went to join Mlle Beauvoisin, with whom he had recently resumed relations. The "siren" had regained all her former power over him and brazenly took advantage of it following his father's death: "He is blind when it comes to that woman," Mme de Montreuil sighed. But the lady apparently failed to live up to expectations, for Donatien did not linger long on the banks of the Rhône. We find him at La Coste on June 15, following a brief stay in Saumane. He inspected the work that had been done and that was still under way, called upon Maître Fage, a notary in Apt, to straighten out his accounts, and informed the community of La Coste that he expected to receive the traditional homage due the new lord. On June 21 the village council considered paying for a mass in memory of the late comte de Sade and recognizing and doing homage to his heir in accordance with custom. The earliest the ceremony could be held, however, was the ninth of August.

On that day, in the presence of Maître Fage, La Coste's two consuls, assisted by four specially selected representatives, "did homage to the high and mighty lord Louis Aldonse Donatien, marquis de Sade,[29] seated in an armchair, [the consuls] kneeling before him, heads bared, without sashes or arms, their hands joined inside those of their lord marquis, who, as a sign of the homage received, released the hands of the aforementioned mayors and consuls and received from each of them and from each of the deputies the customary kiss . . . The aforementioned mayors and consuls and deputies . . . further promised and swore to be, in the future as in the past, good, loyal, and faithful vassals of their lord marquis and his heirs, to keep his secrets, to refrain from doing him harm, to seek his honest profit with all their power, and not to renounce or flee his jurisdiction."[30]

This was a day of the utmost importance, and one we would do well to keep in mind when we come to take up the marquis's political ideas. The ceremony in which the vassal swore "faith and homage" to his lord, which dates from the earliest period of feudalism, had been more or less obsolete in France for at least a century, particularly in this form, with all the marks of submission and respect prescribed by ancient custom. In general the old ceremony had been reduced to the signing of a notarized document recognizing the faith and homage as an established fact. In many cases the lord was represented by a proxy. This was what Donatien's father had done in 1732. To revive such outdated formalities, to insist that the communal authorities of La Coste swear their allegiance in the ancient manner, was to demonstrate a remarkable devotion to feudal rights. All this gives reason to wonder about the marquis's alleged commitment to the "revolutionary" cause.

The marquis's attitude was even more "reactionary" than it might appear: he refused to grant the people of La Coste the reduction of dues that the lord traditionally granted in honor of his "joyous advent." His "reign" thus augured ill from the beginning.

Meanwhile, the restoration of the château was proceeding rapidly, although the new theater was not yet finished. We know little else about what happened during this visit, other than that Donatien wrote his wife that he suffered a great deal from the heat. Was he enjoying pleasures as "active" as during his previous stay? La Présidente was quite anxious to know: "His fortunes have no need, I think, of further shocks. The earlier ones have done him enough harm," she wrote the abbé.[31]

According to local tradition, Donatien also asked to be received officially in Apt, "but the consuls demurred when they learned that their neighbor insisted on receiving virtually the same honors as were accorded to the vice-legate representing the Holy Father in Avignon."[32]

Before leaving Provence Donatien summoned Maître Fage to La Coste in order to express his satisfaction: the notary had arranged for the advantageous sale of certain properties, negotiated new leases, and taken care of many business matters on behalf of his client. The marquis therefore proposed that Fage henceforth take charge of managing his properties. Pleased with the marquis's straightforward way of dealing and assured that the commission would last no more than three years, Fage accepted the proposition. He would soon regret it.

•

Donatien returned to Paris a few days after the birth of his son on August 27, 1767. On January 24, 1768, Louis-Joseph de Bourbon, prince of Condé, and Louise-Elisabeth de Bourbon, dowager princess of Conti, held the infant over the baptismal font in the chapel of the hôtel de Condé. The child was named Louis-Marie.

Mme de Montreuil no doubt hoped that fatherhood would settle the marquis down, but it did no such thing. Soon after his return he again came under surveillance by Inspector Marais, who noted the following in his report of October 16, 1767: "He is pulling out all the stops to persuade Mlle Rivière, of the Opera, to live with him and has offered her twenty-five louis per month provided that she agrees to stay with him at his house in Arcueil on days when she is not obliged to appear on stage. The lady refused, because she has M. Hocquart de Coubron for her benefactor, but M. de Sade is still pursuing her. In the meantime, while awaiting her surrender, he has done what he could to persuade Mme Brissault to supply him with girls to take supper with him in his little house. The lady, who has a pretty good idea what he is capable of, has consistently refused him, but he may have turned to others less scrupulous or unfamiliar with his reputation. He is certain to be heard from before long."[33]

Marais had no idea how truly he spoke. Some four months later, early in February 1768, Sade had his valet bring four girls from the faubourg Saint-Antoine to his Arcueil home. He beat them, then invited them to dinner. Afterward he had his valet pay them a louis; the valet himself received an écu for his services. According to the lieutenant of the constabulary, the occasion was by no means unusual. For fifteen months the marquis had been a source of constant scandal in Arcueil. Night and day he brought home "persons of both sexes with whom he is in debauched commerce." He also had the reputation of being a "very violent man, having insulted and struck several individuals."[34] In June 1767 he had manhandled a coachman who had driven women to the marquis's house and asked to be paid for his services.[35]

•

Donatien at this point seems to have become a prisoner of some blind force within him, which drove him inexorably to the edge of the abyss. "It will not be long before we hear talk of the horrors of M. le comte de Sade," Inspector Marais prophesied.

8

The Arcueil Affair

The Man in the White Muff

Easter Sunday, April 3, 1768, at nine o'clock in the morning on the place des Victoires: a young man in a gray frock coat stands with his back to the grillwork at the base of the statue of Louis XIV. He wears a hunting knife at his side and carries a cane and a muff of lynx fur, a "delightful white muff" in the words of Roland Barthes, who found the object, "placed there no doubt to satisfy a *requirement of delicacy*," fascinating.

A woman meanwhile had left mass at the church of the Petits-Pères and stopped to beg for alms a short distance away from where the man was standing. Rose Keller was around thirty-six, a native of Strasbourg and the widow of an apprentice pastrymaker by the name of Charles Valentin. A cotton spinner without work for the past month, she had been reduced to begging. A passerby stopped, gave her a sou, and continued on his way. The man with the muff beckoned her to approach and promised her an écu if she would follow him. She protested in bad French with a strong German accent: "I am not what you think. I'm not that sort." The man reassured her. It was not at all what she imagined. He simply wanted her to be his housekeeper, nothing more. She would receive a salary and be fed well. She agreed and went with him. He took her to a place near the new market and led her to a room on the third floor whose walls were covered with yellow damask. The furniture included a chaise longue upholstered in the same fabric and several armchairs shrouded in canvas, as was the chaise. After inviting his guest to sit down, the man asked if she would be willing to go to his country house. Where she went made no difference, she said, as long as she could earn a living there. Whereupon the man left her, saying that he had some errands to do and would return for her in an hour.

An hour later he returned with a cab, invited her to join him, and closed the wooden doors behind her, whereupon the driver started off. After a long silence Rose Keller was asked if she knew where they were going. "How could I possibly know, since I can't see anything?" During the remainder of the journey the man pretended to sleep and did not utter another word.

Meanwhile, the marquis's servant Langlois arrived in Arcueil with two prostitutes his master had ordered him to bring. He ushered them into a room near the kitchen. About an hour later Donatien's carriage stopped on the outskirts of the village. After climbing down himself and handing a mysterious package to the coachman, he invited Rose Keller to follow him. It was approximately twelve-thirty in the afternoon. After a short walk the two travelers arrived at a small house on rue de Lardenay. The marquis told the beggar woman to wait a moment, entered the house through the main door, and from the inside opened a small green door for the lady. Leading the way, he proceeded across a small courtyard, climbed a flight of stairs, showed her into a large room, and told her to wait while he went to look for some bread and something to drink. She was to make herself at home. He then left the room, locking the door behind him with two turns of the key. For quite some time Rose Keller remained alone in the shadows, the only window in the room, which opened onto the garden, having been sealed shut from inside. What little light filtered in through the shutters revealed wainscoting, two baldachin beds, and some overstuffed chairs. While Rose Keller inspected the furniture, Donatien joined the two prostitutes that Langlois had brought to the house. An hour later he returned, carrying a lighted candle: "Come down with me, grandma," he said. She followed him into a small study, the door to which he closed behind them. He then asked her to remove her clothes. "For what?" she asked. "For fun," he replied. When she protested that she hadn't come for that, he lost his temper, threatened to kill her and bury her with his own hands, and then left her alone. Frightened, the prisoner began to undress. A moment later, the marquis reappeared, his torso bare beneath a sleeveless jacket and a white handkerchief tied around his head. On seeing that she was still wearing her chemise, he told her to take it off. "I would rather die," she replied. Suddenly he tore it off her and pushed her into an adjoining room with drawn curtains. In the middle of the room stood a bed with a red chintz spread. He threw Rose Keller down on her stomach, and he may also have tied her to the bed with ropes attached to each of her limbs and around her midriff (here the witnesses' statements diverge). He put a pillow over her head and his muff on top of it to muffle her cries. He then grabbed either a bundle of cane or a cat-o'-nine-tails and whipped her until she bled; this was repeated several times.

According to the victim's deposition, the marquis next made small incisions in her flesh with a pen knife and dripped molten sealing wax over her wounds. Seven or eight more times he alternated between cutting and whipping his victim. When she cried out, he brandished a knife and again threatened to kill her and bury her body if she did not quiet down. While she tried to stifle her screams, he then whipped her more savagely than before. She begged him not to kill her because she had not made Easter confession and did not wish to die in a state of sin. Sade then suggested hearing her confession himself and tried to force her to confess to him. The more she begged for mercy, the harder and faster came the blows. Then, all at once, he stopped. Panting like a madman, he emitted frightening sounds, gurgles of suffering and pleasure. The torture had come to an end.

The marquis untied Rose Keller, led her back to the study, and allowed her to dress. A moment later he returned with a towel, a kettle of water, and a basin. In washing and drying herself she left large bloodstains on the linen, which Donatien made her rinse. He then handed her a small vial containing a "brandy-colored" liquid. If she rubbed this on her body, he told her, within an hour no visible marks would remain. She did as she was told, but the substance caused her excruciating pain. While she finished dressing, Donatien went and fetched a plate of boiled beef with a piece of bread and a small bottle of wine. He then took her to the second-floor bedroom. Again he locked her in, but not before telling her to stay away from the window. Above all she was to make sure that no one saw or heard her. She would be released that evening. "Before nightfall," she begged, for she had no idea where she was, had no money, and did not want to sleep in the street. "Don't worry about it," the marquis told her; then he disappeared.

Left alone, Rose Keller tried the door handle, grabbed two covers from the beds, pried the shutter open with a knife, secured a rope to the base of the window, climbed down into the yard, ran to the surrounding wall, climbed a trellis, and dropped to the ground on the other side, scraping her arm and left hand in the process. She then took off down rue de la Fontaine. Langlois ran after her, shouting at her to come back: his master wished to speak with her. He caught up with her, holding a purse full of money in his hand, but she shoved him aside and continued to run, her hair disheveled and her torn chemise flapping between her legs. Along the way she encountered a village woman, Marguerite Sixdeniers, and sobbingly recounted her misfortunes. They were joined by two other women from the village: a Mme Pontier and a Mme Bajou. Terrified by what they heard, the three women took Rose Keller to a building courtyard and there mended her torn clothing. Her skin, they noticed, was covered with bloody gashes "from mid-back to lower thigh." They treated the wounds with lavender water and then accompanied the hapless victim to the home of the *procureur fiscal* (tax prosecutor), who sent them to the château of Charles Lambert, notary and bailiff for the *bailliage* (bailiwick) of Arcueil. Lambert's wife, Marie-Louise Jouette, received them. Rose Keller again began to tell her story, but the sensitive lady was overcome with emotion and had to retire before the tale was finished. The bailiff being absent, Gersant de La Benardière, the lieutenant of the local constabulary (*maréchaussée*), was sent for. He arrived at eight o'clock that night, took the victim's deposition, and had her examined immediately by a surgeon, Pierre-Paul Le Comte, whose report stated the following: "The entire extent of the buttocks and a portion of the back [are] striped with lashes and excoriated with deep and extensive cuts and contusions along the backbone." The damage, in the doctor's opinion, had been done by "a bruising and cutting instrument of some sort." He also noted traces of "melted wax on some of the wounds." Mme Lambert asked one of her neighbors to take the poor victim into her home for the night. She was shown to a cowbarn and given a mattress to sleep on. Two days later Mme Lambert took Rose Keller into her own home.

Meanwhile, the marquis, after saying goodbye to his gardener, left Arcueil at around six in the evening and returned to Paris, where he was staying on rue Neuve-du-Luxembourg.[1]

Good Offices

While the Arcueil police carry on with their investigation, let us shift our attention to the Montreuil household, which found itself in unaccustomed turmoil. Had Donatien confessed everything to his family? Had the provost of Ile-de-France discreetly alerted M. de Montreuil?

In any case, at the Montreuil household all hands were girding themselves for battle, and la Présidente, as determined as ever, seemed ready to do whatever was necessary to save her daughter's honor. The situation was critical, to be sure, but not desperate. Mme de Montreuil immediately took charge of operations.

The first objective was to obtain from the king a lettre de cachet against her son-in-law, which would rescue him from the clutches of the regular judicial system. For this Mme de Montreuil needed her husband's help. Shaking off his customary lethargy, M. de Montreuil immediately approached his most advantageously placed friends. The second objective was to persuade Rose Keller to withdraw her allegations. On April 7 la Présidente called in two trusted advisers: Maître Sohier, an attorney, and the abbé Amblet, Donatien's former tutor and still an intimate family friend. Their mission? To see the girl and induce her to drop the charges; the family was prepared to pay whatever price was necessary. But above all it must be done quickly: time was of the essence.

The two men rushed to a carriage and hastened to Arcueil. Upon arriving at the château, where Rose Keller was still bedridden, they asked to see her. She received them lying down because, she said, she was unable to assume any other position "and unfit for service for the rest of her life." Sohier asked how much she wanted to drop the charges. She stated her price: a thousand écus (three thousand livres), and not a penny less. Sohier was taken aback. Three thousand livres? The sum was enormous, a small fortune. Even if she succeeded in proving her allegations, the courts would never award her anything like that amount. The lawyer then made a series of counterproposals, which Mme Keller rejected one after another. Her offer was final: three thousand livres, take it or leave it. Unable to shake her resolve, the lawyer and the abbé withdrew briefly to talk things over. Sohier then returned and offered her 1,800 livres. Again she refused, and again the two men talked things over. Finally she declared herself willing to compromise, but she would not settle for less than 2,400 livres. Judging the price too high, the mediators went back to Paris to consult with la Présidente, who ordered them to return to Arcueil immediately and settle no matter what the price. Back at the château they found Rose Keller sitting up in bed gossiping with the ladies of the village. "Obviously you're not as sick as you claimed," the attorney noted. "It is to be hoped that you will soon recover." In the end, a statement withdrawing the charges was signed in the presence of Maître Lambert and numerous witnesses. As agreed, the convalescent victim received a payment of 2,400 livres plus an additional seven gold louis "for dressings and medication."

Prisoner of the King

The following day, April 8, a royal warrant arrived ordering that "M. le comte de Sade be arrested and taken to the château de Saumur." Meanwhile, the minister of the king's household informed M. du Petit-Thouars, the warden of Saumur, that he was about to receive a prisoner and advising that the man be "confined, on your responsibility, and under no circumstances whatsoever is he to leave the grounds of the château." In other words, his presence was to be kept secret. The Montreuils were relieved: Donatien was now the king's prisoner and scandal had been avoided, or so they thought.

All that remained was to get rid of the incriminating evidence: whips, ropes, and other compromising items and documents. On April 9, abbé Amblet went to the little house in Arcueil on the pretext of examining the gardener's books; he returned laden with packages. These, he would later explain, contained nothing other than silver and prints that Mme de Sade had asked him to retrieve. But he had noticed nothing out of the ordinary. The place was clean, and the police could be allowed to search.

On April 10 Donatien traveled by postal coach to the place where he was to be held. Still worried about scandal, the family had obtained permission for him to be accompanied by abbé Amblet rather than the police. But rather than travel due south toward the Loire, he headed southeast toward Burgundy and stopped at Joigny on the road not to Saumur but to Lyons. Did he perhaps intend to disobey the king's orders and hide out at La Coste? There is no other plausible explanation for this bizarre itinerary. Soon, however, he gave up this plan, no doubt at the prompting of his former tutor.[2] The abbé must have convinced him that the lettre de cachet was as good as a pardon and that without it he risked trial in the criminal courts. All in all, it was better to spend his time in His Majesty's jails. For once willing to heed good advice, Donatien changed course and headed for Saumur. Before leaving Joigny, however, he wrote his uncle to tell him what had happened:

An unfortunate affair, my dear uncle, has led to my arrest and imminent imprisonment in the château de Saumur. My family has been good enough to come to my defense and urge my release. They obtained permission for abbé Amblet to take me [to Saumur], and he will fill you in about the details of the case. In the name of the misfortune that afflicts me and dogs my steps, I beg you to forgive me all the wrongs I have done you and to bear all this, my dear uncle, with a peaceful spirit rather than the vengeful one I may well deserve. If word of the case gets out in the region, you may deny everything and say that I am with my regiment, where my family is glad to have me spend some time for my own good.[3]

Scapegoat

As the gates of the château de Saumur closed behind the accused, the case erupted in the Parlement of Paris. On April 15, 1768, during a session of the *conseil criminel*, an unidentified member of the court addressed his colleagues to denounce "a horrible crime that took place in Arcueil," of which he mentioned a few details. After deliberating for a time the council ordered that the *procureur général* be summoned at once to report on the facts of the case and the state of the prosecution. In the days that followed, the Parlement ordered the local courts to relinquish jurisdiction in the matter. The *chambre de la Tournelle* (the criminal chamber of the Paris Parlement) took charge of the matter, launched a thorough investigation, and issued a warrant for the arrest of the accused. All the efforts of la Présidente had been for nought: the Arcueil affair was now public, and scandal was inevitable. The man responsible for the Parlement's decision was none other than its *premier président*, Charles-Augustin de Maupeou, who seized the opportunity to avenge himself against his old enemy, M. Cordier de Montreuil. The news caused an uproar among the public and consternation in the family. As long as Donatien was held on orders of the king, his case fell outside the ordinary judicial system. His fate depended solely on the will of the sovereign. But once the Parlement of Paris got involved, the worst was to be feared.

•

I do not wish to exonerate the marquis de Sade of his crimes or to minimize their gravity, as Maurice Heine does when he refers to the Arcueil incident as a mere "spanking," or as Gilbert Lely does when he alludes to the "insubstantial nature of the crime." To whip a defenseless woman is an ignoble act, whatever the torturer's inner drives. If Sade's writings, although a hundred times crueler than his acts, are justified by the rights of the imagination and the freedom accorded to works of the spirit, the same cannot be said for the behavior of the individual. Yet it would be a mistake to ignore the fact that under the Ancien Régime such acts, provided they were committed by members of the nobility, were generally treated as misdemeanors. Every day great lords tortured other human beings, sometimes for money, sometimes not, for the sole gratification of their senses, and no one did anything about it: noble birth was an unfair advantage. Remember, too, that this was a time when educators did not spare the rod for fear of spoiling the child, and the same lords had themselves suffered the stinging pleasures of being beaten at school. Flagellation still had religious significance, moreover, and self-mortification was still practiced in monastic communities. Under these circumstances it may be that whipping, even for lascivious ends, was not as serious an offense as it is today. Respect for the human person and the social progress made by women have profoundly altered our moral views in this regard.

Prostitutes, moreover, constituted a category apart. An eighteenth-century libertine would not have dared treat a relatively respectable courtesan or dancer as he would have treated a common whore, prostitutes being presumed willing to submit to anything. And since Rose Keller was nothing to the marquis but a common street whore, he did not think twice about forcing her to do his bidding: was that not what he paid her for? "Only in Paris and London do these contemptible creatures enjoy such support," he would write later. "When they appear in court in Rome, Venice, Naples, or Warsaw, they are asked whether or not they were paid. If not, the courts insist on payment, as is just. Otherwise, if their only complaint is that they were mistreated, the judge threatens to lock them up if they continue to annoy him with such obscenities. Change your line of work, they are told, or if this one pleases you, learn to put up with its unpleasantness."[4] Sade's attitude toward prostitution is rather surprising, all the more so in that it was not merely opportunistic: Sade always held common prostitutes in contempt. He was harshly critical of Sartine for attaching absurd importance to what these vile creatures said, and he complained that the police paid too much attention to them: "A man can commit every possible abuse and every conceivable infamy provided he takes care with the whore's ass. The reason for this is quite simple: the whores pay, and we don't. When I get out, I too must try to place myself under the protection of the police. I have an ass, too, just like a whore, and I would be most pleased if people took care of it."[5]

•

If the Parlement took an interest in the Arcueil affair, therefore, it may have had less to do with the crime itself than with the personality of the criminal, and particularly with his noble rank. Public opinion, a new force at the time but one with which the weakened central government had to reckon more and more, had long been outraged by the fact that the sexual vices of noblemen were, if not tolerated, at least leniently punished by the courts. Tired of seeing noble offenders get away with their crimes, the public wanted an example to be set, and the marquis de Sade proved a convenient scapegoat. Mme de Saint-Germain grasped the situation perfectly, and it only made her fear all the more for her dear "child": "He is, just now, a victim of the public's ferocity," she wrote the abbé de Sade. "M. de Fronsac's case and many others compound his own. For the past ten years court nobles have committed horrors beyond belief, that is for certain. Remonstrances will be made, or so they say."[6]

Obviously a scapegoat was needed. But why Donatien de Sade and not someone else? Several reasons come to mind. For one thing, Sade never denied his predilections. In fact, he made a show of them, with an innate instinct for provocation. He carried on virtually under the nose of the police, who knew all about his exploits. For another, there was the personal hostility of M. de Maupeou, who worked behind the scenes to dishonor his enemy's son-in-law. No doubt this intrigue played a large part in the marquis's downfall. A seemingly unimportant circumstance also had a major effect on the outcome: the president of the Tournelle, Louis-Paul Pinon, himself owned a country house in Arcueil and happened to have been there at the time of the crime, a fact that had filled him, according to the bookseller Hardy, with "the greatest indignation."

But there was also another reason for the choice of Donatien de Sade, one that previous biographers have failed to emphasize sufficiently: the old enmity between the marquis's father and the court of Louis XV. The suspicions that clouded the reputation of the one-time French ambassador to Cologne, the critical remarks about the royal mistress, the count's scarcely concealed contempt for the king's ministers and courtiers, his reputation as a rake (and even worse, a disgraced and ruined rake)—all these things were not such ancient history that they had been forgotten in the corridors of power. If the king himself seems not to have held the son responsible for the sins of the father, other powerful men did not share their sovereign's forbearance. Louis XV apparently did not care that Donatien had shown no eagerness to pay his respects at court, that he had failed to show up for the signing of his marriage contract, and that he had even spurned the honor of riding in the king's carriage. But others remembered.

Both Heine and Lely believe that the marquis in this period of his life enjoyed powerful protectors, but I do not share their view. In my view, Donatien de Sade was all his life a man apart, without friends, allies, or social moorings. He belonged to no clique or clan and remained isolated at all times, even in the pursuit of pleasure. Unlike Fronsac, Sabran, Jaucourt, and other fashionable libertines, Sade cultivated his enjoyments without company. Except for his valets, who served him sometimes as procurers, sometimes as partners, he is not known to have shared his debauchery with any companion.

In a society like that of the Ancien Régime, where patronage and connections were essential, Sade was therefore a lonely figure. Although he prided himself on his connection to the Condés, they had such a bad reputation themselves that they were of little use to him. By proclaiming his allegiance to them he succeeded only in further discrediting himself. As princes of the blood, they remained untouchable, which only made their enemies keener to wreak vengeance on one of their most notorious henchmen. As early as 1765 Mme des Franches, an old friend of the comte de Sade, said that Donatien's "relations *today* seem usurped; he does so little to sustain them."[7] Socially he had become, like his father before him, and perhaps because of him, a marginal member of the nobility. Though he continued to play the part of a feudal lord in his province, in Paris he counted for almost nothing. And his marriage to a daughter of the *noblesse de robe* was not likely to rehabilitate him, for while "the boar bestows nobility on the sow," as the saying went, the reverse was rarely true. Thus the authorities, under pressure to throw a noble to the wolves, could hardly have dreamed of a better choice. With him there was no danger of a great family or powerful ally turning up to snatch the accused from the long arm of the law on the grounds that he belonged to an ancient race or sprang from a long line distinguished for its fabulous exploits. No one supports a man cut off from his milieu, excluded from his caste, devoid of credit, and unable to offer anything in return. In his distress Donatien's only ally was the king himself. By issuing the lettre de cachet that sent him to Saumur, the monarch had rescued him from the clutches of the Parlement. Now that the Parlement had reaffirmed jurisdiction in the case, the only thing that could save him was royal clemency.

Rightly alarmed by the latest turn of events, the family called all its relatives and friends to arms. The président de Montreuil, who had done everything in his power "to minimize the consequences of this affair," begged the abbé de Sade to come to Paris and take up his nephew's defense, as if that old habitué of the bordellos enjoyed any influence. When asked for help, the duc de Montpezat merely registered "his keen interest" in the unfortunate young man's fate and urged Mme de Villeneuve to do what she could to hasten her uncle's arrival. There is reason to smile at the thought of Madame Piron's client playing the role of providential savior. "It is fortunate for your nephew," the duke added reassuringly, "that he has a wife whose relatives are connected with the Parlement."

The Investigation

Once the evidence gathered in Arcueil had been brought to the criminal chamber of Parlement, the preliminary investigation could begin. On April 19 a warrant was issued ordering that Donatien be brought to the Conciergerie and that his property be seized. Meanwhile, Rose Keller was to be examined within twenty-four hours by court-appointed physicians and surgeons "in order to determine her present condition and the cause and consequences of her injuries." Was the Tournelle aware at this point of the king's order? We cannot be sure, because the two judicial systems, royal and parliamentary, operated independently, and communication between them was not always the best. On the twentieth the police searched the marquis's quarters at the Montreuil hôtel on rue Neuve-du-Luxembourg. In the absence of the accused, who had not been seen on the premises for twelve days, the bailiff left a copy of the arrest warrant with the porter, together with a summons to appear in court two weeks hence. The bailiff agreed not to seize the furniture in the apartment, since it belonged not to the marquis but to M. de Montreuil. That same day, at seven in the morning, two *conseillers* went to Arcueil to inventory the contents of the marquis's house. They carefully inspected all the rooms, searched the drawers, moved cushions, and turned over mattresses but found nothing out of the ordinary: table linen and kitchen towels, candles, drapery pulls, ivory tokens. A locked desk attracted their attention, and they had it opened by a locksmith. It contained "two pieces of green wax, a large inkwell, and a small cardboard box." The cellar contained "an empty wine room, a vinegar room, and a number of stacked wine bottles." There was no trace of what had happened on April 3. But, as we know, the loyal abbé Amblet had already paid a visit.

On April 21 the investigators began their interviews with Rose Keller and the other witnesses: Mmes Pontier, Lambert, Bajou, and Sixdeniers, the procureur Sohier, abbé Amblet, and others. The priest, now aged fifty-three, was still close to his former student. He was, in the Ancien Régime sense of the term, a *domestique* of the marquis's household, and he continued to receive an annual pension of five hundred livres.[8] His deposition, which I cite verbatim, is therefore devoid of credibility. The voice we hear is that of a faithful servant:

> I have known M. de Sade since his childhood, having been in charge of his education. I have known him to have an ardent temperament, which has given him a keen taste for pleasure, but I have always known him to have a good heart, a far cry from the horrors alleged in the complaint. At school he was well liked by his classmates, and he has also been well liked by his comrades in the various units in which he has served. I have seen him perform acts of charity and humanity, among others in regard to a carpenter by the name of Moulin, who died last year after a long illness, during which [Sade] assisted him. The unfortunate man having left several children, M. de Sade took charge of one of them and is paying his board. Thus I cannot believe all the dark deeds of which he is accused.

Since no other document refers to this child or his father, we may assume that the abbé simply made them up. About his trip to Saumur with his former disciple he chose to say nothing.

•

The accused would not be interrogated for three more months, by which time he had been notified of his pardon. Having nothing more to fear, would he have had less to hide? It is tempting to think so. Yet his version of the facts contradicts that of his victim on at least two key points:

1. Did Rose Keller really believe that the marquis was going to offer her honest work, or was she soliciting, as he maintained? To confess to prostitution was to risk imprisonment in La Force. To avoid this, many prostitutes claimed to be unemployed working women, and this may have been the widow Valentin's ploy. Or she may have been one of many part-time prostitutes, who occasionally saw clients to supplement their wages. The fact that she had been at the church of the Petits-Pères before getting "picked up" by Sade suggests that she was indeed a prostitute. The church was well-known as a place where prostitutes solicited clients, particularly on Sundays and holidays: "One can be sure of meeting there any number of beauties, who assault you with their charms and are certainly for hire," notes Inspector Marais. "The minute someone takes the bait, they desert the temple of God and surrender totally to the world."[9] It may be that Rose Keller, having

failed that day to attract any "bites," decided to try her luck on the nearby sidewalks of the place des Victoires.

2. According to Rose Keller, the marquis first tied her to the bed, then beat her with canes and clubs, pausing occasionally to make incisions "with a small knife or blade" and to drip red and white wax on her wounds. Sade admitted that she was lying down but denied having tied her up, and he claimed to have whipped her only with a knotted rope, not with canes or clubs. What is more, he categorically denied making any incisions. He "simply applied daubs of a salve consisting of white wax in various places for the purpose of healing her wounds." In fact, the two allegations are connected. The instrument used would have determined what the victim felt and what the doctors observed. Remember that Keller, lying on her stomach, could not see what was going on behind her back. On April 23 the surgeon Lecomte, who had examined her on the day of the incident, was questioned in detail about her wounds: how extensive, how deep, what appearance, and so on. His answers indicate a clear retreat from his earlier statements:

By excoriation he meant simply that the epidermis had been removed in various places over the entire buttocks and a portion of the lumbar region. As for the contusions, they resembled those caused by canes. As for the cuts, he saw only places where the epidermis had been removed . . .

—Questioned as to whether he recognized any bruises that appeared to have been caused by blows from a blunt instrument.

—Stated that he saw only two traces slightly above the lumbar region on the backbone, without ecchymosis, simply red.

—Questioned as to how many cuts he noticed.

—Stated that there might have been a dozen excoriations resembling cuts.

—Questioned about the size of these cuts.

—Stated that they were the size and shape of a six-sol coin and did not extend below the epiderm.

—It was pointed out to him that it was not natural for cuts to be round, and that he himself had stated in his report to the constable that the subject woman had been excoriated with severe and lengthy cuts and contusions along the backbone.

—Stated that he did not know what instrument had been used to make the cuts, but that they were round, and that the words "severe and lengthy" in his report to the constable referred to the contusions and not to the cuts.

—Questioned as to whether he had seen burn marks on the subject woman.

—Answered in the negative, stating that the subject woman had indeed complained of having had white wax and red wax poured on her but that he had found no sign of red wax and no trace of burning such as would have been caused by the molten Spanish wax allegedly applied to her skinned areas. Stated that he found only drops of white wax on the back, which did not appear to him to have caused any burning.

—Questioned as to whether he had seen traces of ropes having been tied around her feet, hands, and body.

—Answered in the negative.

I have quoted extensively from this important testimony because it was the knife cuts that made the most vivid impression on the general public. Assuming that the surgeon was not bribed by the family (Mme de Montreuil was entirely capable of striking a bargain with him, as she did with Rose Keller), his testimony corroborates the marquis's on at least three points:

1. The victim was not tied up.
2. Given the round shape and general appearance of the wounds, the injuries were caused by the knotted rope used for whipping rather than by the blade of a knife.
3. The traces of wax were not red but white. This is an important point, because red wax, used for sealing, was a mixture of shellac and turpentine and could cause severe burns if applied hot, whereas white beeswax was relatively harmless even when molten. But where did the traces of wax on Rose Keller's back come from?

According to the marquis, the wax was a salve he applied to his victim "for the purpose of healing her wounds." The remedy was a familiar one: ever since antiquity ointments made of oil and virgin wax had been used to treat wounds, chapping, and burns. Another possibility is that the marquis, who held a candle as he flagellated his victim, had dripped wax on her in the heat of the action.

What we are left with is a confession by the marquis that he whipped his victim with canes and/or knotted ropes. Is this not enough? Surely it is, and my purpose, I repeat, is not to exonerate him. But once again, as in the case of Jeanne Testard, the torture was more cerebral than actual. Sade's pleasure came mainly from the terror he inspired in his victim, from his ability to convince her that she would not leave his house alive or to make her think that he was slicing up her flesh. The nature of his perversion was not so much to inflict pain as to inspire terror.

Pierre-Encize

While Donatien, graciously imprisoned at the château de Saumur, quietly waited for events to unfold, the Montreuils again intervened to have him transferred to a more secure place of confinement. On April 23, the minister of the king's household asked M. de Bory, in charge of the château de Pierre-Encize near Lyons, to accept responsibility for the prisoner: "The king's wish is that he not leave his room and that he have no communication with the other prisoners. When he goes out for air and exercise, you will kindly take the usual precautions and see that he is accompanied. Since, however, he is said to be suffering from a fistula and may require treatment prescribed by Brasson, if he needs to see a surgeon in Lyons, you will kindly facilitate the process, and you will also receive the servant who customarily changes his dressings morning and night. However, this servant is not to leave the château."[10] When the marquise asked that her husband be allowed at least to walk about freely inside the fortress, the same minister refused her request on grounds that suggest clearly that the reason for holding the marquis at Pierre-Encize was to protect him more securely from the criminal court:[11] "As for the freedom you wish him to have inside the château," the comte de Saint-Florentin explained, "that is impossible, especially after what has just happened in Parlement, which will not fail to claim him if he is seen in the company of visitors to the château."[12]

Inspector Marais, who was assigned to oversee the transfer, arrived in Saumur toward the end of April and found the prisoner at liberty inside the château, dining at the warden's table. Quite surprised to see the policeman and even more surprised by the purpose of his visit, Donatien inquired as to the reasons for the change. Marais explained that since Parlement had assumed jurisdiction over his case, it was essential "to appear to anticipate the punishment that the seriousness of the crime deserved, and in that way to win the leniency of the tribunal in his favor. He was not to worry and would be treated as well at Pierre-Encize as he had been at Saumur, but the latter was reputed to be too lax." Clearly pleased with this explanation, the prisoner docilely allowed himself to be driven to his new prison. Along the way he spoke at length about the incident and assured Marais that he had done nothing to the woman but whip her, that it had never occurred to him to cut her, "that he could not imagine what had induced the creature to make such a charge, and that he was convinced that if Parlement

ordered an investigation by expert surgeons, they would find no trace
of scars." That being the case, he was unrepentant and regretted only
his detention. "At heart he is still the same," the policeman commented
in reporting Sade's declarations to Saint-Florentin. From the same
report we also know that, despite the precautions taken, news of the
episode had leaked out: in Saumur, Lyons, Moulins, and Dijon, "it
was the story of the day."[13]

Meanwhile, the judicial machine, set in motion by Maupeou and
Pinon, pursued its course. On May 7 the court found Sade in default
for failing to answer the summons (which he hardly could have done,
being imprisoned elsewhere) and again summoned him "by public
outcry" to appear within a week. On May 11, Sade still having failed
to appear after two official trumpeters had sounded their instruments
outside the Montreuil household as well as beside the pillory in Les
Halles, the main staircase of the palace, and "other usual places in
this city of Paris," Master Philippe Rouveau, "the king's only official
crier" named "le sieur de Sade" in a "loud and intelligible voice . . .
as absent and fugitive" and ordered him to appear in person within
one week "to be imprisoned in the Conciergerie" and there "heard
and interrogated . . . Failing which his trial will be held and completed
in default and in absentia." Was the Tournelle still unaware of the
king's order? It seems unlikely. It was merely pretending not to have
heard in accordance with the usual procedure for arrest, violation of
which could have led to dismissal of the charges. "The Parlement does
not recognize the king's prison as valid or adequate," observed the
jurist Siméon. On June 1 Sade was again found to be in default.

Annulment

Once again the marquis's in-laws used their most influential connections and tried in countless ways to obtain letters of annulment, a form
of pardon that entirely effaced the crime and its punishment. This was
a royal prerogative, a mark of the king's omnipotence: the monarch,
and the monarch alone, could pardon whomever he wished. Such a
pardon applied to crimes by nature unremissible and had to be approved by the court.[14] On June 3, after weeks of importuning the king
and his ministers, letters of annulment finally reached the Parlement.
In the meantime, the lieutenant general of police was ordered to transfer the prisoner from Pierre-Encize to the Conciergerie, where the
letters were to be confirmed, after which the marquis was to be returned
to the fortress.

On June 10 Donatien Alphonse François de Sade appeared in court, head bared and on his knees in accordance with custom. He submitted to the two customary interrogations: one in the prison, by the clerk; the other on the witness stand in the court chamber. After taking the oath, he admitted to the principal facts of the case, but in a version, as we have seen, significantly different from that of the victim. Following this deposition, jurisdiction in the case was moved from the Tournelle to the Grand'Chambre, the only section of Parlement authorized to consider royal letters of annulment. The court met that very day with Maupeou presiding and approved the king's decision, which immediately halted the prosecution; Sade was sentenced only to "contribute alms of one hundred livres to be used for bread for the prisoners of the Conciergerie."

Once again la Présidente could pride herself on having saved her son-in-law from a bad pass and having preserved her family's honor. She spent the next two days calling on those who had helped to thank them. On the third day she informed the abbé de Sade of the affair's happy outcome:

After the charges in your nephew's case were reduced, Monsieur, as I had the pleasure of informing you previously, it turns out that the case has not and will not come to trial; it was not a serious enough matter to warrant punishment . . . He was immediately returned to Pierre-Encize, where he will remain as long as the king deems appropriate . . . A disreputable deed, which cannot be condoned, could not have turned out more reputably.[15]

Immediately after the hearing, Donatien was thus returned to Pierre-Encize, where he enjoyed a relatively free existence. The warden, M. de Bory, allowed him to walk about the grounds, although steps were taken to make sure that he could neither escape nor enter into communication with persons outside the prison. Toward the end of July the marquis's wife took up residence in Lyons and obtained permission to see him. In theory she was entitled to only two or three visits during his entire incarceration. But as his term grew longer, M. de Bory proved most indulgent, far exceeding his authority and even holding out hope that the prisoner might soon be released. The family, meanwhile, was working toward that end. Even the prisoner's mother, the elderly dowager comtesse de Sade, broke her silence to ask M. de Saint-Florentin to release her son, in which case he would swear to remain on one of his estates and not return to Paris without the king's consent.

On November 16, 1768, after seven months of captivity, the marquis was set free on orders of the king and commanded to retire to La Coste. On the eve of his release the minister of the king's household issued a warning by way of the dowager countess: "His conduct will determine whether or not he will be allowed greater freedom in the future, and he cannot be too careful about his behavior if he is to make up for the past."

"I leave him to you"

At first the marquise was supposed to follow her husband to Provence: "She has done too much not to complete her work by demonstrating as much devotion to him as possible," Mme de Montreuil observed.[16] But she was pregnant for the third time and preferred to give birth at home. Furthermore, Donatien's financial situation required her to remain in Paris. Since the wedding the marquis had drawn heavily on the household's resources and had squandered 66,000 livres of his wife's dowry in addition to his own income. His Opera girls, procuresses, rentals in Versailles, Arcueil, and Paris, to say nothing of his luxurious life style, soon landed him in financial difficulty. Most of his property had already been mortgaged to pay off debts left by his father. Donatien himself still owed 7,400 livres to his regiment, a debt that he paid off slowly and not without numerous reminders from the minister. In 1767 the couple had been obliged to borrow 14,000 livres from one Jean Gastin; this loan was paid back three months later.[17] On May 26, 1768, Mme de Sade gave up the house in Arcueil. In July she sold, without telling her mother, the few diamonds she owned to pay for her trip to Lyons and six months' arrears in the pension her husband had neglected to pay to the dowager countess. Thus Donatien would depart alone for La Coste toward the end of November 1768, while his wife remained behind to fend off the creditors, some of whom had already brought suit. Asked to send a proxy authorizing his wife to borrow 20,000 livres to settle the most urgent debts, the marquis agreed to a loan of only 6,000 livres, leaving Renée-Pélagie to deal with writs and threats of seizure. Donatien could have taken care of the problem by selling his farm at Cabannes, but he stubbornly refused on the grounds that his wife's dowry was sufficient to cover the deficit. Thus it was la Présidente who came to her daughter's rescue, not without cursing her son-in-law's lack of concern and extravagance in pursuit of his own pleasure. Tired of his selfishness, his stubbornness, and his ingratitude (did he not owe his freedom to her efforts?), she refused to write to him and called upon the abbé de Sade to attest to all that she had done for him and to deplore the way he had paid her back. She assured the abbé that his nephew's repeated faults had killed her "interest in him and hope of seeing him return to the good, which alone had guided me in everything I did in his behalf to repair his misfortunes." Nevertheless, she tried once more to save him by urging the abbé to talk him out of returning to Paris, as he had indicated to his wife he intended to do: "Stop him, Monsieur, categorically, energetically, and by every possible means, from committing this folly, of which I think he is all too capable. Where did he obtain permission to return to Paris? Is he unaware of the obedience and respect due to orders of the king?" She ended her long letter with these disillusioned observations:

I leave him to you, Monsieur. Your consideration for your nephew will determine what you must do for him. For my part, I wash my hands of him. I shall let the torrent flow and concern myself solely with my daughter and her unfortunate children. I want the second one to arrive safely despite the many sorrows its mother has had to bear and without the new ones that her husband still holds in store. Our little one is doing very well and is very handsome, grandmother's prejudice aside. He often kisses his father's portrait in his mother's bedroom. I confess that it pierces my soul.[18]

A Media Event

The Arcueil affair really began only after the curtain fell on the final act of the proceedings in the Grand'Chambre of Parlement. Henceforth the action would proceed in a different theater: the public imagination. Fed by fantasies of every kind, the Sade legend grew inexorably. Despite the obvious effort by the gazettes to tone down the luridness of the crime, the marquis de Sade within a few days became the symbol of absolute evil, the epitome of vice, the monster capable of every crime—an object of universal revulsion. The marquis thus witnessed the creation of a sort of mythic double of himself embodying the darkest of traits, and one way or another he would have to live with it. Somehow he had to come to terms with the character that bore his name, in whom he found it increasingly difficult to recognize himself.

On April 12, 1768, only nine days after the event, Mme du Deffand gave a fairly accurate account of the crime, erroneous in only a few details, to her old friend Horace Walpole. Her letter is noteworthy in that it is the first evidence we have of the argument that Sade was testing a new medication. According to the celebrated correspondent, Sade performed his acts of cruelty solely to test the efficacy of his ointment. "Far from denying his crime or blushing over it," Mme du Deffand wrote, he "claimed to have done a useful thing and to have rendered a great service to the public by discovering a balm capable of healing wounds on the spot. It is true that it had that effect on this woman."[19]

The rumors in circulation were almost universally hostile to the accused. The more they circulated, especially after Parlement assumed jurisdiction in the case, the more new atrocities were added—a fact that did not fail to worry the marquis's supporters. "For two weeks people have been talking of nothing but this ridiculous affair, and they never tire of adding aggravating new details," Mme de Saint-Germain complained in her letter to the abbé de Sade.[20] Strangely enough, despite the press's deliberate playing down of the affair, or perhaps because of it, the case enjoyed an undeniable succès de scandale. Deprived of reliable information, the public evolved a mythology of cruelty in connection with the crime, a mythology that drew on social fantasies and ancient terrors. One pamphleteer noted that "the public outcry that has arisen against the comte de Sade's atrocity has exaggerated his fragile mind's misdeeds, and all sorts of fairy tales have been concocted about him."[21] The gazeteer Marin reported that a "prodigious crowd" attended the session of Parlement at which Donatien made public amends.[22] An association was quick to develop in the public mind between the image of Sade as a cruel nobleman and that of another torturer of illustrious lineage, the part historical, part legendary Bluebeard (Gilles de Retz).

Since the French press was prohibited from discussing a crime that reflected discredit on a respectable family and a superior officer in the king's army, foreign gazettes and clandestine broadsheets moved in to fill the vacuum.[23] The family reacted vigorously. Thus the dowager comtesse de Sade, who generally stayed out of her son's affairs, raised a strong protest with M. de Sartine against an article in the *Gazette de Hollande*: "It is not possible for me to allow you to ignore the most ignoble calumnies that have been uttered against my son. For a time I believed that since you surely must have seen them, you would be kind enough to put an end to them, particularly since I had been assured that people had stopped talking about the business. But I have just learned that the whole unfortunate matter has just been recounted in the *Gazette de Hollande* in the darkest of terms. A scurrilous thing like this is enough to dishonor a person throughout the world. The scoundrels responsible for this horrible offense should be locked up for the rest of their lives, and no one can dishonor a person so closely related to me and not be punished."[24]

Generally speaking, the foreign press and broadsheets all reported the same version of the facts (one that was on the whole fairly close to the truth), but they did not all *say* exactly the same thing. François Moureau remarks that "society can minimize an offense in three ways: it can minimize the responsibility of the actor, deny the seriousness of the crime, or discredit the victim."[25] Apart from the *Courrier du Bas-Rhin* the gazettes reported the name and title of the accused not to accentuate the scandal but to diminish it: since the perpetrator had "the honor of belonging to the highest nobility," the papers worried that the "fairy tales" might "frighten . . . respectable members of his family to the point of making them ill."[26]

Insanity was mentioned as a way of taking the sting out of the crime and diminishing the responsibility of the criminal: "His behavior in this crime clearly proves that he is crazy," observed a columnist for the *Recueil d'anecdotes littéraires et politiques*, who alludes elsewhere to the "effects of a deranged mind," to the "excesses of a frail brain," and to a "sick mind more insane than it is wicked."[27] The same argument was repeated in the *Gazette d'Utrecht*: "It is believed that his mind is unhinged. The family has obtained an order for him to be locked up in the château de Saumur, and the slashed woman has dropped the charges in return for a sum of money."

The allegation that drugs were involved, already reported by Mme du Deffand, was now raised as if to corroborate the charge of insanity. If the marquis poured wax on Rose Keller's wounds, people said, clearly it was not to increase her suffering but to test a miraculous ointment. What was the victim complaining about? Shouldn't she rather thank her benefactor? Wasn't it honorable to serve the cause of scientific research, if only in the role of guinea pig? In the *Courrier du Bas-Rhin* for April 27 we read: "The true reason for the cruel behavior of the marquis de S*** has just been learned. He had obtained from his father a medicine capable of healing wounds within twenty-four hours. Determined to try it out, he used it on a female stranger who had approached him in the street begging for alms. At first he told her that she ought to be ashamed of herself, and when she excused herself by saying that she was out of work, he offered her a job at his country house. He then drove her there and, after forcing her to undress, tied her up and proceeded at his leisure to make deep incisions in her flesh with a sharp knife. Later he applied his balm, which did indeed heal her in twenty-four hours. This comes from a most reliable source." A few days later the *Gazette d'Utrecht* returned to the subject of the Sadeian pharmacopoeia to praise the wondrous efficacy of the remedy, albeit with a modest expression of doubt concerning the method of testing: "The woman, who has withdrawn her charges, has so fully recovered from her wounds that no visible marks remain, which proves the value of the comte de Sade's balm though it does not diminish the atrocity of the means used to test it."[28]

Although the journalists characterize the victim as simple and naïve, they leave some doubt about her character: behind the touching heroine we catch fleeting glimpses of the venal prostitute. All the reports agree that her silence was bought. The *Courrier du Bas-Rhin* went further, suggesting that the marquis had been avenging himself for a certain "present" (venereal disease) that his victim had given him.[29]

But who read the gazettes? To gauge the effects of the scandal on the common people of Paris, we would do better to consult the chronicle of events great and small kept by the good bookseller Siméon-Prosper Hardy. Hardy's journal entry for Friday, April 8, includes a detailed account of what took place in Arcueil five days earlier. A respectable burgher, Hardy had little sympathy for debauched aristocrats, as is evident from the way in which he describes Sade, lists his titles, underscores his connection to the Condés, and repeatedly refers to him as *le comte de Sade*. His bias is particularly evident in the conclusion of his account: "Through powerful connections, royal orders were obtained and it was arranged that the comte de Sade be taken to the château de Pierre-Encize and locked up there. Some people insist, however, that he has been sent abroad. In any case, if the courts do not deal with his behavior, which is so peculiar as to be vile and disgusting, by meting out exemplary punishment, the case will offer posterity one more example that in our century even the most abominable crimes meet with impunity so long as those who commit them are fortunate enough to be noble, wealthy, or well connected."[30]

Arcueil: Theme and Variations

Since fiction often drew on the police blotter for inspiration, it would be surprising if the Arcueil affair had left no trace in contemporary literature. But it was not until the end of the century, with its vogue for crime novels, that the marquis's tortures caught the fancy of *âmes sensibles* (the "sensitive souls" whose tears irrigated the pages of late-eighteenth-century fiction). The story contained any number of elements apt to enchant readers avid for works of fantasy and melodrama. But additional details were added, as though the facts of the case were not horrible enough.

Nicolas Restif de La Bretonne, whose hatred of the author of *Justine* was tenacious and who never passed up an opportunity to attack him, invented out of whole cloth a pseudo-scientific caper in which the marquis allegedly intended to sacrifice Rose Keller's wretched and pointless existence to the science of anatomy. After enticing the beggar woman into an anatomical amphitheater where a large crowd waited, he is said to have proposed dissecting her alive for the sake of science. "What is this wretched female doing on earth? She is good for nothing. We shall use her, as we must, to penetrate the mysteries of human structure." The poor woman, more dead than alive, is then tied down on a table of white marble, while the marquis explains to the audience what results he expects to obtain from the operation. The servants are sent from the room, but just as the would-be surgeon is about to open his victim's stomach, she manages to break free of her bonds and escapes through a window. Later she tells of having seen three human cadavers in the room: one reduced to a skeleton, another emptied of its innards and disposed of in a large barrel, and a third, a man's body, still untouched.[31]

•

Within a few years the Arcueil affair had become a symbol of aristocratic decadence, an epitome of the rotting cadavers of the Ancien Régime. The former marquis had joined the revolutionaries and become a sans-culotte of the Piques section, but Jacques-Antoine Dulaure, a member of the Convention, exposed his true identity in a slanderous text that held Sade responsible for all the corruptions of the deposed nobility and demanded that he be made to pay for the impunity of his peers:

Among the men of this century who have carried on the crimes of the nobility and the horrors of feudalism, we must include the comte de Charolais, who committed murder without batting an eyelash, the comte d'Hornes, who killed in order to steal, and the former duc de Fronsac, today Richelieu, an arsonist, rapist, and scoundrel, cruel even in pursuit of pleasure . . . To all these scoundrels with their châteaux, carriages, red pumps, and red and blue ribbons, we must add the name of the marquis de Sade, whose abominable crimes may outstrip even the most heinous offenses of the other nobles of his time.[32]

The Arcueil affair, with its quintessentially Sadeian plot, inevitably found its place in the marquis's literary work, with the hero himself as narrator. Fiction also offered the best opportunity to justify himself, if only in a brief allusion in the *Président mystifié*, a harsh satire attacking a magistrate in the parlement of Aix: "Above all, remind the judges of Paris, before whom you will be obliged to appear, of the famous adventure of 1769, when their hearts, far more filled with compassion for a hooker's flagellated behind than for the people whose fathers they claimed to be but whom they nevertheless allowed to die of hunger, impelled them to bring criminal charges against a young soldier who, after sacrificing the best years of his life to the service of his prince, upon his return received no laurels other than the humiliation prepared for him by the greatest enemies of the fatherland he had just defended."[33]

In a broader sense, the beggar woman of the place des Victoires was destined to become an obsessive, if diffuse, presence, in all of Sade's writing.

9

Happy Days

Coming from Avignon, Donatien usually took the Apt road and turned right immediately after passing the hamlet of Notre-Dame de Lumières. This was the shortest route. Sometimes he might continue on as far as the old Julien Bridge and cross the Calavon, a route that gradually revealed the rocky spur on which the castle and its tower stood, while on the left gray houses with roofs of ochre tile lay strewn like debris over the slopes of the Luberon Mountains, which formed a natural amphitheater.

To reach the château the marquis would have turned onto a mule trail (called *lou caladou* in local dialect) shaded by oaks that wound a sinuous path among olive trees and vines. This trail led up to the village with its steep, narrow streets, through the Gothic arch of the Clastres gate, and on to the castle ramparts. A few more steps over pebbled ground would have brought him to the austere eastern wall, protected by a moat. After crossing the wide bridge, which rested on two piles and replaced the old drawbridge, he would have passed through a *porte flamande* into a forecourt that once served as a refuge for the lord's vassals in case of an attack on the village. Then, beyond a wrought-iron grill crowned by the Sade coat of arms, he would at last have found himself on the paved court, which was raised slightly above the forecourt and around which several buildings were arrayed. From here the eye could take in the Bonnieux Valley and the Claparèdes plateau, while the Luberon Mountains resembled an enormous eagle sleeping with its wings spread about its body and its head hidden—unless perhaps the village of Oppède, which seemed to have no teeth, formed its stony beak. Sleeping with one eye open, the giant bird looked as though it might at any moment take wing.

"The eagle, Mademoiselle, is sometimes obliged to abandon the seventh region of the air to swoop down on the summit of Mount Olympus, on the ancient pines of the Caucasus, on the frigid larch of the Jura, on the white hindquarters of Taurus, and even, sometimes, near the quarries of Montmartre."[1] In writing these lines the marquis was thinking of the Luberon, as well as of the Chinese pine, cedar, and stone quarries that surrounded his estate.

The château de La Coste had been in the Sade family since 1627, when Jean-Baptiste de Sade, lord of Saumane, married Diane de Simiane, daughter of François, lord of La Coste, La Verrière, and other places. But a parchment in the Apt cartulary mentions the presence of a *castrum* (fortified village) at this strategic location as early as 1038. In Donatien's eyes, this was his fief, in the full sense of the word: a seigneurial estate peopled by villagers over whom he reigned as master, with the right to administer high, low, and medium justice, to collect tolls, and to exact tribute for the privileges of milling grain, fishing, and hunting. It was also a place of pleasure, refuge, and exile. On this November day in 1768 it was above all a place of exile as Donatien stepped through the main gate with the *mistral* wind lashing his face.

•

After such a close call, it was only prudent that Donatien stay out of trouble long enough for the Arcueil scandal to be forgotten. Aside from a few forays into the "houses" of Marseilles, the marquis spent part of the winter languishing within the walls of his castle. But one day, unable to stand it any longer, he began holding parties and balls to which he invited the local nobility, just as before. Many stayed away, for despite the marquis's efforts to avoid it, rumors of the recent scandal had begun to spread in the region, often amplified by gossip. Shunned by good society, Donatien turned to the bourgeois of nearby villages: the Paulets, Appys, Sambucs, and Payans. Many were his own vassals, who wore their Sunday best when they went to see *Moussu lou marquis* in his castle. And when it came to his nephew's parties, the abbé de Sade did not have to be asked twice.

Upon learning of these extravagances, Mme de Montreuil dispatched a furious warning to the abbé in which she did not hesitate to reprimand him for his culpable weakness. She was astonished: rather than redeem his sins by behaving in an exemplary fashion, the madman was throwing parties again: "Balls, comedies, and all that goes with them, and with what actresses!" And all before the eyes of the abbé! Was he unaware of the damage he was doing? "I confess that I would not have been as indulgent as you are. I would have set the hall on fire had I no other way to stop him. The best that can be said for him is that his head is as empty as before, so why expect him to behave consistently."[2]

Dear Fistula!

Donatien had been suffering for some time from hemorrhoids (a "fistula" was also mentioned) that prevented him from riding a horse, a troublesome disability for an officer who dreamed of returning to service. As we have seen, the warden of Pierre-Encize had authorized his prisoner to leave his cell and travel to Lyons for treatment of this "fistula." Acting no doubt at the urging of Mme de Montreuil, who wanted Donatien in Paris for the birth of his child, the dowager comtesse de Sade, using the same pretext, asked the minister of the king's household to allow her son to reside for a period of time just outside the capital on the grounds that the state of his health required emergency care. The reply came on April 2, 1769: "His Majesty, persuaded that you have set before him the exact truth, is willing to allow M. de Sade to return to a country house outside Paris for the purpose of obtaining care necessary for his health and so as to be near emergency assistance, but only on condition that he see very few people and that he return to his estates as soon as his health permits, His Majesty having no intention of revoking his orders in this regard. You may inform M. de Sade of this tacit permission so that he may take advantage of it as soon as possible, given that his current state requires prompt treatment."[3] In fact, the marquis's affliction may have been trying, but it was by no means grave or urgent and hardly required a transfer to the Paris region. He could have found help in Lyons, where doctors had already treated him for the same problem, or in Montpellier. But the family and the minister had agreed on a cover story that would allow the exile to return without arousing public indignation. That, at any rate, is the clear suggestion of la Présidente in her letter to the abbé de Sade: "He is coming to see his wife and family and to obtain treatment for a dangerous infirmity that has recently taken an urgent turn and that requires skilled surgeons and prompt treatment. That is all that is to be told to the public in Provence as well as here when word of his return gets out."[4]

Donatien, however, thumbed his nose at all the precautions and was not even interested in keeping up appearances. No sooner was he informed of the king's decision than he set out not for a country house but for Paris. Having left La Coste on April 23, he arrived in the capital a week later and found his wife in the seventh month of a difficult pregnancy, consumed by worry and exhausted by constant attention to financial concerns. Donatien had in the end sent a proxy authorizing her to borrow 10,000 livres (half the sum needed), but in the meantime the prospective lenders had tired of waiting and invested their money elsewhere. The président de Montreuil had been obliged to come to his daughter's rescue.

Two months later, on June 27, 1769, Renée-Pélagie gave birth to a boy, Donatien-Claude-Armand, who was baptized the following day at Sainte-Marie-Madeleine in Ville-l'Evêque. It was no longer the Condés who served as godparents but the infant's own grandparents, the président de Montreuil and the dowager countess, Marie-Eléonore de Maillé—an incontrovertible sign of the father's disgrace.

In the last letter (dated April 8) that Donatien wrote his wife prior to the birth, he had seemed happy about it and had spoken of "the hopes it gives him and of the docility with which he awaits its effects on him." At the time la Présidente had commented that "the way he conducts himself will determine whether we must fear or hope for what is to come." Since then she had had nothing but praise for her son-in-law, but she dared not allow herself to rejoice too soon. The arrival of a second son appeared to have brought Donatien back to his senses. He was attentive to the marquise and enjoyed taking care of little Louis-Marie, now almost two and "handsome from head to toe." Was this an expression of interest? Feeling? Gratitude? Only time would tell, la Présidente concluded, for she was skeptical about Donatien's conversion and uncertain how he would use his freedom: "I hope that he will not abuse it," she confided to the abbé. "In any case, I have put him on notice that this was the last time that I could or would make an effort on his behalf. I have no doubt, Monsieur, that you are recommending that he display all the reserve and circumspection so necessary in all things for a man in his position. It takes time for the past to be forgotten. I have a hard time making him understand this."[5]

Journey to Holland

Three months later the marquis announced his intention to leave for Holland. Where had this sudden urge to travel come from? Did he feel the need for a change of scene? Did he want people to forget about him? Did he wish to escape his family's scrutiny? Perhaps, or he just may have succumbed to curiosity about a country with which he was not familiar and which was reputed to be one of the richest in Europe in art as well as commerce. In any case, we are able to follow his progress step by step thanks to an account of his month-long travels in the form of seven letters to an imaginary woman.

Having left Paris on the night of September 19, he stopped to sleep at the last way station on the road to Cambrai. The next day he reached Valencienne and from there proceeded to Quiévrain, on the border. He arrived in Brussels on the morning of September 22: "This city is not very pleasant," he noted. "All the streets go up or down. There are few if any beautiful houses and very few public buildings." A week later he was in Antwerp, where he stayed only one night, just long enough to observe that the inhabitants, "full of superstition and bigotry, have miraculously preserved the customs of their former masters, the Spaniards." On October 2 he wrote a third fictitious letter from Rotterdam. The canals, the quays along which trees had been planted, the drawbridges, the handsome walkways, the "groomed and decorated gardens"—all pleased him. But what astonished him most was the extreme cleanliness of the city: "the windows, stairs, and walls gleam like mirrors." And Flemish interiors lived up to their reputations: "It is impossible to imagine the effort the Dutch put into the upkeep of their houses. Before every door there are mats for wiping your feet, and if you were so unfortunate as to enter without observing this ceremony, they would greet you with rage. The stairs and corridors are covered with matting. Even utensils by their nature apt to become dirty such as kitchen andirons and pot hangers are scrubbed and cleaned until you can see yourself in them." So much for the tourist's impressions. As for those of the philosopher, he admired the spirit of tolerance that prevailed here as in the rest of the United Provinces: "All religions are permitted in Rotterdam. Each one has its private temple and practices in complete freedom."

From Rotterdam he traveled to Delft by canal: "There is no more pleasant way of covering distance. Along the entire route you enjoy the charming sight of the most beautiful meadows and landscapes. Truly voluptuous country houses line the canals to the right and left and make for such diverse views that you hardly notice the distance you are traveling." By the same means he traveled on to The Hague and found that city "considerably embellished" by the present Prince of Orange. Although the houses were less than magnificent, the streets were "beautiful, clean, and well placed." As an expert in military matters, he offered his judgment on the maneuvers of the prince's regiment: "I found his troops well maintained and well disciplined, but in general I was not terribly pleased with their maneuvers, which I found cumbersome and slow."

On October 7 Donatien left The Hague for Leyden, which was celebrated for its university but "neither very populous nor very commercial." After a brief stop in Haarlem, he arrived in Amsterdam on the night of October 9. "Those who call this city the rendezvous of nations are correct," he noted. "No other port in Europe is host to such a prodigious number of vessels." Amazed by the city hall, the admiralty, and the "Lovers' Bridge," he expressed disappointment with the theater, a field of endeavor in which he took an intense interest: "There are no French shows. A rather poor Dutch troupe keeps this capital entertained. The theater is fairly large but of the utmost simplicity, though it is as tall as our ordinary theaters. It has only two rows of loges. The parterre is filled with benches, and men and women mingle indiscriminately. I had been told to expect magnificent decorations, but those I found were quite simple. The genius of this nation, in the main confined to commerce, has not supplied a large number of poets. Their theater is limited to two tragedies, and during my stay in Amsterdam I was fortunate enough to see one of them. It is a wretched compilation of extraordinary incidents without motivation or shape. An English-style mélange of the most touching scenes and the most burlesque lines."

On October 18 he wrote from Utrecht, a city "so little populated that grass grows in the streets . . . This city is inhabited by very wealthy people who have retired from trade and who live in idleness." He briefly visited the famous mall that Louis XIV supposedly wanted duplicated at Versailles. The next day he set out for home by way of Antwerp and Brussels, which he reached on October 21. A few days later he was back in Paris.

The marquis probably intended to publish his epistolary account of this journey, but the letters remained unknown until Gilbert Lely discovered the manuscript. They are most notable, perhaps, for their judgments of the Dutch: "I shall simply say that in general they seemed to be good people, keen about business, totally absorbed by the idea of always acquiring new wealth, [and] solely occupied with the means of success. They are quick to do favors when it costs them nothing of their own. They are also phlegmatic, cold, and basically limited when it comes to anything that does not earn a profit. Since the genius of the men forms that of the women, the latter is simple enough that they are not particularly likable. They might be more beautiful, but that is not their fault. One sees few slender waists. They are rather fair, but without physiognomy. Immoderate use of very hot tea and coffee completely ruins their teeth, to the point where it is all but impossible to find four women in Holland with a good set." Beyond this, Donatien makes no mention of having met anyone but does provide an exact accounting of what his trip cost, listing the price of transportation, hotels, inns, and so on. This careful bookkeeping suggests a tourist on a modest budget.

High Society

Throughout the winter of 1769 and the spring of 1770 the Sades seem to have been caught up in a whirl of high-society events. Almost no day passed without a reception. The marquis's datebooks, recently discovered in family archives, list the names of those on whom the couple paid calls and those who visited them. One of these lists is preceded by a curious note in the marquis's hand: "Further visits with Madame, where we were well received"—a suggestion that this was not always the case. Some of his former acquaintances may even have turned their backs on him at this time. Apart from the princes of Conti and Condé, the comtesse de la Tour-du-Pin (a distant relative of Donatien's), the duc de Cossé (the colonel of his regiment), and a few others, there are not many prestigious names among the couple's hosts and guests. There are more of Sade's in-laws (Azys, Evrys, Chamoussets, Toulongeons, Meslays, Plissays, Launays, and Partyets) than there are leading lights of Parisian high society. On Donatien's side the name that appears most often is that of the abbé de Sade. But we also find the "dearly beloved" Mme de Saint-Germain, and M. de Poyanne, formerly Donatien's commanding officer in the carabineers, who did so much for the young man's advancement and who apparently retained his friendship. Among the "men visited" one name attracts attention, however: M. de Saint-Florentin, the minister of the king's household, the very official who signed the royal orders sending Donatien first to Saumur, then to Pierre-Encize, and finally to La Coste before authorizing his return "to the vicinity of Paris." No doubt this was a courtesy call, but it was also an opportunity for Donatien to express his gratitude for all that the minister had done in his behalf.

For the first time in a long while Mme de Montreuil was satisfied with her son-in-law: there had been no scandal since his return to Paris, not even any adventure, to the point where Inspector Marais, who was watching from the corner of his eye, had nothing adverse to say about him. Was he short of resources? Or did he elude the watchful eye of his guardian angel? In any case, la Présidente believed that the time had come to lay the groundwork for his rehabilitation by asking the comte de Saint-Florentin if he could be received at court (where he had not yet set foot). Since Donatien was preparing to rejoin the army and to apply for promotion to the rank of *mestre de camp*, it might do him some good to be seen at Versailles. The merest word or gesture from the sovereign would erase his disgrace once and for all and restore his hopes of a brilliant career. But the minister found this proposal premature:

I wanted, Madame, to sound out the king's thinking about M. de Sade before proposing to His Majesty to allow him to return to court. It appeared to me that the adverse impressions that His Majesty was able to form at various times are still too fresh to be forgotten, and I therefore felt it best not to pursue the matter, for I believed it would probably do no good and that if he were refused, as there is every reason to believe he would be, it would do him a great deal of harm in his regiment. I think that in this matter the only solution is to await the benefits of time.[6]

A Difficult Return

In the last week of July 1770, Captain Donatien de Sade left to rejoin his Burgundy Regiment in garrison at Fontenay-le-Comte. He joined his unit on August 1. Worried, not without reason, about how he would be received, Mme de Montreuil took preemptive action: on August 3 she wrote to the marquise de Paulmy d'Argenson to recommend her son-in-law to the marquise's husband, the minister of state. This important text, for which I am indebted to the present marquis d'Argenson, is worth quoting in its entirety:

I can scarcely hope, Madame, to exist in your memory. It is too long since I have been close enough to you to remind you of my presence and pay you my respects. But it is under the auspices of the kindness that M. le comte d'Argenson[7] showed to M. de Montreuil's family and to mine, and to M. and Mme d'Evry, my sister, that I dare to beg you, Madame, to be so kind as to ask Monsieur le marquis de Voyer to bestow the same kindness on the marquis de Sade, my son-in-law, captain in the Burgundy Cavalry Regiment, presently at Fontenay-le-Comte and under the inspection of the marquis de Voyer.

My son-in-law is in a most delicate position. An unfortunate adventure, into which he was drawn by a hot head and bad company more than two years ago, has attracted all too much attention. Slanderously described in the most distorted way, this act of youthful negligence became a matter of the utmost seriousness. The way in which the case ended in parlement justified his position.

I do not seek, Madame, to excuse actions foreign to the laws of honor, from which he never departed; rather, I wish his actions to be forgotten. Since the king (along with the minister) has been kind enough to maintain his company and to favor his continuing to pay court as in the past, he has been to court several times and attended the marriage of M. le dauphin.[8] Having tried the indulgence of his friends and of the public, he believed he could hope for that of his comrades and would have joined his regiment on June 1 but for deference to the wishes of his colonel, M. le duc de Cossé. His agreement, between us, Madame, has not been easy to obtain, involving as it did particular circumstances and concerns that are difficult to convey in a letter. He has now departed and will reach his unit on the first of the month. The duke is not yet there. In the end, he promised my daughter and me to receive M. de Sade in his home as he does all the other officers, without any distinction that might be disagreeable to him and, in this regard, to set the best possible example: military units usually follow their commanders' opinions. The support of M. le marquis de Voyer would be invaluable on any occasion. For this one I am asking more particularly for his indulgence and for his kindness. Mme de Sade begs you through me, Madame, to obtain them for her husband. By the way in which she has conducted herself she has amply proved her tender devotion to him and has done her duty as all respectable women must. By describing her to you truthfully in this regard, I hope to make her appear worthier in your eyes.

M. le duc de Cossé has told me to expect M. le marquis de Voyer in Fontenay from the twelfth to the fifteenth for his review. If by chance he has already begun his rounds, it would be most unfortunate for M. de Sade if he were to arrive informed only by the unfortunate impressions prevalent for the past year in the mind of the commander and certain personal enemies. In this case I presume to ask for and to count on your kindness. Think, if you will, how important this moment of joining his unit is for his future, on which the future of my daughter and my grandchildren depends—they are dear to my heart. You are a mother, Madame, and it is on that score that I hope you will grant me the pardon of impunity.[9]

Did this letter arrive too late? Did the marquis de Paulmy decline to heed its plea? In any case, things went very badly indeed, as was to be feared. From the moment he arrived in camp Sade met with the hostility of Major de Malherbe, who was commanding the regiment in the absence of its lieutenant-colonel, the comte de Saignes, away on temporary duty in Compiègne. Malherbe refused, on what flimsy pretext we do not know, to allow the captain to carry out his duties. When Donatien protested with his usual vehemence, Malherbe had him placed under arrest. He also forbade his company quartermaster and first sergeant to obey the orders of their superior officer. Donatien immediately informed the comte de Saignes of this harassment. The lieutenant-colonel asked M. de Malherbe to explain his attitude, and the matter ended there.

What happened next? Had Donatien won his case? Did he fight a duel with M. de Malherbe, as he later intimated?[10] Did he leave the military immediately after the incident? All we know is that he remained a while longer in Fontenay. There he made the acquaintance of one Pierre-Benjamin Jallays, a notary by profession and fifteen years older than Donatien. Jallays lived on the rue du Paradis on the outskirts of the town, and for a long time afterward he would remain in correspondence with the marquis.[11]

Although Mme de Montreuil's intervention proved to be of no avail, it is important to recognize its significance. In this matter as in all the others in which she appears to have taken her son-in-law's part, her only purpose was to defend the group to which she belonged. Under the Ancien Régime the interests of one's clan, family, or "house" far outweighed the individual interests of any particular member.

A Sojourn at Fort-L'Evêque

Eight months after this misadventure, Donatien, with the Prince of Condé's support, applied to the Ministry of War for a commission as *mestre de cavalerie* (without salary). In his application he reminded the minister of his previous posts and of the ensignship he had obtained in 1762 but which his "modest fortune had prevented him from purchasing." On March 19, 1771, the minister informed him of His Majesty's favorable response, prompted by "advantageous testimony" concerning his military service. This was the best possible rehabilitation: here he was officially cleansed of his past errors and baptized a virgin subject.[12]

•

On April 17 a happy event brought joy to those close to the marquis: his wife gave birth to a daughter, Madeleine-Laure. The father of three children, restored to his master's favor, Donatien now had only to repair his financial condition. There was every reason to make a new start on life. He was only thirty-one, and the game was not yet over. Mme de Montreuil, detained in her château de Vallery on "essential business," announced the birth to the abbé with this commentary: "We have a little goddaughter by proxy. Do not love her any the less for it, Monsieur. Give her your intelligence and I shall give her my patience, which I feel is the virtue that women need most." Although the two boys kept her busy, she admitted her preference for the elder, Louis-Marie: "Your elder nephew is the prettiest little boy imaginable. The younger one interests me less: he is handsome, but it is too early to judge his intelligence or character—he is barely talking. And then the older one was in my arms, in my safekeeping, during the unhappiest of times . . . [so that] he has inspired a more tender interest."[13]

While Renée-Pélagie recovered slowly after her delivery, Donatien struggled with serious financial difficulties. His parents-in-law refused to advance him additional cash and confined their assistance to protecting their daughter's mortgaged properties. Did he make a quick trip to Provence at this time in search of cash, as Gilbert Lely maintains? It is possible, but in the absence of evidence it is just as plausible to assume that his search for cash was conducted from Paris. Fage, his business agent, was hard put to find the sums needed immediately: "You will concede," the marquis wrote him, "that you will be demonstrating very little zeal to help me out if you cannot manage to put off the three creditors I have indicated to you and to find me the sum of 13,400 livres."[14] As for the future, he was not overly worried: within a year he would receive his stipend from the Estates of Burgundy, along with reimbursement for his company and a "considerable sum" from his wife's dowry. He was also seriously considering selling his farm in Cabannes, near Arles. In Paris, however, his creditors were impatient and threatening to take action. He therefore decided to sell his post as *mestre de camp* to the comte d'Osmont for 10,000 livres. But this was not enough, and the inevitable came to pass: M. de Sade was imprisoned for debt at Fort-l'Evêque. There was nothing dishonorable about this: Fort-l'Evêque was a prison for citizens in temporary financial embarrassment.

We do not know exactly how long this detention lasted, but it was certainly not more than two months, July and August 1771. Donatien left the prison on September 9 after paying an advance of 3,000 livres on what he owed. He was obliged to sign a note pledging on his honor to pay the rest by October 15. A trip to Provence was now essential if he was to find the means to keep himself afloat. Shortly after leaving prison he set out for La Coste, accompanied for the first time by his wife, his sons Louis-Marie and Claude-Armand, and even little Madeleine-Laure, aged five months, with their governess, Mlle Langevin.

The Pretty Canoness

Around a month later the marquis's pretty young sister-in-law Anne-Prospère de Launay, whose health obliged her to spend time in the country, joined the family at La Coste. She came straight from the Benedictine Priory in Alix, near Lyons, where she was secular canoness.[15] Like other communities of canonesses, the one at Alix was primarily a refuge for daughters of the nobility: one had to prove at least four quarters of noble blood to be admitted. The canonesses lived on annuities established by their parents. They did not take vows and therefore remained free to marry and return to the world.

Anne-Prospère was born on December 27, 1751, so she was not quite twenty years old at the time of this visit.[16] Renée-Pélagie had invited her to La Coste on the assumption that she would regain her health more quickly there than in her convent. While convalescing she made herself useful by helping her sister with household chores, making an inventory of her brother-in-law's lace and linen, serving as Donatien's secretary, and acting in plays that he produced in his theater. A previously unpublished letter in her hand to Fage, the notary, was dictated by Donatien, whose secretary added a personal note at the end:

Having been up to now the interpreter of M. de Sade, whom I have just sent packing because I am tired of writing, I shall now speak for myself and beg our dear *avocat* not to forget, as he has done thus far, the four pads of paper I've asked him for. I do not know if the abbé has kept it [sic], but I haven't received any and I'm running short. Send them to me and I shall be most obliged. My brother[-in-law] has told me all about your concern for my health, and I thank you for it. Please come and see us . . . Please, I beg you, remember about the bathtub. I've been ordered to take baths for my health. In order to act on stage, one needs to be in good health—and I badly need my baths to restore mine.[17]

From the moment she arrived Anne-Prospère won everyone's affection, particularly that of the abbé de Sade, who gave her a Corsican pony to ride. She thanked him with a charming note.

The old libertine could scarcely conceal his agitation at the sight of this young beauty, who played the lute for him. He was so captivated by her charms that he openly declared his love for her, easily forgetting the forty-six years that separated them. Offended, the young lady begged him to restrain his ardor. The abbé's reply, written in a jocular, bantering tone, is a clumsy effort to hide his amorous feelings beneath protestations of flirtatious friendship: "No, my dear niece, your uncle will never deny you anything that is in his power. And how could he refuse a favor on which 'your reputation, your honor, and perhaps your life depend?'[18] Those are terrible words, my niece, and for me powerful motives. For in truth nothing in the world is more precious to me than 'your honor and your life.' "[19]

Happiness in Incest

Donatien was no less susceptible to the charms of the pretty canoness. He was in fact strangely stirred by living under the same roof with her. For the first time a living example of the inaccessible virgin was close at hand in the form of this attractive young woman. The woman he secretly desired, the woman he believed to exist only in his dreams, had appeared in the shape of his sister-in-law. How could he resist?

Did he intend the Julie in *Portrait de Mlle de L**** to be a portrait of Mlle de Launay, as Lely suggests? There is good reason to think so. Although the initial might equally well apply to Mlle de Lauris or some nameless mistress, various signs point to the canoness. Rarely did the marquis portray a beloved woman as truthfully, and rarely did he represent his love in a manner that rings so true:

Julie is at that happy age when one begins to feel that the heart is made for love. Her charming eyes reveal this by the most tender expression of sensuality. A curious pallor is the reflection of the desire that is in her, and if love at times gives life to her complexion, only its subtlest flame is evident . . . Julie is tall. Her waist is slender and elegant, her bearing noble, her movements easy and full of grace, as is everything she does. But what grace! How rare it is! It is a grace in which art plays no part. Art? Good God! What could it do where nature has spared no effort? . . . Julie combines the delightfully natural spirit of her age with all the gentleness and sophistication of the most amiable and polished woman. She does more: not content to have an agreeable mind, she has sought to embellish what she was given. From very early on she learned to allow her reason to speak, and, using philosophy to shake off the prejudices

of childhood and upbringing, she learned to understand and to judge at an
age when others scarcely know how to think.

The following passage contains a thinly veiled allusion to Mlle de
Launay's "religious" status, as well as to prejudices that she picked
up in her convent but rid herself of upon discovering love. Since this
description precisely fits Anne-Prospère at the time of her arrival at
La Coste, our doubts as to the identity of the woman in the story
evaporate. This makes the account of her growing passion all the more
interesting:

What discoveries Julie made, and with what keen perception! She saw the
offense to reason and the obfuscation of intelligence in the attempt to paint
as crimes the most pleasant of the soul's emotions and the sweetest of nature's
penchants. What happened? Julie, having noted how they wished to deceive
her heart, allowed it to speak, and soon it avenged the insult. How many
charms her pretty intellect, guided by her heart, now discovered! As the blind-
fold fell away, everything seemed new to Julie, and all the faculties of her soul
acquired a new degree of strength. Everything in her benefited, even her face.
Julie became prettier. What chill spread over her former pleasures, and what
heat over her new ones! The things that moved her were no longer the same.
The cherished bird that she had formerly loved with all her heart, she now
loved only as a bird. Something seemed lacking in her tender feeling for her
friend; it no longer filled her heart as it had seemed to do before. In a word,
it became clear that something was missing. Have you found it, Julie? Can I
flatter myself that you have? . . . Forgive me. I have presumed to write the
history of your soul, when I wanted only to describe it. O, I fear that you may
detect a bit of pride where I should have put nothing but the truth! Forgive
me, adorable Julie! I have dared to speak of my love, when I should have
spoken only of you. But, alas! Allow me to believe that in your eyes as in mine,
those two things will in the future be forever confounded in our hearts.[20]

Did Donatien and his sister-in-law begin a sexual relationship
soon after their encounter? Although there is no certain evidence that
they did, it is not difficult to imagine the marquis's excitement at the
sight of this twenty-year-old virgin, his wife's sister and therefore untouchable, dressed in the habit of her order and wearing around her
neck the gilded cross in eight points (an exact replica of the star of the
Sades) that Louis XV had bestowed upon the canonesses of Alix. At
any rate there can be no doubt that the two felt a violent attraction for
each other. The evidence for this, apart from the *Portrait de Mlle de*

L*** cited above, is a petition to the Châtelet that was drawn up by Gaufridy in 1774 on the basis of information provided by Mme de Sade herself, in which the beginning of the incestuous liaison is described in these terms:

> She [Mme de Sade] was with the marquis de Sade, her husband, on the estate of La Coste in Provence. There she was joined by Mlle de Launay, her sister, on the pretext of keeping her company and breathing a more serene air. Divided between devotion to her husband and affection for her children, she lived there for a considerable time in peaceful conditions that might have gone on untroubled, and her husband's attentiveness prevented her from suspecting that a fatal passion was soon to become the source of a series of woes and misfortunes.[21]

This episode in Sade's life has often been romanticized, and, somewhat carried away, Lely himself gave a sentimental dramatization. Admittedly, the subject lends itself to such treatment, and there is nothing to prevent us from imagining that Donatien and Mlle de Launay fell in love. There are still today good reasons to believe that the affair did take place, and we shall consider them in due course. What is certain, however, is that to an extraordinary degree Anne-Prospère conformed to the marquis de Sade's most undeniable sexual fantasies. A virgin imbued with religious principles, almost a nun, as well as the marquis's wife's sister, she was the very embodiment of purity awaiting its downfall. She was the ideal vehicle for violating taboos, an angel awaiting a fall—the incarnation, in other words, of one of the themes that most obsessed Sade's imagination. Incest, profanation, degradation, blasphemy, sacrilege: everything conspired to stimulate Donatien's erotic reveries to the utmost degree. Mlle de Launay prefigures the pristine purity of Justine upon leaving the convent of Penthémont and before being plunged into the most vile filth. She answered, most delectably, Sade's desperate cry to inaccessible virginity, a cry that Klossowski, who saw it as one of the keys to Sade's work, described as "enveloped and, as it were, encased in a hymn of blasphemy."

Sade always preferred the frenzy of ecstasy to the mere pleasure of existing. His liaison with Anne-Prospère was one of the few times when he had both, when physical pleasure coincided with spiritual delight. The days he spent at La Coste in the company of his wife, his children, and his sister-in-law were certainly among the happiest days of his life.

The Festival of La Coste

Those days were especially happy because Donatien could finally, without impediment, indulge his passion for the theater. He spent most of his time doing just that and involved family and friends in his activities. Although the theater at La Coste could accommodate only about sixty spectators seated and an equal number standing, it had recently been fitted out with the most up-to-date of theatrical equipment. As usual, the fixed scenery represented a salon, which could be covered up by painted canvas backdrops hung from rods. Two of these backdrops portrayed a town square and a prison (ironic souvenir or sinister foreboding?). For lighting there were sixty-five tin holders "for setting candles" and twenty-four fairylights. The windows could be covered over with panels "to make it dark as night." The blue stage curtain was operated from the lobby.[22]

Soon finding the theater at La Coste too cramped for his purposes, the marquis decided to make use of another theater in his family château at Mazan, which he had refurbished during the winter and spring of 1772. Now he would be able to present two different plays alternately in the two theaters. His ambition was to organize a regular troupe under his direction and to move beyond society theater into the world of professionals. Thus far he had entrusted the leading roles to amateurs such as his wife or Mlle de Launay as well as himself, with minor parts given to actors from Aix or Marseilles, generally of the second rank and hired for the occasion. Thus he staged a melodrama "in the English taste" of his own composition, *Le Mariage du siècle*, of which only an outline and a few speeches have survived; but the cast of characters, written in the marquis's own hand, still exists: the heroine, Pauline, was played by the canoness, while Mme de Sade played her confidante and Donatien himself took the part of the comte de Castelli, Pauline's husband.[23] Certain inhabitants of La Coste dreamed of acting in one of the marquis's productions. Young Paulet, for example, the son of a well-to-do family of the village, "would be eager to make his debut in tragedy" but declared himself ready to take on any role. The young man, who worked in commerce in the vicinity of Montpellier, acted as an agent in recruiting actors.

On February 25, 1772, Donatien hired the actor Bourdais and his wife. Throughout the season, which ran from Easter through the first of November, they would play whatever roles Donatien assigned them in exchange for a salary of 800 livres, room, board, and payment of all expenses.[24] Besides being cast regularly as a noble father, Bourdais was made manager of the theater.

The company's repertoire was conventional enough. Its patron took few risks and chose to stage the works of successful playwrights rather than his own plays or works by others as little known as himself. Thus the troupe performed Voltaire, Diderot, Regnard, Destouches, Gresset, La Chaussée, Collé, and even Cahusac and Rochon De Chabannes.

Unfortunately M. de Sade had great difficulty filling his theater. When it became clear that the local nobility was turning up its nose at his plays, he did not hesitate to invite bourgeois of his acquaintance and even opened his doors to peasants, which required the presence of two constables "to prevent disturbances." The abbé de Sade did his best to bring in spectators from Saumane and Mazan with the aid of the *fermier* Ripert.[25] The festival was to have included a cycle of twenty-four plays, the last to be given at Mazan on October 22. But on June 27 it would be tragically interrupted, as we shall see.

Thespis's Chariot

The marquis's passion for the theater was ruinous. When the prudent Fage attempted to point out the folly of such expenditure, he was rudely reprimanded. The abbé de Sade, fully in accord with the notary on the subject of his nephew's expensive whims, told him as much in a letter: "I agree with you about my nephew's passion for the theater, which, as you see, is carried to extremes and will soon ruin him if it lasts. I have said nothing about it thus far, because I feel that my protestations would be wasted. But I am pleased to see that the problem of keeping peace among the actors, their perpetual deceit, the difficulty of finding money to cover these expenses, and the obstacles that constantly crop up to prevent him from gratifying this passion are beginning to disgust him, and I am only waiting for the right moment to strike the final blow. I would have done so already if his wife had been willing to act in concert with me, and if she were less indulgent of her husband's fantasies."[26]

But the person who was most irritated by the marquis's extravagance was of course la Présidente de Montreuil: "I worry about the health of my children, from whom I have not heard for some time," she complained to the abbé.

But I have heard a great deal, from many sources, about the plays and amusements that keep them on the move . . . Such shows, quite simple when performed for one's peers within society, become a matter of great ridicule, to say the least, when one indulges in them without restraint, when one makes a spectacle of oneself before an entire province (which is shocked by it), with people whose profession is to amuse those of M. de Sade's kind and estate when the contract suits them reciprocally, but not to be in parity in the public's eye.

On Tuesday, June 23, 1772, Donatien left La Coste in the middle of the festival for Marseilles, ostensibly to obtain cash. Perhaps family life was beginning to weigh on him as well, and he may have been thinking of amusing himself with the port city's ladies of the night. He took his young valet, Armand, also known as Latour, with him.[27] In theory he was to return by the twenty-ninth at the latest for a performance of the *Philosophe marié* at Mazan. But fate was to rule otherwise.

10

The Marseilles Affair

On the afternoon of June 23 Donatien reached Marseilles, where he stayed at the Hôtel des Treize-Cantons. For the next two days we have no information about his activities, except that he went several times to the brothel kept by a Mme Vachier on rue Saint-Ferréol-le-Vieux to see Jeanne Nicou, a nineteen-year-old native of Lyons.

On Thursday, June 25, he sent Latour to the port district to recruit some "very young" girls for an evening's debauch. In the street the valet approached an eighteen-year-old Lyonnaise by the name of Marianne Laverne and made a date for the following night at eleven o'clock. But when he and his master arrived at the "maison Nicolas" on rue d'Aubagne, it turned out that their quarry had gone for a midnight sail.

On Saturday, June 27, at eight in the morning, Latour knocked at Marianne's door. She had finally returned from her adventure of the night before, and Latour now proposed a new date but this time not at her "establishment," which was too public a place. His master preferred something more discreet. Another prostitute, Marie Borelly, known as Mariette, lived not far away in a building at the corner of rue d'Aubagne and rue des Capucins. Marianne was instructed to be there at exactly ten o'clock. Along with her he had invited two other girls from the "maison Nicolas": Marianne Laugier, known as Mariannette, and Rose Coste, known as Rosette. His master would bring anise candies "to make them fart and take the wind in his mouth."

Jeanne Nicou, who also received an invitation from Latour, refused to go along.

The Marquis de Sade's Little Theater

SCENE 1[1]

DRAMATIS PERSONAE:

MARIANNE LAUGIER, *known as* MARIANNETTE, *age 20*
MARIANNE LAVERNE, *age 18*
ROSE COSTE, *known as* ROSETTE, *age 20*
MARIE BORELLY, *known as* MARIETTE, *age 23*
JEANNE-FRANÇOISE LEMAIRE, *Mariette's servant, age 42*
THE MARQUIS DE SADE, *alias Lafleur, age 32*
His valet, LATOUR, *alias Monsieur le Marquis*

The action begins two hours later. We are in the apartment of Mariette Borelly, 15 *bis* rue d'Aubagne, on the third floor. Enter the mysterious traveler: "average size," "blond hair," "handsome face," "full features." He wears a gray coat with blue lining, a marigold yellow silk vest and breeches, a plume in his hat and a sword at his side, and carries a gold-knobbed cane. He is followed by his valet Latour, who is slightly taller than his master, with long hair, a face pitted by smallpox, and wearing a blue-and-yellow-striped sailor's costume. The marquis enters the room where the four women are waiting and takes a handful of écus from his pocket: "There will be money for everybody!" he shouts, provided they know how to "amuse" him. They begin with a guessing game: whoever guesses how many écus he holds in his hand will go first. Each woman proposes a number, and Marianne is declared the winner. Donatien orders everyone to leave except for the lucky lady and his valet, whom he calls Monsieur le Marquis, while he himself goes by the flunkeyish name Lafleur.

SCENE 2

MARIANNE LAVERNE — THE MARQUIS — LATOUR

The marquis locks the door and orders Latour and Marianne to lie down on the bed. With one hand he whips the prostitute while with the other he masturbates his servant. Then he orders Latour to leave, takes from his pocket a small, gold-rimmed crystal candy box containing pastilles of Spanish fly encrusted with anise-flavored sugar, and offers it to the girl. He tells her to eat a lot of candy, as there is nothing better for producing flatulence. She cannot swallow more than seven or eight. He then proposes that she allow herself to be sodomized either by himself or by his valet, for which he promises her a louis. When she refuses, he hands her a scroll of parchment bristling with misshapen nails and asks her to whip his buttocks with this makeshift scourge. She starts to do as she is told but after three blows feels faint. He orders her to continue; she cannot. He then asks for a heather broom in the hope that it might prove more effective. Marianne goes to the kitchen and asks Lemaire to go and buy one. A short while later she returns, broom in hand, and strikes the marquis several times. Shouting, he begs her to hit harder. Suddenly she stops, feeling sick, and asks to leave. She seeks refuge in the kitchen, where the servant gives her a glass of water. Then, feeling even sicker, she asks for a cup of coffee.

SCENE 3

MARIETTE BORELLY—THE MARQUIS—LATOUR

While Marianne struggles to regain her senses, Donatien invites Mariette and Latour to come in. He undresses the girl, makes her crouch at the foot of the bed, and flagellates her with the broom, then asks that she do the same to him. While she beats him, he uses a penknife to record the number of blows on the wood of the mantelpiece. Then he throws her on the bed and takes her from the front while masturbating his servant, after which Latour sodomizes him. When it is all over, Mariette dresses and leaves the room. Enter Rosette.

SCENE 4

ROSE COSTE, KNOWN AS ROSETTE—THE MARQUIS—LATOUR

This scene duplicates the previous one except for a few minor differences: while Rosette thrashes the marquis with the broom, Latour manipulates him and then allows the marquis to do the same to him. The marquis then offers the girl a louis if she will allow his valet to sodomize her. She refuses and leaves the room, making way for Mariannette.

SCENE 5

MARIANNE LAUGIER, KNOWN AS MARIANNETTE— THE MARQUIS—LATOUR

Mariannette at first submits to the marquis's caresses, but when Donatien prepares to whip her (saying he has twenty-five more blows to administer), she notices the bloody scourge of nails on the bed, becomes frightened, and tries to run. He forcibly prevents her and calls the still shaky Marianne back in, then locks the door. He offers candy to both women. Marianne Laverne refuses, having eaten too many already; Mariannette puts some in her mouth but immediately spits them out. After whipping both girls furiously with the heather broom, the marquis grabs Marianne, throws her down on the bed on her stomach, pulls her pants down from behind, and sticks his nose between the cheeks of her buttocks so as to inhale her wind. He then strikes her a few more times with the broom and orders Mariannette to come to her companion's bedside and watch. Next, he removes his breeches, arouses his servant by touching him, and "lies down on Marianne's buttocks," probably sodomizing her, while Latour does the same to him. Disgusted, Mariannette runs to the window and presses her head against the glass so as not to have to watch any more of this spectacle. The marquis then asks her to masturbate Latour, but she refuses and tries to flee. Marianne, meanwhile, has collapsed in tears. The two girls beg to be allowed to leave. The marquis first threatens them, then gives each one an écu of six livres. He promises them ten more livres if they will go sailing with him that evening.

•

Thus ended what Gilbert Lely euphemistically, and without the slightest irony, called a "Cytherean morning." But the day was still young, and the young marquis still had an ogre's appetite. The morning session was only an appetizer. He would require a more substantial repast by evening's end, for he was to depart for La Coste the next day and had no intention of wasting his final hours of freedom.

Late that afternoon he sent Latour to rue d'Aubagne to fetch Marianne and Mariannette for the sailing expedition, but the girls refused to go with him. The lackey then embarked on a hunt through the brothels of Marseilles. It was essential that he find new flesh for his master before nightfall. Meanwhile, the actor des Rosières called on Donatien, who invited him to dinner. They dined together until Latour returned and whispered a few words in his master's ear: he had found what he was looking for. At around nine o'clock he had approached a prostitute standing in her doorway on rue Saint-Ferréol-le-Vieux and asked to go up to her apartment. She was twenty-five years old, and her name was Marguerite Coste. Latour told her to prepare for a visit from his master. As a token of good faith, he left a handkerchief, then hastened to the Hôtel des Treize-Cantons. Des Rosières was quickly dispatched along with dinner, and the two men set out. Meanwhile, the curtain was rising on the final scene of the drama.

SCENE 6
MARGUERITE COSTE—THE MARQUIS—LATOUR

The scene shifts to Marguerite's bedroom. Night has fallen. The marquis, followed by his servant, rapidly climbs two flights of stairs in a building owned by M. Deboeuf, a master locksmith. He enters the room, dismisses Latour (who withdraws with a distraught look), puts down his cane and sword, and collapses on the bed. Marguerite, meanwhile, pulls up a chair next to the bed and sits down. He immediately offers her his crystal candy box, from which she takes and eats several pieces of candy. He offers more, but she declines. He insists, telling her that he asks all his girls to do the same, and finally persuades her to consume all the contents of the box. In the meantime he asks whether she feels anything in her stomach. He then has her lie down on her stomach, licks her anus, orders her to fart into his mouth, and finally proposes "to enjoy her from behind and in several other ways, still more horrible," all of which she refuses. She consents to be taken but only according to "natural laws." After "amusing himself with her person," the marquis withdraws, leaving six francs on the table.

CURTAIN

Forensic Medicine

Early the next day, as a postal coach bore master and servant away from Marseilles, what was happening to Marguerite Coste would soon set in motion the judicial machinery of the ancient Phocaean capital. Shortly after the marquis had left her the night before, she had felt a powerful burning sensation in her stomach, accompanied by nausea, vertigo, and "a general sick feeling." After lying down, she began to vomit a large quantity of black, fetid matter. The next day she asked her landlady, the widow Ravel, to make her some tea. Finding Marguerite in a woeful state, her bed fouled with vomit, the good woman gave her warm water to drink to help her relieve herself. The victim continued vomiting all day Sunday. That night, she was examined by a doctor, Antoine Roux, who prescribed sweet almond oil, but the vomiting persisted all day Monday. On Tuesday morning the widow Ravel found Marguerite Coste's condition unchanged. Upon learning that a stranger had offered Marguerite candies two nights earlier, Mme Ravel hastened to inform the constabulary, which launched an investigation. That very day, Tuesday, June 30, 1772, Jean-Pierre Chomel, *lieutenant criminel*, went to the prostitute's home on rue Saint-Ferréol-le-Vieux to take her deposition. He found her in bed suffering from spasms of vomiting, during which she continued to bring up black and putrid matter. The policeman collected a sample, which he placed in a bottle and sealed. The royal prosecutor then ordered the surgeon Roux (another Dr. Roux, not the Antoine who had seen her previously), together with an apothecary, to determine the cause of Marguerite Coste's condition by analyzing the material in the sample. He also ordered a search of Mariette Borelly's apartment. During the search, the investigators found two small pastilles in a corner of one room; these were sent to the laboratory for analysis. They also noted a list of figures carved into the mantelpiece to the right of the mirror: 215, 179, 225, 240. Upon questioning, Mariette indicated that the marquis, while being flagellated, had recorded the number of blows he had received —a total of 859 in four sessions in a single morning! And the more powerful blows may have done as much damage as two or even three lesser ones.

On Wednesday, July 1, the physician Longe and the surgeon Roux visited Marguerite Coste at her bedside and found "her eyes sparkling, her face red and inflamed, her tongue moist and covered with white mucus, her pulse strong and rapid." She was in terrible pain. A basin next to the bed was filled with the black matter that she continued to vomit. The doctors palpated her stomach and found it quite tender. Before leaving they prescribed viscous elixirs and enemas.

The next day, Thursday, at ten o'clock, both doctors went to the laboratory of the apothecary Rimbaud, who was assisted on this occasion by his colleague Aubert on orders of the *lieutenant criminel* of Marseilles. All four men then proceeded to analyze the samples. On the surface they found traces of fatty and oily substances, probably from the sweet almond oil. The remainder of the liquid consisted of the various infusions and beverages absorbed by the patient.

The doctors also returned that day to Marguerite's bedside: her gastralgia was less severe but had extended to the lumbar region. The abdomen was not rigid. The stools contained yellowish and bilious material.

On Thursday night the patient's condition remained the same: vomiting.

On Friday, at eleven in the morning, she was still vomiting and her pulse was weak.

Friday night: no vomiting that afternoon.

Saturday morning: bad night, feverish pulse, dry tongue.

These observations led the two doctors to conclude: "1. That these symptoms arise from the laceration and cauterization of the smooth membrane of the stomach and intestines. 2. That this laceration was produced by a bitter, corrosive substance, probably contained in the pastilles that the patient ate. 3. That although the patient is not in imminent danger of death, she is in a very critical, a highly critical condition." The letter is dated Marseilles, July 4, 1772, and signed by Drs. Longe and Roux.[2]

•

While Marguerite Coste convalesces, let us turn our attention to Marianne Laverne, who also experienced the aftereffects of the Sadeian confections, though not as severely as her companion. To be sure, she had consumed fewer of the suspect pastilles. But she too experienced much the same symptoms soon after eating them. These symptoms grew more severe in the days that followed: hematemesis (vomiting blood), followed by extensive vomiting of black and bloody matter "similar to a butcher's rinsewater," which contained stripes of blood and bits of mucus. Other symptoms included a racing pulse, a dry, somewhat whitish tongue, and abdominal pain, particularly in the epigastric region.

On Friday, July 3, the doctors who came to examine Marianne Laverne observed: "Mild excretions from above and below, no more fever. Burning sensation along esophagus, irritated by drinking, pain in loins." On Saturday, the patient was asleep, no fever, lower abdomen "meteorized" (swollen by the accumulation of gas), burning urine. The conclusions of their report were virtually the same as in the case of Marguerite Coste.[3]

As for the analysis, the two master apothecaries André Rimbaud and Jean-Baptiste Joseph Aubert presented a full report of the tests carried out in Rimbaud's laboratory. In the samples taken from Marguerite Coste's effluvia, they found no "mineral substance, arsenic, or corrosive sublimate." They then examined under a microscope the two pastilles found on the floor during the search and saw nothing but an anise seed surrounded by sugar, "artistically done." They detected no bitterness when a piece of one candy was placed on the tip of the tongue. One seed was exposed to flame, but no odor of arsenic was released. The other, placed in two drachmas (roughly 6.48 grams) of limewater, failed to color the liquid. The sample quantity was too small to permit further investigation. Their experiments thus failed to turn up the cause of the vomiting.[4]

Anise and Spanish Fly

The incompetence of the two pharmacists is astonishing. Obsessed by poison, it never occurred to them that the affliction of the two women might have some other cause. Thus they searched in vain for arsenic and limited themselves to an inadequate microscopic examination. Since they were dealing with a known debauchee like Sade, they should immediately have thought of Spanish fly, known since antiquity for its aphrodisiac qualities and, incorporated into pastilles referred to in Italy as *diavolini* and in France as *love pills* or *pastilles à la Richelieu*, commonly used by libertines. The presence of Spanish fly could be detected by a simple blistering test. But Aubert and Rimbaud, when they found no arsenic, declined to press further with their investigation. Even the judges did not mention Spanish fly until later, when the verdict was appealed, but it was surely on the minds of some commentators immediately after the crime. On July 22, 1772, for example, M. de Montyon, the intendant of Provence, responded to a letter from M. de Saint-Florentin, the minister of the king's household, who had in the meantime become the duc de La Vrillière, Saint-Florentin having written because he had heard certain still unsubstantiated rumors and wanted further information: "Another version of this story," Montyon wrote, "and the facts are less terrible and more plausible, is that the young man visited some houses of ill repute, that he gave the girls pastilles with Spanish fly which left them seriously indisposed, and that one of them, who ate more than the others, is close to death. None of the girls has died."[5]

Candy with Spanish fly is also discussed in the personal correspondence of the marquis and his family. He denies having given any to the girls in Marseilles. Commenting on Mme de Sade's petition for a reversal of the decision in the case, Donatien was sharply critical of one passage in the text: "On page 7 you argue that women of this sort cannot and should not know the *etymology, properties, or effects of the Cantharides flies*. This is incorrect. It is a central part of their profession to know this kind of drug, whose properties have the same virtue as their art, and there are, I think, very few who do not know what it is. And it is precisely because they do know that they have seized on it."[6]

Following this line of argument, he attributes the women's affliction to overindulgence at the dinner table, a case that he makes in a notably more playful tone in *Le Président mystifié*: "A mild disturbance of the entrails is a considerable malady in Marseilles as in Aix. And since we have seen a pack of scoundrels, confederates of that strapping fellow there, return a verdict of 'poison' in a case involving a few strumpets with colic, there is no reason for surprise that a case of colic is a serious matter with a magistrate in Provence!"[7]

There can be no doubt that Spanish fly was present in the candies the marquis offered to Marguerite Coste and Marianne Laverne, the only women involved who actually ingested the pastilles. Their symptoms coincide exactly with those produced by Spanish fly. Dr. Pierre Flottes, an accredited expert in clinical and analytical toxicology with whom I have consulted, has no doubt whatsoever that the women were poisoned by powdered cantharides, which can be extremely toxic.

The marquis de Sade surely knew that the use of Spanish fly was dangerous, for all his contemporaries knew it. For proof, one has only to open volume 2 of *L'Encyclopédie* and turn to the article CANTHAR-IDE: "Powdered cantharides applied to the epidermis can cause blisters and lead to burning urine, strangury, thirst, fever, pissing of blood, etc., and make the body's odor stinking and cadaverous. Taken internally, it produces the same symptoms."

Of course Sade was certainly also aware of the aphrodisiac effects of Spanish fly, and surely it was to excite his partners that he gave it to them. His error (I do not go so far as to say *his crime*) was to have administered such a large dose that the women were actually endangered. A normal dose was no more than two pastilles in twenty-four hours. Any more than that could produce a toxic reaction and even death. It is perfectly clear, moreover, why he urged the women to ingest so much: his real purpose was not to produce excitation of the vagina but to stimulate the anal mucus membranes. Since the second effect took longer to achieve than the first, it made sense to double the quantity to accelerate the process, but at the risk of causing internal hemorrhage, renal necrosis, and vesical lesions.

As for the anise, its only function, a byproduct of its aromatic qualities, was to conceal the bitterness of the Spanish fly. Despite claims to the contrary, anise does not cause gaseous distension or flatulence. It is, however, widely used as an antispasmodic. The gas that the marquis inhaled with such exquisite pleasure actually came from spasms induced by the Spanish fly itself. But, reluctant to reveal his secret to the girls, the libertine of the rue d'Aubagne invoked his taste for flatulence to stimulate their appetites: their farts were in a sense his alibi.

It goes without saying that the marquis never sought to kill his victims. There is no need to argue for an absence of criminal intent. We may take him at his word when he exclaims, in an outburst of a sort rare enough with him that it can only be sincere, "Yes, I am a libertine, I admit it. I have thought of everything that can be thought of in that line, but I have certainly not done everything I thought of and surely never will. I am a libertine, but I am not a criminal or a murderer." Furthermore, as Mme de Montreuil pertinently observed, "Why on earth would a man give poison to girls he had never seen or heard of and whose profession offers no occasion for love, jealousy, or benefit of any kind?"[8] In any case, neither Marguerite Coste nor Marianne Laverne died.

Knowing the damage that an overdose of Spanish fly could do to the human body, the marquis still did not hesitate to administer massive doses to his two victims. Was this imprudence, clumsiness, or error? Was it a scientific experiment, as in the case of the salve given to Rose Keller? Or was it simple indifference? What did the life of a prostitute matter to a nobleman? The Arcueil affair had already demonstrated the contempt he felt for those "vile creatures." That a man of his rank could be condemned because of a prostitute was something he could never admit: "These amusements, whose only drawback was at worst the death of a whore, were capital crimes in the last century and in the first eighty years of this one. But people are becoming enlightened, and thanks to philosophy a respectable man can no longer be sacrificed for a hooker. Putting these vile creatures in their true place, people are beginning to feel that, since they are made solely to serve as victims to our passions, it is only their disobedience that must be punished, and not our caprices."[9]

"This divine taste"

While the medical investigation continued, the criminal investigation also moved forward on two startling counts: poisoning and sodomy. Although the judges had been forbidden to investigate matters not contained in the complaint, the key witnesses had already been heard: Marie Borelly, her servant Jeanne-Françoise Lemaire, Marianne Laverne, Jeanne Nicou (who, from the description of the nobleman involved, recognized her regular client), Marianne Laugier, Rose Coste, Dr. Antoine Roux, the actor Sébastien des Rosières, and others, a dozen in all.

None of the interrogated prostitutes admitted to having engaged in sodomy with their client. At the mere mention of the act, all denounced it as "horrible." If it is difficult to believe them (because anal intercourse was a common practice in the brothels of the time and, for the marquis, the only conceivable form of homage to the female body), their reluctance to confess is easy to understand. The penalty for sodomy was reason enough for caution. The punishment provided by law was none other than death by fire: sodomists were burned alive, and their ashes were scattered to the wind. Let me hasten to add, however, that the death sentence was virtually never imposed. It was reserved almost exclusively, moreover, for homosexual sodomy, usually in association with other "crimes."[10] Yet the punishments meted out for sodomy in lieu of death, particularly to creatures as despised as common prostitutes, were frightening enough. Prisons such as Bicêtre and the Salpêtrière were rightly regarded as death's antechambers.

As for the homosexual acts committed by the marquis and his valet and explicitly denounced by the prostitutes, they, too, belong to the repertoire of Sadeian fantasy. The author of *Justine* waxes rapturously lyrical about the joys of passive penetration in the voice of M. de Bressac:

"Ah, Thérèse!" he cried out one day in enthusiasm. "If only you knew the charm of this fantasy, if only you could understand what one feels in the pleasant illusion of becoming nothing but a woman! What an incredible aberration of the mind! One abhors the sex, and yet one wants to imitate it! Ah! How sweet it is, Thérèse, to succeed in this ambition. How delightful it is to be the strumpet of all who want you, . . . to be, one after another in the same day, the mistress of a porter, a marquis, a valet, a monk, to be cherished, caressed, envied, threatened, beaten, now victorious in their arms, now victim at their feet, coaxing them with caresses, reviving them with excesses . . . Oh! No, no, Thérèse, you do not understand what pleasure is for a head constructed as mine is . . . But morality apart, what if you imagined the physical sensations associated with this divine taste! It is impossible to hold on to them. The stimulation is so powerful, the titillations of voluptuousness are so acute . . . [that] you lose your mind . . . you rave. A thousand kisses, each more tender than the last, are not ardent enough to produce the state of intoxication into which the agent plunges us. Wrapped in his arms, mouths glued to each other, we wish that our whole existence could be incorporated into his. We would like to fuse into a single being. If we dare to complain, it is about being neglected. We want him to be more robust than Hercules, to open us up, to penetrate us, so that his precious seed, spewing forth, burning in the depths of our entrails, may by its heat and strength cause ours to spurt out into his hands.[11]

War

From this point on, things moved quickly, unusually quickly for Provence, ordinarily so indolent in the summer months. Without waiting for the apothecaries' report, which he did not receive until the following day, M. de Mende, the royal prosecutor, signed, on July 4, a warrant for the arrest of the marquis de Sade and his valet Latour. On that same day, the last rites were administered to Marguerite Coste, whose condition remained critical.

A day or two earlier, while Donatien was supervising rehearsals of *Adélaïde du Guesclin* and *L'Amant auteur* for performance on July 9 at La Coste, someone came secretly to warn him that he stood accused of poisoning several prostitutes. One of them reportedly had died. Thinking that all was lost, Donatien immediately fled, along with Latour. Mlle de Launay followed her brother-in-law, while Mme de Sade remained behind. No doubt the fugitives hid out somewhere in the region, perhaps with Ripert in Mazan or with Lions in Arles or with the abbé in Saumane. In any case, when the bailiff of Apt, accompanied by several constables, arrived at the château to arrest the marquis and Latour, Fage, the notary, informed the official that the two men had been gone for about a week and that he had heard nothing from them since their departure. The police then questioned the servants and neighbors, who also claimed that no one had seen them and no one knew where they were. The bailiff conducted "a careful search of all the castle's apartments" and left a summons requiring the two fugitives to appear within two weeks' time. As provided by law he then proceeded to "seize and mark" all the marquis's property and sources of revenue: the château, the farms and estates included in his seigneurie, any rents or payments deriving therefrom, and all other seigneurial rights and dependencies. The marquis's steward, Pierre Chauvin, was appointed trustee of this property "with the inhibitions and prohibitions required in such cases."

•

In the meantime Mme de Sade did not stand by idly but tried to imagine all the ways in which her husband might be rescued from the authorities. Her sister, who reappeared after having vanished for a time and from whom she expected at least some comfort, seemed even more devastated than Mme de Sade herself. Renée-Pélagie therefore turned to her mother, la Présidente, for help. But far from wanting to save her son-in-law, as she had always done until now, Mme de Montreuil was firmly resolved to fight him with every ounce of her strength. And what she was capable of we have already seen.

The cause of this sudden reversal was clearly rooted in Donatien's affair with Mlle de Launay. If la Présidente had long remained in the dark about this, her doubts were now gone. Of all the things the marquis might have done to her, this was surely the worst. She had tolerated his debts, his adventures, and his lies. She could even accept that he preferred the company of prostitutes to that of his lawfully wedded wife. Her pragmatic outlook and lack of confidence in the man were hardly compatible with moral zeal. But to have laid hands on Anne-Prospère, to have dared to touch that child, her second daughter, more delicate and fragile than the first—that she could not bear. And this was to say nothing of the risk of venereal disease, always to be feared with a debauchee like Sade. And the scandal—for the incest would soon become public knowledge, would find its way into the gazettes, and the family name would be dragged through the mud. What a disillusionment for la Présidente, who had hoped that this union with the high nobility would bring new luster to that name. "Mme de Montreuil," Maurice Heine wrote, "was not a woman to seek a sterile vengeance, but she would recoil from nothing apt to assuage her anger or protect the material and moral interests of those for whom she was responsible. The arrest and detention of the fugitive seemed to her happily to satisfy both conditions."

Having been abandoned by her mother, Renée-Pélagie decided to act on her own. Following the example set by Mme de Montreuil in 1768, she first tried to induce the two prostitutes to withdraw their charges against the marquis. For that she needed money. She managed to obtain a loan of 4,000 livres, which Ripert, at the urging of the abbé de Sade, agreed to guarantee, and then hastened to Marseilles, taking her sister with her.[12]

The negotiations, hastened along by Maître de Carmis, a Marseilles notary, soon brought results. On August 8 and August 17, respectively, Marguerite Coste and Marianne Laverne signed documents withdrawing their charges in return for substantial indemnities. Mme de Sade had scored a first victory, although in the meantime she had become frightened at the proportions the case was taking on: "Everyone was in the grip of the most extreme prejudice," she would later say. Indeed, the most fantastic rumors were circulating about her husband, heightening tensions and turning against him the opinion of a public ready to swallow the crudest fabrications. For an example of the absurdities that were repeated everywhere, consider the reports Bachaumont received from his correspondents: "Friends write from Marseilles that M. le comte de Sade, who caused such a stir in 1768 . . . gave a ball . . . Into the dessert he slipped chocolate pastilles so good that a number of people devoured them. There were lots of them, and no one failed to eat some, but he had mixed in some Spanish fly. The virtue of this medication is well known. It proved so potent that those who ate the pastilles began to burn with unchaste ardor and to carry on as if in the grip of the most amorous frenzy. The ball degenerated into one of those licentious orgies for which the Romans were renowned. Even the most respectable of women were unable to resist the uterine rage that stirred within them. And so it was that M. de Sade enjoyed the favors of his sister-in-law, with whom he fled to avoid the punishment he deserves. Several persons died of their frightful priapic excesses, and others are still quite sick."[13]

The good bookseller Hardy, normally more circumspect, went even further: the marquis, he said, had been found guilty of "having conspired with his servants to poison his wife on account of the violent passion he had conceived for his sister-in-law."

•

On her way back to La Coste, Mme de Sade suddenly felt an overwhelming sense of discouragement. Never before had she felt at such a loss against adversity. Despite the prostitutes' withdrawal of their charges, she understood that circumstances were now conspiring against Donatien. "His ruin is therefore a foregone conclusion."[14] How could she alone combat the general hostility? How could she make herself heard to a frenzied public? How could she make people see the affair for what it was, an ordinary case of licentious excess? Above all, how could she persuade judges out to ruin her husband to see his side of the case? The obstacles seemed insurmountable, and Mme de Sade felt too tired to go on. Never had she felt her mother's absence more acutely. If only Anne-Prospère could transcend their rivalry as women, if only she could shake off her torpor and work with her sister to save this man with whom both were in love. But the poor canoness wavered between despair, which left her a nervous wreck, and jealous rage toward the unfaithful lover who had just betrayed her in so odious a fashion.

M. de Montreuil's Mission

A few days later, an unexpected visit forced Mme de Sade to set aside these musings. Her father had come to La Coste. M. de Montreuil had in fact set out for Provence on August 7, no doubt at the instigation of his wife. He offered Renée-Pélagie not only moral support but substantial financial aid, advancing her the sum of 3,000 livres on August 25 to help meet any unusual expenses that might arise out of the situation.

M. de Montreuil has left a manuscript account of his journey, none of which has been published until now. The interest of the story makes up for the flatness of the style. Among other things, this text contains the only known description of La Coste in the marquis's time:

La Coste is a château that looks like a fortress, without the slightest regularity. The approaches are quite steep and unpleasant because of the rock slides and the height of the mountain. There is no shelter anywhere near the château, a defect from which Provence in general suffers, there being no patches of wood and very few virgin forests or white oak, the oak of France. There is a good deal of green oak on the mountain. On the estate there are plenty of mulberries, olive trees, and almond trees, but none of these is capable of offering shelter from the great heat of the region . . . La Coste is not a very extensive estate, but it is most seigneurial. The lord receives one-eighth of all that is produced on land in his territory, which is referred to in the canton as the *code huitième*. The steward in charge of all this is a man named Chauvin, a Protestant who lives on the income of the Maison-Basse.[15]

Earlier in his account, M. de Montreuil recorded a visit to M. de Bory, the warden of Pierre-Encize. No doubt he wanted to thank him for services rendered to his son-in-law. It is remarkable, too, that throughout the text le Président remains strangely silent about the Marseilles affair, which was still the news of the day. This discretion is all the more astonishing in that the journal was never intended for publication. Donatien is mentioned only once, in connection with Ripert, at whose home le Président stopped for dinner. Did he meet Donatien there in secret? It seems likely, although he says nothing about it. Nor does he say a word about the two daughters who received him at La Coste. So discreet is M. de Montreuil about the true purpose of his journey that the rest of the text might pass for the diary of an innocent tourist. Is it possible, however, to believe that, at a time when the marquis was facing the scaffold, this visit could simply have been a matter of chance? Is it possible that this old man, by now nearly sixty and of sedentary disposition, would have left his luxurious hôtel on rue Neuve-du-Luxembourg, traveled 430 miles, and braved the furnace of Provence in August, simply for the pleasure of dining with Ripert? There is no reason for the trip other than the necessity to make contact with people who could help: his son-in-law's relatives and allies and above all the men who would judge him. When he took leave of his daughter on September 7, moreover, it was to go to Aix, where the Parlement was preparing to review the sentence handed down by the court in Marseilles. Despite the late hour of his arrival, he went straight to see Maître Gachier, "a well-known attorney of this city," no doubt to consult about what course to take. The following morning, accompanied by the commander of Valence, a M. Gaillard, he went to see M. Johannis, *procureur général* of the new *parlement* of Provence, and then to see M. Mazenod, *président* of the *parlement*, these being the two men on whom the fate of the accused depended. After lunch he left Aix for Lourmarin.[16] Although he says nothing about these conversations, it is not difficult to guess their tenor. M. de Montreuil probably came to an understanding with his colleagues about how to proceed with this affair in such a way as to satisfy justice while preserving his family's interests and honor.

"And their ashes scattered to the wind . . ."

Meanwhile, the pace of court proceedings accelerated. On August 26 the royal prosecutor announced that the testimony of the witnesses, "both those who have been heard and those who will be heard again," had been verified and found credible enough to warrant comparison with that of Sade and Latour, "the accused, absent and in default." On September 2 the prosecutor found the accused "duly convicted, M. de Sade of the crime of poisoning and M. de Sade as well as M. Latour of the crime of sodomy, as charged." Both were sentenced to make public confession on the parvis of La Major, on their knees, head and feet bare, wearing a chemise and a rope around the neck, holding a torch of yellow wax weighing one pound. They were then to be led to a scaffold erected on the place Saint-Louis. The marquis de Sade was to have his head severed, and Latour was to be "hanged or strangled on a gibbet until he is dead."[17] Their bodies were then to be cast into a fire and their ashes scattered to the winds. In addition, the marquis was fined thirty livres and his servant, ten livres.[18]

Donatien was thus to be subjected to a double execution: he was to be beheaded for the crime of poisoning and burned for the crime of sodomy.[19] On September 3 Chomel, the *lieutenant général criminel*, pronounced the final sentence. On September 11, in Aix, the *parlement* of Provence confirmed that sentence and ordered that it be carried out. The next day, September 12, the two men were executed in effigy on the Place des Prêcheurs in Aix. To be sure, this was a symbolic execution, designed primarily to make an impression on the public mind, but in a very real sense it meant "civil death" for the marquis, who from that day on was stripped of all his rights. This civil death would remain in effect until the statute of limitations ran its course, that is to say, for thirty years, the normal period in cases judged in absentia (unless the condemned man appeared before the courts within the next five years).

Can one imagine anything more likely to delight the marquis de Sade than the knowledge that he was to be tortured in public? His jubilation on hearing the news is not difficult to envision. He no doubt celebrated the event in much the same way as a certain marquis whose exploits are recounted by Curval in the *Cent Vingt Journées de Sodome*: "Everybody knows the story of the marquis de ***, who, when informed of the sentence that he was to be burned in effigy, pulled his cock out of his trousers and yelled, 'Fuckgod! Now I'm where I wanted to be, with opprobrium and infamy heaped upon me. Leave me, leave me, I must get off!' And so he did, at that very moment."[20]

•

The marquis was found guilty on two counts, poisoning and sodomy, whereas his valet was convicted of sodomy only. On the count of poisoning, the verdict seems monstrous. The Marseilles magistrates took no account either of the withdrawal of charges by Marguerite Coste and Marianne Laverne, both of whom had recovered fully, or of the apothecaries' conclusions, which, dubious as they may have been, nevertheless exonerated the marquis of attempted poisoning. Although it seems certain today that the incriminated bonbons contained Spanish fly, the subject never came up during the course of the judicial proceedings. Contrary to law, moreover, certain witnesses testified "about acts not mentioned in the complaint," and the complaint itself was not filed by any person, unless it was the judges themselves. Taken together, these irregularities, as well as the haste with which the marquis was judged, suggest that he was condemned in advance.

As for sodomy, the crime, as we have seen, was subject to capital punishment. But throughout the eighteenth century only seven of the thousands of homosexuals known to the police perished at the stake. One was the notorious Benjamin Deschauffours, who was consigned to the flames on May 26, 1726, but he had to answer not just for sodomy but for far more serious crimes as well: the murder of an adolescent, the castration of a young singer, and kidnapping and trafficking in children.[21] A half century later, the *lieutenant général de police*, Lenoir, who would play an important role in the marquis de Sade's fate as prisoner, cited the Deschauffours case as an example of the pernicious effects of class justice: "Here I am bound to observe that at the time this sentence was handed down, Paris harbored, and the police knew of, twenty thousand individuals who practiced the vice for which Deschauffours went to the stake. People wanted a public punishment. It fell not on the most criminal but on the least well protected of the guilty. This is the rule, and this is why the common people can flatter themselves on being more virtuous than the great. The executioner does his work so that it may be so. Pederasty in the long run can be a vice of great lords only."[22]

The judgment against the marquis de Sade can be explained in part by political circumstances, in particular the reform of the *parlements*, and in part by the personal enmity of Chancellor Maupeou. A year earlier, the chancellor, with the approval and support of Louis XV, had exiled the magistrates of all the *parlements* and confiscated their property. This veritable coup d'état provoked vigorous protest, particularly within the Cour des Aides (customs court) in which M. de Montreuil had once served as *président*. The protest was so vigorous, in fact, that the chancellor decided to eliminate the Cour des Aides altogether and exile its current *premier président*, Lamoignon de Malesherbes. On February 23, 1771, he published an edict abolishing the sale of offices and hereditary transmission of official posts, condemning abuses in the administration of justice, and promising "a prompt, pure, and cost-free system of justice." This reform, which rationalized the judicial apparatus and made access to it easier for those it served, incurred the opposition of much of the nobility, though it met with the approval of Voltaire and a few *philosophes*. Finally, and not without difficulty, Maupeou reconstituted a new *parlement*, for the most part composed of reliable men loyal to him. The Aix magistrates who signed Sade's sentence on September 11, for example, discharged their duties under the auspices not of *parlement* but of the Cour des Comptes of Provence. They had been appointed by the chancellor and did his bidding.

The case of Sade could be made an example of the fairness of the new system: this was Maupeou's trump card. The scapegoat wrested from his clutches in the Keller affair was in no danger of eluding him this time. His hands were now free; his sovereign would not disavow him. Thus Sade once again became the stake in a political battle: it was essential, whatever the cost, to demonstrate to all of France that M. de Maupeou's justice was blind to privilege and that birth constituted no rampart against the laws of the land.[23] Once again the chancellor held the ideal criminal in his hands: Sade had been compromised four years earlier in another vice case, and he had chosen to flee arrest, which only compounded his current predicament. His flight was in fact a great boon to Maupeou's minions, for if he had been arrested and haled into court, his appearance might have lessened the severity of his judges and altered their verdict. His mere presence at the trial would infallibly have operated in his favor, because it is easier to condemn an effigy than a man of flesh. Basically, Sade's absence was in everyone's interest, so much so that we may ask if the authorities were not unusually zealous about failing to find him, and if M. de Montreuil's visit to his colleagues on the *parlement* of Aix was not for the purpose of putting the finishing touches on the scenario that was ultimately played out: the execution in effigy, the stripping of Sade's civil rights, the naming of the Montreuils as his children's guardians, the award of his property to his wife, and eventually the marquis's arrest and imprisonment in some forgotten dungeon. What better way to get rid of a troublemaker while saving what could be saved: his fortune and his posterity.

The Lovers of Venice

While he and his valet burned in effigy on Aix's central square, the marquis, traveling in Italy as the "comte de Mazan," found himself in Venice for a romantic idyll with his pretty sister-in-law, whom he passed off as his wife. Some historians have attempted to cast doubt on the notion that Anne-Prospère was with him, but there is now irrefutable proof that the canoness followed Donatien on his Italian escapade. A previously unpublished letter from Sade to Gaufridy, dated July 16, 1793, in discussing the actor Bourdais's claim not to have received payment for his services, contains this sentence: "You see why it is so important that you send me the receipt that Fage received from the actor Bourdais *when I left for Venice in 1772 with Mlle de Launay*."[24]

From Venice the lovers traveled to several other Italian cities, after which the canoness abruptly abandoned the marquis, leaving all her luggage behind. Had she been urgently summoned home by her parents? Had there been a scene between her and the marquis following some transalpine adventure on Donatien's part? In any case, by October 2 we find Anne-Prospère back with her sister at La Coste. Meanwhile, Donatien sailed from Genoa to Nice, where he stayed long enough to deposit his own baggage and that of his sister-in-law. Then, throwing caution to the winds, he went to Marseilles, where on October 16 he received two rolls of fifty louis each from his Parisian business agent, M. de Milly. From there, by horseback, Donatien followed the Turin road as far as Chambéry, where he arrived on October 27, still traveling incognito but accompanied by an unknown woman and two lackeys, whose names we know: one was Latour, his acolyte from Marseilles, and the other Carteron, also known as La Jeunesse (Youth) and nicknamed Martin Quiros, an ingenious fellow but an incorrigible scoundrel who had been in the marquis's employ only a short time. But who was the woman? According to Gilbert Lely, it could only have been Mlle de Launay, who, he claims, must have rejoined her brother-in-law in Nice and traveled with him to Chambéry.[25] But we now know that this cannot have been the case. In his diary M. de Montreuil notes: "I left Paris on October 27, 1772, at nine in the morning, to fetch my daughters, Mme de Sade and Mlle de Launay, at the home of M. le marquis d'Evry, my brother-in-law, where they arrived from Provence with M. d'Evry, who had gone to fetch them."[26] If the canoness was with M. d'Evry and her sister on October 27, she could not possibly have accompanied the marquis de Sade on his trip to Savoy.

In Chambéry the marquis stopped at the Auberge de la Pomme d'Or, where he soon made the acquaintance of a Frenchman, M. de Vaulx. In early November his mysterious companion, whom he introduced sometimes as his wife, sometimes as his sister-in-law, took leave of him. He would later claim that he had "sent her back" to Italy. In any case he had Latour go with her. A few days later he moved into a country house on the outskirts of Chambéry that he had rented for six months from a Savoyard nobleman, M. du Choiri. The region's leading textile merchant, Augustin Ansard, rented him the necessary furnishings, including bedding and drapery.

As the comte de Mazan, "colonel of cavalry in the service of France," Donatien led a discreet existence, never left home (not even for meals, which he ordered from a nearby caterer), and saw no one, with the exception of M. de Vaulx, who became his confidant and took Donatien's part in various disputes with the Montreuils. Toward the end of November, however, a mysterious illness forced our hermit to take to his bed and entrust himself to the care of the surgeon Thonin, who lived near the Pomme d'Or. Thonin prescribed bleeding and visited his patient on several occasions. The marquis now summoned Latour, who had left Chambéry early that month, to replace Carteron at his bedside. Carteron was ordered to set out at once for Paris on a mission for his master to Mme de Sade. Ten days later, Dr. Thonin's patient had recovered sufficiently that the surgeon's visits were no longer required.

In the Lion's Mouth

Drama was as necessary to Donatien de Sade as the air he breathed. Trouble had no sooner left him alone than he hastened after more. What other than such an unusual disposition of mind could have made him write to Mme de Montreuil, whom he considered his most implacable enemy, even as he was concealing his whereabouts from the rest of the world? He seemed driven to put his head in the lion's mouth. In late November or early December his mother-in-law received a letter from him in which he spoke of his "confidence of finding in her a resource against the injustice that pursued" him.

Donatien was lost. Now that she knew where he was hiding, the "iron lady" pressed for immediate action on the part of the minister of foreign affairs, the duc d'Aiguillon, Mme du Barry's protégé yet also head of the *parti dévot*, the party of the devout. Aiguillon asked Count Ferrero de La Marmora, ambassador to France of the court of Piedmont and Sardinia, to ask his sovereign to order the arrest of the marquis de Sade, alias the comte de Mazan. Of course the reasons given were all to the honor of the Montreuil family: to protect the miscreant, already under sentence of death, from himself, for to set foot in France again was to risk his life, and, it was intimated, he was perfectly capable of such a foolish act, "his mind being quite deranged." "His family, which is most considerable, consequently lives in mortal fear that he will sooner or later be arrested, and they see no way to avoid a misfortune other than to put him in a secure place."[27] The family therefore requested that the Piedmontese king order the marquis seized and held under guard in one of his fortresses until such time as his kin wished him to be released. In the meantime the family would pay his room and board.

The king of Sardinia, easily persuaded by such laudable intentions, did not hesitate to issue an order for the arrest of the young lunatic and for his imprisonment in the fortress of Miolans. Naturally the arrest was to be carried out with the minimum possible publicity.

•

On December 8 Donatien as usual was spending the evening home alone with Latour. Suddenly, at nine o'clock, a squadron of police silently surrounded his villa, which was quite isolated from the town, while the comte de La Chavanne, commander of the fortress of Chambéry, appeared at his door along with two adjutants and informed him of the king's warrant for his arrest. When ordered to surrender his arms, Donatien handed over a pair of pocket pistols and a damascened sword. Meanwhile, the police searched the house. They found only a few old clothes, no more than could be held by a clothes rack, but "no letters or papers of any consequence whatever." At length the officer left his prisoner, "as surprised as he was upset," in the safekeeping of the two adjutants, who kept him under surveillance throughout the night. At seven the next morning he was lifted onto a postal coach and accompanied to the citadel of Miolans by four mounted escorts. Latour followed his master on horseback.

11
The Citadel

Perched on a steep promontory twenty-five kilometers from Chambéry, the citadel of Miolans, also known as the "Bastille of the dukes of Savoy," thrust its proud silhouette high above the town of Saint-Pierre-d'Albigny. This eagle's nest, which dominated the valley of the Isère from a height of 780 feet, was encircled by three walls and a double moat. Besides the fort proper, comprising the dungeon and the Tour Saint-Pierre, facing the west wall, one could also make out what was called the lower fort. The dungeon, which served as a prison, was a formidable crenellated square tower with pepper-pot turrets on three sides. Its walls, thrusting straight upward, were relieved by few windows, and these stood more than two hundred fifty feet above the ground. Any attempt to escape from a tower so smooth and steep seemed doomed to failure. Each of the dungeon's three stories contained rooms of various sizes with semicircular vaulted roofs. A spiral staircase led to the terrace, from which one looked out on Mont Blanc, the Roche-Pourrie, the glaciers of La Seillère, the Belledonne range, and the Grande-Chartreuse massif. In the base of the edifice, underneath the drawbridge, lower gates led to a prison of frigid cells illuminated only by the dim light filtering in through a few loopholes: this part of the fortress was known as "Hell." Above this was "Purgatory," consisting of a single room of modest size equipped with a fireplace and a stone bench. The second story, known as "the Treasury," contained two rooms for prisoners, one with a south-facing window and a fireplace. The apartment of the commandant, M. de Launay, was above this. Higher up were two more prisoners' rooms: the Petite Espérance to the north and the Grande Espérance to the south, with a double-barred window that offered a remarkable view of the Alps. This was the room assigned to M. de Sade. Finally, the very top story, which one reached by climbing a flight of seven stairs, was known as "Heaven."

The crenellated and machicolated Tour Saint-Pierre, another square tower, could also accommodate three prisoners. The fort contained twelve additional cells for captives and soldiers, an armory, a kitchen with a monumental fireplace, oven, steamroom, and kiln. There was also a chapel, a vegetable garden, and a well. The lower fort contained a chapel, canteen, powder storage, and supply room for the troops, as well as private gardens, along with one cell for a prisoner who did not need to be locked up and was free to take his meals in the canteen.[1]

The *"Grande Espérance"*

The commandant of Miolans, M. de Launay, was under orders to treat his new guest with all the respect due his birth. Through "politeness" he was to minimize the rigors of imprisonment, but at the same time he was instructed to neglect nothing that might permit his prisoner to escape. M. de Sade occupied the Grande Espérance, the largest and most comfortable cell in the fortress, while his valet took an adjoining room. The servant was even allowed to sleep in his master's cell but was forbidden to leave the fortress. At night the prisoner was securely locked in, and a guard slept in the vestibule outside his door. During the day M. de Sade was allowed to walk about within the dungeon's inner wall, but unbeknownst to him he was always discreetly followed by a guard. At the first sign of suspicious behavior, the guard was to alert the commandant.

The prisoner was allowed to make a fire in his fireplace, to furnish his room to suit his taste, and to make arrangements with the canteen cook about what he liked to eat, but he was strictly prohibited from receiving visits or corresponding with anyone outside the prison. M. de Launay was instructed to hold all letters addressed to the marquis. Donatien was allowed, however, to keep two dogs for company.

The day after his incarceration the marquis petitioned M. de La Tour, governor of the duchy of Savoy, to restore his freedom, of which he said he had been deprived for no reason. "I give my word of honor," he added, "and I am not in the habit of violating such an oath, that I will not leave the city of Chambéry if granted the favor of having it as my place of detention. Won't this equally serve my family's purpose, which is none other than to prevent me from going to France sooner than it wishes, and why then should this favor be denied?"[2] He also asked that he be allowed to correspond freely with the outside world and asked that his servant be permitted to leave the fortress on various errands. On these two points his wishes were granted: henceforth he would be permitted to send and receive mail, provided that all letters received were opened and examined by M. de Launay. The marquis's servant would be allowed to leave the fortress on certain errands, but the usual precautions would be taken "both on exit and on entry."

The Red Chest

Donatien found his captivity increasingly difficult to bear. A visit from Carteron (who was not incarcerated with him) diverted him briefly, but his mood grew more and more bitter with each passing day. The valet, who returned to Chambéry on December 16, was not permitted to see him until the nineteenth. He reported to the marquis on his mission to Paris, where he had delivered certain important letters to Mme de Sade and various friends. No doubt he also brought news of the marquis's children, now reunited with their mother. Sade next ordered his servant to go to Nice to retrieve personal effects he had left there, along with his sister-in-law's baggage. A previously unpublished letter from the marquis offers details that confirm (if further evidence is required) that the canoness did indeed accompany him on his flight to Italy. The letter, dispatched to Carteron immediately after his departure for Nice, contains the marquis's instructions to his servant:

OBSERVATIONS FOR YOUR RETURN

Do not forget that I do not want to have to pay a cent when you arrive. You will go to the Pomme d'Or, store the affairs carefully in my room, then go directly, without dallying, to Chambéry and ask M. le comte de La Tour for permission to bring them to me. You will obtain a written order, and try not to be searched in Chambéry. If you fear a search, put you know what in your pocket.[3] Upon arriving at the fort, give your order to the commandant and bring your cart to the foot of my staircase. There we will sort out Mme de Launay's effects and pack them in a trunk, and the next day you will see to it that this trunk is shipped to Lyons and at the same time cash my letter of exchange, which I do not wish to entrust to anyone here.[4]

The marquis was not the only one concerned about his personal effects. His mother-in-law was also quite anxious, indeed terrified at the thought that personal items and documents belonging to the canoness were in his hands. What would he do with them? To avenge himself might he not reveal his idyll with the young lady to one and all? He had the goods to blackmail Mme de Montreuil and her entire family. La Présidente therefore left no stone unturned in her efforts to regain possession of her daughter's effects. On December 21 she wrote Count de La Marmora:

> We ask that such effects as he may have had with him for his own use or diversion and so necessary for a mind as lively as his be returned to him, with the exception of papers, manuscripts, and letters, regardless of their nature, which his family asks be sent to it, along with a small wooden box or chest, believed to be red in color with copper trim, which also contains papers. If he took this with him into the fort, please try to retrieve it without alerting him and remove any papers it contains.[5]

This chest, which probably contained Mlle de Launay's letters, was not found among the marquis's affairs. Perhaps it was in the trunks he expected to receive from Nice. Nevertheless, Mme de Montreuil was assured that every effort would be made to search any arriving baggage for the missing chest.[6] La Présidente also asked that, in addition to "manuscripts, letters, and other papers," any "wicked, immoral books" that the trunks might contain be seized as well.

Strangely, Mme de Montreuil also expressed the keenest interest in the illness with which her son-in-law had been stricken in November. Could the ambassador of the king of Sardinia provide her with additional information? Dr. Thonin was of course bound by doctor-patient confidentiality, but if M. de La Tour were willing to question him, he would ultimately talk. "It is of the utmost interest to the family," Mme de Montreuil insisted, "to know for certain what to believe about this story." If, indeed, it was a case of venereal disease, her younger daughter would certainly have been infected.

Mme de Montreuil's Prisoner

The marquis de Sade's true jailer at Miolans was none other than his own mother-in-law. She had pledged to assume the full cost of his upkeep: his board, that of his valet, the cost of furniture rental, bedding, table linen, supplies, pocket money, candles, firewood, breeches, stockings, barbers, tips to his guards—everything was charged to la Présidente, accounted for down to the last penny. Bear in mind, however, that her daughter now held the strings to the marquis's purse in her hands, so that M. de Sade was in fact kept in jail at his own expense. He not only paid for his imprisonment but even reimbursed the authorities for the cost of his arrest, including the postal coach that transported him to Miolans. Even the New Year's gifts given to his guards were paid for out of his own funds.

From a distance of more than three hundred miles Mme de Montreuil kept constant watch on her son-in-law's every move. She saw everything, heard everything, controlled everything, gave orders, set limits, tolerated some things, questioned others, scolded, punished, threatened—and demanded obedience. Everyone hastened to do her bidding, from M. de La Tour, the governor of Savoy, to the commandant of Miolans and the ministers of state and foreign affairs in Turin. Her recommendations were as good as orders, and Their Excellencies could hardly have been more eager to satisfy her desires. All paid indirect homage to this woman's intelligence and ability to bend circumstances to her will. If Mme de Montreuil managed so easily to lay down the law, it was partly, as has often been said, because she knew how to terrify but partly too because she knew how to command affection. Her letters reveal some of the secrets of her influence. In them one finds, cleverly combined with the expression of her will, a strategy of sentiment and flattery that skillfully deceived her correspondents— who found her all but irresistible. The compound of flattering mildness, false simplicity, and inflexible energy that we find in her letters tells us more than anything else about her powers of seduction.

La Présidente might thus appear to have been in command of the situation, but she was plagued by a terrible nightmare: the possibility that Donatien might escape. This idea became an obsession, and her repeated exhortations to vigilance come close to neurosis. Nothing was to be done that might in any way facilitate escape. But at the same time she remained keenly aware that her son-in-law was a nobleman and insisted that he be treated "with all the respect and comfort due to his birth and [allowed] such pleasures as may lessen the bitterness of his situation." She also wanted his real name to be kept secret from everyone except the comte de La Tour.

M. de Launay, always obediently attentive when confronting the imperious mother-in-law, scrupulously acceded to her demands: he redoubled his vigilance, tightened the already impressive security of the fortress, and had his prisoner watched day and night so that Donatien could not take a step without his being notified at once. The marquis grew impatient with the constant surveillance, which he regarded as persecution, and besieged the governor of Savoy with complaint after complaint. One day, M. de Launay refused to allow the marquis's valet to deliver a letter from his master. The commandant "persisted in his refusal," the marquis wrote, "with a tone and manners that my birth and military rank scarcely permit me to tolerate." The commandant, for his part, exasperated by his unaccommodating inmate, would have paid handsomely to be rid of him: "I can assure Your Excellency," he wrote the comte de La Tour,

that this seigneur is very dangerous, being as capricious as he is hot-tempered and unsteady, and that he might well make a sacrifice of me by winning someone over with money so as to make his escape, having already made frivolous propositions of the sort to me. For this reason, it would be wise for the relatives to ask that he be transferred to a fortress in France. One cannot be sure of anything with so volatile a mind . . . I beg you to inform the minister of this so as to protect me in case of any eventuality, despite all my precautions.[7]

The poor man also confessed his embarrassment at being unable to report on the content of intercepted letters. He found it impossible to decipher the marquis's handwriting and was in any case not blessed with a memory "fortunate enough" to remember what the letters said.

When la Présidente learned that Donatien was proposing to send reports of his situation to "eminent persons to whom he has the honor of being related," she became frightened and begged Count de La Marmora to examine the contents of these missives: "If they only beg for the goodness and understanding of those in the entourage of the king of France to whom he writes, and attempt to justify his most recent affair, there is no opposition to allowing them to pass. But if they contain false and injurious statements concerning his wife's family . . . it would be cruel to allow these imprudent texts to foist yet another fable on the public and the court, and more dreadful still if he were to have a memoir printed in Geneva, as he threatens his mother-in-law he will."

Meanwhile, early in 1773, the already tense relations between M. de Launay and his prisoner turned poisonous. On January 14 a violent scene erupted between the two men. When the commandant went to Sade's room to inform him of the good news that the comte de La Tour hoped to obtain his prompt release, Donatien received him with an outburst of "the most atrocious invective" in the presence of Lieutenant Duclos, who had become a friend, and the textile merchant Ansard, who happened to be visiting. Prudently, M. de Launay withdrew "to avoid a worse scene" but threatened to put the marquis in a cell with a guard at his door—at Donatien's expense. In reporting the incident to de La Tour, the commandant gave reasons for Sade's enmity. A few days earlier, Donatien had sent a package to his kitchen containing wine, coffee, and chocolate. The officer had returned the package forthwith with the message that he did not accept gifts from anyone. Afraid, however, that some of the guards might prove less scrupulous, he had proposed to lock the marquis in his room, "for otherwise there could be violence, against which I have no security." That same day, Donatien offered his own version of the facts: "We have just had another violent crisis with the commandant," he reported to the governor. "I am not used to being addressed with words like 'Fucker' and 'Bugger,' and M. de Launay's rather indecent way of expressing himself drove me to answer him somewhat vehemently." He asked to be placed henceforth under the sole authority of M. de La Balme, the second in command, "a man of honesty and good manners." This was the only way to avoid terrible rows in the future, Donatien maintained, for "there will always be a veritable danger in placing a man of honor who has received an education under M. de Launay's orders."[8]

Stratagems

On February 14 M. de Sade asked de La Tour to transmit a petition he had just drafted to King Charles-Emmanuel III.[9] The text read:

A mother-in-law guided by most odious self-interest, and who aspires to nothing but my total ruin, profiting from my misfortunes to call down on me all the rigor of the law, to have me condemned, and thus to oblige me to absent myself forever . . . has used the credit acquired through disreputable stratagems to persuade, by roundabout means, Your Majesty's minister in France to serve her in her vengeance . . . Sire, if this unjust woman who wants to destroy me were afraid only of my protests, why would she try to circumvent a deserved punishment? Why would she not have me imprisoned in my own country? She knows full well that the king, my master, would not allow her to.[10]

To believe the marquis, Mme de Montreuil had sought the harshest possible sentence for him and was now seeking to prevent him from reappearing before his judges for the sole purpose of ruining him completely and laying hold of his property.

Meanwhile, M. de Launay remained on his guard. For some time he had been observing suspicious activities in the fortress. These intrigued him, and he reported on them to the governor. The growing intimacy between the marquis and Lieutenant Duclos, with whom he dined almost every evening, particularly worried the commandant. Meanwhile, other information, no less troubling, also came to the governor's attention. The Sardinian ambassador to France informed him on February 26, 1773, that Mme de Sade had just left for Provence, "but there is every reason to believe that she has taken the road to Savoy in order to attempt to see her husband." Such an interview was to be prevented by all available means, for its consequences could prove disastrous. The governor was advised to transmit the necessary orders to the commandant.

•

A short while later, another, less serious incident further disturbed the commandant's repose. This time it was a dispute between M. de Sade and a fellow prisoner, the baron de L'Allée. To dispel the boredom the two men had decided to play a round of faro. The baron, who enjoyed a remarkable flair for winning at cards, took the marquis for twelve louis, exactly the amount he had just received to buy a watch. Since having the watch meant more to him than paying his debt, he begged his partner to postpone payment until the day of his release. The baron reacted very badly and demanded to be paid within the hour. Donatien reported the incident to the governor but added a detail that weighed against the baron and was an outright slur on the honor of de Launay: "I cannot hide from your excellency," he wrote, "that the same M. le baron de L'Allée locked up my servant [Latour], a young man of good family who was recommended to me and who may some day have property, and that he won from him in the same game a hundred gold louis of France in two days . . . Fortune was too decidedly on his side for it not to appear more than likely that he had the knack of controlling it." But that was not all. Although gambling was strictly forbidden within the walls of the prison, M. de Launay did nothing to stop it. Donatien even went so far as to insinuate that he profited from it. In addition, since his servant could not make good his losses, the baron had had him sign a note payable in three years and had done so in the presence of the commandant. As for himself, he readily agreed to pay the twelve louis he had lost, but he asked the comte de La Tour to order that the note for a hundred louis be returned to his young servant, for he would never be in a position to pay such an amount without ruining his family. Of course he also asked the governor to keep secret what he had just revealed. Any indiscretion would expose him to "further difficulties with M. de Launay or to heated quarrels with the baron."[11]

In Paris, meanwhile, Mme de Sade's departure had plunged la Présidente into deep anxiety. To rescue her husband, she believed, Renée-Pélagie was capable of anything. Would she try to see him or to help him escape? No doubt she revealed her worries to the duc d'Aiguillon, because the duke offered Count de La Marmora detailed advice concerning the possible momentous consequences of Mme de Sade's plans. The French foreign minister informed the king of Sardinia's ambassador that "the principal objective" was to see to it that the "comte de Mazan" remained in custody.

Suspicions

In view of Mme de Sade's activities, the commandant of Miolans lived in anxiety, always alert, ready to take action at the first sign of trouble. Convinced that a conspiracy was afoot to abet the prisoner's escape, he tightened his surveillance another notch and tried hard to secure the transfer of Lieutenant Duclos, who was far too familiar with the marquis and whose behavior struck the commandant as more and more suspicious. Having learned the week before that the lieutenant went down from the mountain at a very early hour every morning, he had him followed and discovered that he had been at least once to visit Mme de Sade at Montmélian. M. de Launay therefore urged the governor to transfer Lieutenant Duclos, who was in any case at odds with all his superiors. Otherwise he asked to be relieved of command himself. As long as Duclos was at the citadel, he refused to accept responsibility for what might happen. Another focus of his concern was young Latour, who pretended to be Sade's servant but whom the marquis himself passed off as the bastard son of the duke of Bavaria and who was in fact none other than his "companion in debauch."

Recantations

Despite appearances, Donatien did not remain deaf to M. de Launay's counsel. Since his fulminations had achieved no effect, why not take a gentler approach and try the "submissions" that the commandant was always recommending? He therefore drafted a lengthy memorandum to the comte de La Tour in which he pledged not to receive any more letters "that the whole earth might not read." He then went straight to the subject of his imprisonment and the motives behind it. Why was his family so determined to bury him at Miolans? He saw only one reason, or at any rate only one essential reason, the one advanced by the family itself: his affair with his sister-in-law, "the desire to end a misplaced and unfortunate intrigue." In that case, "they carry their rancor too far," he complained, "because I have quite honestly stated that I renounce, I continue to make the same statement every day, and do so now in the most explicit terms . . . What must I do, Sir, in order to be believed? I beg you to offer me advice. I break off all communication, I offer to return all letters, I swear never to go within a hundred leagues of Paris for as long as they wish, and I promise to suppress any memorandum, petition, or injurious statement that might undermine or interfere with an establishment on account of which they fear me and yet which I desire perhaps more than they. They still do not believe me. What then must I do?"[12]

Although no name is mentioned here, the final lines of this letter fairly clearly imply that an offer had been made for the hand of Anne-Prospère and that Donatien would do nothing to prevent the marriage, to which he looked forward more eagerly than anyone else. The man she was to marry was Antoine-François, vicomte de Beaumont. A better match could not have been found: the young man belonged to a very old family, and his uncle was none other than the archbishop of Paris, Christophe de Beaumont, the man who condemned Rousseau's *Emile* and to whom Rousseau later addressed his famous letter. Rigid, rigorous in the extreme, and a powerful enemy of the Enlightenment, this prelate was engaged in a never-ending war against *philosophes* and libertines. The scandal that would erupt if his own nephew were to marry the sister-in-law and mistress of a debauchee under sentence of death for attempted murder and sodomy was not difficult to imagine. The family reportedly would consent to the marriage only on the express condition that Sade remain imprisoned for life.[13]

A short while later, Mme de Montreuil asked Count de La Marmora to thank the authorities for the "firmness and politeness" they displayed toward her daughter on her mission to Savoy, but she reiterated her wish that M. de Sade "not inundate the public with his dreadful writings and memoirs, which only aggravate his wrongs." Such a course was essential "to his true interests." Apart from this, la Présidente too seems to have embarked on the course of conciliation, going so far as to intervene with Launay to save Lieutenant Duclos.

Even toward Donatien the tone of her letters became noticeably milder. Had his recantation reassured her? Did she now feel that she had attained sufficient power over him? Or was it simply that Anne-Prospère was about to marry, thus removing the principal cause of her anxiety?

The Grace of the Sacrament

Launay now reported that M. de Sade had "begun to humanize himself." He had finally realized that his attacks on la Présidente and unremitting rebelliousness were only delaying his release. "I see no signs that he plans to attempt an escape," the commandant noted, "although I continue to take the same precautions as before."

A veritable metamorphosis had taken place: the ranter had suddenly turned into a humble penitent, anxious for the prize of pardon. On April 1 he submitted to M. de La Tour a petition couched in the humblest of terms. That same day de Launay informed the governor that Sade was displaying growing confidence in him, although he seemed "very worried and melancholy about his detention." When Easter came, the marquis, after discharging his duties as a Christian, "suddenly changed his mood and behavior." Not content, M. de La Tour reported, simply to beg the commandant's forgiveness for all that he had said and written against him, "he begged to be allowed to make amends, in [Launay's] presence, to several of the officers and cadre of the garrison who had been frightened at times by his outbursts." The governor's report concluded: "This change for the better seems to me to be a clear effect of the grace of the sacrament."[14]

The Escape

Every night M. de Sade took dinner in his room with the baron de L'Allée, with whom he was now reconciled after earlier disputes. But since the meals brought to them from the distant canteen generally arrived cold, he asked for permission to dine in the canteen with his companion. The commandant saw no reason to object and ordered that they be served in a room in Lieutenant Duclos's apartment adjacent to the canteen. Off this room was a small storage room, generally locked, where the cook kept supplies and in one corner of which there were latrines. Sade knew this part of the fortress well because he had often visited his friend Duclos in these very rooms. He had noticed that the window of the latrines was the only one without bars in the entire edifice. It was large enough, moreover, for a stout man to pass through. The window overlooked the rear of the fort, on the mountain side, from a height of roughly fourteen and a half feet.

On the night of April 29, the marquis's messenger, Joseph Violon, while prowling in the yard around the dungeon, found a way to engage in a brief conference with him. The following day, anticipating that he would be up all that night, the young man slept until four in the afternoon at a cabaret in Saint-Pierre d'Albigny. Then he headed for the fort and took up a position just underneath the latrine window.

That night, at seven o'clock, the marquis de Sade and the baron de L'Allée went as usual to dinner in the canteen. They were served by Latour, who, after making sure that the cook and his staff were eating dinner and would not need to go to the storeroom, stole the key and hastened to his master's cell, where, after lighting candles, he left on the table two sealed messages addressed to M. de Launay. He then quietly rejoined the two friends, who continued their tranquil dinner. At 8:30 the three prisoners entered the storeroom and proceeded to the latrines. M. de Sade carefully folded his frock coat and placed it, along with his hat, on a chair. He then climbed out the window, followed by the two others. Violon, who was waiting below, had brought a small ladder to help them down. With the young Savoyard as guide, the fugitives rapidly made their getaway under cover of darkness, heading for the French border.

At around nine o'clock, the marquis's guard, who had just finished dinner, returned to his post at the prisoner's door. Seeing light through the keyhole, he assumed that the two friends were playing checkers. Rather than take M. de L'Allée back to his room as he was supposed to do, he let the men continue to play. M. de Sade greatly disliked being interrupted in the middle of a game, and just the night before he had raised quite a fuss when the guard had come for the baron. Since everything appeared to be normal, the guard decided to take a little nap, lay down fully clothed on his bed (remember that his room was next to the marquis's), and fell into a deep sleep. At three in the morning he awoke with a start and again peered through the keyhole. The candles were still burning. Suspecting that something was up, he ran to alert M. de Launay. The commandant jumped out of bed, ran to the prisoner's room, had the door opened, and found no one inside. Next to the dying candles, he found two letters with his name on them: one from the marquis de Sade, the other from the baron de L'Allée. Feverishly he opened the first and to his amazement read these words:

Sir,

If anything can spoil the joy I feel in freeing myself from my chains, it is my fear
that you may be held responsible for my escape. After all your decency and
kindness, I cannot conceal from you the fact that this thought troubles me.

This jubilantly derisive tone continues throughout the letter. Sade
offered his word of honor that the commandant had not abetted his
escape: "Your vigilance delayed it by several days," and "I owe [my
success] solely to my own stratagems." After a few ironic remarks
concerning the commandant's "efforts" and "attentions" to improve
the prisoners' sad lot, the tenor of the letter turns threatening. There
must be no attempt to recapture him: "Fifteen well-armed men with
good horses are waiting for me below the château," he warned, "and
all are resolved to sacrifice their lives rather than allow me to be re-
captured." These mercenaries, supposedly recruited and armed by his
wife and ready for anything, were pure fiction, though surely Sade
would have liked to escape in such a fashion, like the hero of a novel.
But the purpose of the story for now was simply to intimidate M. de
Launay. If the commandant sent the garrison after his escort, there
was a danger of "massacring a lot of people" and of causing even
"more to be hacked up," and in any case the marquis would not be
taken alive: "I shall defend my liberty if it costs me my life." Ever the
romantic!

The marquis ended his letter with a mocking expression of thanks:
"All that remains, dear commandant, is to thank you for all your
kindness. I shall remember it all my life. I hope only to have the
opportunity to persuade you of it. A day will come, I hope, when I shall
be permitted to give full expression to the feelings of gratitude you
have inspired in me, and with which, my dear commandant, I am
honored to be your most humble and obedient servant. [signed] The
marquis de Sade."[15]

The fugitive had also taken pains to prepare a detailed inventory
of the objects left behind in his cell, some items of which appear to
have been abandoned with sarcastic intent. In addition to a wooden
bed, a potty chair, a mattress, linen, silver-plated arms, and six maps
that had decorated the walls, the list included a bidet, a porcelain bowl,
a cup and saucer, a glass, two towels, and a chamber pot. A "brand
new" blue frock coat and a pair of stockings had been left at the site
of the escape and would have to be retrieved from the cook. And there
were also "two sleeping dogs, one all black, the other with white marks,
to which I am quite attached."[16]

12

The Fugitive

Commando Raid at La Coste

The night had just fallen on the village of La Coste, which cowered uneasily at the base of its château. Aureoled in moonlight, the château's main tower stood out in silhouette against the winter sky, enveloped in a vast silence. Suddenly an indistinct murmur could be heard, apparently coming from the direction of the road. As the source of the noise drew nearer, one could make out the sound of hoofbeats mingled with the clatter of spurs. The light of many torches revealed a troop of horsemen passing through the Lower Gate and advancing on the château. The troop commander, wearing a police uniform, rode at the head of the column. Seven constables, readily recognizable by their uniforms, formed his escort, and three brigades of Marseilles deputies brought up the rear.

Using ladders they scaled the castle walls, broke down the gates, and forced their way in. Terrified, Mme de Sade ran out to meet the invaders. Their officer, pistol in one hand, sword in the other, and an expression of "frenzy painted on his face," demanded, "with the most dreadful oaths" and "the most indecent expressions," to know where her husband was. "I must have him, dead or alive," he screamed. The poor woman "saw barbarity before her eyes. Her feelings alternated between horror and terror." She told the officer that M. de Sade was absent. "This word was the signal for the most terrifying furor." The troops split up. Some guarded the approaches to the château, while others searched the rooms, weapons in hand, ready to wreak havoc at the first sign of resistance. One even brandished an iron tool for picking the locks on doors and furniture. When it became clear that the marquis was nowhere to be found, the assailants' frenzy increased. Pouring into his study, they made a shambles of it in seconds, slashing family portraits, while their officer, more infuriated than his troops, tore into chests and armoires, seizing papers and letters. In the wink of an eye he separated the documents he wished to keep from those he did not and tossed handfuls of the rejects into the fireplace; the rest he confiscated. Mme de Sade stood by helpless, clutching a tobacco box of shell rimmed with gold and embellished with a miniature, probably a portrait of her husband, in the hope of saving it from the general devastation. Catching sight of this object, the officer snatched it away and denounced the marquis in the coarsest of terms, which only spurred his men to still greater fury. Some of them threatened to kill the marquis and deliver his body to Mme de Montreuil.

At last the horde withdrew, "having had its fill of cruelty and infamy." On their way back to the village, some of the troops began shouting, "He's captured! We have the bugger!" This was to forestall a possible (though highly unlikely) riot in the village. All this took place on the night of January 6 and the early hours of January 7, 1774.

·

But where had Donatien gone? At dawn on May 1, 1773, M. de Sade and the baron de L'Allée, accompanied by their young guide, came within view of the French border. Exhausted from their all-night march, they decided to rest in the small village of Chapareillant, and the marquis availed himself of the opportunity to write a short note to the governor of Savoy: "The extreme cruelty of a mother-in-law who has no authority over me and the lies, deceptions, and frauds with which I have been hoodwinked for so long are my only reasons for embarking on this perilous course. Your kindness, Sir, leaves me with some regrets. I am sorry to have been so unworthy of it, but the horror of my situation mattered more, and it became impossible for me to hold out any longer. The violence in my blood resists punishments of this type. They are incompatible with me, and I prefer death to the loss of my liberty."[1]

At this point the trail goes cold. While Mme de Montreuil and her daughter both clamored for Donatien's personal effects, especially the letters left behind at Miolans after his escape, the fugitive led a nomadic existence. We know only that he went to Bordeaux and that from there he asked his mother-in-law to send him the funds he would need to flee to Spain. Was he in Cadiz in July 1773, as Mme de Sade told the comte de La Tour, or was this information intended to cover his tracks? What is certain is that by the autumn of 1773 he was back in La Coste. He rarely ventured outside the walls of the château and spent long hours walking in the park or reading in his study, ready to flee at a moment's notice. On the night of January 6, 1774, he was warned about a half-hour before the police arrived that they were coming to arrest him, and he managed to make his getaway.[2] For the next several weeks he hid either in Ripert's "*grange*," his home, or with one or another of the local farmers.[3]

The Plot

Renée-Pélagie saw immediately who was behind the police operation: her mother. Mme de Montreuil had acted at the behest of the Beaumonts, the family of Anne-Prospère's suitor. "The latest scene," Donatien wrote Ripert, "had no other purpose than to remove Mlle de Launay's letters, the family of the archbishop of Paris having insisted on this ceremony before giving her the marquis de Beaumont, his nephew, for her husband. You may spread this news everywhere," the marquis perfidiously added, "along with the story of the expedition, which has caused so much talk. You should use it to cut off any nasty rumors that may circulate about me."[4]

By dint of much effort, la Présidente managed to persuade the king to issue two related orders to M. de Sartine, the *lieutenant de police*, on December 16, 1773: one was for a search of the marquis's château and seizure of all his papers, the other for his arrest and incarceration at Pierre-Encize in view of the old lettre de cachet issued at the time of the Arcueil affair. Mme de Montreuil immediately contacted Inspector Goupil of the Paris police, with whom she had already met several times at her home, for the purpose of planning the raid scheduled for the night of January 6. The purpose of the raid was to arrest the fugitive and seize any papers in his possession—and nothing more. Above all there was to be no violence. The violent events of that night were not ordered by Mme de Montreuil (violence was not her style). The police had simply run amok, as police are wont to do from time to time.

This ill-advised adventure wound up costing Mme de Montreuil a small fortune, for Goupil's bill for his services came to no less than 8,235 livres, 12 sols.[5] This expense, combined with other costs associated with her daughter's situation and the care of her grandchildren, proved a strain even on the Montreuils' substantial resources. "I find myself, as it happens, in the most urgent distress as regards Mme de

Sade," she confided to her friend Mme Necker. "You know, quite apart from more serious misfortunes, that her husband left his affairs in disarray, with the income from land alienated for a number of years and creditors, in Paris as well as Provence, tired of waiting and gone to law. The entire family, moreover, has to be kept alive. I have done all I could, but I am drained. The January business cost me more than 8,000 livres, for nothing as you know, and surely no one will ever reimburse me."[6]

The Secret Agent

Mme de Montreuil received assistance from various people in Provence other than Inspector Goupil. There can be no doubt that Maître Fage was one of them. I have found a dozen of his letters to la Présidente, which make an overwhelming case against him. It should be pointed out, however, that Fage also did his utmost to dissuade Mme de Montreuil from ordering the police raid, although in the end he gave his consent and even participated himself. If we are to make sense of his sometimes ambiguous reactions, we must bear in mind that his relations with the Sades had deteriorated over the winter of 1773. Fage had become exasperated with the lord of La Coste's "mischievous dealings," for Sade made endless demands, paid for services rendered with salvoes of insult, and showed little inclination to pay his debts to the notary. Things had reached the point where by the end of the year Fage's resignation seemed imminent. By contrast, Renée-Pélagie and Donatien berated the scribe as though he were a common servant while harassing him with their demands for money. Their disrespect was only compounded by the fact that they knew him to be in correspondence with la Présidente and strongly suspected him of spying for her. They were not mistaken. His letters, which are published here for the first time, clearly reveal his allegiance to Mme de Montreuil. He found in her an attentive ear, a person to whom he could complain and submit his requests for reimbursement of sums advanced out of his own funds. In exchange, he kept la Présidente regularly informed of what her daughter and son-in-law were up to. On December 9, 1773, he wrote: "Although my greatest crime is to be in contact with you, and although your only knowledge of what is going on comes from me, I am nevertheless at your service here. If I should be fortunate enough to find an opportunity to be of some service to you, I would seize it most eagerly."[7]

The notary's relations with the Sades underwent an abrupt change during the winter of 1773. On December 21 he wrote his patroness:

"I am in the midst of a terrible crisis. La Coste deals with me in the most violent manner, although my dealings with them [i.e., the Sades] are as honest as can be. You are not unaware of the facts, Madame. Here is the fruit of my efforts: this copy of a letter I received a moment ago will convince you of my sad situation." Enclosed was a letter from the marquis, who promised the notary a thrashing: "Please, Sir, do not expose me to such scenes. You will surely have an unpleasant one if you fail me, for I shall immediately climb on my horse and come prove to you that no one fools with me with impunity. In the name of God, let us both avoid such dreadful and vexing things. I have nothing to lose! The pleasure of vengeance is today the only pleasure I know, and I warn you, you will make me savor it in tragic fashion if you offend me by failing to honor arrangements that I swear to you must be irrevocable."

Fage comments: "Do not leave me in this sad situation, Madame. You are my only resource. You see that they are furious with me. Some of my letters have undoubtedly reached them. But what can they find in them other than my views for their benefit and for the order I should like to bring to their affairs? I had no other purpose in writing you. You must see that justice is done, and how little I deserve the treatment I have received."[8]

Concerning the fate of his letters to la Présidente, a matter that tormented him more than he let on, Mme de Montreuil was able to offer reassurance: "Rest assured, Sir, that none of the letters that you have written me have passed, or could have passed, from me to strange hands; I have them all. Thus if any were intercepted, it can only have been from your own post. In any case, when one is guided by reason and honesty, as you are, and as I am, one can hold one's head high."[9] In the margin of this letter Fage wrote: "Secret. To keep."

Fage's Betrayal

Ten days later Fage's relations with Sade had improved for reasons we do not know. Upon learning that Mme de Montreuil planned to have the marquis arrested, he tried to dissuade her:

You will no doubt grant that between this house and myself there is a veritable lovers' mania, disagreements serving only to augment the love of lovers. We are in precisely the same situation. The words "cher avocat" and "avocat de Dieu" are again current, having been substituted for the "Monsieur" that they used to affect to use in almost every sentence. Once again we are on familiar terms and the best friends in the world. Please God that it continues! Surely any obstacle will not come from my side. My dealings toward them are the same as ever, and with your assistance I shall always go beyond the impossible in their behalf.

At this point an anonymous letter arrived, informing the Sades that Madame de Montreuil had obtained a warrant for her son-in-law's arrest. Neither Donatien nor Renée-Pélagie took the warning seriously. Fage witnessed the scene, which he faithfully reported to la Présidente, not without apprising her of his reservations:

They [M. and Mme de Sade] showed me an anonymous letter warning that you had obtained an order from the king for M. de Sade's arrest. You have its contents, signed by me and abbé Gardiolle. This warning is most genuine. This warning was unanimously regarded as a counterfeit for the purpose of intimidation. They cannot imagine that at a time when you are flattering them with the fondest hopes concerning their affairs, especially as to their management, that you would have solicited an order like the one of which they have been informed.

If you will allow me, Madame, to tell you what I think and what my devotion to the person compels me to say, I will point out that if this order is as genuine as they assume it is counterfeit, the house will be still further disrupted and hatred exacerbated to an extreme.

The disruption is inevitable. You know the personalities better than I. To begin with, it is certain that Mme de Sade will do all she possibly can to get him out of trouble . . . Furthermore, I strongly doubt that they will ever succeed in capturing him . . . In any case, if it were to be carried out by someone from Paris, he will be obliged to stay here for a long time if he hopes to capture him . . .

Arranging his affairs and later finding ways to limit his expenditures and cut off all dissipation seems to me a more proper and useful course of action. There is first of all nothing to fear about his leaving La Coste: his only occupations there are walking in his park, spending time with some workman, or closeting himself in his study to read. Once the amount he had to spend had been established, there was no need to say more. As to his attachment to Mme de Sade, he has never seemed more constant to me. There was even reason to hope that he would remain calm for a fairly long time.

About all of this, Madame, you are more perspicacious than I, and if the thing is as it has been represented, then surely you must know what you are doing. My only wish is that this not lead to something worse and that in order to avoid one evil you are not courting a greater one.[10]

Mme de Montreuil paid no attention to this advice and continued to work with Inspector Goupil on the plans for January 6. She wrote, however, to Fage asking for his help, for without him nothing could be done. After much beating around the bush, the notary finally gave in, but not without informing la Présidente of his deep worries:

Ah, Madame, what a cruel mission you assign me! I shall never be able to resolve myself to be an instrument in the arrest of a person whom I cannot abandon regardless of what he may have done. What will become of that respectable lady [Mme de Sade]? What dreadful disorder do I foresee? And how difficult it will be to put all of this behind us! You cannot imagine how deeply I am affected, and how concerned I am for the interests of all parties. I cannot, however, avoid going to Aix. A letter from the intendant summons me there, and I am leaving tomorrow with the person who brought me your letters. I tell you again, this is a very sad commission for me. At a time like this I wish I had never known this house. God forgive this family . . . No, I will never take part in this. You must be satisfied if I simply do nothing contrary to your interests. Upon my return from Aix I shall be honored to tell you more about it.

For the rest, I beg you, Madame, to write me a letter that I can communicate in which it appears that I disapprove of the order and wrote you about it on the basis of the knowledge I obtained from the anonymous letter, and which also contains the reasons that compelled you to request the order. I will then have the means to make them understand that they have only themselves to blame. It will be of great help to me in dealing with Mme de Sade.[11]

This letter should not be taken at face value. If the notary protests too much, it is because, being a prudent man, he wants to cover himself against any future recriminations. The future is always unpredictable: what if his letters should come to the attention of Mme de Sade? It might be best to demonstrate a virtuous indignation against her mother's plans. And, two precautions being better than one, Mme de Montreuil wrote him a letter exonerating him of any involvement in the affair. I have found a copy of this letter in la Présidente's hand:

I cannot hide from you, Sir, my surprise at the heat with which you disapprove the order warned against by the anonymous letter of which you signed a copy. I do not deny being aware of it, nor do I deny that this was the greatest service that, under the present circumstances, the ministry could have rendered to the two families and to M. de S[ade] himself. There was a general outcry against his public residence in his own home, and the style that Mme de S[ade] used toward many people, which was [known] to have been inspired by him, embittered attitudes and failed to prove any change in either his way of thinking or his behavior. If they had followed the advice I have been giving them for a year, this course of action would not have been necessary despite my vast grounds for complaint. However, with such individuals, who always want to lay down the law and have their way in everything, [even resorting to the most infamous stratagems],[12] there is no way to follow a plan or to do any good at all.

No doubt, Sir, you are unaware of many things—that I see. Otherwise you would regard as a great boon what you now regard as a great evil. Despite all the *very serious*[13] matters I have to complain about, as regards both of them, I have nevertheless concerned myself with ways to liquidate this most vexing matter, and the memoir I discussed with you is not ideal.[14]

Finally, on January 6, the police searched La Coste in the manner described earlier. Upon learning of the failure of the mission to arrest the marquis, Fage panicked. He realized that he had been used and let his patroness know that he resented it. On the day after the bungled commando raid he wrote:

You have utterly compromised me by attempting to associate me with the operation in question. I participated only with the greatest reluctance, and it would have been more prudent, for the good of the operation, if I had taken no part in it. It was a partial failure, despite all M. de Goupil's diligence, zeal, measures, and precautions. The plan could not have been better, and no other was as likely to succeed. But the nameless person from Paris whom you know and a warning given a half-hour before the arrival at the château led to the failure of the mission. As for papers, I am bound to compliment M. Goupil, who carried out his mission with all possible scrupulousness and attention. He was, moreover, quite successful, with respect not only to that portion of the papers in which you were interested but also to another, which it is in your vital interest to preserve, as I shall be pleased to demonstrate to you at another time.

I am now going to busy myself with calming the unfortunate lady [Mme de Sade]. I would not have left her yesterday if she had not had Sieur de Vaulx de Montélimar with her in her home, a man who as you know has the lady's interests at heart. I already have some assurance from him that he will try to persuade her to obey the king's orders. Everyone would be equally inclined to do so but for the fear that the imprisonment may be perpetual. One thing is crucial for success: to make sure that funds sent to pay the most pressing debts are sent elsewhere, so that they do not fall into his hands and facilitate his escape to a foreign country. It is true that in that case I fear for the china and silver. I shall, however, do my utmost to save it . . . I am afraid that some papers may still be missing and that some were taken away. I could, with patience, try to get hold of them. Rest assured of my diligence in that regard, and after examining the documents that will soon reach you, let me know what may be missing.[15]

Where would it end? Not content to play the spy and participate in police raids, the notary here volunteers to spirit away his clients' papers. Disloyalty, villainy, and deceit appear to have been the primary traits of this generally unsympathetic character.[16] It is certain, moreover, that he misappropriated Sade's funds. Taking advantage of the sorry state in which the marquis left his finances, Fage manipulated his client's property as he pleased, and for his own benefit. The marquis had been stripped of his civil rights, Mme de Sade paid little attention to business matters, and Mme de Montreuil was far away. No one was about to look over his shoulder, unless of course he resigned his commission and his role as proxy was taken over by someone else. He would then be obliged to return the marquis's books and render an accounting. That is why his attitude continually alternated, for tactical reasons, between exasperation (whether feigned or real) and expressions of fidelity, which he swore burst spontaneously from his lips. At times he announced he was on the verge of dropping the whole business: he was ruined, scorned, mistreated, tired of "wicked dealings," and so on. But at other times he changed his tune and resolved in spite of everything to remain at his post out of pure "devotion" to "that respectable lady," Mme de Sade, to "the unfortunate man to whom she is wedded," and to the whole family, which he claimed he could not abandon without misgivings.

But he who plays with fire often burns himself in the end. Persuaded that Fage had betrayed them, M. and Mme de Sade decided once and for all to get rid of him. Mme de Montreuil, who had her own doubts about his honesty, refused to take up his cause. She had received, moreover, an anonymous letter, dated February 21, 1774, warning her against the notary's financial mismanagement: "Mme la Présidente de Montreuil is urged to delay transmittal of the 4,500 francs that M. Fage so emphatically requested for Sieur Boze, because there is ample reason to believe that this is a double payment, that he paid Mme de Gadagne twice, and that he dared to make four entries of 4,500 francs in his accounts instead of two, which would amount to a swindle of 9,000 livres. Sieur Fage is a known swindler who must be sacked."[17]

On February 3 Mme de Sade notified Ripert, her local steward in Mazan, that owing to "very serious matters of discontent" she had decided to cut her ties to M. Fage. Hence he, Ripert, was henceforth to render accounts not to the notary but to her alone, commencing with the most recent lease.[18] To succeed Fage she had chosen one of his colleagues, an Apt notary generally known simply as "Monsieur l'avocat." His name was Gaspard François Xavier Gaufridy, "attorney at the bar and royal notary of the city of Apt." We have encountered him before: the reader will recall Donatien's former playmate, the boy of his own age who had accompanied him and his little cousin Pauline on walks at his grandmother d'Astouaud's. Indeed, no one seemed more capable of restoring order to the marquis's affairs, for Gaufridy's father, Marcian Gaufridy, had at one time been the administrator of the marquis's father's property.

The Emigré

Ever since the police raid on La Coste, the marquis de Sade had been a hunted man, forced to seek a new refuge every day and convinced, with good reason, that his mother-in-law would doggedly pursue him to the bitter end, regardless of the cost. As long as he remained on French soil, the danger of arrest hovered over him. In early March of 1774 he therefore decided to emigrate to Italy and commissioned Ripert to find him the necessary funds. In a letter to the provost of Mazan he gave detailed instructions about how to obtain the needed cash.[19]

Monsieur le Curé

On March 11, the marquis traveled by carriage as far as Pont-Saint-Esprit. To avoid being recognized, he had donned the cassock of Ripert's brother, a priest. In this same disguise he traveled down the Rhône as far as Marseilles. The journey went well except for one minor incident, which must have delighted Donatien. While crossing the Durance, the ferry's rope broke and the craft drifted in the current for some time. Thinking that their final hour had arrived, the passengers threw themselves at the feet of the "curé" to make their last confession.[20]

Little is known about Donatien's time in Italy. We do not even know what cities he stayed in. But he soon found himself short of cash,

as we know from Mme de Sade's letter of May 12, 1774, to Ripert
mentioning a need for an additional 1,500 livres:

What I am going to add here from M. de Sade, my dear Ripert, is of the utmost
secrecy. You must not speak of it to anyone. After arriving safely at his destination and paying in advance for rent, furniture, and so forth—for abroad
one has nothing but the money in one's hand—someone recognized him.
Unwilling to trust to this person's discretion, he left secretly that night for
another location, which meant incurring additional expenses, so that, given
the exchange of currency, he finds himself short by 1,500 livres of what he
needs for the time remaining. He will not need it until August, but I must
dispatch this sum by early July if it is to reach him in time. So, my dear Ripert,
oblige me, I beg you, without speaking of this to anyone. If pledges are needed,
I will give them, and I will pay back the sum no earlier than six months or a
year from now, as required. Above all do not speak of this to anyone, lest it
get back to my uncles, who would scream like eagles.[21]

These "uncles" were of course the abbé de Sade and the *commandeur*, who represented the family's interests as long as the fugitive's
civil rights remained forfeit. In order to secure the sum of 1,500 livres,
Renée-Pélagie declared her willingness to pawn "a vermilion bowl [or]
a silver coffee pot. If that will not do, a jewelry box or silver medallion.
All these things are worth infinitely more than I am asking."[22] Concerned only with sending this money to Donatien, she forgot about the
creditors, who in the end lost patience: on May 29 she complained
that the Jew Beaucaire, not content with demanding his due in writing,
"came and made a terrible row in the château." Not finding her there,
he made his presence abundantly known in the town.[23]

Meanwhile, M. de Sade pressed his steward to do whatever had
to be done to obtain the money he wanted, offering a pretext scarcely
more credible than his wife's: "What is more, my accounts were totally
wrong," he wrote Ripert on May 29, 1774. "I forgot a trivial little item:
my food. All these calculations prove to you, my dear friend, that I
need money. Kindly leave no stone unturned to amass the sum, and
do not expose me to the horrible inconvenience of running short in a
foreign country, where, having neither resources nor recommendations, I already pass for being far too much of an adventurer."[24]

Mme de Sade Files a Complaint

Just before her husband's departure for Italy, Mme de Sade had put the finishing touches on a memorandum in which she accused her mother of having organized the January 6 raid. She then had the memorandum incorporated in a formal petition by Gaufridy and sent it to the Châtelet (a sovereign court in Paris). In all likelihood it was Donatien himself who drafted this petition, whose style bears little resemblance to that of his wife and still less to the notary's mishmash prose. On the point of leaving La Coste, he hastened its dispatch. Gaufridy, as was his wont, took his time, which earned him this reprimand (the first in a long line) from the furious marquis, now in Italy:

I cannot tell you, Sir, how sorry I am that you allow my affairs to languish so long. That is not what you promised me. My mother-in-law was to have been subpoenaed the week after my departure, but the attorney is just now preparing his objections. Truly things are going well. I think that the whole world is joined in a conspiracy against me, and that it has been decreed that I shall not find a friend or protector anywhere. It would be very dangerous if I were to convince myself of this truth. It would drive me to furious extremes. When the court denies me my rights, I shall make my own rights, and instead of serving me by these delays, one will have plunged me into irreparable misfortunes. That is what your negligence will bring me, Sir, and that is what I shall receive for having given you my complete confidence.[25]

•

Mme de Sade's petition retraced one by one all the "misfortunes" that had befallen her husband since the beginning of 1772, in each instance denouncing her own mother, la Présidente de Montreuil, as the sole author of the marquis's difficulties. The violence of these attacks, the passionate eloquence of the prose, the imprecatory style, even the rhythm of the sentences bear the mark of Sade's own hand. Mme de Sade begins by stating that she has been forced to

resort to the protection of the law to repel the most flagrant harassment that ever existed. An innocent victim of the most sacred attachment reclaims rights of humanity that have been insulted for too long . . . Daughters of Heaven, Justice, Truth, Tenderness, Compassion! You alone can tell us by what fate it comes to pass that you no longer preside over the feelings, actions, or dealings of Mme de Montreuil, and by what prestige injustice, calumny, fury, and cruelty succeed you in dominion over her heart! . . . The man she is persecuting is not a criminal, but a man whom she envisages as refractory to her orders and desires. But must such motives be the premise for an insult to humanity, for a neglect of all due respect, for the misfortunes of a daughter and affectionate wife, for the infamy that stains respectable kin, and for the shame that will perpetuate itself in an unfortunate family, the sad fruit of an engagement on which her mother bestowed her seal of approval?[26]

Addressed to Chapote, a prosecutor at the Châtelet and a "gentle, honest young man with a well-furnished mind," this petition seems to have yielded no result. Four months later Mme de Montreuil still had not been subpoenaed. By contrast, the king's order that the marquis be imprisoned at Pierre-Encize remained in effect despite the failure of the January 6 raid. On March 25 the duc de La Vrillière relayed the king's order to Sénac de Meilhan, the intendant for Provence, urging that it be carried out "with all the necessary vigilance and circumspection."

Dashed Hopes

On May 10, 1774, at 3:30 in the afternoon, the candle that had been burning in the king's window was extinguished: Louis XV had died of smallpox at the age of sixty-four amidst general indifference. The end of his agony, which had begun on April 27, had been impatiently awaited, because all of France hoped that the new reign would usher in a period of prosperity.

All of France—and especially the marquis de Sade. The lettre de cachet signed by the old king was no longer valid under his successor. The time of persecution, manhunts, fear, and adventure was over. M. de Sade was once again a free man, or almost. But Sade failed to reckon with the diligence of la Présidente, who hastened to obtain new orders in the young sovereign's name from the duc de La Vrillière, the only minister of the former government still in place. The duke managed to obtain these new orders without difficulty (Louis XVI was too devout to leave a libertine of Sade's ilk on the loose) and on October 21, 1774, sent them to Sénac de Meilhan together with this previously unpublished letter:

On 25 March last I sent you, Sir, orders of the king to have the marquis de Sade arrested and taken to Pierre-Encize. Since they were of course of a relatively remote date and issued by the late king, I felt that it was best, since they have not yet been carried out, to obtain the king's orders once again, and

His Majesty has kindly granted them. You will find them enclosed herewith. His Majesty hopes you will see to it that they are surely and swiftly carried out . . . It is my impression, moreover, that the officer of the constabulary to whom you have entrusted execution of these orders has not been as diligent as he promised you he would be. I am assured that the marquis de Sade has frequently left his place of hiding, that he has appeared in Marseilles, that he has stayed there for days at a time and, I am told, publicly attended the theater.[27]

Three days later La Vrillière alerted la Présidente that, obedient to her wishes, he had transmitted the order for her son-in-law's arrest to the intendant of Provence. But Sénac de Meilhan saw serious problems with the duke's plan and submitted a plan of his own, which seemed likely to work. We do not know the substance of this plan, but we do know, from another previously unpublished letter from the minister of the royal household to the intendant, that the operation was likely to cost the Montreuils a considerable sum of money. But what did it matter, provided that M. de Sade was rendered permanently harmless:

Sir, I delayed answering the letter you took the trouble to write me on 30 October last only because I was waiting for the family of the marquis de Sade to decide on the means by which you propose to have him arrested. It is indeed, I think, the only way that offers hope of success. The family, after hesitating for a time, has finally decided to make use of it. I therefore ask you to transmit the king's orders to Sieur Ouvières, officer of the constabulary of Marseilles, commissioning him to carry out the orders in exchange for a fixed sum to be paid to him. I have already warned the family that it would cost at least a thousand écus, but they are supposed to see us to make the necessary arrangements, both to agree on the price and to ensure payment. Since it appears that this expedition will require Sieur Ouvières to absent himself from Marseilles for what may be a fairly long period, you will kindly write to inform the provost general that he is to be granted leave.[28]

The "great affair"

The death of Louis XV had another consequence that was to prove most advantageous to Donatien. On the advice of his mentor, the comte de Maurepas, Louis XVI in the early summer of 1774 embarked on a fundamental restructuring of his government ministries. On June 2 the duc d'Aiguillon resigned his post as minister of foreign affairs and turned his portfolio over to the comte de Vergennes. On July 19 the young king handed the enlightened public, and particularly the party of the *philosophes*, a substantial prize when he appointed Turgot minister of the navy in place of Bourgeois de Boynes. One month later, on August 24, he struck a major blow, dismissing Maupeou and Terray and appointing Turgot *contrôleur général des Finances*. Thus Sade's worst enemy, the man who had wanted his head two years earlier, now found himself condemned, like the marquis himself, to exile. And to complete Donatien's revenge, a joyous populace hanged the former chancellor in effigy in the streets of Paris.

Maupeou's departure was interpreted as a sure sign that the *parlements* would soon be reinstated. This issue had been a constant source of political turmoil since the death of Louis XV. The "patriot" party, hostile to Chancellor Maupeou, portrayed the *parlements* as the people's natural champions against the arbitrariness of royal authority: the king, they claimed, was a representative and not a master. The patriots presented themselves as defenders of the fundamental laws of the realm, laws that the chancellor had violated. But they met with opposition from the *dévots* (the religious party) and the champions of absolutism. Though aware of the fact that to reinstate the *parlements* threatened to weaken his authority, the king ultimately conceded that the monarchy could not exist without its sovereign courts and that Maupeou would have to be sacrificed. The latter tried to defend his work by submitting to Louis XVI a memoir justifying his reforms, but Maurepas prevailed by reminding the king that enlightened public opinion sided with the magistrates of the *parlements*. In the end the king called upon Maupeou to surrender the seals of his authority. His successor, Miromesnil, a relative of Maurepas's, immediately submitted a plan for the reinstatement of the *parlements*, which earned him a reputation, in the eyes of the multitude and of the "patriot" party, as "the man of the hour, the restorer of the laws." Finally, on November 12, 1774, after much shillyshallying, Louis XVI held a *lit de justice* (a solemn assembly in which the king, seated on cushions, issued a sovereign edict) reinstating the parliamentary magistrates who had been driven from their courtrooms by his grandfather.

This measure offered Donatien an unhoped-for chance to persuade the *parlement* of Aix to overturn the judgment against him handed down by Maupeou's men. If successful, he would regain his freedom and civil rights and lay the scandal to rest. Even before the royal edict was issued, Renée-Pélagie, who, like everyone else in France, knew that the old *parlements* were soon to be restored, was quick to take action. On her husband's advice, she, together with her sister, left La Coste for Paris on July 14. Although her destination was the hôtel de Bourgogne on rue Taranne in the faubourg Saint-Germain, she asked Gaufridy to address all correspondence to "Carlier, tailor, rue Saint-Nicaise, in Paris. This man is reliable, and the *hôtels garnis* (boarding houses) are not, all of them answering to the police." Her mission was to advance matters with respect to both her petition against her mother and Donatien's appeal. The two cases were closely linked, moreover, for success in the appeal would depend on the fear that the petition continued to inspire: "Without the case in the Châtelet," Renée-Pélagie asserted, "we would never have got to the end of it, and it is very easy to see, no matter what they say, that [the two cases] are closely intertwined." Things dragged on interminably: kindly Chapote, the royal prosecutor, told everyone that Renée-Pélagie was mad and allowed her complaint against la Présidente to molder. The appeal was not to be presented for several more weeks. Meanwhile, expenses continued to mount, creditors still threatened, and la Présidente carried on with her vendetta against her son-in-law. What is more, an astonishing revelation found its way to Mme de Sade's ears: "I have been told," she wrote Gaufridy, "that my mother was madly in love with M. de Sade and that she was much angrier with me than with him. I answered: 'That's all I need!' " Finally, it was confirmed that M. de Beaumont's family would approve his marriage to Mlle de Launay only on condition that Sade would "remain in prison forever, and [they] want the minister's word. This is a shameful demand," Mme de Sade opined.[29]

From Italy, where he was dying of boredom, Donatien followed his wife's activities and observed the difficulties she encountered, particularly with his mother-in-law, who stubbornly refused to come to any accommodation: "Grant us, Sir, that Mme de Montreuil's mania not to conclude this business is most extraordinary. For what does she have to gain? [She will] perpetuate the dishonor of this unfortunate affair and of her daughter and grandchildren, sow frightful disorder with the property, and make me personally lead the saddest, most miserable life, because, believe me, it is never pleasant to be in a country where you are obliged to hide constantly and to play all sorts of roles so as not to be recognized. I assure you that this is a form of torture I knew nothing of and which I find quite hard and most disagreeable."[30]

In the meantime Renée-Pélagie continued her consultations, which led her to some rather optimistic conclusions: the reinstatement of the *parlements*, it appeared, was imminent, and the magistrates she had been to see had given her every reason to hope. Even with her mother things seemed less difficult: "My mother is a lioness, but even so some of her methods are not likely to lead to much. So no matter what she says, I think she will come to terms."[31] As for a reversal of the verdict, her view was that it was not likely to be granted unless Donatien denied everything: "For the big case, we shall file for reversal and deny everything: the flies [i.e., the bonbons laced with Spanish fly] are not proven, and, in the review, the second count [sodomy] can be set aside. This will require a favor, it is true, but people assure me that it won't be at all impossible to obtain. Provided they keep their word, which we shall see as events unfold."[32]

In early September these hopes were confirmed: the former *parlement* of Aix would hear the appeal in six weeks. A request to quash the lettre de cachet would not be filed until the verdict had been overturned and the arrest warrant withdrawn. For now, the thrifty, commonsensical Renée-Pélagie suggested, the best course would be for Donatien to return home "rather than remain abroad spending large sums." As for the case before the Châtelet, there had been no new developments: the complaint against Mme de Montreuil remained in limbo: "The esteemed royal prosecutor is an intelligent man but one who pounces on you and is full of sophisms. This is intolerable when one wants to pursue a reasoned argument, and with him my view is that there is nothing useful to be done except to remain firm and let him talk."[33] She preferred dealing with Sartine, the *lieutenant général de police*: "He is more engaging and better at following through."

Tender Prey

Exactly when Donatien left Italy for France is not known, but it was probably in the last two weeks of September.[34] He did not return directly to La Coste but made a detour through Lyons, where his wife joined him. The couple took advantage of their time in the ancient capital of the Gauls to hire household staff, including a young "secretary" for M. de Sade, a youth around fifteen years of age, almost a child. Naturally his parents were not told that their son's future master and the man condemned to death in Aix were one and the same. This deception was not difficult to carry off, because there was more than one nobleman in Provence who bore the name Sade: there were, for example, the Sades of Eyguières, Mazan, Tarascon, and Saumane. On the same day the couple hired a twenty-four-year-old chambermaid by the name of Anne Sablonnière, also known as Nanon, and five young girls, some natives of Lyons, others of Vienne, and all roughly the same age as the young secretary. We do not know for sure whether the girls' parents gave their consent or were even aware of their hiring by the Sades. Later Sade would claim that it was Nanon, "official madame" of the city of Lyons, who bagged this prey for him.

To hire seven new servants at a time when the Sades were in the midst of a catastrophic financial crisis, when the marquis's income had been garnished by the courts and the family silver pawned with Jews in Mazan, might seem at the very least an ill-considered move. But the real puzzle is Mme de Sade's attitude to this latest turn of events. Knowing her husband, she must have had an inkling that the young Ganymede of a scribe and the slender nymphets would satisfy certain very particular needs. Nevertheless, she saw to it that they were sent to La Coste and left vulnerable to the marquis. What are we to think? To begin with, that Mme de Sade, who had inherited if nothing else her mother's pragmatic spirit, preferred to keep scandal confined within the walls of her home rather than allow it to erupt outside. It was better to bring the flesh Donatien required to him than to allow him to prowl about like a wild animal in search of prey. Her husband's procuress and guardian of his fantasies, half jailer and half madame, she thus began a long dialogue of complicity with the "monster," a dialogue in which she no doubt gratified his most private perversions while at the same time developing her singular ability to collaborate with "evil," to invert its codes, to provoke the impossible, and ultimately to subvert established values. And she did this not with resignation but with the gleefulness of one discovering rebellion.

November came: like a sinister dream the fortress of La Coste slowly faded into the long night of winter, a ghost ship adrift, lights extinguished, compass gone, lost in the fog, and carrying a strange crew to parts unknown.

13

"My stupid childish amusements"

No Exit

What went on behind the walls of La Coste during the winter of 1774–75 we know only from hearsay, but it is not difficult to imagine. If the marquis had yet to conceive his great Silling fantasy, that winter was at least a harbinger of things to come, a living first draft of the finished work. Inside the château roles were assigned in accordance with a strict hierarchy of service, a ritualization and codification of erotic function. In this theater of lust actors and spectators were one. At the pinnacle of the hierarchy were the lord and his wife, with the young staff arrayed below. All the servants were experienced, and all were aware of the master's whims and quick to gratify them. Just below the lord and lady stood the Swiss chambermaid Gothon Duffé, a "callipygous" Protestant and the brood mare of the marquis's stable. Next came her lover, Carteron, known as La Jeunesse (Youth), who had abandoned his wife and children for Gothon's ass, said to be the most beautiful "to have escaped from the Swiss mountains in more than a century." Next came the mysterious Jean and then the frightening Saint-Louis, a foulmouthed drunkard who "tells masters and servants alike to go to the devil." After these two came Nanon, the new recruit, who soon became Saint-Louis's protégée. Bringing up the rear were the young secretary and the five serving damsels. To their number we must add two other girls "of an age and condition not to be sent for by their parents." One was a dancer from Marseilles, Mademoiselle Du Plan, who lived in the château "publicly and without incognito" with the title of governess. The other came from Montpellier and was called Rosette. She remained in Sade's service only two months before returning to her native city. Two or three cooks or kitchen maids along with a niece of Nanon's rounded out this amorous phalanstery. All told some twenty people remained shut up throughout the winter in this isolated château behind walls built recently on the marquis's orders, all of them subject to the master's authority and docile instruments of his desire.

One marvels at this remarkable reconstitution and transformation of "carceral space" for the sole purpose of protecting pleasure from outside attack, at this symbolic delineation of the territory of liberty within the confines of an inviolable prison.

•

In the center of the seraglio was Sade, the master of ceremonies, the director or rather disciplinarian of his troupe, as vigilant with those who served him in debauch as with those who acted on his stage, for order is necessary to the "derangement of the senses." Sade prescribed the configuration of postures, the distribution of pleasures over this or that part of the body. He arranged groups, composed scenes and tableaux vivants, varied attitudes, determined partners, sketched perspectives, suggested gestures, couplings, and refinements, controlled emissions, and in short established the "protocol" of the ceremony.

This "order necessary to lechery, that is, to transgression," as Roland Barthes once called it, also determined how the lord of La Coste spent his time. The almost monastic asceticism of this way of life, as Sade himself described it to Gaufridy, was no mere libertine's ruse. There is no falsehood in Sade's letter, only discretion:

We are therefore expecting you on Tuesday, my dear attorney . . . I beg you to come early, in any case for dinner, which is at three o'clock. You will oblige me by observing this same custom whenever you come to see us this winter. Here is the reason for it: we have decided, for a myriad of reasons, to see very few people this winter. As a result, I spend evenings in my study and Madame busies herself with her ladies in an adjoining room until bedtime. In consequence of which, come nightfall, the château is locked up tight, the lights are extinguished, the kitchen is closed, and often there are no more provisions.[1]

In silence and solitude, safe from prying eyes, the Sadeian liturgy unfolded in all its splendor. Real life and fantasy, La Coste and Silling, coincided.

Endgame

The orgy lasted no more than a month and a half. In early January of 1775 the children's families filed charges of "abduction . . . and seduction," and a criminal investigation was begun in Lyons. The little girls had no complaint with Mme de Sade. On the contrary, "they spoke of her as being compromised herself, and the first victim of a frenzy that can only be seen as madness." But they "furiously" accused the marquis.[2] Of course accusations were not enough. Proof was required. Perhaps tall tales, based on the marquis's reputation, were being told in order to extort money in exchange for silence. Unfortunately for Sade, the evidence against him was palpable: the children's bodies bore marks confirming their reports. And the young secretary, André, came away with a case of the pox for which the marquis was particularly unwilling to bear responsibility: "I summoned that little vixen Madelon," he wrote to Gaufridy, "and I assured her that she was the one who gave André the pox and that if she did not take immediate steps to pay for his cure I would have her driven out of the village as a whore, and I will. She is going to Apt. So tell her in no uncertain terms that I do not intend to pay for this malady."[3]

There is no certainty at all that Mme de Sade took part in the orgy. Her tolerance was not without limits. If she submitted to sodomization, her desire to satisfy her husband surely went no further. Furthermore, the marquis himself was not indiscriminate and refrained from certain sexual practices with certain partners. Clearly, he, like other libertines of his time, practiced flagellation only with prostitutes working in the lesser houses, those at the bottom of the sexual hierarchy, and he never would have tried it with an Opera girl or a courtesan of the prominence of Mlle Beauvoisin or Mlle Colet, much less with his wife or with certain other mistresses such as Signora Moldetti or Sarah Goudar, about whom we shall presently hear more. None of these women ever complained of physical violence on his part. By contrast, the girls from Lyons and Valence were anonymous victims, perfect for the marquis's needs. As for Renée-Pélagie, the only "frenzy" she ever had to endure was of a moral kind: being forced to witness, under her own roof and practically before her eyes, the spectacle of her debasement.

Blackmail

No sooner was the criminal investigation begun than Mme de Sade left for Lyons with Gothon to try once again to nip the affair in the bud. There could be no question of returning the "little chicks" to their parents as long as their bodies continued to bear marks of their abuse (contusions or incisions). To allow the wounds time to heal, the girls were sent to various places and warned not to talk. Three were entrusted to convents in Caderousse and Jumiège, and the nuns were warned against paying any attention to their ravings. Another stayed with the marquise but soon escaped, causing her mistress enormous worry. The most seriously abused of the girls was taken in great secrecy to the abbé de Sade, to whom she recounted the atrocities she had endured. When the abbé refused to keep her any longer and threatened to send her back to Vienne, the marquise, writing at her husband's dictation, bluntly reminded him of certain facts of a nature to silence his scruples. Her letter makes it clear that advancing age had by no means obliged the hermit of Saumane to settle down:

When, this past year, Provence resounded with rumors that you were hiding a girl in your château at Saumane, a creature, people said, snatched from her parents, whose attempts to retrieve her your secretary, acting on your orders, opposed, pistol in hand; when, quite recently, two women from Lyons came and looked me up there to complain of some very bad treatment they claimed to have received at the château of Saumane; I quieted things down, kept everything under wraps, and did all I could to demolish such odious calumnies. I hope that you will be good enough to do the same in this case, to demolish this girl's statements, and above all to prevent her from returning to Vienne, since it seems that your intention is to have her driven there, which would be dangerous, because she is telling, right and left, any number of horrid tales. Keep her with you where she will be happier because she will have her freedom, which I was obliged to deny her in my home for reasons of policy that have turned it into a kind of prison, but which are very different from what you appear to assume and in which that nephew, whom you are so pleased to insult, to call a madman, and so on, has no part.[4]

Thus the abbé was obliged, for a time at any rate, to remain silent, though he was by no means convinced by the marquise's flat denial of any wrongdoing, a denial obviously inspired by Donatien. A month later, exasperated by the child's presence and even more worried about the risk to himself, the abbé begged Gaufridy to take the girl off his hands as soon as possible. He was keeping her at Saumane, he said, only out of forbearance "for people who deserve none from me and with whom I do not wish to have any further dealings."[5] But his request went unanswered. The dear child would remain with him until she had fully recovered. In the meantime Mme de Sade urged him not to allow the girl to be examined by a doctor.

La Présidente Takes a Hand

Given the gravity of the situation, Renée-Pélagie felt that she had to consult with her mother. Mme de Montreuil could not stand idly by when the family honor was once again threatened—this time more gravely than ever, and with the appeal still pending. Her reaction was swift. She contacted the prosecutor in Lyons and, on February 11, wrote to Gaufridy, whom she did not yet know but in whom she placed full confidence. Her position was clear: the children should be returned forthwith but, she added, "with precautions" designed to avoid later trouble. Put plainly, this meant that the girls were to be fully healed before being sent home. As we know, these precautions had already been taken, and Mme de Sade claimed to be in possession of "certificates of good health." Accordingly, M. Gaufridy was asked to take the children back to their parents but to be sure to ask for "valid, binding releases sufficient to avoid any future vexation on this matter." Better still, he should return the children to their parents in the presence of the royal prosecutor and the very priests who had written to Mme de Sade asking that they be sent home. "This is a delicate mission," la Présidente concluded. "Do not entrust it to anyone other than yourself and, to aid you, one other person whom you can trust . . . It is up to you, Sir, to settle all this with prudence, in keeping with the knowledge you possess."[6]

The notary was reluctant to return the girls himself and allowed things to drag on. He delayed so long, in fact, that one day a woman by the name of Lagrange turned up at La Coste to demand her child. Gaufridy took her to his home and mollified her "with sweet talk and clothes." Meanwhile, la Présidente's contacts with the royal prosecutor had borne fruit: the investigation of the incident was about to end, or so it appeared. But what worried Mme de Montreuil most was the girl in Saumane, "because of the gossip." To remove the child from the abbé's home would, she thought, be dangerous "and could become very serious." But there were also drawbacks to leaving her where she was. What was needed was "a well-chosen convent or reliable person in an isolated spot where she can be answered for, and good treatment if she doesn't let her tongue run loose to persuade her that it is in her own best interest to say nothing, because what she might say would work against her and harm her later on."[7] In the meantime it would be extremely risky to turn her loose. She must be kept under surveillance, treated well, and not allowed to see anyone until the whole business was settled.

But la Présidente did not lose sight of her principal objective, namely, reconsideration of the 1772 decision of the court. She railed against the abbé de Sade, who was dragging his heels on pointless moral grounds. He was a fine one to set himself up as a judge! "My mother is furious with M. l'abbé de Saumane," Renée-Pélagie wrote, "because, maintaining as always his stoic tranquillity, he continues to refuse to go to Aix as she explicitly asked him to do. This stubborn refusal to serve his nephew is all too ridiculous and totally unmasks him, fully justifying all our efforts against him."[8] Nevertheless, the abbé persisted: "No, Sir, I will not go to Aix to make an absurd request of the general prosecutor. I will not make this trip until a council decree has been obtained reassigning jurisdiction in the case and submitting it to the *parlement* of Aix. This is my family's view, and I shall abide by it, disturbed though I am that it does not coincide with the ideas of that woman, who regards us as automata designed to carry out her will and who rails constantly against me and what she imagines to be my wrongs."[9]

Undeterred by the abbé's obduracy, Mme de Montreuil worked energetically for her son-in-law's rehabilitation. She was afraid, however, that some new folly would ruin everything, and most of all she feared the influence Donatien had over his wife. "If everything that people say is true," she confided to the notary, "what might not happen from one moment to the next? Oh, I have only too many reasons to expect the worst! No matter what happens, you see, she never utters a single complaint. She would allow herself to be chopped up into pieces before she would agree to anything she believed might hurt him. And would it hurt him if she were to protect herself? On the contrary, it would save her from misfortunes that might redound to his disadvantage and that will not occur if there is no basis for them."

On the central issue, clearly, Mme de Montreuil had not changed one iota. Allow the verdict to be overturned? Fine. She was ready for anything that might cleanse the family escutcheon and save her grandchildren's future, but on the express condition that the marquis be locked up under a valid lettre de cachet. Aware that Renée-Pélagie would adamantly oppose her husband's arrest even if it were in her own interest, yet incapable of understanding the passion that was rapidly bringing her daughter close to the edge of the abyss, la Présidente cast about for ways to protect Mme de Sade from her weakness while nursing the vain hope of rescuing her from the spell of which her mother believed she was the victim. This did not prevent Mme de Montreuil from analyzing the relations between Sade and his wife with great lucidity: by giving in to his whims and facilitating his crimes, la Présidente believed, the marquise was in fact hastening the ruin of the man she loved. Without her he would be less daring and would run fewer risks. "In his château with her he believes he is invulnerable and totally secure and permits himself whatever his heart desires. Elsewhere he restrains himself more. And even there, if she were not present he would lack the means to gratify his deviant desires and therefore would have none of a dangerous kind . . ."[10]

Some Books, a Harpsichord, and a Cabbage

M. de Sade, meanwhile, did not appear to be unduly worried about the future. The closing of his erotic theater had surely occasioned a pang of regret, but he still had Gothon and Nanon as well as the young secretary, not to mention the girl in his wife's care. This was enough to stave off boredom while waiting for things to improve. Cloistered in his château, he spent long hours reading in his study, mainly histories of Provence. Gaufridy came expressly to lend him one, "a little coarse (*gaulois*) as to the style," he remarked, but still a source of "great pleasure." He tried to find a work that Antoine de Ruffi had published in 1655 on Gaspard de Simiane, lord of La Coste, and asked the notary to purchase for him a new history of Provence printed in Paris. Shortly thereafter he learned that there was to be an auction at the Sablières and remarked that if there happened to be a harpsichord for sale, large or small, he wanted it set aside for him. For whom was this instrument intended? So far as we know the marquis played no instrument and had little interest in music. Was it perhaps for Mme de Sade? "If there are any books for sale," he continued, "let me know what is to be had." As for his reputation in the region, it made him smile: "I pass for the *werewolf* of these parts. Poor little chicks with their words of *terror!*"

But the major concern of those who lived in the château was still food. Generally speaking, it was the marquise who oversaw the operation of the household. Her notes to the notaries Fage and Gaufridy, who were truly jacks-of-all-trades, willing even to do the marketing for the mistress of the house, are filled with orders for meat, fruits, and vegetables. From them we know that the meals served at the château were for the most part typical Provençal cuisine. When supplies ran short, as they did from time to time, the marquis took up his pen to protest: "Sir, M. Perrottet tells me you had an excellent market. I congratulate you. But we poor wretches, far from the splendors of town, have had nothing but a miserable cabbage, and poor Gothon, who says that Apt is bursting with excellent things that you do not wish to share with us, is ready to launch an all-out attack if you don't take pity on her tomorrow by sending chard, cauliflower, asparagus, fava beans, peas, carrots, parsnips, artichokes, truffles, potatoes, spinach, rape, radishes, chicory, lettuce, celery, chervil, watercress, beets, and other vegetables."[11]

Dark Clouds

While M. de Sade enjoyed his pleasant ambles, Mme de Montreuil continued her efforts to obtain a reversal of his conviction. The major difficulty was how to do this without the convicted man's surrendering. Similar cases had to be found in order to make an appeal based on case law. "Tell Mme de Sade again," la Présidente wrote to Gaufridy, "that they mustn't imagine that the job is such an easy one, and that persecuting me in an insulting manner as they have done so far is not the way to hasten things along." The magistrates in Aix seemed well disposed, but they wanted orders from the court before taking action. In Paris la Présidente met again with the minister of justice, M. de Miromesnil, who offered expressions of good will but was afraid to appeal to the king's authority in the Council of Dispatches "because one ought not besmirch the imagination of a young prince with an account of the details of this proceeding, which in any case would indispose him altogether too much against the person concerned. It is better to avoid mentioning it to him if one can."[12]

Meanwhile, on May 3, 1775, M. Bruny d'Entrecasteaux, *premier président* of the *parlement* of Aix, simultaneously informed the heads of the two younger branches of the Sade line, Sade-Eyguières and Sade-Vauredone, provost of Saint-Victor in Marseilles, that their kinsman, the marquis de Sade, was in La Coste, "where he is engaging in a variety of excesses with young people of both sexes, whom he has caused to be abducted chiefly from Lyons, where charges have been lodged against him."[13] This action on the part of the newly recalled *parlement* may seem surprising, for it appears to ratify the hostility of the previous body. Perhaps the family was engaged in some maneuver to force Donatien into exile. At bottom Mme de Montreuil would have been happy to have seen her son-in-law banished to some far-off place and even left free, provided he ceased to be talked about. But it was too much to hope for: "If he keeps quiet and his wife stops compromising herself and making things easy for him in a manner unworthy of her and of him, after a while people will stop thinking about him. But are they sensible enough, either of them, to adopt such a course? I doubt it. And if they are together, there will always be reason to fear the same things."[14] And this certainly was not the resolution the abbé de Sade hoped to see: he personally wrote to the minister of the king's household on May 18, 1775, to ask that his brother be arrested. His demented actions, the abbé maintained, had disrupted society and repeatedly alarmed his family.[15]

More serious problems were still to come. On May 11 Anne Sablonnière, known as Nanon, whom the marquis had gotten with child, gave birth in Courthézon to a baby girl, Anne-Elisabeth, whose paternity she attributed to her husband, Barthélemy Fayère. Aged twenty-four and "well-equipped for bed," Nanon ably played her part in the Sadeian orgies at La Coste. "The wench served the main dish after the little girls provided the spices," as Paul Bourdin nicely put it.[16] The baby was sent to a wet nurse in La Coste, while the mother remained with the Sades. But on June 20, after a violent scene with the marquise, Nanon fled the château like a wild hysteric, screaming "a million impertinences," and took refuge in the Maison-Basse. Mme de Sade panicked, for this was a woman capable of the most vile things, dangerous in word as well as deed. Had it not been for her, there would have been no scandal about the little girls. What if she now threw in her lot with the "Lyons cabal" that was out to destroy the marquis? La Présidente had already been trying for some time to have her interned. It would take "at most two more weeks," she informed her daughter in a letter received the night before, recommending that in the meantime the marquise not let Nanon out of her sight. What could be done now to neutralize the threat until the lettre de cachet promised by Mme de Montreuil arrived? How could Nanon be prevented from telling her story in Lyons or Aix? Giving in to panic, the marquise resorted to a bit of underhandedness justified only by her desire to save her husband: she accused Nanon of having stolen three silver plates. Wasn't this the best way to stall for time? "I implore you to see that this case succeeds, for it is more important than you can imagine," she informed Gaufridy. "Try to prevent her from going to Lyons. This is very important . . . If Blancard could possibly give us a man to drive her in security to Paris and place her in my mother's hands, I should be glad to pay for the journey . . ."[17]

Sensing the danger, Nanon sought refuge with Father Alexandre de Nerclos, prior of the convent of Jumiège, who agreed to receive her. A few days later, however, the marquis sent three servants to seize the woman on the pretext that she had stolen forty livres. But this stratagem failed, and the prior complained of the marquis's high-handedness to the abbé de Sade, recommending that the abbé have his nephew imprisoned for the rest of his life. "He is convinced that the marquise is no better than her husband, because no one from their house made Easter [Communion] and because she allows her young male servants to maintain commerce with a married Lutheran woman."[18] As for the rest, he assured the abbé of his belief that he had been able to squelch the hostile rumors.

•

Indubitably there seemed to be a vast conspiracy against Donatien. Just a few days after the Nanon affair, the young secretary's mother arrived from Aix to reclaim her son with "the devil's own fury." This was odd, for until now this woman had always advised her son to devote himself to his master and serve him well. "It is clear," the marquis concluded, "that they are working in secret against me . . . They want this child too, undoubtedly so they can have him make further false statements." This must, he thought, be some low trick of the royal prosecutor in Lyons, who had lulled his mother-in-law with enticing promises while proceeding underhandedly to do him in. Fortunately Maupeou's men no longer controlled the *parlement* of Aix: "If we still had the old imbeciles, this would be a case for drawing and quartering—at the very least." But with an *avocat général* like M. de Castillon, "very wise, very honest, and very reasonable," there was nothing to fear, or so the marquis believed. Years later he would discover some of the darker aspects of this affair. In fact, M. de Castillon had "bared his fangs" to the mother and her son, had dictated a "tissue of horrors," and "they said and wrote what he wanted." Furthermore, the marquis added, "the child was under the thumb of a very greedy mother, who believed that by having him say a thousand dreadful things she would assure herself of a steady income. She knew about the hundred louis in Arcueil."[19] Can we credit this new interpretation of the facts, which, taken from his *grande lettre* to Mme de Sade (1781), postdates the events by six years? It is extremely difficult to distinguish truth from falsehood in the long and pitiful self-defense that the marquis called his "general confession" and in which he was careful to conceal any circumstances liable to be held against him, most notably the physical torture, which he vehemently denied but of which other sources offer abundant proof. He rejects, moreover, the testimony of one witness after another. Nanon's confession? Nothing surprising there: to justify her own actions this "procuress" tried to shift as much blame as she could to the man she took as her accomplice. The bones found in his garden? Mlle Du Plan had decorated a cabinet with them, for a joke, and then deposited them there. This was only partially false: the bones had probably been used as props to terrify the little girls in the La Coste orgies: Sade liked to mix the macabre with the erotic and was not averse to sowing terror among his young companions. The secretary's deposition? The boy was a servant: "therefore, as a child and a servant, he cannot be believed."

On July 5, 1775, Renée-Pélagie breathed a sigh of relief. A lettre de cachet ordering the imprisonment of Nanon Sablonnière in Arles had finally arrived from Versailles. La Présidente, who had personally chosen the Arles house of correction as the place of imprisonment, hoped that the royal orders contained "everything necessary: *humanity but also secrecy and security.*" Finally she was rid of the harpy once and for all. Meanwhile, Nanon's daughter grew weaker with each passing day for want of milk: the wet nurse had simply "neglected" to say that she herself was four months pregnant. On July 30 the infant died at La Coste at the age of ten weeks.

Donatien felt the vise tightening. He no longer felt safe even in the château. The notoriety surrounding the "affair of the little girls" had done him considerable damage, and there was a danger that the police would attempt another raid, which this time might prove costly. The time had come to make a getaway. Once again he turned to Italy in search of refuge, freedom—and pleasure.

From La Coste to Florence

On the afternoon of July 17, 1775, he set out on the Alpine route along with La Jeunesse and Louis Charvin, the postmaster of Courthézon. The three men spent the night two leagues from Céreste (Alpes-de-Haute-Provence) in a "rather nice house where we were fairly uncomfortable, since the people here are not in the habit of living communally and did so only to help us out." The next day they had lunch in Peyruis and slept in another farm house near Sisteron. On the nineteenth, despite the dreadful state of the roads, they made it in one stretch as far as La Saulce, three leagues short of Gap.

Early on the morning of July 25, after an arduous journey, the marquis arrived in Turin, where he stayed at the best hotel in the city. On August 3, 1775, the marquis de Sade, or rather the "comte de Mazan," finally reached Florence, the first major destination of his journey. Here at last he was free, or so he believed, for despite the pseudonym the French police had not lost track of him. Inspector Marais had a network of informants in Italy who kept him apprised of the fugitive's movements. A certain Pitrot, dancer in the Comédie-Italienne, alerted Paris of the "count's" arrival in Florence and remarked on his visits to various Italian courts. In Rome it was a French actor who was assigned to keep an eye on our traveler. Donatien spotted the informant and gave him a thrashing, but this did not prevent the man from following him as far as Naples. When the marquis returned to Grenoble another informant, the son of a chimney sweep who claimed to be a Savoyard officer and who had known Donatien at Miolans, reported on his every move.[20]

Doctor Mesny

As a conscientious and cultivated tourist, M. de Mazan had attentively read the accounts of other travelers who had preceded him, including Cochin, Lalande, and abbé Richard, whom he shamelessly plundered (as Stendhal would do later) for his own *Voyage d'Italie* while contemptuously correcting their slightest error. An ungrateful hairsplitter, he sputtered with rage at the authorities' ineptitude, ignorance, lies, and bad taste. Poor abbé Richard came in for particular ire. Did he confuse the Bologna bridge with the entry to the city? Sade noted the error with contemptuous disdain: "All the details this man gives of his travels reflect roughly the same taste. I leave it to you to judge what credence they deserve."

The day after his arrival in Florence, Donatien went to the home of Dr. Barthélemy Mesny, to whom he carried a letter of introduction from Marquis Pietrobono di Donis, a distant cousin of his and the father of Mme de Valette, who lived in Mazan. A native of Lorraine, now in his sixties, physician to the Grand Duke of Tuscany as well as a naturalist, archaeologist, and collector, Dr. Mesny was justly reputed to be one of the most learned men in the city.[21] He immediately offered to serve as Donatien's guide. The marquis's gratitude is evident in this flattering portrait of his cicerone: "Do not forget, Madame Countess, among the curiosities of Florence, the private natural history collection of Dr. Mesny of the General Military Hospital. This savant has gathered together what his fortune and various gifts have enabled him to acquire. The collection includes shells, fossils, petrified wood, minerals, ancient and modern medals and coins, all remarkably interesting."[22]

Seduced and Abandoned

Never having learned Italian, Donatien was chagrined to discover the language barrier: "It's the devil's own work to make oneself understood here," he confided to Gaufridy. "Not a soul speaks French, and I am still a long way from speaking Italian. I am working at it like a devil, though. Signor di Doni claims that I will never succeed without an Italian mistress, and I assured him (as I assure you) that I certainly won't be taking his advice."[23] In fact Donatien dreamed constantly of finding a pretty tutor. His first opportunity came at the home of the learned doctor.

Dr. Mesny had five daughters: one was married to a Tuscan podesta; another was a nun; a third was married to a French painter; the fourth, Mme Moldetti, was married to a customs official; and the youngest, Françoise, still lived at home with her parents.

It was not the youngest daughter who attracted our libertine's eye but rather the beautiful Chiara Moldetti, aged thirty and already the mother of five children and pregnant with a sixth. "She lived in the Piazza San Spirito in Florence," he would later recall, "the next to the last door on the left when you face the church. She had four boys and a girl and was pregnant with a sixth child. Her eldest son was vile, but the next eldest was not bad, rather like Latour. The two youngest boys seemed destined to be good-looking. The little girl was with a wet nurse and soon to return home. The Moldettis' country estate stood on a hill a half league from Poggio a Caïno, a royal house."[24]

Chiara was seized by a violent passion for the French nobleman, to which he seemed to respond. He swore eternal love until she became his mistress, which did not take long, but very soon thereafter he tired of her and tried to get rid of her. Events then followed the classic pattern: the more she clung to her unfaithful lover, the more he shunned her, sometimes going days without visiting or writing. The poor woman wailed, begged, and pleaded for a word or sign of hope, all to no avail.

Moving evidence of this affair has survived in the form of ardent letters from this woman seduced and abandoned. Of the dozen or so previously unpublished letters, all in Italian (proof that Donatien had made rapid progress in the language), I cannot resist citing a few lines: "I love you, my love, and I swear that in the future I will do whatever you like. Forgive one who loves you with the most ardent sentiments of a sincere heart . . . I see clearly that unhappiness is all that is left to me . . . Ah, cursed Naples! And Rome, which I can no longer bless! These two cities will have been the death of me. This time I expected a tender letter full of those sentiments that I once knew in you and that I clearly see I have lost! . . . How you make me quake with rage and pain at receiving so cold and undeserved a letter when I was expecting just the opposite . . . Ah, my treasure, if you abandon me I can only say that you sought this pretext for that very purpose, and I will know that your heart is one of the most barbarous and insincere that ever was, for this will mean that you never loved me."

Nevertheless, Donatien would serve, by proxy, as godfather to Chiara's child, born in December 1775. As for Dr. Mesny, who was fully informed about his daughter's affair, he understood her quite well, all the more so because he had never held his son-in-law in particularly high esteem.

Sarah Goudar

At around the same time Donatien made the acquaintance of a most unusual individual, one of those shadowy figures often seen in the antechambers of ministries and the corridors of embassies. This one was a Frenchman by the name of Pierre-Ange Goudar. Casanova, who knew a thing or two about scoundrels, called him a "famous roué" and "henchman of the devil," as well as a "wit, pimp, cheat, police spy, false witness, double-dealer, brazen adventurer, and ugly mug." The two men had known each other for some time and had done each other favors. Goudar's past, like everything else about the man, was shrouded in thick layers of mystery. According to the biographical dictionaries he came into the world in 1720, but in fact he was born in Montpellier twelve years earlier, in 1708. Virtually nothing, or at any rate nothing certain, is known about his childhood and youth. Indications are that he was in Reggio in 1744, then in Parma, but subsequently he vanishes without a trace, only to turn up again first in Constantinople, then in Isfahan. What did he live on? No one knows. In 1746 he was in Venice. He published a number of books: *L'Aventurier français* (1746), which is autobiographical; *L'Histoire des Grecs*

(1757), which is facetious and cynical; *La Paix de l'Europe* (1757) and *Charles I*ᵉʳ, *roi d'Angleterre* (1757), which are political and historical; and *L'Anti-Babylone* (1759), a polemic. Then he turned up in London in 1761, where he met Sarah, a bar girl in a tavern, who was sixteen and quite beautiful. Casanova, who witnessed their first meeting, recounted it in these terms:

> Idle as I was, in a country where I did not know the language, I considered myself almost fortunate to have Goudar, who introduced me to the most celebrated courtesans in London, especially the illustrious Kitty Fisher, who was then just beginning to go out of fashion. He also introduced me, in a tavern where we were drinking bottles of strong-beer, which is preferable to wine, to a waitress, sixteen years old and a true prodigy of beauty. She was Irish and Catholic, and her name was Sarah. I wanted her as conquest or acquisition, but Goudar had his eye on her and actually ran off with her a year later. Ultimately he married her, and this is the same Sarah Goudar who made a name for herself in Naples, Florence, Venice, and other places, and whom we ran into again four or five years later, still with her husband. Goudar had hatched the plan of substituting her for Mme Du Barry, Louis XV's mistress, but a lettre de cachet obliged him to go seek his fortune elsewhere. Good old days of the lettre de cachet—alas, you are no more![25]

In 1767 the couple settled in Naples, where Goudar gave language lessons and passed himself off as a man of letters. In fact, his sole means of support were gambling, his wife's charms, which he exploited with talent, and his activities as a secret agent, which earned him not only wages but also protection from people in high places. In those days there were spies aplenty in the minor Italian courts, where the French and the Hapsburgs vied bitterly for influence. By way of intrigue our man successfully infiltrated the king of Naples' entourage in the hope that Ferdinand IV would not long hold out against beautiful Sarah's sultry glances. He was more successful than he hoped: his wife soon found herself in the royal bed, and Goudar himself was heaped with favors.

After Sarah became the mistress of a gambling casino on the Posilippo, the irresistible Englishwoman invited Casanova to join her there one evening. His jaw dropped when he saw the former bar girl:

> Sarah was neither surprised nor embarrassed to see me, but I was petrified. She was dressed in the most elegant manner, looking remarkably well and receiving even better, with manners at once as simple and as noble as can be,

speaking elegant Italian, reasoning well, and ravishing in her beauty. I was dumbfounded, for the change in her was prodigious. Within a quarter of an hour we witnessed the arrival of five or six ladies of the highest rank and ten or twelve dukes, princes, and marquis, along with foreigners of all nations. Before dinner was served to a company of thirty, Mme Goudar sat down at the harpsichord and sang several songs in a siren's voice and with an assurance that did not surprise the other guests, who knew her, but that astonished me and my traveling companions, for she was excellent. Goudar had worked this manner of miracle. This was the fruit of the education he had given her over a period of six or seven years.[26]

Soon, however, the wind began blowing from another quarter. In September 1774 the Goudars were suddenly plunged into disgrace. Ferdinand IV, king of the Two Sicilies, enjoyed a reputation, by no means usurped, as a complete imbecile. Rumor had it that he was almost retarded and utterly dominated by his wife, Marie Caroline, the sister of Marie Antoinette of France, a well-known sapphic who was domineering and fickle and much given to wild orgies and enduring grudges. In any case, Ferdinand expelled the Goudars from the Court of Naples. What had gone wrong? Had the queen suddenly fallen into a jealous rage, as Casanova claims? Had Ferdinand and Marie Caroline become rivals for Sarah's affection? In any event, the monarch seized on the first pretext to rid himself of the adventurer. In 1769 Goudar had published an impertinent broadside entitled *Naples: What Must Be Done to Make the Kingdom Flourish Again*, and it hadn't caused him the least bit of trouble. Four years later, however, the same work was deemed infamous and publicly consigned to the flames by the royal executioner, while its author was given twenty-four hours to leave Naples along with his wife. Ange and Sarah first sought refuge in Florence, then wandered from city to city for several years, living as best they could while enduring expulsion from one place after another for libertine excess.

•

It was shortly after his arrival in Florence that Sade made the acquaintance of Ange Goudar, perhaps through Dr. Mesny. Their relations were short-lived, because the marquis left the capital of Tuscany for Rome on October 21. Those few weeks were long enough, however, for the marquis to become Sarah's lover, and later he would call her one of the three most beautiful women in Florence, along with Countess Albany, née Princess Stolberg, wife of the pretender to the British throne, Charles Edward Stuart, and Lady Cooper, a young Englishwoman of eighteen.[27] In the marquis's eyes Sarah outshone the two others "owing as much to the beauty of her face as to the superiority of her figure and the cultivation of her mind."[28]

La Dolce Vita

On Saturday, October 21, 1775, at three in the afternoon, M. de Sade left Florence, and on October 27 at eleven in the morning he arrived in Rome. On the recommendation of Dr. Mesny he looked up Signor Lucattini, who served as his guide and introduced him to the city's antique dealers. Our traveler ruined himself with purchases of objets d'art and never missed an opportunity to acquire an ancient medal for his friend Mesny. He also made the acquaintance of the scholar Cosimo Alessandro Collini, whom Dr. Mesny had never mentioned although he was a man of considerable learning. Then aged fifty, Collini had once been in the service of Voltaire, whom he had assisted in the composition of various works. He retained the great man's esteem after leaving his service, and the two corresponded regularly. Collini soon became the tutor of Count von Sauer in Strasbourg, and then in 1759 he was named court historiographer by the Elector Palatine, Charles Theodore. Later he became director of the natural history laboratory in Mannheim.

•

At the behest of Pierre-Ange Goudar, Donatien was received in November 1775 by Cardinal de Bernis, at that time the French ambassador to Rome and a good friend of Casanova's. A letter from Goudar alludes to this meeting: "Let me know how you were received by Cardinal de Bernis. If you saw him on a good day and his heart has given him no trouble, you probably found him quite amiable, all the more so in that he has not forgotten that he once lived in a furnished room at Butte Saint-Roch, a room that went for twelve livres under the terms of the poor ordinance. It is rare that furnished rooms provide Rome with cardinals who become ambassadors of France."[29]

In the absence of any evidence, we can only imagine the dialogue between Sade and the libertine prelate, who had once shared two Venetian nuns with Casanova and honored a princess in the cellars of the Vatican. What an inspiration for the future author of *Justine*! Perhaps their conversation was one of mere courtesy, but in that case why would Donatien have gone out of his way to arrange the meeting? The comte de Mazan had no apparent reason to see the French ambassador. Or did he?

In the *Histoire de Juliette*, the heroine of which is of course none other than Donatien himself in feminine disguise, Cardinal de Bernis plays a key role. It is to his home that Juliette goes upon arriving in Rome: "I had letters for Cardinal de Bernis, our ambassador at that court, who received me with all the gallantry of the charming emulator of Petrarch." Five months later, it is Bernis who introduces her to Pope Pius VI, Clement XIV's successor on the throne of Saint Peter.

Given what we know of the man, it is certain that Donatien did everything he could to obtain a private audience with the pope. He would have done so for nothing more than the ironic pleasure such a meeting would have occasioned. The implacable enemy of the Church meets face-to-face with the leader of all Christendom: what a joke! In his preface to *Juliette*, André Pieyre de Mandriargues tried to imagine this interview with the sovereign pontiff: "Did Sade really meet him? It is possible, and it would be droll." Hilarious, in fact. And less implausible than it might seem. For if the *Histoire de Juliette* and the *Voyage d'Italie* are read in parallel, it becomes tempting to reverse their respective functions. If the *Voyage* fills in some of the Italian background of *Juliette*, then perhaps *Juliette* fills in some of the (deliberate or inadvertent) lacunae scattered throughout the *Voyage*. In other words, the novel may reveal, beneath the mask of fiction, what was left unsaid in the (supposedly) authentic narrative.

If Donatien did not have a private audience with Pius VI, he was at least part of the crowd at his coronation.[30] He sent a description of the ceremony, evidently quite vivid, to Dr. Mesny.[31] And when Mme de Sade heard the news, she hastened to spread it around Provence: her husband had seen the pope with his own eyes. His conversion could not be long in coming now![32]

Meanwhile, Sade, to whom any such ideas were foreign, had immersed himself in the pleasures that Rome had to offer to anyone who knew how to find them. Behind its pious facade, the city harbored as much perversity as any in Italy. A letter dated December 5, 1775, from Goudar, whose reluctance to say too much suggests a great deal, tells us that our catechumen had found plenty to divert him in the shadow of Saint Peter's: "I see that you are having a lot of fun in Rome, where you have a great deal to have fun with, but you have to like that kind of fun."[33] Given the connotations of "having fun" (*s'amuser*) in the language of the libertine, particularly when repeated so emphatically, we can be sure that Donatien was indeed not bored.

·

We cannot leave Rome without mentioning young Giuseppe Iberti, whom Sade affectionately called "the little doctor of Rome" and who was surely the dearest and most intimate of his Italian friends. Dr. Mesny had warmly commended Iberti, "who, as you say, has the talent to please and converse with you."

Well placed in Roman society, Iberti generously allowed his French friend to take advantage of his illustrious acquaintances. It was through him that Sade came to know Duchess Honorine di Grillo, a woman of barely twenty years married to a man of sixty and "as much a virgin with that old animal as when her mother took her from the Ursuline convent in Bologna to hand her over to him."[34]

Not content to take Sade to visit monuments and galleries, Iberti willingly responded to the marquis's requests by assuming more delicate tasks, such as looking into the amorous life of Roman society and scandals involving prelates. The Vatican archives, to which he had access, were a source of abundant anecdotes, which he hastened to communicate to Donatien, not hesitating to take enormous risks to please his friend. But one cannot rummage through the secrets of the popes with impunity. One day, a letter from the marquis to his young Aesculapius fell into the clutches of the Inquisition. The poor man was arrested as he left the Duke di Grillo's and thrown into solitary confinement by the Holy Office. It was only thanks to the influence of the Venetian ambassador that he was released four months later, and then on the express condition that he never, on pain of death, reveal what had happened to him. The poor young man nevertheless continued to furnish the marquis with information on certain matters. "I will work on your description exactly as you give it," he wrote soon after leaving his cell. "Rest assured that I will take all necessary pains. You are only too worthy, and I promise you all my attention. But, as far as the amorous details are concerned, excuse me. I am surrounded by spies. As for my letters, I fear that they may be opened en route. Be careful not to send anything in response except this: that you have heard my palpable woes. My God, what an abyss of misery lay in store for me! The more circumspect your letters, the better. You too were unwittingly the cause of my misery."[35] Twenty years later the marquis de Sade would honor the memory of the "little doctor from Rome" by giving him a part in the *Histoire de Juliette*: "You are the only person in these Memoirs whose name I have not sought to disguise. The role of philosopher that I give you here suits you so well that you cannot fail to forgive me for revealing it to the entire world."[36]

A Sojourn in Naples

Toward the end of December, Donatien left Rome and set out for Naples, where he arrived sometime in the first few days of 1776. He was welcomed by Dr. Mesny's son-in-law, a French painter by the name of Tierce, who took it upon himself to find suitable lodging and other facilities.

In Naples the marquis continued his explorations with the same voracious appetite as in Rome and Florence. He set out to see everything, to learn about everything, to judge, to admire, to criticize, to love, to hate—in short, to surrender totally to an insatiable curiosity that took him not only to museums, galleries, churches, palaces, and libraries but also to caves, crypts, and catacombs, and even inside volcanoes. He was not satisfied merely to contemplate works of art and monuments ancient and modern; he also observed customs, politics, religion, government, and social life. The beauty of women, the ways of society, the quality of the theater, ways of eating, drinking, dressing, praying, and conducting oneself in the world—nothing left him indifferent. He wanted to grasp the whole past and present of this civilization, to embrace it all in a unique and universal vision. His aims were vast, a reflection of his extraordinary imagination, but his reach exceeded his grasp.

Thus his first ambition as a writer was grandiose and extravagant. With his "great work" in mind Sade hastily took notes by the side of a road or in some inn and complemented his research with information gleaned from his correspondents Mesny and Iberti. A monumental work, intended for the public but not destined to be published until the twentieth century, thus took shape. Tierce collaborated closely with the author: he reviewed the notes and recorded his observations in little notebooks with numbers referring to the works described. Sade paid considerable attention to these remarks. Often the painter accompanied him on his walks, sketch pad in hand, and made drawings of buildings or landscapes. A hundred of these drawings recently turned up in the Sade family archives. They transform the *Voyage d'Italie* into a veritable travelogue.

Secret Identities

In January 1776 an incident occurred that would have been comic had it not caused serious trouble for the marquis, ultimately leading to his return to France: the so-called Teissier affair.

Rumor had it that a man named Teissier, a salt-tax collector from Lyons, had fled to Italy with 80,000 livres in stolen receipts and that he was hiding in Naples under an assumed name. The French chargé d'affaires, M. Bérenger, became convinced that Teissier was none other than the comte de Mazan and ordered an investigation. This confronted Donatien, who did not dare own up to his true identity, with a serious dilemma. Since he styled himself a colonel, the investigators consulted M. de La Bourdonnaye, a French officer with a thorough knowledge of the officer corps, who stated that he had never heard of a staff officer named Mazan. The marquis was thus obliged to reveal his true name. He showed letters of recommendation from his cousin di Donis and others, but the authorities did not believe his story. They asked for additional proof of his identity and threatened to have him arrested if he did not return to France at once. In the meantime he was placed under surveillance by the Neapolitan police, and his correspondence was subjected to detailed scrutiny. A portrait that he sent to Mme de Sade was intercepted, for example, and sent to Lyons to see if it resembled the fugitive Teissier. Donatien was suspected all the more because he had steadfastly refused to be introduced at court. In short, the misunderstanding was total, and so serious that Mme de Sade, alerted to what was happening, briefly considered coming to Naples herself to rescue her husband from this sad pass. She asked him how long it would take and how much it would cost to travel to Naples by sea, and whether horses could be brought on board. In the meantime she sent him a note for 1,200 francs that she had borrowed from her mother, but he was unable to cash it because he had passed himself off as a bachelor. Donatien, meanwhile, attempted to use his contacts' influence.

Oddly enough, the man who came to his rescue was the prince di San Nicandro, the grand master of the Court of Naples. With his letter of recommendation Donatien went to see Bérenger, who received him coldly and claimed not to recognize either the handwriting or the signature of the letter. This was exactly what Sade expected. "Very well, sir," he responded, "I shall return immediately with the grand master himself . . ." When the chargé, realizing too late that he might have committed a gaffe, appeared embarrassed, Sade taunted him with sarcasm, noting how brilliantly he discharged the duties of his post and remarking that in a job like his it was impossible to be too circumspect. Meanwhile, he headed for the door, assuring the official that he was going directly to the grand master to report on his visit.

"Who is this scoundrel?" the prince exclaimed upon learning of Donatien's conversation with Bérenger. "I shall speak to him this morning at court and teach him how to live!" The effect was almost immediate. A few hours later Bérenger personally appeared at the marquis's door. Donatien dismissed the servant who had come up to inquire if he was home: "Tell your master, sir, that I am not here, and that I shall call on him to take me to court on the first day after the king returns from the hunt." Having delayed for so long, he had finally decided to introduce himself to the Court of Naples—in a colonel's uniform.

No sooner was this decision taken, however, than he panicked at the thought of the affront he was risking. What if he were publicly unmasked? What if he were banished as a thief? "I am scared to death that this appearance is a foolish mistake," he confessed to his wife. "I have allowed myself to be led on and forced to act by people who do not know the whole story, and I should not have been so weak . . ."[37]

It appears that Donatien did actually appear at court, for otherwise he would not have mentioned it to Dr. Mesny or received the elderly savant's irony-tinged reply: "It is not essential for a person traveling, in order to become a philosopher and enjoy the miracles of nature, to be presented to a king . . ."[38]

The marquis left Naples for good on May 5, 1776, still accompanied by La Jeunesse and Charvin. After a brief stay in Rome (May 12–18), the trio proceeded on to Grenoble by way of Velletri, Lorette, Bologna, and Milan.[39]

14

Attempted Murder

Mme de Sade's Troubles

During the marquis's absence, a period of more than a year, Mme de Sade found herself confronted with extremely serious problems, which she attacked with an energy one would not have suspected in a woman reputed to be weak and timid. Crushed by debt, beset with worries, forced to deal with Nanon's threats, the flight of the little girls, the appellate proceedings, the slowness of the courts, the apathy of the abbé de Sade, and the hostility of her mother, she was further obliged to make sure that her darling husband did not lack for anything, to send him linen for twenty-four shirts, and to see to it that he received the money he needed, even if it meant pledging her silver as collateral.

From the house of correction in Arles where she was being held, Nanon especially was a source of mortal alarm. When Antoine Lions, steward of the marquis's farm at Cabannes, went to Arles to try and persuade the prisoner that her punishment was no more than she deserved and that in any case the prison looked quite "decent" to him, he was met with a torrent of insult. Not content to spew forth a "thousand horrors," the prisoner threatened to kill herself in order to draw attention to the injustice of her imprisonment and the wickedness of the nuns, who refused even to allow her to write her parents. For two hours Lions attempted to reason with her, to no avail. "I fear, as do the nuns, some sinister event," he confided to Gaufridy. A few days later M. Des Galois de La Tour, intendant of Provence as well as *président* of the *parlement* of Aix, ordered an investigation of conditions in the prison. Had the unfortunate Nanon's complaints been heard outside the prison walls? In any case, Lions consulted with the mother superior about an appropriate response. Meanwhile, Mme de Montreuil approached the minister and the intendant in the hope of avoiding a scandal. Within a week the matter was settled to the family's total satisfaction: Nanon would remain in jail until M. de Sade was rehabilitated. In the meantime she was treated to impressive sermons and urged to confess. Between outbursts of rage she asked for news of her daughter, of whose death no one had dared to inform her. Lions planned to wait until Easter before broaching the matter: "She will be more likely to listen to reason," he thought. On his last visit, February 23, 1776, she had seemed calmer. In fact, she nursed the hope that when the bishop of Arles, Monsignor Du Laud, came for his pastoral visit, he would take an interest in her case and intervene in her behalf. "I think he is too cautious to get involved," the steward confidently predicted.

Another subject of concern was the "little girls," who had been sent to various places. The abbé de Sade had tried to unburden himself of his by sending her to the hospital in L'Isle-sur-Sorgue. The marquise assumed the cost of her upkeep but urged that the girl be allowed to speak to no one. Within a few weeks she had fully recovered. The abbé then took her out of the hospital and sent her to live as a boarder in Ripert's home, where she would be more comfortable than in Saumane and "less apt to speak with strangers." At this point, however, another of the girls escaped from the convent of Caderousse and set out for Lyons. Two young men came looking for her, one of them claiming to be her godfather. On July 26 the girl entrusted to Ripert also ran away. Before returning home she had filed a deposition with a judge in Orange, where she spent eight days "yapping." Mme de Sade strongly suspected Ripert of having arranged the whole thing. A third child, little Marie, whom the marquise had kept in her service as a scullery maid, came down with a *queue de rougeole*, which necessitated eleven visits to the family physician, Dr. Terris. To prevent the disease from spreading she was sent away from the château, despite her tears. Two days later the doctor found her dead. Elsewhere things were also going badly, and poor Mme de Sade was beset with troubles. Her dispute with the priest and the bishop turned venomous,[1] Gothon fell ill, a vindictive neighbor killed six turkeys he found in his fields, not a penny was to be found in the château, and a pack of creditors was baying at the gates. Renée-Pélagie no longer knew which way to turn first.

To top things off, the "great affair" dragged on interminably. All the coming and going to Aix did little to advance matters. The magistrates of that city, though supposedly not hostile to the appeal, were awaiting orders from the court. Miromesnil did not wish to involve himself in such delicate negotiations, and no one was willing to speak to the king for fear of shocking him. In short, things had reached an impasse. The abbé de Sade gleefully rubbed his hands. He had correctly predicted that nothing would be done until his nephew surrendered himself. M. de Castillon and Judge Siméon now confirmed his view: the case was "full of errors," to be sure, and the sentence was unjust, as was the arrest warrant, but resisting arrest was illegal. In order to review the case and overturn the verdict, "either surrender or seizure of the convicted man" was essential "to cleanse the record of the charge of flight to avoid punishment." The abbé was exultant in a letter to Gaufridy: "Do me justice, Sir, and admit that I have always spoken in these very terms on all points, thereby drawing down upon myself the wrath of Madame de M[ontreuil] . . ."[2]

The abbé correctly surmised that M. de Sade had no intention of surrendering to the authorities. He had only recently set foot on French soil and planned to return to his estate. After arriving in Grenoble on June 18, 1776, he remained for several days, long enough to hire a young "secretary" by the name of Raillanne to replace the one who had left. Knowing his client's epistolary intemperance, Reinaud, Sade's attorney, remarked ironically that the new secretary would "have to be one hell of a literary man." From Grenoble the marquis went to Courthézon, where he left Charvin, the postmaster, and then on to La Coste, where he arrived on June 26 or 27. After spending a few days at home, he returned to Grenoble and dismissed Raillanne, who had failed to satisfy him (in what respect we do not know). In his place he hired another young man by the name of Malatié or Lamalatié, who had been recommended by Mme Giroud, a bookseller.

Works and Days

After settling in at home in the summer of 1776, M. de Sade resumed his regular activities with perfect peace of mind, as if nothing had happened and he was now out of danger. He had always believed that nothing would happen to him as long as he remained on his own estate. Cloistered in his château, within magical walls that he believed to be impregnable, he divided his time between reading and writing. He bought the books he needed (a church history, a Virgil in Latin with a French translation) and sent other volumes to the bindery along with prints to the framer. But mostly he worked on his great work and continued to receive documentation from his Italian friends, especially Dr. Mesny, who found in these little services a way to make ends meet. Sade hoped to publish his *Voyage d'Italie* in the expectation that it might open the way to a career as a man of letters or, rather, a *philosophe*, for what he intended to give the public was no mere travelogue but nothing less than a philosophical treatise.

Donatien spent the entire summer at his work table, behind partially closed shutters in his study, with his books and manuscript. The days passed slowly in silent torpor, with their meager ration of news, domestic chores, and planned visits. By early autumn the monotony had begun to weigh on him, and boredom set in. Soon he could bear it no longer; an irresistible need to do something had taken hold of him. On October 15 he ordered the horses hitched up and headed for Montpellier, where he would remain until November 1.

Mademoiselle Justine

In Montpellier he saw Rosette, who had spent two months at La Coste with Mlle Du Plan. Rosette introduced him to one Adélaïde, whom she persuaded to go with the marquis with the assurance that she would have nothing to complain about "except the loneliness." No sooner was this bargain concluded than Donatien set out in search of another girl to serve as a scullery maid. He mentioned his need to Father Durand, a Recollect friar he knew, who discussed it with the Besson sisters, daughters of the Montpellier gardener. They in turn proposed the job to Catherine Treillet, aged twenty-two, the daughter of a blanket weaver and reportedly very pretty. The three young women set out for the Hôtel du Chapeau-Rouge, where the marquis was staying. Mlle Treillet, who was making forty écus in Montpellier, asked for fifty to work at La Coste. Sade promised that and more if he was pleased with her work.[3] All that remained was to obtain her father's consent. M. Treillet consulted Father Durand, who offered him all the reassurance he wanted: his daughter could not hope for a better position. As for morals, he, Father Durand, could guarantee that the Sade household was a veritable convent. The deal was closed. The next day Catherine went to work for her new master. Father Durand himself accompanied her to La Coste. On his return the friar laid to rest any lingering doubts on M. Treillet's part: his daughter had shed a few tears before entering the château, but Mme de Sade had immediately consoled her. By the time the marquis returned to Provence two or three days later, the

young woman had apparently settled into her new situation. She took
even less time to get used to the marquis. Undoubtedly she did exactly
as she was told, for Donatien lost no time in rebaptizing her with a
name more appropriate to her status as servant-mistress: Justine!

•

Mme de Sade does not appear to have gotten excited about this new
recruit any more than she had about those who had preceded her or
those who would come after. She had already seen so many! What is
more, the marquise was no whimpering victim. If she had ever played
that role, she had abandoned it long ago. By now she knew that she
would never have any control over her husband's desires, and that if
she persisted in an unequal struggle she would lose. Having jettisoned
pride and jealousy, she loved Donatien for what he was in his innermost
self, which she alone knew. She loved him passionately, to be sure,
but without idle sentimentality, without weakness, and without relin-
quishing her lucidity or relaxing her vigilance. Her love was pragmatic,
effective, and active, and with it went unflagging devotion. But it was
also anxious, constantly on the alert, ready to intervene at the first sign
of trouble. Renée-Pélagie was too well aware of what this devil of a
man was capable of not to be afraid of it. Once he surrendered to his
instincts, Donatien would not listen to anyone or anything. He threw
all restraint, all control, all caution to the winds and banished the very
notion of danger from his mind. It was against this devil-may-care
attitude, which could almost be characterized as suicidal, that Renée-
Pélagie fought an unending battle. She fought to save him—and not
in the selfish hope that he would one day come back to her. If it ever
occurred to Mme de Sade to "convert" Donatien, it was to bring him
to God, not to herself.

What worried her most at the moment was the outrageous amount
that the marquis was still spending on "household staff." When he
returned home after a two-week absence, the situation deteriorated
still further. Renée-Pélagie had no idea how she was going to maintain
such a large staff through the winter. She was short of wood and
clothing, and there was no glass in her windows, so that she had to
take to her bed against the cold. Soon food threatened to run short.
There was not enough bread, meat, or spices. In the meantime the
creditors were becoming more and more threatening. Upset by her
daughter's plight, Mme de Montreuil finally sent 1,200 livres to Gaufridy, who was warned that he would be "obliged to render an accounting" and that the funds were to be used only for the château's
subsistence and doled out as needed. Mme de Sade recognized her

mother's nastiness at work: if Mme de Montreuil wished to help her, why didn't she send her the money directly? What did she mean by using the notary as an intermediary? Did she take her daughter for a beggar in need of alms? "These convoluted arrangements of hers make no sense, and there will be a lot of trouble for you if you acquiesce," she wrote Gaufridy, "for then I shall have to send you to the butcher, baker, servants, and so forth. I haven't a cent, and with all that I can expect I'm short a thousand écus of what I need to make it through the winter."[4] The marquis, who suffered from no such scruples, was enraged chiefly at the thought that this manna might escape him, and he protested to Gaufridy, who refused to lend him so much as a sou of the 1,200 livres his mother-in-law had sent. Donatien resorted to emotional blackmail, a tune he generally played extraordinarily well: "I have the impression, moreover, that you're much keener to worm your way into her good graces than to be useful to me. It's very simple: this is the system in fashion, and you must respect it. I won't complain, especially since I expected as much."[5]

Offended Youth

Toward the middle of December M. de Sade informed Father Durand that he would require additional servants. He needed a chambermaid, a kitchen helper, a hairdresser, and a secretary. The priest immediately set to work. Within a few days he had recruited a secretary named Rolland, a hairdresser from Paris, a chambermaid by the name of Cavanis, and a foreign-born woman to work in the kitchen. He drove the new help to La Coste in his wagon. On the night of their arrival the marquis offered them dinner, then locked them in their bedrooms. During the night he went from room to room seeking favors in return for a purseful of money, apparently without success. The next morning three of the four new servants declared that they did not wish to remain another day in the château. Father Durand drove them back in his wagon, except for the new scullery maid, who preferred to remain in the marquis's service.

As soon as they reached Montpellier they informed Treillet of what had happened in the château. Outraged, he let Father Durand have a piece of his mind. Durand admitted that he had heard talk of M. de Sade's escapades but swore to high heaven that he believed the man had repented. There were even rumors that he had converted and that he had met the pope in Rome. When the weaver mentioned going up to La Coste after his daughter, Durand did all he could to stop him.

But when he saw that the man was determined, he gave him a note for the marquis. Treillet left the priest, however, and went directly to the superior of the Recollects, to whom he recounted the story. The superior unsealed Father Durand's letter and found that it contained just the opposite of what Treillet wanted. He forced Durand to rewrite the letter and then banished him from the monastery. Equipped with the new letter, the father of "Justine" set out for La Coste, arriving at the gates on January 17, 1777.

•

At this point let us break off this account, which is based entirely on Treillet's deposition, and turn the floor over to the marquis, who denied the weaver's allegations point by point: his statement is "false and full of slander," the marquis stated in his preamble. "This man is clearly a scoundrel and a liar." As for the facts, he denied them one by one:

—Treillet characterized his daughter as "very pretty." This description was woefully inaccurate, according to Sade.

—Concerning Durand's letter: "This letter is counterfeit, and Father Durand has never been allowed to prove it. What is more, Treillet could not have seen it, since he does not know how to read."

—Concerning the young servants and the infamous night at La Coste: "A servant took them up to bed. M. de S. did not even go with them. He stayed to converse with Madame and Father Durand, and they locked themselves into their rooms until the next morning at four, when the same servant went up to wake them for the departure."

—Concerning the offense to morality:

I have only one thing to say on this point. Supposing I had found these people (who were nature's own horror as to age and looks), but supposing I had found them worthy to satisfy [my] desires, it is likely that, given their offer to work for me and to remain in my house, I would have kept them. And having decided to keep them, I would not have made an assault on their modesty in the middle of the night. I would have had plenty of time during their stay. If, therefore, as was certainly the case, I decided that very night to send them away, given my scant need of their services and the fact that I never asked for them, it is more than likely that I would never have gone and exposed myself by insulting people whom I knew would be leaving the next morning and whom I would thus be putting in a position to lodge charges against me. Did I not foresee that these people would feel ill-used for having been obliged to make this pointless journey? Would I have compounded their resentment by insulting them during the night? To have committed such an error I would have to have been stark raving mad, and I most certainly did not do it. As for the purseful of money, no one knows better than M. Gaufridy that at that time I hadn't a cent.[6]

Whom are we to believe? We know from experience how coolly Sade could retail lie after lie. We have caught him in flagrant untruths so often, we have so frequently heard him protest his innocence in tones of sincerity when his guilt was undeniable, that it is hard to believe him now. In any case, his argument is unconvincing to anyone who knows him well. The imprudence of his behavior? He often recognized imprudence only after the fact, and we know that under the sway of desire he never took precautions. As for the ugliness of the servants, he is certainly exaggerating. And even if he were not, ugliness, as Lely noted, was something that Sade was quite capable of finding attractive, assuming that he shared the odd taste he ascribed to the libertines in *Cent Vingt Journées de Sodome*:

Beauty is the simple thing, ugliness the extraordinary one, and all ardent imaginations probably always prefer the extraordinary thing in lust to the simple one. Beauty and freshness are never striking but in a simple sense; ugliness and degradation deliver a much more solid blow; the turmoil is more vigorous, hence the excitement more keen. Hence it should come as no surprise that plenty of people would take their pleasure with an old, ugly, and even stinking woman than with a fresh and pretty girl, any more than it should come as a surprise, I say, that a man would rather walk on the rough and arid terrain of mountains than on the monotonous paths of the plains.[7]

A Pistol Shot

On January 17, 1777, between noon and one o'clock, Treillet (according to his version of events) appeared at the château gate, letter in hand, and asked to speak to the master. A servant told him that the marquis was not present. He asked to see the marquise. She appeared a moment later, and he introduced himself as the father of her cook. Mme de Sade then whispered a word into the servant's ear, and both withdrew after asking the visitor to wait. A short while later M. de Sade appeared, shouting insults and threats. After telling Treillet that his daughter ought to regard the opportunity to work for him as a stroke of good fortune, he called "Justine." She rushed in and, crying, threw her arms around her father's neck. But the marquis wrenched her from his arms, pushed her roughly into a storeroom, and locked her in before her father could utter a single word. Sade then grabbed

Treillet and bodily hurled him out the door, swearing that he would have the weaver thrown into prison if he did not leave his property immediately. In any case, he added, Treillet's daughter had pledged to work for a year and had not fulfilled her contract.

Treillet claimed that this scene had been witnessed by three masons working at the château: Bontemps, from Roussillon, Perrin, from La Coste, and an apprentice. The following day, January 18, Sade sent a resident of La Coste by the name of Paulet with the following message for Treillet: if he agreed to leave his daughter at the château, he and his fourteen-year-old son could both come to work there as watchmen. "Justine" sent her father twelve livres by the same messenger. She had slipped him another twelve livres previously, just before they were parted.[8]

Treillet may have been telling the truth, but he omitted one small detail: the shot he fired at the marquis at point-blank range. On this specific point the marquis is to be believed. Here is his version of the facts:

A dreadful thing has just happened here, my dear attorney . . . Friday morning at the stroke of noon someone rang at the gate. The servant announced the father of Justine, my cook. This man approached in an insolent manner and said that he had come for his daughter . . . He then trotted out all the usual insults, and so forth. His insolent attitude had made me rather hot under the collar. But I listened to him attentively and then said, 'If you have come for your daughter, sir, here she is. Talk to her as much as you like, but no foul language. If you have come to take her away, your request will not be denied, but would you kindly wait until I have had time to find another?' Whereupon our man took his daughter by the arm and forcibly dragged her toward the door. I then seized the man myself, without anger or violence of any kind (for, having come down from my study, I had at that point no cane or hat or anything else in my hand), and led him to the main gate, telling him that this was no way to go about his business and suggesting that he go down to the village, where someone would consider his request and report on the decision. I uttered these last words just as the scoundrel stepped on the threshold of the main gate. At that instant, without responding or showing excitement, he fired a pistol at me two inches from my chest, but fortunately for me only the primer went off. The man then fled. You can imagine my terror and that of the whole household.[9]

Afterward, the marquis continued, Treillet had gone about the village spreading nasty rumors, while Justine allegedly attempted to see her father again so as to "settle his raving mind." He initially refused, we are told, for fear that he was being drawn into some sort of ambush but finally went to the appointed place, just outside the château gate, in the company of his two witnesses, Perrin and Bontemps. "The conversation, which I will not relate, was most heated," the marquis went on, "for the man carried on with his foul language while the girl went on trying to calm her father down and dissuade him from his purpose." Finally, according to Sade, Treillet fired a second shot into the courtyard when he thought he heard the marquis's voice.

Later Donatien would deny that witnesses had been present when Treillet had burst into his home: "I wish there had been!" he exclaimed. The story of his having asked the father and son to work for him as watchmen was, he said, a pure invention. "Watchman, him! Yes, in order to calm him down, his daughter and M. Paulet may have proposed something of the sort, but the rest is false."

On January 18, the day after the assault, Viguier, the deputy judge of La Coste, opened an investigation into allegations that Treillet had violated the decree of the *parlement* of Provence prohibiting the carrying of arms by "artisans, peasants, and other individuals of common rank." Two days later Treillet left La Coste for Aix with the intention of filing charges of his own. The marquis considered his departure a victory.[10]

"This troubled state of affairs"

Treillet went to Aix to file charges against the man he considered to have assaulted him. Aware of the danger, Sade dispatched Gaufridy to deal with the authorities. The strategy was to forestall the father of "Justine" by filing a suit against him forthwith. The notary refused to act, however. His client's idea struck him as poor if not downright dangerous. To go after Treillet was to stick one's head in the lion's mouth: it showed that the marquis was afraid of what the man might do. The best strategy, according to the notary, was to do nothing, and certainly nothing eye-catching; furthermore, the girl must be sent home. But this, the marquis indicated, was out of the question. Would he have to make his own soup to keep order in his household? "Today a stranger comes demanding his daughter with pistol shots. The day after tomorrow, a peasant will come asking for his day's pay with rifle shots!" Was he not to bring charges against an attempted murderer? Was he to allow himself to be shot at without uttering a word in reproach? He might as well acknowledge his guilt! In his heart of hearts, was this not what Gaufridy believed? "Tell the truth with your usual forthrightness: like the public, which deems me guilty because I am unfortunate, you believed I was not innocent enough for you to defend me publicly. That is a fact, and even if you will not admit it, I am nevertheless convinced that it is the case." In any event, the lord of La Coste would not allow any man to insult him with impunity. His peasants needed to be taught a lesson: "I could hardly bow down before a man who began by insulting me, for this might have set a very bad example, particularly on my own estate—an estate like this, moreover, where it is so essential that the vassals be obliged to show respect, the need for which they are only too likely to forget from one moment to the next." And here is what our future "sans-culotte" had to say on the same subject a little later on: "I have come to the conclusion that all the Costains are beggars fit for the wheel, and one day surely I shall prove my contempt for them and reveal my thoughts. I assure you that if they were to be roasted one after another, I would furnish the kindling without batting an eyelash. When the time comes I will not spare them—they can count on it."[11] Treillet must therefore be prosecuted "with the utmost zeal."

But it was too late. The weaver had already filed charges and submitted to Castillon, the *procureur général*, a deposition detailing his allegations and accusing the marquis of having kidnapped his daughter (but omitting any mention of pistol shots). At this news Sade heaped further abuse on his notary. There was not a minute to lose. This Treillet must be stopped immediately: "Otherwise you will prove to me that people here are out to ruin me and nothing else." Gaufridy finally decided to approach an attorney in Aix by the name of Mouret, but Mouret warned him that the *procureur général* took a very dim view of the marquis de Sade and that the case might go against him:

Even if it were true that this lord was as indifferent as you say he is toward the girl in question, and even if she were as much a vestal as her ugliness persuades you she is, the very grounds on which her father came to claim her required that she be handed over to him at once . . . No monthly or yearly contract can take precedence over a father's claim on his daughter. He alone has legitimate rights over her. The master deprived of her service can claim only [monetary] damages. But when the demand is based on grounds as powerful as the corruption of the daughter by her own master, all claims must cease, and the father is authorized to take his daughter wherever she may be, even by force . . . This affair, which you hope to keep quiet, has already attracted a great deal of notoriety and may have very serious consequences. I should be pleased if in your reply you assure me that this girl has been escorted by reliable individuals to her father in Montpellier, for I see nothing other than this prompt remedy, if *faithfully executed*, that can calm this troubled state of affairs.[12]

The "black pit"

The only remedies the marquis de Sade ever believed in were his own. In the present circumstances he saw only one: to leave for Paris. He therefore ordered two carriages to be prepared: one for him and La Jeunesse, the other for Mme de Sade and "Justine." To believe his version of events, Justine had flung herself down at the feet of her mistress and begged to be taken with her. Shortly after arriving in the capital on the night of February 8, following an exhausting journey over wretched roads in frightful weather, Donatien learned of his mother's death, which had occurred three weeks earlier, on January 14, without anyone's having notified him.

In Paris he went to stay with his former tutor, the abbé Amblet, on rue des Fossés-Monsieur-le-Prince, while Renée-Pélagie spent the first night in the dead woman's apartment at the Carmelite convent on rue d'Enfer. The next day she moved into the hôtel de Danemark on rue Jacob.

On February 13, 1777, at nine in the evening, while Donatien was visiting his wife in her bedroom there, Inspector Marais arrived, lettre de cachet in hand. An hour later the marquis was locked up in the dungeon of Vincennes. On the morning of February 15 he was transferred to room 11, which was called "a room with a view" because it projected beyond the walls of the fortress.

•

Sade could not have been unaware that in going to Paris, he was delivering himself bound hand and foot to Mme de Montreuil, who would show no mercy. He knew that the capital was a huge trap ready to snap shut. Reinaud and Gaufridy had understood this, as had Gothon, who had tried to persuade him to stay at La Coste. How, then, are we to explain this determination to hasten his ruin? Once again we are at the heart of a troubling enigma, a behavior pattern that I earlier explained as the manifestation of a suicidal impulse. Sade would later claim that he had made this journey only to be at his mother's bedside, and he accused Mme de Montreuil of having seized the opportunity to have him thrown into prison: "Of all the possible means vengeance and cruelty might have chosen, Madame, you must agree that you chose the most horrible of all . . . But, apart from the care my mother required, my second purpose [in coming to Paris] was none other than to implore you and calm you down, to come to an understanding with you, to take decisions in connection with my case that you would have approved and counseled."[13]

Mme de Montreuil swore by all the gods that she had nothing to do with her son-in-law's arrest: "He accused me of having betrayed him! Me! When I knew nothing about it, when the minister had known about it for six days, and they were even keeping an eye on me on account of him!"[14] Yet she could not suppress an exultant cry upon learning that he was behind bars: "Things could not be better or more secure: it was about time!" She also explained to Renée-Pélagie that her husband's imprisonment was essential to expediting the appeal procedure. Marais had tried to convince his prisoner of this on the way to Vincennes. We are asked to believe, in other words, that the lettre de cachet fell from the sky at an opportune moment to grease the works in Sade's favor without anyone's having asked that it be issued—a species of "divine surprise." The man named in the letter did not believe a word of this, and it is easy to understand why. His relations with his mother-in-law had never been worse. Less than a month earlier, on January 17, Mme de Montreuil had received "ten big pages of threat and invective" from her daughter (but dictated, of course, by the marquis). "If I wanted to avenge myself or punish him for it," she wrote to Gaufridy, "I would bring them to the ministers who can appreciate, better than I, their behavior and mine and the justice of his complaints and reproaches." Then, expressing her thought more clearly, she adds: "If they attack me as they threaten to, I have the means to respond, and I have no fear of anything in the world. Too bad for whoever forces matters to a head so as to bring the *evidence* to light."[15]

Given that threat, it took no great leap of the imagination to picture la Présidente on the alert and ready to pounce on her prey, as Reinaud did with gusto in a prophetic letter sent to his colleague and kinsman Gaufridy just five days before Sade's arrest: "I can't get out of my head the idea that Mme de Montreuil's letter is a final trap, especially coming after the last futile effort. The marquis is stepping like a fool into the black pit. It seems to me that his mother-in-law, tired of seeing her secrets revealed, is planning a subtle maneuver to take by cunning what she cannot have by force. Upon my word, before the month is out our champion will be behind bars in Paris."[16]

Despite la Présidente's indignant denials, everything does indeed suggest that she was the one who handed her son-in-law over to the police. Mme de Sade was in no doubt about her mother's treachery: "I cannot forgive her for having had him arrested or for making a mystery of things about which I should at least have been informed," she complained to Gaufridy.[17] And the abbé de Sade, who had only just recovered from a nasty cold, found the news rejuvenating: "The man has been arrested and locked up in a fortress near Paris. So now I am at peace, and I believe that everyone will be happy."[18]

Letters of Blood

"The blow so dazed me, so dumbfounded me, that in truth I do not yet know where I stand." Gripped with panic, Mme de Sade, who had watched as her husband was led away, at first turned to her mother for help. "Without anger, without rage," Mme de Montreuil simply repeated that she was not the person responsible, that she was incapable of treachery. To others, however, la Présidente was astonished by her daughter's blindness: "She suspects me of self-interest or prejudice," Mme de Montreuil confided to Gaufridy, "and I shall leave her to be enlightened by others against whom she ought not to harbor such suspicions. How can she be as blind as she seems? That is what I find difficult to imagine, for in the end she must have seen, understood, and been *convinced* on her own that it was not all slander."[19]

Renée-Pélagie next turned to the minister of justice. But the minister, who was concerned solely with the appeal procedure, let her know, not without cynicism, that Donatien's imprisonment meant that he could at last begin his job: "Now that it is possible for me to work, I shall do so." Meanwhile, Renée-Pélagie was quietly advised to remain calm and not make a fuss over the case. She was promised that she would soon receive satisfaction, even beyond what she hoped, and that she would be told where her husband was being held. For the moment she had no idea: believing that he was in the Bastille, she prowled around that fortress. But the drawbridges were always raised, and the guards prohibited any loitering in the vicinity. She had no news of the prisoner. The minister assured her only that he was in good health and wanted for nothing, not even a servant to wait on him. Three months thus elapsed with Renée-Pélagie in ignorance and anxiety but fiercely determined to free Donatien. "Nothing will make me change but my husband's welfare," she assured Gaufridy. "That is my sole aim; the world is nothing to me without that."[20] In the meantime she was allowed to write him. Her letters were transmitted to him by the police. Two days after his arrest she sent him this note: "How did you spend the night, my dear friend? I am truly suffering, although they tell me you are well. I will not be happy until I have seen you. Stay calm, I beg you."[21]

On March 8 the first letter from the prisoner arrived:

Since the dreadful moment when I was plucked so ignominiously from your side, my dear friend, I have been constantly subjected to the cruelest of suffering. I am forbidden to reveal any details of this to you, and all that I can tell you is that it is impossible to be more wretched than I am. I have actually spent seventeen days in this terrible place. But the orders that held me here must have been very different, for the manner in which I was kept bears little resemblance to that in which I am kept today. It is absolutely impossible for me to endure such cruel conditions any longer. Despair has taken hold of me. At times I no longer know who I am. I feel that I am losing my mind. My blood is boiling too much to bear so terrible an embarrassment. I want to turn my rage against myself, and if I am not out of here in four days I am absolutely certain that I shall smash my head against the walls. My decision is firm, and with that I shall satisfy your mother, who told Amblet that my death was the best available way to end my affair. I am unhappy that I am obliged to speak to you like this, my dear friend. I know how much this decision will hurt you, but it is firm, and I permit you to look upon me as a coward if I do not keep my word. If my life is still dear to you, go throw yourself at the feet of the minister, or if necessary the king, and ask them to give your husband back. Can they refuse you? By harassing me as they are doing, they are only abetting your mother's cruel purposes . . . They will not fail to tell you, to put an end to your importunings, that this detention is necessary to dispose of my case, but I hope that you will not be duped by this idle pretext, which is your barbarous mother's way of hiding her vengeance under false colors . . . If a lettre de cachet had been necessary, they had only to issue one allowing me to leave the kingdom. I asked for nothing more, and they would have achieved the same end without resorting to such cruel means.[22]

This correspondence continued without letup throughout the sixteen months of the marquis's incarceration. Mme de Sade was authorized to send only "open," that is, unsealed, letters. When their content failed to please the authorities, they were returned forthwith. The same rules applied to Donatien's letters: "In what he writes me, they cut, erase, and rearrange," the marquise complained. They therefore resorted to invisible ink, which enabled them to communicate a little more freely. Renée-Pélagie regularly informed her husband of her efforts in connection with the "great affair" (to which she referred in their private code as the "pumps from Constantinople"), for which she held out hopes of a quick settlement. In the meantime she urged patience, a "style," she remarked, "which is not to M. de Sade's taste, and I sense how hard it is for him to go on hearing such things after more than seven months."[23] What caused him to suffer most was the uncertain duration of his incarceration: "So tell me any date for an end to this, for to set no limit is deliberately to reduce me to the depths of despair . . . What have I done to be treated so barbarously? Why punish me without hearing me? Why deprive me of hope and reduce me to having death as my goal and sole desire?"[24]

M. Thibault de Sade has made available thirty-six previously unpublished letters that the marquis wrote in this period to his wife and la Présidente.[25] There is little variety in their content: supplications, outbursts of hatred and suffering, moving calls for compassion, threats to commit suicide if not released, and imprecations against Mme de Montreuil, who is pleasantly characterized as an "infernal monster," "venomous beast," "bloody trollop of a mother," and so on. Meanwhile, madness lurked in the wings, as the marquis's mind, "constantly fatigued by the same object, hastens to plunge wholeheartedly" into the abyss. In January 1778, however, he paid his respects to la Présidente and begged her to put an end to his torture. The letter (dated January 5, 1778) would be nothing out of the ordinary were it not for the fact that it is written in blood. This detail (which suggests a remarkable fetish: blood does not lie) is reason enough to reproduce it in part:

Yes, Madame, yes, it is a heart that you deprive of hope, that you are pleased to rack with pain with your obstinacy to conceal from me the details of my arrest—it is, I say, this very heart, beaten down as it is, that nevertheless offers you good wishes as sincere as the afflictions with which you lacerate it. Madame, in the name of all that is dearest to you, deliver me from the horror in which I find myself . . . Allow yourself to be moved by these tears and by the bloody characters in which I have deliberately written this letter. Know that this blood is yours, because today it gives life to creatures that you cherish, who hold you so close, and in whose name I implore you. I shall drain it to the last drop if necessary, and until you have granted me the favor I ask of you, and I shall use it to ask again and again for the same thing . . .[26]

Meanwhile, Renée-Pélagie tirelessly petitioned the minister for permission to see her husband. Her presence would at least make his captivity more bearable. But all her requests were met with the same implacable refusal. Her thoughts then turned to organizing an escape, and she confided her plan to Gaufridy: if the appeal required Donatien's presence in Aix, that would be the moment to strike. In case she herself were prevented from acting, she asked the notary to do so in her place and then to hold the fugitive "locked in a room in a secure place. You could write me a letter in which you would merely indicate that he had left for Paris with his driver, and the signal would be that the address would not be in your handwriting. It is better to have the keys in one's own hand than to ask for them."[27]

But how far could the notary be trusted? Had he not remained in contact with Mme de Montreuil? Had he not been instructed to keep her informed of everything that went on at La Coste? To bolster his confidence la Présidente had even promised him that his letters would be burned the moment they had been read. It seems likely that Gaufridy was not altogether pleased with this role, although he apparently allowed himself to be won over by the imperious lady's flattery as well as her reasoning. Sade would later accuse him, quite unjustly, of treachery. He could find no sarcasm stinging enough to berate his advocate, forgetting that Gaufridy had shown him letters before sending them to la Présidente and that he had done nothing contrary to Sade's interests. If he had searched the marquis's study at La Coste, was it not for the purpose of removing compromising documents? Others tried to persuade him that he was doing his friend an inestimable service, and he may have believed them.

"Writing" or "Mechanisms"?

As for la Présidente and her daughter, the ambiguity was total. Mme de Sade felt obliged to go easy with her mother, to feign moderation, deference, and even trust: "I can take no other course if I hope to succeed," she told Gaufridy. But in secret she confessed: "Once out of her grip, I would rather till the earth than fall into her clutches again." So far from being fooled, however, Mme de Montreuil was annoyed and worried by what she called her daughter's "blindness." This she found even more difficult to comprehend after learning from Gaufridy that some highly compromising items had been found hidden in a secret room at La Coste: "every trace must be annihilated a hundred feet beneath the earth along with anything that might . . .

serve to justify past or future allegations." She did not know exactly what was involved: "Is it writing? Or machines or mechanisms used for all I know on more than one occasion? Or shreds of papers?"[28] These "papers" terrified la Présidente most of all—no doubt they consisted chiefly of Donatien's notes on various scabrous subjects. One such "scrap" concerned the young secretary. It had flown out the window, and neighbors had picked it up. Where had it come from? Were there others like it? And what about the "furniture" with the "far-fetched" sculpture that had caused "so much pain?" What had happened to it? Apparently it had been smashed, because debris were found. Where, exactly? Was Nanon aware of the loss of the papers? "This information is essential for deciding how to proceed with her." What a lot of concern for some scribbled notes and a few sticks of wood. Gaufridy was urged to launch an immediate investigation (a request somewhat at odds with his nonchalant nature). Did Mme de Sade know about any of this? "If she does," her mother remarked, "she is beyond imagining, yet other aspects of her conduct become imaginable. If she does not, this is not the time to enlighten her, but that time will come."[29] Mme de Montreuil confessed that she could not understand Renée-Pélagie's attitude at all: "I cannot yet unravel what she is thinking . . . Does she act out of an invincible infatuation? An excessive sense of duty? Or the fear that she may one day be punished for efforts she might be suspected of not having made? In this respect she is impenetrable for everyone."[30]

The Council of Dispatches

After much maneuvering, la Présidente succeeded in having the case examined by the Council of Dispatches on September 26, 1777, and signs from the three principal ministers who sat on the council were favorable. A petition to be presented to the king at the council meeting was drafted by Joseph Jérôme Siméon, *avocat* in the *parlement* of Aix. After a brief statement of the facts, Siméon came to the accusation proper, which he declared to be "devoid of any kind of probability" and to have been brought before the court "by a person of base condition, the servant of a prostitute and an accomplice in her offenses." The petition further noted that the chemists had found no trace of poison in the pastilles and that two of the women involved had acknowledged the marquis's innocence, having withdrawn "all charges and demands for damages" before Maître Carmis on August 8, 1772.

As for the crime "that offends both nature and morality," the *avocat* deemed the charge inadmissible because this count was "absolutely foreign to the charge that was the sole grounds for the search and investigation by the authorities." Two decrees of the *parlement* of Provence (dated May 8, 1677, and April 18, 1766) forbade judges to hear witnesses concerning matters not contained in the complaint, with dismissal of the charges the penalty for failure to observe this restriction. Nevertheless, the same *parlement* had heard as witnesses "the very individuals who had made depositions against the absent accused: ruined women who drew infamous recompense from their crimes made numerous slanderous charges against a man of quality in the hope of gratifying the most vile interest, and [such witnesses] cannot ever deserve the confidence of the court." On these grounds the marquis de Sade asked the king to dismiss the charges against him and overturn the verdict of the Marseilles court, thereby preparing the way for further appeals.

Despite the *avocat*'s eloquent peroration and the hopeful indications prior to the meeting, the Council of Dispatches refused to overturn the Marseilles verdict on the technical grounds that it had jurisdiction only in administrative cases, criminal matters coming exclusively within the purview of the Privy Council or the Bureau of Appeals.

Thus the decision was clear: M. de Sade would have to appear in person before the *parlement* of Aix. His wife saw this as an opportunity for an escape and even began to lay plans for such an eventuality.[31] But Mme de Montreuil worked to make this appearance unnecessary so as to avoid a confrontation with the prostitutes from Marseilles, "which is always an unfortunate and embarrassing thing," but above all to forestall any possibility of escape. The only way to do this was to claim that madness prevented the marquis from appearing in person, thus clearing the way for him to testify before a commission empowered to hear evidence. This was the basis of la Présidente's instructions to Gaufridy in February 1778: "De S[ade], who was already insane (*aliéné*) at times when he was placed in security about a year ago, is today totally insane. In this unfortunate state he cannot appear either of his own volition or on command of the authorities. In any case, what information is to be had from a demented man?" She asked that a guardian be appointed to represent the interests of the marquis and his family. This plan, she added, "appeals to the minister here, because it is legal and has no drawbacks."[32]

The Abbé's Estate

Meanwhile, on December 31, 1777, the abbé de Sade died at his house in La Vignerme at the age of seventy-two. Without waiting for his death Mme de Sade had asked Gaufridy to have the château sealed in order to prevent any seizure of his effects. He did in fact leave a quite complicated estate encumbered by heavy debts, to say nothing of a Spanish woman living in his home with her daughter, to whom he had just sold La Vignerme.

Shortly before his death he had drawn up a will in favor of his brother, the grand prior and *commandeur*. Knowing the abbé's debts, his brother had insisted on an inventory prior to accepting the inheritance. The estate consisted essentially of a library, a few bronze medals, and a natural history collection. Sensing an opportunity, the grand prior arranged for a general inventory of the contents of Saumane and La Vignerme in March 1778. Virtually all the furniture, along with the château itself, of which the abbé was only a tenant, belonged to the marquis personally. Pretending to believe that these properties were part of the abbé's estate, the *commandeur* had everything that appeared to be of any value moved to his own residence at Saint-Clou, near Mazan, had trees uprooted and planted in his own park, seized the silver, sold the carriage and horses, and even went so far as to receive cash payments that the farmers of the priory of Bonnieux owed to their late prior. In other words, he picked the place clean. What is more, he would never repay one sol of his brother's debts, which amounted to 6,087 livres, 14 sols, not to mention the 6,000 livres advanced by the marquis, and he even neglected to pay for his brother's burial.

As for benefices once held by the abbé of Ebreuil, Mme de Sade thought that they were admirably well suited to her son Claude-Armand, who was a postulant of the Order of Malta but had yet to prove his mettle. She immediately inquired whether he might retain the benefices by becoming a knight. But the replies she received to this and other, related questions were so discouraging that in the end she surrendered the benefices to abbé Charles de Sade-Vauredone, provost of Saint-Victor of Marseilles.

"When will I get out?"

"Tell me, tell me, or I will smash my head against the walls that contain me! Tell me, do not take my soul from me piecemeal, do not shred it piece by piece as you are doing . . . My despair is exploding. It is violent, my expressions portray it for you, you see it. I am no longer in my right mind, my dear friend. The horror of a fate of which they will not allow me to glimpse any end is too much for me to bear, and I cannot take any more . . ."[33]

"Oh, my God, how unhappy I am! . . ."[34]

Day after day, month after month, Sade's letters are a litany of alternating rage and despair, of tenderness and hate, of invective and supplication, repeated ad nauseam. And these verbal flashes are merely the prelude to the melodrama of the next thirteen years, one of the most wrenching monologues in all of literature. The months from February 1777 to June 1778 were the marquis de Sade's apprenticeship in prison. He discovered its torments and anguish but also its resources, above all that of frustration, which would sustain his writing: the most freewheeling literary oeuvre the world has ever known was born in and of the horror of imprisonment.

For the time being, apart from physical and moral suffering that he details, not without obvious self-indulgence, for pages on end, the marquis claimed to be preoccupied chiefly with the "great affair," whose resolution and, with it, he thinks, his eventual release seem to recede further into the future the closer he believes he is to attaining it: "I know only too well that what I need is patience," he wrote his wife, "and it is precisely because of that that I complain about your attempts to divert me, that I complain about the ridiculous letters you have written me, some of which I will show you some day, in reading which the most suspicious, most darkly pessimistic spirit would have given a hundred to one that he would be released the next day."[35]

While awaiting that happy day, he prepared his defense, certain that he was in the right or at least careful to appear certain, because he knew that his letters were being read by the prison censor. To his wife he wrote: "I offer to prove in *the most authentic* and *invincible manner* that there is nothing against me but the most frivolous appearances and not one serious charge . . ."[36]

Preparation for Departure

Finally, on May 18, 1778, the marquis was visited by a certain M. Bontoux, Mme de Montreuil's envoy, who came with a letter of recommendation from la Présidente and a memorandum prepared by two attorneys engaged to handle the case, Maîtres Siméon and Pazery. The memorandum discussed the two courses of action open to the defendant: to reappear in court or to follow the procedure for insanity. When Donatien protested at the idea of passing himself off as mad, Bontoux insisted, emphasizing that there was no other way to avoid going to Aix. The marquis replied that he had no objection to going provided he was allowed to travel without an escort.

All that remained then was to settle the means of his transfer and obtain the necessary legal documents allowing him to appeal the decision of the *parlement* of Provence despite the expiration of the legal limit of five years. La Présidente also had Bontoux warn her son-in-law that a lot had happened since the original incident, that the minister knew about all these things from various complaints filed against the marquis, and that he therefore must not count on being released even if the judgment was overturned.

Immediately after Bontoux's departure, the marquis sat down and prepared a long list of "Objections, Reflections, and Demands" concerning his imminent trip to Aix, which list he dispatched to his wife on May 20. Was the trip prudent? Was it not foolhardy to offer up a head that one had been condemned to lose? Did he not have secret enemies in the province, who might take advantage of the opportunity to do him in? He wanted his wife to be allowed to travel with him, for otherwise he feared a trap. He wanted to know what formalities would be observed in Aix. He asked that Gaufridy meet him on his arrival. And he asked for assurances that he would be released immediately if the court decided in his favor.

The Journey to Aix

Not only did Mme de Sade not travel with her husband, she was not even notified of the date of his departure. Mme de Montreuil chose to say nothing in order to prevent her daughter from interfering. On June 22, when the marquis was already en route, Renée-Pélagie still believed him to be in Vincennes and was worried by his silence: "Since you wrote, my good friend, that you were too busy to answer me, I have not had any news . . . I am in pain and will remain so until I have a note from you to reassure me."[37]

Inspector Marais was assigned to accompany the prisoner to Aix. The carriage left Vincennes on June 14 and came clattering into Aix on cobblestone streets shortly after dusk on Monday, June 20.[38] Since it was too late for the prison formalities to be completed, the policeman and his prisoner spent the night at the Auberge Saint-Jacques. The next afternoon the marquis appeared at the royal prison of Aix "in obedience to the court and to cleanse the record of his flight to avoid punishment," and the inspector turned over to the warden the order the king had issued on June 11 at Versailles.[39]

15

On the Run

The Trial

During the twenty-three days he spent in the jails of Aix, Donatien repeatedly assailed Marais with "a thousand personal requests, despite the fact that he is treated as well as a man of quality can be in prison." He wanted to make gifts to all his fellow prisoners "to prove his good heart." The inspector resisted as many of these whims as he could, "but you have to give in from time to time."[1] Donatien in any case was quite comfortable and managed not only to spend twelve livres with the Conciergerie's caterer but also to conceive an idyll with a young prisoner, Mme Doyen de Baudoin, whom he called his "Dulcinea in the mirror" and to whom he sent love letters through the attorney Reinaud, fittingly dubbed the "messenger of the gods."

The appellate hearing began on June 22 when Sade's petition to the *parlement* of Provence, couched in almost the same terms as Siméon's memoir to the Council of Dispatches, was read aloud to the court. Conducted with unusual speed, the proceedings lasted no more than three weeks. Of course the parties had agreed on a settlement in advance, and the family continued its pressure on the court. The commandeur de Sade, for example, wrote the *premier président*, M. Des Galois de La Tour, on June 25 that his family, "which is honored to be related to all of Provence," would certainly not have suffered such an insult if "we had not seen judges who had the confidence of all estates" suspended from their functions—in other words, if his nephew had not been judged by Maupeou's men. "Libertinage deserves punishment," he continued, "but not the same punishment as for a crime.

And the faults being personal, you should have punished the libertine alone. If I were less acquainted with your kind regards for the family, or if I doubted your equity, I should have hastened to Aix for the honor of making my case to you. But you are too enlightened for me to feel a moment's fear about the judgment you are going to render."[2]

The Verdict

On Tuesday, June 30, at eight in the morning, Inspector Marais arrived at the Conciergerie and from there accompanied Donatien in a sedan chair, its windows covered by curtains, to the Jacobin convent in which the *parlement* was meeting. The court having assembled, the prisoner was ushered in. He made a move to kneel, but the *premier président* signaled that he was to stand. Maître Joseph Jérôme Siméon then delivered a moving summation, after which M. d'Eymar de Mont-meyan, the royal *procureur général*, enthusiastically ratified its argu-ment. After deliberation the *parlement* overturned the Marseilles verdict on the grounds that "the alleged crime of poisoning was totally unproven" and ordered a new trial on the charges of debauchery and pederasty alone, with all the witnesses to be heard again. After the session, which lasted nearly two hours, Marais escorted the marquis back to prison. "At least two hundred people had gathered to see M. de Sade as he entered and left the hall of justice, but they were dis-appointed because the curtains of the sedan chair had been drawn as a precaution. The marquis," Marais noted, "did not seem greatly moved by this first session."

Just after the hearing, Gaufridy met with the *premier président* and the *procureur général*, who unofficially suggested that he go at once to Marseilles to meet with the prostitutes and "persuade them to destroy anything in their depositions having to do with sodomy." Inspector Marais, to whom we owe this information, added this comment: "This M. Gaufridy is a clever man, greatly devoted to the house of Sade, and an attorney who appears to have Mme de Montreuil's full confidence in this case, and this secret agreement cannot be in better hands. I myself will leave today for Marseilles to lend him a discreet hand if the need arises." Gaufridy thus went to Marseilles, where he liberally dispensed money that la Présidente had sent him by way of the Sade d'Eyguières. He treated the women in the case to food and drink and splendidly entertained the city's surgeons and apothecaries, "who said they were enchanted with the way they had been dealt with."[3]

While the witnesses were interrogated, Mme de Montreuil tried to influence the members of the *parlement.* "I impatiently await the end of it all," she confided to Gaufridy. "Not without some anxiety— not for the individual, because on that score I have been given every assurance regarding dangerous opinions or information, but I sincerely hope that no taint remains. Six days ago I wrote to the heads of *parlement* most emphatically on that point. Those who were able to write me did so in the most upright and flattering manner."[4]

Finally, on the morning of July 14, 1778, after a public interrogation of the accused, the *parlement* of Provence issued its definitive verdict. Citing only the crimes of "debauchery and immoderate libertinage," the court ordered that Louis Aldonse Donatien de Sade be "admonished behind the bar, in the presence of the royal *procureur général,* to behave more decently in the future." He was further prohibited from "inhabiting or frequenting the city of Marseilles" for three years and sentenced to pay a fine of fifty livres "applicable to prison charities and court costs." He was then to be released from prison.

To Sade this verdict meant one thing and one thing only: he was free. The bad dream was at an end. One more day and he would be able to return to La Coste and satisfy as before his insatiable appetite for life. He had just turned thirty-eight.

But before the next day dawned he was awakened in his jail cell at three in the morning by Inspector Marais and invited to return with the policeman to Vincennes. The marquis was aghast: had not the court's decision the day before restored his freedom? What he had failed to reckon with was the lettre de cachet issued on February 13, which had been reconfirmed by an order of the king dated July 5 and which had been in Marais's pocket for twenty-four hours.

•

The Sade escutcheon was cleansed of the blemish on the family honor. The marquis was to be returned to his cell. Order had been restored. Well played, Madame la Présidente!

The Escape from Valence

At dawn on July 15 a four-seat berlin lumbered out the gate of the Aix prison carrying Donatien, Inspector Marais, Marais's brother Antoine-Thomas, and two policemen. In order to avoid passing through the marquis's estates the carriage took a roundabout route by way of Tarascon to Valliguières, where it was decided to spend the night in an inn.[5] There Donatien attempted an escape that he had contemplated en route, but he was unable to carry out his plan.

The prisoner and his four guards left Valliguières at dawn on July 16 and continued northward. At nine-thirty that night the carriage pulled into the courtyard of an inn on the outskirts of Valence called the Logis du Louvre.[6] After being shown to his room, Donatien went to the window overlooking the highway and remained there leaning on the sill until Marais invited him to sit down to dinner. A table had been set up in the prisoner's room. But Donatien declined the invitation: he had no appetite and would go without eating. While his four companions dined, he paced back and forth. At length he informed Marais's brother that "nature called." Thomas Marais accompanied him to the toilet, located in the corridor, and waited for him at the head of the stairs. After five or six minutes, the marquis emerged, advanced stealthily toward his guard, pretended to stumble, freed himself from the man's grasp, ran down the stairs, and hurried out the gate and onto the highway. Thinking that he was still in the inn, the Marais brothers and the two policemen searched the premises from top to bottom and then searched the nearby houses, sheds, stables, hayloft, cellars, and other possible hiding places. The marquis was nowhere to be found. Marais then ordered the postmaster to alert the local constabulary, only to be told that this was impossible because the city gates were closed at this late hour. The inspector then sent his brother and one of the policemen out to reconnoiter the road in the direction of Montélimar and the other policeman to scout in the direction of Tain.[7]

At first light the next morning, July 17, the inspector gave a description of the fugitive to M. Thiays, the commander of the constabulary. A dozen constables were immediately dispatched to search houses within two leagues of the city, while mounted deputies were sent to watch roads leading to bridges across the Rhône. The search continued until nightfall without turning up any trace of the marquis. Marais then summoned the assessor of Dauphiné to the inn. That magistrate, assisted by his secretary and the rector of the university, prepared an inventory of the personal effects the escaped prisoner had left behind. On top of his trunk, the key to which he had taken with him, were two night bags. The first contained, among other things, a pair of yellow morocco slippers, a linen dressing gown, a shirt with pegged cuffs, a handkerchief, a pair of white lisle stockings, a bag of powder, and cotton breeches. The other linen bag contained miscellaneous items: a case containing a glass goblet, a container of salve, beef marrow in a small porcelain receptacle, a shabby case containing a silver dish and teaspoon, two new candles, a small bell, a soap box, a sponge in another box, a copper basin, and some clothing: "a camlet habit with yellow lining, steel buttons, silver braid, two English frocks, . . . a flannel-lined calico dressing gown, a black hat with braid in the English style, [and] two flannel jackets." Everything was sealed "with hot red wax" and turned over to Inspector Marais for safekeeping.[8]

•

And our man? Having given his escort the slip, he first hid in a wooden shed adjacent to a threshing ground a quarter of a league from the city. From there two peasants escorted him to Montélimar. "After traveling about a league," he later recounted, "we changed our mind and returned to the Rhône in search of a boat but found none. Finally, toward daybreak, one of us slipped into Vivarais, where we found a small craft that took me to Avignon for a louis."[9]

After arriving in the city of the popes at around six o'clock, Donatien went to his friend Quinault's, had supper with him and his wife, and ordered a carriage prepared. He set out that same night, traveled all night long, and reached La Coste at nine in the morning, exhausted but gleeful. No sooner had he arrived than he scribbled this note to Gaufridy: "I am here, all in, dying of fatigue and hunger. I scared Gothon to death. I will tell you the whole story: it's a novel. Please come see me as soon as possible. Please send by return courier lemons and all the keys. Please bring me the two packets of papers that I gave you for safekeeping, especially the larger one. I am going to eat and go to bed, and I embrace you with all my heart."[10]

"The end of our troubles"

While Donatien savored his first days of freedom, his family rejoiced that their shame had been definitively and legally laid to rest. His wife, who had only just learned that he had been in Aix and won his case but who still knew nothing about his escape, wrote him on July 18: "I am assured, my good friend, that you are pleased with the way your case is turning out. If so, why not tell me about it yourself. You cannot doubt that I am pleased to see us approaching the end of our troubles."[11]

When Reinaud, the lawyer, learned of the marquis's escape, he immediately offered his warm compliments: "My dear Sir, I was expecting a clever stroke, and you will agree that those two little packets on your belt fulfilled their purpose well. I am pleased to congratulate you . . . Nothing surprises me except that you were able to humanize those watchdogs. The older one must have been a delightful sight! I can picture him with his head down . . ."[12]

A *"pure friendship"*

Seized by a kind of vertigo at his newfound freedom, Donatien burned to see and discover everything at once, as if he were compelled to make up for an absence of sixteen months in a few hours' time. Unable to sit still, he dashed about, bubbled over with plans, and amused himself like a child with whatever came to hand. He dashed off a note to Gaufridy: "I tell you nothing because I have too much to say. We absolutely must spend several days together . . . Tell me what people are saying. I don't think any other arrival of mine has caused so much talk. When will you come? I have seen everybody. We are on the most intimate terms with the curé. I think he is in love with me."

In his rapture he even enjoyed playing the moralist. A tenant of his apparently had slept with Jeanneton, the daughter of the watchman Sambuc: "The Chauvin affair seems quite filthy to me," he complained. "There is a furious rage against him. I have a lot to tell you on this score."

To add to his euphoria, he had found on arriving at La Coste a delightful woman, Marie-Dorothée de Rousset, who was employed as a governess. The daughter of Antoine de Rousset, a notary from Apt, she may have been a playmate of the young Donatien in Saumane, although she was four years younger. She and her brother, M. de Rémerville, had participated in a village festival in honor of the young officer in 1763. It was Mme de Sade who had the idea of inviting her to live in the château to serve as mistress of the household. Marie-Dorothée caught the marquis's eye the moment they met. It was not so much her face that pleased him, for she was on the whole less pretty than Mme de Sade, but her wit. Lively, playful, given to mockery, never at a loss for a repartee, unrivaled in the art of verbal fencing, she had an astonishing knack for keeping the marquis amused. They could often be seen together conversing on a stone bench. Their conversations call to mind learned jousts between combatants equally adept at games of love and language. Mlle de Rousset met the libertine's advances with the smiling charms of friendship. So far from losing his temper, as he might have done with a woman of cantankerous virtue, the marquis became caught up in this passionate, intelligent woman's sinuous dialectic. Not insensible to her partner's charms, she was nevertheless able to divert his passions from the sexual to something at once deeper and lighter, something that resembled love but without love's gravity. With the physical instincts reined in, it was possible to surrender unreservedly to the pleasures of the spirit. The couple's conversations in shady bowers at La Coste heralded their future correspondence: a mixture of amorous teasing, philosophy, and affectionate complicity in which the most audacious allusions met with a smiling indulgence that drew their sting. What Donatien felt for this young and desirable woman, whom he affectionately dubbed "Milli," was unlike anything he had known before: her infinite charms, which went to his head with the force of chilled champagne, fed a sensuality that was purely verbal. "She is a very dear and most respectable friend. It is impossible to feel a greater obligation than I feel toward her. Her upright and sensitive soul is ideally suited to make one savor deliciously all the charming sentiments of a pure friendship. I am and always will be very devoted to her. She has conducted herself like a good and candid friend through all this, and gratitude has always held great sway over my soul."[13] There were few other women to whom the marquis paid such handsome homage.

"Dulcinea in the mirror"

These conversations with Mlle de Rousset did not, however, make Donatien forget the face he had glimpsed in a mirror at the Conciergerie of Aix. The attorney Reinaud passed the marquis's messages on to the woman, still in prison, and kept him apprised of the latest news concerning his "Dulcinea." The first letter concerning Mme Doyen de Baudoin was dated July 23: "A few days ago the beautiful prisoner sent me an ambassador and a letter that you may read: M. de Sade is her guardian angel and consequently her motto. What a diabolical impression you made on this woman through a reflection in a mirror! One wonders what effect direct contact might have had! My answer gave her all the satisfaction she could have hoped for. Her case concerns me. But she is not pretty, I tell you, she is not! Her confidante told me so. But the ball has been tossed and must be parried."[14]

A few days later Sade sent her a small amount of money and a letter, assuring Reinaud that "her mail is not tampered with, she receives everything you send." So Reinaud's response must have come as a surprise:

Well! Monsieur le marquis, your letter, delivered by my secretary as received, was intercepted, opened, and read at the Conciergerie. The money was passed to the Baudoin woman, however, at which time she was told that a letter from M. de Sade had come with it but that she would not be allowed to see it. The woman immediately offered excuses and said she had not written to you . . . One of the guards came to complain to me. He showed me the unsealed letter and forced me to read it . . . I pleaded, begged, threatened, cajoled: nothing could make him give me back the letter . . . Returning to the subject again and again, I finally persuaded him to tear it up in my presence. And it was in fact shredded into a thousand pieces . . . I need not tell you that strict orders have been given that the Baudoin woman is not to receive so much as a note that has not first been read by the Conciergerie.[15]

Following this incident, the marquis probably took Reinaud's advice to break off a correspondence that had become far too dangerous for the young woman.

A Cabal

Strange rumors concerning Gaufridy began to reach the marquis's ears. Mlle de Rousset, Canon Vidal from Oppède, and various residents of La Coste reported grave suspicions concerning Donatien's trusted agent. Was someone trying, as Mme de Montreuil believed, to discredit Gaufridy so as to assume control of the marquis's thoughts and affairs? Possibly. In any case, the slander achieved its purpose. Already displeased with the notary on account of his secret correspondence with Mme de Montreuil, Sade was easily persuaded of his treachery. But for the time being he kept his suspicions to himself, because he still needed Gaufridy and because Vidal and Mlle de Rousset both counseled patience. Yet he could not refrain from taunting the man: "I have always admired your remarkable tact in keeping me apprised of your correspondence with Mme de Montreuil," the marquis wrote, adding, with cruel irony, that one day la Présidente would show him all her letters from Gaufridy and that he would joyfully recognize "the tender signs of friendship and constant proof of sincere fidelity." He greatly enjoyed putting his victim on the hot seat: "By the way, my dear advocate, I shall put it to you as you put it to me: 'You always concur,' you say, 'in whatever may be useful and advantageous to me.' But how broadly is this to be construed? Madame de Montreuil regards it as most useful and advantageous that I go to prison. I regard the opposite as most useful and advantageous. Do you think as she does or as I do? . . . As you see, my question is merely a joke, intended simply to show you that one can place on any sentence any interpretation one wishes."[16]

Later, in letters to his wife, the marquis takes a much harsher tone toward the notary, going so far as to suspect him, on the basis of gossip and slander, of having urged Nanon to give evidence against him: "Surely nothing here comes close to the vileness of Gaufridy's behavior. I wrote you about this, but you did not deign to respond because you and your mother were blind on the subject of that scoundrel . . . This is how the monster acted!"[17]

"Like a lioness"

When Mme de Sade finally learned from her mother that the case had ended well but that her husband was still locked up (she still knew nothing about the escape), she and la Présidente had a "terrible scene," which she described in these terms to Gaufridy: "On the subject of the detention, she stated her intentions with a revolting haughtiness and despotism that infuriated me. As a result, I am as little pleased as if nothing good had happened. She gave me to understand, however, that M. de S[ade] would get out, but not right away. Whereas before the case was resolved she told me that the *families* (one of her favorite words) would never put up with his release. What irritates her most is seeing that my ideas and propositions come from me and not M. de S, who she used to think told me what to say as if I were a parrot."[18]

That same day she confided in Reinaud that she planned to meet her husband on the road to the Bourbonnais but was afraid that it might be too late: "I am sending an anonymous agent to find out if Marais is back. If he is not, I shall hasten to the highway."[19] Informed of Donatien's escape a short while later, she sent him an affectionate note: "Do you believe now that I love you, my good little friend whom I adore a thousand times over? Take good care of your health, and do not allow yourself to want for anything. Have someone write me letters not in your hand, and in the white space between the lines you can write in invisible ink. I will do the same."[20]

Mme de Montreuil's rage on learning that her son-in-law was in La Coste was only magnified when her daughter announced that she planned to join him there. La Présidente breathed fire and seriously threatened to have her daughter arrested if she did not change her mind: "She is like a lioness on the subject," according to Mme de Sade. She would never permit her daughter "to be debased and compromised again as she had been in the past by going to be with her husband, unless a *lengthy* period of good behavior proved that it was safe. If her affection or her blindness compels her to go," the irascible old woman threatened, "the government will assist us in every way for a cause so respectable and so just. Let her be of service to him if she must, but let her stay in Paris."[21] Knowing that her mother was quite capable of calling on the authorities to prevent her from leaving, Renée-Pélagie decided to take up residence in the Carmelite convent on rue d'Enfer, where she lived in what had been the apartment of the dowager comtesse de Sade. From there she did what she could to have the lettre de cachet rescinded. Meanwhile, Donatien urged his wife to join him as soon as possible, "her presence being essential for a thousand reasons," and Mme de Montreuil felt that she had to warn her daughter once again: "Your honor belongs to your family. As a mother, I must protect you from falling once again into the dangers we have known. And if you do not wish his freedom to be disturbed, do not risk causing him to fear for yours. You must listen to me, and the truth of what I am saying will be easy to demonstrate as well as dangerous for M. de S[ade] if it comes to that."[22]

"Stupidities and platitudes"

Meanwhile, clouds gathered over La Coste. Dark threats reached the marquis. An anonymous letter arrived from Paris advising him to be on his guard. "The usual stupidities and platitudes," Donatien replied. "I suspected as much. All this little mystery is just another farce, and they no more want to recapture me than I wish to drown myself."[23]

On the evening of August 19, while walking peacefully in his park with Milli Rousset and M. Testanière, the curé of La Coste, Donatien heard someone walking "in an agitated manner" in the adjacent woods. "Who is there?" he shouted, but received no answer. He walked over to the source of the sound and found his watchman, the elder Sambuc, "his mind somewhat clouded with wine" yet still lucid enough to warn his master, "with a striking look of perplexity and terror," to flee at once because the tavern was beginning to fill with people "with highly suspicious faces." Milli Rousset immediately went down to the village to find out what was going on. An hour later she returned to the château and swore to the marquis that it was only a group of silk merchants passing through and that there was nothing to worry about.[24] Still uneasy, however, the marquis decided to take refuge that night with Canon Vidal in Oppède. Milli was to forward his mail and send him two dispatches daily to keep him abreast of the latest developments. As the reports grew more alarming, he left Oppède and took refuge in an abandoned farmhouse more than a league from the village. Extremely anxious and expecting the police to arrive at any moment, he could not sit still. Even if it meant being arrested, he had to leave this wretched hiding place. When Canon Vidal came to see him on Sunday, August 23, he found the marquis in a highly agitated state.

"What's the matter with you?" he exclaimed.

"Nothing. I want to get out of here."

"Are you uncomfortable?"

"No, but I want to go."

"And where do you want to go?"

"Home."

"You are mad! I definitely won't go with you."

"I am not asking you to. I can make it quite well on my own."

"Think it over, I beg you."

"I've thought it over. I want to go home."

"You are blind to the danger. You refuse to see what is in the letters."

"Sure, sure, it's nothing but fairy tales. There is no danger. Let's go."

"But wait at least four days!"

"I won't, I tell you. I want to go."

Seeing that he could not prevent the marquis from leaving, the good canon accompanied him to La Coste, where he arrived in a state of exhaustion. So as not to disturb his rest no one pointed out how imprudent he had been, but the next day they urged him to return to his hideout. He refused. On August 25 he received a letter from his wife, who informed him of the sale of his post as *lieutenant* for the provinces of Bresse, Bugey, Gex, and Valromey to his cousin, Jean-Baptiste-Joseph-David, comte de Sade d'Eyguières. "It sold for what it was worth," Donatien observed simply. "It is only a transfer of title, and it makes absolutely no difference whether I take my 18,000 livres of income from this source or from a piece of land that I may buy. As for the title and the honor, I have little desire for either. They have made me too many enemies."[25]

"What an effect, great God! What an effect!"

At four in the morning on Wednesday, August 26, Gothon rushed into her master's bedroom "naked and all in a lather" and shouting, "Run for your life!" Donatien, convinced that thieves were out to cut his throat, leapt out of bed, rushed out the door, climbed in his nightshirt up to the third story, and locked himself in a storeroom. Suddenly shouts could be heard in the stairway, steps drew near, and someone yelled, "Murder! Fire! Thieves!" The door to the storeroom was battered down, and Inspector Marais burst in, backed by four Paris watchmen and six gendarmes from Provence. The soldiers seized the marquis. A sword was pressed to his body and a pistol to his temple while Marais cursed him in the crudest of terms for his escape from Valence. How had he done it? "Talk, talk, little man!" he screamed. "Talk, you who are about to be locked up for the rest of your life for . . . things done in a small, dark upstairs room where dead bodies were found."[26] The marquis was then bound hand and foot and taken to a police wagon, which immediately set out for Paris, while Sambuc and the priest Testanière, awakened in the middle of the night, looked on dumbfounded. The journey took no fewer than thirteen days. The whole town of Cavaillon saw the lord of La Coste pass through in the custody of his guards. In Avignon, where he had numerous relatives, more than three hundred people stood on their doorsteps and witnessed his shame.[27] "What an effect, great God! What an effect!" he would recall later, in reporting the episode to his wife. "After receiving the compliments of the entire family, after hearing their entreaties to come visit and receive their kisses and congratulations, after letting it be known publicly that it was all over and that, my judgment having been rendered, whatever punishment might follow could only be punishment for a crime . . . after all that, I say, to see oneself arrested in one's own home with a fury, a zeal, a brutality, an insolence that would be out of place with the lowest of scoundrels from the dregs of the populace, to see oneself dragged, bound, and garroted in the midst of one's entire province and in the same places where one had just publicly announced one's innocence and the decree that confirmed it!"[28]

During a two-day stopover in Lyons, M. de Sade seized the opportunity to send instructions to Gaufridy. He was to get what he could out of Saumane and hold on to La Vignerme. Above all he was not to let go of the late abbé's library or natural history collection. As for La Coste, he was to take the farm from Chauvin and give it to Sambuc, a relative of the watchman, to whom he had promised it for the sum of 5,600 livres. He was to sign no lease in excess of six years: "It is foolishness to sign nine-year leases."[29]

Finally, after thirteen long days on the road, at eight-thirty in the evening on September 7, 1778, the marquis de Sade arrived at Vincennes, still in the custody of Inspector Marais. He was formally admitted to the prison, and the door of cell 6 closed behind him.

•

Meanwhile, Mme de Sade, who had just learned of her husband's arrest, felt she had been betrayed by everyone, beginning with her mother. Lonely, bewildered, not knowing whom to trust, she implored Mlle de Rousset to join her in Paris. Not knowing if her friend was already en route, she took the chance of writing her a long letter in which she poured out all her bewilderment, disgust, and desire for vengeance:

My God! What a blow for me! Into what abyss of pain have I fallen now? How am I to escape, whom can I trust, whom can I believe? It is absolutely impossible, given what I have been told and what has been done, to find a basis for judgment or a solution. The vexations, the falsehoods, the air of good faith about certain heads whose nature is not to deceive—all this absorbs me, yet I cannot see a glimmer of a way out. If you have written to my mother giving details, you have done very well, but if you are en route, that is better still. Since this event I no longer see her, and I have sworn eternal hatred and vengeance in writing if within three days she does not arrange for me to rejoin my husband wherever she has had him transferred . . . I am tired of having been deceived by everyone for the past eighteen months. The ministers are truly stone walls. Maybe they would like me to settle for writing him wretched little notes to be opened by the police. I have no intention of falling into the same difficulties as before: I have suffered too much.[30]

Equally upset by what had just happened ("I am really sick," she confessed), Mlle de Rousset urged Gaufridy to plead on the marquis's behalf to la Présidente: "Remember the poor, suffering man and serve him with Mme de Montreuil; excuse his faults. He is your friend, he sincerely likes you, you can do a lot to shorten his term in prison. Do so, I beg you, and do not forget to send me any news the moment it arrives."[31]

Cat Fight

Marie-Dorothée arrived in Paris in early November and found lodging at the Carmelite convent with Mme de Sade, who lavished tokens of affection upon her ("I am really a spoiled child who willingly submits," she said). Nevertheless, this loyal friend of Mme de Sade never lost sight of the goal of winning the marquis's freedom and asked for an interview with la Présidente, who received her "with all possible solicitude, decency, and confidence," but their conversation, to judge by Mlle de Rousset's marvelous account, resembled a confrontation between "two cats about to fight, the aggressor creeping forward on velvet paws but not without showing its claws from time to time to spur its adversary on. Once the battle had begun, despite the seeming calm, we went at it until I was ready to spring. Then, in the fog of ideas and the heat of combat, I saw quite positively that M. de S[ade] was loved and that the heart was racked by knowledge of where he was."

Mlle de Rousset began with "a somewhat exaggerated" portrait of the suffering the prisoner had endured at Vincennes for the past eighteen months. "He is much more comfortable than he was the first time," la Présidente replied. "He has company, he is as free as can be to write, and he has all possible comforts. But what can be done? It is not up to me."

"Oh, I am well aware of that. I come to you only to ask how to go about it. I am no longer familiar with Paris; you know it much better than I. I need some consolation. What better place to find it than with a loving mother?"

The two women next broached the delicate subject of Donatien's "wrongs": "He admits them," Mlle de Rousset alleged, "but he cannot make up for them where he is now."

"Oh! Mademoiselle, if you only knew what he promised me in the past! You cannot imagine the oaths he took in the very room we are in now."

"I believe it. He had every intention of keeping his promises. The man is weak, Madame, as you know. His age and his misfortunes have brought about many changes."

"I hope so! But tell me, Mademoiselle, would you answer for him?"

After a moment's reflection, Mlle de Rousset lowered her eyes and "without unseemly heat or hesitation" gave her answer: "Yes, Madame."

"Nevertheless, his family is against him. No one has yet made the slightest move to ask for his release."

Seizing this opportunity, Marie-Dorothée mentioned her own communications with Donatien's aunts, Mme de Villeneuve and the abbess of Saint-Laurent, who very much wanted his release. "The *commandeur* and the aunts in Cavaillon are surely of the same opinion," she ventured.

"They have every right to ask for [his release]," Mme de Montreuil replied. "I do not oppose it, but my daughter has asked for it several times, and always to no avail. As for the government's reasons for acting this way, if I knew them it would certainly not be appropriate for me to discuss them. I believe that [my son-in-law's imprisonment] is a wise precaution against the escapades in which he has so often compromised himself."[32]

The Recluse and the Prisoner

After leaving la Présidente Mlle de Rousset lost no time in writing Gaufridy to urge that he enlist the family's support in the effort to win the prisoner's release: "You, his attorney, will write that his affairs cannot be put in order without him. In the meantime I will work on the aunts and cousins in Avignon and various others."[33] Obviously she was seriously deluded about the intentions of Donatien's relatives in Provence. Apart from the abbess of Saint-Laurent and cousin Henriette, all the nuns backed Mme de Montreuil, whose firm resolve they admired and toward whom they felt boundless gratitude for her zealous defense of the family honor. The *commandeur* shared the nuns' view. Here, for example, is part of a letter from Gabrielle-Eléonore de Sade, abbess of Saint-Benoît in Cavaillon, to la Présidente, dated January 29, 1779: "I am extremely close to Mme de Sade . . . I wish that she could feel the need to keep him locked up a while longer." A few weeks later she wrote another letter in which not a trace of ambiguity remains: "I am truly distressed by Mme de Sade's stubbornness. She may well be asking for trouble by demanding, with as much imprudence as importunity, her husband's freedom. I have no problem with her attempting to excuse his escapades in the eyes of the public: she is only doing her duty. But I wish she could appreciate all the consequences, and I wish she could see, from the consequences [his actions] have already had, others that might yet ensue. Misplaced pity must not disturb our plans, which are dictated by prudence and necessity. My nephew's freedom cannot and should not reward anything other than his good conduct. After his repeated relapses, we must have moral certainty before returning him to society, so as not to make ourselves responsible for any future escapades in which he might indulge, which, being irreparable, would only complete our despair."[34]

16

Time Stands Still: 1778–1790

"Monsieur le 6"

No matter where the prison, the prisoner's lot is always the same: inside the prison walls history comes to a halt; time's mechanism goes awry. The prisoner is suddenly plunged into "uchronia," into a world where time does not exist. The carceral city is "another world." Like the utopian city it respects a cosmogony of its own, with rhythms that are regular but alien to the uninitiated. It possesses its own cycles and values, its own laws, its own regime, even its own algebra, and through these the logic of incarceration is reproduced *ad infinitum*. During Sade's twelve years in prison, first at Vincennes, later in the Bastille, his life became nothing more than a perverse contest between submission to the tyranny of the place, whether compelled or feigned (or perhaps willingly accepted), and never-ending rebellion. Of course there are also the mirages of an imagination capable of elaborating the most luxuriant creation ever conceived within the four walls of a prison cell. In prison the marquis de Sade identified exclusively with the written word. He existed in language only. The hazards of life vanished, to be replaced by *signs*. Sade's letters are the only evidence of the activity of his mind. From now on we must direct our questions to them.

Imprisonment inevitably entails a change of identity. Donatien exchanged, for an indeterminate period, his noble status for a number that he applied to himself in a letter to Mlle de Rousset: he became "Monsieur le 6." The "gentleman in six" complained strenuously about his new living conditions. Even though his beard had been trimmed and some of his linen had been returned along with a few books and a letter from his wife, he felt that he was far less comfortable in cell six than he had been in cell eleven. Not only could he not light a fire during the winter, but he was invaded by rats and mice, which allowed him not a moment's respite. He asked for a cat to get rid of them but was told that animals were prohibited: "How stupid you are!" he protested. "If animals are prohibited, then rats and mice ought to be prohibited too!" In 1783 he asked for a dog to keep him company, if possible "a young pup, so that I might enjoy the pleasure of bringing it up, either a spaniel or setter."[1] He also complained that his cell was "extremely damp and unhealthy, one can barely see the sky, and all the air passages are blocked up to prevent escape . . . I want a room on an upper story, I don't care which one provided one can light a fire there during the winter, which is impossible in this one, and as long as there is air and a view. That is all I ask." Another serious problem for an unrepentant slug-a-bed like Sade was that he was awakened every morning at six. After repeated requests he succeeded in putting an end to this early wake-up. Last but not least, he wanted permission to walk about the prison yard: this was the subject of his most emphatic entreaties.

And therein hangs a tale: this much-coveted permission was withdrawn and reinstated a hundred times, as punishment or reward for the prisoner's behavior. For his jailers it was a wonderful way to control him, but for Sade it soon became an obsession, an idée fixe. When permission was denied, he screamed in pain, cursed his tormentors for the pleasure they took in torturing him (the *sadist* is always the Other), threatened, raged, and moaned until the privilege was restored. But soon he would be slapped with punishment again (on the flimsiest of pretexts, to be sure), and his hysteria would begin anew. Throughout his twelve years in prison the marquis's walk and the date of his release remained his two major obsessions. It was not until December 7, 1778, after three months' confinement, that he was authorized to take the air twice a week and to receive paper and quills as needed. Over the next year the number of authorized walks was increased to three and then four per week. This privilege, admittedly substantial relative to the normal prison regime, failed to satisfy him completely, however: "For my health I have the greatest need to take the air at least an hour a day, and that is what I am asking for," he wrote his wife.[2] His request was finally granted on April 25, 1780, on orders of M. Le Noir, *lieutenant de police.*

•

But for certain restrictions, M. de Sade was not too badly treated at Vincennes—better, in any case, than he was willing to admit. His wife took it upon herself to supply him with whatever he needed in the way of material goods. She had clothing made for him by his regular tailor, Carlier, saw to it that he did not lack for body and household linen, and procured countless commonplace items to satisfy his requests, or, rather, his demands, for he was generally vociferous and impatient at the slightest delay: among the items he ordered were candles, sponges, stomachers (another idée fixe), head bands, cologne, wax pellets, a "goblet in its case," a "calico cap," a thirty-minute sand timer, paper, and quills. When necessary he had errands run by his turnkey, a stout lad who answered to the name of Lavisé. Mme de Sade regularly reimbursed any sums that were advanced to him at Vincennes or, later, in the Bastille.

Sade's Menus

In prison the marquis's needs were reduced to basics: to protect himself from cold, hunger, and pain. The power of his imagination could not reveal itself until these basic needs were met.

Renée-Pélagie's letters offer meticulously detailed information about the prisoner's eating habits, which appear to have been somewhat different from those of the free man. The differences reflect compensation of two kinds: on the one hand a desire to improve on ordinary prison fare, and on the other hand a use of food as symbolic compensation for the loss incurred through prison alienation. Mirabeau, who spent a few months with Sade in the dungeon of Vincennes, described the prison fare: "Here is what [prisoners] are served all year round. Boiled meat and an entrée for dinner, the entrée being pastry every Thursday; a roast and an entrée for supper; a pound of bread and a bottle of wine per day, and two apples at one of the meals on Thursdays and Sundays . . . Most of the time they find horrible nasty things on their plates. They dine at eleven in the morning and have supper at five in the evening . . ."[3]

In fact, Donatien observed a very different regime thanks to the food provided by his wife or purchased by Lavisé. By paying bonuses to the chefs, he could order anything he wanted. Here, for instance, is part of the weekly menu he submitted to the chief cook at the Bastille:

Dinner:
—An excellent soup (I will not repeat the adjective:
the soups must always be excellent, morning
and night)
—Two succulent and mouth-watering breaded veal
cutlets
—A porridge
—Two cooked apples

Supper:
—Soup
—Four fresh eggs

Dinner:
—Soup
—Succulent half chicken
—Two small vanilla custards
—Two cooked apples

Supper:
—Soup
—A small hash of the leftovers from the morning's
chicken

Dinner:
—Soup
—Sausages
—Two very tender leaves of chard in gravy
—Two cooked pears

Supper:
—Soup
—Apple fritters

As this sample suggests, there was nothing extravagant about the
menu. It was a harmonious, balanced diet that stressed quality of ingredients over quantity. The suppers even seem unusually light, no
doubt to avoid indigestion and insomnia. Cooked apples or pears were
served every day to ease an intestinal function disturbed by lack of

exercise. The diet was also simple (avoiding sauces and stews and using few if any spices) and inexpensive (never more than eight sols per meal). As for alcohol, M. de Sade made moderate use of it, preferring a good bottle of wine to any brandy.

Apart from the meals served in his room, the marquis received numerous gift packages. His wife had certain dishes that he loved delivered from outside: eel pâté, brochettes of plump thrush or warbler wrapped in bacon and vine leaf and ready for roasting, pâté of marinated tuna fish, ham, and so on. As for butter, Donatien would accept only one kind, a Breton product known as "beurre de l'Enfant Jésus."

Sadeian Sweets

The marquis de Sade's palate was most keenly excited by pastry and sweets. He was capable of wolfing down frightening quantities, and in the solitude of his cell he sometimes indulged in veritable orgies of meringues, biscuits, macaroons, preserves, marmalades, jellies, syrups, marshmallows, fresh and preserved fruits, and candied chestnuts.

Chocolate inspired an irresistible passion. He loved it in all its forms: in cream, in cakes, in ice cream, in bars: "I asked . . . for a cake with icing," he wrote his wife, "but I want it to be chocolate and black inside from chocolate as the devil's ass is black from smoke. And the icing is to be the same."[4] Madeleines awakened no memories in him but did make his mouth water.

Needless to say, these sugary debauches, combined with lack of exercise and enforced immobility, soon caused him to gain weight. Within a few years he became close to obese, a change about which his wife worried endlessly: "He is doing well but putting on a lot of weight," she wrote to Gaufridy.

"I am suffering"

He repeated his complaint to anyone who would listen, but to believe him no one took him seriously. Not even his wife, to whom he continually complained that his woes were real and that everyone neglected them: "Truly, Madame, I think you suppose that I complain for no reason . . . to make myself interesting . . . Yes, Madame, I am suffering, and what is worse, more and more every day." Did she want an example of his jailers' inhumanity? For several days he had been racked by a dreadful cough.

Last night, after feeling much worse for several days, I had the idea of writing a short note to the surgeon [M. Fontelliau], in which I asked him for a new remedy that I hoped might bring me some relief. I went to bed and fell asleep feeling a little calmer in the hope that they might bring me what I had asked for. "So," I said on waking the following morning, "did you bring what I asked?"

"Quiet," I was told, "I am returning your note."

"My note?"

"Yes, sir, your note: you wrote to the surgeon, and that is a crime. All requests are to be addressed to the warden."

"And the medicine?"

"Oh, the medicine! When you have the right address—"

So! What do you say to that? Is it nice, is it kind, is it tender? But to be fair, it is clear that the fault does not lie with the lackeys who follow the orders, and I save my curses for the gross imbecility of those who give them . . .

Does the eye of the government not perceive such abominations? Is there no one to reprimand a nobody capable of subjecting a proper gentleman to every form of tyranny, to every whim that passes through his imbecile imagination? . . . I would rather have both hands cut off than fail the nation by not enlightening it about such abuses . . . Oh! I shall unveil them all, all the horrors, all the odious schemes, all the conspiracies hatched by greed and rapacity! I know them all now, I have learned of them at my own expense: all of France must know them too.[5]

•

The marquis de Sade had always suffered from hemorrhoids. Compulsory inactivity only aggravated the malady, which he treated exclusively with cocoa butter pomades and turpentine-based salves. "When I am sitting down, I simply cannot get up without crying out in pain," he confided to his wife. To ease his pain, Renée-Pélagie ordered a special cushion, a round leather seat with a hole in the middle: "By not putting pressure on your rump, this will relieve you," she told him.

His chief complaint, however, involved his eyes. To be sure, long nights of reading and writing had done little to improve his eyesight, which was already deficient prior to his imprisonment. To protect his eyes from the dust he asked his wife for "what they call goggles," that is to say, not eyeglasses but glass lenses affixed to a half-mask made of leather. In the Bastille as well as at Vincennes Sade was seen by the most famous oculists of the time, the Grandjean brothers (Henri, the elder, was the king's surgeon-oculist) and Dr. Demours *fils*. Despite iris powder, eyewash prepared from elder blossoms, seawater showers, footbaths, bleeding from the arm, application of leeches, and cataplasms of chervil "cooked like spinach," the marquis's inflammations were frequent and a constant worry. He feared losing his sight more than anything else. If he were unlucky enough to require an operation while in prison, he insisted on having a female nurse at his side: "I would die of impatience if nothing else if I were cared for by a man." Especially since the male nurse would come from one of the military hospitals, "a filthy, stinking old soldier! With my delicacies, my vapors, and my anxieties when I am ill! That is all it would take to kill me on the third day."[6] Dr. Demours wisely recommended that Donatien avoid reading too much and refrain from work and prescribed knitting "so as to distract without tiring you," but it seems unlikely that the marquis traded his quill for knitting needles.

Mister Prickly

"Imperious, angry, furious, extreme in all things, with a disturbance in the moral imagination unlike any the world has ever known—there you have me in a nutshell: and one more thing, kill me or take me as I am, because I will not change." Such was the accurate portrait Donatien painted of himself in a letter to his wife. What we already knew of his irritability, his impatience, and his cantankerous nature enables us to imagine him as the most disagreeable of prisoners. The loss of freedom would only have exacerbated his customary faults while at the same time aggravating his persecution complex. Mlle de Rousset had given him the jocular nickname "Monsieur le Fagot d'Epines" (Mr. Prickly). For him, indeed, everything was an occasion for scandal. Not a day passed at Vincennes or in the Bastille when he did not provoke a row, often on the flimsiest of pretexts. On June 26, 1780, for example, his jailer, he said, had committed "a very blatant act of impertinence intended to provoke," causing Donatien to fly into a rage so violent that he fainted; after lying unconscious for some time, he began spitting blood, and this continued until the following day. The guard claimed that the prisoner had struck him, but Donatien denied the charge, acknowledging only that he had made a gesture as if to strike the man. In any case, M. de Rougemont, the warden of Vincennes, withdrew permission for the marquis's walk and denied him the small services he was customarily allowed. This led Donatien to write to his wife, asking her to "complain to the minister about the vile treatment to which he was being subjected in the dungeon."[7]

The School for Hatred

After a few months at Vincennes the marquis de Sade was feeling the usual effects of imprisonment: rampant fantasy, feelings of abandonment, raving Manichaeanism. Under the withering effect of imprisonment, he cultivated a vision of the world familiar to all who have been incarcerated. Most significantly, he learned to place under the head of Evil everything that was associated in any way with, or even merely reminiscent of, free society. We have encountered his verbal violence before, and we have seen him vent his brutality on his jailers. But such violence and brutality are as nothing compared with the contents of his prison letters, veritable philippics in which hatred rises to the level of eloquence and execration attains tragic grandeur. One would have to conjure with the name of Louis-Ferdinand Céline to find similar energy in denunciatory verve. Freely mixing falsehood with truth, slander with tattle, and indignation with bad faith, Sade charges his enemy with frenzied joy, pummels him with sarcasm, and riddles him with insult before striking the exuberant fatal blow. I shall cite only one example, because it seems to me representative of his genius for invective and because it brings together in one place all the favorite targets of his disgust: Mme de Montreuil, M. de Sartine (the former *lieutenant général de police* who became minister of the navy in 1774), and the warden Rougemont:

It is not the role of vice or of the most unmistakable horror of vice to reform or punish vice. That is the sole task of virtue, and of virtue of the purest kind.

It is not the role of the présidente de Montreuil, *cousin, niece, kinswoman, granddaughter*, and *godmother* of all the vile bankrupts of Cadiz and Paris; of the présidente de Montreuil, niece of a scoundrel driven from the Invalides by M. de Choiseul for his thefts and embezzlements; of the présidente de Montreuil, who has, in her husband's family, a grandfather hanged in the place de Grève; of the présidente de Montreuil, who has given seven or eight bastards to her husband and pimped for all her daughters—it is not her role to harass, punish, or repress defects of temperament that cannot be mastered and have never harmed anyone.

It is not the role of Dom S[arti]nos,[8] found one fine morning in Paris, whence he came no one knows, much like those poisonous mushrooms that spring up suddenly in a corner of the woods; of Dom S[arti]nos, who was found in the end to have sprung from the left side of the Reverend Father Torquemada and a Jewess seduced by the aforesaid in the prisons of the Inquisition of

Madrid, which he directed; of Dom S[arti]nos, who increased his fortune in France only by sacrificing men as cannibals do; who, being *maître de requêtes*, had the unfortunate man of whom I spoke broken on the wheel solely because his glory depended on showing he had not been wrong and, indeed, was incapable of judging incorrectly; of Dom S[arti]nos, who, in a somewhat higher post, invented odious forms of harassment and tyranny over the pleasures of the public in order to provide "lascivious lists" of a nature to warm the little suppers in the Deer Park,[9] and who, to court each reigning party, caused to perish, either in torture or in prison, more than two hundred innocent persons, as reckoned by the very same persons who abetted his infamous acts; of Dom S[arti]nos, finally, the most political scoundrel and outrageous crook on whom the light of heaven ever shone, and perhaps the first, since abuses were tolerated, to have conceived of keeping a whore with prisoners—no, it is not the role of such a dreadful fraud of a criminal to censure or correct or persecute errors that were the source of his own fondest delights in the days when he was robbing the king of five hundred thousand francs annually out of the million he was given to furnish the court with "lubricious details" and who, in those days, not only stole with impunity but also infamously abused his office to compel unfortunate creatures to indulge in the very vices he seeks to persecute today.

It is not, in short, up to the little bastard Rougemont; to that abomination of vice personified; to that rogue in breeches and doublet who, on the one hand, prostitutes his wife in order to have prisoners and, on the other hand, causes those prisoners to die of hunger in order to have a few more écus and the means to pay the infamous henchmen of his debauches; to that queer fellow, finally, who, were it not for the caprices of fortune and the pleasure he takes in knocking down those who ought to be raised up and raising up those who are made only to crawl; who, but for that, I say, would perhaps be only too happy to be my errand boy had we both remained in the places for which heaven intended us—it is not up to a lowlife of this sort to set himself up as a censor of vice, and of the very vices that he possesses to a far more odious degree, because one becomes more contemptible and more ridiculous when one tries to molest in others what one possesses a thousand times over in oneself; it is not up to the halt to mock the lame, nor to the blind to lead the one-eyed.

So be it, and I salute you.[10]

As we might expect, Donatien's most vengeful epithets were reserved for his mother-in-law: "No, I do not think it is possible to find a creature in the world more abominable than your unworthy mother," he wrote to his wife. "Not even hell vomits up anything close, and I am convinced that it was on women of her ilk that the imagination of the priests fathered the Furies."[11]

Poor Renée-Pélagie did all she could to stem her husband's epistolary rages, warning him that reprisals were still possible because his letters were read by a police agent before being passed on to her. "How ingenious you are, my dear friend, at tormenting yourself!" she wrote. "Calm down, and, more important, don't write anything that can harm you. I won't hide the fact that the letters in which you display bitterness and anger and say many things you do not believe harm your interests, embitter the minister against you, and prevent people from listening to my entreaties. Though I tell the truth, which is that you do not believe what you write but succumb at times to pain and despair, they say that they can judge you only by what you write and that as long as you write in this tone, they will continue to hold a very bad opinion of you. So, my good friend, write no more of these sentences that do you harm. Follow my advice, which is inspired by my burning desire to be reunited with you very soon."[12]

Martin Quiros

We must not think, however, that prisoner Sade lived immersed in a sea of gloom. At times high spirits would take hold of him, and a playful frenzy as unpredictable and as extreme in its effects as his fits of rage would lend a remarkably jovial tone to his letters. Mme de Sade heard little of this earthy humor, which was directed mainly to those who could appreciate it, primarily Carteron, also known as La Jeunesse or "Martin Quiros," a nickname the marquis chose because it reminded him of the servants' names in picaresque novels. The jovial valet was not without wit or learning. He was capable of dropping such names as Caesar, Hercules, Varius, and Don Quixote and contrived, not without success, to make his master smile in the depths of his cell. Nothing amused the marquis so much as his valet's clowning. The letter in which "Quiros" told the story of the eruption of Vesuvius on August 8, 1779, filled him with joy, particularly since it called to mind salacious memories of a hermit the two men had encountered on the mountain's slopes and of a certain sausage with a notably obscene flavor, not to mention the rumbling of the earth itself, something that always carried an erotic charge in the Sadeian symbolic repertoire: "It is most unfortunate (and we were most fortunate) that it [the earthquake] did not happen while we were there. The poor nuns! There are quite a few who won't have minded this accident too much! Ah, I also pity my poor hermit, the one we met half way up, you remember, sir, where we ate a certain sausage that you kept for so long and didn't want us to finish. Remember, remember that devil of a sausage!" In the same letter Carteron complains that he has no work and begs his master to send him a manuscript to copy: "Send me some work, I beg you, for I am growing dull from stupidity. I have no books and nothing to write. Dumb you left me and dumb you will find me."[13]

Space unfortunately does not allow quoting from Carteron's other missives. All reveal such drollery, such naïveté, such a sense of farce and mystification, and such a perfectly Molieresque image of his relations with his master that one might think one was listening to a figure from the stage. The marquis's responses are even more valuable, because they reveal a little-known aspect of his verbal genius, and one of no small importance: his grotesque inventiveness, his gift for parodic caricature. Take, for instance, his reply to "Chevalier Quiros," an astounding piece of low comedy enlivened by the dizzying rhythm of the prose, as the author seems to relish the spectacle of his own words:

Martin Quiros . . . You're being insolent, my son! If I were there, I'd give you a pounding . . . I'd pull off your f***ing false toupee, which you patch up every year with tail hairs from the nags on the Courthézon-Paris road. How would you fix that, you old monkey? Come on, speak up, how would you do it? . . . So try . . . try to keep quiet a little, I beg you, because I'm tired of having been insulted for so long by the rabble. True, I'm like a big dog, and when I see that pack of mongrels and bitches baying after me, I lift my leg and piss on their noses.

So, you motherf***ing ape, with your face full of crabgrass dripping with blackberry juice, you prop for Noah's vine, you rib from Jonah's whale, you used match from a bordello's tinder-box, you rancid ha'p'ny candle, you rotten cinch from my wife's donkey . . . You old pumpkin pickled in bedbug juice, you third horn on the devil's head, you with a face as long as a cod with two oysters for ears, you madame's old shoe, you dirty red linen of Milli Printemps [Mlle de Rousset], if I had you in my clutches now, how I'd rub your dirty face in it, your cooked-apple mug that looks like burning chestnuts, to teach you to lie like that.[14]

"The way I think"

Between crises of rage and despair, M. de Sade had moments of introspection, whose fruits he revealed afterwards to his wife. At such times we must listen especially carefully to what he says, when he

suddenly drops his tone of vindictiveness and complaint either to phi-
losophize about his own fate or to distinguish, as in the following
passage, between our conduct, which depends solely on us, and our
desires, which none of us can control:

Morals do not depend on us; they have to do with our construction, our organization. What is within our power is the ability to prevent our venom from
spreading, so that what surrounds us not only does not suffer but does not
even notice it . . . One cannot create virtues for oneself, and *in those matters*
one is no more the master free to adopt this or that taste than one is the master
free to adopt, concerning a system, this or that opinion, or to make oneself
brunette when one is born a redhead. That is my eternal philosophy, and I
shall never depart from it.[15]

Elsewhere he says, magnificently:

I respect tastes, fantasies. However baroque they may be, I find them all respectable, both because one is not their master and because the most unusual
and bizarre of all, if well analyzed, can always be traced back to a principle
of delicacy. I shall be glad to prove this whenever you like: you know that no
one else analyzes things as I do.[16]

In another letter to his wife he again declares his singularity vis-
à-vis the world as proudly and superbly as if he were throwing down
a gauntlet:

My way of thinking, you say, cannot be approved. What difference does it
make to me? The truly crazy person is the one who thinks in a certain way
for the sake of others! My way of thinking is the fruit of my reflections. It
grows out of my existence, my organization. I am not the master who can
change it. And if I were, I would not change a thing. The way of thinking that
you reproach is the sole consolation of my life. It alleviates all my suffering in
prison, it constitutes all my pleasures in the world, and I am more attached to
it than I am to life. The cause of my misfortunes is not the way I think; it is
the way others think.[17]

Signals and Lemon Juice

It was only after a separation of four years and five months that the
marquis was authorized, on July 13, 1781, to receive a first visit from
his wife. The visit was not to be private, as he had hoped, but in the

presence of a policeman, Boucher, in the council hall. Soon the marquis's visiting rights were subject to the same manipulation as his walks. At the first indiscretion, the first misplaced word in one of his letters, his visits were cancelled. The authorities adopted a particularly meddlesome attitude in the summer of 1783. But thanks to the baron de Breteuil, appointed in November as minister of the royal household for Paris and determined to improve conditions in the prisons, Mme de Sade's visits to her husband became more frequent starting in January 1784. This accounts for Donatien's sustained homage and expression of "extreme deference" to this minister, whom he deemed "worthy of respect in a thousand ways."[18]

•

But visits were not the whole story. Most of all there were letters: hundreds of them, an epistolary soliloquy unique in all the world's literature and carried on without interruption through twelve years of captivity. "Hard upon the brief flashes of gaiety," Mlle de Rousset confided to Gaufridy, "we endure storms, the hail from which riddles our hearts through and through." The marquis's usual tone was one of rage and despair, lamentation, reproach, and sarcasm: in this key he was a virtuoso.

Donatien was authorized to correspond only with his wife, and that correspondence was closely monitored. The prisoner was required to submit each of his letters unsealed to Officer Boucher, who "red-penciled" the passages most critical of the prison administration. If a letter struck the policeman as wholly unacceptable, he did not hesitate to rewrite it in his own hand, preserving only the most mundane passages from the original: requests for linen or candles, for example. Not surprisingly, Donatien's attacks on Boucher were frequent: "The abbreviator, that profound scrutinizer to whom they give my letters to excerpt, a hapless fellow whose first profession was to scrape the mud from people's boots, sometimes makes phrases; he has a good time, he amuses himself, in order to show that he has as much wit as he once had agility in his fingers when his shop was on the Pont-Neuf, and consequently this penman (*plumitif*), as Voltaire says, frequently has me saying a million things as stupid as he is."[19] In the middle of another letter to his wife he offers this warning: "Mr. Scribbler, whoever you are, contemptible animal bribed by our torturers to increase our suffering, you who have contrived with M. de Rougemont to suppress any letters disclosing his dark and dreadful misdeeds and who would deserve as he does to be hanged if there were any justice in France, if the preceding apology displeases you, read it for your profit, cut it or scratch it out, and pass the bottom of this page on to my wife so that I might at least have what I need."[20] Sometimes he even wrote two notes at once "to facilitate the learned operation of the *scrutinizers, abbreviators, commentators,* and *reformers* of [his] style."[21] One direct consequence of the double reading of his letters was a style of double meaning, the author never losing sight of the indiscreet third party who surreptitiously intervened between himself and his wife. As Philippe Roger notes, "the first recipient [of the letters] therefore consisted of his detested guardians as a group: the warden, the minister, the police, the copyists, in a word, the 'jail' . . . Thus he may also, if not primarily, have felt compelled to write to his jailers as much as, if not more than, to the *real* recipient."[22]

Censorship forced the Sades to resort to a thousand ruses to circumvent the vigilance of Officer Boucher. Invisible ink now became one of their regular tools. They used an ink made from lemon juice and wrote either in the white space between lines or at the end of an otherwise innocent letter. During visits Mme de Sade also slipped tiny notes into her muff, and these became another means of communication. They also employed various subterfuges, including hints, double meanings, metaphorical allusions, and, quite often, code names: the marquis sometimes used the names Moïse (Moses) and Oreste (Orestes), while M. de Sartine was referred to as l'Ours (the Bear) and La Jeunesse as Jacques; that "vile scoundrel" Albaret, who had gone to work for Mme de Montreuil, became Cadet de la Basoche, while Milli Rousset changed sex to become M. Hélène, and La Coste was rebaptized Nérac.

•

But Sade's cryptomania went even further: witness his strange use of "signals." Throughout his imprisonment (and only during this period) his letters were filled with numbers to which he attributed mysterious meanings. The minute he was released, the numbers immediately disappeared. During the eleven years of freedom he enjoyed from 1790 to 1801, for example, there is not one "signal" in his correspondence. But the signals reappear as if by magic when he enters Charenton in 1803. The origins of this bizarre arithmetic have been a source of constant puzzlement. Did Sade find it in some cabalistic treatise, or did he invent it out of whole cloth? The answer is still unknown. Perhaps he adapted for his own purposes a code taken from some work on the secrets of the Templars or the Rosicrucians, about which he was quite curious.[23] For the time being this is the most plausible hypothesis.

In the initial stages of what was to become a veritable obsession, the marquis attempted to guess the date of his release by interpreting the figures in his correspondents' letters. In the words of Maurice Heine, "the impossibility of gauging the arbitrary will [of the authorities] led Sade to base series of calculations on the most improbable data. Everything struck him as an indicator of fate, or perhaps an occult clue that had somehow escaped censorship. His mind fastened desperately on the number of lines in a letter or the number of times a particular word was repeated or even on a similarity of sound that called to mind a certain number."[24] Soon this method of divination extended to the most routine events of prison life. It allowed the prisoner to calculate, for example, the day on which permission to take his daily walk would be reinstated or the date of his wife's next visit.

As virtually his only correspondent, Renée-Pélagie enjoyed the dangerous privilege of unwittingly providing Donatien with more "signals" than anyone else. The poor woman, who understood nothing of her husband's obscure speculations, became the butt of insults when those signals turned out, more often than not, to be bearers of bad tidings. The marquis also cursed Mme de Montreuil and her "henchmen" for inspiring his wife's dark prophecies. "Your mother must either be dead drunk or fit to be tied," he wrote, "to risk her daughter's life on a 19 and 4 or a 16 and 9 and not to have tired of all that after twelve years. Oh, what an indigestion of numbers that vile woman had! I am convinced that if she had died before the eruption and they had opened her up, millions of numbers would have emerged from her entrails. It is extraordinary what horror this inspired in me in regard to numbers and intricacies."[25] "Recently, because you required a 23, my walk was shortened, 2 to 3 was all I was allowed, and that makes 23. How amazing! How sublime!"[26]

Baffled by this algebra, whose rules and meaning surpassed her understanding, poor Mme de Sade repeatedly insisted that there was no evil intent in her letters: "As for the signals," she swore, "I tell you once and for all that I never send you any . . . You have promised not to search my letters for signals, yet you fail to keep your word. Rest assured, my dear friend, that if I could tell you what you want to know, I would not use signs. I would state things very clearly."[27]

Sade himself acknowledged the apparent pathological character of his obsession in a letter dated December 15, 1781: "I think I fell victim to a fit of madness, and if I behave that foolishly again I shall be convinced, truly, that I am completely mad."[28]

A Dialogue Between Mother and Daughter

Before examining the relations between husband and wife as revealed by their letters, let us glance at what was going on between Renée-Pélagie and her mother. Their recently discovered correspondence, excerpts from which are published here for the first time, give a more accurate picture of their relations than can be gleaned from the marquis's angry outbursts. These letters also offer a less dramatic and surely more subtle portrait of la Présidente's feelings toward her son-in-law. On December 5, 1778, for example, Mme de Montreuil wrote this to Mme de Sade:

I join you, Madame, in urging M. Le Noir and M. Amelot to grant M. de Sade permission to take walks . . . He is repentant, you tell me, and intends to behave properly. I want to believe it, and I hope it is true. But will anyone believe us? Will they grant our request so easily? No. One judges the future by the past, and therefore we must not speak now of freedom, or else, if we do, we must be prepared for a refusal . . . For, finally, Madame, let us speak plainly. You who know a great deal (though perhaps not all)—he certainly did what he did. If he did it in full possession of his senses and in cold blood, he certainly deserves at the very least to be prevented from doing it again. If he was compelled to do what he did by an ebullience he cannot control, by an "indomitable imagination," to use the expression of a great magistrate who has done important favors, it is therefore necessary (for himself, for he stands to gain more than anyone else) that some years pass to calm his blood, cool his imagination, and offer, in a word, reassurance concerning the dangers of his release.[29]

On December 17, 1778, Mme de Sade wrote to Mme de Montreuil:

The more time goes by, the more I worry about M. de Sade, and the more clearly I perceive the wish to cause his death and regret having been too trusting and having allowed myself to be lulled to sleep. If everyone wants only the best, why not allow him to repair the damage quietly, as he had begun to do? Having been arrested despite his good behavior in the most ignominious manner possible, and having been told publicly that he will remain locked up for the rest of his life, has he not every right to think that what his family wants is his death? Is there anything to which such thoughts cannot lead, when in the two years during which he has been held in the harshest of conditions, nothing has contradicted this iniquity? When a misfortune occurs, it will be time to say, "No one could have predicted that" . . . And when my children are old enough to be aware of such things, they will have much to reproach in those who will have cost their father his life or his reason in prison and who will have prevented them from deriving the benefit of the Aix decree, which is rendered null and void by the course that has been chosen.

Ponder these truths well, my dear mama, I beg you. Make them known to the authors of my misfortunes. How pleasant it would be for me to be indebted to you for my life's consolation! The bitterness that fills my days makes me long for the end of my existence. See to it that my husband is returned to me, dear mama. I would then owe you my life twice over, and I remain, with the utmost respect, your most humble and obedient servant.[30]

On January 30, 1779, Mme de Montreuil wrote Mme de Sade:

You may assure Monsieur de Sade, Madame . . . I forgive him from the bottom of my heart for all the wrongs against me for which I might reproach him, and they will not cause me to do anything that might injure or afflict him. I pity his situation and would do him good if I were able to, as I always did at times when he slandered me at will; however, the indelible memory of the past in its entirety forbids me to have any direct contact with him. I owe this conduct to myself, and would owe it to the universe if its eyes were upon me.[31]

Finally, in February of 1779, Mme de Sade wrote this to her mother:

I promised M. de Sade a page of Laure's writing, but I promised more than I could deliver. My sister said that the teacher found it extraordinary that anyone should want a page of the little one's work. Apparently she wants to wait until [Laure] writes like a master. She has no feeling for the pleasure that a father might take from seeing his child's scribbling. Since you have more credit than I, my dear mama, please obtain this page for me.[32]

"Good little boy"

The prison letters reflect the rumblings and eruptions of the volcano named Sade with the precision of a seismograph. Renée-Pélagie, who was as steadfastly tender and compassionate as her husband was at times scornful and unjust, worked hard to persuade him to bear his affliction with patience and to prove that she remained totally at one with him. Early in 1779 she wrote: "You are exasperated, my good friend, with your situation. I beg you to believe me when I say that I am keenly aware of the full extent of its horror. Would that it were in my power to change it! I am deeply moved by everything you tell me, but the others have a bizarre way of thinking of which we are victims. They think that by keeping you there for a time, you will come out as tame as a lamb. They are not aware of all the harm that this is doing to you, your fortune, and your children. So when they give me their stupid answers, I am enraged, and I could take my world by the head and bang it against the wall until they were ready to change their minds. As you see, I am not as mild as you are in the tortures I wish on them."[33]

Renée-Pélagie forgave Donatien for everything, answering even his wounding comments with protestations of love. Once, after he had assailed her with sarcasm in his inimitable manner, she answered immediately: "I know of few, and I mean very few, a rare few, hearts and souls like yours. If you did not on occasion lose your poor head and write some rather disagreeable things, you would be perfect. But you will always be perfect for me. I shall never be able to stop adoring you, even if you heap insults upon my head. I am only too certain that your heart is never in accord with what you write."[34] What is most striking in Mme de Sade's letters is the maternal tone of her affection, her need to reassure, console, and fondle the man she liked to call her "good little boy."

"Cases" and "Flasks"

Renée-Pélagie's devotion to her husband was not limited to supplying him with things he needed or wanted such as clothing, linen, cushions, sweets, candles, and books. Their understanding was such that Donatien did not hesitate to ask his wife for the instruments he needed to satisfy his erotic fantasies in the solitude of prison. Remember that he entered prison at the age of thirty-seven and did not leave until he was fifty. He therefore spent the prime of his life behind bars, deprived of all sexual relations and reduced to masturbation. Thus he was obliged to resort to a variety of subterfuges to dupe desire.

Determined that he should want for nothing, the marquise once sent him, at his request, a sleeve from one of her dresses. On another occasion she sent him a portrait of a young man, which elicited this enthusiastic outburst: "You sent me the beautiful boy, dear turtle-dove. The beautiful boy! How sweet the words sound to my rather Italian ear! *Un bel giovanetto, signor,* people would say if I were in Naples, and I would answer, *Si, si, signor, mandatelo, lo voglio bene.* You have treated me like a cardinal, *ma petite mère* . . . but unfortunately it is only a painting . . . The case (*étui*) then, at least, the case, since you have reduced me to illusions!"

The "cases" and "flasks" (*flacons*) that the prisoner was so eager to receive were none other than artificial organs to be used for simulating sodomization and achieving what the marquis in his private code called *prestiges* or *manilles*. The marquise was charged with commissioning these objects, to be fashioned to her husband's precise measurements, from carpenters in the faubourg Saint-Antoine. Naturally the craftsmen received her orders with knowing smiles: "For the case, I do not know where to order it," she wrote, "because the workers take me for a madwoman when I speak to them of cases of that size. They laugh in my face and do not do the job. They want money in advance lest the thing be left on their hands, so when the work is done you have to take it or lose your money."[35] Two months later she returned to the subject of the troublesome case: "I assure you, truthfully, that I had a great deal of trouble getting the one you have now, and it is smaller than the one you want. None of the workmen want to do it, they take me for a madwoman and laugh in my face. Do me a favor and ask someone else, or have a model made in fir by a wood-turner. They claim they don't have pieces of rosewood or ebony large enough to hollow out and turn something of that size."[36] "Please dispense me from this commission, you will make me very happy," she asked.[37] Her request is easy to understand, all the more so in that Sade was not easily satisfied. He knew exactly what he wanted and made no bones about asking for it:

It should be obvious to you that this bottle is absolutely worthless as a pocket flask. I am therefore sending it back to you. Use it for the measurements of the ones I have been asking Abraham to make for me at his crystal factory for some time now, taking the measurements from the top, not the bottom. That would be much too small. But measured from the top it will be just what I need for my dressing kit. I have taken the exact measurements above the hole, and it is just right. But it needs to be at least three inches longer, although to tell the truth the circumference is the main thing and the one to which I want most attention paid . . . He assured me that he had supplied one of this size to the archbishop of Lyons. Remind him of this. Pay him what he is owed and insist on his services in exchange. The same bottles can also be used on your dressing table, if you like: mornings on your dressing table and nights on my night stand. That is why you must ask him for two. In the meantime, send me a pocket flask. Since this is for the pocket only and not for my dressing kit, it should be of the proper size to fit my pocket. I have sent the dimensions to you: six inches in circumference by eight or nine inches long.

Early in March 1783 he wrote:

The flask that I broke was a good one. I need one like it, and so that it will not break, put it in a rosewood case, and since I want this case to be able to hold something other than the flask, it should be of a larger circumference. That is why I said a six-inch circumference for the case, with a height proportionate to that of the flask, which will be good if it is like the last one.

On March 18 Mme de Sade replied: "Your case is finished at last. I am sending it to you, where you can easily put something else beside the flask." In the margin there is a note in the marquis's hand: "And the whole thing up the ass, quite comfortably, unfortunately too comfortably."[38] Elsewhere, when Renée-Pélagie points out that a six-inch flask is far too long to put in his pocket, he remarks: "The point is that I'm not putting it in my pocket but elsewhere, where it is still far too small."[39]

Driven by his mania for numbers, he faithfully recorded in his *Almanach illusoire* the number of his *prestiges*, that is, orgasms by masturbation with or without accessories.[40] On December 1, 1780, two years and three months after his return to Vincennes, he computed this phenomenal total: "3268 + 3268 = 6536, nearly six thousand six hundred introductions."[41]

"My honey"

In this infernal couple nothing was simple, and certainly nothing concerning the emotions. Donatien especially was subject to sudden changes of heart, veering abruptly from the most jealous passion to the cruelest taunts, from rage to teasing, from confidence to disgust, from eroticism to horror. "And so I've come back to you, my dear friend," he wrote his wife on December 14, 1780, "to you whom I shall love in spite of everything as the best and dearest friend who could ever have existed for me in the world . . . I have received all your packages. This time they are charming, my heart, and I thank you with all my soul: a superb candle, a pheasant worthy of the table of a tower commander, an exquisite orange blossom, and choice preserves. All joking aside, everything is quite beautiful and very good. Keep it up . . . I assure you that my only happy moments come when I think of our reunion. But they are making me wait a fiendishly long time. Oh, it is too long! Truly it is too long!" Less than a week after these conjugal effusions, however, Donatien is again accusing his wife of "abominable lies" and treating her to these kind words: "You are an imbecile who allows herself to be led about by the nose . . . Would that you and your execrable family and their vile servants could all be put in a sack and hurled into the water. Let them come to me at once and tell me all about it: I swear to heaven that it will be the happiest moment of my life."[42]

Donatien discovered that he was powerless to break the ties between his wife and the Montreuil clan. Over the years, in fact, he saw the marquise move ever closer to her mother. Already she relied on her mother to bring up her children, administer her affairs, and act as her moral guide, and it seemed possible that she might soon fall totally under la Présidente's sway. Donatien foresaw the day when Mme de Montreuil would win the relentless struggle for influence over Renée-Pélagie. He therefore sought desperately to rescue his wife from the clutches of her accursed family. This effort explains his recourse to insult, sarcasm, and even emotional blackmail: "I beg you to come see me, and in the meantime take good care of yourself," he wrote in December 1781, "because I love you in spite of everything. I remember that your former soul is the one I adore; the other is factitious, and I hope that you will set it aside when we are back together. For rest assured that while I love you, of course, and want to be reunited with you more than ever, I will never live with a false woman. There are women in the world with whom people believed that I was deeply in love and whom I betrayed or deceived only because I found them guilty of that execrable vice."[43]

At times, though, he spontaneously sent a message whose only purpose was to declare his love, as in this note: "I embrace you with all my heart, my dear friend, and write with buoyant spirits (*gaieté d'imagination*) simply to tell you that I am doing well and to beg you to come see me soon, for I am tired of having gone so long without hugging you."[44]

It is in the famous letter of November 23–24, 1783, which Gilbert Lely compared to the music of Mozart, "who had such a gift for moving us with the dignity of being human," that Donatien revealed the best of those "buoyant spirits" that gripped him sometimes when he thought about his wife. I shall content myself with a mere enumeration of the nicknames, some of them elegant, some simply silly, that he bestowed on his dear Pélagie: charming creature, my angel, my little pet, my honey, my doggie, Mohammed's ecstasy, darling turtle-dove, my little mother, fresh pork of my thoughts, my eyes' soft glaze, my heart's blood vessels, star of Venus, soul of my soul, mirror of beauty, spur of my nerves, image of divinity, seventeenth planet of space, quintessence of virginity, emanation of angelic spirits, symbol of modesty, miracle of nature, dove of Venus, rose dropped from the bosom of the Graces, my baby, favorite of Minerva, ambrosia of Olympus, charm of the eyes, light of my life.[45]

The Role of the Jealous Lover

The mask of the jealous lover is surely the last disguise one would expect the marquis de Sade to wear. Yet he donned that mask and played the role to the hilt, as he did everything else, investing it with all the bellicose energy he could muster. The first crisis came on July 13, 1781, the date of Mme de Sade's first visit to her husband. What had passed between them? After an absence of several years did Donatien perhaps find Renée-Pélagie more desirable than before? So desirable that he suspected her of some dalliance? Or did he choose simply to play the role of the jealous lover for want of anything better to do, as a way to pass the time? That was what the marquise thought when she confided in Mlle de Rousset a few days later: "Since I saw him he has been making me miserable with a thousand fantasies of his own devising. Since he does not know what to do, he is jealous. I can picture your laughter from here. —And of whom, you ask? —Of Lefèvre (he does me a great honor, does he not?) because I told him that Lefèvre had bought some books for him. He is jealous of Mme de Villette, because I wrote him that she had invited me to come live with her . . . Tell me, will you, where he comes up with these things."[46]

Lefèvre, it is worth noting, was a Provençal peasant who had once worked as a valet for the abbé de Sade, who had taught him to read and write. From there he had gone to work in the offices of the marquis d'Albertas in Aix, after which he had moved to Paris, where Mme de Sade had engaged him as a servant. As for Mme de Villette, a cousin by marriage of Renée-Pélagie, she had been born Reine-Philiberte Rouph de Varicourt, and Voltaire had given her away in marriage to his protégé, the marquis de Villette. The Ferney *philosophe* had bestowed on her the epithets "beautiful and good." But her reputation was certainly better than her husband's, despite Sade's characterization of her as a "great fucker and even a little *Sappho*."[47] No one in Paris was unaware of Charles de Villette's homosexual proclivities: he was known as *"voiture à la Villette,"* after a carriage that one entered from the rear.

The marquise naturally denied any guilty relation with her servant, proclaimed the virtue of Mme de Villette, and defended herself against all charges: "Oh, my dear friend, how little you know me if you can suspect me of such a horrible thing! Calm down, I beg you. There is not the slightest foundation to your suspicions . . ."[48]

Three days later she pledged that she would not accept her cousin's invitation: "I reiterate my word of honor that I will not go to stay with Mme de Villette. I am going to look for a convent so as to deprive you of the opportunity to torment me as you do."[49]

After hesitating between two nunneries of Filles Anglaises while searching for a place "that is not too high-toned and where there are very few women," she settled on the convent of Sainte-Aure on rue Neuve-Sainte-Geneviève, where Mlle de Rousset had lodged previously. Her new quarters did not entirely satisfy her, nor did the company, but she made the best of it:

I have the apartment on the second floor on the side of the bakery. It is the best in the house: a large bedroom, a small foyer, and a study. My companion, with whom I spend little time, is a merchant's widow, three years older than I, who has spent her life in convents . . . My other companion is a notary's daughter, twenty years old, a good child but not suited for the convent and susceptible to the good as well as the bad.

There is no shortage of bread, but the food is just enough not to die of hunger. The boarders have no contact with the nuns other than the registrar,[50] the prioress, and the one who brings the food . . .

I am quite comfortable at Sainte-Aure. The convent is very strict and requires regular attendance at prayers. Many women would not enter a place like this and would not be happy here. But I am not afraid of strictness or of people knowing what I do, and I smile at all the childish nonsense and don't worry about it at all.[51]

Three years later the poor marquise was singing quite a different tune about her lodging. The nuns of Sainte-Aure decided to convert the apartments into cells, and she found herself relegated to a "hole" in the attic—she, a woman who owned "three castles that are going to ruin because no one lives in them." She wrote to Gaufridy: "You are the only person who is to know of my change of lodging, because my mother would want me to take something more expensive. Apart from the economy, this convent pleases me because I am alone here.

I am far from all the talk that I disliked and that did nothing to advance matters. I receive visitors in the parlor. That way, no one sees my apartment. This is an annoyance, but I would put up with ten thousand difficulties of this sort if they would grant justice to my husband."[52]

Though anodyne in appearance, Mme de Sade's residence at Sainte-Aure would have serious consequences for her future relations with Donatien. In thinking to rescue her from the bad influence of the marquise de Villette, he delivered her into the hands of an enemy far more to be feared than any imaginary rival.

"My little pet"

This was one of the terms of endearment that M. de Sade used with Milli Rousset, whom he also called Saint, Milli Printemps, and Fanny. Ever since the days when this independent and sensible woman had held her own in witty conversation at La Coste, he had not forgotten her. He thought of her often and worked to reestablish their interrupted dialogue through Renée-Pélagie, who passed on their letters. The marquise, who saw this correspondence as one of innocent banter, showed no signs of jealousy. Yet what emerges is nothing less than a love story. "Milli Printemps" was one of the few people not scandalized by the marquis's adventures, all of which she knew about. Rather than criticize his conduct, she felt only sympathy and compassion for his misfortunes.

Mlle de Rousset, who had become Mme de Sade's confidante and close friend, was not content merely to cheer her up. At times she prodded the poor marquise and criticized her mournful attitude, urging her to show greater courage and determination. But she could also offer assistance and counsel when needed on matters ranging from dealing with the ministries to coping with life's basic necessities. Was it time to prepare a basket of "treats" for the prisoner or to buy him clothing? Milli offered suggestions, ran errands, and scoured Paris in search of the best macaroons or *bottes fourrées*, filled candies in the shape of a boot "wide enough and long enough for a German woman to dance in," according to the marquis's request. She was also around to boost the morale of the marquise, who was treated so roughly by the exigent prisoner that it sometimes drove her mad. Milli frequently intervened between husband and wife. Her sangfroid and irony worked miracles, for she was not a woman to take seriously the marquis's rages and jeremiads. She answered them with just the right distance, tact, grace, and humor to calm his rage without incurring his hatred. "You would vex a wooden Capuchin with your tirades and ill temper!" she wrote him one day. "Women are mad to cling to a curmudgeon like you! We fly into action at the first sign of anything that might please you. We do all that we can to improve things. Monsieur is never happy."[53] This was the usual tone of the "Saint," who steadfastly refused to add her commiseration to Mme de Sade's: "Madame tells me, 'Do not scold him, I beg you, he is unhappy. Tell him something to make him laugh, bawdy stories, nonsense, whatever you like.' But my spirit is not light enough to take that tone today. Your awful letter communicated all its sadness to me. If I wanted to be melancholy, I might even surpass you. My sensibility and my heart have been too sorely tried. I leave you now and will deal with you another time." Forty-eight hours later she wrote: "Two days of rest have dissipated my bile and my ill humor. It would be cruel to force you to share them, although you quench our thirst with long draughts of yours."[54]

The strange thing is that Donatien, who was generally unwilling to tolerate the slightest lapse in the respect he considered his due (and surely no man has ever had less of a sense of humor in this regard), accepted the Saint's impertinence without protest and was so amused that at times he seemed to go out of his way to court it. Only she could call him "Mr. Prickly" and make ironic remarks about his curmudgeonly attitude without provoking so much as a frown. If he tolerated his "little pet's" jokes so well, it was because he recognized her unusual cleverness and wit as well as her remarkable epistolary talent: "Yes, my little pet," he wrote, "like a latter-day Don Quixote I want to break swords to tell the four corners of the world that my little pet is, of all the little female pets breathing between the two poles, the one who writes the best and is the most lovable."[55] In any case, Mme de Sade could trust her friend: if the Saint held Donatien in her toils, it was not to seduce him but solely to force the wretched fellow to pay attention to his wife, to reproach him for his snubs, or to slip in a word of criticism in the course of an amusing tale: "Women are generally frank," she told him plainly. "The marquis de Sade is the only man who does not want his wife to say, 'I am your second self.' But the thought is so pretty and so sweet. If I had a lover or a husband, I would want him to say it to me a hundred times a day. You will never be either, thank God!"[56]

On learning that the marquise was taking guitar lessons, Donatien flew into a rage. Milli responded: "My jokes did not please you! You don't answer them. But do me the honor, Mr. Prickly, of informing me whether your judgment applies to the entire letter . . . Quite seriously, you have no grounds for being jealous of the guitar teacher.

He is a proper man, pious, full of virtue, brilliant with respect to the heart more than the mind, a good friend, and amusing. We see little of him, because his business does not allow him to come. I asked him to give a few lessons to kill time. While busy writing or doing other things, I take pleasure in listening to Madame practice her scales. At least I know she is not bored."[57]

"Poulido caro"

Imperceptibly, however, the tone of their letters shifted to a more amorous key. As playful as ever, they came to reveal something more affectionate, a more intimate complicity, a more overt penchant for flirtation. Saint Rousset was no mean player of a game that was part mischievous, part libertine. She was without peer when it came to spurring her adversary on, catching him out, or arousing his interest, only to chide him gently in reply. If the marquis was more bold, she was by no means his inferior as to wit: the "little pet" excelled at scoring points, teasing, and egging him on, not without coquetry and pirouettes.

Is she not the one who lays the traps? "I have been trying to find out if you have a jealous temperament," she wrote. "Since you do, I shall keep a close watch on myself. But may heaven preserve you from ever having the slightest whim for me! I shall see to it that you are consigned to the devils! . . . You have always seen me grumbling, endlessly moralizing, laughing only far from you. But if you turned the painting around, you would see a gentler face, which is not devoid of grace or a certain jauntiness of countenance that slays men without their noticing. You shall fall into my snare."[58]

And indeed soon trapped, M. de Sade played the sighing lover and wrote pages of amorous poetry intended to dazzle the young Provençale. But the sly lady remained on her guard: "Too much night talk," she answered.

How clumsy you are to expose your powder that way . . . Phoo! I am wrong, you are consistent. "I have known enough women. I've had every kind there is," you say, "and want no more." But later you say: "See if with that morality you want to play with me. Surely you'll be sorry." Sorry I can believe, but I will not be conquered, and if you try to lead me around by the nose, you may very well break yours . . .

Yes we all have a weak side, but you have one too. Which will be more adroit at subjugating the other? We shall see. Do not flatter yourself that your knowledge of the subject is perfect. The women you have had loved and cherished your passions and your money. With Saint Rousset there is nothing to get a purchase on! How will you take hold of her? You will swear to your tender feelings and a few accessories of the sort. Oh, but I know that one and plenty of others besides! Believe me and decline this combat while there is still time! I think I see Tantalus by the side of the river: you will not drink from it, that I can guarantee![59]

And "Tantalus" was indeed dreaming of things other than "tender feelings" when he imagined the saint stretched out on a bed: "Think of me sometimes when you are between two sheets, your thighs open, and your right hand busy—searching for lice. Remember that the other also must be active, for otherwise you have only half the pleasure."[60]

The epistolary commerce between Donatien and Milli was not limited to a desire to seduce on one side and to make sprightly ripostes on the other. There were also dialogue and argument, half-serious and half-clowning; judgments of books; amusing thoughts and jokes; fantasies; and other verbal amusements. And gifts, as on the day when the saint received a package of toothpicks: "My New Year's gift has arrived. Oh, my God, why deprive yourself of toothpicks? This jewel means more to me than a present of fifty louis. You move my soul in a most unusual fashion. Who would have guessed that toothpicks would have such an effect?"[61] Here and there Mlle de Rousset lets slip that she might allow herself to be seduced, but only at her discretion: her will would be the deciding factor. Was it still just flirtatiousness when she made this flat declaration: "You have always recognized my strongly sensual nature. You will certainly never know its full extent. My energy would be as wild as yours if I did not restrain it, but since I told myself once and for all that reason must prevail in all things, I have worried little about whether I am pretty or ugly. My blotches are such that I look like a little fury."[62]

Sometimes, partly for fun, partly because they were both fond of communicating in code, they wrote in Provençal dialect. In these letters Mlle de Rousset gave free rein to her affection for the prisoner to whom she referred as *poulido caro* ("dear chicken"), as if using a language that only the two of them understood created an intimacy favorable to a free expression of emotion.

"Let us stop writing"

Even if Donatien took this idyll seriously, it could not last long. It was impossible for him to enjoy such a temperate, good-humored (and innocent) relationship without sooner or later suffering a violent change of humor. Only a month after addressing Sade in Provençal as "dear chicken," Milli Rousset informed him that she was preparing to return to Provence on business. Was she about to drop him just like that after promising to secure his release? He was outraged: "If you leave before I am free, I shall never see you again as long as I live . . ."[63]

Milli Rousset temporarily canceled her planned journey, but her relations with the marquis did not improve. On the contrary, they turned venomous in the weeks that followed this farewell letter. Writing to Gaufridy, the saint complained of having been betrayed by her friend: "After writing me a great deal of nonsense (and I do not mean the nonsense he sends his wife every day), he very foolishly attempted to compromise me by divulging to the ministries that I was writing to him and giving him secret advice. I was admonished. I could not deny the charges, since the responses that he caused to pass through their hands were full of invective. They pardoned me and absolved me on the grounds that my intentions were good and my heart was righteous . . . Their minds are so set against him that soon we will not dare open our mouths . . . You cannot mention his name without being threatened with brickbats."[64]

Soon the growing acrimony of the correspondence persuaded both Donatien and Milli to put an end to it. The Saint was the first to act: "Look, Sir, let us stop writing. It is not worth the trouble to say harsh things to each other. It only embitters the heart. I do not wish to hate anyone. You will easily forget, will you not? Without much effort. On my side I shall try to outdo you."[65] Donatien also wanted to end the relationship. "After saying harsh and insulting things, he asked me not to write any more," Milli confessed to Gaufridy. "As you can imagine, after being asked so nicely, I had soul enough not to sin again. It has been six months since he stopped asking whether I am among the dead or the living . . . My vengeance shall be limited exclusively to making him forget the friend he has lost. If he thinks about me, he will be punished enough."[66]

Months and months of silence would follow this adventure, surely the oddest and no doubt the most touching of those that marked the life of the marquis de Sade. Despite the wounding and at times cruel darts that anger caused him to launch against his old friend, he would remain to the end sincerely devoted to her. One token of his esteem is the justly celebrated letter of April 17, 1782 (quoted earlier), in which he paid his respects to Mlle de Rousset.[67]

The eagle, Mademoiselle, is sometimes obliged to abandon the seventh region of the air to swoop down on the summit of Mount Olympus, on the ancient pines of the Caucasus, on the frigid larch of the Jura, on the white hindquarters of Taurus, and even, sometimes, near the quarries of Montmartre.

•

On January 25, 1784, Marie-Dorothée de Rousset died at La Coste. Five years earlier she had experienced the first signs of the disease that would claim her life. While living with Mme de Sade in Paris she had begun to spit blood and afterward had felt extremely weak: "I am not yet dead," she wrote Gaufridy on March 3, 1780, "but close to it . . . Yesterday I started on donkey's milk, prescribed for two months, and I shall begin again in September, if I am still alive, and then we shall see if I can travel to Provence to kiss you. Otherwise we shall kiss in the Valley of Jehoshaphat."[68] Despite her illness, she continued, along with Mme de Sade, to work for the marquis's release, sending petitions and letters of recommendation to the principal ministries. She carried on despite the behavior of the man she was trying to help, who poured venom on his wife and referred to the hapless Saint as a "whore." "It takes great courage to persevere with these petitions," she sighed, her patience exhausted. She had begun to despair of success: "There are serious, very serious, allegations that make me fear a long captivity," she confessed one day to Gaufridy.

Whether true or false, they are warhorses that the ministry can trot out to shut the mouths of respectable people. M. and Madame de Maurepas, two princes, and several other people saw and read the charges and then said: "He is well off where he is. His wife is either mad or as guilty as he is for demanding his release. We do not wish to see her."

The various constables who were at the château have given abominable depositions. These men are believed. All M. de S's life is written down on a sheet of paper. (Let us omit the name) is to be hanged! Details that I had thought were known to only a few people but are now public, along with many other things—great God!—that demand the most profound silence, make me fear a long captivity.[69]

On May 19, 1781, Mlle de Rousset, braving the fatigue of a long journey, traveled by stagecoach to Avignon, which she reached, utterly exhausted, on May 28: "I feel awfully weak. I have trouble standing up and am like a person recovering from a serious illness or just coming down with one." She hoped that a few days' rest would put her in a condition to "recognize the cliffs of La Coste."[70] But it was another year before she was able to travel there. She found the château in a state of advanced dilapidation but moved in anyway and spent the winter of 1782 there in frightful conditions: the winds howled through broken windows and crevices in the walls, rain fell into the bedrooms through crumbling roofs, "there are more cave-ins every half hour," and tiles and plaster "are falling with the din of a carillon." Scared to death, Milli no longer dared to sleep in her own room, whose fireplace had collapsed, and preferred a mattress on the kitchen tiles. The kitchen was scarcely more solid than the rest of the château, but it was better protected against the wind. During the following summer she began spitting blood again. She was tired of suffering, she said, but looked upon her fate with serenity: "If I were English," she wrote Gaufridy, "I would blow my brains out. Being French, I am afraid to die."[71] Six months later, she succumbed to her illness, just forty years of age.

A few days later, unaware of the death of his "little pet," Donatien wrote to his wife: "When you write to Provence, give my best to Milli Rousset, and tell her that if I do not write she mustn't hold it against me. She knows why."[72]

Echoes

From time to time news reached him of the death of people he cherished. Gothon—sturdy "Gautruche," as Donatien called her—died of puerperal fever on October 27, 1781, eight days after giving birth to a boy who would be baptized at the marquis's expense. The moment he heard the news, Sade issued instructions to be relayed to Mlle de Rousset: if Gothon had left a will, its terms were to be scrupulously honored, and if she had left a living child, it was to be taken in charge. Donatien assumed Gothon's debts and asked Gaufridy to donate a louis to the church for a service in her memory.[73] Six months later, the marquis paid his former servant this homage: "I was sorry for Gothon. She had her faults, no doubt, but she redeemed them with her virtues and qualities. There are many people in the world who have never known this compensation . . . Gothon was devoted. She was pleasant, prompt, and unobtrusive in her service. She was a good brood mare and fond of her master's stables."[74]

There was also another death, about which no one dared tell the marquis. On May 13, 1781, Anne-Prospère died suddenly in Paris, the victim of smallpox complicated by an inflammation of the lower abdomen. Madame de Montreuil was said to be inconsolable at the loss of her favorite daughter, while Mme de Sade refrained from telling her husband the news. Six years later, thinking that she was still alive, he asked Renée-Pélagie for news of her and received this response, which makes no mention of the canoness's death:

The silence that I imposed on myself so as not to speak to you, my dear friend, about my sister was quite reasonable, for to have broken it out of a desire to satisfy you would only have worried you and caused you to reach false conclusions. This is the last time that I shall speak to you about her. You insist that I answer your questions and swear that you will calm down and never open your mouth about her again, and it is to calm you that I comply with your request:

"Why did she leave my mother's house?"

—The reason has nothing to do with you and does not dishonor you.

"Is she my enemy?"

—No.

"Tell me what kind of house she lives in, without mentioning the street or neighborhood."

—This information, whatever it may be, can only do you harm. It has become pointless to give an answer.[75]

Finally, on May 24, 1785, gentle La Jeunesse died after an illness of six weeks. Mme de Sade informed Gaufridy of his demise: "He was fully conscious at the end and filled with religious feeling . . . Despite his faults, I have missed him, because he was devoted. I have not yet been able to persuade myself to replace him, which won't be an easy thing to do."[76]

"Those dreadful brats"

Although paternal feeling was never, to put it mildly, a strong component of the marquis's makeup, he cannot be accused of indifference toward his children. Indeed, throughout his years in prison he was constantly preoccupied with their fate. And if his manner varied depending on whether he was dealing with Claude-Armand, Louis-

Marie, or Madeleine-Laure (or perhaps simply on his mood of the moment), it was because his feelings themselves were wildly contradictory. Sometimes paternal, sometimes scornful, his sentiments toward his children were never those of an ordinary father.

No description of the contrasting natures of those three "dreadful brats" is more apt than that given by Mme de Sade herself in 1777, when the eldest was ten, the next eldest eight, and the youngest six. In three sentences she drew a portrait of each of them so true to life that their traits were still recognizable twenty years later. The young chevalier, she predicted, would resemble his great-uncle: "If he continues with the character he has," she said, "he will be a most sensible *commandeur*, who will never act unwisely." She could hardly have said more in so few words. And unfortunately Donatien-Claude-Armand made it his mission to fulfill his mother's prophecy. Louis-Marie she described thus: "The elder boy is slightly built. He is healthy, but his quick temper and petulance are without rival." And we shall find the marquis's favorite son, with his nervous, feverish temperament, just as his mother describes him. "My daughter is healthy," Mme de Sade added. "She assures me diplomatically that she is very happy to see me, but I assure you that she is infinitely more fond of the nuns than she is of me."[77] To the end of her days Madeleine-Laure would remain the devout woman of limited horizons that she already showed signs of becoming.

It should come as no surprise that M. de Sade showed little affection for his children. Did he not consider them to be primarily responsible for his misfortunes? To his wife he wrote: "You will repent of what you are making me suffer here on account of those dreadful brats, whom I abhor as much as I abhor you and all your kin. There you have my last word on the subject, and [you can see] the effect that prison has had on me."[78] He cared little whether or not he received their letters, which were written under dictation, or with their mother's hand guiding their own, although he regularly asked about their progress, their health, and their character, all subjects on which Mme de Sade provided him with abundant information. Thus in 1780 he learned that all three children had come down with smallpox. Louis-Marie would bear permanent scars. Otherwise he was doing well in class, especially in Latin, possessed a thorough knowledge of mythology, and was starting Greek; he absorbed grammar and spelling with ease: "His mistakes are mere slips." He wrote well, although his Latin sentences were more elegant than literal, and he devoured whatever books came his way. He wanted to learn everything at once, spoke too quickly, and gave signs of unusually precocious ambition and vanity. Though handsomer and more graceful than his brother, with an open face and an air of goodness "that causes people to devour him with caresses," the younger son was turning out to be very lazy and less talented than his brother, "although he does not lack intelligence."[79]

Of course the children had no idea where their father was. When they asked, Mme de Sade told them he was traveling. To remind them what their absent father looked like, she showed them his portrait: "The elder boy clearly recognized you and stared at your portrait for a long time, which gave me great pleasure. The chevalier also looked hard, but he did not recognize you as well. He was so little when you left us! They said that they would like to see you and to have you live with us . . . I promised them that, when they come back, they will join us, you and me, wherever we may be. My father and my mother adore them. They left satisfied that they would see you in two years, for they find that your trips are very long. Their feelings give me infinite pleasure."[80]

For all his protestations, the marquis had by no means severed his emotional ties to his children. Toward the end of 1780 he asked for their portraits as a New Year's gift. On several occasions he asked Renée-Pélagie for samples of their handwriting in order to check on their progress. Believing that his release was imminent, he insisted on spending a year with his wife and children "before any plan or party estranges them from me, and," he threatened, "it will cost me nothing to destroy any arrangement you may have made contrary to this unique plan. No one has the right to take my children away before I have had a chance to know them, and I swear to you that it will not happen."[81] On rare occasions, bursts of tenderness toward his children would leave him feeling desperate: "I am like a madman," he confessed to his wife one day. "If you heard me speaking to them all alone . . . you would think I had lost my head. Not a night passes when I do not dream about them."[82]

The Marquis de Sade's Ideal Library

Shortly after becoming minister of the royal household, Malesherbes took steps to improve the condition of state prisoners. On August 27, 1775, only a month after his appointment, he released most of those who had been held on lettres de cachet, which his predecessor, the duc de La Vrillière, had used indiscriminately. Shortly thereafter he issued the following instructions to the warden of Vincennes: "No prisoner is to be denied material to read and to write. The alleged abuses they may make of such materials cannot be dangerous, being confined as securely as they are."[83] Donatien de Sade would make abundant use of this right, and he would do so without major impediment, for even after Malesherbes's departure the liberalization of the prisons continued, from the elimination of solitary confinement to the authorization of gazettes and personal libraries (to supplement the prison library). Under Louis XVI it no longer occurred to anyone to deny prisoners the right to read Voltaire.[84]

Along with writing, reading was Sade's most consistent and most liberating activity. Some letters to his wife contained lists of books to buy or borrow from lending libraries, and he was almost as impatient for these shipments as for his other requests. When Renée-Pélagie was slow to send the works he wanted, she was greeted with a torrent of abuse. But after Sade had read the books, she was treated to his piquant and penetrating commentaries, his acute and amused judgments. Almost no book or periodical was excluded by the penitentiary authorities. The only noteworthy exception to this rule was the *Confessions* of Jean-Jacques Rousseau, the first part of which appeared in 1782. Sade asked to read it several times during the next year. His first request came in a letter dated June 15, 1783, in which the virtuous Genevan found himself in some rather odd company: "The *Confessions* of Jean-Jacques Rousseau. Some novels, rather free and rather—you know what I mean. Something to make pretty thoughts come to me in my solitude, in the line of the *Portier des Chartreux* or *Thérèse Philosophe*. All this because prison has its effects, and I feel that I am more or less taking myself in hand."[85] A few days later the marquise wrote back that the *Confessions* "will not be allowed in."[86] In July he tried again: "Do not forget the cap, the goggles, the six blocks of wax, the *Confessions* of Jean-Jacques, and the jacket that M. de Rougemont assures me you have."[87] But the request bore no fruit, leaving Donatien in a rage: "To deny me Jean-Jacques's *Confessions* is another fine thing, especially after sending me Lucretius and the dialogues of Voltaire. This is proof of a truly discerning taste, a profound judiciousness in your directors. Alas, they do me great honor to think that a Deist author could possibly be a wicked book for me. I wish I were still at that stage! Your therapeutic methods are less than sublime, *messieurs les directeurs!* What makes a thing good or bad is one's own attitude, not the thing in itself . . . Take it from there, gentlemen, and have the good sense to understand, by sending me the book I am asking for, that Rousseau may be a dangerous author for clumsy bigots like you yet become an excellent book for me. Jean-Jacques is to me what an *Imitation of Jesus Christ* is to you."[88]

The scandal aroused by the *Confessions* would have been reason enough for Sade to want to read the book. But there was also another reason, one that did not escape the notice of Philippe Roger.[89] Sade was at this point thinking quite seriously about writing his own memoirs. "I want to write—for myself alone, I give you my oath on it—the *Memoirs of My Life*. But since I want to write them only for myself, I do not want anyone else to see them. I am therefore asking you to obtain M. Le Noir's word of honor that the sealed manuscript bearing the title *Mémoires de ma vie*, which I shall show on leaving prison to the person who will examine my papers, will never be opened or confiscated, and to make sure of this I want you to get a signed note, based on the sample I am attaching, for otherwise I will not go to work."[90]

Despite the authorities' tolerance in regard to reading matter, the prisoner could not read everything; certain titles were off limits, not so much out of concern for public morality but as an individual matter, because there was a danger that they would "inflame his mind." One day, for example, Mme de Sade was refused permission to bring certain books into the prison. "When I went to see M. Le Noir about it," she reported, "he told me that all your books had been taken away because they inflamed your mind and caused you to write unseemly things . . . Restrain your writing, I beg you. It is doing you great harm. Make up for this by persevering in a decent way of thinking, one that resembles the depths of your heart, and above all do not write or utter all the strange thoughts that your mind suggests to you and on the basis of which they fervently wish to judge you."[91]

•

Apart from the impressive number of books that Sade was capable of devouring, what is most striking when one attempts to reconstruct the library he assembled in prison is the sheer variety of tastes and preoccupations his reading reveals. If certain works were intended only to satisfy his scientific curiosity (an *Essay on Fluids*, for example, or a *Best Elements of Physics*, or Buffon's *Natural History*), others, such as the *Almanach des spectacles* and scripts of the year's plays kept him abreast of fashions in the theater, an art at which he worked hard to keep himself up to date. Still others were of direct service to the novelist, particularly historical works and travel stories: *Le Voyageur français* by the abbé de La Porte, a "delightful read"; Cook's *Voyages*; histories of the late Empire, the Hanoverian wars, and wars in Beauvais, France, and Malta; and the *Voyages de Bougainville*, to name a few. Novels figured among works of entertainment or "second reading," as he called them. The shelves in the marquis's cell held Marivaux's *Vie de Marianne* and *Le Paysan parvenu*, Robert Challe's *Les Illustres françaises*, Guilleragues's *Lettres portugaises*, and Laclos's *Liaisons dangereuses*, along with all that was new in fiction. He took the greatest pleasure, however, from Voltaire's novellas, which he knew by heart: "The works of such a man cannot be reread too often. I urge you to read them, even if you have already done so a thousand times, for they are always new and always delightful."[92] Naturally he had all the great "classics": Homer, Virgil, Lucretius, Montaigne, Tasso, and Ariosto occupied a proud place on his shelves. Philosophy, too, was well represented, from Nicole's *Logique* to Holbach's *Système de la nature* and its refutation by abbé Bergier. Always on the lookout for recent publications, Sade ordered the twelve volumes of Louis-Sébastien Mercier's *Tableau de Paris* as they came from the printer. He urged his wife to rely on abbé Amblet for the selection of books of all kinds: "On the selection of books, consult no one other than Amblet, I beg you, and consult him even when I ask [for a book by name], because I am not familiar with all the works, and some may be very bad."[93]

Certain authors, such as d'Alembert and abbé Prévost, drew exclamations of admiration: "What a man! What a writer! These are the people I would want for arbiters and judges, and not the imbecile crew that has taken it in mind to discipline me!"[94] Massillon elicited such passion from him that he borrowed the celebrated preacher's rhythms to sing his praises: "My God, my dear friend, how I love Father Massillon's sermons! They lift me up, they enchant me, they delight me . . . It is to the heart that this man directs his maxims. It is the heart that he seeks to seduce, and it is the heart that he continually captivates . . . What purity! What morality! And what a happy mix of strength and simplicity!"[95] By contrast, he had nothing but scorn for a Restif de La Bretonne (who of course returned his contempt in spades). "Be sure not to buy anything by M. Rétif, in God's name. He is an author for the Pont-Neuf and the Bibliothèque Bleue, and it is extraordinary that you should have taken it in mind to send me something of his."[96]

"The ultimate impropriety"

Sade always thought of himself as a writer. Long before his first imprisonment, and doubtless even before his first scandals, he *was* a writer, as were his father and his father's friends and his uncle the abbé. Like many noblemen of the time, Sade made literature without knowing it, or, rather, without making it known, just as he wrote salon comedies and acted in society theaters: for his own pleasure and that of his friends and family, spectators and readers persuaded in advance of his talent and wit. His love letters, light comedies, couplets, quatrains, and occasional verse, all carefully copied by the loyal La Jeunesse, give evidence of this recreational writing. Did he attempt to have these works published at an early date, as some have claimed? Not only is there no evidence of any such attempt, but to have done so would have been out of keeping with the spirit of the time—and with Sade's own conception of nobility. Until the end of the eighteenth century to be an author was to derogate from nobility, and it is hard to imagine a man so jealous of his caste prerogatives engaging in an activity considered debasing by his fellow aristocrats. His earliest "professional" ambitions date from his stay in Italy in 1775–1776, that is, from a time when, having become a déclassé, and virtually broke, he began to think seriously about publishing an account of his travels.

Thus he was an anonymous writer, a writer without a book, long before the imprisonment of 1778–1790. But it was in prison that the Sadeian style was born in all its irreducible distinctiveness. It was in prison (which served as both protection and limitation of his freedom) that Sade liberated his tongue and forged his own style. "It was in the depths of solitude, which horrified him (both in itself and for the sanction it represented), that horror, transformed into an object of desire, originated; here, the irresistible need to write, along with a terrifying, indomitable power of language, was born. Everything had to be told. The first freedom is the freedom to tell all."[97] So it was that Sade the prisoner crossed the line defining what Maurice Blanchot so aptly called the "ultimate impropriety." Simone de Beauvoir remarked that Sade "went into prison a man; he came out a writer." Logically, then, the prison is everywhere in Sade's work. The fortress, the dungeon, the convent, the inaccessible island, the besieged citadel: his imagination rang all the changes on the enclosed space of confinement. But at the same time his writing—that instrument of freedom—became, like his walk and his visits, a means of control for his jailers, who first granted him the privilege only to take it away as one might take away a child's rattle: he was denied "all use of pencil, ink, quill, and paper." "His castration was circumscribed: the scriptural sperm could no longer flow; detention became retention; deprived of both his walk and his pen, Sade swelled up and became a eunuch."[98]

During the first two years of his detention, the prisoner worked mainly on revising the manuscript of his *Voyage d'Italie*, which now comprised an imposing mass of pages recopied by La Jeunesse, while his friend, Dr. Mesny, from whom he hid his misfortunes and who therefore believed he was still a free man, continued to send him the documentation he needed for his work. Already, though, Sade was devoting much of his time to the theater, a consuming, overweening passion that would remain with him to the end. On December 24, 1780, he sketched an outline of his comedy *L'Inconstant* (which would become *Le Capricieux*), for which he began writing verse a few weeks later, on January 8. After "rethinking and correcting" the manuscript on April 5, 1781, he began working on a fair copy, which was completed on April 14. He then sent it to his wife, who, along with abbé Amblet, remained throughout his life his best literary adviser. "Your play is excellent," she told him. "I definitely place it above the other two, which also have their merits. The characters are well drawn . . . This play is sure to win applause, and if the Comédiens-Français were to make any changes, they would be very slight, and I do not even see what they might change."[99] A year later Renée-Pélagie received *Le Prévaricateur* and the final draft of the tragedy *Jeanne Laisné*, followed by a short play in free verse, *La Folle épreuve ou le Mari crédule*. The list of comedies grew longer and longer. *Deux Jumelles*, which Mme de Sade found "quite decent, capable of being performed in a convent, a little cold but not bad," was followed by *Le Misanthrope par amour, ou Sophie et Desfrancs*, which abbé Amblet did not like at all: "After reading it, he did not want to put his opinion on paper, because he said frankly that there was nothing good to say. If this work amuses you, you can carry on with it, he said, but as for appearing in public, he said it cannot be. You wanted him to speak frankly, and frankly that is what he told me."[100] To those who might criticize him for spending his enforced leisure in such "foolishness," Sade answered that the dramatic genre had always been cultivated by "our most famous men of letters" and that in any case he had chosen "that which demands the least paraphernalia and offers the most agreeable diversion." Though still behind bars, he was already dreaming of having his comedies performed at the Théâtre-Français, an idea, he confided to his wife, "so baroque that sometimes I approve of it and sometimes I reject it." In the end, of course, he gave it up.

Since his room was subject to frequent searches, he took infinite precautions to hide his manuscripts from his guards and never sent a copy to his wife without including a note indicating that the text contained no hidden meanings or double-entendres and that any resemblance between the characters and the author or his friends and relatives was strictly coincidental. "Since I portray the difficulties of a very unhappy man after having suffered every possible kind of misfortune myself, it would be very difficult to avoid some resemblance, but I categorically declare that my intention was neither to speak of nor to portray myself."[101] What exasperated him most of all, however, was the confiscation of his drafts: "It is pointless to confiscate drafts of texts when fair copies have been sent out," he correctly pointed out, "and it is foolish to confiscate those that are formless and whose quality, good or bad, consequently cannot be judged, and these are the texts I need most urgently. If any of the works that have been confiscated appear to be finished, whether good or bad, let them keep them if they wish until my release, but have them return the drafts, I beg you."[102]

Donatien did not lack for ideas or projects: memoirs, histories, novels, travelogues—he aspired to try his hand at all the genres, compelled by a persistent urge to write that grew more imperious as hope of liberation faded. While working on his *Dialogue entre un prêtre et un moribond* (summer of 1782), he wrote out the first sketches of *Cent Vingt Journées de Sodome*, which he would finish in the Bastille. He had also begun to contemplate a book on metempsychosis, which greatly surprised Mme de Sade: "I find this subject to be, as farfetched products of the human mind go, one of the easiest to ridicule and madness of the most laughable kind."[103] More curious and far more interesting was his ambitious idea for a "House of the Arts," plans for which he elaborated in May of 1782, while the king's architect Heurtier was building the Salle Favart, a new theater for the Comédie-Italienne. Donatien's plan involved nothing less than the construction of a monumental theater some 260 feet in diameter, around which were to be arrayed twelve paths, each with a separate building dedicated to one of the muses and devoted to a different art. Although this project attracted the attention of several people, including Reufflet-Duhameau, nothing was ever done to bring it to fruition, at least not in its original architectural form. But the marquis continued to dream of bringing all the arts together in one place, a dream that was eventually to be realized in a dramatic work entitled *La Ruse d'Amour* (later *L'Union des Arts*), a series of five one-act plays linked together by a common backdrop.

The Bastille

Early in 1784 the Vincennes prison was officially closed for unknown reasons. Public opinion had been turning increasingly against the state prisons, and the Bastille was big enough to hold all the prisoners previously housed both there and at Vincennes. On February 29, 1784, the three remaining prisoners from Vincennes were transferred to the Bastille: the comte de Solages, imprisoned by his family, the comte de Whyte de Maleville, who was insane, and the marquis de Sade.

Upon arriving at the Bastille Donatien was lodged on "Liberty three," that is, on the third floor of the tower ironically referred to as "Liberty," which, together with the Bertaudière Tower, formed the *bastide* (cell-block) of Saint-Antoine. Each floor of the tower comprised a single octagonal room, fifteen to sixteen feet in diameter and fifteen to twenty feet high. The ceiling and walls were whitewashed, and the floor was brick. Three steps led up to a window secured by three sets of bars. The furnishing consisted of a bed with green serge curtains, one or two tables, several chairs, andirons, a shovel, and a pair of tongs. But the prisoner ordered furniture from outside, carpeted the room as he wanted, and fixed it up to his taste. He had his books, paintings, and engravings brought over from Vincennes but did not regain possession of them until April 29. In the meantime he complained of having been transferred "by force, without warning, without information of any kind, with all this mystery, all this burlesque incognito, all this enthusiasm, all this barely pardonable heat . . . And where was I taken? To a prison where I am a thousand times worse off and a thousand times more constrained than in the wretched place I left . . . I am in a room half as large as the one I had before, where I cannot turn around and which I rarely leave except to spend a few minutes in a narrow courtyard where the air one breathes smells of the guard-room and the kitchen, and into which they escort me with bayonets affixed to the ends of their rifles as if I had attempted to dethrone Louis XVI." Even more annoying, he had not been allowed to take his clothing or pillow or even his "rump cushion." He was forbidden to use knives or scissors. And he was obliged to make his bed and sweep his room: "As for the first [that is, making the bed], fine, because they did it very badly and it amuses me. But about the second [sweeping the room], unfortunately I have no knack for it. It is my parents' fault for not having made that talent a part of my education."[104] And he had other complaints as well: "The meat they serve me is so tough that you cannot swallow a single piece. The fireplace gives me such a headache that, cold as it is, I am forced to do without a fire, and for a servant they have given me a strange fellow as impertinent as any you might meet."[105] Worse yet, they had posted a guard just inches from his pillow, "a man who sleeps all day and who, from the stroke of midnight until eight in the morning, gallops about, smashing, breaking, overturning, screaming, and doing other similarly delightful things."[106] He bemoaned his fate: "Ah, how different this is from Vincennes! At Vincennes the harassment never descended to such minute details as it does here. They did not contrive so assiduously to annoy me over the smallest things."[107] Within a very short time, however, Sade was able to reconstitute more than decent quarters for himself in the Bastille, complete with his entire library and his gallery of family portraits. All his clothes were returned under seal and duly "acknowledged sound and intact" by their owner, as were his cushions, his velvet cap, his glass goblet in its case, and his tin syringe in its box. Finally, his most precious possessions, his papers and manuscripts, were returned to him in a separate carton.

As one might imagine, this transfer to a prison even more sinister than Vincennes did little to improve the marquis's mood. M. de Launay, the commandant of the Bastille, complained bitterly to the *lieutenant général de police* about this "extremely difficult and violent prisoner" who made scenes and lost his temper on the slightest pretext, who wrote "letters full of horrible things about his wife, his family, and us," who repeatedly insulted his guards, and who greeted his wife with "torrents of insults and nonsense." And the warden added: "The truth is that she fears for her life if he should someday regain his freedom." Did Renée-Pélagie really think that Donatien might murder her? Surely Launay was exaggerating, but he seized the opportunity to reduce Mme de Sade's visits to one a month. "This is a favor to his wife and family . . . If he does not abuse the privilege, more frequent visits may be allowed later on." And shortly thereafter Mme de Sade was indeed authorized to visit her husband once a week.

On September 22, 1788, the marquis de Sade was transferred, at his request, to cell six in the Liberty Tower, which was lighter and airier than his previous room. He was also granted the services of a disabled veteran to do his housekeeping and to run errands as well as to take care of him when he was ill. He had new tapestries hung and acquired more comfortable furniture at a cost of a thousand livres, a tidy sum that would be paid by his wife. Things were going well, or at any rate better than before, except that he was assigned a new guard, "that scoundrel Lossinotte, the *stupidest* and most *insolent* valet I have ever seen in my life."[108]

Family Council

On October 5, 1786, at eleven in the morning, attorneys Thomas Gibert and Toussaint-Charles Girard, acting on behalf of the marquis's paternal uncle, the *commandeur*, held a meeting with Donatien in the Bastille's council chamber. Their purpose was to "summon" him to sign a power of attorney in favor of his uncle "or any other relative he may deem appropriate, for the purpose of regulating, governing, and administering, during the time of his detention, his property and affairs as well as those of Mme la comtesse de Sade, his wife, . . . [and] to provide for the maintenance and education of his children, and even their establishment, whether by marriage or otherwise," et cetera. The marquis agreed that someone was needed to administer his properties but argued that no one was better equipped to do so than himself; hence he urged the *commandeur* to request that the minister grant his release and stated his determination never to sign any power of attorney.[109]

Brushing aside this dismissal, the family met in council on June 21, 1787, and under a writ granted by the Châtelet of Paris assumed control of the marquis's property and the education of his children. Donatien was deprived not only of his worldly goods but also of his paternal rights.

This official transfer of control only bestowed the sanction of law on the de facto reality of the situation. It goes without saying that the *commandeur*, a respectable old duffer of eighty-four who owed his nominal position as head of the family council solely to his advanced age and high rank in the Order of Malta, actually wielded no power, having sacrificed all his prerogatives to Mme de Montreuil. In a letter dated July 7, 1787, he pledged to abide by la Présidente's wishes: "I shall make modest use of my power, and never without informing you in advance." And he added: "I shall write Mme de Sade as soon as I can. It was about time that she looked after the good of her children. I shall always be grateful to her for it."[110]

Novellas and Novels

Far from slowing, Sade's literary activity only increased after his transfer to the Bastille. On October 22, 1785, he began turning the drafts of the *Cent Vingt Journées de Sodome* into a fair copy. To avoid having the work confiscated he copied the text in an almost microscopic handwriting onto four-inch sheets, which were glued end to end to form a strip almost forty feet long, filled on both sides. This minuscule volume could easily be hidden in a pocket or a crevice in the wall. The work was completed on the morning of November 27, after thirty-seven days of writing from seven to ten in the evening. The manuscript represents an incomplete version, however, and the author probably would have extended the work had he not lost the precious scroll for good in 1789.

Much has been written about this most unusual novel, Sade's first great work. From Maurice Heine, who, between 1931 and 1935, was the first to publish a text based on a manuscript that he considered to be the first *psychopathia sexualis*, a precursor of Krafft-Ebing and Freud, to Michel Delon, who has just reprinted the work in the Pléiade collection,[111] most commentators have focused on the psychiatric or psychoanalytic character of the book. Following Heine, Jean Paulhan saw the work as an "enormous catalogue of perversions," and Gilbert Lely called it a "medical treatise." Jacques Lacan peremptorily dismissed this view, however: "To say that the work of Sade anticipates Freud, if only as a catalogue of perversions, is a piece of nonsense that has become a literary commonplace, the blame for which can be laid, as usual, at the door of the specialists."[112] Dr. Hesnard alludes to the work's dreamlike character, "in the condensation of erotic aberrancies, in their increasing sexual complexity, in the arithmetic unfolding of dramatic events fraught with an ambivalence between outright abasement and voluptuous fascination."[113] And Jean Gillibert has written that "the Sadeian horror reminds us . . . of our childhood resurrected in dream, of the myth of our childhood, sexual and repressed, the place to which Freud held fast while encouraging us to let go and to press forward into the—impossible—future of our beginning, toward the invention of what we call the Past and which is nothing other than what will yet come to pass."[114] Although it is not the role of the biographer to propose yet another interpretation, it is worth noting that the *Cent Vingt Journées de Sodome* cannot be dissociated from Sade's sexual practice in prison and might be characterized as a record of his fantasies. Beyond the ejaculatory allegory, writing became consubstantial with desire through the ritual of pen and ink.

In the fall of 1786 Sade was working on *Aline et Valcour* and gathering information about Spain and Portugal, where certain episodes of the novel are set. On July 8, 1787, he completed the 138 pages of his philosophical novella, *Les Infortunes de la vertu*, and inscribed this note in the margins of the final page: "My eyes hurt badly during the writing." Shortly thereafter he invited the chevalier du Puget, the king's *lieutenant général* at the Bastille, to a reading of *Jeanne Laisné ou le Siège de Beauvais* before the staff officers in the council hall.[115] On March 1, 1788, he began working on a new novella, *Eugénie de Franval*, which he finished in six days,[116] and on October 1, 1788, he compiled a bibliography of his works, which at that date comprised some fifteen octavo volumes, not counting his clandestine manuscripts.[117]

Charenton

On the morning of July 2, 1789, Donatien Alphonse François de Sade nervously paced his cell. His wife had informed him of the turmoil in the streets of Paris. For several days he had noticed the military preparations inside the fortress: the garrison had been reinforced, cannon had been moved into position, and barrels of powder had been placed on the gun platforms. Clearly something grave was in the offing. Around noon Lossinotte came to tell him that his walk around the towers had been cancelled on orders of the commandant. This news exasperated him no end. He sent Lossinotte back to Launay and threatened to make a dreadful row if the decision was not rescinded. When the guard returned, however, the answer was still no. Beside himself with rage, Sade picked up a long white-metal funnel normally used for emptying his chamber pot into the moat, placed the improvised megaphone in his cell window, and began to shout at the top of his lungs that the prisoners' throats were being cut and that the warden and all his jailers were murderers. Spectators gathered, their heads tilted upward, while the marquis ranted; eventually he called upon the assembled mob to come to his aid by laying siege to the fortress. Guards finally managed to subdue the madman, whom the commandant now sought to get rid of in any way he could, and the sooner the better: "The time has come to relieve us of this person who cannot be controlled and over whom none of the officers can gain any authority," he wrote to M. de Villedeuil, minister of state.[118]

That night, at one in the morning, six armed men snatched Donatien from his bed. Without allowing him time to dress or to take anything with him, they hurled him into a coach and drove him "naked as a worm" to Charenton, where he was to be locked up for an indefinite period. While Mme de Sade slept peacefully, unaware of what was going on at the Bastille, M. Chenon, a *commissaire* of the Châtelet, placed seals on what had been her husband's cell.

Charenton was at that time a hospital for the mentally ill run by

the Brothers of Charity. Louis-Sébastien Mercier praised their administration, their vigilance, and their care but deplored the fact that, in
addition to the mentally ill, they also played host to prisoners held
under lettres de cachet. "It is troubling," he wrote in 1788, only a year
before Sade was transferred to Charenton, "to see the Brothers of
Charity turned into jailers and hospitals transformed into little *bastilles*
. . . Charenton is pleasantly situated; it is not by nature a state prison,
but it has become one, because people are locked up there under lettres
de cachet . . . The prisoners of Charenton are madmen, imbeciles,
libertines, debauchees, [and] spendthrifts."[119]

There is another account of conditions at Charenton even more
precious for our purposes since it comes from the hand of Sade himself,
in a letter written in answer to the attorney Maton de la Varenne:

Laziness, baseness, a taste for dissolution, lust, gluttony, or the need to flee a
world in which one has dishonored oneself—these are the only grounds for
the vocation of a Brother of Charity. Once this axiom is acknowledged, it is
easy to draw the conclusion that an administration run by such scoundrels can
only represent the greatest danger. Someone ought to look into it: that is all
I am asking. Deign, Sir, along with me, to turn your glance this way for a
moment. Deign to follow me into the dank lair that serves as asylum to those
unfortunates whom avarice, greed, ambition, vengeance, and crimes of all
sorts are gobbling up at Charenton even as I write, at a time when our good
Parisians imagine that, the Bastille having been destroyed, despotism is disarmed. Yes, please follow me, I urge you.

Your eyes will discover, if they can see, a dark building buried in the earth
up to its roof, a horrid place arranged in such a way that the air can never
reach the interior and the sobs and screams of the prisoners cannot be heard
by anyone, after seven or eight jailers, led by a nice fat friar with a rubicund
face, looking hale and hearty, have opened the gate to a small courtyard whose
foul exhalations may prevent you from continuing. See, if you can, more than
twenty wretches in full possession of their reason but forgotten for centuries
in this asylum of woe, and whose keepers, in order to magnify the horror of
their position, dare to confound them and lump them together with madmen,
wild men, and epileptics, who infect them, corrupt them, and beat them, and
if they complain the only satisfaction they receive is to be told that they can
take refuge in their dungeon cells if the company is not to their liking. Will
you enter one of those dank cells? You will find four bare, damp walls covered
with insects, with a bed nailed to one wall, a haven for fleas and spiders that
have lain undisturbed for a hundred years. A wretched chair and rotten table
stand close by, and the cell is sealed by a door equipped with a window through

which the poor inmate can be fed without anyone's having to enter. A narrow window, almost always without glass, allows a scant few rays of light to penetrate this dreadful redoubt, which is surrounded on all sides by walls sixty feet high. That is what you will see.[120]

"Our leader is not here"

On Tuesday, July 14, 1789, ten days after Sade's transfer to Charenton, the Bastille was attacked and seized. Commandant de Launay, Major de Losme-Salbray, and an aide named Miray were dragged out onto the Place de Grève and massacred. A kitchen-boy by the name of Desnot managed to sever Launay's head by cutting his throat with a pocketknife, whereupon he placed his trophy on a pike and carried it through the streets. These facts are well-known. Less well-known is the fact that the populace that invaded and sacked the fortress did not spare the marquis's cell. His library of six hundred volumes, his clothing, his linen, his furniture, his portraits, and above all his manuscripts—all were "slashed, burned, carried off, [or] pillaged," in particular the scroll containing the *Cent Vingt Journées de Sodome*, which Sade would never recover.

By an unfortunate coincidence Mme de Sade chose this same Fourteenth of July to retrieve her husband's effects, which remained under seal in the Bastille. The historian Robert Darnton has found former *lieutenant général de police* Jean-Charles Pierre Le Noir's account of exactly what happened that day:

The comte de Sade was transferred in early July of that year [1789] from the Bastille to the place of confinement run by the Brothers of Charity at Charenton. He had left various family papers at the Bastille and asked that they be turned over only to a person whom he authorized with a power of attorney. On the thirteenth he drew up at Charenton a power authorizing his wife to retrieve his papers from the Bastille. Equipped with her husband's power of attorney, she went on the morning of July 14 to see Commissaire Chénon, the official named by the *lieutenant de police* to oversee this state prison. They prepared to go to the prison together. The commissaire had to draw up an affidavit concerning the return of the papers, which Mme de Sade was to receive, but at that moment an insurrection began in Commissaire Chénon's *quartier*, and he was obliged to remain at his post and postpone until evening his visit with Mme de Sade to the Bastille. This incident saved the commissaire and possibly Mme de Sade. But the next day, July 15, the commissaire, while walking on a path through the garden of the Palais-Royal, was assailed by [men and] women of the populace, who attempted to hang him from a tree, saying, "We missed killing you at the Bastille." He removed his wig and showed them his bald head. "What will you do with my old head?" he asked. At that moment he noticed a woman, who said: "Leave him, our leader is not here." After the women had beaten him and placed a rope around his neck, they kissed him and left him there.[121]

On July 19, Mme de Sade, who had taken refuge at Sainte-Aure, informed Commissaire Chénon that she was renouncing all responsibility for her husband's affairs: "If you have not yet used my letter to withdraw M. de Sade's effects from the Bastille without observing the usual formalities in such cases, I beg you to dispose of the items in such a way that I cannot be held responsible for M. de Sade's papers and effects, as I have personal reasons for wishing not to be burdened with them."[122] This was the first sign of independence from her husband that she had ever shown.

"I want him to be happy"

Although the lettre de cachet was universally decried, especially after the famous remonstrances of the Cour des Aides of August 14, 1770, drafted by Malesherbes, it remained a part of French law. True, Louis XVI did not abuse the power, and the baron de Breteuil's circular of March 1784 virtually put an end to the procedure, or at any rate to the familial lettre de cachet, which was both the most prevalent and most arbitrary type. Nearly all the *cahiers de doléances* (lists of local grievances) called for its elimination, and the king himself, in his declaration of June 23, 1789, which can be regarded as the monarchy's last will and testament, declared himself of his own free will in favor of individual liberty and urged the Estates General "to seek and obtain the most suitable means to reconcile the abolition of the orders known under the name lettres de cachet with the maintenance of public security and with the precautions necessary either to protect, in certain cases, the honor of families or to repress incipient sedition or to protect the state from the effects of a criminal conspiracy." But the lettre de cachet was not finally abolished until the National Assembly voted on March 16, 1790, and its decree was ratified by the king on March 26. Article X of that decree states that "arbitrary orders resulting in exile and all other orders of the same nature, as well as all lettres de cachet, are abolished, and none will be issued in the future. Those who were affected are free to remove themselves to whatever place they deem suitable."[123]

Two days later, on March 18, Louis-Marie and Claude-Armand went to tell their father the good news. As an exceptional favor, the Brothers of Charity authorized the marquis to walk and dine with his sons free from surveillance. "I want him to be happy, but I seriously doubt that he knows how," Mme de Montreuil answered her grandsons when they told him they wanted to bring the prisoner the glad tidings themselves.[124] She also wondered whether the language of the decree did not allow the families some room for maneuver: "The way in which it is drafted may yield certain exceptions. The question is whether, under certain circumstances, the families must call attention to them. As things stand, I think, the families should remain neutral and allow the administration or the public party to decide as they deem appropriate. This is the only way to remain above reproach in one's own eyes and in the eyes of others, come what may."[125]

Ten days later, on Friday, April 2, 1790, Donatien Alphonse François de Sade left Charenton a free man.

II

CITIZEN,
MAN OF
LETTERS

17
Free! . . .

"Good day, good works!"

Donatien thus found himself in Paris on Good Friday in the year of
grace 1790 with no other baggage than three poor mattresses, a black
ratteen coat, and one gold louis in his pocket, and with no idea where
to go, where to stay, where to eat, or where to find money.[1] Most of
his friends and relatives had emigrated, and those who remained were
in no haste to offer their hospitality. Renée-Pélagie refused to receive
him in the convent of Sainte-Aure, where she had prudently holed up.
His thoughts then turned to M. de Milly, a *procureur* at the Châtelet
and his former business agent, who was now living in retirement among
his books in a house on rue du Bouloir behind the place des Victoires.
The old man welcomed him with kindness, offered him food and a
bed, and lent him a few hundred francs, enough to get by for a week
or two.

No sooner was his freedom restored than Donatien hastened to
inform Gaufridy of the good news: "I left Charenton (where I was
transferred from the Bastille) on Good Friday. Good day, good works!
Yes, my dear advocate, this was the day on which I regained my freedom. I have therefore decided to honor it for the rest of my life . . .
[and] each time that the forty-fifth day of Lent brings us to another
Good Friday, I shall kneel down, pray, and give thanks . . . I shall
resolve to mend my ways, and I shall keep my word!"[2]

Three days later he again wrote Gaufridy, this time asking for
money. He needed a thousand écus immediately until next summer.
The need was urgent. There were debts to pay and expenses to meet:

for a room at an inn, a servant, a tailor, a caterer, and all the rest. His property, he exulted, was once again his own: the sequestration order had been lifted. Gaufridy would henceforth deal with no one but himself, just as in the good old days. While awaiting the completion of certain formalities, however, Donatien had no choice: if his wife would not help him, he had only his mother-in-law to turn to. She lent him 1,200 livres, which he pledged to repay quickly. This was just enough to pay what he still owed the monks of Charenton and to reimburse part of what Milly had advanced. A few days later Mme de Montreuil lent him another 200 livres, which enabled him to rent a furnished room in the hôtel du Bouloir, near where he was staying with Milly.

•

At the hôtel du Bouloir Donatien's neighbor was a twenty-eight-year-old damsel with a waist slender enough to be spanned by two hands, rather drawn features, and the kind of turned-up nose on which the fates of empires have been known to hinge. Her name was Théroigne de Méricourt, and she was a native of the Netherlands. Once a kept woman, now converted to the revolutionary cause, she had thrown herself wholeheartedly into political activity, crisscrossed the streets of Paris dressed as an Amazon with pistols stuck in her belt, and participated in countless festivals and meetings, speaking out at the Jacobin Club as well as the Cordeliers. With her friends, the mathematician Gilbert Romme (also a tenant of the hôtel du Bouloir) and the physician Lanthenas, she had recently founded the Club des Amis de la Loi, which proposed to offer political instruction to the people. It seems unlikely that Donatien encouraged her in this project, which appears to have been rather remote from his preoccupations, and for the time being he had other worries than the education of the masses. Nevertheless, according to certain sources, a tender friendship joined him to *la belle Liégeoise*. Twenty years later, a contemporary of Sade's who had dined next to him at the table of Charenton's director, M. de Coulmier, heard him say that the only woman for whom he had ever felt a genuine passion was none other than Théroigne de Méricourt, who on the morning of August 10, 1792, had killed the journalist Suleau with her own hands. Full of admiration for her "strongly etched character," he was unstinting in his praise of the beautiful firebrand, whom he reportedly compared to certain biblical heroines. "I assure you," he allegedly added, "that there was something sublime in that girl."[3] Although it is hard to know what credit to attach to this anecdote, it is worth reporting.

The Trappist Syndrome

The man who emerged from Charenton bore little resemblance to the one Inspector Marais had taken to Vincennes on September 7, 1778. Twelve years of detention had changed him beyond recognition. His build was much heavier, and his face had grown puffy: "For want of exercise I have acquired a corpulence so enormous that I can hardly move," he confessed. Meanwhile, strange maladies had appeared, and others had grown worse. His eyes were his most serious problem. Despite Grandjean's care he still experienced severe pain and, at times, worrisome disturbances of vision. Migraines racked his head, and rheumatism and gastritis tortured him constantly. He felt broken and worn out.

The world, too, had changed, and Donatien wondered, not without anxiety, if he would be able to find his place in it after so long an absence. For the past few months especially it seemed that time had suddenly accelerated, hastening History forward at a dizzying pace. The culture had evolved more quickly than the people, as new values toppled the old. Every day unforeseeable developments mocked the prophets, as if the reality of events outpaced the ability to imagine them. How are we to fathom the state of mind of a man who had lived for so many years as a recluse, apart from other men, in static time? The sensibility, the aesthetic, the fashions, even the language of the day were nothing like what he had known. At Vincennes, in the Bastille, at Charenton Donatien had caught only muffled echoes and unintelligible rumors of this immense hubbub. His only news of the great collapse had come from his wife's horrified commentaries and from the carefully censored information that had penetrated the walls of his solitude. A prison, like a convent or a hospital, lives on its own time, a time that seems immobile because its rhythm is the slow beat of boredom. Donatien had lived by that time for more than ten years, growing more and more sluggish as each moment seemed to drag on for an eternity. For more than ten years he had been immersed in prison silence, occasionally interrupted by the squeak of a lock or the scolding of a turnkey. Empty hours, silence, isolation: Sade had needed this material void to bring forth a new language. He had needed this blank page to elaborate the still novel rites of his rhetoric. And he would incarcerate the libertines of his novels in similarly inviolable places (Silling, Sainte-Marie-des-Bois), erecting complicated systems of walls between them and the world in order to protect the secrecy of their rituals.

Now he needed to rediscover the time of the city, the sounds of the city. More than that, he needed to get hold of himself, to rediscover the quotidian after having lived among nightmares, to find his bearings in the midst of a world that he had continually reinvented. His relation to his fellow men had assumed the form of fantasy; now he had to relate once again to real people. It was a painful reawakening, all the more so in that the intensity of his writing practice had only estranged him still further from reality, like a wall within a wall. Prisons and fortresses had become mythical places of incarceration, where drives and instincts enjoyed a reinvented freedom. The Bastille had been transformed into a theater of illusions: no longer a physical asylum, it became an interior asylum, an intangible, magical fortress whose walls were like mirrors reflecting lust.

Once the initial euphoria of freedom faded, Sade was gripped by an intense disgust, not unlike that known to recluses, convalescents, hostages, and others who survive for long periods on hopes of liberation only to feel paralyzed when the gates finally open in front of them: "I have lost my taste for everything," he wrote. "Nothing pleases me. The world that I was insane enough to miss so intensely seems boring . . . [and] sad . . . At times I am seized by a desire to join the Trappists, and I cannot be sure that one fine day I may not disappear, never to be heard of again.[4] I have never been as misanthropic as I have become since returning to the society of men, and if I seem strange to them . . . they can be sure that they have the same effect on me."

If Sade spoke of fleeing the world, of retiring to a monastery (as a manner of speaking, to be sure—he never seriously considered it), and, in a word, disappearing, it was because he hoped to rediscover the void he had known behind prison walls: this finite, structured space had become forever identified in Sade's mind with the voluptuary imagination.

Separation

Renée-Pélagie was no longer there to hear his complaints: she had refused to see him when he left Charenton. When he asked if he might find lodging with her at Sainte-Aure, she informed him in a brief note that she intended to ask for a separation.

She had been thinking about this and preparing herself for a long time. As long as he remained in prison, she could not bring herself to act: he needed her too much. Now that he was free, nothing stood in her way. Her mother had begged her to leave him a hundred times, and each time she had refused—but she had also been tempted. Could she break off relations with Donatien, cease to see him, cease to listen to him, cease to give in every day to his fresh demands, cease to endure his whims, his humiliations, and his irony, and cease to live torn between her husband and her children? Until recently the mere thought of leaving him had frightened her. She had dismissed it with horror as a betrayal unworthy of her. But little by little, under her mother's unrelenting pressure, she had grown used to looking upon separation as a possible if not probable way out, though one whose date she postponed day after day, convinced in her heart of hearts that she would never go through with it. Imperceptibly, however, her mind had begun to change. If it would have been cowardly to have left this man in the past, was it not cowardly now to stay with him? The issue was not her own deliverance or even that of her children but the salvation of her soul. As she approached the age of fifty, Renée-Pélagie felt the need to rectify her relations with God. At Sainte-Aure she had been told so often that this was the price of salvation, that she had already waited too long, that she risked eternal damnation if she continued to share her life with this man a moment longer, that what she had once regarded as a shameful desertion now appeared as a sacred duty. Up to the final moment she had hoped to lead her husband back to the path of religion. As late as June 1789 she still believed in the possibility of his conversion: "My tender friend," she wrote, "if you are sincere, God will not deny you his grace . . . He is a good God. He asks only to forgive, but He knows the depths of the heart. He has changed hearts harder and more culpable than yours . . ."

The prayers of a mother and the admonitions of the Church found an unexpected but crucial ally in the events of 1789. When Renée-Pélagie saw her Christian faith mocked, its priests insulted, its certitudes denied, it was as if the ground dissolved beneath her feet. And all at once, with a power against which she found herself helpless, the human hordes trampling all that she held most sacred took on her husband's features. The Revolution had a face, and that face was Donatien's. It was too much. This Revolution, whose first rumblings he had greeted with exclamations of joy, and in which he would surely take part once he regained his freedom, was about to bury her and her family under the rubble of the old world. The voice that spoke in her now was no longer that of a scorned wife's wounded pride but something graver, something that transcended her, to be sure, but whose ominous foreboding she sensed. A world was sinking fast, and that world was her own. She felt fear. She saw in Donatien the image of her murderer: he wanted her death, he was unleashing against her forces that would seek to destroy her, he was pointing her out to the executioner. In the end, where the combined forces of the Church and la Présidente had failed, the Revolution brilliantly triumphed: Renée-Pélagie would dare to defy Donatien.

Nevertheless, even taken together, her mother's influence, her confessor's voice, and the course of events do not suffice to account for the marquise's change of heart. No doubt this separation never would have taken place had it not also marked the end of a great love. Passion had lifted this woman of limited intelligence and tranquil flesh to sublime heights, compelling her, as it were, to love beyond her means. But when her love died, she once again became the conventional, down-to-earth creature she was, a woman whose husband could no longer make her share his delirium.

And what a life she had led for the past twenty-seven years! Not a day had gone by when she had not had to quail before the most humiliating threats: the police, prison, and scandal from the very first months of her marriage, the blackmail of prostitutes and of La Coste's child victims, and Donatien's rages, demands, and brutalities. Had not the Bastille guards recently been obliged to intervene to keep the prisoner from beating her? Perhaps M. de Launay was not exaggerating when he said that she feared for her life if her husband regained his freedom. Not a single day of the past twenty-seven years had passed without a need to fight: her mother, the creditors, the bureaucrats of Paris, the farmers of Provence. This was a woman whose strength and patience were exhausted, whose aspiration now was to rest. And let us not forget the effects of age: Mme de Sade had just turned fifty, but the ordeals she had endured made her seem ten years older. In recent years her natural tendency toward plumpness had grown more pronounced. Like Donatien, she had gained an enormous amount of weight. Her step had grown heavy, and it was difficult for her to walk. Sensing that her strength was draining away, she had been obliged to hire a valet to accompany her when she went out.

Other factors also weighed on her decision: the future of her children and the protection of her property. Donatien had regained not only his freedom but full enjoyment of his fortune. Having good reason to doubt his talents as a prudent manager, Renée-Pélagie could fear the worst: immoderate expenditures, debts, living from hand to mouth, and in the end certain ruin. And when she thought of her children (those little *Montreuils* being raised by their grandmother), her worries on this score were only compounded.

And there were still more serious things to worry about. The new law also restored all Donatien's civil rights, which meant that he was once again the legal father of his children. This prospect alone was enough to make Mme de Sade quake with fear. The opportunity was too good for la Présidente to pass up. No doubt she found the right moment to press certain decisive arguments: was Renée-Pélagie unaware of the terrifying responsibility she bore? Did she not see that her children's future depended on her decision? Was she prepared to turn them into outcasts, to consign them to a life of misery and opprobrium? Arguments such as these could have moved souls less susceptible than Renée-Pélagie's.

Yet when the moment came to confront her husband, to tell him to his face that she was ending their life in common, she suddenly felt weak. If only he greeted her with his usual sarcasms, her task would be easier. His insults would revive her courage; his harshness would justify her action in her own eyes. But if he came to her in affection, as he sometimes did, would she have the strength to resist? She knew—and had perhaps been reminded—that if she agreed to see him, even for just an hour, she might be lost for eternity. So she wrote him in haste to say that it was all over between them and that she was planning to file for separation. If he needed money, he could write in the future to Gaufridy. For the first time in her life, Renée-Pélagie did not give in to the logic of emotion.

On June 13 she confirmed her intentions in a letter to Gaufridy: she had come to the decision to separate from her husband only after "mature and carefully weighed consideration." As for her grounds, if M. de Sade "looks into the depths of his heart," he could not but acknowledge the justice of her case or recognize that "it cannot be otherwise." If he wished to make a scene, the choice was his: "I shall say only what he forces me to say in my own defense; *but I will say it if he forces me.*"[5]

•

The separation caught Donatien only partly by surprise. For the past few months he had felt his wife slipping away: "Some time ago I began to notice something in Mme de Sade's manner when she came to see me in the Bastille that caused me worry and heartache. My need of her forced me to hide this, but everything about her alarmed me. I could see the confessor's prodding at work, and, to tell the truth, I saw clearly that my release would mark a time of separation."[6] Did he really believe this? Although he knew that Pélagie was torn between her confessor and himself, he nevertheless felt that he was the stronger of the two. She would never risk a leap into the unknown. She had a romantic soul, to be sure, but in the timid and tender manner of a bourgeoise. She lacked audacity, passion, energy, intelligence.

Upon receiving his wife's letter, therefore, Donatien uttered a cry of rage. The Montreuils! Once again, the Montreuils! Always and everywhere, the Montreuils! This was the last straw! "They have forced my wife to separate from me. She did not want to do it. There is nothing they did not invent, nothing they did not do, to sway her decision." All of a sudden his hatred of those "rotten scoundrels" was reignited. At bottom, he believed, the break with Renée-Pélagie was a sordid matter of money. By filing for separation, she would not only lend credence to all the libels against him and heap opprobrium on her own children but also force him to reimburse her dowry: she would reduce him to poverty. And for what? To vegetate pleasantly in a convent, "where some confessor will no doubt console her and smooth her way to crime, horror, and defilement."

"Democratic gallows"

No sooner had he settled into the hôtel du Bouloir than Donatien began thinking of leaving for Provence to resume control of his affairs. But what was happening in the south of France was scarcely an inducement to go there. Since 1789 Provence had been in the forefront of the Revolution; agitation that began in Marseilles and Toulon quickly spread to the countryside. At the first sign of trouble the nobles had emigrated to the Piedmont. A few months had sufficed to empty a city like Aix, which only exacerbated the anxiety of workers dependent for their livelihood on the wealthier segments of the population. A particularly harsh winter encouraged further revolutionary ferment. Grain ran short, bread prices rose, and misery descended on the very poor. In their distress the Comtadins naturally turned to the papal vice-legate for help. Mgr Casoni's only response was "to go cut wood wherever you find it, and take grain wherever there is grain to be had." The peasants followed the prelate's advice. They cut down any trees they found: first the willows, then the mulberry bushes, and finally even the fruit trees. And they took grain from where it was stored, in convent granaries. It was in this atmosphere of discontent and brigandage that news of the insurrection in Paris and the taking of the Bastille reached Provence.[7]

The unique status of the Comtat, as an enclave of papal territory within French borders, left it more vulnerable than any other region to popular uprising. Within the Avignon bourgeoisie there had long been a faction in favor of union with France, and now the common folk, disturbed by the economic crisis and hostile to the papal administration, furnished a ready-made militia in support of the cause.

In the spring of 1790, when Donatien was contemplating leaving Paris, the situation grew even worse. The ravages of poverty and unemployment continued unabated, and beggars filled the streets, threateningly at times, frightening those whose property was vulnerable to pillage. Fears of an aristocratic conspiracy, which was repeatedly detected and denounced, gave rise to the wildest of fantasies and provoked the most violent reactions. Shouts of "To the gibbet!" were heard with increasing frequency in the streets of Avignon. The marquis de Rognes, threatened with hanging for having published a pamphlet deemed counterrevolutionary, was obliged to flee. A month later, Passeri, the legation's fiscal lawyer, was attacked by a mob that surrounded his home: the panic came close to degenerating into a massacre. A few days later, a café in the place de l'Horloge, thought to be the headquarters of the "aristocrats," was demolished by a band of armed men and its proprietor nearly hanged. Arrests multiplied. By June the tension had reached the breaking point. The "patriots" talked of nothing but the counterattack that the enemies of the Revolution were alleged to be planning; the most alarmist rumors circulated. On June 10, with fears still running high, a handful of aristocrats attempted to seize the Palace of the Popes. Shots were fired, and four cannon were hastily assembled into a battery; the ensuing fusillade lasted several hours, causing several deaths. The next day, June 11, the marquis de Rochegude, presumed to have been the leader of the assault, was hanged along with two other suspects in the midst of a howling mob. Horror gripped the city.

All over the Comtat people succumbed to what has become known as the "Great Fear" of the summer of '89. Rumors that bands of pillagers were roving the countryside, sacking castles, burning crops, interfering with the harvest, and taking food from people's mouths had sown terror throughout rural society. The sound of the tocsin spread the alarm from village to village. People threw a few bundles into a wagon and fled. The bravest stayed behind to defend their homes: they armed themselves with rifles, scythes, pitchforks, procured gunpowder, and organized volunteers to keep watch over sheaves of wheat in the fields. It was in this climate of collective psychosis that almost unbelievable news reached the countryside: on the night of August Fourth the nobility and clergy had spontaneously sacrificed their privileges on the altar of *la patrie*.

At La Coste, however, calm seemed still to reign. There had been no acts of vandalism against the château or against the marquis's estates. The Costains had not even seen any point to contesting his privileges. Why should they, since they had accomplished their own little revolution all by themselves? It had taken place without drama, without noise, without violence.[8] Taking advantage of the master's long absences, they had simply chipped away at his properties one by one; townspeople no longer felt any compunction about hunting on the marquis's land. The feudal regime had been cut down to no more than a seigneurial tax known as the *tasque*, which admittedly still imposed a very heavy burden on the community.[9]

What is more, the village retained a certain sympathy for a man whom people looked on as a victim of despotism and who was known familiarly as *le pistachié* (seducer or skirt-chaser). The marquis, for his part, had never shunned contact with his peasants. He bullied them, to be sure, but he knew each of them by name and spoke their language. He was, moreover, critical of his own children for their ignorance of rural society: "They will not go to La Coste, as I do, to the homes of the poor, to inquire about their capabilities, resources, and families, and consequently they will not win [the peasants'] affection. It pains me to see this, but they have something of the Montreuil haughtiness, whereas I would prefer the Sade energy." Donatien always thought of himself as a child of the village. He had never abandoned it as his father had done to live at court. As for his debauches, which everyone in the village knew about, they never frightened anyone. They were talked about, to be sure, in the tavern and on the doorstep, and old-timers whispered that in the old days things used to go on up at the castle, but no one really had it in for him. The sarcastic peasants thought it was all rather funny. Those stories about women were good for a laugh, and a ribald joke or two was not to be disdained when pitchers were brimming with cool *vacqueyras*. The shock was lessened by the fact that Donatien had always prudently avoided preying on the maidens of La Coste and its environs. Furthermore, the dolce vita was too widespread among the nobility of the Luberon to scandalize anyone. No one was more blasé about the mores of the high nobility than their peasants.

In La Coste, an old Waldensian citadel with a mainly Protestant population (roughly fifty-five percent, but as high as eighty percent among householders), religious feeling had been declining steadily, and dechristianization was making headway. For the past half century the local population had been served by a series of priests undistinguished for either virtue or piety. In 1727 the perpetual vicar of La Coste was accused of "spiritual incest and sacrilegious abduction" involving one Anne Gardiolle, his penitent; he was sentenced to be hanged and strangled, after which his body was to be cast into the flames and his ashes spread on the highway.[10]

Despite urgent appeals for charity from the local clergy, not a sou from the marquis's purse ever clinked in La Coste's collection box. In order to survive, the curé was reduced to mercenary activities: the presbytery had been transformed into a breeding house for silk worms, whose odor drove Mlle de Rousset away, and the good father vied with his parishioners for the mulberry leaves he needed to keep his business going.

In such a climate of religious disaffection, the marquis's escapades had long met with nothing more than discreet laughter or tolerant winks. The most devout of the locals affected a distressed, almost piteous, mien. After all, vice was an unwritten privilege of the nobility, and no one in La Coste thought to contest it. What people criticized the marquis for was his failure to contribute to the upkeep of the poor or to fill the offices of seigneurial justice, thereby forcing local citizens to take their disputes all the way to Aix.

Regularly informed by Reinaud of what was happening in Provence, Sade imagined the countryside ablaze and awash in blood and chose to cancel his trip rather than risk perishing on the "democratic gallows." As he put it in a letter to the Aix attorney: "Valence, Montauban, and Marseilles are horror shows, where every day cannibals perform English-style dramas that are enough to make your hair stand on end."[11] It was therefore better to postpone his visit until next spring, "if God and the enemies of the nobility allow me to live."

"Good view, good air"

Before long Donatien forgot about Provence. He had made the acquaintance of a delightful woman, Marguerite Fayard des Avenières (born 1745), who lived apart from her husband, a *premier président* in the finance bureau of Lyons. A woman of wit and talent and an occasional playwright, she had just completed a short comedy in two acts entitled *Pauline*, which, at the time she met Donatien, she was thinking of presenting to the Théâtre-Français. This was not an impure affair as in the old days. Those days were over: the lady was forty-five, and Donatien was fifty. So there was no danger from that quarter: "I dare say, although certainly no sentiment other than friendship enters into our affair, that I forget my woes whenever I am with her." In any case, he felt old, worn out, with no zest for the things that used to set his blood racing: "All that disgusts me now as much as it used to set me on fire." He was barely strong enough to endure his ills: "There are coughs, eye aches, stomachaches, headaches. There are rheumatisms and I don't know what else. All this wears me down and does not, thank God, allow me to think of anything else, and I am four times happier as a result."[12]

Thus, Donatien gradually regained his taste for life. His dark thoughts and his misanthropy soon left him. There was no longer any question of joining the Trappists. Instead he felt an urgent need to speak out, to communicate, as if with one stroke to unleash twelve years' worth of mute thoughts stored up in prison silence. So imperious was his need that at times he caught himself speaking aloud with no one else present. Fortunately, this was a rare occurrence: he did not lack for company. In short, Donatien was happy. He was surrounded by women who offered a calm, gentle enjoyment of sensual pleasures that he had never known: "Good view, good air, good company. I shall bide my time here patiently until spring."

The Somber Tale of a Dowry

Toward the end of May this gentle tranquillity was interrupted by a vexing bailiff's notice. Mme de Sade had acted on her plans and petitioned the Châtelet for a separation. Donatien was in a rage: "All the vile slander that has been spread about me in taverns and wardrooms or compiled in almanacs and broadsheets has gone into this fine memorandum. The most atrocious indecencies are scandalously invented . . . [and] slanderously reported. This is, in a word, a monument of lies and foolishness, as crude and obscure as it is flatly and stupidly written." After consulting with lawyers, he decided not to respond to this "monument of impudence" and to allow himself to be judged by default.

Ten days later, on June 9, 1790, the Châtelet granted the requested separation. One item in the decree attracted his keenest attention: the court "condemned him to pay, return, and restore the sum of 160,842 livres in principal received by him as a dowry constituted according to the terms of their marriage contract."

This was a fortune. Reimbursing such a sum was out of the question. And in any case there was no way of coming up with the funds. He would have had to liquidate part of his property, selling at a loss because all the nobles who had emigrated had put their property up for cash before leaving. The real estate market was currently facing its greatest crisis in French history.

Sade needed a reliable mediator, and he found one in Reinaud, the attorney from Aix, with whom he had long done business. Unbeknownst to Sade, but without ever betraying his interests, Reinaud entered into a lengthy correspondence with Mme de Montreuil and managed to win his way into her good graces. After three weeks of strenuous negotiations in Paris, he succeeded in striking an accord between the two parties, each as wary, as grasping, and as unwilling to make concessions as the other. Finally, on September 23, 1790, the agreement was signed. The marquis acknowledged his debt of 160,842 livres, but Mme de Sade agreed not to insist on reimbursement of the principal or interest during his lifetime; she retained, however, a mortgage on all his property. In return, the marquis agreed to pay her 4,000 livres annually, to be guaranteed by liens on his farmers' production.

Donatien could consider himself fortunate. He did not have to reimburse the entire principal, and the interest he owed was to be calculated on favorable terms (representing no more than 2.5% of the capital annually). Nevertheless, the minute the document was signed, he claimed to have been duped. Shortly before the negotiation, Reinaud had asked Mme de Montreuil for an account of his client's revenues, which only she could supply, since she had been the person administering the marquis's property. According to the statement she produced, the marquis's annual income was 14,000 livres. Reinaud took her at her word and proceeded on the assumption that, deducting the 4,000 livres to be paid to Mme de Sade, Donatien still had 10,000 livres, which was enough to live on quite handsomely. A few days later, however, these figures proved to be incorrect. Gaufridy, who had prepared the statement, had neglected to deduct various pensions and interest payments, which amounted to a total of 6,000 livres. Upon learning of this deficit, Donatien flew into a rage and denounced Gaufridy for dealings "in which bad faith, rapacity, and mischief have presided with such arrogance." He did not blame poor Reinaud at all: "I do him too much justice for that. It is the lot of good people to be dupes. It is better to be a dupe than a scoundrel."

In any case, the marquis would never pay a penny of the annual pension of 4,000 francs that he had pledged to give his wife. When she demanded her due, the marquis fumed to Gaufridy: "The devil take me if I know how to do it! When my poor father said, 'I am marrying my son off to extortionists so that he can make his fortune,' the poor man had no idea that those extortionists, those bankrupts, would ruin me."[13] In order to avoid payment he claimed that his property had been seized, that his land lay fallow, that his estates had deteriorated, that he was perpetually in poverty. The Montreuils were wealthy enough, he calculated, to maintain their daughter and her children. On the other hand—*grand seigneur* to the end—he allowed Gaufridy to send his wife the hogsheads of oil she asked for without insisting on payment.

18
A Playwright's Tribulations

"Interminable Intermissions"

Although his cantankerous nature found full expression in these quarrels over money, Donatien was not wholeheartedly invested in them. He had a hundred other things on his mind. Out of prison this demon of a man seems to have lived ten lives at once. He devoured everything, wolfed it down. Unable to sit still, he raced about town in a sort of feverish rage as if trying to make up for the "interminable intermissions" that had plagued his life. He moved on several planes at once, or, rather, in a nexus of planes that make these intervals of freedom difficult for a biographer to capture. Surely a synoptic table would give a better account of his life than a linear narrative.

For some years now he had been aware of the fact that, socially speaking, he did not exist. Having always avoided all remunerative activity despite his incessant need for cash (a need that he could meet, like any nobleman of his time, simply by taking on more debt), he was one of the first to understand that henceforth everyone would need a profession. After 1789 the risk of being branded a nobleman could no longer be neglected. The marquis needed a career, and what career would suit him better than that of man of letters? The idea pleased him, and he embraced it enthusiastically.

We know what writing meant to him during his long years in prison: it had been an escape, a refuge, a sublimation. It had taken the place of the body, it had liberated the senses, it had expanded space and restructured time. From Vincennes to the Bastille he had written constantly: novels, novellas, stories, essays, anecdotes, travelogues, historical fragments, literary and philosophical treatises (to which he would later give the title *Portefeuille d'un homme de lettres*), some twenty plays, and nearly two hundred letters.

Viscerally attached to his writing, Sade had shed tears of desperation on learning of the disappearance of his manuscripts during the assault on the Bastille. He recounted this drama on numerous occasions, always with pain and always denouncing Renée-Pélagie's criminal negligence, which, he said, had caused the loss of fifteen volumes "ready for the printer." But that was not the worst of it: according to Donatien, his wife had allegedly burned numerous other manuscripts in her possession.

Among the vanished works was the *Cent Vingt Journées de Sodome*, one of those to which he was most attached. Donatien tried to retrieve his lost papers, including the precious scroll, from the police, but to no avail. By chance, the manuscript of the *Cent Vingt Journées* had been picked up in Sade's cell at the Bastille by Arnoux Saint-Maximin, who had offered it to the marquis de Villeneuve-Trans. After remaining in the family for three generations, it was sold around 1900 to a German who had it sealed in a phallus-shaped container; it was published for the first time in 1904 thanks to Iwan Bloch, a Berlin psychiatrist and the author (under the pseudonym Eugène Duehren) of the first biography of Sade. The manuscript did not leave Germany until 1929. In January of that year the writer and critic Maurice Heine, the uncontested dean of Sadeian studies, went to Berlin at the behest of Charles de Noailles to acquire it. Until recently it remained in the possession of the Noailles family, where it could be seen and photographed. It is now owned by a collector living in Geneva.

Not everything was lost in the catastrophe, however. Donatien claimed that he recovered only a quarter of his writings after his release; he no doubt exaggerated his loss. Among the surviving texts, in any case, were *Justine*, *Aline et Valcour*, a dozen plays, novellas, stories, essays, outlines of future works, etc. In short, he already had enough to fill several volumes.

The Obverse of Evil

So M. de Sade now became of his own free will a "man of letters." This title replaced that of "marquis" in all official documents—and a good thing, too, given the circumstances. Donatien hoped that the title "man of letters" would cleanse him of the original sin of nobility: "I fought in the cavalry in the Hanover war. Discovering a taste for literature, I left the service while still young for the writer's study. My current profession is man of letters," he declared in 1794 before the Committee of General Security in an attempt to exonerate himself of his origins. A little later he would make a similar argument to the members of a people's commission: "I am accused of being a noble. This is false . . . Nearly all of my forebears . . . practiced the honorable trade of cultivating the land. My father was a man of letters. I have followed the same career, after having served six or seven years in my youth."[1] At his express request his mail was henceforth addressed to *M. Sade, homme de lettres*, the new profession compensating for the loss of the particule. Not having published anything at age fifty has never prevented anyone from calling himself a writer. And Sade was far from the only person to follow a similar course: how many un-employed nobles used this alibi to save their necks?

•

Donatien expected to win success not with his novels but with his plays. Naïvely he believed that fame could be acquired overnight only in the theater. A book sometimes took years to find an audience, whereas the theater brought immediate rewards. It also brought much greater re-wards, and this was an argument that weighed heavily with Sade. Finally, theater was fashionable. The Revolution had brought with it the triumph of the spoken word, of emotional force, of pathos, of oratory. The spoken word was more prestigious than the written word, and the art of oratory reigned supreme in the street as well as the forum, in the café as well as the public gardens. The law of January 13, 1791, which abolished the monopoly of the Comédie-Française, made it legal for any citizen to open a theater, and many new theaters sprang up in Paris. Where there had been approximately ten in 1789, there were more than thirty-five in 1793. The principles of liberty, declaimed in a grandiloquent manner, found a suitable outlet on the stage.

Sade had not awaited the Revolution to discover his love of the theater. Theater had always been the great, perhaps the only, passion of his life. His father had inspired his taste for it, the Jesuits had fostered it, and he had served his apprenticeship, first at the château d'Evry and later at La Coste and Mazan. He knew the workings of the theater and the specialties it required. Experienced as actor, director, play-wright, and scenery designer, he could have staged a show single-handed. In addition, his youthful affairs had familiarized him with the secrets of the wings, with the charms as well as the dangers of backstage dealings.

The dramatic oeuvre that Sade regarded as his best bet for literary fame and fortune may surprise a reader familiar with his novels. In his plays we find no rapes, no torture, no violence, no lust of any kind. If vice is mentioned at all, it is only to condemn it. Religion is spoken of with respect, and society with deference. In short, the plays are the opposite of *Juliette* or the *Cent Vingt Journées de Sodome*. Without going so far as Gilbert Lely, who called the plays "disgraced offspring," one can hardly fail to be surprised by the gulf between these works, suffused with pious sentiments and reassuring platitudes, and the great novels, buffeted by the hurricane of the instincts. Indeed, this theater is so diametrically opposed to Sade's secret oeuvre that one can hardly help thinking that he had two faces, each the inverse of the other.

Far from marginalizing him, this bipolar aspect of his work ranges him alongside the best authors of the period. In any case it proves, if proof is required, that Sade cannot be reduced to a mere clinical phenomenon. Nothing is changed by the fact that he wrote most of his books in prison: this makes it possible to comment ad infinitum on his obsession with circular space or the various forms of his reclusive fantasies, but it cannot eliminate another of his obsessions, one that was quite real and that Sade shared with his contemporaries, namely, his obsession with the strategy of the mask. What eighteenth-century author did not wear a mask? What does the audacious materialism of Diderot's *Rêve de d'Alembert* have in common with the Greuzian sentimentality of his *Père de famille*? What does the corrosive sarcasm of Voltaire's *Candide* have in common with the teary pathos of his *Zaïre*? In a novel, an essay, or a philosophical tale one can bite and scratch, but on stage one plays the sanctimonious hypocrite: one pulls in one's ideas as a cat pulls in its claws. And what is true of ideas is still more true of morality. An author could not appear on stage unless cloaked in ingenuous probity. Reading, a solitary, private pursuit, justified all the caprices of the imagination. But the public insisted on decent drapery: one did not bare one's heart or body before three hundred people.

Yet if the marquis presented his plays wearing the mask of moralism, he was nevertheless keen to preserve the connection between these theatrical works and the novels. Thus the moralistic Delcour in *Le Boudoir* appears with the same name in *Juliette*. The odious Oxtiern, who attempts to have Ernestine killed by the young woman's father, would be entirely in place in the *Cent Vingt Journées*, as would his speech on women and marriage. The comte de Verceuil has virtually the same name as the Verneuil who tortures Justine. Certain situations occur in both the plays and the novels: the captive wife, for example.

But in the plays she ends up being saved, whereas in the novels she is murdered.[2]

These fairy plays, English melodramas, and tragedies in alexandrines are therefore worth examining as the indispensable complement of Sade's universe, the golden legend without which there might be no dark legend at all.

A Harsh Apprenticeship

Sade's first move as a newly baptized man of letters was to join the Society of Authors, which Beaumarchais had founded twenty years earlier. He hoped to make his mark with a powerful, incontestable work that would take him straight to the pinnacle of the art. And he had what he needed: *Jeanne Laisné ou le Siège de Beauvais*, a tragedy in five acts, written in alexandrines at Vincennes in 1783. The play is a vast historical fresco in which the heroine, Jeanne Laisné, also known as Jeanne Hachette, routs the troops of Charles the Bold at the siege of Beauvais in 1472. Donatien was particularly fond of this patriotic play (patriotism being in fashion at the time), which revived the myth of Joan of Arc while sparing no effect apt to arouse the enthusiasm of the public: heroism and pathos, Sade believed, would rekindle the ardent love "that every Frenchman owes his country."

On May 2, 1790, only a month after his release from prison, he contacted Molé, an illustrious member of the Society and a figure of fashion. Not being a tragedian, Molé could offer no advice about *Jeanne Laisné*, but did introduce Sade to some of his friends, especially Mlle Raucourt. The illustrious tragedian met the author, listened to his play, and urged him to present it to the reading committee of the Comédie-Française. In gratitude Sade promised her the principal role. A few days later, he consulted Mme Vestris, Dugazon's sister, and made the same promise to her. This novice's blunder would cost him dearly. Shortly thereafter, he invited Saint-Prix, the handsome young leading man of the Français, to a reading at Mme de Fleurieu's. Saint-Prix did not mince his words: the play could not be submitted as it stood. It would surely be rejected. Among other criticisms, he reproached the author for writing "lines of comedy." Revisions would be needed, but Sade dug in his heels: he had already revised the piece many times.

Things were at an impasse. Annoyed, Donatien approached Dorfeuille, one of the two administrators of the Théâtre-Français. But Dorfeuille hid behind his associate, Gaillard, claiming that Gaillard was the real decision maker and that his own views counted for nothing. And Gaillard was wont to turn whichever way the wind was blowing: he was subject to so many influences that his reaction could not even be predicted. So Donatien resigned himself to go back to work and make the necessary revisions.

The Grandeur and Servitude of the Dramatic Art

While revising *Jeanne Laisné*, Sade tried his luck with other plays. His drawers were full of them, after all. *Le Boudoir* was rejected by the Théâtre-Français. On September 16, however, *Le Misanthrope par amour, ou Sophie et Desfrancs* was unanimously accepted by the theater's readers' committee. The author was awarded five years' free entry to the theater. All that remained was to set a date for rehearsals.

It is interesting to consider the reasons for the rejection of *Le Boudoir*. The readers' committee of the Français gave none. But a few years later the same play was also rejected by the Feydeau Theater, whose director, M. de Miramond, stated his objections: "The administration of the Feydeau hoped, in applauding the elegant facility of your style, that it would have the pleasure of giving a favorable response to the work you were kind enough to send us, entitled *Le Boudoir ou le Mari crédule*. But it recognized with considerable regret that it could not accept this play, whose substance is not compatible with the rules of propriety and whose characters might create impressions apt to alarm friends of good morals."

This moral condemnation is in many ways surprising, because Sade's play today seems an innocent trifle compared with his other writing. Yet Miramond was not the only one to express such a judgment. The actress Julie Candeille, celebrated for her beauty as much as for her talent, wrote the marquis that "the short play entitled *Le Boudoir* is pleasantly written, but I doubt that the subject, in itself rather free, can be developed on stage without danger. When people gather together, they are of course more severe with respect to the morals presented to them than they are in private. I do not think they will tolerate Mme Dolcour's moral instruction, and I urge the author to exercise his talents on another subject."[3]

Some time later, he submitted *Le Comte Oxtiern, ou les Effets du libertinage*, a three-act prose drama, to the Feydeau Theater. He had written this work not in prison but in the spring of 1791, basing it on a hasty revision of his novella *Ernestine*, whose violence he toned down somewhat to make it suitable for the stage. Not enough, apparently, because Miramond declared that he could not possibly produce a play "based on the most odious atrocity." But less than two months later, Boursault-Malherbe took it for the Théâtre Molière, promising the author to leave nothing undone to ensure its success. Sade was overjoyed!

The recently opened Théâtre Molière specialized in the patriotic and revolutionary repertoire. According to the *Almanach des spectacles de Paris* it was a theater that staged "incendiary and absurd" plays "with all the bloody apparatus of turmoil and riot." Boursault-Malherbe and his theater, the audacious chronicler went on, "dishonored both good taste and good sense" and preached "disorder, licentiousness, murder, hatred, and rage under the false pretense of liberty." It is easy to understand why Sade's tale of a high-ranking Swedish nobleman, a cruel libertine who rapes and kidnaps Ernestine, the daughter of Count von Falkenheim, and has her lover thrown in prison, would have appealed to the theater's director, a sworn enemy of the aristocracy. But what did the theater matter as long as one's works were performed?

The Vengeance of the Comédie-Française

As the Théâtre Molière began rehearsing *Oxtiern*, Sade began to worry about the delay in the production of *Le Misanthrope par amour* at the Comédie-Française. Since the copying of the parts three months earlier, there had been no news. What was going on? He wrote but received no reply. Becoming angry, he raised his voice in protest and began issuing demands, whereupon he received this unadorned note bearing neither a date nor a signature: "This work was accepted by the former Comédie-Française only to provide its author with access to the theater and in the hope that he would substitute another. The administration of the Théâtre-Français cannot permit the production of any dubious work . . ."[4]

Dubious? *Le Misanthrope par amour*? After its unanimous acceptance? Donatien could not believe his eyes. To be sure, the theater had the right to include a play in the repertoire without being obliged to produce it, but it never did. When the work had been accepted a year earlier, no one had characterized it as "dubious." What had happened? The question has long remained unanswered, but it can, I think, be cleared up now with the aid of unpublished documents from the Sade family archives.

While waging a battle on many fronts to have his works produced, M. de Sade took an active part in the work of the Society of Authors.

During the meeting of June 28, 1791, which was held as usual at the home of the group's president, Sedaine, the authors present debated the issue of the daily compensation to be paid to the actors and actresses of the Comédie-Française. Some fixed the amount at 800 livres, while others held that 700 ought to suffice. When the minutes of the meeting were published, Sade's signature figured among the names in the second group. The actors were outraged. Donatien turned pale: might not his "friends" in the Society seek reprisal by boycotting his works? He immediately wrote to the Comédie-Française in his own defense: he was the victim, he said, of an unfortunate error. He never intended to injure the players. On the contrary, he had always come to their defense and indeed had voted for them. He swore that this was true and said he could not understand how his signature had wound up on the other side. His letter was read before the assembled company, whose members seemed convinced and sent him this response (dated August 21) over the signature of the Comédie's secretary, Delaporte: "The Comédie-Française, having listened to a reading of the letter that you did me the honor of sending, has instructed me to assure you on its behalf that it is not concerned about your behavior in the assembly of *Messieurs les Auteurs*, that it wants no guarantee other than your word, and that it cannot doubt that you have warmly defended its interests. Finally, Sir, I am expressly instructed to tell you that the reward it owes your proper and generous actions is one of respect without surprise, since an honest and courageous man like you, Sir, must always act as he thinks."[5]

This was not enough, however, to reassure Sade. The affair had provoked a good deal of turmoil. Despite his denials, his name did indeed appear at the bottom of the minutes. To silence the rumors he would need irrefutable proof of his innocence. He asked Sedaine to provide it: he alone could attest that Sade had taken the part of the actors in the June 28 meeting. But the old veteran of the authors' wars refused to back him up and responded in a half-serious, half-sarcastic manner: "I assure you, Sir, that I cannot recall in the slightest whether you voted to give 800 livres or 700 livres to a company that wants neither accord. It is true that I always attached little importance to the substance of the matter, and that is partly the cause of my distraction as to the variety of opinions. Not that I think that any author who needs the talents of actors should not be greatly afraid of angering them. M. de Beaumarchais signed all these papers, and I know nothing more about it."[6]

To put an end once and for all to the backstage rumors that still mentioned him as an enemy of the actors, Sade decided to publish an official categorical denial in the *Petites-Affiches*. The text, from the Supplement of Saturday, September 24, 1791, reads in part:

To the Editor: September 20, 1791. I beg you, Sir, to insert in your newspaper my formal disavowal of my signature at the bottom of a text entitled "Report to Dramatic Authors on the Salary Proposed by the Comédie-Française." It is true that I was present at the meeting of dramatic authors where this subject was discussed, but it is absolutely false that I placed my name with those of the authors who voted to grant the actors of the Comédie-Française only 700 livres per day. I certify that I signed only that article which, for special considerations, awarded fees of 800 livres per day to the Comédie. Having verified my signature on the document itself, I cannot conceive . . . what error placed it among those who supported the opposing proposition.

The actors of the Comédie did not believe a word of this and concluded that the impertinent marquis deserved a lesson. Hence they decided not to perform *Le Misanthrope par amour*. For consolation, Sade still had his free entry to the theater for five years. Instead of seeing his own play produced, he would be able to applaud the plays of others free of charge.

"Lower the curtain!"

This was a cruel disappointment, but *Oxtiern* was now in rehearsal at the Théâtre Molière, and that offered some comfort. The premiere was scheduled for October 22. That morning Sade placed a notice in the Supplement to the *Petites-Affiches* that had the look of an advertisement. In it he recounted how he had personally met the hero of the play in Sweden (where he had never set foot) and learned from the man's own mouth of the events that he was now presenting on stage. Except for the dénouement, he claimed, the whole story was historically factual. Indeed, this was the play's principal interest: "I felt that this story, as piquant as it is extraordinary, as novel as it is true, would command attention on stage. It is difficult to present a more interesting victim alongside a more odious scoundrel. Whatever success this work may achieve, it will continue to have the merit of being true, and I have always believed that in the theater *truth* yielded a kind of interest that fiction could never claim."[7]

On the night of the dress rehearsal, when the actor playing the role of Oxtiern uttered the words, "Succumb, therefore, perfidious one!

Your lot is to suffer if ours is to rule," certain spectators, exasperated by language that conjured up bad memories of the Ancien Régime, began to yell: "End it! Enough! Enough!" The actors continued, however, despite the increasingly tumultuous atmosphere. The reception must have been lukewarm at best, for a few days later the author confided in Gaufridy: "I have finally appeared in public, my dear attorney. Last Saturday, the twenty-second, a play of mine was performed, with a success—thanks to cabals, machinations, and women about whom I had said disobliging things—that was *quite mixed*. It is to be performed again on Saturday, the twenty-ninth, with changes. Pray for me. We shall see. Adieu."[8]

The proposed changes concerned the text and the cast. Sade eliminated the line that had caused the furor at the premiere. He also asked for changes in the costumes, but the director of the theater opposed this for reasons of cost. One or two of the actors were replaced, which slowed rehearsals because the new actors had to learn their parts. As a result, the second performance was postponed from October 29 to November 4.

That night things went smoothly until the middle of the play. But at the beginning of the second act, a spectator, probably shocked by Oxtiern's cynicism, stood up and yelled, "Lower the curtain!" The actors continued to play, but one of the stagehands felt called upon to obey this unexpected order and lowered the curtain. Half the audience then shouted down the protester and called for his ejection from the theater. When the curtain was raised, however, the other half of the audience forced it to be lowered again. A terrible row ensued between partisans and adversaries of the play. In the end the public called for the author, who came on stage and took a bow amid whistles and bravos.

Two days later, the *Moniteur*, which had never before deigned to mention the Théâtre Molière in its columns, published an account of the evening that included this comment: "There is interest and energy in the play, but the role of Oxtiern is of a revolting atrocity. He is more criminal, more vile than Lovelace and no more likable." In relating this memorable evening to Gaufridy some days later, Sade wrote: "The dreadful furor aroused by [*Oxtiern*] has meant that it will no longer be performed under the same title, and I have delayed the next show. People were at one another's throats. The guard and the constable were obliged to be on the alert each time it was given. I preferred to suspend performance. We are going to revive it this winter."[9]

This plan for a revival must have been serious, because a week after the second performance Boursault-Malherbe signed a new contract with the author. In fact, however, the play was never revived in Paris, but it was performed in Versailles ten years later. We shall hear of it again.

The coming of 1792 brought Sade new hope. The Théâtre-Italien finally decided to begin rehearsal of *Le Suborneur*, which it had accepted two years earlier. In a month, everything was ready and the actors knew their parts. Of course the play was short, one act in verse. It was to be presented as a curtain-raiser along with Grétry's comic opera *L'Amitié à l'épreuve*.

The premiere was set for Monday, March 5. That night the pit seemed more agitated than usual when the curtain went up on the first scene: "A salon with the apartment of M. de Pontac in the background." The first lines were spoken in a hubbub that grew steadily louder as the play progressed. By the fourth scene the noise drowned out the actors, who were obliged to withdraw to the wings. At this point a band of patriots wearing curious red wool caps with forward-curving peaks burst into the theater. Startled Parisians thus caught their first glimpse of the so-called Phrygian bonnet. One of the agitators climbed onto the stage and harangued the public: "Citizens! All patriots must now rally behind our red bonnet. In all theaters the friends of liberty will combat plays by aristocrats!" When calm was finally restored, the actors continued with a different piece, *L'Ecole des parvenus*, with ariettas by Pujoulx and Devienne.

On April 7 a resigned Sade recounted his misfortunes to Gaufridy: "This past month the Jacobite faction closed down a play of mine at the Théâtre-Italien solely because it was written by a *ci-devant* [that is, a former noble]. They turned up in red wool bonnets. It was the first time anyone had seen such a thing. This fashion lasted fifteen days before the mayor suppressed it. But it was reserved for me to be the first victim. I am born for these things."[10]

Justine, *or The Art of "Corrupting the Devil"*

Although Donatien felt a tender paternal affection for his plays (parents often prefer the children least favored by nature), he did not neglect his prose fiction. This was not without ulterior motive: he hoped to derive a substantial income from his novels. Sooner or later he might be obliged to give up his estates, and increasingly he looked upon the profession of man of letters as an honorable "second" career. "Here I am doing all I can to earn a little money through my works," he confided to Gaufridy. Since he had been able to recover certain of the novels he wrote while in the Bastille, why not attempt to exploit them as well?

In early March of 1791 he promised the loyal Reinaud that he would that summer be sending four volumes of a "philosophical novel" that he hoped to have printed by Easter. This was *Aline et Valcour*, the one novel of his for which he would not have to blush and would always feel a legitimate pride. Unfortunately, unforeseen circumstances delayed publication: the work did not appear until 1795. We shall hear more of it later.

On June 12, 1791, another letter to Reinaud announced the imminent publication of *Justine*: "They are now printing a novel of mine, but one too immoral to send to a man as pious and as decent as you. I needed money, my publisher asked me for something *quite spicy*, and I made him [a book] capable of corrupting the devil. They are calling it *Justine ou les Malheurs de la vertu*. Burn it and do not read it if by chance it falls into your hands: I renounce it. But soon you will have the philosophical novel that I shall be sending without fail."

In fact, *Justine* was not entirely a work written on commission as the letter to Reinaud suggests. Sade, the reader will recall, had written a first version between June 23 and July 8, 1787, while still in the Bastille. It was then only a short novella of 138 pages destined to be part of a collection of shorter works. But when further episodes were added to the manuscript the following year, Sade began to think of *Les Infortunes de la vertu* as a full-fledged novel. The publisher Girouard, to whom Sade proposed the work, no doubt saw the profits to be made with such material and asked the author to add still further adventures. Sade did not need to be asked twice: he multiplied the scabrous episodes and tied them together with a chronological thread in the manner of a *feuilleton* (serialized novel). "Spiced up" in this manner, *Justine* became a promising commercial prospect.

The genre was *à la mode*. A veritable wave of licentious fiction had swept across France, mingling titillating visions with the imprecations of revolutionary orators and the *Ça ira!* of patriots. The erotic vein, though apparently so contrary to civic virtue, met with unheard of favor. Sex had never sold so well. People went wild for lascivious scenes and lubricious bodies. It was impossible to find debauches outrageous enough, lovemaking furious enough, or perversions new enough to slake the public's lusty appetite. The erotic and the political had never meshed so tightly. *La foutromanie* (literally, fuckomania) was all the rage, as every day ribald pamphlets mocked the king's sexual impotence, the queen's "uterine furies," and the Jesuits' pederasty (*loyoliser* became synonymous with sodomize, and the abbé "Couillardin" [Father Balling] transformed the church into a bordello). This gutter literature was a long way from the frivolous voluptuousness of the Trianon. Here there was no mincing of words. Degenerate aristocrats were denounced with the robust candor of the patriot, the embodiment of cleanliness and health.

Sade was not the last to denounce this avalanche of obscenity. Apart from the *Portier des Chartreux* and *Thérèse philosophe* none of it seemed worthy of interest: it was all "miserable brochures, conceived in cafés or bordellos, which prove that their authors suffered from two voids at once: one in the mind and the other in the stomach." Concerned not to confound this vile production with his lofty conception of vice, he added: "Lust, daughter of opulence and superiority, cannot be treated except by people of a certain stamp . . . , except by individuals, finally, who, blessed by nature to begin with, are also sufficiently blessed by fortune to have tried themselves what they trace for us with their lustful brushes. This is quite beyond the reach of the rogues who are flooding us with the contemptible brochures I am speaking of."[11] There is no better description of the distance between Sade's work and the ambient vulgarity.

Gilbert Lely, concerned not to bring evidence against his hero (one is tempted to say his *god*), tried to exonerate Donatien of any mercenary motive, but to do so he had to tie himself in knots. To believe Lely, Donatien presumably mentioned his need for money and renounced his novel for the sole purpose of sparing Reinaud, who was too proper to understand, while hiding the "troubling metaphysical necessity" that Lely alleges dictated the writing. As if Sade had ever been afraid of shocking anyone. To put it bluntly, in writing *Justine* Sade *deliberately* went in for pornography in order to be able to publish what was truly close to his heart: *Aline et Valcour* and his plays.[12]

The fact that *Justine* was written to earn money in no way diminishes its importance. It remains one of the most powerful and most striking creations of French literature. Furthermore, Sade never acknowledged any of the works through which he came to embody the urgent demand for freedom, the prophecy of a forbidden life, the constant exercise of refusal, and the spirit of negation pushed to the point of furor—all the things, in short, that make him the absolute rebel. Neither *La Nouvelle Justine* nor *L'Histoire de Juliette* nor *La Philosophie dans le boudoir* were signed with his own name. It is as if the man of letters sought to set himself apart from this other self, his occult and pornographic double, whose writing transcended social and fictional conventions. Is this any reason for *us* to renounce *him* as he renounced his works? No, on the contrary, the more the author intended to distance himself from his work, the more we should be attached to it, or at least intrigued by it. Does not the unconscious of the dream reveal more than reality? And was the "metaphysical necessity" that Lely talks about incompatible with the need to earn money? To divorce self-interest from creation is to oversimplify the creative process and to condemn oneself to awful blindness (born of idealization). Sade may have written masterpieces without knowing it. So what? One cannot require of a writer that he always be worthy of his work.

The marquis must nevertheless have felt a secret pride when he saw for the first time the two calf-bound octavo volumes of *Justine* at Girouard's Bookshop, 47, rue du Bout-du-Monde (End-of-the-World Street, following the course of the old great sewer—what a symbol for those who see Sade as the century's sewerman). Of course his name did not appear on the title page, and his publisher's name had been prudently replaced by the usual notice: "In Holland, by the Associated Booksellers." The first volume contained an allegorical frontispiece by Chéry depicting Virtue between Lust and Irreligion. Within a few days *Justine* was on sale in all the shops at a price of seven livres, ten sols.[13]

We know the reaction of the work's first readers thanks to an article published in 1791 in the *Feuille de correspondance du libraire*:

If, in order to secure love of virtue, one needs to know the horror of unadulterated vice and the atrocities that one can be driven to commit by not knowing how to restrain desire, this book can be read with profit. It is even possible that, terrified by the hideous portrait that the author has been able to paint of the most revolting crimes, the most dissolute debauchees will come to blush at having surrendered to such execrable misconduct and, like the heroine of this novel, return to the path of virtue after having soiled it thousands upon thousands of times. But how can one pretend to such success, when it is demonstrated that of all the corruptions, the most incurable is that of the heart?

This book is therefore at the least very dangerous, and if we make its existence known here, it is for this reason, that the title might lead inexperienced young people astray so that they might consume the poison that the work contains, and we are pleased to alert those responsible for the education of such young people so that they may carefully keep this book away from them, or read from it those passages most apt to revolt them if their imaginations absolutely require strong and terrifying impressions.[14]

This early indictment of Sade's work nevertheless acknowledged its capacity to dissuade those who might be tempted by crime. Of course such strong medicine is to be used with caution, being capable of curing in small doses but of killing if abused. A second critique, which appeared a year later in the *Petites-Affiches*, denied the work even this merit:

Everything that the most deranged imagination can possibly invent in the way of things indecent, sophistic, and disgusting is collected in this bizarre novel, whose title might attract and deceive sensitive and honest souls . . . If the imagination that produced such a monstrous work is indeed deranged, it must be conceded that it is rich and brilliant of its kind. The most astonishing incidents, the most surprising descriptions—everything is here. And if the author of this novel wished to use his intelligence to propagate the only true principles of social order and nature, we do not doubt that he would succeed fully. But his *Justine* is far from fulfilling this laudable goal . . . Young people, you in whom libertinage has not yet blunted delicacy—shun this book dangerous for both heart and senses. You, mature men, whom experience and the calming of the passions have placed out of danger—read it to see how far one can go in derangement of the human imagination. But throw it into the fire immediately thereafter. This is advice you will give yourself if you have the strength to read it in its entirety.[15]

Despite the homage paid to the author's "rich and brilliant" imagination, it is hard not to smile at the critic's expression of horror. True, Ducray-Duminil, the editor of the *Petites-Affiches*, was not noted for his boldness, and his paper faithfully reflected the conventionality of its readers. But still, how could one be shocked by *Justine* at a time when the streets were flooded with the filthiest of pamphlets, when printing presses endlessly restocked the locked rooms in which libraries stored their curiosa, and when "fuckomania" engulfed all of France?

No doubt Sade had transgressed the ultimate limits of erotic discourse. No one had ever gone so far in painting crime (the generic term for all the Sadeian passions), if only by virtue of his obsession with combining different kinds of debauchery. In his rage for the absolute, Sade had lacerated language and shredded the rhetoric of the usual "alcove writers." He pushed the possibilities of orgasm beyond all semblance of plausibility. "The Sadeian scene," Roland Barthes observes, "soon appears to be outside of any reality: the complexity of combination, the contortions of the partners, the lavish expenditure of pleasure, the extraordinary endurance of the victims—everything transcends human nature."[16]

No doubt *Justine* puzzled the amateurs of erotica, the readers of Nerciat and Louvet de Couvray, though perhaps less those of Laclos, even if the metaphorization of the senses in *Les Liaisons dangereuses* is a long way from Sade's plainspoken bluntness. Nevertheless, contemporaries did not hesitate to toss the latter work into the same cesspit as *Justine*. As Joseph Rosny wrote in the *Tribunal d'Apollon*: "The novel *Les Liaisons dangereuses* has done more harm to morals in the past few years than a whole century's worth of works of this type. The infamous novel *Justine* is the only one that comes close to disputing its criminal supremacy as to number of victims."[17] Maurice Heine also drew a parallel between Laclos and Sade, but only in order to call attention to the somber brilliance of their work: "The great figure of Sade, along with Laclos, dominates the last twenty years of his century. And the reasons for this stunning superiority are to be sought above all in a systematically pessimistic philosophical conception that both writers based on a serious knowledge of the world and of man."[18]

Those who regard libertine writing as a stimulus to sexual activity ("books that are read with one hand," as a grande dame of the seventeenth century once put it) are apt to be disappointed. *Justine* does not belong to the pornographic genre in the ordinary sense of the word. The *impossibilia*, pushed to the point of absurdity—or irony—suffice to render the work unsuitable for titillation. The very extravagance of the situations inhibits desire. And Sade's subversiveness has more to do with language than with politics. It is creation, not provocation—and therein lies what is truly revolutionary about it. "Sade's greatness is not that he celebrated crime or perversion or that he invented a radical language for doing so; it is rather that he invented a vast discourse based on its own repetitions (and not on the repetition of others) and converted into details, surprises, voyages, trivia, portraits, configurations, proper names, and so on. The antidote to censorship, in short, was to turn prohibition into the stuff of fiction."[19]

Justine scandalized, to be sure, but above all it frightened. Its publication sowed panic. People quickly sensed that the danger was not to morals alone and that the subversion went far beyond obscenity; the true danger lay elsewhere. That is why contemporaries refused to afford the work the toleration ordinarily granted to licentious writings. *Justine* was rejected in toto and irrevocably. People wanted to see it destroyed. They shunned it as they might flee a barbarian invasion, out of an instinct for survival.

How was the book received when it first appeared? According to Maurice Heine, whose views were seconded by Gilbert Lely, the novel went through no fewer than six editions in ten years, which would indeed represent a considerable success for the period. But these six "editions," which to this day no bibliographer has taken the trouble to compare, may have been simple reimpressions with different dates and formats. In that case the audience for *Justine* would have been considerably smaller than has hitherto been estimated. In truth, it seems impossible today to gauge the book's real impact, much less the number of its readers. What we do know is that the police took no action, which suggests that the work was not widely read. But a few years later, in Year VIII (1800), the editor of the *Tribunal d'Apollon* would chastise the authorities for having underestimated its success: "Active and useful observers of the police," he exclaimed, "here is a case to watch! *You think that the work is not selling? You are in error!*"[20]

One thing for certain is that *Justine* did not make its author wealthy, nor did any of his other books. Contrary to all his hopes, Sade would never live by his pen. But profit, which can rightly be considered one of his major motivations for writing, was not his only purpose. A letter to his younger son reveals that Sade had a clear intuition of his literary posterity: he believed in the immortality of his genius. When, with his usual *tartufferie*, Donatien-Claude-Armand one day expressed indignation over his father's writing, the marquis replied: "But when you permit me or cause me to starve, I shall have to work for a living. In any case, if my works are good, what harm is there? And, my God, do not be sorry to see your name live on in immortality. My works are bringing it about, and your virtues, though preferable to my works, would never do that."[21]

•

If *Justine* did not bring its author the financial rewards he had hoped, it did achieve a succès de scandale. The work marked the birth of the Sadeian mythology, the moment when the word "sadistic" became a curse, a symbol of absolute evil.

19

The Hermit of
the Chaussée d'Antin

"Sensible"

She was an actress, aged thirty-three, pretty, "gentle, pious, extremely respectable," yet easy to be with and as good at preparing a meal as at maintaining useful relations. Her name was Marie-Constance Renelle, but she used the name of her husband, one Balthazar Quesnet, who had abandoned her and her child to set himself up in business somewhere in the Americas.[1] Had Donatien met her in the course of his backstage tribulations? We do not know. In any case, Constance's career on the pines had been short-lived; she is all but unknown to theater historians. What we do know for certain, however, is the day she met Donatien: August 25, 1790. He would remember it to his dying breath.[2]

Yet theirs was no storybook romance. To believe Sade, he attached himself to Mme Quesnet only to escape his solitude and because he needed someone he could rely on: "The loneliness to which Mme de Sade abandoned me when I left the Bastille compelled me to form a bond with someone whose solicitude would replace that denied me by my family. In order to secure the loyalty and attachment of the person with whom I entered into an association, I offered her a contract providing an income of 60 livres annually, to be increased at regular intervals."[3] In other words, Sade would have us think that Constance was nothing more than a paid companion (and a rather meagerly compensated one at that), as well as a confidante capable of managing his household. But given the abundant evidence of his attachment to her, why should we believe him? His obvious solicitude toward her, the care and respect he showed her, argue otherwise. If love played no part in their union, affection at least was not lacking. The truth is that Donatien was never able to distinguish between concern for his interests and the promptings of his heart. His selfishness, which he exhibited with rare immodesty, was almost always coupled with sensitivity toward the other person. Complete cynicism was foreign to him.

There can be no doubt, moreover, that Constance's modesty, honesty, and unhappiness moved him. The one-time *grand seigneur* and the abandoned wife were made for each other. However far apart they may have begun, they were now joined by a common fate. Constance would follow him everywhere, even to Charenton, where she was still at his side when death separated them. Early in their relationship Donatien gave her the nickname "Sensible" (meaning sensitive, emotional). No name could have suited her better, except perhaps her own given name, Constance.

The House of the Sage

Taken by his new conquest, Donatien spent less and less time with Mme de Fleurieu, a woman of letters from whom he had rented an apartment on rue Honoré-Chevalier, where he continued to stay while looking for new lodging. On November 1, 1790, he broke permanently with her and moved into a small house at 20, rue Neuve-des-Mathurins on the Chaussée d'Antin, which he rented for 1,200 francs per year.

The Chaussée d'Antin was then the newest and most glittering section of Paris. There, during the reign of Louis XVI, financiers and roués, great noblemen and people of fashion had built themselves homes at ruinous expense. On the rue de la Chaussée-d'Antin itself stood the hôtel d'Epinay, where Jean-Jacques Rousseau's friend Mlle d'Epinay had died in semi-retirement in 1783; the hôtel Necker; the hôtel Hocquart de Montfermeil, built by Ledoux in 1789; and above all the hôtel of the celebrated Guimard, a dancer and courtesan, better known as the *hôtel de Terpsichore* and also built by Ledoux as well as decorated by Fragonard and the young David, then just at the beginning of his career. This luxurious dwelling, which included a 500-seat theater, had been sold in 1786 to the banker Perrégaux. Mirabeau also lived on this boulevard when Donatien moved into a house nearby. One cannot help imagining the two old enemies from Vincennes meeting at some street corner.

The façade of 20, rue Neuve-des-Mathurins, was more modest than some of its neighbors. It opened onto a courtyard flanked by two low houses, one of which was occupied by Sade. Until the end of the year he lived alone, "like a nice fat priest in his presbytery," with a housekeeper, a cook, and a lackey. "That is my entire staff, my retinue," he wrote to Gaufridy. "Is it too much?" In January of 1791, as planned, Constance left her apartment and moved into Sade's first-floor rooms, which she furnished with her furniture. She had her own entrance on rue de la Ferme-des-Mathurins. Having two addresses would prove most useful later on.

With Constance and his books, Donatien, now fifty-one, aspired to nothing more than the tranquil life of a man of letters. His sole preoccupation was to have his plays produced. His senses, at last assuaged, no longer gave him trouble. His days of folly were over. "Sensible" would not have to endure the same tortures as Renée-Pélagie: "Oh, my friend, never seek to corrupt the person you love; it may go further than you think," she is supposed to have said one day. In reporting this remark, he added these words in homage to his companion: "Adorable woman, allow me to quote your own words: they offer such a good portrait of the soul of the woman who, a short while later, saved this same man's life that I would like to engrave these touching words in the temple of Memory, where your virtues assure you a place."[4] Henceforth Sade would reserve the extravagances of his imagination for his work. He would ask nothing of Constance—not even fidelity. She was hardly a woman to sell such a treasure to the highest bidder. In any case, the libertine was apparently quite dead. When Reinaud expressed worry at the idea of his keeping an actress as a concubine, Sade answered: "Nothing is more virtuous than my little household. To begin with, not a word of love. She is nothing but a good and decent bourgeoise, lovable, gentle, witty, and . . . willing to take charge of my little house . . . Could I live alone with two or three servants who would have robbed me and perhaps killed me? Was it not essential to place a reliable individual between myself and such scoundrels? Could I skim my pot and go over my butcher's accounts while ensconced in my study with Molière, Destouches, Marivaux, Boissy, and Regnard, whom I honor, esteem, admire, yet never equal? Do I not need, moreover, a person to whom I can read what I have just written? Well, then, my companion fills the bill. May God preserve her, despite the astonishing cabal that is working ceaselessly to take her from me! The only thing I fear is that, tired of so many surreptitious *montreuilliques* maneuvers, the poor creature may become disgusted or bored and leave me."[5] These fears were groundless: no one was trying to take Constance from him, and her loyalty proved equal to every trial. But his attitude was typical of his paranoia.

Life in Sade's little retreat was cozy. "He wallowed in comfort," Paul Bourdin waspishly remarked. That is one way of looking at it. But why refuse him the right to dream of a bourgeois existence? After thirteen years of captivity, he may well have wanted something different. What he was looking for, as he toiled in his warm study amid his books and papers and with his eyes resting on his tiny garden, was not so much material comfort as the realization of a philosophical ideal. He borrowed his model from Rousseau. It was in imitation of Jean-Jacques that he exalted the joys of domestic life; it was Jean-Jacques's idyllic union with Thérèse that he had in mind when describing his life with Constance.

Like Thérèse, Constance Quesnet had little literary education but a sensibility that largely compensated for her lack of culture. Like Jean-Jacques, Donatien was in the habit of reading her what he had written immediately after writing it. He took account of her observations, which he sometimes recorded in his *Notes littéraires*. On *Crimes de l'amour*, for example, he noted: "My friend said that in truth the theater sometimes served up equally dreadful traits, but that performance was less dangerous than cold-blooded reading about the same horrors in a novel, and that it was in this respect that she believed my book to be dangerous. She also found my style simple, agreeable, and not mannered."

To polish off this tableau of married life, Donatien took in Constance's six-year-old son, Charles Quesnet, whom he raised according to the boy's mother's principles and taught to revere her. Later he wrote the boy: "I have often told you, a mother is a friend that nature gives us only once, and nothing in the world can compensate us for the misfortune of losing her. Nothing can take her place: the venomous features of men, their blackguardry, their calumnies, their nastiness afflict us unimpeded. We hurl ourselves upon the bosom of a friend or a wife, but what a difference, O my dear Quesnet! We no longer find the disinterested attentions of a mother, that precious sensibility undistorted by any private interest. In a word, O my dear friend, those hands are no longer the hands of nature."[6] This nostalgia for the maternal refuge that he himself never knew takes on a striking resonance. It seems in any case to contradict Klossowski's thesis that Sade was perpetually obsessed with the thought of being smothered by his mother's breast: "His actions and ideas are nothing but the conscious

manifestation of his struggle to free his being from its original envelope," wrote the author of *Sade, mon prochain*.[7] But rejection and regret
are not necessarily mutually exclusive.

Although his sons were no longer in Paris, Sade continued to see
his daughter. Paradoxically, a man said by some to have had no paternal sentiments whatsoever went regularly to the convent of Sainte-
Aure where Madeleine-Laure was a boarder. The wary mother
superior watched over their interviews until one day Sade, exasperated
by her presence, asked to be left alone with his daughter. Mlle de Sade
was hardly attractive. At age twenty she had all the earmarks of an
elderly spinster. Although fairly tall (five foot five), she had a thick
waist, a fleshy, inexpressive face, and a short, flat nose. She was also
cross-eyed. Her father's portrait is unindulgent: "I assure you that my
daughter is quite as ugly as I described. I have seen her three or four
times since. I have examined her quite closely, and I assure you that
in mind as well as figure she is quite simply a fat farmer's wife. She
remains with her mother, who to tell the truth has contributed nothing
to either her figure or her genius. What is more, she is very well off
as she is for what she is to become: for what can be done at present?"[8]
No doubt he occasionally ran into Renée-Pélagie in the corridors, but
husband and wife no longer had anything to say to each other. If they
continued to write on occasion, it was only to exchange notes on business matters, for the most part dry, bitter, and dealing with the countless
issues that remained in dispute between them: old debts, matters of
inheritance, various mortgages, and so on, not to mention the crucial
pension, which Donatien stubbornly refused to pay despite his wife's
endless entreaties.

Money

Sade's relation to money had always been neurotic. From 1790 on,
however, it became obsessive. His demands took a variety of forms,
including begging, threats, blackmail, and insults, and sometimes all
at once. His language was passionate, imperious, and vehement. This
passion would have its martyr, moreover: Gaufridy.

Gaufridy was a man humiliated, pummeled, insulted, trampled,
vilified, and cursed when, as was often the case, the cash failed to arrive
in time or was deemed insufficient. To be sure, he also heard sweet
talk, flattery, and protestations of friendship, sometimes even childhood
memories. But these affectionate interludes were rare, and further
storms invariably followed. With Donatien, asking for money was a

way of asserting power. He dominated Gaufridy and his other agents to the precise extent that he could press his demands upon them. Repeating these demands (the need for money being of course the leitmotif of his correspondence) was tantamount to reasserting his dominance and thus reexperiencing the sheer pleasure of lording it over one's inferior. Donatien was thrilled by his own impatience, because he saw in it a reflection of his power. It was in this dialectic between the need and the demand for money more than in his amorous practices that Sade earned the adjective derived from his name: the (moral) torture he inflicted in this way surely stung no less than several lashes across the buttocks.

In any event, the two things were not unrelated. There can be no doubt that in the realm of the imagination, money—like writing—took the place of now dormant sexual desire. Even with his diminished fortune he had more than enough to live on. But money for Sade was not measured by life's necessities, nor did it gratify an instinctual avarice or greed. On the contrary, he was insanely profligate, lived beyond his means, and borrowed by the bushel. This symbolic squandering was invariably followed by its corollary, want. Expenditure and desire were thus locked in a frenetic circular chase. In Sade one finds a permanent quest for crisis coupled with a subtle strategy of dependence. The same scenario is repeated ad infinitum in an immutable pattern reminiscent of manic behavior: headstrong struggle along with a quest as terrifying and pathetic as the quest for love yet incapable of being satisfied by anything but itself.

Sade's intense preoccupation with the sums of money he was to receive contrasts strikingly with his lack of interest in the actual state of his affairs. His annuities were paid quarterly. Since these payments never sufficed to cover current expenses, he required advances. He would then allege some unforeseen circumstance: a debt in urgent need of repayment, an object to be redeemed from a pawnbroker, an unusual but indispensable purchase, a loss on assignats (paper currency issued by the revolutionary government and circulated at discount), a bill from the tax collector. Gaufridy was ordered to come up with the cash. Were the marquis's accounts in deficit? So what? Did the sums requested exceed his income? He did not care. Did the cost of repairs and other necessities have to be met? Sade did not wish to hear about it. He was owed so much; he wanted so much. When his agent tried to explain, Sade accused him of conspiring against him, of wanting his death. There was no valid excuse for failing to meet his demand. The slightest objection caused him to suffer.

This tenacious indifference toward matters of practical administration put him constantly at odds with those whose job it was to keep
him informed. Was his wheat worth less than in past years? Had
production of oil or wine decreased? What did it matter to him? He
begged Gaufridy not to bother him with detailed accounts and sent
him this sample of the kind of report he wanted to receive:

La Coste *net yield, in pocket* ....
Idem Mazan ....
Idem Arles ....
Idem Saumane ....
Total: ....

Above all, do not drown this information in any dissertation or details. I do
not want details or dissertations. I want to know how much I have, *net*, per
year, *exactly* what income I have in my pocket every year—and *that is all!* Do
not send me one line more than is in this sample.[9]

When poor Lions, his steward at Arles, tried to tell him that his
sheep had not been sheared, he exploded: "As for me, my dear fellow,
I don't give a damn about sheep. Do you think my butcher and my
baker will take as payment my statement that 'Gentlemen, my sheep
have not been sheared'?"

Denial of reality was a permanent trait of Sade's nature. In mon-
etary matters this denial took on truly insane proportions. Sade did not
care a fig for numbers that represented sums to be paid as opposed to
received. In essence such sums did not exist for him. It was up to his
agents to take care of them. If they attempted to broach their problems
with him, he castigated them: scolding took the place of arithmetic.
Gaufridy was so familiar with this behavior that he no longer even
tried to make the marquis listen to reason. Sade had an inimitable way
of claiming his due (for he was *always* owed something). He employed
the whole arsenal of the language of passion to arrive at his ends. If
his expectations were disappointed, he protested that his friendship
had been rejected and said he was left with no choice but to beg or to
commit suicide. Would his childhood friend allow him to die? He
begged, demanded, threatened, and called on Heaven to right the
wrong he had suffered or to rescue him from despair. Did the letter
of exchange finally arrive? Immediately he forgot everything, clasped
his "dear advocate" to his bosom, and swore eternal friendship—which
lasted until the next post, when he once again began hammering away

at his man for his next installment. His behavior is a textbook case of sadomasochistic behavior in which insincerity vies with obliviousness.

The Bad Master

In 1775 Fage had given notice because he could no longer put up with his client's moods. Gaufridy never did give notice; he endured everything right to the very end. Was this weakness? Stupidity? Indifference? I would ascribe it, rather, to lassitude, to natural indolence. Everyone who had to deal with him—not only Donatien but also Mme de Sade and la Présidente—complained of how long it took him to complete even the smallest business transaction (Mme de Villeneuve called him a "dawdler"). But no one ever caught him redhanded stealing the marquis's money. That did not stop Sade from suggesting, however, that he might be abusing the freedom he had been allowed. He frequently insinuated that gossip had reached his ears regarding certain of his agent's misdealings. Naturally he didn't believe a word of this talk and dismissed the slander. He nevertheless questioned the man just to worry him a bit, though fundamentally convinced that he had done nothing wrong. Gaufridy would rise to the bait and dash off a ten-page brief protesting his innocence. Exasperated by a scrawl that he found difficult to read, the marquis would drop the whole matter and never mention it again.

Despite the old and strangely intertwined ties of service and friendship between Gaufridy and the marquis, the agent was not blind to his master's faults. He was aware of Donatien's fundamental injustice, extravagance, selfishness, indelicacy, and fits of rage, and sometimes these traits drove him wild. One day he confided to his colleague Reinaud: "The marquis's behavior . . . displeases me as much as it does you, and I see that it is still the same and there is no hope that it will change. And you must know how difficult it is for me to be involved in the affairs of a man like this, who wants what he wants and whom no argument can dissuade or divert from his course."[10]

Gaufridy and Reinaud were the only people in the world, apart from Renée-Pélagie, who were involved in Sade's private life from day to day. Both men, but especially Gaufridy, saw him as an unbearable paranoiac and a greedy, vicious, totally unscrupulous village nobleman. He went back on his word so easily that it was downright disreputable. One example will suffice: having extracted two letters of credit from Gaufridy, each in the amount of 1,000 livres, with a solemn promise not to cash them until the notary had received the collateral from his farmers, he broke his promise and cashed both letters without notifying Gaufridy, who was obliged to pay out of his own pocket.[11]

Isolism

For Sade, man's nature is to be born solitary: there is, he was fond of repeating, no bond between one man and another. Hence he had little if any understanding of friendship: his attitude toward his agents is the best gauge we have of his relations with "the other." His almost daily correspondence with them after his release from prison defines him as a social (or asocial) being, revealing the full extent of his economic unrealism and fundamentally self-centered attitude. In sexual desire as in social relations Sade never saw the other as anything but an instrument. He even invented the word "isolism" to denote the relation of means to end that he intended to institute with the other. "All creatures are born isolated and with no need of one another," he wrote in *Juliette*.[12] The libertine is obliged to deny the "chimerical bond" that supposedly links him to others, because "this so-called thread of fraternity can only have been imagined by the weak." It debilitates the healthy body and saps its energy—the famous "energy of the Sades."

Unfit for any form of society, cast out, and marginalized, Sade condemned himself to solitude. But, universalizing his own case, he bestowed existential value on it. The only perceptible reality, in his eyes, was that of the subject shut up within himself and hostile to any other subject that might dispute his sovereignty. This indifference to the other necessarily leads to solitary hedonism: "We laugh at the torment of others. What could such torment possibly have in common with us?" And further: "There is no comparison between what others endure and what we feel. The strongest pain in others must surely be nothing for us, and the slightest tickle of pleasure that we feel touches us." In this respect, the masturbatory habits he had developed in prison would seem most compatible with his vision, except that what they lack is precisely the "eye" of the other, of the desperately necessary yet tragically absent *voyeur*.

Sade sums up man's solitary immanence in this pessimistic observation: "My neighbor is nothing to me: there is not the slightest connection between him and me."

20

The Grand Illusion

Man Ray's fantastic portrait of Sade is well known. With the Bastille in flames in the background, the marquis's profile stands out, powerfully sculpted into the very stones of the fortress. This portrait symbolizes a vision of Sade common to the nineteenth and much of the twentieth century. Even today Sade does not merely embody the Revolution, he *is* the Revolution. For some, he was a harbinger of revolutionary excess, which came close to realizing the extravagance of the Sadeian imagination. For others, he drew the violence of his writing from the facts of the period. "O, that worthy couple, Sade and Robespierre!" exclaimed Jules Janin in an outburst of righteous indignation. But since the *ci-devant* marquis only barely escaped the Terror, he immediately adds: "He frightened the executioners of '93!"[1] The biographer Michaud is blunter about the parallel between the infamous debauchee and the bloody patriot: "After dishonoring himself in so many crimes, Sade could hardly fail to support a revolution that in some sense consecrated the principles of those crimes or at any rate protected their authors. Yet he was too proud of his birth, too haughty, too despotic to place himself squarely behind the sans-culottes' banners of equality."[2] The paradox of the libertine nobleman who was nevertheless also a friend of the Terror before becoming its prey is clearly embarrassing to writers like Janin and Michaud, who despise libertinage as much as they detest the Revolution and who affect nostalgia for the Ancien Régime. How did a progressive historian like Michelet react? Where Janin and Michaud had compared Sade's debauches to the violence of the Revolution, Michelet blamed them on the vices of his caste:

That such a man could still live was the best proof of the need to destroy the hideous arbitrariness of the old monarchy. He lived, but in the end, when justice came into this world, the guillotine's first essay was rightfully his. A prisoner of the Bastille, he posed as a victim. People credulously believed these kinds of lies. He was well received, allegedly, by M. Clermont-Tonnerre and the *constitutionnels*; and well received by the men of '93, well enough to preside over his section, that of Les Piques or the place Vendôme, the section of Robespierre . . . Then fifty years of age, a professor *emeritus* of crime,[3] he taught, with the authority of the age and in the elegant forms of a man of his condition, that nature, indifferent to good and evil, is nothing but a succession of murders, that she loves to kill one life to sustain a thousand others, that the world is a vast crime. Societies end with these kinds of monsters: the Middle Ages with a Gilles de Retz, the celebrated child-killer; the Ancien Régime with a Sade, the apostle of murderers.[4]

Surrealism would for a long time bestow its seal of approval on this amalgam. Eluard and Breton gave their blessing to the identification of Sade with the Revolution, which became impossible to challenge: "The Revolution found him devoted body and soul. He was able to set his genius alongside that of an entire people delirious with force and freedom," Eluard wrote.[5] What is more, it was this very identification that allowed surrealism to adopt Sade as its own. He was then called upon, along with Rimbaud and Lautréamont, to undermine tradition: "Sade could not exist without the Revolution."[6] Surrealists derived from his life a "myth of origin" through which to interpret the enigma of their own movement, namely, their relation to sexuality, revolution, and philosophy.[7] He participated in surrealism's ideological struggle with the prevailing aesthetic. What is more, surrealism adopted Sade's implicit terrorism to articulate its own position vis-à-vis Marxism. There was also the no less celebrated Sade/Freud dialectic, which, though challenged by Lacan, nevertheless helped to associate the name of Sade with subversion. Certain surrealists (such as Louis Aragon) were less interested in the ideological cooptation of their hero than in his potential for scandal (highly valued by surrealists and dadaists alike). Sade's name, like the names of Hegel and Lautréamont, was invoked by all who claimed to embody a logic of liberty, dionysianism, and transcendence and who advocated "deliberate scandal, provocation, and demoralization" along with "rigorous, fundamental seriousness and honesty in all words and deeds."[8]

In the worst cases (and there is unfortunately no shortage of examples), the portrait of Sade as a libertarian genius verges on the fraudulent. In 1927 Aragon, Breton, Eluard, Péret, and Unik joined the Communist Party because they wanted to make a genuine contribution to the revolutionary cause. This group enlistment in party ranks all but precluded any further discussion of Sade by surrealists. Atheist materialism was one thing: at the price of minor historical distortion, there was room for dialogue with Sadeian atheism. But there was no way to approach the rest of Sade's political thought without resorting to an extremely naïve or reductionist reading. We may credit Paul Eluard with both naïveté and reductionism and at the same time honor the zeal of the neophyte militant revealed in the article he dared to publish under his name in the communist journal *Clarté* on February 15, 1927, where Sade is presented as a materialist philosopher and precursor of Proudhon, Fourier, Darwin, Malthus, and Spencer, to say nothing of all of modern psychiatry. In order to appeal to an audience that would have been outraged by sexual explicitness, Eluard censored the violence of Sade's writing, quoted exclusively from the political speeches and dialogues, piously eliminated any proposition in contradiction with Marxist orthodoxy, and even went to the extreme of suppressing or disguising certain biographical details. This attempted beatification elicited a howl of protest from Georges Bataille: "Little does it matter to the surrealists . . . that Sade, pusillanimously emasculated by his apologists, assumes the figure of a moralizing idealist."

André Breton appears to have been more critical (or more lucid) regarding Sade's political commitment. For him, "Sade is surrealistic in sadism," thereby equating the truth of the man with the signifier of the myth. As for the rest, it suffices to read this brief excerpt from *La Révolution surréaliste* to measure the extent of Breton's skepticism: "Did Sade, at the height of the Convention, engage in counterrevolutionary activity? It is enough to raise a question such as this to appreciate the fragility of the testimony of those who are no longer with us. Too many scoundrels are interested in the success of this enterprise of spiritual pocket-picking for me to follow them onto this terrain. When it comes to rebellion, none of us should need ancestors. I am bound to point out that, in my view, one should beware of worshipping men, however great they may appear. Except for Lautréamont, I see none who haven't left some equivocal trace of their passage."[9]

•

In the aftermath of World War II, the author of the *Cent Vingt Journées de Sodome* was faced with more serious accusations. The man who had been portrayed as a communist militant was now denounced as an apostle of the extreme right and even of Nazism, with some commentators going so far as to blame him for the death camps. Raymond Queneau had this to say in his *Lectures pour un front*: "It is undeniable that the world imagined by Sade and willed by his characters (and why not by Sade himself?) was a hallucinatory precursor of the world ruled by the Gestapo, its tortures, and its camps. Now, Sade was an integral component of surrealist ideology, for example, and Breton, as early as 1939, displayed a certain embarrassment in the interpretation of his works. The fact that Sade was not himself a terrorist (and Desbordes has clearly explained why) and that his work has a profound human value (which no one denies) does not alter the situation: all who embraced the marquis's ideas to one degree or another must now envision, without hypocrisy, the reality of the death camps, with their horrors no longer confined within a man's head but practiced by thousands of fanatics. Disagreeable as it may be, philosophies end in charnel houses."[10] The explanation for this text can be found in its date: November 3, 1945. Six months earlier the Allies had liberated Buchenwald, Dachau, and Ravensbrück.

A substantial number of intellectuals now cast Sade among the torturers of the Third Reich. In *Les Temps modernes* Simone de Beauvoir asked if Sade ought to be burned, and for Sartre the answer was never even in doubt.[11] Without condemning Sade explicitly, Albert Camus evoked the responsibility of the writer. By reducing man to an experimental object, the founder of the Society of the Friends of Crime had allegedly instructed the theorists of naked power in how to go about their business "when the time came to arrange the schedules of their slaves." "Contemporary history and tragedy," Camus went on to say, "really begin with him."[12]

With *Marat-Sade* (1965) Peter Weiss had an opportunity to redress the balance and reevaluate the stakes of the controversy. After all, the play raised issues that would come up again three years later in the student uprisings of 1968. Yet the misunderstanding persisted in the character of Sade himself, author-actor-spectator in the psychodrama of the Terror. And Pasolini's film *Salo* (1975), which transplanted Sade to Mussolini's Italy, only perpetuated the ambiguity. In 1966 the question became the subject of a debate in the columns of the magazine *Nouvel Observateur* under the title "Should the Divine Marquis Be Burned?"[13] One participant, Pierre Favre, who would publish his *Sade utopiste* the following year, was determined to destroy the myth of Sade the revolutionary. He expressed astonishment at "the strange presence of Sade in all the literature of the left, though one cannot really point to any specific ideological influence. There is good reason to denounce this diffuse, persistent, even insistent presence, because the endless references inevitably create in readers' minds an absurd association between Sade and the thought of the left."

Beginning with an axiom that is dubious at best, namely, that the intellectual left has sought a "guide to action" in Sade's work (the truth of which can be judged in light of all that I have said in this chapter thus far), Favre proceeded to present a point-by-point indictment. His misleading and reductive argument, which was challenged on numerous points by Gilbert Lely and Maurice Blanchot, ended with a coup de grâce: that Sade's ideas had led to Nazism and genocide.

More recently, in an article in *Esprit*, Colette Capitan Peter drew a parallel between the thought of French right-wing thinker Charles Maurras, sadism, and Nazism, based essentially on the contention that "violence" is central to all three doctrines.[14] Philippe Roger has to my mind rightly criticized the arbitrariness and inconsistency of Peter's argument.[15]

And then in August 1989 Elisabeth Badinter, appearing on the television program *Apostrophes*, once again revived the seemingly perennial equation of sadism with Nazism.[16] As a biographer of Condorcet, Badinter might have been expected to show a firmer appreciation of literary subtleties or at the very least a more nuanced understanding of Sade's place among the political philosophers of his time. In any case, it may be worth pointing out that the author of the *Cent Vingt Journées de Sodome* was also the first French writer to protest against the death penalty [which was abolished in France during the tenure of Elisabeth Badinter's husband and collaborator, Robert Badinter, as minister of justice —Trans.].

•

Sade's political thought is far too complex to be hastily summarized and far too fluid to be encapsulated in a series of lapidary propositions. An adequate account would somehow have to capture its incessant movement with all its eddies and currents, to grasp its discontinuities, contradictions, waverings, divagations, and constants. An impartial analysis of the texts is required if any light is to be gained from Sade's political writing.

One thing is clear in any case. Anyone who relies solely on Sade's speeches, petitions, "observations," and other political pamphlets—for the most part occasional pieces written to justify himself or works of propaganda intended to demonstrate his patriotic zeal—will inevitably conclude that he was an apologist for the Revolution. But he himself warns against drawing any such conclusion in the unambiguous confession of opportunism that he made to Gaufridy: "Now, my dear advocate, you ask me what I really believe so that you may adopt the same manner of thinking. Surely nothing could be more delicate than this point of your letter, but the truth is that it would be very difficult for me to answer your question honestly. To begin with, as a man of letters, I find myself obliged to work one day for one party, one day for another, and this establishes a certain mobility of opinion that is not without influence on my private thoughts."[17]

Noble by Blood

Sade had always been hostile to court life. His father, who knew all its pitfalls, had issued a firm warning against its false allures, deceits, constraints, and dangers. Not that these warnings were necessary, because the marquis's independent nature and the scandal attached to his name would in any case have denied him access, especially under a king like Louis XVI, who was far more exigent than his grandfather in matters of morals.

This contempt for the court, generally accompanied by a scarcely concealed opposition to absolutism, was widespread in that segment of the nobility claiming the most ancient roots, and particularly among the ancient provincial nobility, which had never lived in Versailles and which constituted the majority of the order. Ever since Louis XIV, the antiquity of a person's blood line had not been enough to guarantee social preeminence. Other criteria such as wealth, culture, and access to royal favor became relevant, and the recently ennobled who possessed these advantages could gain access to the highest civil and military posts. Not content to subdue the nobility by reducing the power of seigneurs, the monarchical state had created large numbers of new nobles by conferring titles on the most outstanding of its common-born servants. In the resulting system of competing elites, the recent nobility enjoyed the advantage of wealth. And the old nobility felt nostalgic for that feudal paradise, as Sade saw it, "in which seigneurs lived despotically on their lands" and for "those glorious times when France counted within its borders a host of sovereigns rather than thirty million vile slaves crawling before a single man."[18]

One of the major conflicts of the late eighteenth century was that which pitted the seigneur of ancient lineage against the recently promoted nobleman. Bitter and disappointed, the old nobility stopped short of rebellion but did claim historic rights to a share of power. If certain of its representatives even proclaimed themselves antimonarchists, it was not to promote any republican ideal but to restore the feudal system as they imagined it. In 1787–88 the idea of an aristocratic revolution was not unthinkable. The old nobility was unanimous: "France must be de-Bourbonized."[19]

The pre-1789 marquis de Sade had been the very archetype of the nobleman of the sword, proud of his ancestors, jealous of his blood, and nostalgic for his past. Like all his peers, he felt a profound contempt for the nobility of the robe, which had sprung from the bourgeoisie. But he also knew that the *robins*, as they were called, posed a real threat to the old aristocracy because they had both wealth and ideological unity. Sade's contempt found a marvelous target in the Montreuils, who, as *robins* enriched by business dealings, were the very image of all he hated about the recently ennobled: "Tell me," he wrote his wife in July 1783, "I beg you, whether it was my friendly fishwife *Cordier* or my old pal *Fouloiseau* who wanted to deprive me of shirts. One refuses linen to prisoners in the hospital but not to me. How your baseness, the baseness of your origins and of your parents, is apparent in all things! Mommy, when I had so forgotten who I was that I was willing to sell you what I am, my purpose may have been to leave you with nothing but the shirt on your back—but not to do without shirts myself. Remember that phrase, you and your spawn, until I can have it printed."[20]

Sade's class prejudice knew no bounds. Spurred and magnified by neurotic anxiety, it drove his attacks on men of power but dubious background, ministers and policemen such as Maupeou and Sartine, about whom he wrote La Jeunesse in January 1780: "One can speak ill of the government, the king, and religion: all that is nothing. But a whore, Monsieur Quiros, 'zounds! a whore, you must take care not to offend her, or in a moment the Sartines, Maupeous, Montreuils, and other henchmen of the bordello will swoop down on you in *soldierly* fashion to protect the whore and *intrepidly* lock you, a gentleman, up for twelve or fifteen years on account of a whore."[21]

When the chevalier du Puget pointed out to him that "one must not pay attention to what people were," Sade agreed: "That is true when their virtues make you forget their birth. In that case one has to respect them far more than the useless or stupid noble who, offering society nothing but the parchment his ancestors earned, makes his presence felt chiefly by pointing up the difference between himself and his forebears. But when the son of a gardener from Vitry [Losme], of a boatman from Avignon [Miray], and of an overseer of galley slaves [Jourdan de Saint-Sauveur], having barely left behind their low and dissolute origins, bring to the posts in which their ignominy has placed them the shameful vices of their background, everything drives them back, unsuspecting, to the fetid marsh to which nature condemned them, and when they lift their noses up from the ground, they remind me of a filthy, disgusting toad that briefly attempts to escape from the muck only to fall back in and disappear."[22] This unflattering portrait of the common condition dates from 1788. We would do well to keep it in mind.

The same aristocratic haughtiness governed relations between the lord of La Coste and the vassals, peasants, and farmers for whom he nevertheless claimed to feel such great affection. Admittedly, the following lines, quoted earlier, were written the day after old Treillet had fired his pistol at Donatien (January 21 or 22, 1777): "All the Costains are beggars fit for the wheel . . . I assure you that if they were to be roasted one after another, I would supply the kindling without batting an eyelash. When the time comes, I will not spare them . . . Today a stranger comes and asks for his daughter by firing his pistol, tomorrow a peasant will come and ask for his daily wage by firing his rifle. Do they not already give sufficient proof of their independence by going off to hunt, to the mountains, and who knows where else?"[23]

A nobleman's eldest son was destined from birth for a career in the military. This was the only way to get out from under his father's thumb and thus ease the burden on his family. In response to pressure from one segment of the public, an edict of 1781 had reserved officers' commissions for noble sons. The comte de Saint-Germain had opened a dozen military schools, including those at Brienne and La Flèche, to train six hundred young nobles for military careers.[24] In this, too, the marquis de Sade shared the prejudices of his caste. Although he took little interest in the education of his younger son and none at all in that of his daughter, he was deeply concerned about the future of young Louis-Marie, the pride of the family and future of the Sade line. Scandalized at the idea that the boy might serve in a unit unworthy of his name, Sade bitterly blamed his wife: "Nothing can make me consent to my son's becoming an infantry sublieutenant, and he shall not be one. If you allow him to join up against my wishes, I give you my word of honor that I shall force him to quit, and I will stop at nothing to have my way . . . I absolutely refuse to allow him to serve in any unit other than the carabineers."[25]

•

An aristocrat of the high and ancient nobility, steeped in the pride of his caste, sharing its interests, privileges, and aspirations with an untroubled conscience, the marquis was nevertheless aware of the reality of the stakes. With a lucidity that set him apart from other nobles, he knew that the jig was up, that the aristocracy was on its last legs, a victim of the internal contradictions of an economy too closely tied to the land. He had no illusions about his future and sensed that all forces were converging directly or indirectly to bring about the rise of the bourgeoisie.

This consciousness of belonging to a condemned class was not untinged by nostalgia. Though little given to dwelling on the past, he could not restrain his emotions in this 1781 letter to his wife: "Do you know to whom that house opposite the Luxembourg once belonged? Oh, you no doubt know as well as I do. That was the hôtel de Maillé. My grandfathers lived there under Louis XIII. It housed a huge family of Maillés, yet today not even a *sous-fermier* would want it for his hôtel."[26]

More clear-sighted than many others despite his detention, Sade even claimed to have predicted the Revolution. His novel *Aline et Valcour* was published in 1795 with this notice: "Written one year before the Revolution of France." The claim is wholly accurate, since he began writing the work sometime between November 28, 1785, the day he finished the *Cent Vingt Journées de Sodome*, and October 1, 1788, when he mentioned it in the catalogue of his works completed by that date. Thus he could legitimately boast of having predicted the great breakdown of French society as early as 1788—and he did not deny himself the privilege. "What is even more remarkable about this work," the publisher's note proclaims, "is that it was written in the Bastille. The way in which our author, a victim of ministerial despotism, predicted the Revolution is quite extraordinary and should considerably enhance the interest of his work."[27]

Now, it is true that certain characters in the novel prophesied the fall of the Ancien Régime and the advent of a republic.[28] Father Berseuil, for example, tells Déterville that "your modern Babylon will destroy itself like that of Semiramis. It will vanish from the face of the earth as did the flourishing cities of Greece, whose luxury was the sole cause of their demise. And the State, made weak in order to embellish this new Sodom, will sink with it beneath your gilded ruins."[29] A number of similar passages could be cited.[30]

But the very number of seemingly prescient passages in the work should be enough to arouse suspicion. It took no particular clairvoyance in 1788 to foresee what would happen in 1789: others besides Sade had managed it. And his task was made easier by the fact that *Aline et Valcour*, the "fruit of several years of sleepless nights," did not appear until 1795, seven years after it was written. During those seven eventful years, we know that Sade constantly revised his text, as he himself tells us, to keep it "up to date" and give it the kind of "masculine and severe physiognomy that suits a free nation." There can be no doubt that he availed himself of the delay to embellish the work with "prophecies." The predictions are too specific, the advantages of adding them after the fact are too obvious, and the author's winks at the reader are too apparent. What is more, Sade's patriotic zeal in 1788 seems rather surprising, given that he did not hesitate in that same year to characterize the world of the common man as "dissolute," "muck," and a "fetid swamp."

On the eve of 1789 Sade's ideology was still aristocratic and still tempted by hopes of a feudal revival. Not that he thought of feudalism in traditional terms: he was too conscious of the movement of history to wish for a return to the past. Of this the defeat of the aristocrats in *Aline et Valcour* is sufficient proof. He understood full well that the bourgeoisie, better adapted than the aristocracy to the economic realities of the day, would sooner or later become the ruling class. But did that mean that the nobility would have to resign itself to defeat? Not at all. In order to survive, however, it would have to overcome its reluctance and adopt bourgeois values. Like it or not, political pragmatism would compel it to create the conditions for an objective alliance between the two classes: this was the price of the aristocracy's survival. Such an alliance would require the nobility to relinquish certain of its privileges and the monarch to share power. In other words, the foundations of the Ancien Régime would come under attack.

You Said Monarchien?

Following his release from prison on May 19, 1790, Sade summed up his feelings about the Revolution in a letter to Reinaud:

In any case, do not mistake me for an *enragé*. I tell you that I am simply an *impartial*, annoyed to have lost so much, still more annoyed to see my sovereign in irons, and disconcerted by what you gentlemen in the provinces have no inkling of, that it is impossible to do, to continue to do, the right thing as long as the monarch's sanctions are constrained by thirty thousand armed spectators and twenty artillery pieces. Yet with all that I feel but little regret for the Ancien Régime. To be sure, it made me too miserable for me to shed any tears on its behalf. That is my profession of faith, and I make it without fear.[31]

This is an important document, which contradicts those who persist in seeing Sade as the first of the sans-culottes, whereas in fact he was upset to see *his* king reduced to silence and the monarchy cowed by an armed populace. If he feels but little regret for the Ancien Régime, it is because he sees no real contradiction between the aristocratic spirit and liberal demands. There was in principle nothing about the end of absolutism likely to displease him: he had suffered too much at its hands not to applaud its disappearance. Nor could he forget, even if gratitude was not foremost among his virtues, that he owed his release to the Revolution and its abolition of the lettre de cachet. Though certainly a monarchist and devoted to the king's person ("I adore the king," he said elsewhere), Sade nevertheless opposed a policy whose only end was the restoration of the old order. In short, he exemplifies a position that might be characterized as "critical monarchism."

In fact, the party that most closely matched his political philosophy was that of the so-called *monarchiens*. Composed of deputies of the Constituent Assembly including Mounier, Lally-Tollendal, Malouet, and Stanislas de Clermont-Tonnerre, Donatien's cousin by marriage, the *monarchiens* favored an English-style parliamentary regime with a bicameral legislature. Their slogan was "Nation, King, Law" and their symbol was Lafayette. The party theoretician was Jean-Joseph Mounier, a man whom Mme de Staël called "passionately reasonable" and whose anti-absolutist program won the unanimous support of his comrades. Wary of all political upheaval and devoted to the fundamental values of progress and tolerance, the *monarchiens* largely adhered to the philosophy of the Enlightenment. Their ambition led them to favor a program of careful institutional reform under the aegis of an enlightened monarchy, which, they felt, remained the best guarantee of national regeneration. In short, they dreamed of a monarchical revolution that would make it possible to reconcile the rights of princes with the rights of man. "These men shared a common representation of the political order, a common wariness of democracy, and a desire to borrow from the English a model of free government rooted in history, which is to say, based on *inherited rights*, guaranteed not by the substitution of one absolute sovereignty for another but by a redefinition of the balance of power."[32]

Sade's views were not dissimilar to these. As an enemy of the "Jacobite faction," which he always detested, and a proponent of English-style constitutional monarchy, respectful of royal authority, he numbered among those who favored "moderate" reform and therefore found his natural place in the Club des Impartiaux founded in January 1790 by his cousin Clermont-Tonnerre and Malouet to counter the influence of the Jacobins.

Nevertheless, this did not prevent him from obtaining, on July 1, 1790, a card identifying him as an "active citizen" of the Section de la Place Vendôme, later known as the Section des Piques and destined to become one of the most radical of the Paris sections. At around the same time he renounced his particule and adopted the name Louis Sade, which struck him as more democratic. Why *Louis*? According to family tradition, this was the name his father had intended for him to have at birth. But it was a poor choice, for by 1792 many people were trading the name "Louis" for others considered less "monarchist."

As a conscientious member of his section, Sade regularly attended meetings that were held on the average once every ten days at the Eglise des Capucines, but he did not play an active role. He scrupulously fulfilled his duties as a citizen while trying as much as possible to remain out of the limelight, although self-effacement was hardly his nature. Are we nevertheless obliged to look upon his membership in the section as a mark of political commitment? Certainly not. In the beginning the municipal sections included citizens of all orders and all political factions. Moderates wielded considerable influence, particularly in western Paris, where they outnumbered the *enragés*. From wealthy bankers on down to small retailers, from shopkeepers to artisans to people of modest private means, an apparently insurmountable barrier rose against the more audacious revolutionary measures. At the time Sade joined the Section de la Place Vendôme, it had not yet succumbed to extremist fever. His adherence must therefore be interpreted as a measure of prudence and nothing more. There was pressure on everyone to join, and it was the least he could do while waiting to see what happened next.

In any case, many intelligent people believed that the Revolution was over. All that remained was to strike a compromise with the monarchy and embody that compromise in a constitution. Sade could only rejoice at the thought, for his career as a man of letters, the only thing that mattered to him now, depended in large part on civil peace. His ambition was not to change the fundamental laws of the realm but to have his plays produced, even if it meant sacrificing his nobility and pledging his loyalty to the new regime. At first this cost him very little, for he embraced the prevailing ideas of the day. Very quickly, however, the political situation evolved in such a way that additional concessions were required, concessions that carried him further and further from his initial convictions and little by little chipped away at his freedom, to the point where he became a hostage of a Revolution whose inception he had enthusiastically hailed.

•

On July 14, 1790, the first anniversary of the taking of the Bastille, Sade attended the Festival of the Federation. The spectacle of the occasion appealed not only to the citizen but equally to the lover of theater. The staging was grandiose: an immense amphitheater of greenery had been erected on the esplanade of the Champ-de-Mars. Earthen slopes supporting thirty rows of seating had been constructed on all sides. A covered reviewing stand had been set up in front of the Ecole Militaire for officials and ambassadors. The royal podium projected into the center of the theater so that everyone could see the king. At the other end of the esplanade an enormous arch of triumph consisting of three bays, each more than seventy-five feet high, marked the entrance; it provided a magnificent view for the privileged few who managed to find places at the top. It was probably from there that Sade watched the parade, lost in the crowd beneath one of the innumerable colorful umbrellas that made the stands look like a field of peonies. Since morning veritable waterspouts had poured rain on the city. But it would have taken more than a deluge to quench the enthusiasm of the 300,000 *fédérés* from all over France who crowded the amphitheater despite the storm.

Sade recounted the story of that memorable day to Gaufridy:

Such a thing is impossible to recount in detail. You had to see it to describe it. I was in the best places, though that did not prevent the rain from soaking my body for six hours running. This circumstance disrupted everything and caused people to say that God had just declared himself an *aristocrat*. No festival has ever been this orderly, and none has had fewer accidents. One man was killed and two wounded by the cannon, and through clumsiness to boot, but that was all. Nevertheless, this festival, which was supposed to establish love, is going to give birth to discord. There are more rumors than ever.

People are saying that the king was supposed to take the oath on the altar . . .
What platitude! Where would the oath have been healthier or draped in more
august forms than uttered amongst the representatives of the nation? All the
nastiness is coming from the Orleanist party, which desires nothing other than
civil war. We are lost if it triumphs.[33]

There can be no doubt about Sade's mood: he fully identified with
this festival of fraternity, which symbolized unanimity, or, rather, the
illusion of unanimity around the achievements of the Revolution and
the will of an entire people to profess its "patriotism." Yet he was
worried. In the days preceding the gathering on the Champ-de-Mars,
wild rumors had circulated in the capital, sowing panic in both camps:
that of the aristocrats, who trembled at the sight of Paris delivered to
the forces of revolution, and that of the popular masses, who were
afraid that the aristocrats might launch an attack during the ceremony.
No one was immune to this conspiracy psychosis, not even the marquis
de Sade, who ascribed to the duc d'Orléans's blunderings an importance that they certainly did not have but that supporters of Louis XVI
were more than willing to attribute to them. By contrast, Sade seems
to have had no inkling that the king secretly hoped to restore the old
order and was seriously contemplating a counterrevolutionary move.

Sade never bothered to conceal his hatred of the Orleanist faction:
one of the few constants in his labyrinthine political thought, that
hatred achieved particularly vehement expression in part five of the
Histoire de Juliette, in which Count Brahe, grand master of the Swedish
Masons and leader of the conspiracy against Gustav III, inevitably calls
to mind the king's brother, Philippe d'Orléans, grand master of the
Grand Orient lodge of French Freemasons and a notorious debauchee
and professional agitator who took the name Philippe-Egalité during
the Revolution. For anyone who might doubt this, the author took the
trouble to add this footnote: "Stockholm's revolutionary spirit, might
you not by chance have made your way to Paris?"

•

Toward the end of October 1790 the *monarchien* Club des Impartiaux
was supplanted by the Société des Amis de la Constitution Monarchique, of which Sade became a full member. In a surviving fragment
of a letter to Gaufridy, one can read that, "inviolably attached by
friendship and blood to the interests of the comte de Clermont-
Tonnerre, [Sade] could not refrain from joining the monarchical club
of which [Stanislas] is in a sense the leader and initiator."[34] Apart from

his affection for his cousin, a profound community of ideas linked him to this group.

In imitation of the Jacobins, and in order to combat them more effectively, the new club increased the number of its affiliates in the départements and rapidly gained popularity by distributing bread coupons to the indigent. Hostile to both the prejudices of the Ancien Régime and the passions of the reformers, it took "Liberty and Fidelity" as its motto. The law, as the instrument of the king's reign, remained the supreme authority for these monarchists. The Constituent Assembly had declared the prince inviolable and sacred, the throne indivisible, and the crown hereditary in virtue of the Constitution. What the members of the club were defending was this Constitution. They placed all their hopes in the law of the Constitution as the best rampart against the possibility of wicked fiats. They also published a weekly organ, the *Journal de la Société des Amis de la Constitution Monarchique*, the first issue of which appeared on Saturday, December 18, 1790.

Very soon the Jacobins and their friends, generally well informed about the activity of their adversaries, denounced these demagogic maneuvers and launched a campaign designed to reveal the organization's true aims. In particular, it was accused of advocating arbitrary rule and of making handouts to the poor from suspect sources, including the court (which was true). They were even suspected of working to undermine the Constitution. These charges were not completely groundless. Apart from Clermont-Tonnerre himself, Malouet, Boisgelin, Bergasse, and a few others, it is undeniable that the club, headquartered on rue Saint-Antoine, was composed mainly of men nostalgic for the Ancien Régime and convinced that the nobility would always be the ornament and bulwark of the monarchy. Behind the constitutional façade lurked a veritable den of counterrevolution.

By an odd coincidence, the most virulent attacks on the club came from the Place-Vendôme section. On January 24 the section vehemently denounced the actions of the Society, "whose very name [Friends of the Monarchical Constitution] is an insult to the king's true friends, who will always be friends of the Constitution."[35] Soon other sections joined in to demand, "in the name of all Paris," the destruction, *by all means*, of this "seedbed of seduction," where monarchists "offer hungry misery the poison of aristocracy." The affair turned ugly, riots erupted, the Constituent Assembly became involved, Clermont-Tonnerre was jeered by a mob, and club members were attacked with rocks and bludgeons. On March 28, 1791, the municipal government of Paris ordered the club closed. Donatien, who had attended few of its meetings (to believe him, he had joined only to please his cousin), was nevertheless called upon to choose sides. Without batting an eyelash he turned his back on his dear Delphine's husband and rejoined his section.

Brother Donatien

It has often been claimed that Sade at some point became a Freemason. No doubt the fact that his father was a member contributed to the belief that the son must have been as well. But there is no proof that he was ever initiated. Nevertheless, a certain vague similarity of values has lent credence to the idea. Yet even if he had been tempted by the philosophy of the lodges, his militant atheism would have prevented him from practicing rites that still bore too much resemblance to the Christian liturgy. "Natural" as this religion might be, the cult of the "Great Architect of the Universe" would surely have disgusted him. For Sade, as for d'Alembert, Diderot, Condorcet, Turgot and others who refrained from joining the Masonic Order, the Cult of Reason could do without rites of any kind and was to be practiced only in the open.

In any case, it is difficult to imagine Sade in a secret society, living on a footing of perfect equality with his "brothers." Nothing could have been more contrary to his principles than an ideology that abolished all distinctions of birth and status.

Though estranged from the Masons for all these reasons, Sade displayed a keen interest in these "sons of Enlightenment." The portrait he gives of the Loge du Nord in *Juliette* attests to a thorough knowledge of the "royal art," probably derived from his reading (there was an abundant specialist literature available).[36] Masonic ritual clearly interested him, even if he liked to subvert it by subjecting the initiation ceremony to a libertine's fancy: sodomy, prostitution, human sacrifice, orgies, and atrocities of all kinds were included. It is easy to imagine his delight at turning temples of social virtue into altars of perversity. In the end, the only Masonry to which Sade's heroes subscribe is that of the Society of the Friends of Crime. What fascinated Sade in Masonry was not the Masonic ideal but the rigorous rules and protocols on which it was based, its independence from the laws of the state, and its method of subjecting instinct to ritual.

Death of the "Liberator"

On April 2, 1791, Paris was dumbfounded to learn of the death of Mirabeau. Just a few days earlier, on March 28, he had delivered a speech to the Constituent Assembly, his teeth clenched and death already written on his face. That night he had taken to his bed, never to rise again. His friend, Dr. Cabanis, had not left his bedside. The great orator had spent his last night in delirium, his eyes fixed on the window, and had finally succumbed at eight-thirty in the morning, while an anxious crowd waited at his door. The news of his death at the age of forty-three spread like wildfire, and there seemed to be something unnatural in its suddenness. Within hours signs and posters had appeared on the walls of the capital, some accusing the Lameth brothers, others denouncing Barnave. To put an end to the rumors, the public prosecutor for the First Arrondissement ordered an autopsy, which revealed an inflammation of the liver and stomach but not the slightest trace of poison. On the same day Mirabeau's secretary Comps attempted suicide by stabbing himself fifteen times, but he lived to write an article about the episode.

The next day the Assembly decided to bury the orator in the Eglise Sainte-Geneviève, which had just been deconsecrated and rebaptized the Pantheon. The temple of religion had been transformed into an altar of *la patrie*. Mirabeau would have the honor of being the first to be buried there, a distinction that did not please everyone. Marat and the Cordeliers denounced the hero of the moment as an intriguer, but Robespierre defended his memory. A hundred thousand Parisians paid him their last respects, while national guardsmen fired a salvo over the body and dozens of constitutional priests surrounded the coffin.

The marquis soon learned of the death of his old adversary and neighbor, and he described the event to Gaufridy:

There is nothing like the sensation this death has produced here. Crowds of people have invaded the theaters and forced the shows to a halt. Some not quite so enthusiastic about the liberator of France have taken a dim view of these interruptions, and one of the interrupters was dragged into the Palais-Royal, where I have no idea what became of him. It caused quite a stir. I went that night to the Palais-Royal, where grief was clearly visible on people's faces. A lugubrious silence prevailed, and many knots had gathered. The death of the secretary who stabbed himself fifteen times is quite extraordinary. The man was, and still is, suspected of having cooperated in his patron's death. I do not know if time will clear up this dark mystery . . .

Tuesday morning, April 5 . . . The liberator was buried yesterday evening at seven o'clock, or, rather, temporarily laid to rest in the parish of Saint-Eustache before being transported to Sainte-Geneviève to be interred there, under the auspices of the patron saint of Paris. It is just that the *patron* should have the *liberator*. The convoy was magnificent. All possible corporations took part, with M. d'Orléans at the head of the procession. All the bells of Paris pealed. Sometime earlier the *liberator* was opened up to see if he had poison in his entrails, and twelve men of the people were chosen at random from the crowd that had not left his door since his death to observe the procedure. The good Parisians, quite pleased to see that the *liberator* had died of natural causes, stopped threatening to kill all the aristocrats whom they had previously suspected of having caused this great misfortune . . . The street where the liberator died has changed its name and become *rue de Mirabeau*.[37]

The Letter to the King

June 24, 1791. The royal family is returned to Paris under escort following a bizarre escape attempt that had ended in the village of Varennes. Louis XVI's berlin crosses a city stunned into deathly silence. Three hundred thousand Parisians watch it pass without a murmur. The night before, these words had appeared in chalk on the walls of the capital: "Anyone who applauds the king will be bludgeoned. Anyone who insults him will be hanged." Just as the cortège enters the place de la Révolution, a man springs from the crowd, leaps onto the king's carriage, tosses in a letter, and disappears. That man was none other than Donatien de Sade. Or so he would claim three years later, on 6 messidor, Year II (June 24, 1794), after seven months' detention in the jails of the Terror—Robespierre's abattoir had begun to claim growing numbers of victims, and it was a matter of escaping the slaughter.

If the story was invented, the famous letter does indeed exist. It was published by Girouard, Sade's faithful printer, a few days after the king's return from Varennes. According to the author's deposition, the letter made the rounds of Paris. It had even, he claimed, been read out publicly in the Tuileries and from makeshift platforms around the city. Its title was significant: "Address of a Citizen of Paris to the King of the French."[38] Sade wrote not to the "king of France by the grace of God" (the traditional formula) but to the "king of the French" by the grace of the nation and bound to it by contract, an idea that he developed in the body of the text: "If you wish to reign, let it be over a free nation. It is the nation that installs you, that names you its leader. It is the nation that places you on its throne, and not the God of the universe, as people used to have the weakness to believe."[39] His reproaches are those of all Frenchmen supportive of the values of a constitutionally regenerated monarchy but disappointed by the king's conduct: "Say what you would have us think of a man who has betrayed us, who did not shrink from profaning either the throne on which he was seated on the day of the Federative Pact or the altar opposite which he swore the sacred oath that bound him to his nation in the same moment as that nation bound itself to him, with an expression of love and feeling whose spectacle drew tears from all of France, gathered together on one field."[40]

Sade's principal complaint against despotism will come as no surprise: it was the lettre de cachet, that pure product of arbitrary power. Inevitably he must have had his own fate in mind when he wrote: "You complain of your situation; you are moaning, you say, in irons . . . As you reflect on your misfortune in a position that might seem enviable to many others, deign for a moment to think of the former victims of your despotism, of those sad individuals whom your signature alone, obtained by seduction or deception, wrested from the bosoms of their tearful families and plunged forever into the dungeons of those terrifying bastilles with which your kingdom bristled . . . When one has permitted such great evils, Sire, one must learn to endure lesser ones."[41]

Yet Louis XVI was not the only person responsible for those great evils. Joining his voice to those of many emigrés as well as to that of the Jacobins, Sade did not hesitate to incriminate the king's entourage, and above all the nefarious influence of the queen: "If it is true, as seems only too certain, that it was the companion of your fate who gave you such advice, do not expose her any longer to the vengeance of the French. Separate from her. You no longer need her. Send her back to her homeland [Austria], which sent her away only to distill, for a longer period and with more certain effect, the destructive venoms of the hatred it has always felt for France."

Nevertheless, like the majority of the French population, which remained in spite of everything loyal to the monarchical principle, Sade retained his confidence in the sovereign. Even after Varennes, all was not lost if only Louis XVI would agree to play the constitutional game by the rules and heed the counsel of the nation and none other. Sade's "Address to the King" ends on this note: "Hope is rekindled in all hearts at the news of your return. Everyone is disposed to pardon you. Listen to what people are saying, Sire: you are not the one who deceived us; you were deceived yourself; this flight was the work of your priests and courtiers . . . No one is more intimately convinced than I that the French empire can be governed only by a monarch. But that monarch, elected by a free nation, must faithfully respect the law."[42]

Quite pleased with his "Address," Sade sent it to Reinaud, who greeted the missive with irony: "So it is true that you have told the king off! What a conversion of French into Latin! Your piece is well done, coherent, and has nerve. One recognizes your sparkling touch. But beyond the rhetorical devices that you employ with skill and success, I maintain that the author ought to distinguish himself in deed, I mean by example! You abandoned your wife; you would have the king dismiss his; and today, in pleading, you reclaim yours! Put some consistency in things: one is often the reply to one's own objection. But, in favor of the style of your essay, let us forget that you are preaching what you do not practice."[43]

When the Constituent Assembly rejected bicameralism, hopes of an English-style government (with two chambers and a preponderance of royal power) seemed to evaporate, and its proponents became suspect. Although republicanism had begun to gain ground, Sade still dared to support an English solution in his "Address to the King." If he continued to believe in a constitutional monarchy against all probability, it was because he sensed that to reject what was in his eyes the only possible system, the only one he could support without losing his soul, would open the way to unforeseeable disasters.

On September 14 he was bound to acknowledge the obvious: the game was lost. The Constitution to which Louis XVI swore allegiance that day owed nothing to the laws of England, and royalists now felt that their sovereign had given his blessing to the crimes of the Revolution. "Your salvation consists in refusal," Burke had warned the French king. But the king's refusal to accept the Constitution would have signified his disavowal of the policies pursued up to that point by the moderates. In any case, the idea of an English-style monarchy was doomed from the start, for the simple reason that the economic and social condition of the French aristocracy had nothing in common with that of the English aristocracy. It took the political blindness of a Clermont-Tonnerre or the naïveté of a Sade to think that the English system could work in France.

Two months later, on December 5, 1791, Sade wrote to Gaufridy: "I am anti-Jacobite. I hate them to death. I adore the king, but I detest the old abuses. I love any number of articles of the Constitution; others revolt me. I want the luster of the nobility restored, because taking it away solved nothing. I want the king to be the nation's leader. I do not want a National Assembly, but two chambers as in England, which would give the king a tempered authority, balanced by the concord of a nation necessarily divided into two orders; the third [the clergy] is useless, I want no part of it. That is my profession of faith. What am I at present? Aristocrat or democrat? You will tell me if you please, attorney, because I for one have no idea."[44]

This profession of faith strains credulity. The Constitution of 1791, adopted only a short while before, already seemed hopelessly out of date. Democratic ideas were spreading. Robespierre was calling for universal suffrage, Marat was whipping up dissent, a republican alternative was making headway, and meanwhile the king was banking on a redemptive war to save the monarchy. The ship of state was taking on water at an alarming rate. Yet here is Sade dreaming of restoring the luster of the nobility, rejecting the National Assembly, and proclaiming his "adoration" of the sovereign. One can scarcely believe one's eyes. Aristocrat or democrat? We may wager that the good Gaufridy had no difficulty responding. Never before had Sade demonstrated such complete denial of reality. There is even something pathetic in this negation of the irreversible. What did he expect, anyway? Nothing. As always, he closed his eyes to avoid seeing the obstacle. He cast away the cause of his despair and erased it from his consciousness. But too lucid to believe in his own deceits, he knew that terrible things were in the offing, and that he would have to face them.

21

In Torment

Double Language

In Paris a liberal aristocrat, open to reforms and ready for sacrifices, the marquis de Sade remained, in the eyes of his peasants, the great and arrogant feudal lord they had always known. He was even more haughty and contemptuous than before, as if he wished to make it clear what separated him from them at a time when ancestral values were crumbling. Like most of his peers he did not accept the new social relations born of the Revolution. Did the notary of Mazan, a man by the name of Conil, have some rather nasty things to say about the *ci-devant* seigneur? The lord himself offered, through Gaufridy, a riposte that cracked like a whip: "The National Assembly's decree equalizes men, but it neither identifies nor couples man with beast, and Conil, accordingly, sensing distances he affects to forget, ought, rather than write me, *return to the stable, ask for his oats, and shut his mouth.*"

Recognizing the implications of recent events, Sade looked with horror on the revolutionary movements he saw unfolding before his eyes. The letter to Reinaud from which I quoted earlier clearly indicates his mixed feelings of disgust and anxiety at the sight of the popular hordes: "Ah! It is a long time since I said to myself that this beautiful and gentle nation, which ate the maréchal d'Ancre's buttocks off the grill, was merely awaiting the right occasion to exalt itself, to show that, always perched between cruelty and fanaticism, it would recover its natural tone as soon as the opportunity arose."[1] In fact, he did not understand the people at all and never had. Aristocrat that he was, and accustomed to viewing the common man as an irresponsible child, he feared the unpredictability of the people's reactions. He knew that the irrational unleashing of its furor imperiled the existence of his class. If he avoided physical contact with his vassals and postponed his trip to Provence year after year for fear of the "democratic gallows," he nevertheless intended to remain the master of his estates and did not hesitate to reprimand his people when the need arose. Thus, when the revolutionary authorities of Mazan asked him to rebuild the walls of his château, he informed them that he was not about to take orders from "imbecile" villagers. "My father destroyed those walls with the sovereign's permission," he wrote to Gaufridy. "I will repair them only on orders equivalent to those that allowed us to destroy them. If this does not please them, you can give them my permission to pull the château down, and then they can use the stones from which it was built to make their rampart. What is more, they can be sure that neither I nor my race will wish to live in a country that has so horrendously sapped and dishonored itself as this one. We shall go on business to visit our property [and] our farms, but breathe the same air as brigands such as these? Oh, my word, never, never! I hate them at present as much as I used to love them, and I look upon them as imbeciles who, because the French Revolution made it possible for them to enrich themselves, trampled one another in their foolish rush to embrace it."[2]

Apart from the haughtiness of the *grand seigneur* and the feudal tone of the letter, the text interestingly reveals Sade's view that the Revolution could among other things serve as a means of acquiring wealth. Perhaps, at a moment when his own financial situation was at its most precarious, he even thought of availing himself of the opportunity. Blasphemous as this suggestion may seem to some, there is nothing inherently implausible about it. It was not the first or the last time that unscrupulous, pragmatic men would profit from turmoil: war, revolution, occupation. And in matters of money Sade, as we have seen, was utterly ruthless. Since the beginning of the Revolution he had seen speculators of every stripe enrich themselves: buyers of national properties, bankers, merchants, notaries, and ordinary entrepreneurs. Why not Sade? It seems likely that the idea at least occurred to him. What is certain, in any case, is that he thought about protecting his fortune from the various requisitions to which nobles and relatives of émigrés were subject.

I have been able to identify the two property administrators with whom he dealt for this purpose. They were Toussaint-Charles Girard and Jean-François Dufouleur, both Paris notaries whose offices Sade frequently visited from 1790 on and who both paid with their lives for the services they rendered to nobles. Dufouleur perished on the scaffold in 1794 for having saved the fortune of the Leduc de Biéville family by serving as a front.[3] And Girard, the former president of the Section des Amis de la Patrie, would be judged on the same day as his client Donatien de Sade (July 26, 1794) and found guilty of having protected émigré property. Unlike Sade, however, Girard was in fact put to death.[4] Today, however, there is incontrovertible proof that Sade passed money, 15,000 livres to be exact, to Mme Quesnet in the form of a fraudulent note signed in the presence of Maître Dufouleur.[5]

We are thus a long way from the image of Sade as a patriot, friend of the common man, and Jacobin that some people persist in perpetuating. At the risk of disappointing them, let me state clearly that he was nothing of the kind. His personal correspondence proves this abundantly, and there is no reason to doubt what he wrote on this score to Gaufridy and Reinaud, with whom he had no reason to pretend and who in any case shared his views. If his actions sometimes suggest the contrary, and if his political writings—which he himself called "civic productions"—tend to fall all over themselves with displays of republican zeal, the reason is that they were the product of circumstances. Sade was too skeptical about human qualities, too pessimistic, and too immune to the illusion of political morality to believe in the revolutionary ideal any more than he had believed in the Christian one. The only revolution that truly mattered to him, the only one in which he ever believed, the only one in which he would triumph beyond his wildest imagination, was that of writing.

Administrative Error

By 1792 most nobles had fled the country. The emigration proceeded in three successive waves: the first in July and August of 1789, after the seizure of the Bastille and the Great Fear; the second in 1790, owing to the decrees abolishing the feudal regime; and the third in September and October of 1791, triggered by the failure of the flight to Varennes. In all, nearly 150,000 people fled their homes between 1789 and 1800.[6] Sade was among the few who refused exile. Neither the threats he faced nor his innate fear of popular movements nor the failure of the monarchical revolution nor the example of his peers could persuade him to leave. Emigrate? Give up hope of producing his plays? Compromise his career as a dramatic author? He never gave it a thought. Literary ambition outweighed everything else: whatever happened, he would remain in France.

What, in any case, did he have to fear? Was he not wholly above suspicion? His years in the Bastille, his "Address to the King," his section card—were these not incontrovertible tokens of his civic spirit? Citizen Louis Sade, "man of letters," had nothing whatsoever to do with the *ci-devant* marquis de Sade. Let everyone take notice. And if there were some who still dared to doubt his conversion, he would go further. He would become a Jacobin if necessary. And of course his fortune itself was at stake. Sade's only property was his land in Provence, and by virtue of the decrees of October 31 and November 9, 1791, which made emigration a crime of conspiracy against the state, that land would have been seized immediately if he had made a move to leave the country.

Apart from all these good reasons for remaining in Paris, there was also the fascination that the Revolution, in spite of everything, exerted on his imagination. Part of him could indeed identify with it: there was an obscure connection between the liberty of his writing and actual liberty at the precise moment when the latter fell into crisis and created a historical vacuum. But this was coincidence, not identity: Sade's insurrectional energies were not those that had stirred the forces of revolution; indeed, the two were rather contradictory. "And yet," Maurice Blanchot notes, "without the mad extravagance represented by the name, the life, and the truth of Sade, the Revolution would have been deprived of a part of its Reason."[7] In any case, emigration did not have quite the same meaning for Sade as for others. He had been a wanderer, a prisoner, a solitary. Had he ever ceased to be an émigré in his own land? Thus he decided to remain hypocritically at home.

Toward the end of 1792, however, his name appeared on a printed poster in Marseilles among those who had quit the nation's territory. On December 13 of that year "Louis-Alphonse [*sic*] Donatien Sade" was listed among émigrés from the Bouches-du-Rhône. Had someone played him a nasty trick? Or was it an error? Or had he perhaps been confused with his son Louis-Marie? Dumbfounded, Donatien protested to the local authorities, sending petitions, residence certificates, printed documents from the Section des Piques bearing his signature, and affidavits of all sorts attesting to his presence in Paris. In vain. He grew impatient, pressed Gaufridy to act, and finally obtained satisfaction on May 26, 1793.[8]

A month later, however, the case was reopened. On June 25, 1793, the Convention divided the département of the Bouches-du-Rhône, deemed too large, in two, creating the new département of the Vaucluse, which now claimed jurisdiction over Citizen Sade. Through bureaucratic imbroglio, administrative Machiavellianism, or official negligence—who knows which?—Donatien's name appeared on the list of émigrés furnished to the new département. The whole process of having it removed had to start afresh. Thus began a dreadful succession of petitions, letters, and pleas and an exhausting search for witnesses, support, and letters of recommendation that would continue, with tragicomic interludes, for no fewer than ten years. Despite all the evidence that Sade was able to amass of his good faith, he would be found guilty, first of having emigrated, then of having returned illegally to France. All the while, the *couperet* of Damocles hung over his head.

•

Mme de Sade and her daughter also declined to emigrate, probably for economic reasons. Apart from brief stays at their family estate in La Verrière, near Chevreuse, they remained where they were. Donatien's two sons did emigrate, however. On July 13, 1791, Louis-Marie resigned as sublieutenant of the 84th Infantry Regiment, and on September 11 he left France for Germany. Claude-Armand, aide-de-camp to the marquis de Toulongeon, deserted in May 1792 and went to join his brother. Before long the emigration of his children would cause the *ci-devant* marquis serious trouble. He was forced to lie, to swear that he did not know where the boys were, although he was as well-informed of their movements as could be expected under the circumstances.

"Leave my old shanties!"

In March 1792 alarming news reached Donatien from Provence. Violent clashes had taken place in the vicinity of Apt. Gaufridy and his son, both associated with a royalist conspiracy, had taken refuge in Lyons. The marquis was beside himself with worry. He immediately sent his notary this dispatch: "My anxiety will lessen only when I have news of you. Send word immediately, I beg you. Abandon me, quit my affairs, take no further interest in me. If that is what it takes, I agree to it. But love me, save yourself, persuade yourself that you have in me a childhood friend who would sooner see harm come to himself than to you."[9] In an outburst of generosity he offered hospitality to his "dear advocate." Why not seek safety in Paris? His house was small, but comfortable. But if friendship moved Donatien, self-interest also played a part. With Gaufridy absent, his affairs would go to ruin, his rents would go uncollected, his château would be abandoned. A few days later, though, he could breathe again. His agent was back in Apt.

Foreseeing a new attack, Gaufridy had established a garrison of twenty-four men around his house. The marquis immediately offered to share the cost, for he felt to some extent responsible for his agent's situation.

Although the immediate danger had passed, Sade was still worried, and with good reason. Among the Apt rioters were certain of his former vassals from La Coste. Were these isolated cases, or had a majority of Costains embraced violent action? Would the château be attacked? He questioned Gaufridy: "Are all these people angry only with the priests who refused the oath, or is some of their anger also directed against landowners?"[10] The response was quick but hardly reassuring. Sade learned, in fact, that the village Jacobins had voted to destroy the château's battlements. In a frenzy of anxiety he then lodged a protest with the president of the Club de la Constitution of La Coste. After professing his sincere attachment to the Revolution and the Constitution, he went on to deliver an eloquent plea:

If anyone removes so much as one stone of the house that I own within your boundaries, I shall go to our legislators, I shall go to your brothers the Jacobins of Paris, and I shall ask that the following words be engraved on it: "Stone from the house of the man who caused the stones of the Bastille to fall, which the Friends of the Constitution removed from the domicile of the most unfortunate victim of the tyranny of kings. Passerby, add this outrage to the history of human inconsistency!"

Oh, leave my old shanties, Monsieur le président! See my heart, open my writings, read my letters printed and distributed throughout Paris when the ladies of France departed and the king took flight. There you will see whether the author of such texts is a man whose property one ought to be tampering with.[11]

Despite the municipality's reassurances, Sade's mind was not at ease. He had learned to distrust his fellow man and set little store by oaths. Cowardice and self-interest could, he knew, cause the most solemn promise to be forgotten in an instant.

The iconoclastic furor of the people of Provence worried him no less than the burning of châteaux, not so much for religious as for family reasons. On learning that the Franciscan convent in Avignon was slated for destruction, he became concerned about Laura's ashes, which had been placed in the sepulchre of his ancestors. "Would it not be decent to give this celebrated woman an inviolable asylum, such as one of the parishes on my estates? And would this project, uniquely philosophical in my eyes, be seen as aristocratic by the patriots? I

consult you on the facts and beg you to reply. In addition, I believe
that the Celestine fathers have some papers or monuments concerning
Laura. Should they not be retrieved? They have, I believe, the original
of Francis I's poem for Laura.[12] That is a document that I think might
be retrieved."[13]

Despite the turmoil in Provence, Donatien told himself that if an
attempt were made to seize his property, he would stand a better chance
of defending himself on the premises than he would in Paris. This
time his mind was made up: come what may, he would take the stagecoach to Avignon next May (1793), and he would take Constance with
him. He would not stay more than three months. Of course he would
need to find a place to live. This would not be easy, despite his châteaux
in the region. Mazan was uninhabitable, Saumane scared him because
it was too isolated, and it was better not to think of La Coste: this was
hardly the moment to play the returning lord. It would be best to rent
a modest house in the village. But once again events would confound
his plans.

"Forthwith!"

On June 19, 1792, on a motion of Condorcet, the Legislative Assembly
decreed that all genealogical documents preserved in public archives
were to be destroyed. On that very day, at the foot of the statue of
Louis XIV in the place Vendôme, six hundred folio volumes of noble
nomenclature were burned. Frightened, Donatien immediately sent
instructions to Ripert: "Take the greatest care with my estate books
and titles. Here, yesterday, on the place Vendôme, all the titles of the
nobility were burned. This fantasy may catch on in your cantons. Preserve my papers, I urge you, by placing them in a dry place where no
living soul can find them . . . Nothing is more important. Write at once,
forthwith."[14]

Such was the man whom some would portray as a ferocious enemy
of caste! What was M. de Sade thinking of three weeks before the
overthrow of the monarchy on August 10, 1792? What preoccupied
him? What was on his mind? Saving his parchments! "Forthwith!"

"I am alone!"

August 10, 1792, at three in the morning. The insurrectional Commune
organized at the Hôtel de Ville. All night long, the tocsin sounded, as
at the time of the Saint Bartholomew's massacre. From belfry to belfry

the riot had spread, as the monarchy's death knell resounded through the depths of the night. At around six that morning delegates from the Left-Bank sections and *fédérés*, mainly from Brittany and Marseilles, crossed the Pont Saint-Michel without firing a shot. They soon reached the place du Carrousel at the entrance to the Tuileries. Still relatively few in number, they were surprised by the size of the defensive force. Above the palace walls they glimpsed the Swiss Guards in their red uniforms, a substantial contingent of National Guards, their cannon aimed at the crowd, and hundreds of mounted guardsmen. In all, nearly 4,000 men, bolstered by two to three hundred loyal supporters of the king, former bodyguards and noblemen armed with makeshift weapons. Some carried ceremonial sabers, others fireplace tongs.

While the insurgents took up positions and awaited reinforcements from other Paris sections, Louis XVI was acclaimed by a battalion, but on the parade ground behind the château he was jeered. Jeering broke out in the ranks of the cannoneers. Roederer, the *procureur-syndic* of Paris, then urged the king to take refuge in the Assembly and attempted to protect the royal family. After an hour's discussion the sovereign went with his family and Swiss Guards to the Salle du Manège, while the mob massed behind the parade-ground grill continued its catcalls. The Assembly received the king according to protocol and sent him to wait in the official recorder's lodge.

In the meantime the crowd continued to grow. All Paris was now marching on the château. Civilians and military men, *fédérés*, sans-culottes, *sectionnaires*, national guards, workers, bourgeois, Parisians, provincials: nearly ten thousand men armed with pikes and rifles massed behind the fence. Gendarmes, their hats on their *baïonettes*, fraternized with the crowd, and they were soon joined by the Val-de-Grâce cannoneers whose guns were trained on the place du Carrousel. A detachment commanded by Westermann managed to force the royal gates. The attackers poured through this breach and advanced on the great staircase. At that moment a shot was fired from a second-story window. This was the signal. The Swiss opened fire. The insurgents retreated, leaving three hundred dead on the pavement. But masses of people now poured in from the faubourgs Saint-Antoine and Saint-Marceau. The Swiss retreated in turn. The battle turned fierce. The insurgents soon found themselves at the gates of the palace. From within clouds of thick smoke the cannon fired. In the Assembly, Louis XVI, informed of the massacre, issued an order to the Swiss to lay down their arms. But in the confusion, the messenger, General d'Hervilly, failed to convey the order to the troops. Finally, the people forced their way in through the Gallery of the Louvre, slit the throats of most of the Swiss, and entered the royal apartments. A frightful carnage began. The surviving Swiss were stripped and castrated, sometimes decapitated. Others were forced to jump from windows and impaled on pikes. Once taken, the palace was sacked. Everything was smashed, torn to shreds, or burned. And while the celebrating mob pulled down symbols of the monarchy all over Paris, the Assembly decreed that the king was deposed and named a provisional Executive Council.

What was M. de Sade doing during this time? Two years later, on June 24, 1794, he would testify before the Popular Commission that on August 10 a friend had come for him early in the morning; they had both gone to the place du Carrousel and had fought with the Marseillais. His friend had even been wounded. "I was boiling with rage," Sade added, "that the tyrant and his vile wife did not suffer punishment for their crime on the spot."[15] It is difficult to ascribe any credibility to this belated testimony, given while the marquis was in prison and threatened with execution. It is contradicted, moreover, by his emotion on learning of the tragic end of his cousin Stanislas.

Clermont-Tonnerre was a ready-made target for the antimonarchist mob. Was he not the defender of the monarchy, the champion of the royal veto, the pope's man? He had never ceased to advocate an English-style constitution or to support a suspect king. A friend of Lafayette, Malouet, Montmorin, and Necker, he had defended Besenval and opposed Marat, Brissot, and Robespierre. That was enough to have earned him the mob's hatred. To make matters worse, he was also accused of conspiracy, of hiding arms in his home. He was charged with being an active member of the "Austrian committee" and a traitor to the nation. How could he escape the vengeful patriots?

On August 10, at nine in the morning, an enraged band of armed men invaded his hôtel on rue des Vieilles-Tuileries. Plucked from the arms of Delphine, he was dragged off to the Premonstratensian church at La Croix-Rouge, where the section was in permanent session. When questioned, he denied the charges. The commissaires set him free and ordered him to go into hiding. But the need to explain himself was too great; he wanted to address the mob. At first the crowd applauded him, but threats and hostile shouts soon drowned him out. A cook whom he had dismissed for theft and who happened to be present stirred up the horde against his former master. Stanislas was struck about the head with two blows from a scythe. He fled on shaky legs and managed to reach the home of his friend, Mme de Brassac, at the Abbaye-aux-

Bois near the head of the rue du Bac. His pursuers chased him up to the fifth floor, grabbed him, and threw him out the window. His body crashed to the pavement. The frenzied mob then threw itself on the corpse, mutilated it, disfigured it, and dragged it back to his hôtel. At the sight of the still quivering body, Delphine fainted. Stanislas de Clermont-Tonnerre was not yet thirty-five years old.

Two weeks later, Donatien, still shaken by the event, wrote Gaufridy: "The events of the tenth have robbed me of everything: relatives, friends, protection, aid; three hours devastated everything in my vicinity. I am alone!"[16]

Ten years later, thinking back on that tragic day, Sade could not help reflecting on the massacres of Saint Bartholomew: "De Thou, in his fifty-second book, reports that, on the day after Saint Bartholomew's, the women of the court of Catherine de Médicis came out of the Louvre to contemplate the naked bodies of the Huguenots murdered and stripped beside its walls. On the Tenth of August the women of Paris likewise came to contemplate the bodies of the Swiss strewn about the Tuileries."[17]

A Mystification

Nothing would ever again be as it had been before. Donatien knew it. He would now have to provide real proof of *civisme* and attempt to hoodwink the ruling authorities if he did not wish to end up like poor Stanislas. His allegiance to the new regime would be all the more ardent because he had committed various imprudent acts for which he would now need to earn a pardon. They were not much to speak of, really, but in present circumstances the life of a *ci-devant* hung by a thread. His first mistake was to have joined the Sociéte des Amis de la Constitution Monarchique. His second was more serious: he had asked for places for himself and his sons in the king's constitutional guard. That was back in 1791. At the time, the duc de Cossé-Brissac, who commanded the regiment, had wanted no part of him, partly because of his bad reputation, no doubt, but also because he had "too many grounds for grievance against the king." Nevertheless, his name still figured on the list of candidates.[18] But what tormented him most was his sons' emigration, which, if it became known, would subject him to the law's wrath. The authorities had to be thrown off the trail and misled by means of concrete, irrefutable documents: words and appearances no longer sufficed. Since he could not deny the facts, he hoped at least to disapprove of them publicly and thus avoid responsibility. An idea came to him. Why not fabricate documents attesting to his good faith. He therefore wrote three letters, dated August 17 and 18, 1792, and addressed, respectively, to the président de Montreuil, Renée-Pélagie, and his children. In the first he roundly criticized his father-in-law for having forced Louis-Marie and Claude-Armand to emigrate. He thus killed two birds with one stone, seizing the opportunity to strike yet another blow at the *"clique montreuillique."* It is not difficult to imagine the pleasure he took in writing these lines: "Was it to prove your *high nobility* that you wanted your children, your nephews, to join the ranks of the *nobles*? I, sir, never having suffered from this risible folly, never wished for anything in mine other than patriotism and good faith. By emigrating they failed on both counts, and, more than that, they failed me, who always strongly opposed their action, and in the presence of witnesses known to you. For your ambitious other half, Madame de Montreuil, nothing could be simpler than to sacrifice everything and betray everything in an attempt to revive the foul bones of disgusting robinocracy and the pestilential claws of ministers with lettres de cachet."

What pleasant sophistry! To denounce the aristocratic pretensions of the Montreuils, our apprentice sans-culotte used the language of the *grand seigneur.*

To the marquise he repeated his threats and added a new one: "Make them come back, Madame, make them come back and embrace their father's cause. I am a citizen and patriot and always have been . . . If, in a word, they are not back within two weeks, I warn you, Madame, that I shall disinherit them."

The third letter was addressed to his sons, to admonish them for their behavior and summon them to obey or risk their father's curse: "My children, you know that I was always critical of your decision, which you took at the instigation of your mother's family . . . I warn you, moreover, that I am doing my service in my section, that circumstances may place us opposite one another, and that it is not right to take arms against your father."

Of course these letters were never sent to their addressees. In any case they were intended not for their nominal recipients but for any investigators who might be charged with looking into what had become of the children. The protestations of patriotism, the repeated attacks on despotism, the insulting criticism of Louis XVI, and even the edifying tone of the letters all were intended to lend credence to the image of a man utterly and sincerely committed to the new powers.

Dies Irae

In the aftermath of August 10, the revolutionary movement picked up steam. The myth of a vast aristocratic plot abetted by foreign powers revived ancient terrors. Fears of betrayal spread through the capital, and panic, as always, led to repression. The Commune was the first to adopt terroristic policies that in many respects prefigured the Terror of 1793. Under pressure from the sans-culottes the moribund Assembly passed one coercive measure after another: punishment of the "guilty" was the order of the day.

Toward the end of the month alarming rumors further heightened tensions. News of the defeat of French forces at Longwy reached Paris on August 26. On September 2 Verdun capitulated: the road to the capital was open. It was then that Danton, who embodied the unity of the revolutionary forces, climbed to the podium of the Assembly and with his powerful voice issued the famous appeal: "All yearn, all quiver, all burn for combat . . . The tocsin that is about to sound is not a signal of alarm, it is a trumpet call to attack the enemies of the *patrie*. To defeat them, gentlemen, we need audacity, still more audacity, audacity always, and France is saved."

Two hours after this speech, on the afternoon of Sunday, September 2, while the tocsin sounded and the alarm cannon called Parisians to join their units on the Champ-de-Mars, wagonloads of priests headed for deportation were halted and taken to the Abbaye and the Carmelite convent. The ignoble carnage began at once. Some fifty assassins—artisans, cobblers, café keepers, vinegar makers, cartwrights, and locksmiths, joined by *fédérés* from Marseilles and Brittany—conducted a parody of a popular tribunal and then bludgeoned the "condemned" prisoners to death with sabers and pikes. In two hours, 115 priests were massacred in an immense bloodbath. Most were poor country priests who had come to Paris in search of refuge.

Sinister rumors had been circulating since August 25. Everywhere people were saying that the traitors locked up in the prisons of Paris were continuing to plot against the Revolution and that royalists were coming to free and arm all the prisoners, including common criminals, and set them against the patriots. The masses were gripped by panic. Men refused to leave for the front before purging their city of the nation's enemies. The press named "conspirators" and whipped up hostility against them. Marat and above all Fréron exhorted the sans-culottes to carry out summary executions: "The prisons are bursting

with scoundrels," the latter wrote in *L'Orateur du peuple*. "It is urgent
that society be delivered from them at once." On September 3, at the
Abbaye, the princesse de Lamballe fell afoul of the executioners. One
of them stabbed her in the stomach, ripped open her clothing, and
sliced off her breasts and vulva, to the great amusement of the patriots,
who shouted: "The whore! Nobody will go poking her now!"[19] After
cutting off her head and forcing a wigmaker to curl her long tresses,
the mob mounted its trophy on the end of a pike and displayed it
outside Marie-Antoinette's windows at the Temple. The mass "executions" proceeded without letup until September 6. In all the prisons
of Paris, bloodthirsty assassins indulged in the worst excesses: in Saint-
Firmin, the Châtelet, La Force, the Salpêtrière, the Bernardins. More
than 1,200 victims, including women and children, may have died
during the tragic days of the so-called September Massacres.

Immediately afterward, Donatien penned these lines, intended for
Gaufridy: "Ten thousand prisoners perished in the events of September
3. There is nothing to equal the horror of the massacres that were
committed. The *ci-devant* princesse de Lamballe numbered among the
victims. Her head on a pike was offered up to the eyes of the king and
queen, and her unfortunate corpse was dragged through the streets for
eight hours after having been subjected to the filthy indignities of the
most outrageous debauch. All the refractory priests had their throats
cut in the churches where they were being held, among them the
archbishop of Arles, the most virtuous and respectable of men. The
[customs] barriers and theaters are closed, the city is illuminated every
night, and Verdun, I am assured, has been taken."[20]

But as he was about to seal this letter, Donatien changed his mind:
did it not betray too much pity for the victims and too much disgust
at their executioners? If it were to fall into the wrong hands, might it
not give him away? So he folded the sheet and wrote, between the
lines, after "there is nothing to equal the horror of the massacres," the
words, "*but they were just.*" This insert tells us more about his true
sentiments than all his political speeches combined.

"Death in my heart"

The murderous madness spread like wildfire from the capital to the
provinces. The threat of an enemy invasion and the news from Paris
sowed terror throughout the region. With a week's delay the countryside reacted in its turn to the events of August and September. The

peasant insurrection took the form of violent actions against landlords' property: châteaux were sacked and burned, crops laid waste, and sabotage of all sorts was committed. Once again there were bloody riots in the Apt region. The troops charged with smashing counter-revolutionary plots arrested the princes' agent, Monier de La Quarrée, and dismantled his network in the southeast. The monarchist conspirators took flight. Gaufridy, after wandering about the countryside for a time, sought refuge again in Lyons along with his son Elzéar and a dozen other suspects, including his colleague Fage. The marquis, who soon learned of the notary's whereabouts, advised him against remaining in Lyons. To be sure, it offered a safe asylum for the time being, but if the Sardinians turned against France, as was to be feared, the capital of the Gauls would surely suffer. Why the devil not come to Paris? There, at least, Gaufridy's old friend could assure his security: "I am going to speak to you as a friend, and a friend who is offering you everything he can and not what he cannot," he wrote on September 13. "And I am sure that this language is what an honest friend like you wants to hear. I am offering you a bedroom in my home large enough for two beds. Thus, you and your son can sleep there. The room is furnished but has no bed. I will rent you the two beds at a very good price. I shall supply your heat and light. I shall feed you, *you*, and your son may board in the same house for sixty francs per month, which would put your total expenses at roughly eighty to ninety francs per month. I am quite sure it is costing you more in Lyons. Your return will not cost you anything. You will wait for me, and we shall leave together in April."[21] In the same letter he begged his correspondent to stop using various formulas of politeness and to refrain from signing altogether: it was impossible to be too prudent. To be sure, the invitation seems generous, especially in view of the "little household's" meager budget and the risks entailed, but Donatien surely owed that much to his old servant. Gaufridy's zealous service of the *ci-devant* nobleman was part of the reason for his difficulties, as Reinaud would reveal somewhat later: "The devotion he brought to your affairs played no small part in this retreat. He had had frequent visits, sometimes from one side, sometimes from the other, and the incursions into Apt had made him apprehensive about more unpleasant things to come."[22] The notary had even received secret warnings that he ought to drop his client.

Meanwhile, before leaving home, Gaufridy had taken pains to alert the district administrators, who on September 7 warned the municipality of La Coste that there might be serious disturbances. The administrators asked the municipal authorities to "take care that the home of Sieur Sade, who has not emigrated, is not violated."[23]

•

A few days later, at the home of a tavern keeper in the nearby town of Lauris on the banks of the Durance, a villager loudly mocked those "poltroonish Costains" for lacking the courage to attack their former lord's château. In Lauris it was the mayor himself who had given the signal for the attack by hurling the first stones. What were these fools waiting for? Spurred on by the mockery of their companions, the Costains, aided by a few residents of Lauris, decided to strike. On Sunday, September 16, rumors of an impending offensive circulated in the streets of the village. Some said it was scheduled for the following day. As if by chance, Mayor Sambuc chose precisely that night to go to the Bonnieux fair, and the château's caretaker moved out.

The action was to be led by two professional "agitators." One, Ange Raspail, a former pastry maker from Apt and member of that city's people's commission, was locally regarded as an eloquent orator. He was addressed as *commissaire* and never went anywhere without his megaphone. That very morning, he and his companion François Roux had led an attack on the château de Beaureport, the residence of the émigré Saporta. But the Costains' haste thwarted their plan.

The next day, Monday, September 17, at around ten in the morning, several dozen attackers (witnesses put the number at around eighty)—men, women, and children armed with clubs and pikes—burst into the forecourt and court of the château. The national guard, summoned immediately, soon arrived on the scene, but the troops' orders to disperse were greeted with insults and threats. The mob broke down doors and poured into the interior apartments. All the rooms were pillaged and vandalized. The heaviest furniture was thrown out the window. Whatever could not be carried away was smashed to pieces. Windows were shattered, partitions were knocked down, wall paneling and parquet floors were pried loose, and doors were smashed against the surrounding cliffs. The cellars were searched, and the best bottles, consumed on the spot, further warmed the passions of the mob. Some tried to demolish the dovecote. Within an hour the château had been virtually emptied of its contents and strewn with debris.

When Raspail and Roux arrived on the scene a good hour later, they managed to calm some of the hotter heads. A sign of the times: the commune made the leader of the brigands responsible for restoring order and returning the stolen objects. Imbued with a sense of his own importance, Raspail assembled the vandals, gave them a tongue-lashing, reminded them that the property of the former nobleman belonged to the nation, and ordered them to bring what they had taken to the presbytery.

The real reasons for the attack on the château remain mysterious. The challenge thrown down by the men in Lauris may have triggered the event but cannot explain it. According to the faithful Reinaud, the people of La Coste were merely following the example of their neighbors, but he does not rule out personal vengeance as a motive: "The reason for the attack was none other than a mania that had gripped people in several places, the gist of which was the need to destroy dominating fortified castles. They began with the one in Lauris, which is next door. Châteaux in La Tour-d'Aigues and other places met the same fate. There may be something personal in it, what I do not know."[24] Paulet, an officer of the commune and an agent of Sade's, threw all responsibility onto "a few disreputable types from Lauris."[25] Citizen Sade could not be suspected of counterrevolutionary sentiments: his patriotic writings and sectional responsibilities (he had just been named secretary) were well known in the region. What then? Some maintained that hoarders had stored grain in the château, thereby earning the wrath of the peasants. A finger of suspicion was even pointed at Gaufridy. But Reinaud had no difficulty demonstrating that the rumors were false and allaying any doubts the marquis might have had about his agent.[26]

The destruction of La Coste left the marquis feeling sick at heart. "What a loss! It is beyond words. There was enough in the château to furnish six like it! . . . I am in despair . . . Adieu, adieu! I have death in my heart!"[27]

22

The Patriotic Farce

From the time they were created in June 1790, the forty-eight sections of Paris played an ever more important part in the nation's affairs. Going beyond their municipal competence, they intervened in political life in a variety of ways and on issues ranging farther and farther afield from their nominal responsibilities. By November 1790 *Le Moniteur* was so disturbed by this development that it characterized the actions of the sections as "undisciplined." Finally, the National Assembly decided to take steps to prevent a violent minority from imposing its will on the sections. The decree of May 18–22, 1791, laid down rules governing when the sections could meet and restricted their deliberation to matters of municipal administration. The goal was to avoid any conflict of authority with the central government. But the sections refused to abide by the law and insisted on their right to meet freely. Under pressure from the sans-culottes, further heightened by the threat of foreign invasion, the Legislative Assembly finally gave in: on July 24, 1792, it granted the sections authority to sit in permanent session. This did not mean meeting day and night without adjourning. Except in unusual circumstances sessions began at five or six in the evening and ended around eleven, with the agenda being set by the members present.

Another innovation was that when the Assembly decided to make meetings of administrative bodies public as of July 1, 1792, the sections set up podiums in the rooms where these bodies met. Soon bands of agitators were forcing their way in, taking part in debates, and disrupting the proceedings. The result was not hard to predict: frightened moderates abandoned the floor to the extremists.

Though lacking a political program, the sections formulated clear demands. On August 3, 1792, they demanded before the Assembly that the sovereign, "the first link in the counterrevolutionary chain," be deposed and that a "Convention" be convoked.

•

At its inception the Section de la Place Vendôme counted some 1,200 active citizens of the Vendôme-Madeleine district among its members and held its meetings in what had been the Church of the Capuchins, which no longer exists.[1] Initially considered to be one of the most moderate sections in Paris, it was subject to the same evolution as the other sections in 1791 and 1792. Infiltrated by sans-culottes, it was taken over by its most subversive elements and radicalized to the point where it became one of the capital's "reddest" bastions. Robespierre was a member. He was one of the five commissars from the section who joined the Commune's general council on August 10. Another of its members was the notorious François-Nicolas Vincent, known as the "carnivore," an incorrigible *enragé* whose excesses got him arrested along with his equally fanatical friend Ronsin. His signature appears on the residence certificates of Mme de Sade and her daughter.

In September 1792, the place Vendôme was renamed the place des Piques, and the section took on the much more threatening name Section des Piques.

The Sans-Culotte Marquis

Despite—or rather because of—his origins, Sade did not yield the terrain to the partisans of violence but struck a bargain with them. What else could he do? If he withdrew from the section now, he would be accused of having betrayed the people. Not only did he have to stay at his post, come what may, but he knew that he would be obliged to adopt ever more radical positions, because being a *ci-devant* automatically led to his being suspected of *incivisme*. Well might he change his first name, drop his particule, and swear he had never been a noble: no one in his section was fooled. When his good faith was questioned, he pointed to his detention in the Bastille: "Here it is a great honor to have been there. You boast of it, you publish it, and it wins you a kind of respect," he confided to Gaufridy. He loudly proclaimed that he had been a victim of the "tyrant," endlessly recounted his exploit of July 2, 1789, renounced his past, his ancestors, and his children, and multiplied proofs of his republican faith.

Thus far, it is true, Louis Sade had conducted himself as an ideal citizen: a frequent presence at general meetings, attentive, disciplined, careful to take his turn at guard, diligent in carrying out missions entrusted to him, he had yet to slip up. But this was no longer enough. With the rise of the Terror and the onslaught of the sans-culottes, clouds had begun to gather in the sections. Debates were so politicized that there was no longer room for mirth, caution, or indifference. Merely to refuse to serve in public office could be taken as a counter-revolutionary act and might lead to prison or even the guillotine. If he hoped to survive, Sade would have to abandon his neutrality and howl with the wolves. In short, the time had come to act. He was caught up in an implacable mechanism; the die was cast. This was no easy task for a man like him, little given to compromise and thoroughly unfamiliar with popular militancy. Everything set him apart from the typical sans-culotte: his birth, his fortune, his manner—that goes without saying. But above all his manner of thinking. Nothing was more contrary to his nature than the egalitarian and collectivist ideology. Nothing was more repugnant to him than "equality of pleasure," contempt for culture, and legal terrorism. But what aroused his greatest antipathy, what seemed most absurd to him, was the moralism of the common man. The sans-culotte was virtuous: to the militant mind, a disorderly private life was incompatible with an honest public life. One petition demanded that "public prostitutes be held in national houses, where the air should be salubrious, and given work appropriate to their sex." Another called for a law against gambling dens and bordellos. "In order to be a respectable man," the French Republican explained to the citizen of Philadelphia, "one must be a good son, good husband, and good father; in other words, one must combine all the public and private virtues . . . Therein lies the true definition of the word patriotism."[2] The sans-culotte hated the noble not so much because of his birth or his fortune as because of his corrupt morals.

So many loathings to overcome, so many impulses to dominate! Yet Sade was successful. What sacrifices did he have to make? He does not say, but we can easily imagine them. His task was nothing less than to annihilate his own personality, so great was the distance between these lamentable prejudices and the Sadeian idea of insurrection. "Something of Sade belongs to the Terror, as something of the Terror belongs to Sade," Blanchot wrote. This is true. But what did the everyday terror enforced by the sans-culottes have in common with the splendor of Sadeian terror? What did it have to do with the fresh lucidity that springs from reading Sade? With that alliance of clarity and obscurity that troubles us? With those excesses that blind us to the point of making us doubt ourselves? With that *energy*, finally, that "is not force," according to Saint-Just, and without which Sade believed happiness was impossible?

Sade had always dreamed of a regime without law. "The reign of laws is vicious," he wrote in the *Histoire de Juliette*. "It is inferior to that of anarchy. The best proof of what I am arguing is the obligation of the government itself to plunge into anarchy when it wants to remake the constitution. To abrogate its ancient laws it is obliged to establish a revolutionary regime in which there are no laws: from this regime new laws are born in the end, but this second State is necessarily less pure than the first, since it derives from it, since it was necessary to effect this first good, *anarchy*, in order to arrive at the second good, the *constitution of the State*."[3] And this: "It is the multitude of laws that creates the multitude of crimes. Cease to believe that this or that action is criminal. Make no law to repress it, and it is certain that the multitude of your crimes will disappear."[4] And further: "Let us convince ourselves of this once and for all: laws are simply useless or dangerous. Their only purpose is to multiply crimes or to ensure that they are committed in security, owing to the secrecy they impose. Without laws and religion, one cannot imagine the degree of glory and grandeur that human knowledge might have achieved today. It is extraordinary how those odious obstacles have retarded progress."[5] For Sade, therefore, *revolution* ought to mean that pure moment when man's development remains suspended between old and new laws, when the individual attains his true sovereignty, when "being is nothing but the movement of the infinite that suppresses itself and is constantly born of its disappearance" (Blanchot). In the silence of the laws man's only truth appears, to wit, his infinite power of negation, and with it the joyous frenzy of outrage. This is the time—the virtual time of dissolution—that Sade invokes in the name of Insurrection. In place of which the only spectacle reality had to offer was a cold Terror, a petty bureaucracy, and the only orgy the coarse lyricism of the sansculottes. No, the truth is that it was not Sade who outwitted the Revolution, but the Revolution that betrayed Sade.

The Republican Stage

Aware of the fragility of the situation, Donatien energetically threw himself into the popular cause and placed at the service of the nation his only generally recognized skill, namely, his talent as a man of letters. Literary talents are not legion, and Donatien's comrades were glad to have one at hand. Fortunately his licentious works were un-known to the sans-culottes, whose moral sensibilities would have been shocked. All that fellow section members knew about was his perfectly acceptable work as a dramatic author.

Trading the pleasures of libertine narrative for the austerity of the administrative style, Sade began modestly on October 28, 1792, with a report on the hospitals of Paris, which earned him the congratulations of his colleagues. They were so happy, in fact, that they decided to print his "Observations" and send them to the other forty-seven sections.[6]

A few days later, on November 2, his "Idea on the Law's Mode of Sanction" received a similar welcome. The section unanimously voted to have the work printed and sent to the other sections, with an invitation to "express their wishes as soon as possible on this important subject."[7] Gilbert Lely considered this the most substantial and original of Sade's political pamphlets. "A powerful love of liberty radiates from every paragraph," he observes.[8] What was the work about?

After the overthrow of the monarchy on August 10, a new con-stitution was needed. Sade therefore proposed a version of direct de-mocracy in which sovereignty would effectively be exercised by the entire nation and not merely by its representatives. The influence of Rousseau's *Social Contract*, whose political ideas were just beginning to be picked up by the petite and moyenne bourgeoisie, is apparent. Nevertheless, in Sade's version of direct democracy, the collectivity of citizens had only the power to "sanction" the laws, that is, the right to accept or reject them; the power to formulate and promulgate laws remained the prerogative of the nation's deputies.

Curiously enough, Sade's text invoked the principle of monocam-eralism ("sovereignty is ONE, INDIVISIBLE, INALIENABLE"), where-as only a year earlier he had professed his profound attachment to English-style bicameralism. But there is nothing surprising about such a change of heart, nor about his vibrant (and misleading) reminder of his fidelity to the revolutionary ideal: "I love the people; my works prove that I established the present system before the cannon that brought down the Bastille heralded its coming." We have already seen how, prior to 1789, the marquis de Sade characterized the people for whom he now manifested such solicitude. He ended with this lyrical flourish: "The happiest day of my life was the day I believed I witnessed the rebirth of the sweet equality of the golden age, the day I saw the beneficent limbs of the tree of liberty festooned with the debris of throne and scepter." It is hard to know which to admire more, his effrontery or his humor.

Our hero plainly found his (quite successful) pastiche amusing and was pleased with his imposture: "Do you know that I now enjoy great credit in my section," he exulted to Gaufridy. "Not a day goes by without my services being employed. The brief text enclosed herewith, which was much appreciated, gives proof of this.[9] I have also been appointed to serve on the section's hospital committee. There are ninety-six of us. Everything is to be redone, and I assure you that our task is a very difficult one. We must study, work, compile. I have scarcely an hour to myself." He ended with a brief lesson in patriotic conduct:

You can prepare a brief memorandum in my name and send it, provided you do not end with these words: "So they even look upon you as a citizen." This aristocratic phrase would land any man who uttered it here on the gallows. One sees clearly, gentlemen of the *départements*, that you are not yet EQUAL TO the Revolution.

Otherwise, my hope that you will soon return to Provence means that I will not write to anyone until I have heard from you. I can well imagine that the agents of *seigneurs* have come in for trouble, but I do not expect to hear that you have been bothered on my account, since my role has never been in doubt, my patriotism, proven during ten years in the Bastille, can never be questioned, and it is, in a word, certain that I have no further aristocratic pretensions and am up to my neck in the Revolution, heart and mind.[10]

The ruse is transparent: the republican peroration was included only to deceive the enemy in case the note should fall into the wrong hands. "You must be prudent in your letters, and never did despotism unseal as many as liberty is opening now," the marquis observed in 1790.[11] He spoke as an expert, for this was a little game he played many times. After gaining influence within his section, for example, he did not hesitate to open mail addressed to Mme de Montreuil. When Reinaud realized what was happening because of a "lost" letter to la Présidente, he alerted her at once: "I believe I have proof of what was until now only a suspicion . . . Our correspondence is being intercepted, you can be sure of it. I do not accuse the post; I believe it to be loyal, but I cast my eyes on M. Edas [an anagram for Sade that Reinaud regularly used to refer to the marquis], who is in your section, and I do not think I am mistaken. Or, if I am, I do not err without reason."[12] Sade was not a man to shrink from such indelicacy, and there is every reason to believe that there were other victims besides Mme de Montreuil.

•

Once he became an actor performing his own life, the marquis was condemned to repeat the comedy of his political commitment without letup. He was marvelous in the part: no one suspected him, and, as can be sensed from the tone of his letter, it filled him with joy. The Revolution, which had shut down the work of playwright Sade when the sans-culottes in their red caps halted the performance of *Le Suborneur* on March 5, 1792, now thrust the actor onto the republican stage in a tailor-made role.[13]

But the best farce, as even Sade agreed, was his appointment to serve on an investigating jury (*juré d'accusation*). On April 8, 1793, in an astounding turnabout, his name appeared on a list of twenty citizens of his section appointed to a special jury to investigate a case of counterfeit assignats. The one-time criminal had become a judge. This new mask enchanted him: "You'll never guess! . . . I am a *judge*, yes, a *judge*! . . . Member of an investigating jury! Who would have predicted that? . . . As you see, my mind is maturing, and I am beginning to acquire wisdom . . . But congratulate me, and above all do not fail to send money to *monsieur le juge*, or I'll be damned if I don't *sentence you to death*! Spread the news around at home, so that at last they come to recognize me as a good patriot, for I swear to you I truly am, heart and soul."[14]

Two months later, on June 16, his section entrusted him with an official mission: he was to appear before the Convention to read an address he had written. On behalf of his comrades he called for repeal of the decree that established a revolutionary army of the interior in Paris, consisting of six thousand men to be paid forty sols per day each. This decree had been passed in the wake of the popular uprisings of May 31 and June 2, which had led to the fall of the Girondins, swept the Montagnards into power, and triggered the federalist movement, characterized by some as "counterrevolutionary." At a time when war was raging in the Vendée and the struggle with the coalition of monarchies was intensifying, this latest uprising added to the threats hanging over the Republic. Denounced by Sade as impolitic, unjust, and dangerous, the decree, he argued, threatened to create a Pretorian guard in Paris that an ambitious usurper might one day turn to his advantage. The author of the petition also suggested various reforms pertaining to the organization of the army. Taking a modern view of national defense, he proposed replacing both the professional army

and the practice of hiring mercenaries with an army of citizen con-
scripts: "Only the citizen of Paris has the right to defend his city," he
proclaimed. "And the city that can raise an army of a hundred and
fifty thousand men at the first beat of the drum has no need to pay
mercenaries who, for the very reason that they are paid, are unworthy
to defend it."[15]

"That is how I avenge myself"

The previous year, after a search that the law permitted in homes of
suspect individuals, the Montreuil residence on rue de la Madeleine
had been sealed. The owners had been away at the time. When they
returned, they asked that the seals be removed. "Now, since they live
in my section," Donatien reported, "I am about to be named commissar
in charge of overseeing the removal of seals, and I assure you that if
I find any trace of aristocracy, as I do not doubt I shall, I will not spare
them." But he immediately added: "Did you have a good laugh,
lawyer?"[16] He was joking of course.

On the evening of April 6, 1793, the aged président de Montreuil
came in person, without warning, to see his son-in-law at the Section
des Piques. No doubt he came at the behest of his wife, who wanted
to sound out Donatien's intentions and solicit his help in case things
took a turn for the worse. The past month had seen the establishment
of the Committees of Surveillance and the Revolutionary Tribunal.
The witch-hunt was on: aristocrats, relatives of émigrés, refractory
priests, and, more generally, anyone with any reason to be hostile to
the faction in power were subject to indiscriminate arrest. The Montreuils felt threatened. In a panic they desperately sought support wherever they could find it. At that point their thoughts turned to the
disgraced son-in-law whom they had once had thrown in prison but
who now exercised important responsibilities within their section. They
would find him, argue that it was a matter of saving the grandparents
of his own children, and hope to convince him that in the tragic circumstances old bitterness ought to be laid to rest. If need be, they
would invoke class solidarity, the *union sacrée*. After all, were they not
all slaves in the same galley, facing the same taskmasters? If they had
to humiliate themselves in front of Donatien, so be it. Between shame
and the guillotine the choice was clear.

La Présidente had presumably been prepared to sacrifice herself.
Was she not the true head of the family? At bottom she might even
have found a mission like this one rather to her taste; it was certainly

in her style. Mme de Montreuil never felt so comfortable as in adversity. She gave unstintingly of her energy and courage. The vanquished queen throwing herself at the feet of her adversary: she would have been perfect in the part! One can imagine the scene. She would have played it with a dolorous grandeur that would have produced the most striking effect. But would Donatien have been moved? Perhaps not. Given the doubt, it was better to send her husband. Conciliatory and amiable, with no real personality of his own, the old président had never clashed directly with Donatien. So the mission fell to him.

And so, the unexpected visit. The two men had not seen each other for fifteen years, and it is not difficult to imagine the embarrassment on both sides. After all that had happened, Sade certainly did not lack good reasons to show the old duffer the door. Given his impetuous character, we may even wager that he burned with the desire to do just that. The old man was there, in front of him, "in his sights." For once he—the outlaw, the black sheep of the family—was in a position of strength. So what happened? Did he become terrified? Did he imagine he was looking at the Commendatore's statue? He received his father-in-law with deference and chatted with him for an hour, like two old friends happy to see each other again. Did they discuss the past? Did Sade repent? Did Montreuil concede his wife's wrongs? We will never know. "It went as pleasantly as could be," Donatien recounted that same night. "I expected him at any moment to invite me to come visit him."[17] One can scarcely believe one's eyes. Less than a month earlier, on March 13, to be exact, Mme de Sade had severely dressed him down for his repeated attacks on her parents: "Sir, I have already been pleased to inform you that, since you do not pay me what you owe, it was impossible for me to pay anything on your account. *In regard to my family, it has nothing to do with your affairs. And if you attack it, it will always respond with the truth, as we* [sic] *have always done.*"[18]

•

Shortly after the September massacres, at the very moment the patriots were sacking the château at La Coste, Sade was appointed secretary of his section for the first time. Less than a year later, on July 23, 1793, he became its president. No more walk-on parts for Sade: he was now moving into the leading roles. Still, the importance of a sectional presidency should not be exaggerated. The presidency rotated on a weekly, sometimes a daily, basis. So, even though Sade ironically remarked to Gaufridy that he had been "promoted again—now I am president of my section," it was not, strictly speaking, a promotion but rather a mark of confidence or of gratitude for services rendered.

On August 1 the citizen-president performed his inaugural function, informing the inhabitants of the section of the wishes of the département of Paris in regard to the festival that was to be held in honor of the new constitution. Landlords and principal tenants were required to paint the following words on the facades of their buildings: Unity—Indivisibility of the Republic—Liberty—Equality—Fraternity —or Death; in addition, they were asked to fly a tricolor banner topped by a liberty bonnet on their building's roof.

The next day, an incident during a section meeting forced Sade to resign his post. What happened? Wearing a red cap, as sectional etiquette required, he was presiding over the general assembly when a sudden attack forced him to step down from the podium. "I am devastated, exhausted, I am spitting blood. I told you that I was president of my section. My meeting was so stormy that I could no longer bear it. Yesterday, among other things, after twice being obliged to withdraw, I was forced to give up my chair to my vice-president. They wanted me to put a horrible, inhumane measure to a vote. I did not wish to do so. Thank God, now I'm out of it."[19]

What "horrible, inhumane" measure was he talking about? The Terror was raging, "horror" was everywhere: one has an embarrassment of riches to choose from. The night before, the Convention had passed a decree ordering that the sepulchres of the kings of France at Saint-Denis be opened on the first anniversary of the fall of the monarchy (August 10, 1793). At the same session the deputies ordered the destruction of the Vendée and the transfer of Marie-Antoinette to the Conciergerie, where she was to be held pending her appearance before the Revolutionary Tribunal. Was the Section des Piques asked to support these measures? Or was it a matter of approving the execution of a "suspect"? This time, Donatien had cracked under the pressure; his nerves gave out. He was capable of swallowing any number of patriotic pills, so long as it was a matter only of giving his word or committing something to paper. The game rather amused him, because he liked masks. But the spectacle, the very idea of the guillotine caused him to vomit with disgust. Among the many paradoxical things about the author of the *Cent Vingt Journées de Sodome*, not the least was his quivering fright in the face of acts that he described so complacently in his writing. The Tenth of August and the September massacres had revolted him. But what he was now being asked to do was beyond his strength. If "murder for pleasure" appealed to him because it gratified the imagination, institutional murder disgusted him because it was nothing more than the odious expression of abstract principles. "The guillotine," he would write to Gaufridy on January 21, 1795 (two years to the day after the execution of Louis XVI), "*the guillotine before my eyes* has caused me a hundred times more pain than all the bastilles imaginable ever did."[20] As Jean Paulhan remarked, "the true sadist is perhaps the one who rejects the easy alternative of sadism and who cannot admit that no one is asking him to act out his mania."[21]

During the same memorable August 2 meeting of his section, he saved the lives of his wife's parents by having their names placed on a "purification list." Perhaps that was the reason for his illness. "If I had said a word, they would have been treated severely. I kept quiet: that is how I avenge myself."[22]

One would have to mistake our man quite badly to be astonished by this gesture. To be sure, no one was ever more vindictive, violent, or cynical than he. But no one has ever caught him in an act of cowardice either. He was not a man to strike his enemy when he was down. Convinced that there was such a thing as an ethics of blood, he would have judged such an act as unworthy of a gentleman, especially if directed against *robinocrates* like the Montreuils, for whom he felt nothing but contempt. Transferring his superiority of birth to his superiority of the moment, which he owed to his position as section president, he inflicted on the Montreuils the cruelest possible vengeance by saving them from death. Was this an act of admirable clemency or supreme disdain? Here we would do well to recall what he wrote to Gaufridy a year earlier: "The Montreuils are my greatest enemies. They are also acknowledged scoundrels, criminals whom I could ruin with a word if I chose. But I take pity on them. I pay them back with contempt and indifference for all the harm they have done me." Another, perhaps an even more important, reason for his action may have been that his horror of the scaffold got the better of his resentment.

•

On May 30, 1794, the président and Mme de Montreuil, now deprived of all political support, were imprisoned as parents of émigrés. Both were liberated when the Terror was overthrown on the Ninth of Thermidor, but the président died in Paris six months later, on January 15, 1795, in his eightieth year.

The "Martyrs of Liberty"

The incident of August 2 appears to have been quickly forgotten. In any case, it did not prevent Sade from submitting for his colleagues' approval one month later (on September 29, 1793) a "Discourse to the Shades of Marat and Le Peletier," which he had written especially for a ceremony being organized in honor of the two "martyrs of liberty." The general assembly, "applauding the principles and the energy of this discourse," voted to have it printed and sent to the National Convention, all the départements, the armies, the constituted municipal authorities of Paris, the forty-seven other sections, and various popular societies.

The ceremony honoring Marat and Le Peletier took place on Wednesday, October 9. After a lengthy procession marked by speeches at a number of locations along the way, Citizen Sade slowly climbed the stairs leading to a platform in the place des Piques (the ci-devant place Vendôme), where he took up a position between busts of the two heroes, which had been borne ceremoniously in the procession and placed there on display. Looming above vapors of incense that shimmered all around him, imposing, ponderous, his plump face bearing the stamp of gravity, Donatien de Sade recited his homily. His voice resounded in religious silence: "Citizens. The most cherished duty of truly republican hearts is the recognition due to great men."[23]

Lely's verdict is clear: "This is Sade's most disappointing political text." In any case, it is not the most eloquent. With an untroubled conscience (though possibly not without humor) Sade rose to new heights of bombast, his patriotic lyricism inflated to the point of caricature: "Marat! Le Peletier! . . . The voices of centuries to come will only add to the homages that the generation now in bloom is paying you today. Sublime martyrs of liberty, already installed in the Temple of Memory," et cetera.

The author of the Cent Vingt Journées de Sodome could not have uttered such inept lines without a dark and icy snicker (to himself of course). No one was better than Sade at concealing mockery in order to savor it in solitude. We can imagine his secret delight at seeing his pastiche acclaimed. What foolishness! And what revenge for the playwright whose work had been hooted off the stage to hear applause break out among the people crowded together on the vast stage of the place Vendôme.

Passing from the "victim" (as he termed Marat, the bloody vampire of the Terror) to his "executioner," Sade failed to shake the lead from his tongue. The subject was one that might have inspired him, though. A woman proud of her crime: there was material in that to feed the fantasies of the creator of Juliette. But, troubled perhaps by the image of a maiden carrying the murder weapon in her bosom, he could do no more than align his periods in perfect imitation of the sans-culotte style: "Timid and gentle sex, how can it be that hands so delicate gripped the dagger sharpened by seduction? . . . The barbarous murderer of Marat, like those mixed creatures of uncertain sex vomited up by the infernos to dispirit the male and female sex alike, directly belongs to neither one. May her memory forever remain shrouded in a funereal veil. Cease, above all, to present her effigy to us, as some dare, beneath the enchanting emblem of beauty. Too credulous artists, smash, reverse, disfigure the traits of this monster, or show her to our outraged eyes only amidst the furies of Tartarus."[24]

Behind this hodgepodge we recognize one of Sade's hobbyhorses, his horror of the androgyne. Unworthy of her sex, Charlotte Corday is relegated to a place among the hermaphroditic monsters.

Meanwhile, another woman was on Sade's mind. A week to the day after his speech, on Wednesday, October 16, 1793, Marie-Antoinette's head fell onto the scaffold. In the solitude of his study he made this entry in his notebook: "WORDS OF ANTOINETTE AT THE CONCIERGERIE: 'The ferocious beasts who surround me every day invent some new humiliation to add to the horror of my fate. Drop by drop they distill in my heart the poison of adversity; they delight in counting my sighs, and while waiting to batten themselves on my blood, they slake their thirst with my tears.' "[25]

Is it necessary to point out that Marie-Antoinette never spoke these words? By placing them in her mouth, Sade was applying them to his own fate. He identified with the humiliated sovereign as she fell beneath the executioner's blade.

•

After the October 9 apotheosis, Donatien was certain that he held his audience and confident, perhaps too confident, of his dramatic genius. He had so thoroughly entered into his character that at times he lost himself in his own game. But what he gained in assurance, he lost in circumspection. Absorbed, impassioned, sometimes amused by the autobiographical drama he was improvising day in and day out, certain details began to escape him. Trivial things to be sure, but in the lion's den the slightest slip could prove very costly. As skillful an actor as he was (and we know his passion for the profession), he occasionally lost control of his nerves. We saw it happen during the meeting of August 2, when he had to step down. Fortunately, the incident was not repeated. Nothing more was said about it in the section, at any rate not in Donatien's presence. But one senses that from that day on he became more vulnerable, at the mercy of a moment's imprudence. Fatigue was no doubt gaining on him, and his ability to concentrate was dwindling. Worst of all, he felt that he was being watched more and more closely. Robespierre exhorted the people to remain supremely vigilant: "Citizens, you will have peace only as long as you keep your eyes open for all treason and your arms raised against all traitors." Beyond the duty of vigilance, there was also a duty to denounce conspiracy and treason. With the Terror spying on one's neighbor became a civic duty, an obligation that could not be shirked by any citizen worthy of the name. Not to denounce a suspect was to subject oneself to charges of treason. The sections were infested with informers who would sell their mothers and fathers for a hundred-sol assignat.

"Let us adore the virtues!"

Although atheism was already openly professed by several members of the Convention and the Paris authorities, notably Chaumette, the Commune's prosecutor, and Hébert, the journalist of *Père Duchesne*, it had yet to be consecrated in public ceremonies. The Convention's commissars in the départements were the first to set the example. Others soon followed.

On November 15, six sections proclaimed before the Convention that, having ripped away the veil of error, they renounced all religions other than the cult of liberty. The Section des Piques was one of the six. In a signal honor, Citizen Sade was named to draft the petition. More than that, it was he who stepped to the rail ahead of the seven other delegates to read the text to the Convention.[26] Did the eight men deck themselves out in the priestly trappings that other delegations had worn on similar missions? It is hard to imagine our man lending himself to such a masquerade. As an uncontested master of transgression, he knew better than anyone that such puerile games could sap its substance. In such mockery there was an implicit acceptance of religion that he could not countenance. Profanation of the sacred conferred meaning on it, something Sade had always denied.

We must therefore try to imagine him in his usual costume, wearing his red cap, speech in hand, moving slowly toward the center of the area reserved for petitioners to the Convention. After adjusting his spectacles and clearing his throat, he began reading amid the hubbub that never ceased in the vicinity of the rostrum. Fortunately, the text was short. After ten minutes, he withdrew, to applause from the audience. The Convention awarded his project "honorable mention" and decided to publish it in the bulletin and send it to the Committee of Public Instruction.

For the first time in his political career he had been able to express some of his firmest convictions. On the subjects of the death of religious superstition and dechristianization, all he had to do was develop long-held ideas. An atheist "to the point of fanaticism," as he liked to describe himself, he simply followed his natural bent. Hence there was nothing at all coerced in his declaration to the representatives of the nation:

The reign of philosophy is at last destroying that of deceit. Man has finally seen the light, and, destroying with one hand the frivolous playthings of an absurd religion, with the other he is erecting an altar to his heart's most cherished deity. Reason is replacing Mary in our temples, and the incense that used to burn at the knees of an adulterous woman will from now on be kindled only at the feet of the goddess who broke our chains . . . The philosopher has long laughed in secret at the apish antics of Catholicism, but if he dared to raise his voice, it was in the dungeons of the Bastille, where ministerial despotism soon learned how to compel its silence. How could tyranny fail to bolster superstition? Both were nurtured in the same cradle, both were daughters of fanaticism, both were served by those useless creatures known as the priest of the temple and the monarch of the throne; having a common foundation, they could not but protect each other.[27]

These lines summarize Sade's position on religion rather well. This was a subject on which he never varied. Atheism was one of the permanent linchpins of his thought. Twenty years earlier, in his *Voyage d'Italie* (1775), he was already mocking piety and fetishism and laughing at "holy tomfoolery" and the "sacred baubles that superstition dares without blushing to offer to the credulity of the weak."

As for his other hobbyhorse, the alliance between the throne and the altar, which he so violently condemns in the "Petition," his attitude in *Aline et Valcour* (1795) is identical, albeit without the oratorical pathos: "Theocratic stringency always bolsters aristocracy. Religion is nothing but the instrument of tyranny. It supports it; it lends it strength. The first duty of a free government, or of a government that regains its freedom, is without a doubt the total destruction of all religious obstacles. To banish kings without destroying the religious cult is to cut off but one of the hydra's heads."[28]

It is curious to observe that Sade's thinking coincided with the Revolution in only two of its phases, namely, the period of constitutional monarchy and that of dechristianization, and that both were remarkably brief. One led to the Terror, the other to the Cult of the Supreme Being.

By contrast, the second part of Sade's "Petition" was totally in contradiction with his thought, for he detested the pagan cults as much as the Christian one for which the Terror sought to substitute them. After celebrating the "martyrs of liberty," now he was called upon to sacrifice to the deities of Reason and Morality. Once again overcoming his repugnance, the author of the *Cent Vingt Journées de Sodome* set to work laying the foundations of a new religion dedicated to—Virtue. "Let us adore the virtues," he proclaimed to the Convention. "Filial piety, greatness of soul, equality, good faith, love of fatherland, charity, and the other virtues—let each of these, I say, be erected in one of our former temples, let them become the sole objects of our homage. We shall learn to respect them, to imitate them, by worshipping them."[29]

Carried away by atheistic fervor and a desire to speak well, Donatien had just committed an enormous error. Without intending to, he had defied the government. At the very moment when the Committee of Public Safety led by Robespierre was trying to halt the progress of atheism and end the proliferation of secular cults, Donatien had done his best to extol the end of superstition and to celebrate the birth of the goddess Reason. Nothing could have annoyed the committee more. Its members believed that superstition could not be rooted out by persecuting believers or profaning churches but only gradually, through the steady progress of enlightenment. The violent destruction of churches might pointlessly inflame popular sentiment, thereby supplying the enemies of the Republic with weapons and spreading scandal throughout Europe. There was also suspicion that the dechristianizers were a front for a plot against the Revolution fomented by the Hébertistes. On November 21, 1793, less than a week after Donatien's speech, Robespierre called a halt to the anti-Christian campaign.

Sade may have realized that the wind had shifted. In any case he understood that the "Petition" had been ill timed. To be sure, the Convention had applauded it, but that did not allay his fears. On the contrary, the more the people, backed by the Commune and the sections, revealed their anticlericalism, the more the revolutionary government would feel justified combatting it. Particularly since the

Convention itself, which had initially encouraged the dechristianization movement and welcomed burlesque parodies of Catholic ritual in
its chamber, had begun to change its tune. Shocked by the debauchery
and bad taste of the anti-Catholic demonstrations, the deputies had
grown tired of anticlerical agitation. Donatien should have realized
this. He also should have been listening when, only twenty days before
he delivered his speech, the Committee of Public Safety had castigated
the antireligious violence of André Dumont in these terms: "The coun-
terrevolutionaries must not be given the opportunity to say that we are
violating the freedom of religion or making war on religion in itself.
Seditious and unpatriotic priests must be punished, but the title of
priest as such should not be overtly banned."[30] M. de Sade also should
have asked himself about the attitude of those "comrades" in his section who chose him as their official delegate to the Convention. Had
they wished to send him to the scaffold, they might not have acted
differently.

Had he gotten wind of any specific threat? It seems likely that he
had, because he spent the following days preparing his defense, as if
he sensed imminent danger, as if he felt a need to gather in advance
all documents tending to prove his loyal devotion to the Revolution.
He asked Paré, the minister of the interior, to supply him with a copy
of the letter of July 3, 1789, in which warden de Launay had reported
to the minister his rebellious act and his call to the people.[31] And he
renewed his counsels of caution to Gaufridy: "Put 'citizen' in your
letters. If they were opened, [omitting the word] would be enough to
arouse suspicion, and neither you nor I are made to be suspects."[32]

I Shall Father Others

A few days later, on learning that a law was being prepared against
the relatives of émigrés, he sent Gaufridy the text of a petition to the
Convention intended to protect him from the proposed new measures.
It looks a lot like a plea in self-defense. Recalling his harangue of July
2, 1789, for the hundredth time, Sade touches up the portrait so much
that it becomes a heroic caricature. To hear him tell it, he had taken
the Bastille single-handedly by bellowing through his funnel: "I pop-
ularized treason; I revealed to the inhabitants of Paris the atrocities
being prepared against them in this château. Launay believed me to
be dangerous. I have the letter in which he asked minister Villedeuil
to remove me from the fortress, whose treason I wished to prevent
whatever the cost . . ."[33]

Finally, he asked, what could a man do if his own sons betrayed him? The answer was simple: have more children. So Donatien, with a straight face, promised the deputies of the Convention that he would father new children whose patriotic ardor would make up for the desertion of his two sons. Père Ubu could have done no more.

23

The Prisons of
Liberty

The Arrest

On 18 frimaire, Year II (December 8, 1793), at ten in the morning,
two men appeared at 20, rue Neuve-des-Mathurins with a warrant for
the arrest of Citizen Sade, whom they found in the company of Mme
Quesnet. He was expecting this visit and did not seem very surprised
when Juspel and Michel Laurent, two commissars from the revolutionary committee of the Section des Piques, showed him an order to
seal the premises. "Citizens," he told them, "I know nothing better
than obedience to the laws. Do your duty."

He then opened his drawers, collected the papers in them, and
took them to his second-floor study, although he asked if he could
retain some documents on his person. Juspel examined them, saw
nothing but testimonials to his patriotism, and allowed Sade to keep
them, but not before duly affixing his initials. Sade then asked the
official to pass on to his printer Girouard three pages of the manuscript
of *Aline et Valcour*, which he was then in the process of revising. "Since
this work was written three years ago, it is no longer up to date," he
explained. The policeman did not deny this request but said that he
would have to consult his superiors.

The officers inquired whether Sade was married to Citizen Quesnet. "No. She lives below me, but she has her own apartment." The
two men were not fools: having seen the poor woman's panic, they
divined the couple's intimate relations and decided to take a look
around the lady's rooms. Finding nothing suspicious, they allowed her
to remain in her apartment, sealed the door to Donatien's study and

the bedroom opposite, and took the prisoner to the jail known as the Madelonnettes.[1]

The Madelonnettes

The former convent of the Filles de la Madeleine, 6, rue des Fontaines-du-Temple, had only recently been converted to a jail. Until April 1793 it had still served as an asylum for more or less reformed prostitutes. Short of inmates immediately after its conversion, the new jail saw its population grow suddenly after the "law of suspects" was passed in September 1793. Cells were arranged along the walls of four fifty-foot corridors. But these soon proved insufficient. Planned to hold 200 prisoners, by October the Madelonnettes housed more than 280, some crowded into the last remaining space in the attic.

When Citizen Sade arrived on the afternoon of December 8, there was no room for him. He was therefore given a bed in the latrines at the end of the corridor. The place was so filthy and stank so badly that the doors had to be kept closed lest the stench spread to the rest of the prison. Sade would spend six weeks here.

Like the other prisoners, he found a little consolation in the humanity of Vaubertrand, the warder with the vaudeville name, a kind, sensitive man always on the lookout for an opportunity to ease the lot of one of the "suspects." No doubt Sade was also pleasantly surprised to find a number of familiar faces. Of the thirteen actors of the Théâtre-Français who remained faithful to the monarchy, his friends Molé, Saint-Prix, and Saint-Phal were in the Madelonnettes (the actresses were in Sainte-Pélagie). Another inmate surely brought back memories: Charles-Pierre Claret de Fleurieu, minister of the Navy under Louis XVI and brother-in-law of his former patroness. Last but not least, we can imagine his satisfaction at finding among his companions in misfortune certain of his former persecutors, such as the comte Angrand d'Alleray, aged seventy-eight and formerly *lieutenant civil* of the Grand Châtelet, and the last *lieutenant de police*, Thiroux de Crosne, both of whom ended on the scaffold.

Like all the prisons of the Terror, the Madelonnettes received the cream of Ancien Régime society. But for the misery of the surroundings it was possible to believe that one was in a salon of the faubourg Saint-Germain. There were men as distinguished as abbé Barthélemy, the archaeologist and numismatist; the marquis de Boulainvilliers, the last provost of Paris; the marquis de La Tour du Pin-Gouvernet, minister of war in 1789; Saint-Priest, brother of the former minister of the interior, General Lanoue; and others. While awaiting execution, the prisoners played music or composed verses to set rhymes. One night a quartet by Pleyel was performed; the next night, songs were sung in honor of the amiable Mme Vaubertrand and her little boy, a charming child of four. Since there were no women in the Madelonnettes, the warder's young wife was hailed as an angel. The prisoners talked of common friends, recalled happier days, discussed books, wrote, painted, and composed verse. Within the dank walls of a prison, they recreated the society of another age.

•

On the day of his incarceration, Donatien issued this appeal to the Section des Piques:

Citizens,
I have been arrested without being informed of the reasons for my detention. I throw myself into the arms of my fellow citizens, hopeful that, because my patriotism is known to them, they will not want me to languish in irons. For ten years I was a victim of the despotism of tyrants. I cherished the Revolution as my liberator. Can it be that the nation that broke my chains three years ago is today putting me in new ones? No, citizens, you will not permit it. I beg you to ask for my release only if I am not guilty. If I am guilty, it is just that I should be punished. But, citizens, I am not, I swear it, and given that certainty, you will not refuse to take an interest in your unfortunate fellow citizen.

SADE[2]

Ce octodi 18 frimaire [December 8, 1793]

The section, meeting in general assembly, decided to transmit Sade's letter to the Committee of Surveillance, which simply noted that "Citizen Sade has been placed under arrest pursuant to an order of the police administration" before moving on to the next item of the agenda.[3]

One would have had to be remarkably naïve to have expected any help from that quarter. Clearly it had been this very Committee of Surveillance, that of Sade's own section, which had denounced him. He had no doubt been under observation for several weeks. Perhaps he had suspected it. By this time he surely understood the truth. Thus, his letter was nothing but a tactical maneuver intended to demonstrate his good faith. Not to have written it would have been tantamount to acknowledging his guilt—and accepting his defeat.

Having received no response from his esteemed colleagues, his next move was to approach the Committee of General Security, which is to say, Robespierre's police, the most redoubtable organ of the Terror. On December 29 he dispatched a lengthy missive professing gratitude and loyalty to the Republic. Once again he alluded to his exploit of July 2, 1789 ("one of the finest proofs of *civisme* a republican can provide") and rehearsed his record of service. He asked to have the seals removed from his apartment, his papers examined, and a verdict rendered as to his guilt or innocence.[4]

Ten days passed without an answer. Nothing was happening. No government could have behaved in a more high-handed manner. Like thousands of other citizens, Donatien had been arrested under the notorious "law of suspects," which had been adopted by the Convention on September 17, 1793, on a motion by deputy Merlin de Douai. If ever there was a scurrilous law, this was it. It decreed that all enemies of the Revolution, avowed or presumed, were to be arrested and held until the country was at peace. The lawmakers had been careful to leave the definition of the word "suspect" vague enough to encompass as many people as possible. Included within the category were émigrés and all their relatives "who have not continually demonstrated their devotion to the Revolution." The law also targeted all public officials removed from their posts and anyone without a certificate of civic spirit. It affected as well "those who by their conduct, relations, words, or writings have shown themselves to be supporters of tyranny or federalism and enemies of liberty." In other words, the law spelled the end of freedom of opinion and expression. Last but not least, "those who cannot give proof of having performed their civic duties . . . or of honest means of support" were also categorized as "suspect."

•

Unsure of how long he would be held or even whether he would get out of prison alive, Sade found it difficult to contain his impatience. Unwilling to break all ties to the outside world but unable to act in his own behalf, he delegated his faithful Constance, the only person in the world in whom he had absolute confidence, to represent him officially in all circumstances. A document signed on December 22, 1793, in the presence of Maîtres Dufouleur and Thion, who had come to the Madelonnettes, named Mme Quesnet his "general and penal proxy" empowered to receive all monies due him, discharge his debts, retrieve his mail, and use all sums in her possession "in whatever manner she deems appropriate."

On January 8, 1794, M. de Sade was plunged into the deepest anxiety by the news that his printer and publisher Girouard had just been guillotined. True, the man had made no secret of his royalist sympathies. He had surreptitiously distributed counterrevolutionary broadsides, and his proof-mark bore a *fleur de lys*. It was he who had published the very subversive *Gazette de Paris* by the journalist Du Rozoi, who had perished on the scaffold in 1792. On learning of Girouard's execution Donatien could not help thinking of the proofs of *Aline et Valcour* languishing in the unfortunate fellow's shop on rue du Bout-du-Monde.

During the evening of January 12, 1794, the police at last came and removed the marquis from the Madelonnettes and accompanied him to his home, where the seals on his apartment were broken and his papers searched. The operation took several hours. Fourteen letters from the provinces (probably from Gaufridy) were seized, and Sade was transferred to the Carmelite prison on rue de Vaugirard. It was shortly past midnight.

Saint-Lazare

The Carmelite convent at 70, rue de Vaugirard, had been the scene of a particularly bloody episode of the Revolution. It was here that 115 priests were murdered during the September massacres. Like a number of other religious establishments, the convent was converted into a prison during the Terror. More than 700 detainees passed through its gates during this period, including Alexandre de Beauharnais and his wife Joséphine [the future wife of Napoleon —Trans.], the comte de Soyécourt, and Mme de Custine. Donatien stayed only eight days, barely long enough to glimpse the fetid corridors, the disgusting dining hall, and the prisoners wandering about like ghosts, "dirty, their legs bare, with handkerchiefs around their heads, their hair uncombed and their beards grown long." He was locked up with six prisoners suffering from severe fever, two of whom died after he left.[5]

On January 22, 1794, he was transferred to Saint-Lazare, which had also recently been converted to house "guests of the Republic." Once a leprosarium, this building, which stood at the site of what is now 107, rue du faubourg Saint-Denis, later became the Convent of Priests of the Mission and had served even under the Ancien Régime as a prison for tipsy priests and youths of good family addicted to gambling or libertinage or in danger of *mésalliance*. All its inmates had been "privileged" individuals whose relatives could afford the exorbitant cost of room and board. The buildings of the convent, with their cells, dining halls, exercise areas, and courtyards, constituted the largest prison in Paris, and in January 1794 the purveyors of Terror decided to make use of it. The food here was particularly foul: abominable bread and adulterated wine sometimes provoked fatal maladies. Sade would remain in this prison for only two months, not long enough to make the acquaintance of the poet André Chénier, who did not enter until June 9, though he did meet another poet, Roucher, who spent his enforced leisure time writing his wife letters brimming with details of prison life. Among the numerous aristocrats held at Saint-Lazare, Donatien saw Mme de Maillé, a cousin, and her sixteen-year-old son François.

The painter Hubert Robert entered Saint-Lazare on January 30, a week after Donatien, along with his friend Roucher. Both had been transferred from Sainte-Pélagie, where they had shared the same cell. Sade could not help being struck by the new inmate's unusual appearance, for he invariably wore a quilted silk housecoat and carried a sketchbook and pencils. Perhaps Donatien was present when the painter captured the notorious "Germinal" wing, a heated common room shared by many prisoners, on canvas; the painting can be seen today in the Musée Carnavalet. Perhaps he paused behind Robert's back to admire the chiaroscuro. Perhaps he himself appears in the painting, a dim silhouette wandering among the shades.

The Accusation

It was not until three months to the day after his arrest, on March 8, 1794, that the Committee of Surveillance of the Section des Piques finally voted to send the Committee of General Security its "Report on the Political Conduct of Citizen Sade." From this report it emerges that the two principal counts of the indictment against him were these:

1. In 1791 he had asked to serve with the duc de Brissac, at that time captain of the royal guard.[6]

2. "He is in all respects a most immoral man, highly suspect and unworthy of society, judging by the remarks against him in volume III of *L'Espion anglais* or volume I of the *Liste des ci-devant nobles* [Dulaure], page 89, no. 28."

Incredibly, nothing had been found against him other than gossip taken from *L'Observateur anglais* (which dated from 1778) and Dulaure's notice embroidering on the Arcueil affair, now some twenty-five years old.[7]

The offer to serve in the constitutional guard would seem to have been a relatively minor offense. To be sure, people had been condemned for less: examples abound. One often-cited case was that of Citizen Bernard-Marguerite Descours, who went to the national abattoir for having served as aide-de-camp in Brissac's guards. But Donatien had never actually served in the unit (for the reason mentioned above), and he had given ample "proof" of *civisme* in his section. He was not exactly an ordinary citizen. As late as three weeks prior to his arrest he was representing his comrades before the Convention. Today we know that the section had then grasped the nature of his double game and resolved to destroy him. The question was how to get rid of a man in whom one had displayed so much confidence. The committee therefore dug up the old Brissac affair and rummaged through yellowing gazettes to unearth ancient crimes of vice. These items were then disingenuously arranged to sustain a case against Sade.

The remainder of the report tells us more about the real reasons for his disgrace. The committee surely would not have proceeded as cautiously against another man. Robespierre's justice was hardly scrupulous, to put it mildly, about questions of law. But with Sade the authorities were dealing with an adversary of some magnitude, a man hitherto regarded as an ally, a former secretary and president of his section who accordingly had the means to defend himself. In this case the section had been too credulous for too long to be able to attack him on such (apparently) fragile grounds as these: "Since he appeared in the section, he has feigned being a patriot since August 10. But [his comrades] were not fooled. He unmasked himself, *primo*, with a petition contrary to revolutionary principles and to the formation of the revolutionary army decreed by the Convention . . . [And he was] an enemy in principle of republican societies, continually making in private conversation comparisons based on Greek and Roman history in order to prove the impossibility of establishing a republican government in France."[8] The misunderstanding is grotesque—and tragic. While M. de Sade played at being a sans-culotte, his comrades played at being *faux naïfs*. The whole affair smacks of a commedia dell'arte.

Just what was Sade accused of besides libertinage and a willingness to serve in the royal guards? Opportunism and moderatism—and from the point of view of the Committee of Surveillance, these charges were perfectly justified. As for the petition against the revolutionary army, remember that Sade had drafted it at the behest of his section, which in fact had delegated him to read his text to the Convention.

As for the malicious allusion to the cultivated mind taking his examples from the Greeks and Romans, it was characteristic of the sans-culotte's permanent suspicion of the "intellectual." Sade's outspoken skepticism of the republican form of government was a more serious matter. He had given clear expression to that skepticism three years earlier in his "Address to the King": "No one in the world is more convinced than I that the French empire can be governed only by a monarch."

•

The indictment that prosecutor Fouquier-Tinville would bring against Sade a few months later also mentioned "intelligence and correspondence with the enemies of the Republic." The charge was probably based on eight to ten letters from Gaufridy, which had been seized at Sade's home and "which the imbecile members of the revolutionary committee find suspect." Over the previous two years, relations between Sade and his agent had indeed taken a dangerously political turn. While Sade was playing the patriotic card, Gaufridy, who had initially remained true to his royalist convictions, moved gradually toward Girondism at first and, later, federalism.

After the Tenth of August Gaufridy's activities moved into a militant phase: the notary personally joined in the monarchist conspiracy in Apt led by the marquis Monier de La Quarrée against the coalition government of Girondins and Montagnards. But when Monier was arrested in Grenoble, Gaufridy thought it prudent to beat a retreat to Lyons, where he went with his son Elzéar. As we saw earlier, Sade at this time generously offered him a place to stay in Paris. Gaufridy, for no reason other than his usual ineptitude, felt called upon to send his benefactor a warm letter of thanks, even at the risk of compromising the recipient. He never managed to eliminate from his letters the expressions of deference that his client and friend inspired. In spite of everything his correspondence preserved all the polite formulas of the Ancien Régime. And the word "citizen" came so uneasily to his pen that his correspondent constantly had to remind him of his duty— without much success.

In the wake of the Parisian insurrections of May 31 and June 2, which drove the Girondins from power, Elzéar Gaufridy enlisted in the départemental army. A month later, on July 25, General Carteaux entered Avignon at the head of the Convention's army after routing the federalists. Gaufridy had no choice but to flee again. With his colleague Fage and several other residents of Apt, he left for Toulon, the stronghold of the federalist movement in Provence, and there ranged himself behind the white banner with the *fleur de lys*. Meanwhile, Toulon was proclaiming Louis XVII king, surrendering its forts to the English under Admiral Hood, issuing an appeal to the comte de Provence as regent of France, and reverting to the laws of the prerevolutionary period.

On December 19, however, Dugommier, along with a young artillery captain by the name of Bonaparte, captured Toulon. The Army of the Republic gave the royalist anthill a swift kick. Recognized by two Apt natives among the troops, Gaufridy and his comrades were arrested and escaped the guillotine only by producing fake residence certificates issued by sympathetic municipalities.

Despite the circumstances the notary continued to correspond with the marquis through a friend from Apt. Naturally, these letters from a notorious royalist could not fail to attract the attention of the Committee of General Security. Thinking that he was making a shrewd move, Sade issued his agent certificates of *civisme* like this one, dated October 13, 1793: "Your patriotism is recognized, my dear advocate. Your sentiments are secure. Why are you looking for peace and quiet outside your home? One who, *like you*, has nothing to reproach in himself should stay home. Only those who leave are suspected, and I assure you that it reflects badly on you that you are always going off like this. Leave that to others, whose civic spirit is not as fully recognized as yours."[9] This naïve expedient only further compromised Sade without absolving his correspondent in the least.

Other "errors" also counted against him: his intervention on behalf of the Montreuils (and possibly other aristocrats), his indisposition on August 2, when he had been obliged to give up the presidency of his section, and probably other lapses of which we know nothing: an involuntary reaction, a word dropped in the course of a conversation, an intercepted letter, a grimace, a smile. That was all it took at the time to find oneself a suspect.

Maximilien and Donàtien

Yet while these grounds for suspicion seem sufficient, they do not explain everything. Sade's arrest on December 8, 1793, also grew out of less visible but no doubt more important considerations. There was of course the moral issue. Although Dulaure's exposé, published in Year II, alluded to ancient affairs, it nevertheless had the effect of reviving interest in Donatien's scandalous life, reminding those who had forgotten and instructing those who had never heard of it. Dulaure did not mince his words: "This man, whom prison saved from the scaffold, whose irons were a favor, was somehow confused with those unfortunate victims whom ministerial despotism held unjustly. This execrable scoundrel is living among civilized men and dares with impunity to number himself among the ranks of citizens."[10]

The novel *Justine*, published anonymously in 1791, was soon attributed to him. The Committee of Surveillance of the Section des Piques had to know that he was the author, and this presumption must have outweighed all others under a government imbued with the puritanism of its leader. Nothing disgusted the Incorruptible more than libertinage. There was no better token of the aristocracy's decadence, and nothing more alien to the aspirations of the people.

Robespierre and Sade! The former, trussed in stiff virtue, could not help feeling contempt for his overstuffed fellow *sectionnaire*. Sade, the archetypal voluptuary, had surely filled him with insurmountable disgust from the moment they met. Clearly they had met. How could they not, having frequented the same haunts for at least two years? Sade was a noted playwright, and Robespierre, the former director of the Arras Académie des Belles-Lettres, an admirer of Rousseau, and the author of long-forgotten literary memoirs, prided himself on his cultivated mind. By an odd coincidence, Robespierre's first essay, a dissertation written for the annual prize competition of the Metz Academy, dealt with the following question: "What is the origin of the view that all the individual members of a family share a portion of the shame associated with the punishment inflicted on a person guilty of a dishonorable crime?" M. de Sade, at the time a prisoner in the Bastille, might have offered some judicious advice on this theme.

Robespierre's antipathy must have changed to hatred when he learned of the "Petition" that Sade had read on November 15 at the bar of the Convention. A week later, he responded from the podium of the Jacobin Club not only to Sade but to all who believed as the marquis did that God was dead. His words had an ominous ring. One sentence above all whistled like the blade of the guillotine in the *ci-devant* marquis's ears: "Atheism is aristocratic." The orator continued in a calm, clear voice: "The idea of a Great Being who watches over oppressed innocence and punishes triumphant crime is essentially popular." These words presaged the famous speech on the "Relation of Religious and Moral Ideas to Republican Principles" of 18 floréal, in which Robespierre established the Cult of the Supreme Being as the state religion.

Once atheism had been outlawed, the adepts of the "encyclopedist sect" became the nation's worst enemies, guilty of having "launched a sudden, violent attack on religion in order to establish themselves as ardent apostles of nothingness and fanatical missionaries of atheism."

Would free thought henceforth be permitted in matters of religion? The answer was as terrifying as it was vague: "Woe unto those who seek to dampen sublime enthusiasm!" The new national religion would allow men to be free only insofar as they were good: "Command victory," Robespierre proclaimed, "but above all return vice to the depths of nothingness. The enemies of the Republic are the corrupt." Sade was one of these "corrupt men" that Robespierre had always combatted and whom he now intended to purge from the Republic. Sade had thus made himself a suspect by his way of life, his writings, and his fanatical atheism far more than by any specific action: atheism was his central conviction, his dominant passion, the measure of his freedom.

"If atheism wants martyrs, let it say so," he proclaimed, "and my blood is ready." Robespierre took him at his word.

M. de Sade's "Confession"

On March 18, 1794, ten days after the section issued its report "on the political conduct of Citizen Sade," Donatien submitted a written defense to the Committee of General Security. This was couched in the form of an administrative questionnaire, with questions and answers, in which truth was mixed with lies, errors (deliberate or not), omissions, and denials. For example, concerning "his profession before and after the Revolution," he wrote: "We are natives of a small town in the ci-devant comtat of Avignon, where my ancestors were variously farmers and merchants. I have never been noble, [and] I can prove it whenever you wish." Only the most extreme desperation could have led the marquis de Sade to deny his ancestry in so cowardly a fashion. And there was much more in the same vein.

We have heard it all before. Sade rehearsed the story of his appeal to the crowd outside the Bastille, his internment at Charenton, and his eventual release. He again professed his love of liberty, his hatred of tyrants, and his loyalty to the nation. He gave a detailed accounting of his services to his section, not omitting his moment of glory: the speech in honor of Marat and Le Peletier. In the midst of his brief he slipped in this invocation to himself, which in retrospect takes on a double meaning: "Sade, remember the irons that the despots made you wear, and die a thousand deaths rather than live under a government that would allow them to be used again!" He spoke truer than he knew.

The Maison Coignard

On 7 germinal, Year II (March 27, 1794), Sade was taken under guard from Saint-Lazare to Picpus. The document authorizing this transfer mentions "for reasons of illness" without further details.

The house that stood at what is now the corner of boulevard Diderot and the rue de Picpus had once belonged to Ninon de Lenclos. It had been sublet for a short time to one Eugène Coignard, who had converted it into a hospital, this being a lucrative business at the time. Nearby, on rue de Charonne, a former mirror maker by the name of Jacques Belhomme had created a similar establishment as early as 1769. At first things had been difficult. Business had been slow, and over the years the hospital population had dwindled to only thirty-seven. Then the Terror came, and suddenly people were being turned away: affluent "patients" thronged the hospital and fought over its rooms. Soon the space proved insufficient, and it became necessary to rent another building next door. Jacques Belhomme had struck it rich: he took in wealthy "suspects" incarcerated in various Paris prisons who somehow managed to pass themselves off as sick. In return for exorbitant room and board, most of these privileged individuals escaped the guillotine; the rest at least enjoyed better treatment while awaiting their fate.

The Maison Belhomme was located in a comfortable hôtel with a pretty garden. There were no bars or fences, and patients could receive visitors. Of course there were intermediaries involved in ransoming these high-class inmates and negotiating with the authorities to have them transferred to the "hospital." Fouquier-Tinville is suspected of having participated in this kind of arrangement, but there is no proof. What is certain, however, is that corruption was rife at all levels: members of the Committee of General Security, their agents, informants, judges and juries of the Revolutionary Tribunal, and police officals were all involved.[11] The negotiations were almost always conducted orally and in the greatest secrecy. There is little prospect of ever coming across a written record. That is why the history of these private hospitals, or *maisons de santé*, during the Terror is so full of gaps. What is more, it was not only a matter of corruption; some members of the government used their influence to protect their imprisoned friends. The Maison Belhomme was honored by the presence of some of the wealthiest prisoners: Philippe-Egalité's wife, the duchesse d'Orléans; Radix de Sainte-Foix, Louis XVI's secret adviser; Portalis; Pétion's widow; Mlle Lange, creator of the role of Pamela in the comedy of the same name; the actress Marie-Antoinette Mézeray of the Comédie-Française; and the comtesse du Roure, to name a few.

When Eugène Coignard opened his home on rue de Picpus, he hoped to rival that of Belhomme, and he came close to realizing his dream. The home prospered from the day it opened late in 1793.[12] By December 28 it housed no fewer than 166 inmates, far more than it was built to hold. In January Coignard was forced to rent from Citizen Riédain an adjoining property, a former convent of canonesses. Among the earliest inmates of this new subsidiary, Coignard was delighted to receive his neighbor and former rival, none other than Jacques Belhomme, who had been sentenced to six years in irons for having abused his position a little too blatantly.[13] So long as they did not try to escape through the gate, the inmates of the Maison Coignard enjoyed the same advantages as those of the Maison Belhomme: fresh air, a large garden, comfort, decent food, and comparative freedom. They could receive newspapers and keep up with current events. Every day the last page of *Le Moniteur* listed the names of those who had been executed. Thanks to the services of the "good doctor" Coignard and various intermediaries, many *ci-devants* kept their heads on their shoulders: the duc de Brancas-Villars and his wife, both quite elderly; the marquis de Boissy; the philosopher Volney, author of *Les Ruines, ou Méditations sur les révolutions des empires*; Choderlos de Laclos; and of course the marquis de Sade.

As a form of preventive detention, these discreet "hospitals" were the best chance a "suspect" had of being forgotten by the authorities, provided of course that he or she could afford to pay the exorbitant room and board and the blackmail demanded by the intermediaries. For Donatien this must have been an issue. But fortunately Marie-Constance was on the job. With tireless devotion she moved heaven and earth, called on deputies she knew in the Convention, notably Goupilleau de Montaigu, and managed to borrow the sum demanded and get her friend transferred out of Saint-Lazare for reasons of health. Sade would later pay deserved homage to the "adorable woman" who "with the most courageous energy . . . saved his life" by rescuing him from the "revolutionary scythe."[14]

On arriving at the Maison Coignard, Sade felt in familiar surroundings, just as he had in the Madelonnettes and Saint-Lazare. The prisons of "liberty" were remarkably similar to those of "tyranny," and our man had spent enough time in the latter to know how they worked. The prison world held no secrets for him; this was the only advantage he had over his companions in misfortune, but it was a significant one. At the very least he was spared the usual anxiety of the novice.

At the Foot of the Scaffold

On the sixth of thermidor (July 24, 1794), the clerk of the Committee of Public Safety sent Sade's dossier to the Revolutionary Tribunal under a cover sheet bearing the following note: "Aldonze Sade, ex-noble and count, man of letters and cavalry officer, accused of conspiracy against the Republic."[15] Two days later, Fouquier-Tinville issued an indictment against twenty-eight individuals, including Donatien; his niece, Mme de Maillé, aged thirty-nine; his notary Toussaint-Charles Girard; and Jean-Pierre Béchon d'Arquien, aged forty-seven, "ex-count, . . . ex-lieutenant of musketeers, ex-chevalier of the order of the tyrant," and a patient at the Maison Coignard. The indictment against Sade included the following charges: "Sade, ex-count, captain of Capet's guards in 1792, maintained intelligence and correspondence with the enemies of the Republic. He continually fought against the republican government by arguing in his section that such a government was impracticable. He has proved himself to be a partisan of federalism and a supporter of the traitor Roland. Finally, it appears that the proofs of patriotism he attempted to provide were intended only to obstruct the investigation into his complicity with the tyrant's conspiracy, of which he was a vile satellite."[16]

The next day, 9 thermidor, the bailiff of the Tribunal, carrying an order containing the names of the twenty-eight accused, went to various places of detention around Paris to take them into custody. But five of them failed to appear, among them "Aldonze Sade." The other twenty-three were taken to a hearing of the second section of the Revolutionary Tribunal under Judge Scellier. After a summary trial, all were condemned to death with the exception of a farmer by the name of Aviat-Turot, who was acquitted, and Mme de Maillé, who broke down during the session. Three days earlier, her seventeen-year-old son François had mounted the scaffold as an accomplice in the alleged Saint-Lazare conspiracy. Upon catching sight of the men who had condemned him, the room in which he had uttered his last words, the seat in which he had been seated, perhaps the very one in which she herself would sit, the poor woman had been seized with convulsions so violent that Scellier had not dared judge her in that condition and had had her removed from the courtroom. She was transferred to the Conciergerie, from which she would be released after the fall of Robespierre.

That left only twenty-one condemned victims. No sooner was their judgment pronounced than they were loaded into tumbrils and taken to the barrière du Trône.

Early on the morning of that same day, 9 thermidor, a rumor had begun to spread through Paris: Robespierre had just been arrested and taken to the Committee of General Security along with his younger brother Augustin and Saint-Just, Lebas, and Couthon. Trouble had broken out at various places in the capital. Fouquier-Tinville was alerted: the majority in the Convention might change at any moment. Would it not be more prudent to delay the execution? Going through with it might outrage the people of Paris, already drenched in blood. "Nothing should halt the course of justice," the public prosecutor declared. The convoy therefore continued on its way. At about three in the afternoon the tumbrils rolled out of the Palais de Justice and proceeded to move through Paris in a southeasterly direction. On the rue du faubourg Saint-Antoine, where only yesterday insults had been hurled at the condemned, the crowd finally dared to make its voice heard. People gathered around the condemned prisoners and began to unhitch the horses from the wagons. The gendarmes of the escort hesitated and looked at one another, about to give in. The condemned, sensing a glimmer of hope, again felt the blood flow in their veins. At that moment four horsemen rode up at a gallop, led by Hanriot, commander-in-chief of the National Guard, half drunk and roving the streets of the capital attempting to rouse the people in favor of Robespierre. Saber blows dispersed the crowd, and the gendarmes were ordered to continue on their way. Wheels began to clatter over the pavement once again, and the condemned, having endured their tragic, abortive reprieve, were taken to the place of execution and promptly decapitated.

That night, as every night, M. de Sade heard the groaning brakes of a tumbril stopping outside the gates. He went to the window and glimpsed the shadows of the gravediggers dancing in the torchlight. As they unloaded pale corpses by the shovelful, he felt a shiver run down his spine: nothingness had just grazed him with its black wing.

•

If Sade managed to cheat fate, it was not because of some obscure design of Providence, nor was it, as Gilbert Lely believed, due to the "number and crowding of the prisons" or the "disorder in the dossiers." Nor was it the negligence of the bailiff charged with taking the prisoners into custody who, after failing to find Sade at Saint-Lazare, supposedly "forgot" to call his name at Picpus. Sade had been transferred there exactly four months earlier. That was enough time for his dossier to have been brought up to date. When the bailiff came for the comte Béchon d'Arquien, also held at the Maison Coignard, Sade was supposed to have gone with him, but at the last minute it had proved impossible to find him. Or, more precisely, no one had looked for him. The bailiff had not even called his name. On the list, alongside the name "Sade," he had been content to write, "Absent." Given the mess that prevailed in the Revolutionary Tribunal in those days of Thermidor, an absence was more than plausible; in any case it was an excellent alibi.

It was no accident and no mistake that Donatien escaped death: someone in high places wanted him to. Why? How? To begin with, he had paid dearly, as we have seen. "My detention has ruined me," he wrote to Gaufridy.[17] On leaving Picpus he said that he was "besieged on all sides by people who lent me money during my detention."[18] He admitted to debts of 2,000 écus, or 6,000 livres: a considerable sum, which we may assume had gone to pay his ransom. In addition, Constance had done all she could to win his pardon. She had friends not only in the Convention but on the Committee of General Security, from which Donatien would boast a few months later of being able to get what he wanted: "I am fairly certain of this committee's justice and gratitude," he wrote to Audibert, his farmer in La Coste. And speaking of Gaufridy, still in trouble with the authorities: "I can now help him out with the Committee of General Security. Have him tell me what he wants me to do, and I will do it."[19] There can be no doubt: he owed his life to Sensible and to her alone. She was the one who arranged the necessary loans; she was the one who used her contacts; and she was the one who obtained his release. Sade would never forget it.

Even prisoners heard news of Robespierre's downfall on the very day it occurred. The next day, 10 thermidor, they were relieved to learn that the head of the "Incorruptible" had fallen to the guillotine's blade. Now that the nightmare was over, Donatien could finally look forward to an early release from Picpus. On 18 thermidor (August 5), the Convention decreed that all citizens held on grounds not mentioned in the law of suspects would be liberated, and the Committees of Surveillance were ordered to forward copies of the grounds for holding those not released to either the prisoner himself or his family. Twenty days later, the Section des Piques sent the Committee of General Security a certificate of *civisme* concerning their colleague, this one very different in content and tone from that of March 8: "We, the undersigned, citizens of the Section des Piques, certify that we know Citizen Sade and that we have seen him fulfill various functions both in the section and in the hospital with zeal and intelligence, and we attest that nothing has come to our attention that would call into question his adherence to the principles of a good patriot or cast doubt on his civic spirit . . ."[20]

Scarcely a month after the death of the dictator, the wind had shifted: the section had changed sides. Like all of France, it had entered the Thermidorean era.

In the meantime the indefatigable Constance crisscrossed Paris summoning her friends to have Donatien released as soon as possible. On October 11 a deputy, Bourdon, promised to intervene in the case. Two days later, the Convention's Committee of Security and Surveillance ordered his immediate release. On October 15 he finally left the Maison Coignard after 312 days of detention and returned to his house on rue Neuve-des-Mathurins.

Just as four years earlier, Gaufridy was the first person with whom he shared his joy: "At last my torment is over, and the Committee of General Security, in seeing that justice was finally done, has even shown me a great sign of esteem by asking me to remain in Paris, even though I am an ex-noble, because of my patriotic works, with which the Committee wishes me to continue nurturing the public spirit."[21] He did not forget to pay his respects to the woman who had supported him throughout his long ordeal: "Finally, my name had just been placed on the list, and I was eleventh, when, on the eve of my doom, the sword of justice fell on France's new Sylla. From that moment, everything improved, and thanks to the ardent and eager concern of the wonderful companion who has shared my life for the past five years, I was finally delivered on 24 vendémiaire last."[22]

24
At Bay

Two Orphan Girls

For the ten and a half months he had been in prison, M. de Sade had maintained absolute secrecy about his incarceration, leading his agents in Provence to believe that he was living with a friend in the country. On his instructions mail had been addressed to him by way of Mme Quesnet, rue de la Ferme-des-Mathurins. Such caution was perfectly justifiable, moreover, for the slightest indiscretion might forever compromise the return of his sequestered property and the removal of his name from the list of émigrés. Nevertheless, despite his precautions, the rumor spread in the Vaucluse that he was in prison and would not be getting out any time soon. He immediately denied this report, offering assurances that, far from being out of favor with the authorities, he had become the government's official poet: "Gaufridy informs me that someone told him I was in prison," he wrote to Quinquin. "I have only one thing to say in response: if I were in prison, would I be sending you all certificates of residence, as I have just done? As you must know, I would not be able to obtain them if I were in prison. And if I were in prison, I would not be doing what I am doing right now at the behest of the Committee of Public Safety, namely, writing a patriotic comedy in five acts in verse to be performed at the Theater of the Republic."[1]

During this period the long-suffering Gaufridy fared little better than his employer. Regarded as an outlaw because of his opinions, he had been forced once again to flee along with his son Elzéar, but he continued to manage the marquis's property from afar. He regularly received letters from Donatien by way of Reinaud, who served as an intermediary. Gaufridy's absence irritated Donatien. What foolishness, to run away at the first sign of trouble! Especially now, when he needed him so badly. He had to be persuaded at all costs to return. With his new connections Sade was in a position to put in a good word for the notary with the Committee of General Security. If Gaufridy would just tell him what needed to be done, he would do it.

Around the middle of November a visitor from Avignon newly arrived in Paris came to dinner at Sade's home and brought him news of the scribe: "Gaufridy is a long way from Apt. You may not see him again for a long time." Donatien's hopes began to fade. At that moment a valet brought him a letter. After unsealing it, he uttered a cry of joy: it was from none other than his friend Gaufridy, back home at last and in need of assistance: could Goupilleau be persuaded to intervene on his behalf? The same letter also brought the sad news that Reinaud had just died.

The notary's freedom being at stake, Donatien immediately contacted Goupilleau (de Montaigu, as he was known), a former delegate to the Vaucluse, a deputy of the Convention, and a personal friend of Constance. Sade sent him a petition on behalf of Gaufridy and also asked Goupilleau to intervene with the Committee of General Security, of which he was a member. Mme Quesnet, meanwhile, approached a number of people. Victory took no more than a month to achieve: Gaufridy would be bothered no longer.

Until recently the price paid for the scribe's tranquillity remained a mystery. Now, thanks to a previously unpublished letter, we know: M. Goupilleau de Montaigu was to receive, in exchange for his services, two young orphan girls from the Apt region. It would be a simple matter to persuade their grandmother that they would receive a much better upbringing "under the eyes of their protector" than at home in the provinces. "They will be in a better position to receive the favors to which their misfortune so amply entitles them," Sade hypocritically added.[2] Gaufridy would not wish to deny his benefactor this small service. In any case, it was business as usual: M. Goupilleau always took his compensation in kind.[3]

The New Paris

Once free, Donatien appears to have given up politics for good. His letters avoided current events, apart from an occasional allusion to topical matters, often connected with his own interests: his farmers were not paying, his income was not arriving on time, his property was not leased, the price of food was going up and the value of the assignat was going down. The need for money became his sole obsession. Meanwhile, as his income fell and the threat of confiscation loomed larger, the management of his estates came to seem an unbearable burden. He dreamed of shifting the responsibility to Gaufridy. The notary knew his affairs better than anyone else and enjoyed his full confidence. He had long been thinking of appointing a chief steward to manage all his property. Gaufridy had always avoided the issue, insisting that he was up to his neck in other work but actually fearing (for reasons we can understand only too well) that he would be reduced to slavery. He was too well aware of his client's despotic moods to surrender himself body and soul.

Instead of politics, Sade was now devoting more and more of his time to literature. Relieved of administrative responsibilities and once again an ordinary member of his section, he could devote himself entirely to writing. With his newfound freedom he worked on finishing old pieces, begun before his incarceration, and starting new ones. Two important books would appear in 1795, *La Philosophie dans le boudoir*, which drew heavily on recent events, and *Aline et Valcour*.

Unambiguously denouncing the excesses of the Robespierrist regime that had condemned him to death, Sade entered into a new compromise with the Thermidorean reaction. Despite his antibourgeois prejudices, the power of money just now establishing itself seemed more bearable, all things considered, than that of the Terror. It was without enthusiasm but with no particular aversion that he followed the debates over the Constitution of Year III, whose principles one of its drafters, Boissy d'Anglas, described as follows: "You must finally guarantee the property of the rich . . . Civil equality: that is all the reasonable man can demand . . . We ought to be governed by the best: the best are the best educated and those with the greatest interest in preserving the law. But for a few exceptions you will find such men only among those who, owning property, are attached to the country that contains it, to the laws that protect it, to the tranquillity that preserves it."[4]

The sans-culottes and the popular movement were eliminated from the scene. France, still oppressed by all that it had endured for the past two terrible years, again felt social and domestic life stirring within its bosom. Paris breathed again. Gaiety and the taste for amusement brusquely reasserted their rights, while the political transformation of the capital proceeded at a rapid pace. One section after another passed into the hands of moderates. The Section des Piques,

once notable for its Jacobin fanaticism, now took a surprising ideological turn. The high aristocracy had disappeared with the monarchy,
and nobles had scattered abroad. Those unwilling to emigrate had
been decimated by the Terror. Those who remained in the country
were obliged to conceal their names and forfeit their property; their
chief desire was to disappear into oblivion. The bourgeoisie openly
resumed its pursuit of long-standing objectives: economic freedom,
respect for private property, and property qualifications for voting. In
this respect Thermidor "harked back to 1789."[5] Salons reopened their
doors, balls were held everywhere, theaters drew large crowds, luxury
again dared to rear its head, and ostentatious display flourished un-
checked: Mme Tallien launched a vogue for dressing in the manner
of the ancients; Mmes Hamelin and Récamier outdid each other in
curvaceous sartorial elegance; the *muscadins* strutted about the Palais-
Royal, closely shaved, perfumed, and clad in gloves and tails but armed
with bludgeons and ready for battle; they wore their hair in *cadenettes*
(long braids associated with a martial spirit). A ferocious appetite
gripped the French: "Gluttony is the basis of present-day society,"
Mercier noted in *Nouveau Paris*.

Offices, power, consideration—all changed hands. Yet never had
society witnessed such violent contrasts. While parvenus and stock-
jobbers reigned in the capital and speculation ran riot and insolent
fortunes piled up in strongboxes, the nation endured the most desperate
poverty. The collapse of the assignat led to a dizzying rise in the prices
of the most essential items: the bread ration decreased steadily, meat
went up every day, and the markets were empty. Distressing sights
were everywhere: lines forming in front of bakeries at one in the morning; poor wretches too weak to walk left to die on the sidewalks; and
suicides beyond counting, with mothers even leaping into the Seine
along with their children. The winter and spring of 1795 saw the
culmination of the ruin of small shopkeepers, people living on private
incomes, and government employees.

M. de Sade, Job Seeker

No sooner was he released from Picpus than M. de Sade resumed his
familiar litany: his back was to the wall, he was ruined, he was buried
in debt, his health was in a tragically precarious state. With winter
coming he lay shivering in his bed, besieged on all sides, with nothing
more to hock. Desperate at last, he begged Gaufridy to send him
enough to live on. "If you do not come to my aid immediately, I shall

have to blow my brains out." This was not the first time the marquis had threatened to take his own life, so the notary did not panic. A month went by. When nothing arrived, Donatien drew a bitter parallel between his own diligence to save his friend and Gaufridy's "lethargy" when the marquis asked for money.

For once, though, Donatien was barely exaggerating. There can be no doubt that his economic situation had deteriorated badly. The end of the command economy, from which he had expected great things, had presumably profited only the "merchant aristocracy" and the speculators. Far from reaping the profits of the new regime, Donatien suffered severely from its consequences. The explanation is simple. For one thing, all his property had been provisionally sequestered during his detention, and certain parcels remained sequestered even after his release. For another, when his harvests were sent to the national storage depot in his district, he was awarded the lowest possible price: thus he received six livres per quintal for his hay, when it was worth forty.[6] Finally, despite his insistence on being paid in hard cash, nearly all his income came to him in the form of assignats, and the value of this paper money had declined steadily, from 31 percent of face value in July 1794 to 20 percent in December and then to 8 percent in March 1795. The louis, meanwhile, was rising steadily, from 700 livres in June to 1,200 in September and 1,800 in October. This runaway deflation of paper currency further exacerbated the rise in food prices. The influx of food diminished, reserves dwindled, and the black market flourished.

In this widespread depression M. de Sade's fate was similar to that of many small landowners dependent on the income from their land, which now came in the form of worthless paper. His living conditions became desperate: "I am writing this in a fairly warm room, yet the cold that we are experiencing is such that (something I have never seen before) my ink freezes as I write, and I am forced to keep it in a bain-marie. And there is no wood. A load sufficient for two months is all you can get, and it costs forty francs. Everything is the same: with twenty-five francs a day you die of hunger."[7] The winter of 1795 was one of the harshest on record. The Seine remained frozen for several weeks in a row, preventing shipments of food from arriving: "We have already surpassed the cold waves of 1740 and 1709. You cannot imagine how cold it is, and we are short of everything. Even water costs more today than wine used to."[8] In the same letter Sade reported the death of the président de Montreuil, who had passed away the week before, on January 15, 1795.

Soon out of money and without news from Gaufridy, Sade decided to apply for a job and sent a curriculum vitae to the *conventionnel* Jacques-Antoine Rabaut-Pommier, who at one time had been one of Marat's bitterest enemies. Sade, Marat's erstwhile apologist, enumerated his skills, mentioning his aptitude for negotiations, a profession "in which his father spent twenty years," his knowledge of certain parts of Europe, and his literary gifts. He could be of use "in the composition or editing of a work of any kind or in the operation or administration of a library, office, or museum." In conclusion he wrote: "Sade, who is not without talents, is, in a word, asking you to find him a job. His profession of true patriotism and his eagerness at all times to be of use to his country should tell you that he will discharge the responsibilities of any position you may be kind enough to obtain for him with aptitude and intelligence."[9]

Not surprisingly, this letter went unanswered. Sade was fifty-six, had never worked in his life, and had a long criminal record, an ambiguous political itinerary, and a difficult personality: even the most favorably disposed person in the world might be discouraged. As for his literary references, they amounted, thus far, to an obscene novel, a number of rejected plays, a few others hooted off stage, and a few occasional speeches. On top of all that, his children were émigrés, he was separated from his wife, and he was living on dubious terms with a woman: none of this was likely to inspire confidence.

Literary Comeback

Having been unlucky in the theater, Sade could legitimately pin his hopes on his novels. As it happens, the eight volumes of *Aline et Valcour* had just been published, and we know what a hard road it had been. Written in the Bastille between 1785 and 1788 and revised by the author after his release, the book had initially been scheduled to appear in 1791. On March 6 of that year the author had announced that it would be printed by Easter. On June 12 he said that publication was imminent. But thirty months later it still was not finished. The reader will recall that when Sade's house was searched on December 8, 1793, Donatien had asked one of the policemen to pass three pages of manuscript on to his publisher Girouard. Unfortunately, Girouard was executed a few months later.

On December 5, 1794, the marquis asked the government to return to him "any printed portions of this novel from Girouard's shop." Although he had been paid for the manuscript, he reserved "substantial rights over the copies." In any case he wished to make some minor corrections so as to give the work "that male and severe physiognomy that is appropriate to a free nation." Last but not least, the work was "the fruit of several years of sleepless nights, and," he said, "I shall never reap the rewards if you do not, by returning it to me, put me in a position to have it published."[10] It would not appear until August 1795, when Girouard's widow at last published it in eight elegant volumes illustrated with etchings.

The first copies were for Gaufridy. On August 26 Sade wrote him: "Please let me know how I may send you, postpaid, two copies of a work in eight volumes that I have just had printed; one for you, the other for your best friend. This work, from which people say they expect a great deal, may interest you. I shall send it as soon as I have your answer."[11] Certainly Sade himself expected a great deal from the book, not only for his reputation as a writer but also in improved living conditions. Why shouldn't he live by his pen, after all, if there was no other prospect of employment? Two days later he sent Lions a publicity message to be communicated to all the booksellers of the region. No doubt he hoped that his notoriety in Provence would add to his sales:

You are hereby informed, Citizen, that a work entitled *Aline et Valcour, ou le Roman philosophique*, eight volumes (in-18), handsome characters, embellished with engravings, has been published in Paris by the widow Girouard, Maison Egalité. Wholesale price: 100 livres, stitched.

Copies are being snapped up at a rate that should encourage you to hasten your order. In case you should wish to procure copies, kindly submit your order to Citizen Lions, your agent in Paris, and the number of copies you request will be shipped to him. Answer at your earliest convenience if you wish to order.

11 fructidor, Year III [August 28, 1795][12]

Was *Aline et Valcour* really being snapped up by readers? M. de Sade was no doubt exaggerating somewhat. Yet bibliographers have identified no fewer than three successive editions, which is proof of a certain success. What is more, the work inspired imitators—a fairly good sign. An obscure hack by the name of Ménégault borrowed from "L'Histoire de Sainville et de Léonore" for a counterfeit entitled "Valmor et Lydia," which he later reprinted verbatim under the name "Alzonde et Koradin." These two identical works were taken word for word from an episode of *Aline et Valcour* that takes up almost two-thirds of the novel. The plagiarist, by the way, had several other exploits to his credit, and these would eventually earn him terms in the work-house and penitentiary.[13]

•

In the same year, 1795, two small volumes were published under the titillating title *La Philosophie dans le boudoir*, with a notice that it was a "Posthumous Work by the Author of Justine." The point of the attribution is clear: the *Philosophie* was deliberately being cast as a work in the licentious genre of *Justine*, a "dangerous" book, for the sole purpose of attracting a clientele. And to spice things up still further, Sade included this epigraph: "Mothers will prescribe the work for their daughters." But if, as in the case of *Justine*, the purpose of the book was commercial (and how can anyone deny that it was?), the grandeur of its conception makes us forget its lucrative intent. To be sure, erotic scenes abound. Dolmancé and Saint-Ange try to outdo each other in obscenities. Spurred on by the questions of their young pupil Eugénie, they engage in nothing less than an erotic contest to see which of them can carry perversion to its uttermost extreme, whether in word or deed. The theory of pleasure—the alpha and omega of all things—gives rise to extensive discussions illustrated by practical exercises in frenetic depravity. The text builds in a crescendo toward the scene in which a valet by the name of Lapierre, afflicted with the pox, seizes Eugénie's mother Mme de Mistival, has intercourse with her, and then sodomizes her in order to pass on the disease. Then, to make sure that no noxious effluvia can escape her body, the two libertines take needle and thread and sew up its various orifices.

These "exploits" divert the reader from seven didactic dialogues dealing, in a disjointed, freewheeling manner, with questions such as religion, nature, morals, crime, and revolution. Embedded in rather arbitrary fashion within the body of the text, the pamphlet entitled "Français, encore un effort, si vous voulez être républicain," which Sade attributes to Dolmancé, does not contradict the ironic intention announced by the title. This part of the work amounts to nothing less than a reductio ad absurdum of the theory of revolution and a radical mockery of Jacobin philosophy. Sade avails himself of the opportunity to cross swords with two of his bêtes noires: Christianity and the death penalty. He returns, with greater freedom than had hitherto been possible, to his vehement attacks on the God of the Christians, and his scorn spills over onto Robespierre's theism: "We want nothing more to do with the fantastic author of a self-moved universe. We want nothing more to do with a god having no extension who yet fills all space with his immensity, with an omnipotent god who can never do what he wants, with a sovereignly good being who sows nothing but discontent, with a friend of order in whose government everything is in disorder. No, we want nothing more to do with a god who deranges nature, who is the father of confusion, who moves man at the moment when man indulges in horrors: such a god makes us shake with rage, and we relegate him forever to the oblivion from which the infamous Robespierre wished to rescue him."[14] Condemned to death a year earlier for similar remarks, Sade is here clearly taking posthumous revenge.

As for capital punishment, Sade shared the view of marginal "utopians" opposed to the death penalty, such as Morelly, who in his *Code de la nature* (1755) suggested replacing it with life imprisonment. For Sade, the death penalty was the ultimate crime, because the law that prescribed it lacked even the excuse of passion, madness, or desire. The state kills by reason; it is thus guilty of cold-blooded institutional murder, which nothing can justify. To those who invoked the alleged deterrent value of capital punishment, Sade replied: "The second reason for abolishing the death penalty is that it has never prevented crime, for crimes are committed every day at the foot of the scaffold. This penalty should be eliminated, in a word, because there is no calculation more erroneous than that involved in putting one man to death for killing another, since the obvious result of this procedure is that instead of one man less, there are suddenly two, and such arithmetic can be familiar only to executioners or imbeciles."[15] Sade did not conceal his hopes of influencing the legislature, then at work drafting the "Code of the Year IV." To be sure, it took less courage to publish these lines after Thermidor than during the Terror. It is interesting, however, to find the "infamous marquis" standing alone against the death penalty, after the disciples of Rousseau and noble Nature had caused so many heads to fall in the name of virtue.

Sectional Stew

Did Donatien truly hope to get rich through his books? That is perhaps putting it a bit strongly. He hoped only to earn enough to get by or at least to delay his slide into poverty, whose specter was looming on the horizon. Prices were rising at a frightening rate, and Donatien was having a hard time keeping up. What used to cost fifteen sols now cost fifteen francs. Worse still, the uncouth shopkeeper threw your purchases in your face. "Many items have gone up even more," he complained. "For example, the preserves, oil, and candles that I asked you for have increased thirtyfold. Wine is just about the only thing that has merely tripled. Luxury items are unbelievable: a dog, six hundred francs; a horse, thirty, forty, or even fifty thousand francs; a ride in a carriage that used to cost twenty-five sols is now a hundred francs; a cloth coat is a thousand écus." Accordingly, he cut back his expenses to a minimum: "Sectional stew, sectional bread, vegetables five days a week, not one show, not one fantasy, [just] my lady friend, a cook and myself."[16] But day by day his situation was growing more precarious.

Gaufridy was staggering under Sade's demands for money. The marquis hammered away at him but received no response. He threatened Mme Gaufridy: if her husband persisted in his silence, he, Sade, would move in with them. Then they would have to feed him. Still nothing. For once the notary was not guilty of negligence. If he remained unresponsive, it was because he had just lost his eldest son Elzéar, and his heart was no longer in business. Upon learning the sad news, M. de Sade responded in his own way: "I can imagine your regrets and your sorrow and sincerely pity you for the terrible loss you have suffered. But, my dear and good friend, while crying for the dead, do not allow the living to perish: that is the point to which your terrible negligence has reduced me. My money, I beg you for it."[17]

Another death cheered him: that of his elderly relative, M. de Murs, whose inheritance he had always coveted. But his joy was mixed with livid rage against Gaufridy, who had not even notified him: "Yes, it is five months since M. de Murs died and I am the person who, by law, is to inherit from him, yet you tell me nothing! . . . Oh! My friend, your behavior is inconceivable, and I see none of your feeling for me in it! . . . Is it possible, great God, that you have fallen asleep over this matter? Make haste, I beg you. Go with the law in hand, and it all belongs to us! If you let this drag on, the nation will take it all, and I will have nothing."[18]

He was not wrong about the law. Since the old man had emigrated, his will was invalid, and his natural heirs, the demoiselles de Chabrillant, forfeited their rights; so it was written in the law, and M. de Sade was highly legalistic—when it came to others. What could be more natural than for Sade, the father of émigrés, to attempt to rob the daughters of an émigré of their property? But he was wasting his time, as it turned out: the late M. de Murs's fortune would not fall into his clutches. Cynicism did him no good, or at any rate he lacked the knack for making use of it. It was a shame, because at bottom he had all the gifts of a stockjobber. He could have made a fortune out of other people's hunger, as the Turcarets did under the Directory. He did not lack the effrontery, the unscrupulousness, the selfishness, or any of the other essential qualities of the speculator. With a little more hypocrisy and a little less clumsiness, he might have been riding in a carriage on the boulevards with a crimson complexion and a pot-belly. But he was too contemptuous of money for that; if he sometimes gave in to greed, he never yielded to the lure of profit.

Now, however, only one way out of his difficulties remained: to sell his property.

Father and Son

Apart from these material difficulties, Sade was also concerned about his status as the father of émigrés. The decrees of 25 brumaire and 12 floréal (November 15, 1794, and May 1, 1795) ordered that émigrés who returned to France should promptly be brought to trial along with their accomplices. All were subject to the death penalty, applicable within twenty-four hours after sentencing without reprieve or appeal. Sade's elder son Louis-Marie had returned to Paris, while his younger son was in Malta as a knight of the Order. Donatien immediately improvised the following scenario, which he sent to Gaufridy with instructions to spread the story as widely as possible:

One day, a month ago, my elder son entered my bedroom. I do not need to describe for you what mixed emotions of fear, surprise, and joy I felt on seeing him.

"Father," the young man said as he embraced me, "neither my brother nor I ever emigrated. He has been in Malta for five years serving his Order, and the laws on emigration have no bearing on knights [of the Order]. As for me, father, guided by the same considerations as my brother, and neither of us knowing which party, yours or mother's, to choose, I quit the service. I love the arts, and I have made such progress in them that today I am earning a living from engraving and botany. I have traveled all over France to mountains and picturesque sites. In short, I have worked. I have come back, and come back provided with all the papers and certificates necessary to convince you of the truth of what I am saying. I am living in the Section des Tuileries, I am working every day in the museum, and I am doing my sectional service. If anyone dares to accuse me of emigration, they will see how I respond. At the first opportunity I personally will write to Citizen Gaufridy to assure him that if anyone ever dares to accuse me of this crime, I have documents to dispel any doubts."

And if doubts remained, if anyone dared to invoke the Convention's decrees in the notary's presence, he was to respond as follows:

—It is very fortunate for M. de Sade that his children are not in that situation.
—But how can that be? People said they had emigrated.
—The accusation is false. I defy you to find them on any list. The younger one is in Malta, and a knight of that Order does not emigrate by going to his post. The elder boy is with his father. He traveled within France, learned something about engraving and botany, and is earning his living that way. He is a member of the Section des Tuileries and will provide proof of all this whenever you like.[19]

In the future, as a measure of prudence, Sade would refer to his children as *Vogel* (German for bird). One wonders why he chose that particular word.

•

Louis-Marie had always been Sade's favorite of his three children. He was the least "Montreuil," the closest to his father in tastes and sensibility. An engraver by trade, musician, writer, and not bad looking, he shared a number of character traits with his father: impetuous, querulous, and insincere, he had Donatien's talent for setting everyone against him, beginning with his own mother, whom he irritated no end; his brother was secretly jealous of him, and his uncles and aunts were critical of his foul language and vehement temper. The sudden tantrums that erupt in some of Louis-Marie's many letters to his family concerning the président de Montreuil's inheritance are strikingly reminiscent of Donatien's tone in writing to his notary. And like the marquis, Louis-Marie squandered money by the barrelful, a failing that elicited this disillusioned comment from Mme de Sade: "If he continues in this way, someone will have to feed him, as they do his father." And like Donatien the boy was a libertine, constantly running off to parties and balls and always gambling, and he had lost count of his female conquests. Once, he even slept with a former mistress of his father's, a beautiful creole identified only as Mme Raynal de S*** and known as Mimi, a painter and woman of easy virtue.[20] The marquis was furious and stopped at nothing to separate the pair.

Louis-Marie's closest friend was a young officer from Carpentras named Alexander Cabanis, in whom young Sade confided about his love affairs. Cabanis tried to lead his friend back to the straight and narrow, encouraging him to rejoin the army and above all to go to

Avignon to pay his respects to his great-aunt Villeneuve. The elderly lady had never let go of the youth and had even expressed a desire to make him her heir, because she preferred him to Donatien's other children. Time was of the essence, since the lady was more than eighty years old. But Louis-Marie's mind was on other things: the promise of an inheritance was nothing compared with a night in Paris. In the end, however, he did go to see Mme de Villeneuve. And once more M. de Sade lost his temper, for he was again in rivalry with his son, this time over money.

Relations between father and son could not have been more tumultuous. Undoubtedly they had too much in common to get along; their clashes were frequent and severe. Between disputes, however, Donatien did not hide the fact that at bottom he was fond of Louis-Marie, despite, or perhaps because of, his bohemian, adventurous, devil-may-care side. "I love him dearly. I am sure that he will always be happy with what I leave him but not with the position from which I shall be leaving him his fortune. Energetic, a lover of the arts, concerned solely with painting and music, this young man does not hide the fact that once peace comes, he wants the whole world for his fatherland. If I did not discourage him, he would leave immediately for New England."[21]

In the bloody showdown of 13 vendémiaire with the royalists, Louis-Marie served with Bonaparte. His father, aware of this and having heard no news of his son's condition, feared for his safety, as he revealed to Gaufridy. But once the danger was past, he waited for the boy to step out of line again so that he might administer another tongue-lashing. Their relations were passionate and vehement, a mixture of love and hate.

A Bluff

Ever since his release from Picpus, Donatien had been thinking of selling his property in Saumane known as La Grand'Bastide. The moment seemed opportune, because land, after several price increases, "is now as valuable as gold." Sade wanted thirty to thirty-five thousand francs for the property and commissioned Gaufridy to conduct the negotiations. Shortly thereafter the notary located buyers willing to pay forty thousand francs: his brother-in-law Archias, a merchant from Aix, and his partner, a man named Arnaud. Sade received a deposit of 22,276 livres in the form of two letters of exchange. So far, so good.

A short while later Sade received an offer of forty-five thousand

francs from a Sieur Villars of L'Isle-sur-la-Sorgue. He immediately
called a halt to the prior deal. If Messieurs Archias and Arnaud wanted
the farm, all they had to do was improve on this new offer. Sade,
meanwhile, promised not to cash the letters of exchange until a contract
was signed. Then he changed his mind: the offer, he decided, was still
too low, real estate was going up, there was no shortage of buyers, and
it would be foolish not to take advantage of the situation. So he wrote
to Archias, telling him that he had just sold the farm himself for sixty
thousand francs and was returning the first letter of exchange, the
smaller of the two, worth 9,022 livres, forthwith. He chose to keep the
other, in the amount of 13,254 livres, in order to "avoid the costs and
dangers of sending it." Gaufridy would reimburse Archias directly out
of revenues he was expecting. "I am unhappy," Sade hypocritically
added, "not to have been able to conclude the deal with you. If it had
been a question of only a thousand écus, my confidence in and friendship for Gaufridy would certainly have led me to overlook the difference, but fifteen to twenty thousand livres was worth looking out for."[22]
This was an outright lie. Sade had not sold his farm. He was simply
bluffing in the hope of driving the price up still further. In the meantime, however, he had pocketed part of the deposit.

Three days later, he returned to the attack and with a perfectly
straight face sent the following letter to Gaufridy: "There is not a
Provençal in Paris who does not make me an offer daily, and I swear
I had one today for sixty-five thousand livres, but I will not use it to
break the deal with you; your buyers can have the farm." Out of pure
goodness, in other words, he was willing to sell his land to Archias
and Arnaud, but not for less than sixty-one thousand livres, and on
condition that the deposit of 13,254 livres be regarded henceforth as
a loan, naturally without interest, in exchange for which the marquis
would relinquish his claim on the next harvest from the sold property.
Sade outdid himself this time in cynicism, impudence, and deceit. At
first the buyers were simply staggered by such outright dishonesty and
frowned at the deal, but in the end they agreed. The contract was
signed in the presence of Maître Forest, an Apt notary, on March 31,
1795.

At this point Gaufridy realized that the marquis had outwitted
him, to say nothing of embarrassing him in front of his brother-in-
law. As usual Sade saw only his own interest. As well as Gaufridy knew
him, he could not restrain his bitterness: "I would never have thought
that you would aggravate my sorrows." Not yet recovered from the loss
of his son three months earlier, he was all the more pained by his

friend's betrayal. But Sade, for his part, rubbed his hands together in glee. Delighted at having gotten the better of the two partners and persuaded that he had swindled them, he shamelessly expressed his pleasure to the notary and then added a friendly tap on the shoulder: "Come, now, my dear citizen, stop your frowning and stop accusing me of no longer trusting you . . . Feel happy again, regain your confidence and your friendship, and above all keep up the good work."[23]

Let the righteous reader be reassured, however: Messrs Archias and Arnaud had struck a good bargain nevertheless, and Donatien wound up being swindled. Given the runaway inflation of paper money, the proceeds from this sale quickly evaporated.

"Take her pulse"

Still short of cash, Sade thought of getting rid of Mazan, which meant little more to him than La Grand'Bastide. To tell the truth, he got the idea from his aunt Villeneuve. In February 1795 she had proposed him an annuity of fifteen thousand livres, payable in advance, in exchange for the right to live in the château. She was tired of Avignon and needed peace and quiet. The marquis howled with outrage. Fifteen thousand francs? Was she joking? He would require at least seventy thousand. Mazan, year in and year out, brought him four thousand francs. It would therefore yield the full amount of the annuity in roughly four years of the elderly woman's life. The marquis claimed, moreover, that he had been on the verge of letting Mazan to a farmer for eight thousand francs a year. And his aunt, he said, still had ten years to live. The calculation was simple. Seventy thousand, not a penny less! Of course if she paid in gold, he would let it go for thirty thousand, or even twenty-five, but that was his final offer. Take it or leave it. But wait, Mme de Villeneuve could strike an even better bargain if she wished. She was rich and had two daughters. Why not buy Mazan "in perpetuity"? Her daughters would enjoy its fruits after she was gone. Sade was willing to settle for a hundred thousand francs in hard cash or two hundred fifty thousand in assignats, and he promised a bonus of two thousand gold écus to his steward Quinquin if he closed the deal. But what if the old lady had only two more years to live? In that case the annuity would be the better deal, and Sade would have blown his chance. So he dashed off a hasty note to Gaufridy: "Go see her at once and *take her pulse*, and if you think she cannot last two years, close the deal on the spot."[24] If twenty-five thousand francs seemed too high, he said he was ready to come down to twenty thousand. If she refused, let the château with its courtyard and grounds be sold for the best price. But the fruit orchard was to be preserved: "It's a veritable Peru." If no buyer appeared, he would have the buildings demolished brick by brick and sell off the stones, timbers, and hardware. He hoped to get a million francs out of it, enough to repay his debts and buy himself a country house near Paris. A utopian dream!

Gaufridy Steps Aside

Time passed, and Mazan did not sell. Mme de Villeneuve gave up on the idea. To add insult to injury, she also refused to give her nephew the silver to which he was entitled from the late abbé's estate. Donatien swallowed his anger for fear of losing the old lady's inheritance and once again set out in search of money, whatever it might take. The quest became an obsession. To be sure, his situation was becoming more critical by the day. Prices were continuing to rise, and the steady decline of the assignat was reducing his income to nothing. To top it all off, Gaufridy no longer answered his letters, if he so much as bothered to read them. The ingrate had forgotten his dear friend Sade at a time when the marquis was dying of hunger, bedridden, ravaged by fever, without money to pay for treatment. Pleas, reproaches, injunctions, and threats fell in avalanches on the notary's office. As if M. de Sade were the only person in the world! As if he, Gaufridy, didn't have other clients to attend to! But M. de Sade didn't care a whit about all that: those who had the honor to serve him were expected to devote themselves fully to the task twenty-four hours a day. They had not just a duty but a vocation to serve him.

Determined to reduce his caseload, Gaufridy took his second son Charles into the business as his assistant, and to start the boy out his father assigned him the marquis's affairs. The father may have been relieved, but the son was terrified of the ordeal that lay in store. Though annoyed at first, Sade eventually started the apprentice scribe off with a clean slate. But the younger Gaufridy was not as ready to bow and scrape as his father had been. He knew whom he was dealing with and had no intention of allowing himself to be eaten alive. Nor was he about to put up with the marquis's insolence. When the first harsh words came, the novice dug in his heels, which earned him this lesson: "For God's sake, do not get angry when I get angry, for if we are both angry who will patch things up? If you fail to send money, permit me to scream and rage as if I were being skinned alive; your sole response in all circumstances should be a letter of exchange."[25] M. de Sade used rage as a form of spiritual hygiene; anger freed him from his humors.

The Sale of La Coste

Sell La Coste? The marquis had thought about it a few times but never very seriously. Now, however, his back was to the wall. His finances had been deteriorating steadily since the beginning of 1796. In less than a year the proceeds from the sale of La Grand'Bastide had melted like snow on a warm day. In March he had had to abandon his comfortable nest in the Chaussée-d'Antin, whose rent had become too heavy a burden. Together with Mme Quesnet he rented a country house in Clichy-la-Garenne opposite the château stables. Though a bit far from Paris, it cost only three hundred livres per year.

On September 9, 1796, without warning, Sade signed a purchase–and–sale agreement for La Coste and all its dependencies with Joseph-Stanislas Rovère, a member of the Conseil des Anciens, for the price of 58,400 livres plus an under-the-table payment of 16,000 livres. The new owner promised to leave the stewardship of the property in the hands of Gaufridy, whom Sade had praised warmly, hoping thereby to win himself a local ally. This was a miscalculation: the notary was not a man to serve two masters.

•

As soon as he was informed of the promise to sell, Gaufridy warned M. de Sade of the difficulties that would not fail to arise in attempting to close the deal: La Coste was mortgaged; Mme de Sade's claim on the marquis's property by itself totaled 199,000 livres, the amount of her dowry plus the interest that her husband had failed to pay her for the past six years. The sales contract would therefore have to stipulate that any monies paid by Rovère would be rolled over into real estate so that Mme de Sade might take out a lien on the new property. Donatien, who had hoped to obtain a little cold cash out of the deal, received none.

Saint-Ouen

On October 14, 1796, exactly twenty-four hours after the sale of La Coste, Constance Quesnet paid 15,000 francs to become the owner of a house at 3, place de la Liberté, in Saint-Ouen. On April 20, 1797, the couple moved into its new home along with Mme Quesnet's son.

When Mme Quesnet resold the property with her furniture on

July 5, 1802, the notary Normand had a detailed inventory prepared. Thanks to this document, we can for the first time reconstruct the setting in which Donatien spent his final three years of freedom with his beloved Sensible.

The carriage entrance opened onto a grassy courtyard with fruit trees between two projecting wings of the house. On the first floor a dining room with papered walls featured a fireplace in a niche and, in the center, a round walnut table capable of seating twelve. This led to the salon, which had a marble fireplace, a yellow canapé, six chairs stuffed with straw, two large armoires, a mahogany console, a sofa, four matching armchairs, and numerous other items. Among the other rooms, Sade's bedroom had "arabesque" wallpaper and a marble fireplace, six chairs, a commode, a small armoire, and a veneered writing desk. The marquis's study was lined with bookcases, which were the only items of furniture that Constance would not sell.

Though not particularly luxurious, the house does leave an impression of bourgeois comfort. The partly urban, partly rural furnishing (many of the chairs being filled with straw) was characteristic of country houses near Paris at the time.

The Lord's Homecoming

Though the owner of two new estates and a house, the marquis nevertheless lacked what was really essential. Obliged to roll over the money derived from the sale of La Coste, he had been unable to keep a cent for himself, and buying the house in Saint-Ouen had put a new dent in his finances. What could he do to extract hard cash from his remaining property? All his possessions had liens against them, but he needed to sell one without being forced to reinvest the proceeds. In other words, he had to get around the troublesome regulations governing the sale of mortgaged property—no mean feat.

Suddenly an idea came to him. He had found a way to sell his land without a contract, but he absolutely had to have three thousand francs before May 1. Only his friend Gaufridy could help him out. There was not a second to lose. If he missed the deadline, it would be too late. Those three thousand francs were more essential to him than the air he breathed. Once the deal was closed, he would leave the notary in peace. He swore that he would never ask him for another cent. He also promised that he would not use the money to travel to the south of France, as rumor had it that he would: "No, no, no, a thousand times no, whatever the tellers of false tales may say, the money is not for going to Provence." Two weeks later he turned up at Gaufridy's door with Mme Quesnet on his arm. The notary was not surprised. Rovère had warned him of the marquis's arrival.

It was exactly nineteen years since the marquis had last set foot in Provence—at the time of his dramatic arrest on August 26, 1778. The entire Gaufridy family—Mme Gaufridy and her sister Mme Archias, the boys Charles and François, the girls Benoîte and Gothon, and even the grandmother—gave the marquis a warm welcome. The notary fell into his old friend's arms. If neither found it easy to recognize the other, there was plenty of emotion on both sides.

Once the effusion was over, however, it was down to business for M. de Sade. For the sake of convenience (and to avoid gossip) he left Constance with the notary and went alone to Saumane, the first stop on his journey and the first hitch in his plans, seemingly insignificant to begin with—but within a short time things had degenerated into a scandal. With Donatien the slightest incident could take on ridiculous proportions. At issue in this case was a trivial sum, 29 francs and 14 sols, which one of the marquis's debtors had paid, in accordance with the law on émigrés, to the collector of the Domaine National, a man by the name of Noël Perrin, for payment into the Public Treasury. The irascible marquis sent two outraged letters in quick succession to the unfortunate Perrin, accusing him of theft and demanding that the money be returned immediately. If not, Donatien would denounce him to the Directory and see to it that he got the punishment he deserved. The official, however, was not intimidated and filed charges against his accuser with the criminal court of Avignon, which found his allegations against Perrin "false and libelous." Since the petitioner, "in his capacity as collector, all of whose actions must be above reproach, cannot allow such charges to be spread," the court condemned Citizen Sade to pay, in addition to court costs, a fine of 1,500 francs to the communal charities of Avignon. Clearly the Republic did not toy with charges of defamation of public officials in the performance of their duties, especially when the accused was a former noble.

M. de Sade couldn't have cared less about the guilty verdict (he had seen others). What troubled him, though, was the fine of 1,500 francs. It could not have come at a worse moment. He tried to arrange things by signing a notarized retraction, in which he disavowed his charges against Citizen Perrin and acknowledged that he was "an honest and decent man who had always performed the duties of his office with distinction." Perrin agreed to drop the matter provided that the defendant pay his costs and make a contribution of 24 francs to the hospital in Carpentras. Sade thus got out of this scrape at small cost, but it failed to teach him much of a lesson. Availing himself of the opportunity, he proclaimed once again that he had never emigrated, that his name had been removed from the list of émigrés from the Bouches-du-Rhône, but that it still appeared on that of the Vaucluse. The collector's mistake was therefore perfectly comprehensible, and the man was only doing his duty.[26] But the affair alerted the authorities, who reprimanded the notary Quinquin of Mazan for having neglected to sequester the marquis's property in that city. Mazan was in fact located in the Vaucluse, a département that officially listed Sade as an émigré. The oversight was immediately rectified, making it impossible for Donatien to sell so much as a square inch of land in the commune of Mazan. In short, things were in a total mess. The Perrin affair had "set this whole train in motion." Sade had no doubt expected a very different sort of welcoming gift to greet him on his return home.

When the former marquis arrived in Mazan, there were incidents. A "crook" even swindled him out of twenty-five louis. Shortly after Donatien's departure, the man was found murdered, his body buried under a pile of rocks. The municipal council came as a body to visit the former lord of the place and left a sheriff's deputy on the premises to ensure that his taxes would be paid. An opportunist to some, a "terrorist" to others, an undesirable to all, M. de Sade could scarcely avoid recognizing that his presence in a Provence still caught up in turmoil was in many ways unwelcome. If he had expected to be received as the prodigal son, the residents of the area soon disabused him. Their welcome was anything but warm. He nevertheless used his time to confirm Gaufridy's nephew Roux as his proxy in place of Quinquin, also known as "the Widower." A Jacobin extremist, this "Widower" had feigned devotion to the marquis while managing his property but had in fact been conducting business dealings behind his back. Donatien also sorted out what remained of his family archives, which had survived the sacking of La Coste only to be mauled in Mazan.

As for La Coste, Donatien had nothing to say. If he made a pilgrimage to his former home, he left no written record of it, perhaps because he was not at his best in dealing with emotion. Or perhaps he decided not to visit a place that for him was too full of memories and that he no longer owned. Is it assuming too much to suggest that he was afraid of his past? Had his sensibility degenerated to the point where we cannot imagine him facing the steep hill atop which the desolate walls of his castle loomed skyward, meditating on the fickleness of fate? His silence, in any event, is strange.

As his travels continued, Sade gradually became aware of a thousand hitherto unsuspected difficulties. Seen from Paris, the situation had seemed fairly clear. Did he need money? All he had to do was holler and let Gaufridy figure out how to come up with it. Were creditors demanding to be paid? Were farmers not paying what they owed? What of it? From a distance the obstacles seemed to vanish. But reality close up was something else entirely. The creditors were no longer a myth, nor were the farmers vague ghosts. The Riperts, Audiberts, and Quinquins all had faces, and accounts were no longer merely numbers on a page. Alone, in a hostile environment, faced with problems of which he had previously heard only faint echoes, he now had to negotiate with one man, sign a compromise agreement with another, allow himself to become bogged down in pointless legal maneuvers with a third, and waste his time in hopeless activity.

M. de Sade's Lottery

In the end he decided to leave for his principal destination, the Beaucaire fair, where he planned to carry out the ingenious strategy he had conceived in Paris and for which he needed 3,000 francs. The idea was simple. Since he could not sell his land, he would put up his estates as the stakes in a lottery. Abracadabra and presto! And since the farm at Cabannes, located in the Bouches-du-Rhône, had not been sequestered, he would begin with it. Gaufridy's complicity being essential, the marquis begged the notary to accompany him, but the old man begged off on grounds of fatigue. The marquis then asked if he could take Gaufridy's sons, Charles and François. The notary resisted at first but ultimately gave in. Charles went ahead to attend to the customary formalities, and on July 23, the day after the official opening of the fair, M. de Sade arrived on the scene together with young François. At last his problems were over. He would go home with his pockets full, put his affairs in order, and replenish what it had cost him to buy the house in Saint-Ouen. But in the event, not a single ticket was sold. Sade's disappointment was as great as his illusions had been grand.

Still, the public's lack of interest in a farm of this size is strange. Might Gaufridy have been behind it? The notary, as we have seen, was no longer inclined to indulge Sade's extravagances (or what he considered extravagances). He felt himself charged with a superior mission: to rescue Sade from his demons, to slow his precipitous fall. And above all to save his children's inheritance. So skillful was Mme de Sade at reminding him of his "duty" that he sacrificed his client's interests without giving them a second thought. He felt no compunctions about instructing Charles to see to it that the Beaucaire lottery failed. And he felt no compunctions several months later about preventing the sale of Cabannes.

But on that occasion Sade had foreseen everything: the sale would be concluded secretly, and Renée-Pélagie would know nothing about it. In any case, she had never had the property surveyed, and his children had no idea what it was worth. As for the other creditors, the deal would be closed before they noticed a thing. And in any case they could be swindled by introducing a phony prior claim: the sale could be backdated and a straw man brought into the picture, an alleged creditor who would put a lien on the proceeds, pocket them, and then return the cash to Donatien under the table. Mme Quesnet had played the role to perfection in Paris. Why shouldn't Gaufridy do it in Provence? But the notary refused. With Mme de Sade pulling strings from afar, he thwarted the plan by brandishing dozens of liens, enough to discourage even the most eager buyers. By paying an indemnity he even managed to get the farmer Lombard, who had purchased several fields from the marquis, to relinquish his claims. This feat earned him the marquise's congratulations: "I would be upset if you thought I was not grateful for what you did to prevent a sale not in M. de Sade's interests or those of his children . . . You can be certain that I will not compromise you in any way."[27]

The libertine *grand seigneur* and his sidekick, the prudent accountant, were a fascinating, indeed an almost mythical, pair. One was like the reincarnation of Don Juan, while the other might have been Sganarelle.

Toward the end of the journey Sade learned that a group of youths had broken into his château at Mazan and demanded that it be demolished. It was definitely time to go. When it came time to part, Donatien and Gaufridy embraced, tears in their eyes. No doubt both men vaguely sensed that they were seeing each other for the last time: Donatien would never again set foot in Provence.

25

Sade's
Misfortunes

At bottom Donatien was not unhappy to return to Paris. Not only had his plans come to nought, but he had been able to gauge his native region's hostility to him personally. There could be no doubt that the "good peasants" he had known in another era had changed dramatically. To them he was now the class enemy and nothing more. What was the good of playing the sans-culotte in Paris only to be accused of being a despot on the lands of one's ancestors? And then he was beginning to miss Sensible, who had stayed at Gaufridy's while he traveled; he was glad to be reunited with his "dear friend, whose life is dearer to him than his own."

In the postal coach taking them back to Paris, however, the two suddenly quarreled. At least that is the account offered by a certain Bonnefoy, formerly a surveyor from Colombes, who had lent the couple the money for the trip and who was traveling with them in the same carriage. Bonnefoy's story is at odds with everything we know about the couple's affectionate relations, but it is worth quoting anyway:

There was some testiness en route, but not as much as I would have thought. They both told me that they would not be living together for long, and what I have learned since my arrival confirms this. I am counting on seeing them tomorrow for the last time. It is truly to be hoped for M. de Sade's sake that he separates from her, or that she separates from him. She is the nastiest woman alive. That she is as false as a counterfeit coin hardly surprises me. When a woman has spent the better part of her life in theaters in the provinces as well as Paris, she is capable of playing comedy in any and all circumstances. I do not think that M. de Sade will leave his relationship with her as he came into it. I am much afraid that he fails to perceive her wiles. She is clever and has stout young fellows to look after her interests. And he, to top it all off, has the same reputation in Paris as in Provence.[1]

This Bonnefoy was Rovère's henchman, a professional slanderer, and later the presumed author of anonymous letters attacking Sade— in short, an out and out scoundrel whose every move was dictated by his patron back in Paris. His plan was to discredit the marquis and his companion in Gaufridy's eyes, if necessary by means of baldfaced lies. This was the reason for the venomous report to the notary. Bonnefoy's testimony to the contrary notwithstanding, the journey had passed without the slightest difficulty. I have found the marquis's own account among his unpublished papers, and it contradicts Bonnefoy's version point by point:

Fair weather, nice road, *Sensible's charming mood* [my italics]. No panic or swooning whatsoever on the part of this dear lady, who never frowns except on occasion to say, "Oh, how annoying it is to leave Provence! What a respectable, charming, delicate friend I am losing in M. Gaufridy. When will I see him and his charming family again?" And then she makes a hundred plans to come back and see you in two years. So you see, as I was saying, everything went as well as could be expected.[2]

New Threats

The coup d'état of 18 fructidor, Year V (September 4, 1797) crushed the right and put a new Directory in power. In its wake sixty-five suspects were sentenced to be deported to Guiana: among them, the former director Barthélemy, Pichegru, forty deputies of the Conseil des Cinq Cents, and thirteen deputies of the Conseil des Anciens, including Joseph Rovère, who would soon succumb to the rigors of the climate without ever having set foot in his château at La Coste.

A new wave of Jacobinism swept across France. In the wake of the coup the Directory saw to it that the councils passed a whole series of laws against émigrés, against the royalist press, and against priests, who among other things were obliged to take an oath to hate royalty. M. de Sade once again felt seriously threatened. Not only was there a danger that his remaining property would be sequestered, but under Articles XV and XVI of the law on émigrés, any individual whose name appeared on any list and had not been definitively removed was required to leave the territory of the Republic or risk arrest and trial before a military commission. Overnight the marquis once again found himself declared an outlaw.

He learned the bad news at a way station on the road to Paris:

Everything was going well until Cosne, a small town in the Bourbonnais two days from Paris by coach, when, upon arriving at the inn, Sensible, always full of melancholy forebodings, asked the mistress of the place about the news from Paris. "The news is excellent, Madame, very good," the terrifying creature replied. "We're finally rid of the deported nobles—fifty leagues from the borders for all of them, and their property confiscated!" Though feeling faint, Sensible replied, "What charming news, Madame. Yes, Madame, we shall have a good supper, for such decrees are made for rejoicing, and we want to celebrate." But I leave it to you to imagine what it was like the moment we were alone, given our dear friend's precious soul.[3]

Upon returning to Saint-Ouen, Donatien sent the minister of police, Doudreau, a detailed account of the confusion surrounding the presence of his name on the list of émigrés from the Vaucluse, along with a dossier of five hundred documents attesting to his uninterrupted residence in Paris: excerpts from jail registers, notices and minutes of meetings of the Section des Piques, certificates of residence and non-emigration from the département of Paris, and so on.[4] It was all wasted effort: Doudreau was removed from office a few days later. Sade then decided to aim higher.

Blunder

Following the coup d'état the new strong man was undeniably the vicomte de Barras. Descended from an old Provençal family, Barras had served as a deputy of the Convention and had voted in favor of the king's execution. Having rapidly enriched himself with bribes, he drew the ire of Robespierre and joined the opposition to the Terror. But his political career did not really begin until after the Ninth of Thermidor. On 13 vendémiaire, Year III (October 5, 1795), he crushed the royalist insurrection with the aid of his friend Bonaparte and shortly thereafter found himself among the five directors invested with executive authority by the Constitution of Year III. He now began leading the life of an oriental satrap, surrounded by loose women and parvenus in an atmosphere of utter debauch. "King Barras," as he was known, lived in high style in his château de Grosbois, where he indulged tastes worthy of an opulent, generous, and spendthrift prince. In the aftermath of 18 fructidor he found himself at the head of a sort of triumvirate along with Reubell and La Revellière-Lepeaux.

This was the man whom Donatien would attempt to interest in his fate. After all, their backgrounds were similar: both Provençal nobles, perhaps even vaguely related (to believe Barras), and equally depraved, they had followed similar political trajectories though at different levels. And now Sensible proposed approaching the great man with a report exonerating Donatien of the charge of emigration. At first he agreed, but at the last moment he took fright. Barras, whom the marquis believed to be from Avignon although he was in fact born in the Var, surely knew about his past: everyone in the region had heard the stories. Might he not refuse to help? "Does Barras, who is from Avignon, know me? And if so, how does he know me? And what will he do based on such impressions as he may have of me? In any case, I have my innocence and my excellent revolutionary conduct going for me, so I can hold my head high . . . But the old adventures . . . in the eyes of a man from the region? . . . Anyway, I was in view under Robespierre, and the *ancien* did nothing then. We must hope that he will do nothing again now."[5]

Sade's fears were well founded: Barras did not have to hail from Avignon to have heard of our man and judge him adversely. The director devoted no fewer than two pages of his memoirs to the man now seeking his protection, and it is clear from what he says that Donatien could not have made a worse choice:

If anything could justify a prison like the Bastille, I should think it would be almost compatible with my principles of legal order to say that the marquis de Sade fully deserved to have been locked up in it . . . This is not the place to recount the story of this personage, so extraordinary that one might look upon him as an anomaly in the midst of the human race. The system that he did not shrink from setting forth in works that were not devoid of talent had been preceded, in various places, by a hideous practice that had provoked universal horror, yet he had managed to avoid the sanction of the law . . . According to this system, the pleasures of the senses do not consist in the reciprocity of agreeable sensations but rather ought to be based on the greatest pain in the object chosen to satisfy the passions. For him it was not enough to obtain the most powerful expression of this pain through rape and violence visited on both sexes; he professed, in addition, that sensuality could not do without blood and carnage. He wished the pleasures of his lubricious fantasies not to stop at torture but to continue until his victims were dead . . . And as if it were not enough to have applied the depravity and ferocity of his system in nature, M. de Sade felt it necessary, so as not to leave that system in a state of imperfection, to trespass on life's final consolations and overturn all the limits of morality. So that to attract proselytes, to entice and harden them in his criminal ways, he attempted to demonstrate, in the forms of the novel, with all the prestige of eloquence and the rigor of logic, that the woes of this world are reserved to what we call virtue and that the crowns of felicity belong to vice; and that it has been so ever since Adam, and will always be so.[6]

When it came to libertinage and political morality, the vicomte de Barras was scarcely in a position to be lecturing the marquis de Sade. But that was one more reason to refuse his support: defending another man's reputation does little for one's own.

Barras merely added his usual note to the marquis's request: "Prompt report." The police noted that the different first names appearing in Sade's various residence certificates constituted an obstacle to removing his name from the list of émigrés. Unless he could produce a certified document attesting to his true name and aliases and establishing that he was indeed the person whom the administration of the Bouches-du-Rhône intended to strike from the list of émigrés with its decree of May 26, 1793, it would be impossible for the minister to issue a favorable report to the Directory.

In fact, nothing was more difficult than to have a name removed from a list of émigrés, even with irrefutable proof of never having left French soil: it was too much in the government's interest to maintain its hold on sequestered property. Sade's case was far from unique: hundreds of citizens had been wrongly listed as émigrés, among them poor Monge, whose name had been placed on a list in the Côte-d'Or at a time when he was minister of the navy in Paris.

The Last Card

Unable to sell his land or collect his revenue, caught in a stranglehold, Sade's thoughts turned to Renée-Pélagie. Wouldn't the best solution be to transfer ownership of all his property to her while retaining for himself the right to what it produced? That would solve all his problems, free him from the burdens of management, and assure him of a regular income. He sent this proposition to M. de Bonnières, a lawyer and former deputy who was acting as his wife's business agent. Rather than present himself as a man in need of a favor, Sade painted a glowing picture of the advantages that Bonnières's client would derive from the operation and even managed to slip in a few insolent, if heartfelt, gibes at his former wife, such as this homage to Constance: "Citizen Quesnet, with whom I am lodged, has different claims on me. When my property was confiscated under Robespierre, she paid for everything in the house and furnished all provisions for a year. The solitude in which Mme de Sade left me on my release from the Bastille obliged me to associate with someone whose solicitude would take the place of that denied me by my family."[7] But Renée-Pélagie knew him too well to be taken in; she divined Donatien's distress and knew that he was playing his last card.

She mulled over the offer for forty-eight hours before informing M. de Bonnières of her decision: it was negative. Donatien then decided to approach her directly, without an intermediary. This time he dropped all pretenses. He no longer concealed the fact that the arrangement he was proposing was for him a matter of life and death. His letter, recently discovered in family archives, is rather pathetic in its almost supplicating tone:

M. de Bonnières writes me, Madame, that you are refusing me the only thing that can save me from the frightful difficulty in which I find myself, and that your refusal is based on three grounds, which I shall transcribe word for word from his letter, with my response to each underneath:

The scarcity of hard currency.

Well, Madame, I am not asking you for any.

The modesty of your income.

I am asking you only for mine. So what difference does the modesty of yours make?

Last but not least, your fear that you will not be able to honor fully the commitments you might make to me.

But, Madame, you are not making any. You will pay me when you receive [the income from the properties]. If you experience delays, I shall experience them also.

Since the objections you raised with M. de Bonnières have no foundation whatsoever, I beg you, Madame, to enter into an agreement that does not hinder or disadvantage you in any way, the refusal of which will reduce me to misery and plunge me into despair.

Everything, in a word, comes down to this:

I shall transfer to you, or to my son, the bare property of everything I own in Provence, with these two provisos: that you, or he, shall scrupulously pay me the income during my lifetime, and that you and he shall authorize me to dispose of my national acquisitions in order to compensate those who will take care of me in my final years.

I appeal to your soul, to your sensibility. Must I fear a refusal?[8]

Renée-Pélagie deliberately shunned this offer of dialogue in which Donatien attempted from the first to appeal to her heart. But this was a language she no longer understood or wished to understand. She therefore had M. de Bonnières draft a reply, in the form of a torrent of figures indicating that Donatien's debt to his client now amounted to 367,000 livres in principal and interest, including her father-in-law's debts, the reimbursement of her dowry, and the endowment that her husband had constituted for her. In other words, M. de Sade's liabilities far exceeded his assets. But Renée-Pélagie had a counteroffer, whose intent was nothing less than to strip Donatien of the last of his worldly goods: he was to transfer to her *full* ownership (as opposed to bare property) of his land, in exchange for which she would pay him the *net* income, that is, the revenue remaining after deduction of interest due, real-estate taxes, and so on. Negotiations ground to a halt.

A Pornographic Monument

From now on M. de Sade's chief concern was to make sure that he and Sensible had enough to live on from day to day. Deprived of his principal sources of revenue, he had to earn a living and pay his bills. In short, he needed to find work. The marquis had nothing against work; in this respect he shared none of the prejudices of his caste. We saw earlier that he had attempted to find work, but without success. And the only thing he knew how to do was write—which he did not stop doing.

Despite the torments of many kinds he had suffered since his release from Picpus, he had not allowed a single day to pass without taking up his pen. He covered page after page without stopping, almost without revising, and the pages grew into volumes and the volumes into stacks. There was no reason for his writing to stop. He could go on this way until he died. But one day, driven by need, he took everything he had written to the publisher Massé on rue Helvétius. Massé rubbed his hands together with glee: he had every reason to.

Sade had just presented him with ten volumes of boundless licentiousness illustrated with obscene engravings. It was the most ambitious pornographic enterprise ever assembled. The title of the work was *La Nouvelle Justine ou les Malheurs de la vertu, suivie de l'Histoire de Juliette, sa soeur*, and it was published sometime in 1797 (we do not know the month).

This monument (in every sense of the word) was also (perhaps primarily) a speculative venture in publishing. It was attuned to the taste of the day: the Directory had brought with it a thirst for quick, violent, destructive pleasure. No other period in French history ever witnessed a comparable relaxation of moral standards, except perhaps the Regency, which the Directory in its way emulated with even greater brutality and cynicism than the original. Women, it seems, had never been so easy. The example was set on high: for every earnest Mme de Condorcet or faithful Mme Récamier, how many women, recently liberated by divorce, indulged their every whim and passed from one man to another—from power to money or from money to power. From the top to the bottom of society, prostitution became a regular feature of the landscape.

No description of the close association of politics, vice, and cash can rival Talleyrand's account to a friend in America of life in Paris: "Balls, shows, and fireworks displays have replaced prisons and revolutionary committees . . . The women of the court have disappeared, but the women of the newly rich have taken their place and are followed, like their predecessors, by trollops who vie with them for the prizes of luxury and extravagance. Around these dangerous sirens buzz frivolous swarms of wits, once called fops but today known as *les merveilleux*, who talk politics while dancing and sigh after royalty while eating ice cream or yawning at a fireworks display."[9] And Mallet du Pan added that "the capital is divided between the madmen and the crooks."[10]

Nowhere in the world was lust on more immodest display than in Paris, and nowhere more in Paris than at the Palais-Royal. What was the cause of this corruption? Insufficient policing—and the baleful influence of the marquis de Sade! Such, at any rate, was the opinion of Citizen Picquenard, the police official who prepared this report for Merlin de Douai, the president of the Directory:

Citizen President,

Paris is enjoying the most perfect tranquillity, but it is impossible to hide the fact that the Republic is paying dearly for this, since it exists only at the expense of morality. It is impossible to form an adequate idea of the public dissolution and depravity . . . The so-called Palais Egalité, but still the Palais-Royal, has for the past two weeks especially been the gathering place for all that is revolting in the most audacious obscenity. The pederasts have moved in, and at ten in the evening they publicly perform under the canopy of the Circus the odious acts of their infamous turpitudes. I am obliged to tell all, Citizen President: several children of the masculine sex have recently been brought in to head-quarters. The oldest of these children was barely six, and all were infected with the venereal virus. These unfortunate little ones, whose statements cannot be listened to without trembling with horror, were brought to the Palais-Royal by their mother to serve as instruments in the most infamous and horrifying debauch. The lessons of the execrable novel *Justine* are put into practice with unprecedented audacity, and the efforts of the watch are virtually powerless against this pestiferous mob of scoundrels of every kind.

Female prostitution is at its height. Not even the most senior police in-spector can remember ever having seen so large a number of public women.[11]

The *Nouvelle Justine* and *Juliette* could hardly have been better timed, and of course they sold best under the arcades of the Palais-Royal. Sade staunchly denied being the author of the works, just as he had denied writing *Justine* in 1791, and for the time being no one thought of disturbing his peace. The work would not be seized until a year after its first publication.

I have not been able to find any critical notice in the press of the time, except for one mention, or, rather, denunciation, from the satirical—and venomous—pen of Colnet du Ravel, a bookseller, au-thor, journalist, pamphleteer—and police spy:

If you have read *Justine ou les malheurs de la vertu*, you no doubt believe that not even the most depraved heart or the most bizarrely obscene imagination could conceive anything so offensive to reason, chastity, and humanity. You would be wrong. This master of corruption has just outdone himself by bringing out the *Nouvelle Justine*, which is even more detestable than the original.

I know the identity of this infamous author, but his name will not besmirch my pen. I also know the identity of the bookseller who has taken it upon himself to sell this disgusting product: may he blush at his association with the shame surrounding a scoundrel whose name calls to mind what is most hideous in crime.

> *Quo non mortalia pectora cogis*
> *Auri sacra fames!*[12]

I place licentious works such as the one I am denouncing to the authorities in the same class as attacks on the government, because if courage founds republics, good morals preserve them. Their ruin almost always leads to the fall of empires.[13]

Sales

Auri sacra fames! It was certainly not a desire for riches that made the marquis run but simply the eternal problem of survival. The new Justine apparently failed to earn enough to keep her author alive, even with the help of her sister Juliette. Having paid off the most urgent debts, he found himself once again with an empty purse. Never one to lack for ideas, Donatien now came up with an ingenious plan to sell his plays, which lay in cartons gathering dust. True, Paris had stayed away or thumbed its nose, but perhaps the plays would find their audience in the provinces. It was worth a try. Theatergoers were certainly less demanding in Nantes or Besançon than in the capital; the public was less blasé. Those provincials suffered from a shortage of entertainment. The marquis was sure they would hasten after the boon he was about to bestow on them.

In his finest style he therefore drafted a letter to the directors of ten provincial theaters, proposing a dozen "new" plays, some of which, having been "honored with acceptance by the boards of some of the finest theaters in Paris, have long since earned me entry to their performances." Sade offered to sell the rights to all twelve masterpieces "for the modest price of 6,600 livres, or a mere 550 francs each."[14] For a "Sade festival" this was essentially giving them away. But nobody wanted them.

"Carrots and beans"

On September 10, 1798, Sade and Mme Quesnet, having come to the end of their resources, were forced to leave Saint-Ouen and separate until things improved. Constance went to Paris to live with friends, while Donatien went to live with one of his farmers in the Beauce. But not for long, because his "impetuous creditor" Païra ("will pay" in French!) attached the income from his farms. Because Sade's host no longer owed him anything, he told him flatly that he could no longer stay there. Sade then took refuge in Versailles, one of the least expensive cities near Paris and one where he could easily find credit; he moved into "the back of an attic" of the Burgeat house at 32, rue Satory, with Charles Quesnet, now aged fourteen, and a serving woman: "We eat a few carrots and beans, and we keep warm (not every day, but when we can) with twigs that we buy half the time on credit. Our misery is such that, when Mme Quesnet comes to see us, she brings us food from her friends' houses in her pocket."[15] Shortly thereafter, Sade became a boarder of Brunelle, a restaurateur, who lived at 100, rue Satory. He was still there when winter came, "without wood, without candles, without provisions of any kind, relegated to the home of a wretched innkeeper who, out of charity, is willing to give me a little soup." Partly to avoid his creditors, but partly also because he did not dare give his real name (which was well known in Versailles, where he had once lived on the same rue Satory and where his father had died and was buried), he called himself "Citizen Charles."

He had nothing to live on but the forty sols per day he earned as a prompter in the city's theater and with which he also had to feed and raise Constance's son. But taking care of the boy, he said, "is a small thing in compensation for the trouble, care, and expense to which the poor mother puts herself every day, running all over town on foot in a horrible season both to placate the creditors and to have my name removed from the list. Truly, this woman is an angel sent by heaven so that [I] do not succumb utterly to the plagues visited upon me by my enemies."[16]

The Dragon and the Pants-Shitter

Sade's destitution was such that, swallowing his pride, he once again approached his wife. Not without difficulty, he finally persuaded M. de Bonnières to arrange a meeting between Renée-Pélagie and Mme Quesnet. Better than anyone else Constance would be able to describe his misery to Mme de Sade and persuade her to take pity on him. But Louis-Marie learned of the impending meeting, hastened to de Bonnières and gave him "the bloodiest dressing down," and then rushed to his mother's side and persuaded her to change her mind.

The rest is not difficult to imagine. Donatien frothed with rage: his son wanted him dead; the boy was a "monster," a "dragon," "the greatest egoist and troublemaker who ever lived." And what was the unworthy parricide doing in Provence? Undoubtedly intriguing and conspiring—and Gaufridy was welcoming the boy into his own home.

But good news had just arrived from Provence. Thanks to Sade's agent Citizen Bourges, the Vaucluse département on February 4, 1799, had ordered an end to the sequestration of the marquis's property, "as well as reimbursement of revenues therefrom received by the collectors of the Domaines Nationaux," but on condition that Sade "not be allowed to alienate his real estate or demand restitution of the fruits collected up to the date of his final removal from the list" and that he "pay the costs of maintenance and management to this date and put down a negotiable bond covering the value of his movable property."[17]

However far-reaching, this decision was not about to put money in Donatien's pocket: the creditors were just waiting to pounce on his estates in the Comtat. But it was a first step toward final removal of his name from the émigré list. In any case, the deputies from the Vaucluse were in favor of the move, as were some of those from the Bouches-du-Rhône; his friend Goupilleau was backing his request, and Barras had added his recommendation in the margin. The only thing still missing was an affidavit certifying his identity, which the authorities in Bouches-du-Rhône still refused to issue.[18]

Only Gaufridy could take care of this problem. He would have to go to Aix forthwith, dropping everything else. As long as his property in the Bouches-du-Rhône remained sequestered, Sade would be reduced to begging. But Gaufridy dragged his feet as always. M. de Sade thundered, accused the notary of "unforgivable and cruel apathy," and in the end threatened to throw himself into the arms of his son Louis-Marie and give him all the property in return for a pension. Then Gaufridy would see what it was to deal with a hard man. Then he would see how he was treated. "You will have nobody to blame but yourself."

No answer. Three months later, Sade sent a still more angry reminder. What was the "pants-shitter" waiting for to repair his "criminal" negligence? And what about the money? Insults fell on the poor man like hailstones: he was cruel, cowardly, hypocritical, lazy, and selfish. Sade ended with an ultimatum: if within a month he still had received nothing, he would come in person, armed with two pistols, one for each of them.

Gaufridy allowed the storm to pass without uttering a word. Now Donatien, on the brink of apoplexy, and in any case having nothing more to lose, not even friendship, dispatched the most terrible letter he had ever sent to Gaufridy. The notary read it with tears of rage. This time it was too much. Never before had the marquis dared to go so far: "Send me enough to live on or you will have great misfortunes on your conscience. You will bear the blame for them; the Supreme Being is just; he will make you as miserable as you are making me. I hope for it; I ask God for it every day. Your son François is a swindler. He finds my misfortune amusing . . . I know full well that rogues and scoundrels will spirit my letter out of your hands. Oh, how I scorn and despise and wish for public vengeance against such lowlife, people capable of smothering my cries! . . . You are reducing me to the very depths of misery, and you are quiet. May heaven in its just vengeance make you suffer what I am suffering . . . and it will . . . when I hear of it, I will say, 'I am avenged.' . . . You are a torturer."[19]

For the first time the elderly scribe felt real anger. He was used to curses falling on his own head but not on the heads of his children. No, it was definitely too much. And since he was now being handed an opportunity to break with the marquis, something he had dreamt of doing for years without ever having dared to act, why not take advantage of it? Gaufridy therefore concocted eight pages of gibberish to justify his resignation and dispatched it within the hour.

Donatien immediately realized that he had gone too far and asked Mme Quesnet to patch things up. Gentle Constance urged the notary to reconsider his decision: "Forgive a man who is in despair and who exhausted the last of his resources two years ago." In any case, he acknowledged his errors; his letter, he confessed, had been "a bit strong," because he had listened to his head rather than his heart. "Where can he find someone like you, a friend for forty years? It is impossible. You will plunge him into despair if you cease to be his friend. So I beg you, on my own account, my dear citizen, not to abandon poor M. de Sade. He is too unhappy for that."[20]

Gaufridy, touched by Constance's letter, agreed to resume his management of Sade's affairs. In any case, his sons Charles and François would be doing the work from now on, because he, Gaufridy, was in semi-retirement. Donatien received his pardon "with tears of joy." He wrote his "dear old friend": "Please honor me again with your love and your letters, and accept my most sincere apologies for having offended you . . ."[21] This was the first and the last time in the marquis's life that he ever offered anyone an apology. In any case, this interlude of comity was short-lived: the squabbling about anything and everything soon resumed. The marquis's temperament did not improve with age and misery but only grew more bitter.

"I am not dead"

On picking up *L'Ami des Lois* for August 29, 1799, Donatien was staggered to read the following article: "We are assured that de Sades [*sic*] is dead. The mere name of this infamous writer breathes a cadaverous stench that kills virtue and inspires horror: he is the author of *Justine ou les Malheurs de la vertu*. Not even the most depraved heart, the most degraded spirit, the most bizarrely obscene imagination could conceive anything so offensive to reason, decency, or humanity."[22]

The author of this obituary, François-Martin Poultier, known as Poultier d'Elmotte, an erstwhile Benedictine monk who had pursued a second career as a journalist, had founded *L'Ami des Lois* in 1796. By his own admission no slander was too vile for him to print if it could sell newspapers.

The next day Sade caused a short note of protest to be published in various papers: "I do not know, citizen, why it pleased Poultier to kill me off while at the same time declaring me to be the author of *Justine*. Only the habit of murder and slander could have driven him to publish such detestable lies. I beg you to publish both the proof of my existence and my categorical denial of responsibility for the infamous book *Justine*."[23]

But another, even more scurrilous article appeared about a month later in *Le Tribunal d'Apollon*, a stupid and nasty paper whose subtitle deserves credit for frankness if nothing else: "Insulting, biased, and defamatory broadside. By an Association of Literary Pygmies." The same article cited a passage from Bachaumont's *Mémoires secrets* (1783) recounting the Marseilles affair.[24] Any revival of a past that Sade was doing all he could to bury threatened to block forever the restoration of his sequestered property. The attack was too serious to allow it to go unanswered. He therefore published a vitriolic reply to his ill-tempered critic in *L'Ami des Lois*:

No, I am not dead, and what I ought to do is take a stout club and impress on your fleur-de-lysed shoulders unambiguous proof of my existence. I would probably do it, too, but for fear of infecting myself by coming too close to your rotten corpse . . . It is false that I am the author of *Justine* . . . So bark, bray, scream, distill your venom: you are like a toad, unable to spit your poison past your nose, so that it always falls on you rather than on those you wish to defile.[25]

The Return of Jeanne Laisné

Sade had never altogether recovered from his failures as a dramatic author. To him they seemed to reflect an injustice for which he periodically demanded reparations. On October 1, 1799, he tried his luck once more, asking Goupilleau de Montaigu, whom he knew well by this time, to use his political influence to "have whoever is in charge at the Théâtre-Français order" the "immediate" rehearsal and performance of *Jeanne Laisné*. The moment seemed particularly propitious for a production of this tragedy, which had previously been refused by the same theater. In the final months of its agony the Directory was trying in every possible way, and in particular through dramatic performances, to revive republican sentiment, and theaters were being turned into schools of patriotism. A memo circulated to theater impresarios advised them to stage "dramatic works most likely to inspire hatred of kings and devotion to the Republic."[26]

Goupilleau probably took some half-hearted steps to gratify Sade's request, but in vain. A month later, Sade tried again. He proposed to read the play himself to Goupilleau and others: "Sade would be happy for Citizen Goupilleau to invite others as competent to judge as the citizen-representative himself. If the play meets with their favor, the government should order its performance as a patriotic production. Otherwise, nothing will be done, and the ideal moment for the performance will pass."[27]

The Bottom of the Abyss

While the press attacked him and Goupilleau played hard to get, Donatien was still starving to death in Versailles, and Charles Gaufridy was still refusing to send him a penny. The young scoundrel had received some money, but he had used it to pay taxes even though land seized by the government should have been exempt. To excuse himself the scatterbrained youth sent Sade a screed as nonsensical as those of his father, signing himself "your dear son." The marquis's reply was curt: "I do not think I slept with your mother, my dear Charles."

When the Theater of Versailles closed, Donatien lost his sole source of income. He picked up a few sols here and there "by writing petitions for the public," but not enough to live on. Constance, who had sold "her very last nightgown," had been working in Paris but had recently fallen ill. Need was forcing him to "new depths," Sade confessed to Gaufridy: "Yes, new depths. Must I own up to one? . . . Tremble . . . Despair that your dawdling is responsible for this . . . Well, then, my friend . . . my dear advocate . . . I have been reduced to selling the furniture and effects from my son's room because I had no bread! . . . *I stole it!*"[28] We have no other information about this theft. Was it his older son's room or Armand's? Where and when did it happen? It may be that Sade made the whole thing up to encourage greater diligence in the notary. Winter was coming on, and before long Sade expected to find himself on the streets because he was nearly a year behind in his rent. In early December 1799, so as not "to die on a streetcorner," he checked into a hospice, where he slept with the ill, the indigent, and other homeless people, and from now on he would live on public charity.[29]

A few days later he learned that by a decree of 19 frimaire (December 10, 1799) the département of the Bouches-du-Rhône had finally lifted the sequester. There was not a moment to lose. Once again he berated young Gaufridy, who then left immediately for Arles only to return empty-handed. The former and current farmer of the property together owed 6,600 livres but failed to pay a penny. Gaufridy had not even seen them: freezing to death, he had been in a hurry to return home. "Poor little abbé Charles!" the marquis ironically commented. "Clearly he is a soldier of the pope. He does not go out in bad weather. And I? Wasn't I more to be pitied than you? Without a fire, in the hospital, with nothing to eat but a pauper's dinner! Truly, you make me laugh!"

•

The year is 1800: a revolution was ending and a new century beginning, bringing with it immense hope. The Eighteenth of Brumaire (the date of Napoléon's coup d'état) marked the end of the Directory and the birth of the Consulate. On that day Napoleon Bonaparte celebrated his wedding with the French nation: from now on the destiny of France would be incarnated in the man whom Chateaubriand would later call a "fatal prodigy." Stendhal was discovering Milan with the army in Italy; he was seventeen. Beethoven was just finishing his First Symphony. Cuvier had published his first *Lectures on Comparative Anatomy*. In Tours a chubby-cheeked toddler was taking his first steps: his name was Honoré de Balzac.

The old man in the hospice at Versailles approached the nineteenth century with indifference, and the century would pay him back with contempt. True, the republican era also ignored the new century: by the official calendar it was Year VIII of the first century.

With no clothes to wear, short of necessities, and sick and bedridden to boot, M. de Sade was dying of cold and hunger. Meanwhile, that "wet chicken" Charles Gaufridy was fobbing him off with words: "Equivocal phrases full of lies, nonsense, contradictions, etc. M. l'abbé has a cold, his horse stumbled, he is afraid his mama will whip him when he arrives, and his friends reprimand him. 'And the money, you inept, ill-tempered man, the money, the money?' 'Oh! The farmer has it!' 'You devil, couldn't you go and get it? Go there from Marseilles and give it to the banker, to be sent to me with all urgency?' 'Oh, no! It was too cold. My father wrote a letter.' And lightning does not strike people so treacherous and vile as to take such advantage of other people's credulity and misery! The Gaufridys—like father, like son! For the last time I tell you I am desperate!"[30]

"Embrace me, my dear advocate!"

No doubt he was painting things darker than they really were. He was not averse to melodrama, as we have seen. Nevertheless, the state of his finances (if not his health) does indeed appear to have been desperate. He became an embittered man. His demands grew tyrannical, and relations with Gaufridy turned poisonous. The recent incident had left deep wounds on the notary and his two sons, wounds only partially scarred over and apt to reopen at any moment. And the marquis could be relied upon to provide an occasion. He did so on February 20, 1800.

On that day Constable Cazade, who while keeping the marquis under "surveillance" had developed some sympathy for him, came to inform him that two sheriff's deputies had been stationed at his house in Saint-Ouen because of arrears in his tax payments. Meanwhile, a bailiff arrived with a warrant for the marquis's arrest owing to two unpaid bills made out to his innkeeper. Fortunately, Cazade intervened and managed to delay execution of the warrant for one week. But poor Constance, who witnessed the scene, came down "with a dreadful fever that kept her in bed while I lacked the means to give her the most urgently needed medication or even so much as a cup of bouillon," and it was two days before she was on her feet again. Donatien shared his anguish with Charlotte Archias, Gaufridy's sister-in-law, a "pious and sensitive soul," adding: "A dreadful prison will be my asylum, and a cold tomb that of my worthy and respectable friend!"

Then, in an outburst of mad rage, Donatien took up pen and paper and for the first time dared to come right out and accuse Gaufridy of theft: "It is quite clear from your manner that my money is in your hands and that you are using it for your own profit . . . I warn you that the people who are going to come after you will know how to make you cough it up." Two weeks later, when still no money had arrived, the marquis threatened to go to Apt and challenge the elder Gaufridy to a duel. One can just imagine the two old men crossing swords in the marketplace. Don Diègue versus Don Gormas!

Relations were at the breaking point, and M. de Sade lost no time in forcing a showdown. On May 1 he sent Charles this warning: "I am going to bring suit against your father if I have not received the specified amount by the aforementioned date, because your father, to whom I delegated only the power to make my farmers pay up, has no power to skim from or delay my payments, and all to oblige crooks who are no doubt rewarding him for his efforts."[31] This was more than the Gaufridys could bear. Stung by these accusations, Charles's father, only too happy to give up his place, tendered yet another resignation, "convinced that I shall no longer be exposed to such insulting and threatening letters, which, far from encouraging me to act, only sap all desire to do so." The notary availed himself of the opportunity to pour out his heart. For the first time he dared to mention the "disgust" he felt rising in his gorge when he opened the marquis's missives. "Thus I was afraid of the days when the mail arrived, and the first disagreeable words that I read in your letters caused me to stop reading and set them aside. I had reached that point. Everything is now out in the open."[32] Not quite everything—for Donatien, thinking that Gaufridy had succumbed to a momentary vexation, once again turned on the charm: "I beg you to remain in charge of my affairs . . . Embrace me, my dear advocate, with as good a heart as I embrace you, and I assure you that the leaven of hatred will vanish from our souls." Donatien thought he knew Gaufridy well: he would not, he calculated, be able to resist the language of the heart. Already, in October 1799, he had written: "I love you, my dear advocate, yes, I love you, and have loved you for a long time. No matter what people say, no one will ever disrupt my relations with you."[33] But those relations were now disrupted for good. This time Gaufridy would not change his mind. Besides, he was now seventy years old, and his only thoughts were of retirement. Sade therefore replaced him with Etienne Laloubie, whom we have met before, for he was also known as Citizen Cazade, the former constable who had been assigned to keep the marquis under surveillance. He had conceived such a passion for Donatien that he now quit public service to go to work for him—a decision of wild imprudence.

The Disciple

In fact, this Laloubie was not a steward like the others. His relations with Sade soon attained a degree of intimacy whose precise nature remains murky. In any case, the marquis appears to have been charmed by this enterprising young man, who eagerly delved into his accounts, visited his farmers in Provence, settled his disputes, and in general presented him with optimistic assessments. This was quite a change from Gaufridy's somber prognostications. Donatien pardoned Laloubie's fatuousness, boasting, and reforming zeal, which he put down to youth. Meanwhile, Laloubie, for his part, did not conceal the fascination the elderly libertine held for him. Apart from the material benefit he derived from managing the marquis's properties, he also acquired certain principles of philosophy and morality by which he set great store. Their relationship was in every sense one of master and disciple. Did it go further than that? People around them whispered that it did, and there was nothing implausible in the suggestion. In any event, Sade taught the young man to live an unfettered existence and freed him from his prejudices; in short, he revealed Laloubie to himself. In return, the apprentice libertine treated him with affectionate deference in his letters. Sprightly and confident, those letters exhibit a remarkably free tone with the man Laloubie familiarly called "my general."

"In sum, all things considered, *my general*," Laloubie wrote Sade,

I am all the more inclined to accept your reasons because they seem to me to be dictated by genuine friendship. I therefore agree with you quite frankly that I was for too long the dupe of the foolish statements and observations of certain individuals who seemed to want to establish themselves at all costs as censors of everything in spite of common sense and all laws natural and human.

Please rest assured, dear and honest friend, that, like you, I shall from now on wean myself from all those fine talkers who seem jealous of an intimacy that is foreign to them. It will be a rare day in summer, as the proverb says, before they catch me in their toils again, for I am determined henceforth to act only on the basis of my own views or those of my true and good friends.

I propose to come see you tomorrow or the next day at the latest, and we shall then have the pleasure of conferring at our leisure about any subject that may interest you. Meanwhile, I beg you to give my regards to my dear godmother, whom I embrace with all my heart, as I do you.

The Crimes of Love

On April 5, 1800, M. de Sade returned with Sensible to his house in Saint-Ouen. Clearly his financial situation had improved, thanks largely to sales of his books. *Oxtiern* had been published by Blaizot in Versailles. More important, Massé had brought out a collection of eleven short stories written in the Bastille in 1787 and 1788. The collection was entitled *Les Crimes de l'amour* and prefaced by a brief essay on the novel. Although these stories belonged to a long tradition of picaresque adventure,[34] the reader of *Justine* or the *Cent Vingt Jour-*

nées will find in them none of the Luciferian grandeur or poetic genius of the Sadeian novel.

This was the first time that Sade had allowed a book to appear under his own name. The title page of *Aline et Valcour* bore only his initial: "By Citizen S***." But *Les Crimes de l'amour* carried the inscription "By D. A. F. Sade, author of *Aline et Valcour.*" At a time when the press was launching unbridled attacks on him and repeatedly identifying him as the author of *Justine*, he took full credit for these two "avowable" works. The reason is easy to guess. Sade was more than ever in search of literary respectability and was chiefly interested in shedding his reputation as a pornographer so as to assume the position of full-fledged "man of letters." He therefore shunned all forms of excess, whether sensual or linguistic: in these stories bloody acts, whether heroic or tragic, are consistently set within a moral framework. Rather than pose as an apologist for evil, he denounced its heinousness and perils. His great criminals, Franval and Oxtiern, expiate their sins in suffering. Yet there is nothing equivocal about the rationalist morality that he takes as his touchstone, for "it assumes that obscure forces constantly overwhelm human consciousness and freedom."[35] In any case, an attentive reading reveals a delight in transgression and acknowledgment of the omnipotence of desire on almost every page.

A Caning

Sade's contemporaries were not all taken in. In particular, a journalist by the name of Villeterque, seeing no difference between *Les Crimes de l'amour* and *Justine*, blasted the work in memorable terms: "A detestable book by a man suspected of having written one even more horrifying . . . What possible utility is there in these portraits of crime triumphant? They stimulate the wicked man's maleficent inclinations, they elicit cries of indignation from the virtuous man who is firm in his principles, and in the weak man they provoke tears of discouragement . . . I could not read these four volumes of revolting atrocities without indignation. One is not even compensated by their style for the disgust they inspire; the author's style in this work is pitiful, always extravagant, full of sentences in bad taste, misconstructions, and trivial reflections."[36]

Stung to the quick, Sade answered with a twenty-page pamphlet entitled "The Author of *Les Crimes de l'amour* to Villeterque, Hack."[37] As Gilbert Lely aptly puts it, this diatribe was "a *grand seigneur's* cane brought down hard on the back of an insolent lackey." And the blows struck home:

I have long been convinced that insults dictated by envy or other motives even more vile and conveyed via the foul breath of a hack ought not affect a man of letters any more than the morning cackling of barnyard animals ought to disturb a tranquil and reasonable traveler.

I hereby summon Villeterque . . . to PROVE that I am the author of this still more HORRIFYING book. Only a slanderer casts suspicion this way, without proof of any kind, on the probity of an individual . . .

Villeterque . . . hack Villeterque, where, then, does crime triumph in the stories? Ah! If I see anything triumphing here, it is truly nothing other than your ignorance and your cowardly desire to defame!

Villeterque, you have raved, you have lied, you have piled nonsense on top of slander, ineptitude on top of fraud, and all to avenge the penny-a-liners in whose company your tedious compilations so justly place you. I have taught you a lesson and am prepared to teach you others if you insult me again.

Despite his age and suffering, the marquis clearly had lost none of his verve.

26

Charenton

Ambush

On March 6, 1801, the police raided the offices of publisher Nicolas Massé on rue Helvétius. Sade, who had come to discuss business with his publisher, witnessed the raid. Among the papers seized were certain of his manuscripts: the *Boccace français*, the *Délassements du libertin ou la Neuvaine de Cythère*, and a "political" work, *Mes Caprices ou un Peu de tout*, together with printed volumes containing additions and corrections in the marquis's hand: a copy of *La Nouvelle Justine* and the final volume of *Juliette*.

Meanwhile, another search was conducted at the home of an individual "known to have intimate relations" with Sade, according to the police report, which mentioned no name. It was probably Etienne Laloubie.[1] Nothing suspicious was found.

When the policemen were done with their search at Massé's, they produced a warrant authorizing them to take Sade to Saint-Ouen. On the way he stopped to get his keys from Constance on rue des Trois-Frères. When she saw him flanked by gendarmes, her heart sank, but she swore never to abandon him. The group then set out at once for Saint-Ouen, north of Paris. After a minute inspection, the police seized some licentious plaster casts, three paintings, and a tapestry "depicting the most obscene subjects, mostly taken from the infamous novel *Justine*." All these items were taken to the prefecture of police, along with the marquis and Massé. On arrival the two men were separated and Sade was placed in solitary confinement, no doubt to avoid a scandal.[2]

The next day the two men were questioned by Constable Moutard, an erstwhile bookseller now working for the police. The questioning continued on March 8. Donatien was confronted with the manuscript of *Juliette* and acknowledged that it was in his handwriting, but he professed to be only the copyist and not the author. He had been paid for his work, he declared. When asked where the original was, he gave no answer. The policeman, apparently ill informed as to his circumstances, then expressed surprise that a man of his station should have taken work as a copyist "of such a frightful work, and for hire."[3] In the meantime Massé had been freed after twenty-four hours, having revealed the name of the warehouse where the stocks of *Juliette* were stored. A thousand copies of the work were destroyed and a dozen others seized, along with volumes of *La Nouvelle Justine*. Over the next few weeks there were further searches at bookstores, printers' shops, and binderies.[4]

The "Mousetrap"

The depot of the prefecture, often referred to simply as "the Depot" or "the Mousetrap," was a dark crypt as dank as a sewer. Day and night it sucked up the scum of the city and funneled them into three holding tanks, or *salles*, depending on age and sex; only later were the prisoners, not yet "accused," grouped by crime. To enter this wretched receptacle, fifteen feet underground, almost at the level of the Seine, one passed through a half-sunken door, reminiscent of the entry to a tomb. Inside there were massive columns, brick walls, and stone benches. The roof, a ribbed vault that aped a Gothic arch, served as an echo chamber, amplifying the noise from the Quai de l'Horloge.

It was in this foul pit that Sade waited in vain to be judged. He was relatively well treated, handled even with "respect and decency," but he was not allowed any visitors. Mme Quesnet came several times, both alone and with Laloubie, but failed to see him. On the eighth day he learned that the prefect had sent his dossier to the minister of police. Finally, on March 16, after ten days' detention, he was advised that his case would be disposed of within twenty-four hours. The next day, however, nothing happened. On Constance's advice Sade consulted a lawyer, Maître Jaillot of Versailles. On March 21, he was still in "the Mousetrap" but had been transferred to a common cell. On the thirtieth, he was questioned again and shown a letter that he denied having written. On his way back to his cell he managed a furtive embrace with Constance. Finally, on April 2, the prefect Dubois, after consultation with the minister of police, came to the conclusion that an indictment and trial "would provoke a scandalous furor not likely to be redeemed by a sufficiently exemplary punishment" and decided to have the marquis de Sade "deposited" in Sainte-Pélagie "to punish him administratively" for having written the "infamous novel *Justine*" and the still more dreadful *Juliette*.

Zoloé

Clearly Sade had fallen victim to the violent campaign the press had for months been waging against him. By naming him as the author of *Justine* the newspapers had alerted the authorities, which since the inception of the Consulate had been particularly sensitive to moral issues. But there may also have been another reason for his incarceration, one about which the authorities had good reason to be unusually discreet.

In July 1800 an anonymous *roman à clef* had been published in Paris. The work was a vicious attack on some leading figures of the day: Josephine (portrayed as Zoloé); Mme Tallien, popularly known as "Our Lady of Thermidor" (Laureda); Mme Visconti, the wife of the Italian diplomat; Bonaparte (dubbed Orsec, an anagram for *Corse*—Napoleon was Corsican); Tallien (Fessinot); and Barras (Sabar). An engraved frontispiece portrayed the three heroines, Josephine, Mme Tallien, and Mme Visconti, wearing loose tunics and removing their masks before the spirit of History.[5] The satire opened with this bittersweet portrait of Josephine-Zoloé:

Zoloé, though pressing the outer limits of her fourth decade, affects to please no less than if she were twenty-five. Her prestige has crowds of courtiers dogging her steps and more or less compensates for youth's absent graces. She has a very subtle mind, a character supple or proud depending on the circumstances, a highly insinuating tone, and a consummately hypocritical ability to dissimulate. Along with all that is seductive and captivating she enjoys an ardor for pleasure a hundred times greater than Laureda's, a usurer's avidity for money, which she squanders with the alacrity of a gambler, and a dizzying love of luxury grand enough to swallow up the revenue of ten provinces.

Zoloé was never beautiful, but at fifteen her coquetry was already refined, and that flower of youth that so often serves as a passport to love and great wealth had hitched a swarm of admirers to her chariot.

Far from scattering upon her marriage to the comte de Barmont [Alexandre de Beauharnais], who had advantageous connections at court, the suitors to a man swore not to lose heart, and Zoloé, sensitive Zoloé, could not bear to make them violate their oath. From this marriage came a son and a daughter, today devoted to their illustrious stepfather's fortune.

Zoloé hails from America. Her possessions in the colonies are immense. But the turmoil that has devastated those mines, so fertile for Europeans, has cut her off from the product of her rich estates, which is so necessary here to sustain her prodigious magnificence.

Did the author truly believe, as some maintained, that Bonaparte would read *Zoloé* as a well-intentioned warning from an admirer whose only wish was to open the First Consul's eyes to the treachery of his entourage? It seems unlikely. In any case, it was soon rumored that the author could only be the marquis de Sade himself. While the police followed him and gathered information about his every word and deed, he remained totally in the dark.

Meanwhile, his publisher Massé, manipulated by the police, asked him to come to his office on March 6, 1801, to discuss a possible new edition of *Justine* and *Juliette* and to bring the manuscript with him. An unsuspecting Sade fell into the trap. We know the rest.

Was he or was he not the author of *Zoloé*? Yes, according to Apollinaire, Dr. Cabanès, and Jean Desbordes. No, to believe Gilbert Lely, who failed to recognize the Sade "manner" in the work: "The sentence structure and vocabulary, as well as the narrative pace and form, bear no resemblance whatsoever to this writer's style. The extremely slack and careless diction infallibly point to a professional satirist and to that advent of vulgarity in our literature for which the period of the Revolution is noted." Except for the final point (Lely never missed an opportunity to pour scorn on the Revolution), I am generally inclined to accept his verdict. It is true that *Zoloé* is not worthy of Sade's pen; it abounds with smutty language and vile slander not at all in keeping with his style.

In that case, the man whom the Consulate's police placed in solitary confinement was the author of *Justine* and *Juliette*, period. But then why not try him like any other accused criminal? By throwing him in prison without a trial, the authorities risked making a martyr of him, a political prisoner jailed for his opinions. The prefect Dubois offers an answer: "I had the honor of reporting verbally to His Excellency, who, being aware of the offenses that Sade had committed before the Revolution and convinced that such punishments as might be meted out by a tribunal would be insufficient and not at all proportional to his offense, was of the opinion that he ought to be put away in Sainte-Pélagie and forgotten for a long time."[6]

In other words, Sade's imprisonment had been ordered by the minister of justice himself, and on account of a novel that for four years had been sold freely under the arches of the Palais-Royal, a novel that anyone could examine and read and that, to believe Restif and Mercier, was selling like hotcakes. Why had it taken so long for the government to crack down? There is only one possible answer to that question: the infamous *Zoloé* had yet to be published. It was *Zoloé* that provoked the ire of the First Consul and compelled the police to act. The fact that (as I believe) it was not written by Sade changes nothing: it was enough that it was attributed to him. Officially, Sade would never be indicted, and the name *Zoloé* would never be uttered outside ministerial offices.

Ex Officiis Imperatoris

The marquis de Sade was thus a victim of the extralegal arbitrariness characteristic of Napoleon's reign. With the inception of the Consulate the prisons became colonies of helots living beyond the pale of society, like lepers deprived of citizenship and stripped of their rights. The authorities saw a *corpus delicti* and imposed punishment. But they refused to permit normal judicial proceedings: there was no trial, no cross-examination of witnesses, no summation, no protracted investigation. Protesters were dispatched without fuss, without scandal, without public debate. They were declared mentally ill and locked away in asylums for the rest of their lives. The procedure was simple and effective: Napoleon used it to send the poet Désorgues to Charenton at the same time as Sade for having written this innocent refrain:

> *Oui, le grand Napoléon*
> *Est un grand caméléon.*

[*Yes, the great Napoleon is a great chameleon (turncoat).*]

It was also said that, when offered a lemon ice cream at the Café de la Rotonde, Désorgues had refused by saying, "Je n'aime pas l'écorce" (a pun on *l'écorce–les Corses*: I do not like the peel—I do not like Corsicans). This ill-advised play on words, together with the two wretched lines of verse, earned Désorgues confinement in an asylum until he died in 1808.

Hundreds of other people, known and unknown, would join him in prisons rebaptized asylums, confined as lunatics even though they had never been seen by any alienist. The system was based on a very simple maxim: one had to be crazy not to adulate the Emperor.

Sainte-Pélagie

Under the Ancien Régime the convent of Sainte-Pélagie housed wayward girls whom ladies of the court such as Mme de Miramion and the duchesse d'Aiguillon sought to rehabilitate. In 1790 its gates were opened, along with those of all other religious establishments. Nuns and penitents were forced to quit their cells. Two years later the Paris Commune converted the building into a prison. In September 1793 it became a major prison for political prisoners. Nearly 350 people were held in its dank cells. It was here, before mounting the scaffold, that Mme Roland hastily wrote her admirable *Memoirs*.

By the time Donatien passed through the rue de la Clef gate on April 2, 1801, the state of the buildings had changed little, but the atmosphere was very different: the odor of death no longer clung to the walls, and the cells now housed young troublemakers and insolvent debtors. Constance immediately came to visit. She had obtained permission to see Donatien three times per *décade* [instead of weeks, the Republican calendar divided the year into ten-day units known as *décades* —Trans.]

On May 20, 1802, Sade, the indefatigable petitioner, asked the minister of justice either to grant him his day in court so that he might defend himself before a panel of magistrates or else to set him free. He repeatedly insisted that he was not the author of *Justine*, indeed swore by all that he held most sacred that he had not written the book:

For fifteen months I have been moaning in the most dreadful prison in Paris, whereas according to the law no accused person may be held more than ten days without being brought to trial. I ask to be tried. Either I am or I am not the author of the book that is imputed to me. If I am convicted, I wish to endure my punishment. But if not, I want to be free.

What is this arbitrary partiality that smashes the guilty man's fetters while crushing the innocent beneath oppressive chains? Is this what we have sacrificed our lives and fortunes for twelve years to achieve? These atrocities are incompatible with the virtues that France admires in you. I beg you not to allow me to remain their victim one minute longer.

I want, in a word, to be *freed* or *judged*. I have the right to speak this way. My misfortunes and the laws give it to me, and I have every reason to hope that you, in particular, will grant my request. Greetings and respect.[7]

The Pelagian Mysteries

One day, a prisoner by the name of Hurard Saint-Désiré, a poetaster and would-be man of letters, decided along with two fellow sufferers to found a literary society within the walls of the prison. The three lost no time putting their plan into practice, and Hurard was assigned to draft an invitation to be circulated to certain carefully selected inmates: "Sir, everyone here seems to be in his private study, and boredom is beginning to overtake us. You are invited to appear tonight at six sharp in room no. 9, on the fourth floor, to plan a dinner meeting under the aegis of provident friendship. Only those who, like you, Sir, possess talents of some kind will be admitted."[8]

With a membership limited to nine, like so many muses, the society thus formed was dubbed the *Dîners de Sainte-Pélagie*. Citizen Sade was not only a member of this group but soon became its president.

But Sade's activities in Sainte-Pélagie were not limited to composing verses for meetings of this literary society. He also attracted attention for his sexual obsessions and his attentions to young men imprisoned for various minor offenses such as student pranks, disturbing the peace, and so on. One day in March 1803 he fell into conversation with some young rowdies who, after causing a disturbance at the Théâtre-Français, had been sent to Sainte-Pélagie for a few days and whose cells were located on the same corridor as his. Were his propositions a bit too bold? Did he make indecent gestures or touch one of the youths or threaten somebody? In any case, this time a decision was made to transfer him to Bicêtre. The police report on the incident is characteristically lavish in detail: "A search of his cell turned up an enormous instrument that he fabricated with wax and used on himself, for the instrument retained traces of its guilty insertion."[9]

"Libertine Dementia"

"A terrible sore on the body politic, a large, deep, bleeding sore that cannot be looked at without averting one's eyes. Down to the very stench of the place, which one can smell from four hundred yards away, everything alerts you to the fact that you are approaching a place of confinement, an asylum of misery, degradation, and misfortune." Such was Louis-Sébastien Mercier's view of Bicêtre in 1783, when it was still known as "the rabble's Bastille." At once hospital, madhouse, and prison, Bicêtre concentrated the dregs of humanity within its walls. Madness and syphilis rubbed shoulders with misery and crime. The elderly, the sick, the epileptic, the parasite-infested, the mentally retarded, the syphilitic, the indigent, and the vagabond lived cheek by jowl with the thief, the pickpocket, the swindler, the prostitute, and the murderer, like rats in a cesspit. The prisoners were housed in dark, tiny cells built one on top of the other, some buried as deep as twenty feet below the ground and enveloped in total darkness.

Closed in 1790 when religious orders were banned, Bicêtre had opened its gates once more under the Directory, this time as a mental asylum. Living conditions had improved noticeably. Thanks to the efforts of the psychiatrist Philippe Pinel, the windowless cells disappeared, but the place still suffered from an execrable reputation.

The marquis entered Bicêtre on March 15, 1803, but did not remain there long. Afraid that detention in such an infamous place would discredit the family name, Mme de Sade and her children urged the prefect Dubois to transfer him somewhere else. After considering the fort of Ham and Mont-Saint-Michel, Dubois ordered that Donatien be sent to Charenton. Since M. de Sade was in possession of all his mental faculties, sexual obsession was cited as the grounds for his detention: "This incorrigible man was in a perpetual state of libertine dementia." In the meantime, M. de Coulmier, the director of the asylum, was given special instructions intended to forestall any attempt to escape. The cost of keeping the alleged madman in the asylum, set at 3,000 francs per year and payable quarterly, was assumed by his family. This fee covered care, meals, lodging, laundry, and surveillance.

On the eve of his transfer from Bicêtre, Donatien wrote M. de Coulmier to offer all possible assurances as to his future conduct. He promised to earn the director's respect and to "de-persuade" him of his bad reputation. On April 27, 1803, a policeman named Bouchon accompanied Sade to Charenton.

François Simonet de Coulmier

M. de Coulmier became *régisseur* of Charenton on September 22, 1797, and later *directeur*. The man is worth pausing over for a few moments. His intelligent administration and noble compassion eased the marquis's final years, and that alone would be enough to earn him our attention. But beyond that, his innovative treatment of the mentally ill, which earned him much hatred, vituperation, and calumny during his lifetime, cries out for reparation. It is not too much to say that

Coulmier was one of those who brought the asylum into the modern era.

Born in Dijon in 1742, he was a sickly child. His parents' financial reverses left him with no choice but to take holy orders, and he donned the Premonstratensian habit at Chambrefontaine on February 19, 1764. When the Estates General met in 1789, he was elected a deputy of the clergy and became a champion of the poor. On June 6 he brandished a piece of black bread in calling for passage of a bill to do something about the high price of grain and the wretched condition of the impoverished. On June 21 he quit the Second Estate (the clergy) and joined the Third. Over the next few years he was active in charity and hospital work, and his success earned him his nomination to head Charenton in 1797. He was then fifty-five years old, two years younger than Donatien de Sade.

He found the asylum in deplorable condition: buildings dilapidated, furniture looted, trees uprooted, garden plots rented to private individuals. Only sixteen beds remained in the institution and only 264 francs in its cash box, but there were no inmates. The most urgent task was thus to repair the premises, and Coulmier threw himself into it with great vigor.

Under his leadership the facility grew rapidly. He had a new wing built for female patients, a second new wing for men, and segregated patients by diagnosis (hypochondria, melancholia, folly, mania, idiocy). "Wild, agitated, and disruptive" patients were isolated in special wards. The number of inmates grew steadily: 202 were admitted to the hospital between 1797 and 1800, 434 between 1800 and 1805, and 1,007 between 1805 and 1810.

The institution's reputation grew along with its size, but the director's generous and liberal spirit earned him stinging reproaches. The entire medical faculty plotted against this defrocked priest whom the authorities had dared to appoint to such a position despite his lack of a medical degree.

Luxury Clinic or Death Camp?

Possibly inspired by the ideas of Pinel but in any case quite similar to the methods taught by the celebrated alienist, the therapeutic regime instituted by Coulmier and his chief physician, Dr. Jean-Baptiste Joseph Gastaldy, favored "moral treatment" over the combination of diet, bleeding, purgatives, and antispasmodics all too commonly employed at the time to treat all mental illnesses, regardless of the locus, origin, or nature of the particular patient's malady. At Charenton the individual nature of each affliction was taken into account, and treatment was supposed to be humane. Charles-François Giraudy, the hospital's assistant physician, made this point in the description he gave of Charenton in 1804, only a year after Sade's admission:

The *maison nationale de Charenton* is the first in France to be dedicated exclusively to the treatment of the alienated; the first where the presence of incurables is not harmful to those still susceptible of cure; where the patients are not in all cases deemed to be totally devoid of judgment; where they are not exposed to brutality or bad jokes or to the frightening use of chains or to other inhuman forms of treatment; where one finds none of the errors accredited by blind empirical routine, no trace of false prejudice; in a word, the first where the new principles of mental medicine can be faithfully applied in practice . . . This establishment, owing to its nature and situation, is destined to become one of the finest monuments of charitable works in all Europe.[10]

To some this portrait may seem all too idyllic. That would hardly be surprising. Giraudy had written it for the minister of the interior, to whom it was sent after an official inspection visit to Charenton on April 5, 1804. The reality was no doubt less glowing. But does that mean that the place was a torture camp? For that is how it was described by the former cavalry officer Hippolyte de Colins, who was sent to study horse medicine at the Imperial Veterinary School in Alfort. Extremely curious about what went on at nearby Charenton, he managed to win the confidence of the personnel and over a period of weeks visited all the buildings, closely examining every nook and cranny (or so he claimed) and recording his observations in a report completed in June 1812 and soon sent to the minister of the interior. To believe this report, Charenton was at once a prison, a death house, and a torture chamber. Inmates were housed, according to Colins, two or three to a cell no more than ten feet across. The cells on the ground floor were actually more than a foot below the surface. In them the guards placed poor wretches deemed to be "unclean" or deserving of some punishment. "There nearly all of them sleep on nothing but straw, many without covers . . . The second and third floors are arranged in the same way, and although they are less damp, they are scarcely less unhealthy owing to the pervasive filth. The walls are dirty and covered with garbage that has been there for years. In many cases one breathes contaminated air emanating from the patients in an atmosphere that is not replenished by adequate circulation of the air. And this problem is compounded by the stench from the latrines, which are nearly all located at the intersections of corridors and apt to give forth unbearable odors at the slightest change of weather."[11] Colins further denounced the use of the douche: "a powerful column of water driven by a very considerable and very tall mass of liquid, which gives the patient a violent shock, arrests his breathing, and generally serves only to irritate him." To round out this account, Colins described in detail an even more terrifying torture known as the "surprise bath." The blindfolded patient was seated on the edge of a tub, then grabbed by the hair and suddenly forced backward into cold water, his head being held below the surface for several seconds. The patient was then "removed and placed for five or six minutes on the douche chair."[12] The doctors at Charenton no doubt expected miracles from the shock due to this sudden immersion, but their colleague Esquirol deemed the treatment useless and traumatic; he called it the "terror bath."

Despite its minute detail, Colins's report is to be regarded with caution. Even Esquirol, who used it in preparing his own report on Charenton, was more moderate than his predecessor.[13] Although he criticized Coulmier for his anarchic administration, his passion for secrecy, and above all his love of spectacle, he expressed only minor reservations about the quality of care. Apart from the notorious "terror bath," none of the methods truly scandalized him, as bizarre or barbarous as they may seem: the wicker dummy, for example, in which raving lunatics were confined, or the wooden box in which suicidal depressives were made to lie down (no doubt to give them a foretaste of the coffin). He simply expressed satisfaction that by his time such things had been eliminated, taking this as a sign of progress: "For us the straitjacket is enough," he declared. Indeed, his most severe criticisms were aimed at the installations, which he found haphazard, and the theatrical performances, whose effects he feared. Reading him, one has the impression that Charenton was still the most up-to-date of psychiatric hospitals.

And Esquirol was not alone. Dr. Ramon, a man of extreme integrity and exemplary moderation, judged Coulmier's administration in these terms: "M. de Coulmier reigned despotically over everything, but this despotism was by no means austere or harsh, and it can be said that M. de Coulmier was beloved by all his administrees, employees, and pensioners. His was, in short, a paternal government, but a rather relaxed one."[14] Like his colleague, Ramon was critical not so much of the therapeutic methods, where he found little to complain about, as of the general atmosphere at Charenton. His criticism focused chiefly on Coulmier's lax discipline: the director of Charenton had tolerated, if not encouraged, loose and "rather unbuttoned" morals in a place that hardly lent itself to such carrying-on. "Gatherings, balls, concerts, and theatrical performances were organized . . . There were banquets, balls, concerts, and stage performances to which large numbers of outsiders were invited, including men of letters and many theatrical celebrities, chiefly actors and actresses from the boulevard theaters."[15] The time was ripe for Sade to make his appearance.

M. de Sade Arrives

Confined as a "police patient," to use the bizarre bureaucratic formulation, the marquis de Sade was by this time sixty-three years old. He already knew Charenton, having served time there during the first eight months of the Revolution. A sympathetic attachment soon developed between Coulmier and the new inmate. The two men had a common taste for women and libertinage, a pronounced penchant for pleasures of all kinds, and a boundless passion for the theater and everything connected with it: dance, balls, and spectacles of every sort—to say nothing of pretty actresses and intimate suppers. Their ensuing friendship was not without stormy patches. How could it have been? Sade's tyrannical character, further exacerbated by confinement, his impatience, his perpetual jeremiads, and his paranoia—all these things only grew worse with age. Coulmier, for his part, found himself in a delicate situation, torn between his favorite inmate's demands and the strict supervision of the minister to whom he was accountable. By 1805 he was in open conflict with chief physician Royer-Collard, who found it impossible to tolerate the presence in the hospital of the all-too-notorious author of *Juliette*. Add to this the slander and intrigue that was always brewing in this small, closed community and it becomes easy to see why Coulmier's mood was not always serene.[16]

•

From the first, M. de Sade enjoyed a privileged situation. He was housed in the right wing of the hospital, on the third floor, where he occupied a pleasant room with an adjoining library whose windows overlooked a patch of green on the Marne side of the building. To reach the room one passed through an antechamber equipped with a study. The quite commonplace wall hangings and furniture reflected the occupant's indifference to such things. The room contained a miserable low-canopy bed with curtains of "poor calico," a bergère upholstered in yellow Utrecht velvet, an old desk of blackened wood, a marble-top commode done in veneer, a mirror mounted on a gray-painted wooden stand, an old folding screen, two straw-stuffed chairs, and a fireplace with andirons, shovel, and tongs. On the walls hung a portrait by Nattier of the marquis's father, Jean-Baptiste, in arms, along with four miniatures: Eléonore de Maillé, his mother; Mlle de Launay, his much-beloved sister-in-law; his elder son Louis-Marie; and the picture of Mlle de Charolais in Franciscan habit.

M. de Sade was free to stroll about the grounds at will; he kept an open table, received certain other patients, paid them visits, and lent them books. Apart from his freedom, therefore, he seems to have lacked none of the ingredients of a tranquil existence—not even family life, for in August 1804 Constance joined Sade at Charenton with special permission from Coulmier, who informed Claude-Armand of his action: "Your father is doing marvelously well and seems quite pleased that I have allowed Mme Quesnet to enter the hospital as a boarder. I have acceded to this arrangement in the hope of improving the situation of M. de Sade, who apparently wants it. I shall be delighted to do whatever may be agreeable to him so long as he does not abuse it."[17] Admitted to the hospital as a "free boarder," Constance occupied the room adjacent to Donatien's and passed for his illegitimate daughter.

"Sodom destroyed"

Despite the many advantages that Sade enjoyed over his companions in confinement, whether mental patients or "political" prisoners like himself, he was nevertheless subject to close surveillance. His room was regularly inspected by the police, who were authorized to seize any licentious manuscripts they found. On May 1, 1804, the prefect ordered a search of Sade's papers and informed him that "if he continues to rebel, he will be transferred back to Bicêtre." The prefect also asked M. de Coulmier "to punish him by keeping him confined when he fails to obey your orders."[18]

In theory the marquis was not allowed to leave the asylum. On Easter Sunday 1805, however, M. de Coulmier permitted his pensioner to go to the parish church of Saint-Maurice to deliver the bread for consecration and take up a collection (an unusual occupation for an unbeliever). Two days later, the director was severely reprimanded by the prefect of police: "This individual was transferred from Bicêtre, where he was supposed to remain for the rest of his life, only to assist his family in settling his affairs. He is a prisoner in your institution, and you may not and must not under any circumstances or on any pretext allow him to leave without my express written authorization. And how could you fail to foresee that the presence of such a man in public would inevitably inspire horror and provoke disorder?"[19]

On June 5, 1807, the police again searched Sade's cell, this time on orders of the minister himself, "to determine whether sieur de Sade, confined at Charenton, was writing a licentious work in which people in office may be treated with criminal indecency and there may be discussion of an event linked to foreign policy."[20] In the course of their search the bloodhounds turned up "many papers and instruments of the most disgusting libertinage," evidence that the marquis had not given up his masturbatory habits. Dubois reported the results of the search to minister Fouché: "I was informed that a female by the name of Quesnet, who passes for de Sade's daughter and mistress, was a boarder in the same hospital. I therefore gave orders to search her apartment as well. And it was there that a manuscript was found . . . entitled *Les Entretiens du château de Florbelle.*" And he added: "The work is disgusting to read. It seems that de Sade aimed to surpass the horrors of *Justine* and *Juliette.*"[21] This literary monument, which Gilbert Lely aptly termed a "Sodom destroyed," was taken to the prefecture along with an armful of other notebooks in the same hand. Sade would never see them again: *Les Journées de Florbelle*, as the play later came to be entitled, would be consigned to the flames after his death on orders of prefect Delvau and at the request of his son Claude-Armand, who personally witnessed the auto da-fé.[22]

Dubois's report, which was discovered only recently in the National Archives, also yields an astonishing revelation. Among the letters received by the marquis since his confinement, "there are several written by a single hand that prove he has disciples as horrifying as their master. The writer describes scenes of libertinage that have recently occurred and boasts of having administered potions that produced an appearance of death lasting several hours in women who were then used in every possible manner, tortured, and forced to drink three enormous bottles of blood. I hope to discover the author of these letters and of these crimes. I have reason to believe that he will not elude the searches I have ordered." Did Dubois succeed in identifying this mysterious adept? For us the enigma remains unresolved.

As for the "libertine and impious fragments" by Sade himself, Dubois was content to offer only one example. Since we cannot read this text in Sade's own version, we give the policeman's: "The author describes his first adventure in libertinage, before embarking on a career in which he made such rapid progress. He relates that, after being sodomized from five in the morning until eight, and guided, as always, by the principle that causes him to choose a mélange of sacrilege and libertinage, he went to confession and communion before devoting the rest of the day to all that is most dreadful in debauchery."[23] These few lines make us regret all the more the original text, which is probably lost forever.

"Groaning . . . in irons"

It will come as no surprise that Sade, with his mania for filing petitions, took an active role in seeking his release. Until death finally put an end to his efforts in 1814, he protested his imprisonment in every possible way. A year after his admission to Charenton he had Mme Quesnet write a letter to the minister of justice, no doubt counting on his tender friend's naïve prose and uncertain spelling to move the magistrate. But the "Great Judge," as Constance called him, remained adamant.

Then new hope arose. On May 18, 1804, Sade learned of the creation of a committee of seven members chosen by the Senate from among its own ranks to examine the cases of individuals not tried by the courts within ten days of their arrest. The committee had been in existence for only a few days when Sade sent its members a letter vehemently protesting his detention: "For forty months I have been groaning in the cruelest, most unjust irons." Seeking the cause of this persecution, he continued: "I see it in a frightful coalition of kin whose attitudes and opinions I did not wish to share during the Revolution . . . They cleverly took advantage of the fleeting moment of credibility offered by their return to France to do in the only member of their family unwilling to follow them." Here was something new. For the first time Sade named his own children as his oppressors (for it is clearly to them that his letter refers). Now that the Montreuils were gone, his children would serve as his scapegoats.

When the senatorial committee declined to act in his case, Donatien decided to appeal directly to the minister of police, Joseph Fouché. He received no response. Three months later the prisoner asked the same minister to authorize him to go to Paris if business required his presence there. He observed that such authorization should be granted all the more readily since Charenton was not officially a prison.[24] His request was refused. Undaunted, Donatien submitted another request in June 1806: he asked to be let out twice a week "to attend to business" and gave his word of honor never to stay away overnight and never to avail himself of the privilege except in an emergency. The minister responded in a brief note to Coulmier: "The ex-marquis de Sade and his execrable works are too well known to enter into any detail on his account. It is already a great deal that sieur de Sade enjoys a manner of liberty within the institution. But if he were so much as to be seen outside, it would cause a public scandal."[25]

"Innocent Games"

If theatrical performances were a part of Coulmier's plan of "moral treatment," he nevertheless relied in large part on Dr. Gastaldy, Charenton's chief physician, to put that plan into effect: "We searched together for ways to divert [our patients] with innocent games, concerts, dancing, and plays in which the roles were filled by patients . . . These occupations kept them active and warded off melancholy ideas, an all too common source of madness . . . This moral treatment, approved by the most respectable people, by outsiders who eagerly sought tickets so as to see for themselves the influence of the arts on the moral as well as the physical, eventually succeeded in establishing Charenton's reputation."[26]

Coulmier prudently omitted the name of one person who nevertheless played an essential part in his theatrical program: the marquis de Sade. As playwright, actor, organizer, director, scenery designer, and "press agent," Sade in fact became the true "artistic director" of the Charenton theater until it was closed down in 1813.

•

The first necessity was an appropriate place for these group therapy sessions to be held. At the marquis's suggestion, Coulmier accordingly had a real theater built just above the women's ward, a theater with a stage, wings, loges, an orchestra pit, and parterre. Opposite the stage, projecting out over the audience, was the dignitaries' box, reserved for the hospital director and his guests. On either side of this box rose tiers of seats, twenty for men on one side, twenty for women on the other; these were reserved for patients of the hospital, selected from among the least disturbed of the inmates. Mme Quesnet had a box of her own with seven seats. The remaining space was sufficient to accommodate roughly two hundred invited guests. Performances began early in 1805.[27]

The news quickly spread through Paris. Received skeptically at first, the idea soon aroused curiosity and then genuine interest among certain society intellectuals. Abetted by an element of snob appeal, an invitation to a play at Charenton soon became the height of chic. People vied with one another for the honor of attending and sang the praises of the strange marquis who had had the extraordinary audacity to present madmen on stage. Women from the most elegant circles crowded the performances.

Our marquis was exultant. Although the bulk of the troupe was made up of patients, the stars were actors and actresses from Paris, and Sade directed rehearsals with the help of a professional, Mme Saint-Aubin of the Opéra-Comique. When necessary he served as stagehand or prompter, no task being too small for his talents. On premiere nights he rushed about like the host of an elegant dinner party receiving distinguished guests. While Sensible did the honors of the house, the marquis dispensed tickets and fluttered about among the principal players and dancers. After the show he invited the prettiest actresses to supper.

Performances were held once a month, and generally two pieces were staged: operas, dramas, or comedies. Sometimes there was a ballet as well, and on holidays a fireworks display.

The Festival of Friendship

Sade wrote several plays for Charenton, only one of which has survived. If his views on the therapeutic value of theater coincided with those of Coulmier, it would nevertheless be presumptuous to conclude that he was the inventor of psychodrama, as is all too often claimed. Psychodrama today is generally used only in treating neurosis. Participants are not asked to perform works written by playwrights but rather to improvise scenes based on past or present emotional conflicts; these performances are monitored by therapists, who subsequently offer interpretations. Thus modern psychodrama "differs in many ways from the theater of Charenton, but there is one principle common to both: that mental illness originates in the passions, to use the language of the past, or in pathogenic disturbances, to use that of the present, disturbances that at some point turned the psychic processes in an abnormal direction. By reliving these painful and pain-causing experiences from the past, one hopes to repair their harmful manifestations."[28]

In any case, there is no evidence that Sade ever wrote or selected plays for Charenton with the actors' maladies in mind. His practice was thus a far cry from what Peter Weiss imagined in *Marat-Sade*, a play that caused a scandal in the 1960s when the role of Charlotte Corday was played by a catatonic, that of Jacques Roux by a sexual deviant, and that of Marat by a paranoiac, each actor being chosen on the basis of his or her psychosis.

"A shameful ruin"

Much of the information we have about the performances at Charenton comes from accounts left by visitors. One of these, Auguste de Labouisse-Rochefort, today deservedly forgotten but once known as the "poet of the hymen" owing to his ardor in celebrating the sweet pleasures of marriage, has left a fascinating account of a performance he had the opportunity to attend on July 5, 1805. The theater was not very large, he noted, and the size of the stage was in keeping with that of the theater. "Upon arriving in the orchestra, I sat next to a group of ladies and young men, whose conversation was as animated as it was confused . . . There was chatter about philosophy, fashion, the fine arts, jealous lovers, vexing people . . . But then someone tapped on the stage with a small gavel. This was the signal to begin . . ."

What Labouisse saw next was a performance of *L'Impertinent* by Desmahis, a one-act play in free verse ideal for staging in the drawing room. The play, "which belongs to a most frivolous genre, demands extreme perfection in the principal role." Alas, the actor who played "the Impertinent" had "none of the easy, graceful tone that the pit applauded in Fleury." He was "very big, very fat, very cold, very heavy, a large mass, a vulgar, short man whose head seemed a shameful ruin" (to give a literal prose translation of Labouisse's account in rhymed verse).

As the reader will have guessed, this clumsy, elephantine comedian who had not even learned his lines was none other than the marquis de Sade. To be sure, he was no longer really of an age to play the part, and his obesity was hardly appropriate to foppish conceit. Nevertheless, Labouisse's portrait is surely a caricature.[29]

Mademoiselle Flore

Another visitor to Charenton was a novice actress by the name of Mademoiselle Flore, who went there in the hope that Mme Saint-Aubin might further her career. We are indebted to her for this interesting portrait of Sade:

This man, whom I regarded as a kind of curiosity, like one of those monstrous creatures they display in cages, was the notorious marquis de Sade, the author of several books that cannot be named and whose titles alone are an insult to taste and morality, which is supposed to make you think I haven't read them. It seemed that his face was the emblem of his mind and character. I can see it still, and I have a memory for faces as well as names. He had a fairly handsome head, rather long, an aquiline nose, open nostrils, a narrow mouth, and a protruding lower lip. The corners of his mouth turned down in a disdainful smile. His small but brilliant eyes lurked beneath thick, jutting brows. His creased eyelids covered the corners of his eyes, like a cat's. His exposed forehead formed an oval at the top. He wore his hair tucked up in the style of Louis XV and slightly curled on the sides, all of it perfectly powdered, and it was all his though he was seventy-four years old at the time.[30] His figure was erect and tall, and his noble bearing was that of a man of high society.

Forgive me for having given so lengthy a portrait of a man who has enjoyed an infamous celebrity. He still had grand manners and great wit.

A Vaudevillian at Charenton

Armand de Rochefort, a journalist, songwriter, and author of numerous vaudeville pieces, was also a guest at Charenton. He had been invited to celebrate the birthday of Coulmier, whom he called *Coulommiers* and described as a sort of gnome with gnarled legs. The date was October 6, 1812, and Rochefort was twenty-two at the time. Before the show he had been invited to a gala dinner with more than sixty other guests. Seated to his left was "an elderly man with a nodding head and burning eyes. The white hair on his head gave his face a venerable air that commanded respect." Rochefort continued: "He spoke to me several times with such warmth and variety of intelligence that I liked him a great deal. When we rose after dinner, I asked my neighbor on the right who this engaging man was, and he answered that it was the marquis de S***. At which I drew back as terrified as if I had just been bitten by the most poisonous of snakes. I knew that this wretched old man was the author of a monstrous novel in which the madness of crime in all its forms was published in the name of love. Indeed, I had read this infamous book, which had left me as disgusted as if I had just witnessed an execution in the place de Grève, but I had no idea that I would one day see the creator of that work seated at the table of the director of a public institution."

After dinner, the company moved to the theater for a performance of Marivaux's *Fausses confidences*. Before the curtain went up, there was music, "flawlessly performed" though played by lunatics.

The play ended "amidst applause, surprise and astonishment . . . After the miracles I had seen, I needed to leave this place before I could be sure that I had preserved my own reason."[31]

Surprise and uneasiness: these were the chief reactions of those invited to witness the performances at Charenton, and it was for precisely these reactions that they came. Pernicious though such pleasures may seem to some, they are nevertheless revealing of what is eternally fascinating in the confrontation between reality and illusion. Long before Nietzsche, Sade showed that dramatic art was not the fruit of Apollonian clarity alone but also the progeny of Dionysus, the god of drunkenness, madness, and hubris—in a word, of excess.

27

Twilight

Wolf among Sheep

Dr. Joseph Gastaldy enjoyed a considerable reputation as a gourmet. He presided over the famous *Jury dégustateur* (Tasters' Jury), and Grimod de La Reynière listed him in his *Almanach des gourmands*. This passion for fine dining would prove lethal. On December 20, 1805, following a dinner at the home of Cardinal de Belloy, archbishop of Paris, during which Gastaldy consumed four helpings of grilled salmon, he was forced to take to his bed and died ten days later.

This fatal indigestion was to have serious consequences not only for the administration of the hospital but also for the lives of its inmates, and particularly for M. de Sade. Coulmier and Gastaldy shared similar ideas about psychiatry. They had launched the theater experiment together, and each held the other in the highest esteem. The future of the institution now depended on the choice of a new chief physician. By law it was Coulmier's prerogative to propose a candidate.

The interior minister wanted the position to go to Dr. Royer-Collard, a distinguished alienist and the brother of politician and philosopher Pierre-Paul Royer-Collard. To Coulmier this was not a pleasant prospect, for he was familiar with the doctor's imperious character and influence in high places. He therefore sounded out M. Thouret, the director of the medical school, but received an evasive reply. Pressed by the ministry, Coulmier thought it shrewd to propose Royer-Collard but asked that the surgeon Deguise be named "physician in residence" and adjunct to Royer. Deguise, a former student of Gastaldy's, lived near the hospital and was thus available in emergencies. The minister approved this arrangement.

Problems arose immediately. To begin with, Royer-Collard complained that the late Gastaldy's honoraria now had to be shared by two people. Coulmier agreed to pay him a bonus of a thousand francs but on condition that he visit Charenton three times a week rather than two. Royer-Collard agreed to Coulmier's terms, accepted the advance, but continued to make two visits a week. What is more, he chose to begin his visits at nine in the morning rather than six, which disrupted the hospital routine by delaying administration of the patients' medication and depriving them of their walks. Royer also found a hundred ways to annoy his colleague Deguise: he set his public consultations for Tuesday, knowing that this was the day Deguise had scheduled his, reproached the surgeon for using "a series of active means" in treatment, and threatened drastic reforms.

A Controversy over Patient Records

The most serious conflict between Royer-Collard and Coulmier involved patient records. On this point the new chief physician was not entirely in the wrong. He asked the hospital administration to send him each patient's file containing the usual information: name, place of birth, age, occupation, family status, wealth, diagnosis, duration of hospitalization, course of the psychosis, medications prescribed with an indication of the effects of each, and so on: "in a word," the physician wrote, "any information that may shed some light on the patient's situation and contribute to more effective treatment. This is a prerequisite for the practice of my ministry. Without this assistance I should be forced to resign."[1] This would appear to have been a legitimate request on the part of an alienist interested in following the individual history of each of his patients. But the director general saw it as a form of police inquisition and categorically refused to honor the request. "As you know," he wrote in his reply to Royer-Collard, "there is a cruel prejudice against the disease that we treat at Charenton. Unjust though it is, it exists nonetheless . . . Would it not be most imprudent of me, honored as I am by the confidence of the government and entrusted with family secrets, to allow such records to be kept in the custody of a private individual, where upon his death they might attract the curiosity of the public, his relatives, or his servants? No, Sir, this idea is so terrifying from the standpoint of society's interest that you have no choice but to withdraw an inappropriate request that duty, honor, and conscience oblige me to deny."[2] Accustomed to running his institution with a free hand, M. de Coulmier this time exceeded his authority. There was no fundamental reason why the chief physician's request for assistance should have seemed anything but routine, and in the end Coulmier would no doubt have given in had he not become increasingly distrustful of Royer in the interim. From the moment Royer had taken the job, Coulmier had seen him as an enemy. He would never change his mind.

A Privileged Client

The man, it must be conceded, scarcely inspired sympathy. Quick to take offense and austerely virtuous, he cast a critical eye on everything that was being done at Charenton. Soon after he took up his post, his thin silhouette could be seen slinking along the hospital's corridors. He prowled from ward to ward, notebook in hand, noting abuses, irregularities, and neglect. Two things scandalized him most of all: the privileges enjoyed by certain inmates and the lunatics' theater. M. de Sade accordingly became his favorite target.

Indeed, the marquis's mere presence at Charenton would have been enough to disgust him. Righteous to the core, Royer could not stand the sight of the elderly libertine, active and energetic and independent in his ways, directing the theater, calling the shots, and enjoying enormous privileges under the director general's indulgent gaze. And then there was Sade's liaison with Mme Quesnet, whom he passed off as his daughter (whence the rumors of incest that circulated around the hospital for a time), to say nothing of his flirtations with the young actresses who came from Paris to appear in his shows or of his elegant suppers or his sometimes questionable, if not downright inappropriate, behavior with certain patients and staff members over whom he wielded dangerous influence.

The chief physician was not the only one outraged by all this. Other inmates found M. de Sade's arrogance equally difficult to bear. More authoritarian than ever in his old age, he was as gruff with them as he would have been with his own lackeys. One of them, a demented former cook by the name of Thierry who had played minor parts in various plays, dared to complain one day to M. de Coulmier:

Sir, allow me to explain, as promised, the scene I had with M. de Sade.
He told me in front of M. Veillet to do something necessary for the dec-

oration [of the theater], but when I turned my back on him in order to go fetch what he wanted he suddenly grabbed me by the shoulders and said, "Be so good as to listen to me, you urchin." I calmly told him that he was wrong to speak to me in this way, because I was simply carrying out his orders. He denied this and said I had turned my back on him out of impertinence and was a queer duck in need of fifty lashes, which he would be happy to administer. Then, Sir, I lost patience and could not help answering him back in the same tone he had used with me. I should inform you that for the past few days I have stopped going to M. de Sade's because I am tired of his brutalities. He has been kind to me in the past, I grant, and for that I repaid him with my eagerness to please and be useful to him in any way I could.

Society is an exchange of benefits, and I dare say in all honesty I have done as much for M. de Sade as he has done for me. For all he ever gave me was a few dinners. I am tired of being mistaken for his valet and of being treated as such. It was only out of friendship that I offered him my service.

As a result, M. de Sade may stop giving me roles in plays . . .[3]

Not badly argued for a supposed lunatic.

The protection the marquis received from the director also caused some gnashing of teeth, as we learn from a letter to the interior minister. It was sent by a rather odd personage by the name of Eude Gaillon, a former subprefect of the Eure, who had been afflicted first with "absences of feeling" and later, by his own account, with "temporary insanity." Hospitalized at Coulmier's hospital "on the basis of the reputation this institution enjoyed in the past," Gaillon passed several tranquil months at Charenton until the day he learned that the man living just below him was none other than the notorious marquis de Sade. Suddenly an irresistible feeling of disgust took hold of him: "I was not in control of my reaction at the mere sight of him," he wrote. "I was later astonished to learn that such a man was an intimate of M. de Coulmier, who soon gave me proof of this. One day in his office he asked me why I did not keep company with M. de Sade, as he was willing to do with me. Quite astonished, I replied that he had done no more than greet me politely and that I had done the same in return, but that it would be impossible for me to associate with such a man. He became angry and dared to say to me that we can see flyspecks in another man's soup yet overlook paving stones in our own. I left him with the remark that the observation was far more pertinent to him than to me. A few days later I was insulted in the park by Sade, and when I complained to M. de Coulmier I met with a cold reception.

Since that time he has made life at Charenton so unpleasant for me that I wrote my family asking them to get me out."[4]

Other inmates were probably just as offended by Coulmier's favors to Sade. Many objected to the marquis's imperious and brutal behavior. As he grew older, he scarcely became more accommodating. His tyrannical nature made itself felt everywhere. His presence at the hospital became a permanent source of conflict and scandal. Other inmates could not forgive either his haughtiness or his privileges. Not a day went by, for instance, when he did not have guests for lunch, thereby arousing the jealousy of other inmates. He appeared to be exempt from all obligations and, not being a lunatic, escaped even the medical authorities. It was too much. Royer-Collard swore to put things in order, and he kept his word. In the meantime, however, an unforeseen event turned the prisoner's life upside down.

A Forced Marriage

On May 31, 1808, Claude-Armand arrived unexpectedly at his father's door and informed him of his intention to take a wife. The young lady in question was a distant cousin from the Eyguières branch of the family, Louise-Gabrielle-Laure de Sade, daughter of Jean-Baptiste-Joseph David de Sade d'Eyguières and Marie-Françoise-Amélie de Bimard. Donatien had little sympathy for the father, who had succeeded him in 1778 as *lieutenant général* of Bresse and Bugey. But the circumstances required him to put on a good face. It was not easy these days for a young man with a noble name to find a wife. It was even more difficult when the young man's father was in Charenton. In these early years of the nineteenth century many people still looked upon madness as hereditary, to the point where the children of the mentally ill, and even distant kin (one could never be too prudent!), almost never found mates. This prejudice was one of those that Coulmier cited as grounds for refusing to reveal the inmates' identity to his chief physician. Sade's elder son, Louis-Marie, who had not found a wife at age forty and who would die a bachelor (he was not the marrying type), had asked his father to obtain a "certificate of cure" so that he might marry the girl whom Mme de Sorans and Delphine de Talaru, Clermont-Tonnerre's remarried widow, had turned up for him. The young lady was assured an income of five thousand livres, an unexpectedly good match. But her parents had said: "The father is in Charenton. If it is for madness, we want no part of the son. If it is for a book, it doesn't matter to us."[5] As for Madeleine-Laure de Sade,

"Sainte Laure" as Mme de Bimard called her, no suitor ever asked for her hand, nor did she have, so far as we know, the slightest amorous adventure. She spent her life in prayer, avoided society, was reduced to servitude by her own servant, and died in 1844 at the age of seventy-three.

Since Donatien saw no impediment to his son's marriage, all that remained was to sign the papers. Claude-Armand wanted this done immediately at the offices of the Charenton notary. But Coulmier refused to allow the prisoner to leave the hospital. Well, all right, then, summon the scribe to the hospital and the papers could be signed there. But the notary said that was impossible: such a solemn document could only be signed in his office. The director was consulted again, and this time he gave his approval, on condition that the marquis's departure be delayed until nightfall, after eight-thirty. In the meantime, the marquis and his son set to work drafting the contracts. Meanwhile, however, an express dispatch arrived from Louis-Marie, asking to see his father the following day. Donatien set a time and returned to work with his younger son. Suddenly Louis-Marie appeared. He had been too impatient to wait for his father's reply. He told Donatien he had to speak to him at once: it was urgent. The two men withdrew, leaving Armand alone. Louis-Marie then revealed that the marriage was a trap. The moment the papers were signed, the marquis would be removed from Charenton and locked up in a fortress. He had heard talk of Ham or possibly Mont-Saint-Michel. The marquis then returned to his room and told Claude-Armand that he would not sign anything that night, that he would have to think things over. His son was to return the next day.

On the following day, June 1, Armand hastened to hear his father's decision. Donatien approved the marriage and even said he was prepared to give his consent, but on one condition: his son would have to sign a notarized document guaranteeing that he would be kept at Charenton and provided with decent resources. He insisted, moreover, that this agreement be drafted immediately. Caught by surprise, Claude-Armand sat down and wrote these words at his father's dictation:

I affirm that neither I nor any member of my family will tamper with my father's liberty or tranquillity. I declare that, on the contrary, I shall do everything in my power to see to it that he remains unmolested where he is if I cannot obtain a more agreeable sojourn for him, and I promise to search unremittingly for one, in view of his desires and of the needs of a man of his age and health; and that, in any case, I shall shortly conclude our business dealings, from which I expect to receive full ownership of his property in exchange for an annual pension of 5,400 livres payable anywhere and immune from distraint, of which 1,200 livres shall be diverted at his death to Mme Quesnet for her to enjoy as long as she lives, unconditionally, and in full and entire peace, in such place as it may please her to reside. And this pension too shall be immune from distraint and inalienable.

Armand raised his head, thinking that the exercise was over. But the marquis forced him to add this postscript: "This is all that M. de Sade can do. He is well aware that nothing can prevent his son from proceeding as he wishes. If, however, his [younger son's] actions confirm the suspicions of M. de Sade *père*, he will make them public and immediately reveal them to his elder son and any remaining kin, and he will beg them in the most forthright and energetic manner to preserve an unfortunate old man from the consuming sorrow in which some would wish to envelop his tomb and, further, ask their help in bringing execration and public obloquy on the authors of such a gruesomely perfidious deed."[6] Claude-Armand was of course unable to put his signature to such an agreement. He simply told his father that he would discuss it with his prospective in-laws. Then he complained bitterly of his brother's "meanness" and "lies." On June 2 he again stopped briefly at Charenton to reassure the marquis "concerning all his fears of the night before" regarding his eventual transfer. He was in a great rush, he said, to reach Echauffour before Louis-Marie.[7]

In fact, his disappointment was immense. Not that he needed his father's consent to marry: at thirty-nine he was well past the age of majority. But his father's accord was indispensable if he was to receive the gift his mother had promised him when he married. And this was precisely what worried Louis-Marie and prompted his peculiar behavior. The reader will recall that the elder son had always been the child Mme de Sade liked least, just as he was his father's favorite: the latter was only partly the cause of the former. Louis-Marie had no doubt that his mother would favor his younger brother, and that is why he attempted to prevent his father from consenting to the marriage.

But there may also have been another reason for his action, one that I was fortunate to discover only recently. Louis-Marie's great-aunt Mme de Villeneuve had, during her lifetime (she died in 1798 at the age of 83), thought of marrying him to the same Gabrielle-Laure whom Claude-Armand now wished to marry. This comes from a letter that his friend Alexandre Cabanis wrote while visiting the elderly woman in Avignon: "She told me that she had thought of setting you up six years ago with your cousin Sade d'Eyguières, about whom you are asking for information. All I can tell you for the moment is that the father, the mother, and the daughter are émigrés. But wait a few days."[8] With his usual negligence Louis-Marie did not follow up on this letter and never regretted it. But now, after his recent setbacks, his sanctimonious little brother had just snatched away a remarkably good match, and this was too much to bear. He therefore decided to drop everything and return to the army. At age forty-one he had all but given up hope. When he confided his woes to Cabanis, his friend tried to dissuade him: "I am sorry about all your suffering and regret to see your brother marrying before you. But I think you are partly to blame. You never could make up your mind about your various marriage plans, and you never could bring yourself to settle on the choices you made or others made for you. You have been in the army twice, and you quit just when you might have found employment. You are past forty, and it seems to me that it is a little late to hope to resume a military career. It takes youth, health, and vigor to make war."[9] But Louis-Marie's mind was made up: three months later he rejoined the ranks of the Grande Armée, and on January 25, 1809, he was commissioned a lieutenant in the Second Battalion of Isembourg.

Meanwhile, at the château of Condé-en-Brie, Mme de Bimard, the future mother-in-law, anxiously awaited the marquis's reply: "Right now I have just one object in mind," she wrote Claude-Armand. "It comes from the heart, it consumes me entirely, and I forget whether I have business elsewhere. I shall remember when this thing is all finally over and done with."[10] She shivered at the thought that the plans might collapse. For she wanted this marriage perhaps even more than Claude-Armand did and was extremely eager to see it concluded.

Her disappointment on learning of the marquis's refusal is easy to imagine. And it was all the fault of that good-for-nothing Louis-Marie! Mme de Bimard now took matters into her own hands. Energetic, cunning, restless, and meddlesome, in the classic mold of the "Sadeian" mother-in-law, she discussed the matter with eminent acquaintances, spoke to one Poirier, a "powerful friend in the magistracy . . . who knows the presiding judge and all the judges in the lower courts," gathered advice, took consultation, collected information, and pondered various ways of countering the opposition of M. de Sade *père*. The first priority was to avoid going to court.

Finally, after mature deliberation, an idea came to her, one of which she was inordinately proud: "I was inspired," she said. What

was it? Very simple. Since the marquis de Sade had never been deleted
from the list of émigrés or amnestied, his civil rights remained forfeit.
The moral (if it can be called that): his consent was "worthless and
unnecessary." Quite elementary: all it took was an idea.

It is hard to believe one's eyes. Of all the Sades, Donatien Alphonse
François was the only one who had remained in France throughout
the Revolution. Mme de Bimard had emigrated; her husband, M. de
Sade d'Eyguières, had emigrated; Claude-Armand had emigrated. All
had emigrated except Donatien. And now they were invoking his alleged emigration for their own ends! Even more mind-boggling, these
nobles, who had fled the Terror to escape its laws, were now availing
themselves of the very same laws that had been promulgated against
them and their peers. It is almost unbelievable. What is more, Mme
de Bimard herself was not entirely unaware that her behavior was
contradictory: "Someone might perhaps object that these laws are out
of date," she confided to her future son-in-law. "More than anyone
else we should hesitate to invoke revolutionary laws, but when they
remain in force or have been extended, we must abide by them without
fear of criticism." What a smoothly hypocritical way of saying that the
end justifies the means.

Mme de Bimard's outrageously cynical but highly ingenious
scheme met with the approval of Claude-Armand and his mother. All
that remained was to put the plan into practice. First, the police were
consulted to make sure that the marquis's name was indeed still on
the list of émigrés. Next, Mme de Sade was asked to sign a petition
to the minister of justice informing him of the situation. The minister's
answer arrived on June 21. What it lacked in equity it made up for in
clarity: "A person whose name appears on the list of émigrés and who
has not been amnestied forfeits the civil rights accorded to every French
citizen under the Napoleonic Code. His wife, henceforth free, no longer
has need of [his] authorization, and his children, if they wish to marry,
should proceed as they would if their father did not exist."[11] The coast
was clear: Claude-Armand could marry whenever he wished, and his
mother could dispose of her property in any way she chose.

But Donatien had not said his last word. On June 20 he decided to
make a formal objection to his son's marriage. On June 24 a bailiff
served notice of this objection on Claude-Armand, Gabrielle-Laure,
and the town hall of Condé where she had elected domicile. On July 9
Mme de Bimard notified the prefect of police that her future son-in-law
intended to ask the courts to quash the objection, "but, given his desire
and that of his respectable mother and of the family he is about to enter

that his father's name be heard no more in the tribunals and that no notoriety recall it to memory, all of us join in asking whether it might not be possible to discover who is controlling M. de Sade's poor mind so as to prevent them from influencing him and so as to persuade [M. de Sade] to adopt the only reasonable course remaining open to him, namely, to withdraw his ill-advised opposition."[12] In other words, get his elder son away from him and stifle his objections to the marriage.

The authorities took the hint: on July 20 a constable claiming to have been sent by Dubois took M. de Sade from the hospital to the offices of Maître Finot, a Charenton notary, to sign a document withdrawing his objection to the marriage. What else could he do? Now that the justice ministry was involved, there was little chance of winning a lawsuit. In any case, the bride and groom could easily have circumvented the opposition, since on July 23 a lower court authorized Mme de Sade to make "any gift she wished" to her younger son, and on July 29 another decision declared Sade's opposition to the marriage "null and void, being made by a legally incapacitated individual."[13]

Donatien was forced to admit defeat. On August 2 he formally consented to his son's marriage in a document entirely written in his own hand.[14] The civil marriage of Claude-Armand and Gabrielle-Laure was held in the town hall of Condé on September 15, 1808, and their union was blessed the same day in the château's newly restored chapel.

The Specter of Ham

Police minister Fouché ordered an investigation into Sade's behavior at Charenton, with Dubois in charge. The prefect found that M. de Sade maintained relations with various people inside the hospital "and even with individuals from outside." But how could this be prevented, given that the institution was not a prison? It was also true that he gave speech lessons to the actors and actresses who performed in the theater the director had authorized. When questioned about this, M. de Coulmier "admitted the fact and even said that in this respect he was much obliged to de Sade, since he regarded comedy as a means of curing alienation of the mind and was therefore happy to have a man in his hospital capable of training for the stage alienated individuals whom he wished to treat with this kind of remedy." Dubois's report concluded with this recommendation: "If de Sade's stay in the Charenton hospital is a kind of scandal, if it leads to almost inevitable abuses, I feel that there may be grounds for having him transferred to either the château at Ham or any other state prison, where he would be kept at his family's expense. This man, who has corrupted public morals with his impious and libertine writings and who has blackened his name with innumerable crimes, cannot return to society without danger."[15]

Upon receiving this report the minister ordered Sade's transfer to Ham.[16] Dubois immediately informed the family of this decision. Armand was on the point of signing his marriage contract. The old man at Charenton was no longer in a position to oppose the marriage or anything else. Why, then, exile him to such a remote place? It would be a bother for all involved. And as far as social honor was concerned, it was better, from the family's standpoint, to have the marquis confined at Charenton for "libertine dementia" than to have him locked up in a fortress as a common criminal. The family therefore sent the prefect a petition citing "the prisoner's infirmities and age" and pointing out that "being settled in Paris, it would find it more difficult, and the modesty of its fortune would deny it the means, to offer him the care that nature and humanity require." Coulmier attached a favorable note. Dubois dispatched these documents to the minister on September 9, together with a personal note of his own: "The considerations noted by the family would strike me as powerful arguments if they concerned a man other than de Sade. But unless he is kept in a locked cell; unless all communication with individuals inside and outside the prison other than members of his family is forbidden; unless he is denied ink, pens, and paper; I feel that the decision of September 2 should be maintained." In the margin Fouché's secretary noted: "Maintain decision."[17] Thus Sade would go to Ham.

A few days later, Armand approached the prefect once again. A draft of his letter, with Mme de Bimard's corrections of his spelling errors, has survived. In it Sade's son asks the prefect to persuade the minister to rescind his order. If that could not be done, he asked that the prisoner at least be allowed to spend the winter quietly at Charenton and that the transfer be delayed until the following spring.[18]

A month passed during which no decision was taken. M. de Sade's family then submitted another petition for postponement of the transfer, accompanied by a medical certificate signed on October 22 by Dr. Deguise, who indicated that his patient "was afflicted with acute and diffuse rheumatism particularly in the area of the chest. Also, palpitations, etc., in the chest or in the head: whence dizziness that causes him to stumble. Furthermore, his right leg tends to swell, especially at night. M. de Sade's plethoric condition requires special care, and there would be reason to fear for his life if he were to change his habits and manner of living."[19]

To some this certificate may seem to have been drafted expressly to put pressure on the minister. I do not share this view. At sixty-eight the marquis had witnessed a rapid deterioration of his health over the previous few months. He himself had compiled a full and precise accounting of his ills, probably for Dr. Deguise, in which he complained of troubles affecting his stomach, throat, teeth, and head; of spasms and shivers; of "disgust and total prostration . . . I have completely lost the use of my left eye, and my right leg, extraordinarily swollen, causes me almost continuous pain, especially when I tire it."[20]

With help from highly placed friends of Mme de Bimard, the family's petition finally brought results. On November 11, 1808, the minister of police granted the family's request and postponed the marquis's transfer to Ham until the first fortnight of April 1809.

One month before this deadline, however, the minister received two new petitions asking that the prisoner be kept at Charenton for the remainder of his life. The identity of the first petitioner is well known: she was Mme de Talaru, the marquis's dearly beloved cousin Delphine and the former wife of the unfortunate Stanislas de Clermont-Tonnerre; in 1802 she had taken a second husband, Louis Justin Marie, marquis de Talaru, a man with connections to the greatest names in France. On the morning of March 9 she went in person to see Fouché and ask him to "issue orders forthwith to allow M. de Sade to remain indefinitely at Charenton, where he has been for eight years and is receiving the care his health requires."[21]

The second petition, previously unknown, came from the indefatigable Mme de Bimard. It was dated March 19, ten days after Mme de Talaru's petition, and from it we learn that it was to Mme de Bimard that Donatien owed the postponement of his original transfer. This time she asked that the transfer order be permanently rescinded: "I am in your debt, Sir, for postponing the order to transfer M. de Sade to the château of Ham. If you can now have the order rescinded, how could I ever repay you?"[22]

On April 21, Fouché rescinded the transfer order and authorized Sade to remain at Charenton for the rest of his life.[23]

"Our infernal family"

A few weeks later, the marquis learned that his elder son had been killed in Italy. On June 9, 1809, Lieutenant Louis-Marie de Sade had been en route to join his unit at Otranto. At Mercugliano in the province of Avellino he was ambushed by Neapolitan rebels, who shot him in the head. A briefcase was found near his body containing a quantity of papers, his passport, a letter of exchange from Mme de Sade in the amount of 1,200 francs, and a portrait of a lady. When M. de Sade received the papers from the minister of war, he placed them in a large gray envelope on which he wrote in big letters with a rather shaky hand the words "Papers found on my son after his death."

It was ten days after Louis-Marie's death before the marquis heard the news, because on June 17, in a petition to the emperor, he still spoke of his son "who is distinguishing himself in the army." We know virtually nothing about his reaction. On June 2, a week before the tragic ambush, he had celebrated his seventieth birthday. Age often has the faculty of attenuating certain emotions, especially those associated with death, as if the proximity of one's own demise inured against that of others, even one's own children. Had Donatien experienced such a numbing of the heart? It is impossible to say. Generally mute in the face of great pain—the death of his father, for instance, or the sale of La Coste—he may have preferred silence now too. Sade never indulged in self-pity except when it was in his interest or it amused him to do so (and often self-interest and amusement were much of a piece). He never mouthed grand words without a cynical or ironical wink. He never uttered a cry, except in anger. He never felt pity, especially not for himself. Such was the essence of the libertine, whose impassiveness may be compared with the stoicism of the dandy.

So—not a tear from the marquis. Not a word in mitigation or relief. Nothing accessible. Not even an allusion to what had happened, except for a stinging rebuke to Claude-Armand for having told his mother the news too soon: "Are you aware that your behavior is vile and that you are about to add a further tinge of horror by informing your mother of her son's death, which you need not do for another year? But you want it to be said that you killed both your father and your mother, one with misery, the other with pain. Patience, patience, your son will avenge you. Remember that such atrocities never go unpunished."[24]

Of the two boys Louis-Marie had been Sade's favorite, the one to whom he had felt closest. In many ways their relations had not been unlike Donatien's with his own father. Cold and unyielding, utterly without affection, Louis-Marie had been a libertine in morals and in spirit, and he had a keen eye. His father's selfishness, his mother's weakness, his sister's doltish mind, his brother's hypocrisy, his uncles' and aunts' greed—all these things had been a part of what he once called "our infernal family."

Prisoner of the Emperor

Charenton, June 17, 1809

Sire,

Le sieur de Sade, the father of a family in which, for his consolation, he sees one son distinguishing himself in the army, has for nine years, in three consecutive prisons, been leading the most miserable life in the world. He is in his seventies, almost blind, and afflicted with gout and with rheumatisms of the chest and stomach that cause him horrendous pain. Certificates from the physicians of Charenton, where he now is, attest to the truth of these statements and give him warrant at last to ask for his freedom, in exchange for which he offers his solemn promise that he who grants it will never have grounds to regret it. He dares to declare himself, of Your Majesty, Sire, with the greatest respect, the most humble and obedient servant and subject.[25]

Gilbert Lely was rightly outraged at the sight of "a prince of the language" thus obliged to humiliate himself before the "bloody impostor." But Sade was playing his last card, the only one capable, he believed, of shaking the emperor's resolve—the card not of compassion but of shame at the indecent spectacle of a sick old man kept in chains. Napoleon turned to the privy council on state prisoners for advice, and on July 12 he received this report:

DE SADE: He acquired an appalling celebrity through the novel *Justine*, of which he has been adjudged the author. He was preparing to publish a still more infamous book when the police, in Year IX, seized the manuscript and proofs. He could have been tried before the courts, but it was feared that the trial might be scandalous, and he remained in prison.

My respect for Your Majesty does not allow me to enter into any detail concerning his conduct at Sainte-Pélagie and Charenton, where he has been held. This man appears to be in a perpetual state of lascivious furor, which constantly compels him to monstrous thoughts and actions. He also preaches crime in his speeches and writings. He is an unnatural being, and no effort should be spared to keep him out of society.

The commission is of the opinion, and I propose to Your Majesty, that he should be held in detention and denied all communication with the outside.[26]

These recommendations were reflected in the note that Coulmier received from interior minister Montalivet on October 18, 1810: "Le sieur *de Sade* shall be placed in a *completely separate room*, so that *all communication*, whether *inside* or *outside*, *on any pretext whatsoever*, may be *denied*. The greatest care shall be taken to deny him *all use of pencils, ink, quills, and paper.*"[27]

Irritated by these instructions, Coulmier forthrightly replied that his institution was not a prison and that it was impossible for him to keep M. de Sade in an isolated cell, all the "disciplinary cells" (*loges de force*) having been converted to private rooms. Furthermore, he added, "I should consider myself most unfortunate to use my time persecuting a man who, though no doubt guilty of many things, has long since demonstrated, through his consistent behavior, his desire to put his mistakes behind him . . . In view of my birth and the various positions and responsibilities with which I have been entrusted, I am honored to head a humanitarian institution, but I should feel humiliated to be made a jailer . . . I should like simply to point out that M. de Sade is doubly unfortunate, in that his bad example not only justified his children in leaving him with no resources but also permitted them to profit from his detention by stripping him of everything he had."[28]

At the marquis's request Mme de Talaru went to Montalivet to ask that his recent measures against her "uncle" be moderated. She cited his poor health and his need to breathe fresh air and see people. She also reassured the minister concerning the rumors that Sade's works were soon to be published in Leipzig: the stories were false; the possibility had never even been considered. The minister agreed to allow the prisoner to walk in the park but not at the same time as other patients; he could also visit Mme Quesnet, provided she was alone. Shortly thereafter, Sade received permission to speak to three persons of his own choosing; all others were to be excluded from conversation with him. Little by little, through one concession after another, he succeeded, with Coulmier's support, in chipping away at the restrictions and eventually in regaining the full freedom he had previously enjoyed.

•

In affixing his signature to the order maintaining Sade's detention, Napoleon was not merely carrying out a routine official duty. The author of *Justine* was not entirely unknown to him: he was familiar with the book and with Sade's reputation and detested both. On Saint Helena the former emperor of the French vented his wrath once more:

he "said that as emperor he had heard a summary and thumbed through the most abominable book ever engendered by the most depraved imagination: this was a novel which, even at the time of the Convention, he said had revolted public morality so that its author had been locked up and had remained so ever since, and he believed he was still alive."[29]

Mme de Sade's Last Summer

On July 7, 1810, at ten in the morning, Renée-Pélagie Cordier de Montreuil, the separated wife of the marquis de Sade, breathed her last at her château of Echauffour in Normandy. She was sixty-nine. Long since crippled and deaf, she had gradually lost her sight owing to a cataract. Since her condition did not allow her to attend her son's wedding, she had sent a proxy to represent her. Nor had she taken part in the interminable negotiations leading up to the marriage, contenting herself with signing documents and following Mme de Bimard's lead. Since January 1807 she had rented an apartment in a convent on the quai de la Tournelle, where she stayed during her brief visits to Paris. But for most of the year she lived in Echauffour with her daughter. When the latter died in 1844, she was buried at her own request alongside her mother. Their ashes still rest in the tiny village cemetery. On the tombstone one can still read the engraved names of Renée-Pélagie and Madeleine-Laure de Sade, followed by these words: "Both as virtuous as they were benevolent."

Last Writings

The marquis's papers have no more to say about his wife's death than about his son's. He was preoccupied with more immediate matters: paying his board, finding paper and ink, and writing—tirelessly darkening sheet after sheet with his hand, sometimes as firm and regular as in the past, sometimes, as when fatigue overcame him and thick effluvia glued his eyelids shut, shaky and barely recognizable.

For three years he had regularly kept a journal in small notebooks. One of them had been seized in the aftermath of the order of October 18, 1810, and Sade had asked Coulmier to give it back along with other seized items, "including both paper and quills." Nothing was returned. Another notebook was seized in 1814. Yet there was nothing reprehensible in these hastily scribbled, disorderly, unpunctuated pages, nothing but fragments of sentences in an old man's tired, hesitant hand. There were also many initials and many aliases and above all numbers by the hundreds, scattered among the words, arrayed in columns: dates, hours, sums of money, and a minute accounting of his days in captivity, indefatigably precise week after week and month after month.

This journal is an esoteric work, barely intelligible for all its codes and ellipses. From the moment he had been admitted to Charenton Sade had succumbed once more to his mania for "signals." Once again, as in the Bastille, numbers spoke to him in an oracular tongue whose meaning escapes us. Not only did they predict the future and reveal the good or evil intentions of people close to him; they also had the power to portend or arouse sexual desire.

Sade's interpretive mania alone might have justified his presence among the lunatics had Dubois not preferred "libertine dementia" as an excuse. The marquis recognized that his obsession struck some people as bizarre. "I think that, apart from the revolting absurdity of the system of figures that certain obsequious individuals use against me, it has the further disadvantage of making me seem a universal object of derision, a person who can be mocked with impunity, a considerable disadvantage from which my children probably never suffered. In any case, it is a minor triumph of stupidity over intelligence; that is all they have, and they must be allowed to keep it."[30]

Sade's only real diversion was the theater, which continued to occupy much of his time despite Royer-Collard's efforts to shut it down. When not staging the works of other playwrights, he revised his own and had the texts copied by other patients. He had not abandoned his ambitions as a writer of drama, and never would. To the end of his life he sought, with pathetic persistence, to have his plays performed in Parisian theaters. In 1813 he resubmitted *Jeanne Laisné* to the Comédie-Française, claiming that it had been received "subject to revisions" twelve years earlier, a statement we know to be false. A reader gave the work a withering review, mercilessly pointing out historical errors, improbabilities, melodramatic effects, and the mediocrity of the prosody (supported by quotations of dubious alexandrines); the report concluded that the work was unsuitable even for presentation to the theater's readers' committee. It is no insult to Sade's genius to ratify this judgment. The play was unplayable and has remained so.

Sade consoled himself by writing occasional verse for Charenton's festivals. On October 6, 1812, he wrote a cantata in honor of the visit of Cardinal Maury, archbishop of Paris. We do not know if the prelate was pleased with the homage he received. In any case, hospital officials

chose to conceal the true identity of the author and attributed the work
to one of the institution's female inmates.[31]

•

Sade continued to produce. In 1812 he wrote a "heroic" novel entitled
Adélaïde de Brunswick and based on an eleventh-century tale. In 1813
he revised his *Histoire secrète d'Isabelle de Bavière.* In 1814 he gave the
manuscripts of both works to his valet Paquet and instructed him to
find a publisher, but apparently no one took either work, for *Isabelle*
was not published until 1953 and *Adélaïde* until 1964.

It was also in 1813 that the two brief volumes of *La Marquise de
Gange* came out with no author's name on the title page. This, too,
was a historical novel, based on the tragic story of Marie-Elisabeth de
Rossan, marquise de Gange, whom Louis XIV had nicknamed "la
belle Provençale" and who had been brutally murdered by her two
brothers-in-law.[32] The innocence of the heroine, the cruelty of the
subject, and the atmosphere of dark eroticism in which certain of the
scenes unfold—all cried out for fictional treatment, and Sade was not
the only writer to use the story.

As we have seen, the marquis's sons took no pride in their father's
writings. They never spoke of his work without embarrassment or in
anything but veiled terms. Yet the tragic fate of *la belle Provençale*
managed to move the heart of Claude-Armand: "I greatly enjoyed
reading *La Marquise de Gange,*" he confessed to his father.[33] His letter
was dated November 17, 1814: two weeks later the marquis de Sade
was dead.

"You have lived too long!"

"It is a savory pleasure," Gilbert Lely wrote, "to imagine Sade for the
first time leafing through the five octavo volumes of *Le Génie du Christianisme.*" We no longer need to imagine it. Thanks to previously
unpublished sources, we now know that Donatien did indeed receive
Chateaubriand's work. Indeed, it was at his express request that Mme
de Bimard sent him a copy on May 2, 1811, along with a note from
which she deliberately omitted the word "cousin" (for who could say
what might happen if anyone should discover her connection with the
monster?):

Our little René left yesterday with his father. I hope that by now the angelic
child has arrived safely.

Rest assured of my concern for your situation. What actions I may take

are solely up to you, my [cousin]. Be always what we want you to be, so that
we may say: "Now he is as he always should have been. Restore his freedom,
give him back to his family." In closing, my [cousin], I offer you, with my
customary frankness and heartfelt sincerity, good wishes born of genuine
devotion.[34]

She did not have to wait long for an answer. Two days later, Sade
sent her one of the longest and finest letters he ever wrote. Suffused
with dark irony, here is the elderly prisoner's last word, his spiritual
testament, never before published:

Charenton, May 4, 1811

I cannot but thank you most sincerely, my dear cousin, for the handsome
present you have just given me. I assure you that I value it highly, and *Le
Génie du christianisme*, which comes to me on wings of virtue, spirit, and grace,
cannot fail to produce all the beneficial effects you hope for. But what are these
expressions, my dear cousin, with which you accompany your delightful gift?
Though you say it in words far kinder and more spiritual, what you are telling
me literally means: *you will get out when you are good.* But I dare put it to
you: can one really speak this way to a wretched old man laid low by illness
and imprisonment? Either I am what I ought to be, or I shall never be. Taking
the first horn of the dilemma (the only true one), if I am what I ought to be,
and I am, what is the use of making me suffer so long? And taking the second
horn, why torment me if there is no hope? For then there is nothing but cruelty
without profit. Do reason, morality, and religion permit such means? When
Christ immolated himself for our sake, was it not to redeem our sins? Therefore,
he did not want us to suffer in vain, since he gave his life so that we might be
spared the inferno. Why do those who persecute me preach a God whom they
do not imitate? And have I not ample reason to complain still more bitterly
when I see that the foolish fears people have about me are based solely on
slander? In the beginning I was made to suffer as the author of a book I
disavowed a hundred times in all my other works, in twenty newspapers, and
in five interrogations. For there was no other way to justify the truly absurd
length of so flagrant a detention, a *length* that, because it arouses suspicion of
other crimes, dishonors both my family and myself. I continued, they say, to
write, as if they did not know that the papers seized at Charenton, forming a
sequel to the book in question, had ceased to exist twenty years earlier. —I
managed the theater in the institution where I am kept, and that theater was
a breeding place of horror. —Would they have tolerated it, authorized it,
frequented it for six years had it been such? Could it have healed nearly fifty
patients had it resembled such a thing? Would officials have come to praise

me and thank me for my trouble had they found immorality in this amusement? —But I seduced young people of both sexes . . . Who are they? Where are they? Let them speak. I defy them to make such hideous charges. Listen, at least, to the head of the institution in which these offenses allegedly were committed, and see what he says.

What, then, have I done to suffer so long? —Eh, wretch, what have you done? Don't you see? *You have lived too long.*

Well, then, my dear cousin, may my persecutors be patient. Woe and despair are opening my coffin, I am preparing to enter it, and I surely will not live for as many years as have elapsed since they began tormenting me. Let them not carry barbarity to the extreme of not allowing me to expire in an asylum other than this one, made for dementia, epilepsy, and rage; let them fear no more from a man in whom the total exhaustion of both moral and physical faculties should absolutely allay their terrors. —With what ardor would I not then hurl myself upon the bosom of a religion which, instead of offering me tyrants and tortures, would proffer me nothing but consolation and virtue? Yes, my dear, kind cousin, what it takes to convince is examples, not torments. We hate the very opinions of those who mistreat us. We adopt, we revere, we cherish those of our benefactors. The sympathetic creature who, with one hand, wipes our tears in the name of a God whom he presents us with the other, is always sure to persuade us. If chains or serpents surround the One he gives us, we draw back, we turn away, we detest, and we shed tears over humankind.[35]

And what did he think of *Le Génie du Christianisme*? Did he so much as bother to read it? Be that as it may, the book's author elicited no particular respect. To Sade, Chateaubriand was one of the "godly rabble" along with men like Geoffroy, Genlis, Legouvé, Luce de Lancival, and other "henchmen of the tonsured gang."[36]

Daily Vexations

Meanwhile, life at Charenton continued, bitter and punctuated by vexations and disappointments. The battle was never-ending and tiresome. Not a day went by without Donatien's finding some grounds for complaint or protest. He wanted free access to his room key; he wanted permission to take his walks whenever he wished without being followed; he wanted to converse at will with three inmates of his own choosing, in return for which he promised "to speak to no one else"; and each time his paper and pens were taken from him, as they were periodically, he had to ask for them back. The inmates on the floor above made too much noise; he lacked sufficient wood for winter; his supply of candles was inadequate; his young servant Maniard had been sent away when it was alleged that Sade had tried to corrupt him, and they would not let him have the fellow back.[37] He did not care to be served "by a lunatic, an informer, or a fellow who delivers corn plasters." His farmers in Provence had forgotten about him. He hadn't enough even to pay his barber. And he was short of everything, thanks to his son, who had failed to pay his board. His letters to Claude-Armand, a long series of complaints and recriminations, cast a brutal light on relations between the old man of Charenton and the lord of Condé-en-Brie: "You are the reason why no one pays me," Donatien charged one day, "and your unforgivable cruelty causes you to close your eyes to all I am suffering. To put it in a nutshell, M. de C, having received nothing, is on the verge of refusing to feed me, and I have neither stockings nor breeches nor shoes. I am sick and need drugs that the hospital does not provide. Since I cannot buy them, I must suffer without relief. Will you love the child your wife is carrying if one day he treats you in this fashion? Eh, well, I solemnly promise you that this will come to pass."[38]

These cries of despair, distressing as they are, should not mislead us. The reality was far less tragic than M. de Sade indicated. He was always more than happy to exaggerate his misfortunes to arouse compassion. It amused and delighted him, especially if it sent his son into a rage. Claude-Armand took it as a personal affront whenever the old man asked to be pitied. So despite his hardhearted selfishness, he never let his father go without the basic necessities, not out of filial love but out of human respect, so as to keep up appearances. His letters to the notary Boursier show how scrupulously he responded to his father's needs, from arranging for a subscription to the *Journal de Paris* or the *Courrier de l'Europe et des spectacles* to providing extra wood for heating during harsh winters. Armand also paid his father a monthly allowance of 150 francs for pocket money. This was not much but enough to cover minor expenses. Nevertheless, it failed to prevent the marquis from crying poverty, at the risk (surely not unintended) of shaming his son. Ordinarily close-mouthed about his private affairs, Armand one day remarked to Corbin, his mother's former secretary, that his father was constantly getting him into trouble "because of his manners and his obsession with asking everyone for money."[39] This was true. Not only did he borrow wherever he could; he publicly accused his son of penny-pinching and announced to all the world that the boy was starving him to death. "Of all the rules of arithmetic, subtraction is the one he knows best," he wrote one day to the same Corbin. One can imagine the confusion of poor Armand, so worried about what people might say and afraid of nothing so much as being taken for his father's tormentor.

Brought up by his grandmother to respect the bourgeois virtues, Claude-Armand was merely abiding by the precepts the Montreuils had taught him. Cold in heart and mind, devoid of imagination, which he feared more than anything else in the world, jealous of his respectability, he never suspected that there might be a life other than the cozy, disciplined, protected one that was his first at Echauffour and later at Condé-en-Brie. Hence the instinctive repulsion he had always felt toward his father. Nothing but the hazards of birth attached this mediocre soul to that sublime adventurer. Yet Armand assumed the burden of caring for his father, if only to avoid a transfer to Bicêtre and the ensuing stain on the family's honor. He gave his alms of 150 francs per month only so that he might have a clear conscience, for he owed his father nothing: had he not inherited his mother's claims? It was to him, now, that his father was in debt for the full amount of his mother's dowry plus the accumulated interest, by this time amounting to some 200,000 livres. In other words, the marquis would remain for the rest of his life his son's hostage, just as he had once been his wife's.

·

Despite the relative freedom he enjoyed at Charenton, Sade remained a prisoner in the eyes of the law and thus subject to constant searches and questioning. Besides the police raids that disrupted the life of the hospital and upset the patients, Sade was subject to periodic interrogations, whose dates he carefully recorded along with a word or two of commentary. On March 31, 1811, it was comte Jolivet, *conseiller d'Etat*, who "wrangled a bit" with him. On November 14 he was again questioned by comte Corvietto, the inspector general of state prisons, who was "very kind and very decent." On March 31, 1813, it was comte Appellius, "or a name something like that," who came to see him. M. de Sade found him "very stiff, but very short."[40]

"I am not happy"

The marquis was not a man who allowed himself to be beaten down. In the face of adversity he had always demonstrated uncommon energy. Yet there were days when he felt his strength abandon him and when melancholy, repressed as though it were a shameful weakness, surreptitiously took possession of his soul. At such times his reveries naturally carried him back to the places of his childhood, La Coste and Saumane. He was even surprised to find himself thinking kind thoughts about his old friend Gaufridy.

The aged notary was still living in his house in Apt. He was now seventy and enjoying a tranquil retirement. Since the letter that ended their relationship, he had heard nothing from the marquis and was unaware of his internment at Charenton. Claude-Armand still maintained business relations with Gaufridy's two sons, Charles and François, however. Accordingly, we can imagine the elderly notary's emotion when he was given an envelope addressed in his old friend's hand. That handwriting—how could he have forgotten it? At one time the mere sight of it had been enough to make him tremble. Now, however, the marquis did not moan, did not bluster, did not threaten. He merely asked Gaufridy to look after Mme Quesnet's interests and "just claims" on his property. He also wanted his former attorney to help him unravel the suit his wife had brought against Rovère's widow, whose purpose was nothing less than to gain possession of the properties purchased with the proceeds from the sale of La Coste. And he asked for the return of a manuscript of memoirs of his life, "highly inaccurate and without form," which he had seen in the possession of François Gaufridy and which François had been unwilling to return. "I absolutely disavow this manuscript, and I beg you to see that it is returned."

Then, toward the end of his letter, he came to more personal matters. For the first time he surrendered to sincerity and revealed his distress:

How are you and yours doing? Have good things happened in your family, places for your boys, marriages for your girls?

How is the good and honest Madame Gaufridy? And you, my dear advocate, you, my life's contemporary, my childhood companion, how are you?

. . . A few details about La Coste, about those I loved, about the Paulets, etc. Is it true that Mme Rovère reserves the château for herself? What state is it in? And my poor park—can one still recognize anything of mine there?

How are my relatives in Apt?

Perhaps, now, you might like a word about me? Well, then! *I am not happy*, but I am well. That is all I can say to the friend who, I hope, still asks after me.

To you for life.

SADE[41]

Down with the Theater

For M. de Coulmier the years following Gastaldy's death were among the most difficult he had ever known. Not only had his relations with Royer-Collard steadily deteriorated to the point where the two men studiously avoided each other and communicated only by writing, but the hospital suddenly found itself in the midst of a severe financial crisis. The poor director was able to measure the depths of his disgrace when Montalivet visited the hospital in 1810: the minister's face expressed nothing but stern disapproval.

In January 1812 Montalivet assigned an auditor, M. Froidefond de Belleisle, to examine Charenton's accounts. Coulmier, at one time the abbé of the Premonstratensian abbey of Abbecourt, had always kept the books of the hospital as he had once kept those of his abbey, in the form of a simple running account. The auditor asked for a summary statement grouping all receipts and expenditures by category for the entire period from Year XI to 1809. Thus fifteen years worth of accounts had to be redone, a heavy burden for a man of seventy-one, who would somehow have to manage the whole job by himself since his bookkeeper had just died unexpectedly. But he did what was required and received a final discharge from his financial administration.

That left the major issue of the theater. Despite the hostility of the chief physician, the prefect of police, the interior minister, the political and medical authorities, and others who loudly denounced what they considered to be a "scandal," Coulmier stood fast. Faithful to Gastaldy's theories and to his own convictions, he fought off the attacks, ignored the polemics, and continued to put on plays. What is more, he left Sade in charge of production, a decision that might well be regarded as a provocation. In 1810 the marquis was still submitting lists of guests for his approval, which shows that the public had not tired of the productions.[42]

Despite Coulmier's stubborn persistence and the continuing interest of a large audience, the enterprise seemed unlikely to survive for very long: too many enemies were determined to put an end to it. Most alienists looked upon it as an interesting experiment but remained skeptical about its therapeutic value. The great Esquirol, Pinel's disciple and successor at the Salpêtrière, believed that certain plays could have a tranquilizing effect but denied that they were therapeutic. He was especially critical of the Charenton theater, and his criticism was not unfounded, since he had conducted similar experiments with his own patients without conclusive results: "I took several lunatics in my care to the theater: quiet maniacs, calm monomaniacs, and melancholiacs. I chose lighthearted plays apt to produce calming impressions but incapable of stimulating dangerous ideas or passions. I inquired about each patient's taste and encouraged them to look forward to this distraction for a considerable period. I never saw one cured by the theater."

His chief criticism of the organizer of the Charenton festivals, the "all too notorious de Sade," was that he used deception and aggravated the patients' maladies: "This theater was a lie," he would later write.

The lunatics did not act; the director deceived the public. Everyone was taken in: the important and the unimportant, the learned and the ignorant—all wanted to attend the plays performed by the lunatics of Charenton. For years all Paris went to see them, some out of curiosity, others to judge the effects of this wonderful method of healing the mentally ill. The truth is that the method did not cure.

The lunatics who attended these theatrical performances attracted the attention and curiosity of a frivolous, unserious, and sometimes mean public. The bizarre attitudes and bearing of these unfortunate individuals drew mocking laughter and insulting pity from the audience. What more did it take to wound the pride and sensitivities of these poor souls, or to disconcert the intelligence and reason of those few who retained the ability to be attentive? Favor decided which patients would attend the shows. It gave rise to jealousy, disputes, and bitterness. This led to sudden outbursts of madness, to recurrences of mania and fury.[43]

Unfortunately, the celebrated alienist obtained his information at second hand: we now know that all of it was taken from Hippolyte de Colins. Esquirol followed Colins in condemning the hospital's theatrical venture. It was the cavalry officer who was responsible for the (false) report that Coulmier had come up with this ingenious scheme only to draw crowds of spectators from Paris. Colins was the first to criticize the plays for their allegedly pernicious effects on patients. And Esquirol did not merely follow Colins's argument point by point; he actually lifted entire sentences from it. Neither Lely nor Daumas (who published Colins's report) nor Dr. Ramon (who had the text) pointed out the disturbing similarities between the two documents; they are enough to discredit the psychiatrist's account.

Meanwhile, the authorities, alerted by Royer-Collard's report concerning the theater's "harmful effects" on the imaginations of certain patients, repeatedly raised their concerns with Coulmier and his inmate impresario. It appears that the marquis's arguments succeeded in calming the investigators' fears. Recall that in the letter to Mme de Bimard quoted above, he mentioned having "cured nearly fifty patients" and claimed that government officials had come to praise him and thank him for his efforts. "Two members of the government came yesterday," he wrote. "They seemed pleased to see me, asked me what I wanted, listened to my requests, . . . [and] praised me for my efforts in curing patients by means of theatrical productions. They insisted that I show them certain trifles I had composed on this subject, which they approved, requested, and received with gratitude."[44]

The Last Season

Oddly enough, the blow that finally did in the theater of Charenton was struck not by the authorities or the doctors or even the awe-inspiring Royer-Collard but by the patients themselves, or at any rate certain of the patients, who were dismayed that balls and parties were being held in an institution where they lived in miserable conditions. One of them, whose name remains unknown, complained directly to the minister of the interior. The vehemence of his petition probably reflects the state of mind of many of the other inmates:

Excellency, What would you say about a hospital where balls and concerts are given two or three times a week, and splendid dinners on occasion, while the wretched patients are treated like criminals, most of them sleeping on straw like dogs with a small piece of tattered cloth for a blanket? Yet that is all they have to protect themselves against the rigors of the climate. How many, Excellency, must be claimed by the cold? Alas, if the dead could speak, how many people would sign my little petition![45]

Dated January 29, 1812, this letter was added to the already full dossier of protests the ministry had received against M. de Sade's performances. The situation could not continue. For the seven years the theater had been in existence, petitions had continually poured in to Montalivet's offices. A decision had to be made. Hippolyte de Colins's report, discreetly brought to the minister's attention, only encouraged him in his plan to shut the theater down. Shaken by the many protests and above all by Colins's diatribe, Montalivet on May 6, 1813, ordered a halt, "until further notice," to "the balls and concerts that are given in the Charenton hospital."[46]

On this stage where the curtain now fell for the last time M. de Sade had fully experienced the joy of the theatrical illusion. An asylum, a makeshift stage, an audience of madmen and voyeurs, a cast of lunatics: the essence of the theater restored at last. This theater was a place not for social entertainment or a display of masks but a physical necessity, an instinct, a compulsion to deceive.

The New Order

Coulmier tried in vain to have the minister's order rescinded. The closing of the theater struck him as a grave offense to the memory of his friend Gastaldy. He said as much in a letter to Montalivet and even petitioned the emperor, but to no avail.[47]

A year later, on April 11, 1814, Napoleon signed his abdication at the palace of Fontainebleau. On May 3 King Louis XVIII made his solemn entry into Paris. On May 5 he formed his first government and awarded the ministry of the interior to Montesquiou, an ardent defender of the monarchy during the Revolution and under the Empire. On May 31 the new minister appointed M. Roulhac de Maupas director general of Charenton, replacing M. de Coulmier, who, on resigning, received an extraordinary bonus of 35,589 francs 19 centimes, as much in reimbursement of monies advanced as in "consideration of the sacrifices of all kinds that he has made."[48] These events, apparently distinct, were in fact closely related. Although Coulmier was seventy-three, he was still perfectly capable of serving in his post, and it goes without saying that he was a victim of the political upheaval that took place in the spring of 1814. The regime established by Louis XVIII could not have as head of what was now the *maison royale* of Charenton a priest who had once sworn allegiance to the republican constitution and who, to make matters worse, had been defrocked, served in the Constituent Assembly as a *montagnard* deputy, and behaved in a morally dubious manner.

Nor was the choice of M. Roulhac de Maupas an accident. An erstwhile lawyer with no particular talent, he owed his appointment to a marriage that inevitably worked in his favor: he was the husband of Henriette Royer-Collard, the chief physician's eldest daughter. And it is worth noting that the doctor's brother, Pierre-Paul Royer-Collard, a zealous monarchist, had for a time served as the abbé de Montesquiou's right-hand man. Everything fit together.

Shortly after taking up his position, on September 7, 1814, to be exact, the new administrator sent the abbé de Montesquiou a six-page report on his illustrious inmate. After rehearsing the circumstances and purpose of his detention, the proposed transfer to Ham, the intervention of Mme de Talaru, and the questionable laxity of his predecessor, Maupas came to the present situation: while acknowledging the marquis's medical problems, justifying his need for fresh air and exercise, he expressed doubt that the minister's intention was to allow him to communicate with other inmates, to have access to paper and pens, or to have his works copied and sent outside the hospital.[49]

Given that surveillance at Charenton was impossible and that Sade's health did not permit imprisonment in a penitentiary, Maupas saw only one possible solution: move him to another institution. In the margins of the first page of the report, the minister wrote in pencil: "To the château d'If if possible."

On October 21, 1814, Montesquiou asked comte Beugnot, director general of the royal police, to come to a decision about M. de Sade: "I beg you, Monsieur le comte, to examine ways of removing M. de Sade as promptly as possible from Charenton and sending him to a place where he can no longer do harm to society."[50] In less than two months Sade would be gone—for good.

M. de Sade's Last Adventure

At several places in Sade's journal one finds a mysterious sign, a sort of slashed zero rather like this: Ø. As the reader may have guessed, this was an erotic symbol denoting sodomy. One finds it linked to both names and masturbatory fantasies, and often there are numbers jotted down in close proximity. For example, under the date July 29, 1807, we find: "Night, idea Ø at 116, 4th of the year." On January 15, 1808: "Prosper comes with idea ØØ. This is his third visit and the second by his maid, who forms Ø for the first time." March 4, 1808: "Idea ØØ appears the v. of 9 months." For the year 1814 the sign was applied solely to a very young girl from whom he received frequent visits and whom he designated by the initials *Mgl*. Her name was Madeleine Leclerc.

Here we enter on the least glorious phase of the "divine marquis's" life. This is no longer the dashing nobleman of Arcueil or the bold libertine of Marseilles or even the tempestuous prisoner of Vincennes and the Bastille counting up his *prestiges*, but an old man trying to rekindle his senses through intimacy with a sixteen-year-old girl.

Madeleine Leclerc was the daughter of a nurse in the hospital, where she herself worked as an apprentice seamstress or laundress.

When the elderly inmate noticed her for the first time on January 9, 1808, at a time when Mme de Quesnet was ill, she was just a little girl, not yet twelve. Thanks to the marquis's maniacal passion for numbers, one scholar thought he could establish November 15, 1812, as the date of Madeleine's first visit to his room. But an unpublished document suggests that it may have been earlier, prior to March 31, 1811, the date of M. Jolivet's first visit. In fact, the day after the inspector's tour of the hospital, the marquis wrote, or rather dictated to his son (whose handwriting is recognizable), an answer to various charges lodged against him. In particular, he denied having relations with a young boy and a little girl:

The slanders that have been made up about the young man are false. He has received nothing from me but very good advice, and if he left the hospital, it was because the director discovered that he had a regular affair with a girl on the staff.

As for the little girl, the daughter of a hospital nurse placed by her mother with Mme Quesnet, she works only for Mme Quesnet, not for me.[51]

The young man was the same Maniard who had worked for Donatien until Coulmier threw him out. And the little girl could only have been Madeleine Leclerc, at the time aged fifteen.

For the period from July 18 to November 30, 1814, we have detailed information about the relations between these unusual lovers from surviving fragments of Donatien's journal. M. de Sade did not fail to count, with his usual mania for detail, each of the young lady's *chambres* (his code word for sexual relations), and often he added interesting details: for example, on July 21, "Mgl. was quite upset, she almost could not get over it, and in general was cold throughout the Ø, which ended almost as soon as it began." On September 2: "Mgl. came to do her 88th of the total and her 64th *chambre*. It was easy to see that she had been sick, she was still feeling the effects. She had cut the hair on her cunt."

Rather than recoiling in horror, Mme Leclerc encouraged her daughter to satisfy the marquis's senile demands in exchange for a few coins (*figures*, the marquis called them). The proceeds from this barely veiled prostitution helped to pay the bills, and the price only heightened the ecstasy of the hard-core libertine, who had always preferred to pay for his pleasure. Strangely, these modest retributions did not preclude a kind of feeling on both sides. The girl felt an attachment to her protector, a kind of affectionate indulgence such as one might feel toward an elderly uncle given to pinching backsides. The marquis, for his part, was jealous of his young friend, kept a close eye on the company she kept, and ordered her not to go to balls, parties, or baths. Little by little, he took on the role of an attentive teacher, giving the adolescent elementary lessons in reading, writing, and singing.

And how did Mme Quesnet react to all this? After a few stormy scenes and "outbursts of temper" it appears that gentle Constance resigned herself to the situation, though without ceding anything to the usurper. She knew that no one could take her place in Donatien's heart and no doubt told herself that this was his last fling. Why should she destroy this final illusion, as ridiculous as it might seem? M. de Sade was full of plans for the day he might regain his freedom, an eventuality of which he harbored no doubt. He envisioned making a new life for himself with a ménage à trois. He would set up housekeeping with Madeleine and Constance and keep both women for himself. At last, he would have affection and pleasure together in one place. He discussed this plan with Mme Leclerc, who gave her consent on certain conditions. First, he would have to find work for the little girl. Why not in the theater, where he still had contacts? Donatien suggested. The mother turned up her nose: the pay was too low. All right, then, she could stay at Charenton until he found something better.

Of course he was not totally taken in and suspected that Leclerc and her daughter were putting him on. Perhaps he even wondered sometimes whether he would ever leave the hospital alive. But soon his vital energy gained the upper hand, and his thoughts would turn once more to his imminent release and the new life he would lead then, a fantasy in which he believed with the same indomitable energy, the same stubborn certainty, the same fervor as ever.

"This is my testament"

Donatien de Sade was not a man to let events get ahead of him. The reader will recall that he had already drafted his will once during the Terror in anticipation of the republican scaffold. Twelve years later and vulnerable to the perils of old age, he had no intention of being caught unprepared. So on January 30, 1806, at the age of sixty-six, he committed his last wishes to paper, placed the sheets in an envelope, sealed it with his red wax seal, and then inscribed these words: "This is my testament, which I entrust to the safekeeping of Monsieur Finot. D. A. F. Sade."

The first three articles concerned Sensible. "Wishing," he wrote, to attest to this lady, insofar as my feeble powers permit, my extreme gratitude for the care and sincere friendship she has shown me from the twenty-fifth of August one thousand seven hundred ninety until the day of my death—and having demonstrated those feelings not only with tact and disinterest but even more with the most courageous energy, since, under the regime of the Terror, she snatched me from the revolutionary scythe only too certainly dangling above my head, as everyone knows—I hereby give and bequeath, in virtue of the motives set forth above, to the aforementioned *dame* Marie-Constance Reinelle [*sic*], in her married name Quesnet, the sum of twenty-four thousand livres *tournois* in currency legal tender in France at the time of my decease . . . so as to constitute for her an income sufficient for her food and maintenance, said income to be paid to her in quarterly installments every three months, and inalienable and immune from distraint by whosoever it may be, it being my further wish that the property and sale of said property revert to Charles Quesnet, son of the aforementioned *dame* Quesnet, who shall become owner of the whole under the same conditions, but only after the death of his respectable mother . . .

Donatien further bequeathed to his faithful companion "all furniture, effects, linen, clothing, books, and papers" in his possession at the time of his death, with the exception of his father's papers, "designated as such by labels placed on the bindings," which were to be given to his children.

By the fourth article he bequeathed to Finot a ring valued at 1,200 livres "for his trouble and care in executing this act."

The fifth and final article contained his last wishes. M. de Sade expressly forbade an autopsy, although one was required under Charenton's regulations.[52] He also set forth in great detail his wishes concerning burial, a sign of the importance he attached to what became of his material remains:

Fifth and last: I absolutely forbid my body to be opened on any pretext whatsoever. I most emphatically ask that it be kept for forty-eight hours in the room where I die, placed in a wooden coffin that shall not be nailed shut before the expiration of the forty-eight hours prescribed above, at which time said coffin shall be nailed. During this period a dispatch shall be sent express to M. Le Normand, a lumber dealer on boulevard de l'Egalité, number 101, at Versailles, asking him personally to fetch my body with a wagon and with that wagon to escort it to the forest on my estate in Malmaison, commune of Emancé, near Epernon, where I want it to be placed, without ceremony of any kind, in the first copse on the right in said forest when entered from the direction of the old château via the main road that divides it. A grave shall be dug in this copse by the farmer of Malmaison under the supervision of Monsieur Le Normand, who shall not leave my body until he has placed it into said grave. In this ceremony he may, if he wishes, request the company of those of my relatives or friends who, without pomp of any kind, may wish to show me this final mark of attachment. Once the grave has been covered over, it shall be strewn with acorns so that eventually the site of said grave will be refilled, and the copse will grow as thickly as it did before, so that the traces of my grave will disappear from the surface of the earth as I trust my memory will disappear from the memory of men, except for the small number of people who were kind enough to love me to the very end and of whom I take a very fond memory with me into my grave. Done at Charenton-Saint-Maurice in full possession of mind and body this thirtieth of January one thousand eight hundred six.[53]

The Flight of the Eagle

On November 11, 1814, the medical student L.-J. Ramon, aged nineteen, joined the staff of Charenton as an intern. In the course of his visits to patients, he more than once encountered an elderly man, a lonely, aloof figure with a massive silhouette, whom he would remember all his life: "I frequently met him in the corridor adjacent to his apartment, walking alone with a slow, heavy step and dressed in a highly negligent manner. I never saw him talk with anyone. As I passed by, I used to greet him, and he would respond to my greeting with a cold politeness that ended any thought of entering into conversation . . . Nothing could have made me suspect him of being the author of *Justine* and *Juliette*. He had no effect on me other than that of being a haughty and morose old nobleman."

That same November 11, M. de Sade wrote a letter to Pépin, his farmer in Saumane. He wanted to know if the cutting of the forest at La Garrigue had been completed. If not, the farmer was instructed to speed up the operation so as to derive "the best possible profit." A part of the proceeds was to be used to pay for urgent repairs to the château. The marquis awaited the rest with extreme impatience: "The need I have for this money is beyond words."[54]

This was probably M. de Sade's last business letter. If so, his last letter went to Saumane, the only property he had left, and whose vaults still bear, engraved in the stone, the eagle with wings spread, membered, beaked, unguled, and crowned. The old man thus reached out to the child that was. The cut wood, the money, the farmer: this was his shorthand for what had not been swept away into oblivion, for all that remained in his memory: the hot summer behind closed shutters, the small court dominated by the raised watchpath; the large, shady rooms; the great paneled staircase; the vast park where in clear weather you could see beyond the foothills of the Comtat as far as the peak of Saint-Loup, the Aigoual, and the Cévennes.

•

In the days that followed, the marquis's health took a marked turn for the worse. Violent pains in his lower abdomen and testicles made a diet imperative. He was forbidden to drink old wine. On November 26 he asked the assistant physician Ramon to adjust his suspensory bandage. His private parts were horribly painful, especially at night when he touched them. On Sunday, November 27, Madeleine Leclerc visited him for the ninety-sixth time and stayed for two hours. He detailed his pains for her, and she seemed "most sensitive" to them. "She had not been to any balls and promised not to go to any. She spoke of the future and said she would turn eighteen on December 19. She lent herself as usual to our little games, promised to come back next Sunday or Monday, thanked me for what I was doing for her, and made it clear that she was not deceiving me and had no desire to."[55] On Wednesday, the thirtieth: "They have put a truss on me for the first time." These are the last words written in the marquis's hand. Thursday, December 1: his condition worsened. He could no longer walk. He suffered an attack of "prostrating gangrenous fever." He was transported to a two-room suite, probably because it was more convenient, and entrusted to the care of a servant. On Friday, December 2: Claude-Armand visited his father that afternoon. On seeing his condition he asked Dr. Ramon to take charge of his care. Although Ramon's duties as "first student" did not require him to stand vigils, the young doctor promised to watch over the marquis. At dawn he went to see his patient. As he entered the room, he ran into abbé Geoffroy, the house chaplain, who was leaving. The clergyman seemed if not edified at least pleased with his visit. The dying man had asked him to come back the next day. The intern then took up his place at the bedside of the marquis, whose breathing, noisy and difficult, became increasingly labored. Ramon had him swallow a few gulps of an infusion and a potion against "pulmonary congestion in the form of asthma." Suddenly, at about ten in the evening, shortly after having administered this drink, the doctor noticed that the sounds had stopped. Surprised by this silence, he approached the bed and leaned over the old man's body. Donatien de Sade's mortal race was run: the eagle had returned to the "seventh region of the air."

Epilogue

Late in the morning of December 3, 1814, while the body of the marquis de Sade lay in the hospital chapel, two members of the staff went to the *mairie* to file the death certificate. At the stroke of noon they affixed their signatures to the bottom of the document, along with that of Maître Finot, the deceased's notary and executor, who had some time earlier been elected mayor of Charenton-Saint-Maurice.

On the same day, Roulhac de Maupas informed the *directeur général de la police* of the marquis's death: "Since M. Armand de Sade, his son, was present, I do not believe that civil law requires seals to be affixed. As for further steps to be taken and in regard to public order, Y[our] E[xcellency] will judge whether precautions are needed and will deign to give me my orders. I am sufficiently confident of the younger M. de Sade's scrupulousness to presume that if there are any dangerous papers among his father's possessions, he will destroy them on his own." Despite this letter, the marquis's room would be sealed on December 5 at the insistence of Maître Finot.

The marquis was given a *religious* burial in the cemetery of Charenton, "at the far eastern end, almost on the banks of the Saut-du-Loup separating the cemetery from the forest of Vincennes. The grave was covered with a stone on which no name was engraved and which had no ornament other than a simple cross."[1] We do not know the date of the ceremony (most likely December 6) or the names of those who attended.

It has been widely repeated that none of the provisions of the marquis's will were respected at his death. To those who feel that his wishes were betrayed, it may be useful to point out the following facts:

1. The estate at Malmaison that the marquis de Sade expressly designated as his final resting place had been sold four years earlier on June 23, 1810. It was therefore impossible to respect his wishes.[2]

2. In keeping with his request, his body was not autopsied as required by hospital regulations. Claude-Armand personally intervened with M. Roulhac de Maupas to prevent the dissection of his father's corpse. Dr. Ramon's testimony is explicit: "Sade's cadaver was perhaps the only one I did not open from late 1814 to 1817."[3] The same witness reports that it was not until a few years letter—"I cannot assign a specific date"—that "when, owing to a need to excavate the cemetery, Sade's grave was one of those requiring exhumation, I did not fail to attend the operation."[4]

3. In an act of insidious, posthumous revenge by religious fetishism on a rebellious soul, the cross erected at the marquis's grave was the only serious affront to his wishes. May these words of the author of *Justine* efface this insult: "Let us renounce the ridiculous theory of the immortality of the soul, made to be scorned as relentlessly as that of the existence of a God as false and as ridiculous as it is. Let us abjure with equal courage both of these absurd fables, the fruits of fear, ignorance, and superstition."

•

When Sade's body was exhumed, Dr. Ramon asked for and received Sade's skull. There can be no doubt about the authenticity of the relic.[5] The vogue for phrenology was then at its height. A fervent adept of this discipline as well as the equally fashionable doctrine of magnetism, young Ramon was about to prepare the marquis's skull for analysis when he was visited by Dr. Spurzheim, a German disciple of Gall, whose courses he had attended in Vienna early in the century. Spurzheim asked for the precious object. Eventually Ramon gave in to his entreaties, and Spurzheim promised to return it along with several molds that he planned to have made. He left to give courses in England, Germany, and America and died some time later. Ramon never saw Sade's skull again. But during the few days it was in his possession, he studied it carefully and drew the following conclusions:

Excellent development of the top of the cranium (theosophy, benevolence); no exaggerated prominences behind and above the ears (no combativeness— organs so developed in the skull of du Guesclin); cerebellum of moderate size, no exaggerated distance from one mastoid process to the other (no excess in physical love).

In a word, if nothing made me suspect Sade, with his grave and I would almost say patriarchal demeanor, of being the author of *Justine* and *Juliette*, the inspection of his head would have caused me to absolve him of responsibility for such works. His skull was in all respects similar to that of a Father of the Church.[6]

The original of this skull may be regarded as definitively lost. Some think it may be in Germany, others in America. But Thibault de Sade, always attentive to matters involving his ancestor, has located one of the molds made for Spurzheim in the anthropology laboratory of the Musée de l'Homme. On its left side it bears this inscription in red letters: "Marquis de Sade. Coll. Dumoutier no. 529." Dumoutier was the teaching assistant who prepared the hall for Spurzheim's lectures. Thus in all likelihood it was Spurzheim who analyzed the marquis's skull in these terms:

The cerebral organization of the marquis de Sade, considered in relation to phrenology, is one of those frequent examples in which one finds the most disparate contrasts. The excessive development of certain organs whose faculties have very different purposes suggests that they had acquired the highest possible degree of activity and must have been responsible for this bizarre man's most glaring traits of character. Under the influence of a wise and enlightened will, the effect would have been that of the noblest and most generous passions. But the contrary occurred: the harmony that governs the sublime combinations of the intellectual faculties and human feelings had ceased to exist in him. Whether as a result of changes in the organization of his brain or through the influence of circumstances in the external world, the result was such a depravity in the morals and philosophy of the marquis de Sade that they consisted of the most amorphous composite of vices and virtues, acts of charity and crime, hatred and love. Born of the most shameful passions and imbued with sentiments of opprobrium and ignominy, such a monstrous conception would, if it had not been the work of a madman, have rendered its author unworthy of the name of man and forever sullied the memory of his posterity.[7]

EPITAPH OF D. A. F. SADE,

PRISONER UNDER EVERY REGIME

BY HIMSELF

Passant,
Agenouille-toi pour prier
Près du plus malheureux des hommes.
Il naquit au siècle dernier
Et mourut au siècle où nous sommes.
Le despotisme au front hideux
En tous les temps lui fit la guerre;
Sous les rois, ce monstre odieux
S'empara de sa vie entière.
Sous la Terreur, il se maintient
Et met Sade au bord de l'abîme.
Sous le Consulat il revient,
Sade en est encore la victime.[8]

[Passerby, kneel down to pray beside the unhappiest of men. He was born in the last century and died in the present one. Despotism of hideous mien made war on him in all ages; under the kings, that odious monster took hold of his entire life. Under the Terror, it persisted, and put Sade at the brink of the abyss. Under the Consulate, it returned, and Sade was still its victim.]

Notes

Bibliography

Index

Notes

* All references, unless otherwise indicated, are to this edition. It contains the complete scholarly apparatus, with references to archives and to other sources, which has been omitted from the 1982 edition.

† References to Sade's writings are to this edition—now being reissued by the publisher Jean-Jacques Pauvert—except for the *Cent Vingt Journées de Sodome* and *Aline et Valcour*. For these two works, references are to the text established by Michel Delon (Sade, *Œuvres*, vol. 1. Paris: Gallimard, "Pléiade," 1990).

Prologue

1. Noël Marmottan, *Le Pont d'Avignon, le petit pâtre Bénézet* (Cavaillon: Imprimerie Mistral, 1964), and Jean-Paul Clébert, *Guide de la Provence mystérieuse* (Paris: Sand, 1986).

2. Joseph-François de Remerville, *Histoire de la ville d'Apt*, 1690. Bibliothèque Mazarine, Ms. 3442–3445.

3. If so, she would still be a member of the Sade family by her mother, Laure, daughter of Hugues de Sade, who married Henri de Chabaud.

4. Abbé Jean-Antoine de Pithon-Curt, *Histoire de la noblesse du Comtat Venaissin, d'Avignon et de la principauté d'Orange, dressée sur les preuves* (Paris: Veuve de Lormel et fils, 1750), 3 vols., vol. 3, pp. 168–73.

5. Discovered by the abbé de Sade and reproduced in his *Mémoires pour la vie de François Pétrarque*, vol. 3, pp. 83–85.

6. This anecdote, which appeared as Scève made his intellectual debut, is hotly contested today. It is seen primarily as a sign of his commitment to a new poetic form.

7. For a recent summary of the state of the question, see Enzo Giudici, "Bilancio di una annosa questione: 'Maurice Scève e la scoperta della tomba di Laura,' " *Quaderni di filologia e lingue romanze. Ricerche svolte dall'Universita di Macerata*, vol. 2, Edizioni dell'Ateneo, 1980, pp. 3–70. The author raises serious doubts about Laura's kinship to the house of Sade.

8. In the Sadeian imagination the myth of Laura is linked to the shade of Justine and all the other virgins who fill the marquis's novels. "For Sade," Pierre Klossowski writes, "the image of the virgin is, through the reaction it causes in him, already an image of his own cruelty, which it prefigures and provokes." A paradoxical creature, the virgin is an object of desire that excludes possession. She thus spurs the male drive and turns it against procreation. In the Sadeian experiment her function is therefore defined as an inversion of religious ascesis.

9. By charter of January 11, 1416.

10. See Father Ménestrier, *Le Véritable Art du blason et l'origine des armoiries* (Lyons, 1671).

1. A Don Juan

1. Arch. Sade. Unpublished text.

2. Pierre Klossowski, *Sade, mon prochain* (Paris: Seuil, 1947), pp. 189–201. See also Gérard Mendel, *La Révolte contre le père* (Paris: Payot, 1974), pp. 102–10.

3. *O.C.*, vol. 3, p. 391.

4. *O.C.*, vol. 14, pp. 368–69.

5. Gaspard-François de Sade (1669–1739) was the first of the family to take the title marquis. He styled himself the marquis de Mazan.

6. From Sister Marguerite-Félicité de Sade, nun of Saint-Bernard de Cavaillon, to the marquis de Sade. (Arch. Sade. Unpublished letter.)

7. September 18, 1721. (Arch. Sade. Unpublished letter.)

8. A portrait by Nattier of Mlle de Charolais in this costume hung in the gallery of the château de La Coste until September 1792, when the castle was sacked and it disappeared. I believe I have located this painting. Several similar portraits of Mlle de Charolais are known to me, including a miniature in the collection of Xavier de Sade,

a painting from the school of Nattier in the Musée des Beaux-Arts de Béziers, a portrait attributed to Natoire in the Musée de Versailles, and another miniature in my possession.

9. Arch. Sade. Unpublished letter.

10. Arch. Sade. Unpublished letter.

11. Voltaire, *Correspondance* (Paris: Gallimard-Pléiade), vol. 1, p. 123.

12. Marie Victoire Hortense de La Tour d'Auvergne, née Bouillon, married Charles Armand René, duc de La Trémoïlle, first gentleman of the king's bedchamber (who died of smallpox on May 23, 1741, at the age of thirty-three). The duchesse de Bouillon occupied the apartment at Versailles just above the queen's.

13. Arch. Sade. Unpublished letter.

14. Probably an allusion to the duc de La Trémoïlle, who commanded this regiment.

15. Arch. Sade. Unpublished letter.

16. Ars., Ms. Bastille 10255. Unpublished document.

17. On the repression of homosexuality under the Ancien Régime, see my *Les Bûchers de Sodome* (Paris: Fayard, 1985).

18. Arch. Sade. Unpublished letter.

19. Soon to be published by Fayard along with unpublished works by the marquis and other family papers.

20. Arch. Sade. Unpublished letter.

21. Born August 18, 1714, she married the prince in 1729.

22. Arch. Sade. Unpublished text.

23. Voltaire, *Correspondance*, vol. 1, pp. 433 and 1389 (note).

2. A Broken Career

1. Arch. Sade. Unpublished letter.

2. The initiation of Sade and Montesquieu was reported in the *British Journal*, Saturday, May 16, 1730. On the comte de Sade's mission, see also Pierre Chevallier, *La Première Profanation du temple maçonnique* (Paris: Vrin, 1968), pp. 31–32.

3. René-Louis de Voyer, marquis d'Argenson, *Journal et Mémoires*, ed. E.-J. B. Rathery (Paris, 1859–67), vol. 3, p. 260.

4. On this question see Victor L. Tapié, *L'Europe de Marie-Thérèse, du baroque aux Lumières* (Paris: Fayard, 1973), pp. 27ff., and *Recueil des instructions aux ambassadeurs et ministres de France*, vol. 28: "Etats allemands, tome II—Electorat de Cologne," (Paris: Editions du C.N.R.S., 1963), pp. 159ff.

5. *Mémoires de la vie galante, politique et littéraire de l'abbé Aunillon Delaunay du Gué, ambassadeur de Louis XV près le prince électeur de Cologne* (Paris, 1808), vol. 2, pp. 131 and 136. The *domino* was a long, hooded robe that one wore to masked balls.

6. Ibid., vol. 2, p. 124.

7. *Recueil des instructions aux ambassadeurs et ministres de France*, vol. 28, p. 221.

8. Arch. Sade. Unpublished document.

9. The letter began: "Sire. Monsieur le comte de Sade has informed me of the orders he received from Your Majesty for his return." Some months later, the count returned the letters of recall to his secretary Baumez, who had remained in Bonn. (Arch. Sade. Unpublished document.) "Letters of recall" were customarily sent to an ambassador to be remanded to the prince recalling him.

10. Aunillon, *Mémoires*, vol. 2, letter 14, pp. 106–9.

11. D'Argenson, *Journal*, vol. 4, p. 244.

12. Arch. Sade. Unpublished letter.

13. The count included a detailed account of his arrest in a letter to an unknown correspondent. Arch. Sade. Unpublished letter.

14. Voltaire to the comte de Sade, June 1745. Arch. Sade. Unpublished letter.

15. Arch. Sade. Unpublished letter.

16. Arch. Sade. Unpublished letter.

17. The two men had long known each other as companions in debauch. The maréchal was in Montpellier in December 1744 to preside over the Estates of Languedoc.

18. Arch. Sade. Unpublished letter.

19. Arch. Sade. Unpublished letter.

3. Uprooting

1. See the "Plan général de l'hôtel de Condé et de ses dépendances," A.N. N IV Seine 21.

2. *Description nouvelle de la ville de Paris et Recherche des singularités les plus remarquables qui se trouvent à présent dans cette grande ville*, 5th ed. (Paris, 1706), vol. 2, p. 291. The princes of Condé occupied this hôtel until 1764, when Louis-Joseph de Condé sold it to Louis XV for 4,168,107 livres, 15 sols. The king had it leveled to make way for the Théâtre de l'Odéon and its surrounding district.

3. Edmond Jean-François Barbier, *Chronique de la Régence et du règne de Louis XV* (Paris: Charpentier, 1885), vol. 1, p. 275.

4. Mathieu Marais, *Journal et Mémoires sur la Régence et le règne de Louis XV* (Paris, 1863–68), vol. 3, pp. 18–19.

5. *Mémoires du maréchal-duc de Richelieu* (Paris: Firmin–Didot, 1889), p. 278.

6. Duc de Luynes, *Mémoires* (Paris: Firmin–Didot, 1860–64), vol. 4, p. 201, and vol. 7, p. 385.

7. *Aline et Valcour*, in Sade, *Œuvres*, vol. 1, ed. Michel Delon (Paris: Gallimard, 1990), p. 403.

8. Archives de la commune de Saumane, Registre BB 6 (1743–61), copy, author's collection, unpublished.

9. *Aline et Valcour*, p. 403.

10. Appointed by royal commission on January 26, 1744, confirmed by papal bull on December 7 of the same year, he took possession of his abbey on January 24, 1745.

11. From the abbé to the comte de Sade, 26 January [1745]. Arch. Sade. Unpublished letter.

12. May the author be allowed a personal reminiscence? I visited this underground dungeon some years ago at the same time as a tourist couple with a small daughter in tow. At one point the little girl became lost in the darkness and began to scream. The frightened mother began searching in all directions, flashlight in hand, and echoes of the little girl's name could be heard reverberating through the vaulted chambers: "Justine!"

13. *Les Cent Vingt Journées de Sodome*, in Sade, *Œuvres*, vol. 1, pp. 57–58.

14. Voltaire, *Correspondance* (Paris: Gallimard), vol. 1, p. 443.

15. *Lettres de la marquise du Châtelet*, ed. Theodore Besterman (Geneva: Institut et musée Voltaire), vol. 1, p. 250: letter 137 to Francesco Algarotti, August 27, 1738.

16. All the titles mentioned here figure in an inventory of the abbé de Sade's library (forthcoming).

17. This cartulary was destroyed when the château de Mazan was sacked during the Revolution. The abbé had drawn up an inventory, which is today in the family archives. A note in the marquis's hand states that "this important collection was transported to Mazan during the Revolution of '89, '90, '91, etc., at the urgent behest of Pélagie de Montreuil, wife of Louis Aldonze Donatien de Sade. All that was possible was done to rescue it from the furor of the thieves who beset the nobility at that time, but it was not to be. When calmer times returned, Donatien de Sade went to Provence, gathered what he could of the remains of these important papers, and had them locked up in drawers in the cartulary of Saumane, where he left them with the intention of putting them in order when circumstances permit. Done by me at Saumane, July 26, 1797. [signed] Donatien de Sade." Arch. Sade and Lely, *Vie*, vol. 1, pp. 10–11.

18. Sade mentions the abbé Boileau and Meibomius in the *Histoire de Juliette*, *O.C.*, vol. 9, p. 288 n.

19. Letter of 1765 to his aunt Gabrielle-Eléonore, abbess of Saint-Benoît de Cavaillon, reproduced in Jean Desbordes, *Le Vrai Visage du marquis de Sade* (Paris: Editions de la Nouvelle Revue Critique, 1939), p. 42.

20. See Dr. Charles Bidet, *D'Ebreuil à Châteauneuf. La vallée de la Sioule, Ebreuil et son abbaye* (Clermont-Ferrand: G. de Bussac, 1973), pp. 93–94, 115.

21. Sade, *Œuvres*, vol. 1, p. 403.

22. The abbé de Sade.

23. Letter from the comte de Sade to his uncle, Jean-Louis de Sade, prior of Sainte-Croix de Maulsang and provost of the church of L'Isle-sur-la-Sorgue, November 11, 1752. Arch. Sade. Unpublished letter.

24. Engravings by Lemaire and Boulée of the scenery used in tragedies staged at Louis-le-Grand can be seen in the catalogue of *Petits et grands théâtres du marquis de Sade* (Paris Arts Center, 1989), pp. 36–37.

25. *Instruction pour les maîtres des écoles chrétiennes*, p. 27.

26. D'Argenson, op. cit., vol. 1, p. 18.

27. For further details see Lever, *Les Bûchers de Sodome*, pp. 322–33.

4. "A most unusual child"

1. Arch. Sade. Unpublished letter.

2. Jean Levesque de Burigny (1692–1785) was the author of many works, including a *Life of Erasmus* (1757) and a *Life of M. Bossuet* (1761). His brother, Louis-Jean Levesque de Pouilly, vicomte d'Arcis-le-Ponsard, owned an estate next to Mme de Longeville's.

3. Anne-Charlotte de Salaberry, marquise Romé de Vernouillet, was a striking beauty whom the maréchal de Richelieu honored with his assiduous attentions.

4. Mme de Raimond to the comte de Sade, July 1753. Arch. Sade. Unpublished letter.

5. My italics. Somewhat later Mme de Raimond interpreted Donatien's silences as reflecting inattentiveness to others and attributed this to his timidity: "What do you have to say about our child? About his coldness? I am bothered by it, because a person who does not appear to be somewhat considerate is slower to please. This will come when he sees you and loses the timidity of youth." (Mme de Raimond to the comte de Sade, July 16, 1756. Arch. Sade. Unpublished letter.)

6. Mme de Raimond to the comte de Sade, September 8, 1753, Arch. Sade. Unpublished letter.

7. *Faut-il brûler Sade?* (Paris: Gallimard, 1972), p. 33.

8. Mme de Raimond to the comte de Sade, September 8, 1753. Arch. Sade. Unpublished letter.

9. Mme de Raimond to the comte de Sade, September 22, 1753. Arch. Sade. Unpublished letter.

10. At least in the beginning, although their relations cooled somewhat later on.

11. Mme de Saint-Germain to the comte de Sade. Arch. Sade. Unpublished letter.

12. *O.C.*, vol. 14, pp. 267ff.

13. Ibid., p. 270.

14. *L.M.L.*, vol. 3, p. 71.

15. Letter of February 3, 1784, in *L.M.L.*, vol. 3, p. 177.

16. Allusion to the comte de Clermont's affair with the celebrated dancer before she became Grimberghen's mistress.

17. October 1, 1753. Arch. Sade. Unpublished letter.

18. Comte de Sade to marquis de Surgères, February 24, 1754. Arch. Sade. Unpublished letter.

19. Comte de Sade to marquis de Surgères, February 1, 1755. Arch. Sade. Unpublished letter.

20. One very young "bib colonel" was carried in the arms of one of his grenadiers in the attack on Port-Mahon.

21. "Place where young men learn to ride and sometimes to handle weapons, to dance, and to perform on horseback." (*Encyclopédie*, vol. 1, p. 57, col. a).

22. *Aline et Valcour*, in Sade, *Œuvres*, vol. 1, p. 403.

23. In 1498 King Louis XII organized several companies of light cavalry (or light horse). A century later, in 1599, Henri IV rewarded the light horse for their courage during the Italian Wars and wars of religion by including them in his guard. Under Louis XIII they wore breastplates and helmets as defensive weapons and carried épée or saber and pistols for offensive weapons. Louis XV equipped them with muskets in 1745.

24. From the abbé to the comte de Sade, October 20, 1754. Arch. Sade. Unpublished letter.

25. Mme de Raimond to the comte de Sade, October 11, 1755. Arch. Sade. Unpublished letter.

26. *Extraordinaire de la Gazette*, June 27–28, 1756.

27. *Aline et Valcour*, in Sade, *Œuvres*, vol. 1, p. 404.

28. Marquis de Poyanne to the comte de Sade, September 23, 1756. Arch. Sade. Unpublished letter.

29. Mme de Raimond to the comte de Sade, August 3, 1756. Arch. Sade. Unpublished letter.

30. Arch. Sade. Unpublished letter.

31. Arch. Sade. Unpublished letter.

32. Mme de Raimond to the comte de Sade, [April] 1757. Arch. Sade. Unpublished letter.

33. Arch. Sade. Unpublished letter.

34. Antoine de Pas, marquis de Feuquières (1648–1711), was the author of *Mémoires sur la guerre*, first published in 1731 and reputed to be one of the best manuals of

strategy of the period. It contains abundant information and numerous judgments generally expressed in a very free style.

35. Marquis de Poyanne to the comte de Sade, May 18, 1758. Arch. Sade. Unpublished letter.

36. Arch. Sade. Unpublished letter.

37. Arch. Sade. Unpublished letter.

38. There is little information about how this court aristocrat conceived of his role as a lord of the manor. This draft of a letter to the curé of Saumane may give some idea: "The misery that comes of several bad harvests makes me afraid that my Saumane peasants may suffer this winter, which arouses my compassion. But my charity does not extend to those who prefer the idle life and who would rather beg than work. I wish to relieve those reduced to poverty by the shortage of work, and to that end I urge you to say in your sermon that I will give work to all who have none and who are willing to work for a reasonable wage, and that they may quit this employment whenever they find it possible to earn more elsewhere. They need only see M. Planchon, who will tell them what there is to be done." Arch. Sade. Unpublished letter.

39. Comte de Sade to Mme de Raimond, December 31, 1758. Arch. Sade. Unpublished letter.

40. August 4, 1758. Arch. Sade. Unpublished letter.

41. *O.C.*, vol. 16, p. 34.

42. Letter to Mlle de Rousset, [May 12, 1779], in *L.M.L.*, vol. 1, p. 69.

5. A Fine Marriage

1. B.N. Ms. N.a.fr. 24384, f⁰ 305. L.a.n.s. Reproduced in Lely, *Vie*, vol. 1, pp. 58–59, with several misreadings and undeciphered words.

2. B.N. Ms. N.a.fr. 24384, f⁰ˢ 304–5. L.n.s. The writing is not Donatien's. In the margin in his father's hand one can read: "Copy of the letter he wrote to the abbé, who is staying with me, and about which I am very angry because I did not want anyone to know what he had done." Reproduced in Lely, *Vie*, vol. 1, pp. 57–58, with several misreadings.

3. Arch. Sade. Unpublished letter.

4. The term *brevet de retenue* actually designated the document by which the king granted a certain sum to the holders of nonhereditary offices or their proxies.

5. From M. de Montmorillon, August 6, 1759. Arch. Sade. Unpublished letter.

6. Comte de Sade to M. de Montmorillon, August 1759. Arch. Sade. Unpublished letter.

7. M. Auban de La Feuillée to comte de Sade, October 8, 1759. In the margin one can read this note by Donatien: "This was a marriage for me." Arch. Sade. Unpublished letter.

8. Duc de Choiseul to comte de Sade, May 20, 1761. Arch. Sade. Unpublished letter.

9. Mme Beauvau-Bassompierre to comte de Sade, June 21, 1761. Arch. Sade. Unpublished letter.

10. The post of standard-bearer (*guidon de gendarmerie*) was highly prized and very expensive. Henri d'Alméras mistakenly placed this episode in 1762, and Lely repeated the error.

11. M. de La Ronce to comte de Sade, November 12, 1761. Arch. Sade. Unpublished letter.

12. Comte de Sade to Mme de Raimond de Longeville, August 16, 1761. Arch. Sade. Unpublished letter.

13. Duc de Choiseul to comte de Sade, November 12, 1761. Arch. Sade. Unpublished letter.

14. Duc de Choiseul to comte de Sade, December 7, 1761. Arch. Sade. Unpublished letter.

15. Louis-Joseph de Condé to comte de Sade, December 15, 1761. Arch. Sade. Unpublished letter.

16. A note in the marquis's hand reads: "How I put him to the test with that one!"

17. *Oeuvres diverses*. Ms. Arch. Sade. Reproduced in Lely, *Vie*, vol. 1, pp. 59–62.

18. B.N. Ms. N.a.fr. 24384, f°s 279–80.

19. From duc de Cossé to comte de Sade, November 12, 1761. Arch. Sade. Unpublished letter.

20. Those unfit for combat were assigned to sedentary posts such as commanding fortresses, supervising duels, and so on.

21. Arch. Sade. Unpublished letter.

22. B.N. Ms. N.a.fr. 24384, f°s 287–88.

23. Underlined in text.

24. B.N. Ms. N.a.fr. 24384, f°s 279–80.

25. Actually he had six children.

26. In the year of his son's marriage to Marie-Madeleine de Plissay (August 22, 1740), Jacques-René Cordier de Launay purchased from the marquis de Pont-Saint-Pierre the baronial estate of Echauffour in Normandy and the dependent *seigneurie* of Montreuil-Largillé. Claude-René then took on the name Montreuil. The acquisition of the *seigneurie* did confer a noble title on him, but not nobility itself, which was associated with his office.

27. The Order of Malta maintained several convents for women that dated back to the time of the Hospital of Saint John in Jerusalem. Only the daughters of noble families were allowed to enter. The most important were in France: one in Toulouse and two others in Martel and Beaulieu in the Lot. Members of these communities were known as lady canonesses of Malta.

28. From the comte de Sade to the abbé, March 17, 1763. B.N. Ms. N.a.fr. 24384, f° 281.

29. He was appointed to that post on May 24, 1743, and occupied it until July 17, 1754, when Jacques Charpentier de Boisgibault succeeded him. At the time of his daughter's engagement to the marquis de Sade, his only title was honorary president.

30. Born in 1720, Marie-Madeleine Masson de Plissay belonged to a family of the robe ennobled by its office at the end of the seventeenth century.

31. Maurice Heine, op. cit., pp. 335–36.

32. In 1754 he married the second daughter of the marquis de Villette and Thérèse-Charlotte Cordier de Launay, sister of the président de Montreuil. He was therefore a cousin by marriage of Renée-Pélagie, the future marquise de Sade.

33. Nephew of the président de Montreuil and cousin of Renée-Pélagie.

34. B.N. Ms. N.a.fr. 24384, f°s 310–11.

35. Paris de Montmartel, guard of the royal treasury and banker to the king.

36. Jacques-René Cordier de Launay, special treasurer for war in the cities of Berghe and Furnes and father of the président de Montreuil.

37. Paternal grandmother of the future bride.

38. Renée-Pélagie's aunt on her father's side.

39. From the comte de Sade to the abbé de Sade, B.N. Ms. N.a.fr. 24384, f⁰ˢ 310–11.

40. From the comte de Sade to the abbé de Sade, May 15, 1763. B.N. Ms. N.a.fr. 24384, f⁰ˢ 302–3.

41. B.N. Ms. N.a.fr. 24384, f⁰ˢ 314–15.

42. B.N. Ms. N.a.fr. 24384, f⁰ˢ 310–11.

43. B.N. Ms. N.a.fr. 24384, f⁰ˢ 306–7.

44. Stands for *chaude-pisse*, slang for venereal disease. Sade's contemporaries did not distinguish between *la vérole* (pox, or syphilis) and what we now call gonorrhea. They looked upon the latter as *la vérole récente*, as opposed to *la vérole confirmée* or *invétérée*. The distinction was not made until the very end of the eighteenth century. The only known treatment was mercury, although in the 1760s bichloride of mercury, which was easier to apply, came into use.

45. Sade, *Oeuvres diverses*. Ms. Arch. Sade. Reproduced in its entirety in Lely, *Vie*, vol. 1, pp. 68–71.

46. B.N. Ms. N.a.fr. 24384, f⁰ˢ 277–78.

47. B.N. Ms. N.a.fr. 24384, f⁰ˢ 448–49.

48. Arch. Sade. Unpublished document. There is no extant portrait of Mme de Sade, or of the marquis for that matter, other than the well-known pencil drawing by Van Loo. The engraving preserved in the Cabinet des Estampes of the Bibliothèque Nationale that several authors claim is of the marquise does not appear to be authentic. It is a medallion engraved in the nineteenth century, crudely made, and the identification is in my opinion suspect. The height of four foot ten is given in the units of the time, which do not correspond to our feet and inches: according to our measurements she was five foot two.

49. B.N. Ms. N.a.fr. 24384, f⁰ 267.

50. From the comte de Sade to the abbess of Saint-Laurent, ca. May 15, 1763. B.N. Ms. N.a.fr. 24384, f⁰ˢ 262–63.

51. From the comte de Sade to Gabrielle-Laure de Sade, May 2, 1763. B.N. Ms. N.a.fr. 24384, f⁰ 267.

52. Lely, *Vie*, vol. 1, p. 87.

53. Maurice Heine, op. cit., pp. 336–37.

54. B.N. Ms. N.a.fr. 24384, f⁰ˢ 406–7.

55. Excerpt from the "Registre des Actes de mariage de l'an 1763." Dispatch of September 28, 1810. Arch. Sade. Unpublished document.

6. *"Wild as the wind"*

1. Comte de Sade to abbé de Sade, August 16, 1763. B.N. Ms. N.a.fr. 24384, f⁰ˢ 308–9.

2. Comte de Sade to his sister Gabrielle-Laure, June 9, 1763. B.N. Ms. N.a.fr. 24384, f⁰ˢ 275–76.

3. Comte de Sade to abbé de Sade, October 20, 1763. B.N. Ms. N.a.fr. 24384, f⁰ˢ 289–90.

4. Mme de Montreuil to abbé de Sade, October 20, 1763. B.N. Ms. N.a.fr. 24384, f°s 410–12.

5. Comte de Sade to abbé de Sade, June 2, 1763. B.N. Ms. N.a.fr. 24384, f°s 308–9.

6. The contract stipulated that "the fees and emoluments of [this] office are due to the aforementioned lord [Donatien de Sade], husband-to-be, *from March 4, 1760, onward*." (A.D. Vaucluse, J. 87.)

7. From Mme de Montreuil to abbé de Sade, September 14, 1763. B.N. Ms. N.a.fr. 24384, f°s 414–15.

8. From Mme de Montreuil to comte de Sade, September 24, 1763. Arch. Sade. Unpublished letter.

9. Mlle de Rousset to Gaufridy, November 27, 1778, in Paul Bourdin, *Correspondance inédite du marquis de Sade* (Paris, 1929), p. 129. This appreciation was written fifteen years after Donatien's marriage, proof that la Présidente remained attractive at the age of nearly fifty-five.

10. The manuscript, a small folio bound in vellum, is currently in the possession of Prof. François Moureau of the University of Dijon, who allowed me to consult it freely.

11. Comte de Sade to abbé de Sade, June 2, 1763. B.N. Ms. N.a.fr. 24384, f°s 308–9.

12. B.N. Ms. N.a.fr. 24384, f°s 414–15.

13. B.N. Ms. N.a.fr. 24384, f°s 410–12.

14. *Aline et Valcour*, letter 3, in Sade, *Œuvres*, vol. 1, p. 397.

15. *La Philosophie dans le boudoir*, in *O.C.*, vol. 3, pp. 406–7.

16. Prince de Ligne, *Mémoires, Lettres et Pensées* (Paris: François Bourin, 1989), p. 696.

17. *La Philosophie dans le boudoir*, in *O.C.*, vol. 3, pp. 406–7.

18. Ibid., p. 416.

19. *L'Aigle, Mademoiselle* (Paris: Georges Artigues, 1949), p. 101.

20. B.N. Ms. N.a.fr. 24384, f°s 410–12.

21. This account scrupulously follows the original text of Jeanne Testard's deposition, which was discovered by the bibliophile Jean Pomarède and reproduced by Gilbert Lely in *O.C.*, vol. 12, afterword, pp. 643–50. By a strange coincidence, it was the same commissioner, Hubert Mutel, who was assigned to investigate the debauches of the abbé de Sade on May 25, 1762.

22. The marquis would meet Rose Keller years later at this very spot.

23. Arch. Sade. Unpublished letter.

24. Ibid.

25. *L'Amateur d'autographes*, 1866, pp. 355–56.

26. B.N. Ms. N.a.fr. 24384, f° 312.

27. A.N. O^1 406, no. 361.

28. Sade, "Premières Oeuvres," in *O.C.*, vol. 16, pp. 23–25.

29. Lely, *Vie*, vol. 1, p. 118.

30. Ibid., pp. 148–49.

31. Ibid., pp. 149–50.

32. Ibid., pp. 150–51.

33. Camille Piton, *Paris sous Louis XV* (Paris: Mercure de France, 1911–14), vol. 2, pp. 206–7.

34. B.N. Ms. N.a.fr. 24384, f°s 454–56.

35. Lely, *Vie*, vol. 1, pp. 153–54.

36. Piton, *Paris sous Louis XV*, vol. 2, pp. 147–48.

7. First Scandals

1. Camille Piton, *Paris sous Louis XV*, vol. 2, p. 196.

2. Ibid., vol. 2, p. 208.

3. On December 13, 1765, Inspector Marais noted that "Mlle Beauvoisin has just gotten over her miscarriage," implying that conception took place around March 15.

4. Unpublished letter in author's private collection.

5. From Mme de Montreuil to the abbé de Sade, May 20, 1765. B.N. Ms. N.a.fr. 24384, f°s 442–43.

6. Piton, *Paris sous Louis XV*, vol. 3, p. 61.

7. From Mme de Montreuil to the abbé de Sade, July 17, 1765. B.N. Ms. N.a.fr. 24384, f°s 452–53.

8. Jean Desbordes, op. cit., p. 42; transcription G. Lely, *Vie*, vol. 1, p. 126.

9. Letter from the marquis to the abbé de Sade, October 18, 1766, in Jean Desbordes, op. cit., p. 43.

10. From Mme de Montreuil to the abbé de Sade, August 8, 1765. B.N. Ms. N.a.fr. 24384, f° 456.

11. From Mme de Montreuil to the abbé de Sade, August 26, 1765. B.N. Ms. N.a.fr. 24384, f° 460.

12. Lely, *Vie*, vol. 1, pp. 131–32.

13. From Mme de Montreuil to the abbé de Sade, November 7, 1765. B.N. Ms. N.a.fr. 24384, f°s 457–58.

14. Camille Piton, op. cit., vol. 3, pp. 61–62 and 70–71.

15. Ibid., pp. 72–73 and 305.

16. Lely, *Vie*, vol. 1, pp. 136–37. This letter is one of those that the marquis had copied and bound in his *Oeuvres diverses*, which proves that he ascribed more literary than autobiographical value to it.

17. Mme de Montreuil and the abbé de Sade seem to have been the only people aware of this tryst: "He spent four days in Melun with the object of his current infatuation," the abbé wrote la Présidente. "He assures me that he has poured out his heart to you about this weakness and even that he wrote you from Lyons about his stay. I would like to know if this is true, because such confidence in you would please me and give me hope for the future." Letter from the abbé de Sade to la Présidente de Montreuil, June 1, 1766, in Lely, *Vie*, vol. 1, pp. 137–39.

18. See the well-documented work, with illustrative drawings, by Henri Fauville, *La Coste. Sade en Provence* (Aix-en-Provence: Edisud, 1984), pp. 55–69.

19. From the abbé de Sade to la Présidente de Montreuil, June 1, 1766, in Lely, *Vie*, vol. 1, pp. 137–39.

20. Ibid.

21. Lely, *Vie*, vol. 1, p. 156.

22. Ibid., pp. 157–58.

23. Arch. Sade. Unpublished document, with a marginal note in the marquis's hand: "Pretty fragment."

24. Arch. Sade. Unpublished document.

25. From the comte de Sade to Gabrielle-Laure de Sade, June 20, 1765. Arch. Sade. Unpublished letter.

26. From Mme de Montreuil to the abbé de Sade, January 30, 1767. B.N. Ms. N.a.fr. 24384, f°s 418–19.

27. From Mme de Montreuil to the abbé de Sade, April 19, 1767. Lely, *Vie*, vol. 1, pp. 141–42.

28. Maurice Heine, op. cit., p. 234.

29. Note that the consuls of La Coste restored the marquis's authentic given names for the occasion, probably at his request.

30. Henri Fauville, op. cit., p. 72.

31. B.N. Ms. N.a.fr. 24384, f°s 461–62.

32. Henri Fauville, op. cit., p. 72.

33. Camille Piton, op. cit., vol. 3, pp. 243–44.

34. Deposition of Jean-François Vallée, *procureur fiscal* for the *bailliage* of Arcueil, April 16, 1768; see Maurice Heine, op. cit., pp. 166 and 182–83.

35. Another example of brutality was recently turned up by Arlette Farge in the course of her research in eighteenth-century judicial archives: "On January 18, 1766, a complaint was filed concerning a dispute that took place on the place des Victoires between a master and a coachman, one of whose horses had been stabbed with a sword. We are told that Paul Lefèvre, a public coachman, saw 'a cabriolet hitched to a horse in which rode a gentleman whom he discovered to be the marquis de Sade and his servant,' and that he stopped to let his client out, which prevented the cabriolet from continuing on its way. A dispute ensued. The marquis de Sade, having left his carriage, 'hit the horses with his sword and stabbed one in the stomach.' The affair was settled amicably. The marquis de Sade (it was indeed he) paid 24 livres for 'injury to a horse' and lost service. The marquis's signature appears at the bottom of the legal document. What an unexpected pleasure to discover Sade stuck in traffic in the place des Victoires between a coachman and his cabriolet." Arlette Farge, *Le Goût de l'archive* (Paris: Seuil, 1989), pp. 84–85.

8. The Arcueil Affair

1. This account is a faithful reconstruction of the facts based on the depositions given by Rose Keller and other witnesses and published for the first time by Maurice Heine (op. cit., pp. 158–203). I owe no less a debt to Gilbert Lely, although my account differs from his in a few minor points. See his *Vie du marquis de Sade*, vol. 1, pp. 170–96.

2. This escape attempt was reported in the *Recueil d'anecdotes littéraires et politiques* on April 24, 1768, and was not really contradicted by later articles (see May 23). Bibliothèque Mazarine, ms. 2383.

3. From the marquis to the abbé de Sade, Joigny en Bourgogne, April 12, 1678, in Jean Desbordes, op. cit., pp. 53–54.

4. *Aline et Valcour*, "Histoire de Léonore," in Sade, *Œuvres*, Pléiade, vol. 1, p. 863.

5. Letter to Mme de Sade, July 1783, in *O.C.*, vol. 12, p. 393.

6. Letter from Mme de Saint-Germain to the abbé de Sade, April 18, 1768, in Lely, *Vie*, vol. 1, pp. 224–25.

7. Arch. Sade. Unpublished letter.

8. Receipts preserved in family archives.

9. Camille Piton, *Paris sous Louis XV*, vol. 3, p. 124.

10. Lely, *Vie*, vol. 1, p. 228.

11. Sade used this episode in *Aline et Valcour*. See Sade, *Œuvres*, vol. 1, p. 410.

12. Lely, *Vie*, vol. 1, p. 228.

13. Letter from Inspector Marais to the comte de Saint-Florentin, minister of the royal household, April 30, 1768. B.M. Reims. Ms. Collection Tarbé: XVIII, 222. Reproduced in Lely, *Vie*, vol. 1, pp. 230–31.

14. Letters of annulment (*lettres d'abolition*) were not granted for duels, premeditated murder, or abduction. When they concerned a nobleman, they had to be approved either by a sovereign court or a royal bailiff or seneschal. Their effect was to expunge the crime from the books, so that prosecution of the accused could not continue.

15. From Mme de Montreuil to the abbé de Sade, 13 June 1768. B.N. Ms. N.a.fr. 24384, f°s 420–21.

16. Letter to the abbé de Sade, November 19, 1768. B.N. Ms. N.a.fr. 24384, f°s 438–39.

17. Affidavits of April 18 and July 30, 1767, signed before Maître Gibert in Paris. Arch. Sade. Unpublished document.

18. From Mme de Montreuil to the abbé de Sade, March 2, 1769. B.N. Ms. N.a.fr. 24384, f°s 424–27.

19. *Letters of the Marquise du Deffand to Horace Walpole* (London: Methuen, 1912), vol. 1, pp. 417–19, 443.

20. Letter of April 18, 1768. Lely, *Vie*, vol. 1, p. 225.

21. *Recueil d'anecdotes littéraires et politiques*. B. Mazarine, ms. 2383, article of April 20, 1768.

22. *Gazette à la main*: B.H.V.P., ms. 627, article of June 12, 1768. This manuscript gazette was sent to Colonel Count Assolinski, residing at Porte Saint-Denis.

23. See François Moureau, "Sade avant Sade," in *Cahiers de l'U.E.R. Froissart*, Université de Valenciennes, no. 4, Winter 1980, pp. 19–28.

24. Lely, *Vie*, vol. 1, pp. 231–32.

25. Op. cit., p. 22.

26. *Courrier du Bas-Rhin*, April 20, 1768, p. 250.

27. *Recueil d'anecdotes littéraires et politiques*. B. Mazarine, ms. 2383, articles of April 13, 17, 20 and May 23, 1768.

28. *Gazette d'Utrecht. Supplément*, May 3, 1768.

29. *Courrier du Bas-Rhin*, April 20, 1768.

30. Siméon-Prosper Hardy, *Mes Loisirs, ou Journal d'événements tels qu'ils parviennent à ma connaissance*. B.N. Ms. F.fr. 6680.

31. Nicolas Restif de La Bretonne, *Les Nuits de Paris ou le Spectateur nocturne*, 1788–1794, 194th night. Sade, for his part, never hid his contempt for "this author of the Pont-Neuf and Bibliothèque bleue" (that is, whose works were sold in cheap editions from bookstalls and by itinerant hawkers).

32. J.-A. Dulaure, *Collection de la liste des ci-devant ducs, marquis, comtes, barons, etc.* (Paris: L'Imprimerie des Ci-devant Nobles, Year II of Liberty, 1790), no. 31, pp. 5–8, no. 32, pp. 1–4.

33. "Le Président mystifié," in *Historiettes, contes et fabliaux. O.C.*, vol. 14, p. 208.

9. Happy Days

1. Letter to Mlle de Rousset, April 17, 1782, in *O.C.*, vol. 12, p. 349.

2. From Mme de Montreuil to the abbé de Sade, March 4, 1769, B.N. Ms. N.a.fr. 24384, fᵒˢ 440–41.

3. Lely, *Vie*, vol. 1, pp. 242–43.

4. B.N. Ms. N.a.fr. 24384, fᵒˢ 446–48.

5. From Mme de Montreuil to the abbé de Sade, June 29, 1769. B.N. Ms. N.a.fr. 24384, fᵒˢ 422–23.

6. From M. de Saint-Florentin to la Présidente de Montreuil, March 24, 1770. Lely, *Vie*, vol. 1, p. 245.

7. The former minister of war had died five years earlier, on August 22, 1764.

8. La Présidente was certainly mistaking her dreams for reality, for five months earlier, on March 24, 1770, M. de Saint-Florentin had informed her that her son-in-law was considered an undesirable at court. It is possible, however, that the king's position had changed in the meantime.

9. Argenson archives (letter made available by comte Xavier de Sade).

10. Eight years later, from the dungeon of Vincennes, he wrote his wife: "If you will recall certain circumstances, different to be sure but in which the purpose was the same, honor and life, you will see that life has never meant anything to me when my honor was compromised. Remember that time and the letters received previously, with the certainty they implied of the likelihood that I would remain. Did I change my position? . . . And why? Because my honor required it." (To Mme de Sade, May 20, 1778. Arch. Sade. Unpublished letter.)

11. See Dr. Jean Artarit, "Sade et la Vendée," in *Annuaire de la Société d'émulation de la Vendée*, 1985, pp. 111–21.

12. The original brevet was signed by the king and Monteynard (secretary of state for war) and dated March 13, 1771. Arch. Sade.

13. From Mme de Montreuil to the abbé de Sade, April 27, 1771, B.N. Ms. N.a.fr. 24384, fᵒˢ 448–49.

14. J. Desbordes, op. cit.

15. This information comes from the président de Montreuil's diary (F. Moureau collection): "Anne-Prospère Cordier de Launay, born on December 27, 1751, canoness of Alix in Beaujolais."

16. Lely believed that her birth date was somewhere between 1743 and 1745, but information from the président's diary corrects this misimpression (see previous note). The same source tells us that the lady was baptized (as Jeanne-Prospère) in the Madeleine of Ville-l'Evêque.

17. M. Lever collection. Unpublished letter.

18. The phrase in quotes is underscored in the manuscript.

19. B.N. Ms. N.a.fr. 24384, fᵒ 324.

20. *Oeuvres diverses*, fᵒˢ 125 rᵒ–130 vᵒ. Reproduced in Lely, *Vie*, vol. 1, pp. 280–82.

21. B.N. Ms. N.a.fr. 24384, fᵒˢ 595ff.

22. Information taken from the inventory of La Coste prepared in 1769 by Maître Fage and published in H. Fauville, op. cit., p. 86.

23. See Sade, *Théâtre*, ed. Jean-Jacques Brochier, vol. 1, pp. 82–83.

24. The contract is in Lely, *Vie*, vol. 1, pp. 252–53.

25. A letter dated January 15, 1772, from the marquis to one Girard de Lourmarin reveals, by its obsequiousness, how desperate the marquis was to attract an audience.

26. Bibliothèque Ceccano, Avignon, fonds Jouve, ms. 6 600, f° 82, in Fauville, op. cit., p. 89.

27. The man is generally believed to have sprung from noble stock. It was even rumored that he was the duke of Bavaria's bastard son.

10. The Marseilles Affair

1. The account given here is based on court documents. The originals have vanished from the départemental archives of Bouches-du-Rhône, where only the texts of decrees remain, but a copy made by Marius Garcin for Alfred Bégis, a legal scholar and collector, who annotated the text, is preserved in the Archives de la Société du Roman philosophique (Inventory number 13. Dossier of 46 folio pages). Maurice Heine, who discovered this invaluable document, published it in an article in the journal *Hippocrate*, no. 1, March 1933: "L'affaire des bonbons cantharidés du marquis de Sade—27 juin–12 septembre 1772," which Gilbert Lely reproduced in his edition of Maurice Heine, *Le Marquis de Sade* (Gallimard, 1950), pp. 120–54.

2. Heine, op. cit., p. 132.

3. Heine, op. cit., p. 133.

4. Ibid., pp. 133–34.

5. A. D. Bouches-du-Rhône. Police. Ordres du roi. C. 4156. The letter from the duc de La Vrillière, dated July 15, 1772, along with Montyon's response can be found in Heine, op. cit., pp. 121–22.

6. "Réflexions et notes sur la requête en question," to Mme de Sade, April 21, 1777, in *O.C.*, vol. 13, pp. 124–30.

7. *Historiettes, contes et fabliaux*, in *O.C.*, vol. 14, p. 196.

8. From Mme de Montreuil to Gaufridy, March 12, 1776. Arch. Sade. Unpublished letter.

9. *La Nouvelle Justine*, in *O.C.*, vol. 7, p. 318, note.

10. From the early Middle Ages an imposing and more or less persistent judicial apparatus was erected against the "crime" of sodomy (homosexual or heterosexual), but its existence is in some ways misleading. The severity of the punishment served mainly to frighten people and deter them from committing the crime rather than punish those who did. Through the end of the eighteenth century, the law was extremely repressive, but its effects seem to have been astonishingly limited. Of the seventy-three trials for sodomy catalogued to date, only thirty-eight led to actual executions, two of which involved women. In addition, there were ten sentences involving banishment, galley slavery, or imprisonment of one sort or another, eight executions in effigy (the guilty parties remaining at large), two fines (one involving a woman), ten acquittals or dismissals (three women), one suicide, and four cases in which the sentence is unknown. Thus from 1317 to 1789 there were thirty-eight executions for the crime of sodomy, a very small number compared with the number of witches and charlatans of various kinds executed in France during the same period. Furthermore, at least a dozen of the thirty-eight executions involved individuals accused of rape, kidnapping, or murder in addition to sodomy. See Maurice Lever, *Les Bûchers de Sodome* (Paris: Fayard, 1985).

11. *Justine ou les Malheurs de la vertu*, in *O.C.*, vol. 3, p. 111.

12. B.N. Ms. N.a.fr. 24384, f°ˢ 328–31.

13. Bachaumont, *Mémoires secrets pour servir à l'histoire de la République des Lettres en France, depuis 1762 jusqu'à nos jours, ou Journal d'un observateur* (London, 1771–87), 36 vols., vol. 6, July 25, 1772.

14. "Requête de Mme de Sade," B.N. Ms. N.a.fr. 24384, f°s 595ff.

15. M. de Montreuil's diary, François Moureau collection, unpublished.

16. Ibid.

17. This was an act of clemency, because it allowed the victim to avoid the misfortune of being burned alive. Authorization was granted by way of a *retentum*, which allowed the executioner to strangle the condemned man and consign only a body already dead to the flames. The large crowds that attended executions were prevented from seeing the subterfuge by the thick smoke generated by the fire.

18. Heine, op. cit., pp. 146–47.

19. "The punishment for sodomy cannot possibly be harsh enough to expiate a crime for which nature blushes," wrote the jurist Antoine Bruneau in 1715.

20. *O.C.*, vol. 13, pp. 279–80.

21. See Lever, *Les Bûchers de Sodome*, pp. 335–81.

22. Jacques Peuchet, *Mémoires tirés des archives de la police de Paris* (Paris, 1838), 3 vols, vol. 1, p. 289.

23. Ironically, the marquis's father had done an important favor for the chancellor's father, René-Charles de Maupeou, by obtaining an infantry brigade for one of his sons. His letter of thanks is in the Sade archives.

24. The words in italics were underlined by the marquis.

25. Lely, *Vie*, vol. 1, p. 283.

26. M. de Montreuil's diary (op. cit.).

27. Letter from the Count de La Marmora to Lascaris, minister of foreign affairs in Turin, November 20, 1772, published in Lely, *Vie*, vol. 1, p. 364.

11. The Citadel

1. This description is based on Auguste Dufour and François Rabut, *Miolans, prison d'Etat* (Chambéry: Société savoisienne d'Histoire et d'Archéologie, 1879), vol. 18; Dr. Paul Sérieux, "L'internement du marquis de Sade au fort de Miolans," *Hippocrate*, Sept.–Oct. 1937, pp. 385–401 and 465–82; and Heine, op. cit., pp. 346–49.

2. Letter from the marquis de Sade to the comte de La Tour, December 10, 1772, reproduced in Lely, *Vie*, vol. 1, pp. 373–74.

3. Probably letters from Mlle de Launay.

4. Maurice Lever collection. Unpublished letter.

5. "Mémoire de la famille du marquis de Sade," December 21, 1772, in Lely, *Vie*, vol. 1, pp. 380–82.

6. "Réponse du comte de La Tour au Mémoire du 21 décembre," ibid., pp. 387–89.

7. Letter from M. de Launay to the comte de La Tour, January 1, 1773, ibid., pp. 392–93.

8. Letter from the marquis de Sade to the comte de La Tour, January 14 or 15, 1773, ibid., pp. 404–5.

9. A week later, on February 20, 1773, the king died, leaving the throne to his son, Victor Amadeus III.

10. "Au roi," ibid., pp. 418–19.

11. Letter from the marquis de Sade to the comte de La Tour, February 27, 1773, ibid., pp. 427–29.

12. From the marquis de Sade to the comte de La Tour, ibid., pp. 445–48.

13. See the letter from Mme de Sade to Gaufridy, July 29, 1774, in Paul Bourdin, op. cit., p. 14. The marriage never took place.

14. Letter from the comte de La Tour to the chevalier de Mouroux, April 17, 1773, Lely, *Vie*, vol. 1, p. 468.

15. Letter from the marquis de Sade to M. de Launay, April 30, 1773, ibid., pp. 470–72.

16. "Etat des effects laissés à Miolans," ibid., pp. 473–75.

12. The Fugitive

1. From the marquis de Sade to the comte de La Tour in Lely, *Vie*, vol. 1, pp. 475–76.

2. Much later Fage would claim that he had warned M. de Sade of the conspiracy that was forming against him, which seems unlikely given his participation in the assault on the castle.

3. In the local dialect the word *grange* referred not to a barn but to a house occupied by a relatively well-to-do farmer.

4. Letter from the marquis de Sade to Ripert, March 2, 1774, printed here with the kind permission of M. Thierry Bodin.

5. Details in Desbordes, *Le Vrai Visage du marquis de Sade*, pp. 136–38.

6. From Mme de Montreuil to Mme Necker (draft). Arch. Sade. Unpublished letter.

7. From Fage to Mme de Montreuil, December 9, 1773, Arch. Sade. Unpublished letter.

8. From Fage to Mme de Montreuil, December 21, 1773. Arch. Sade. Unpublished letter.

9. From Mme de Montreuil to Fage, January 1, 1774. Published in Desbordes, *Le Vrai Visage*, p. 133, under the impression that the letter is to Gaufridy, on which basis he accuses the latter of betrayal.

10. Fage to Mme de Montreuil, December 31, 1773. Arch. Sade. Unpublished letter.

11. Fage to Mme de Montreuil, January 3, 1774. Arch. Sade. Unpublished letter.

12. Bracketed words crossed out in the original.

13. Italicized words underscored in the original.

14. Mme de Montreuil to Fage (draft), January 12, 1774. Arch. Sade. Unpublished letter.

15. Fage to Mme de Montreuil, January 7–8, 1774. Arch. Sade. Unpublished letter.

16. Fage attempted to justify his actions in a text written in 1797 (twenty-three years after the fact), in which he claimed that the marquis owed him 6,156 livres, 4 sols, and 2 deniers. See A. D. Vaucluse, Etude Geoffroy, Apt. Divers 81.

17. Arch. Sade. Unpublished letter.

18. B.N. Ms. N.a.fr. 24384, f° 55.

19. Marquis de Sade to Ripert, dated "La Coste, March 2, 1774," which is probably false, since Sade announces that he will arrive on March 1. The letter is in the private collection of M. Thierry Bodin.

20. See Mme de Sade to Ripert, March 19, 1774, and the marquis de Sade to Ripert, May 29, 1774. B.N. Ms. N.a.fr. 24384, f°s 11 and 58.

21. From Mme de Sade to Ripert, La Coste, May 12, 1774, B.N. Ms. N.a.fr. 24384, f°s 64–65.

22. Mme de Sade to Ripert, La Coste, May 18, 1774. B.N. Ms. N.a.fr. 24384, f° 66.

23. Mme de Sade to Ripert, La Coste, May 29, 1774. B.N. Ms. N.a.fr. 24384, f°s 68–69.

24. Marquis de Sade to Ripert, May 29, 1774, B.N. Ms. N.a.fr. 24384, f° 11.

25. Letter published by Emile Lizé, "A travers les chiffons d'Alexis Rousset," in *Revue d'Histoire littéraire de la France*, 1978, no. 3, pp. 439–40.

26. B.N. Ms. N.a.fr. 24384, f°s 595ff.

27. From the duc de La Vrillière to Sénac de Meilhan, October 21, 1774. Arch. Sade. Fonds Bégis. Unpublished letter.

28. From the duc de La Vrillière to Sénac de Meilhan, February 26, 1775. Arch. Sade. Fonds Bégis. Unpublished letter.

29. Bourdin, op. cit., p. 14.

30. From Sade to Gaufridy, no date, in Bourdin, op. cit., pp. 13–14.

31. From Mme de Sade to Gaufridy, no date, ibid., pp. 14–15.

32. From Mme de Sade to Gaufridy, no date, ibid., pp. 15.

33. From Mme de Sade to Gaufridy, no date, ibid., pp. 15–16.

34. On October 10, 1774, he wrote a letter to Ripert in which he revealed that he was at La Coste. B.N. Ms. N.a.fr. 24384, f° 1.

13. "My stupid childish amusements"

1. From the marquis de Sade to Gaufridy, undated, in Bourdin, op. cit., p. 16.

2. Letter from Mme de Montreuil to Gaufridy, April 8, 1775, ibid., p. 31.

3. Henri Fauville, *La Coste. Sade en Provence*, pp. 105–6.

4. The abbé de Sade obliterated parts of the letter that he deemed compromising. The few fragments deciphered by Lely mention a girl named Rose, whom the abbé allegedly impregnated. Lely, *Vie*, vol. 1, pp. 552–54.

5. From the abbé de Sade to Gaufridy, March 28, 1775, in Bourdin, op. cit., p. 29.

6. From Mme de Montreuil to Gaufridy, February 11, 1775, ibid., pp. 26–27.

7. From Mme de Montreuil to Gaufridy, March 9, 1775, ibid., pp. 27–28.

8. From Mme de Sade to Gaufridy, March 14, 1775, ibid., p. 28.

9. From the abbé de Sade to Gaufridy, April 8, 1775, ibid., p. 32.

10. From Mme de Montreuil to Gaufridy, April 8, 1775, ibid., p. 32.

11. From the marquis de Sade to Gaufridy, undated, ibid., p. 32.

12. From Mme de Montreuil to Gaufridy, April 29, 1775, ibid., p. 33.

13. Maurice Heine, op. cit., p. 239.

14. From Mme de Montreuil to Gaufridy, July 26, 1775, in Bourdin, op. cit., p. 39.

15. Maurice Heine, op. cit., p. 239, and Lely, *Vie*, vol. 1, p. 560.

16. Bourdin, op. cit., p. 20.

17. From Mme de Sade to Gaufridy, June 21, 1775, in Bourdin, op. cit., pp. 35–36.

18. Heine, op. cit., p. 240.

19. "Ma grande lettre," to Mme de Sade, February 20, 1781, in *O.C.*, vol. 12, pp. 272–73.

20. See the letter from the marquis to Mme de Sade, March 1785, in *L.M.L.*, vol. 1, pp. 83–86.

21. Many families with origins in Lorraine had lived in Tuscany since the Grand Duchy was assigned to François of Lorraine, the husband of Maria Theresa (1738).

22. *Voyage d'Italie*, *O.C.*, vol. 16, p. 160.

23. From Sade to Gaufridy, August 10, 1775, in Bourdin, op. cit., pp. 39–40.

24. *Voyage d'Italie*, manuscript, "Premier volume de Rome," p. 162. Arch. Sade. Unpublished document.

25. Casanova, *Mémoires*, ed. Robert Abirached (Paris: Gallimard, 1985), vol. 3, p. 281.

26. Ibid., pp. 841–42.

27. The amorous nature of the relations between Sarah and Donatien is evident in letters from Dr. Mesny to the marquis published for the first time in the appendix to the French edition of this book.

28. *Voyage d'Italie*, *O.C.*, vol. 16, p. 164.

29. Ange Goudar to Sade, December 5, 1775, in Maurice Lever, "Ange Goudar: quatre lettres au marquis de Sade," *Dix-huitième siècle*, no. 23, 1991.

30. Clement XIV's successor, Giovanni-Angelo Braschi, ascended to the throne of Saint Peter on February 14, 1775, under the name Pius VI, but he did not officially take possession of his pontificate until December of that year.

31. Dr. Mesny to Sade, December 19, 1775. Arch. Sade. Unpublished letter.

32. Bourdin, op. cit., p. 58.

33. Lever, "Ange Goudar."

34. *Histoire de Juliette*, in *O.C.*, vol. 9, pp. 101–2.

35. Lely, *Vie*, vol. 1, p. 571.

36. *O.C.*, vol. 9, p. 133.

37. To Mme de Sade. Bourdin, op. cit., pp. 54–55.

38. Dr. Mesny to Sade, February 6, 1776. Arch. Sade. Unpublished letter.

39. The return trip from Naples to Courthézon took fifty-seven days, thirty-five in travel, twenty-two in rest.

14. Attempted Murder

1. The priest had forbidden the schoolmistress to teach without the bishop's permission and had required the village authorities to enforce his decree, an action that Mme de Sade felt violated the *droits du seigneur*.

2. Bourdin, op. cit., pp. 46–47.

3. Treillet deposition from Arch. Bégis, in Lely, *Vie*, vol. 1, pp. 588–90.

4. Mme de Sade to Gaufridy, December 27, 1776, in Bourdin, op. cit., pp. 59–60.

5. Marquis de Sade to Gaufridy, ibid., p. 60.

6. Ibid., pp. 64–65.

7. Lely, *Vie*, vol. 1, pp. 579–80, and Sade, *Œuvres*, vol. 1, pp. 51–52.

8. Lely, *Vie*, vol. 1, p. 590. In the margin Sade noted: "If his daughter had time to give him twelve livres, they had time to talk, so everything on this page is false."

9. Sade to Gaufridy, undated, in Bourdin, op. cit., pp. 60–63.

10. B.M. Reims, Ms. Collection Tarbé XVIII, document 224. Unpublished letter.

11. Sade to Gaufridy, undated, in Bourdin, op. cit., pp. 66–68.

12. From Mouret to Gaufridy, Aix, January 30, 1777, ibid., pp. 78–79.

13. Lely, *Vie*, vol. 1, p. 599.

14. Mme de Montreuil to Gaufridy, August 13, 1778, in Bourdin, op. cit., p. 121.

15. Mme de Montreuil to Gaufridy, August 13, 1778, in Bourdin, op. cit., p. 77.

16. Reinaud to Gaufridy, February 8, 1777, ibid., pp. 79–80.

17. Letter of April 6, 1777, ibid., p. 83.

18. Abbé de Sade to Gaufridy, ibid., p. 80.

19. Mme de Montreuil to Gaufridy, February 25, 1777, ibid., p. 80.

20. Mme de Sade to Gaufridy, March 19, 1777, ibid., p. 80.

21. Letter of February 15, 1777, in *L.M.L.*, vol. 2, p. 101.

22. Arch. Sade. Partially unpublished letter.

23. Mme de Sade to Gaufridy, undated, in Bourdin, op. cit., p. 90.

24. To Mme de Sade, early January 1778. Arch. Sade. Unpublished letter.

25. Copied and annotated by Gilbert Lely, who quoted fragments of them, these letters have never been published in their entirety. They will appear in a forthcoming edition of the complete correspondence that I am editing.

26. Arch. Sade. Unpublished letter.

27. Mme de Sade to Gaufridy, June 4, 1777, in Bourdin, op. cit., pp. 86–87.

28. Mme de Montreuil to Gaufridy, June 3, 1777, ibid., p. 86. Mme de Montreuil is no doubt alluding to a device used to facilitate penetration that was in common use among libertines of the time and that Sade described in L'Histoire de Juliette, O.C., vol. 8, pp. 563–64.

29. Mme de Montreuil to Gaufridy, June 3, 1777, in Bourdin, op. cit., p. 86.

30. From Mme de Montreuil to Gaufridy, December 20, 1777, ibid., p. 93.

31. See her letter to Gaufridy, February 16, 1778, in Bourdin, op. cit., pp. 101–2.

32. Mme de Montreuil to Gaufridy, February 1778. Previously unpublished.

33. To Mme de Sade, January 20, 1778. Arch. Sade. Unpublished letter.

34. To Mme de Sade, March 1778. Arch. Sade. Unpublished letter.

35. To Mme de Sade, early January 1778. Arch. Sade. Unpublished letter.

36. To Mme de Sade, March 1778. Arch. Sade. Unpublished letter.

37. Mme de Sade to the marquis, June 22, 1778. Arch. Sade. Unpublished letter.

38. The costs of the journey were paid by Mme de Montreuil.

39. Bourdin, op. cit., pp. 104–5.

15. On the Run

1. Inspector Marais to *lieutenant de police* Le Noir. B. M. Reims, coll. Tarbé, XVIII, 222–28.

2. Commandeur de Sade to *président* Des Galois de La Tour, June 25, 1778, in Bourdin, op. cit., pp. 106–7.

3. Bourdin, op. cit., p. 97.

4. Mme de Montreuil to Gaufridy, July 14, 1778, ibid., pp. 108–9.

5. See Lely, *Vie*, vol. 1, pp. 627 and 643–50.

6. Lely, *Vie*, vol. 1, p. 628.

7. According to the version of the story the marquis told Gaufridy, Inspector Marais himself abetted the escape. See his letter to Gaufridy of "July 18 at eight in the morning" in Bourdin, op. cit., pp. 109–12.

8. According to Marais's deposition. See Lely, *Vie*, vol. 1, p. 647.

9. Lely, *Vie*, vol. 1, p. 649.

10. Marquis de Sade to Gaufridy, undated [note in Gaufridy's hand: "received July 18"], in Bourdin, op. cit., p. 109.

11. Arch. Sade. Unpublished letter.

12. Reinaud to the marquis de Sade, July 23, 1778. Arch. Sade. Unpublished letter.

13. Marquis de Sade to Gaufridy, September 1, 1778, Bourdin, op. cit., p. 124.

14. Arch. Sade. Unpublished letter.

15. Reinand to the marquis de Sade, late July or early August 1778. Arch. Sade. Unpublished letter.

16. Bourdin, op. cit., p. 119.

17. To Mme de Sade, between September 7 and 27, 1778, in *O.C.*, vol. 12, pp. 153–54.

18. Mme de Sade to Gaufridy, July 27, 1778, in Bourdin, op. cit., p. 114.

19. Letter of July 27, 1778, ibid., p. 114.

20. Ibid., p. 112. Though undated, this letter must be subsequent to those of July 27 cited above.

21. Mme de Montreuil to Gaufridy, August 1, 1778, ibid., p. 116.

22. Mme de Montreuil to Mme de Sade, August 13, 1778, ibid., p. 121.

23. Marquis de Sade to Gaufridy, August 8, 1778, ibid., p. 118.

24. Raising silkworms was a specialty of La Coste and surrounding villages.

25. Letter to Gaufridy, September 1, 1778, in Bourdin, op. cit., p. 123.

26. Mlle de Rousset to Mme de Montreuil, August 28, 1778, Bourdin, op. cit., p. 126.

27. From a letter dated August 26, 1778, probably a mistake for August 27, in Bourdin, op. cit., p. 122.

28. To Mme de Sade, between September 7 and 27, 1778, in *O.C.*, vol. 12, p. 152.

29. See Lely, *Vie*, vol. 1, pp. 262ff.

30. Mme de Sade to Mlle de Rousset, September 7, 1778, Bourdin, op. cit., p. 125.

31. Letter of September 5, 1778, ibid., pp. 124–25.

32. Letters from Mlle de Rousset to Gaufridy, November 27, 1778, and Mme de Montreuil to Gaufridy, December 8, 1778, ibid., pp. 128–30.

33. Mlle de Rousset to Gaufridy, November 27, 1778, ibid., p. 129.

34. Letter of April 29, 1779. Arch. Sade. Unpublished letter.

16. Time Stands Still: 1778–1790

1. Sade was quite fond of dogs. He kept several at La Coste and was attached to the two setters he had while in prison at Miolans.

2. *Monsieur le 6*, p. 83.

3. Mirabeau, *Des Lettres de cachet et des prisons d'Etat. Ouvrage posthume composé en 1778* (Hamburg, 1782), pp. 53–54.

4. To Mme de Sade, May 9, 1779, in *L.M.L.*, vol. 1, p. 67.

5. To Mme de Sade, December 2, 1779, in *O.C.*, vol. 12, pp. 225–28.

6. To Mme de Sade, March 4, 1783, in *L.M.L.*, vol. 3, pp. 128–30.

7. Lely, *Vie*, vol. 2, p. 69.

8. Antoine-Raymond-Jean Galbert de Sartine (1729–1801) served as *lieutenant général de police* for Paris from 1759 to 1774.

9. Louis XV delighted in reading police reports concerning his subjects' debauches.

10. To Mme de Sade, May 21, 1781, in *L'Aigle, Mademoiselle*, pp. 67–70.

11. To Mme de Sade, July 3, 1780, in *L.M.L.*, vol. 3, pp. 47–48.

12. From Mme de Sade to her husband, December 31, 1781, in *L.M.L.*, vol. 2, pp. 308–9.

13. From La Jeunesse to Sade, September 14, 1779. Ars., ms. 12455, f°ˢ 558–63.

14. B.M. Avignon, ms., Requien, 11886.

15. To Mme de Sade, 1782, in *Monsieur le 6*, pp. 225–26.

16. To Mme de Sade, November 23–24, 1783, in *O.C.*, vol. 12, p. 412.

17. To Mme de Sade, early November 1783, in *L'Aigle, Mademoiselle*, p. 117.

18. To Mme de Sade, after January 10, 1784, in *O.C.*, vol. 12, p. 424.

19. To Mme de Sade, early November 1780, in *L.M.L.*, vol. 3, p. 65.

20. To Mme de Sade, May 20, 1780. Arch. Sade. Unpublished letter.

21. To Mme de Sade, June 25, 1777.

22. Philippe Roger, "Sade épistolier," in *La Fin de l'Ancien Régime. Manuscrits de la Révolution: Sade, Rétif, Beaumarchais, Laclos* (Paris: Presses Universitaires de Vincennes, 1991), pp. 50–51.

23. See Roger G. Lacombe, *Sade et ses masques* (Paris: Payot, 1974), chaps. 1–4.

24. Heine, op. cit., p. 215.

25. *L.M.L.*, vol. 1, p. 44.

26. To Mme de Sade, sometime after April 21, 1781, in *O.C.*, vol. 12, p. 234.

27. From Mme de Sade to her husband, March 6, 1779, in *L.M.L.*, vol. 2, p. 182.

28. To Mme de Sade, December 15, 1781, in *L.M.L.*, vol. 3, pp. 102–3.

29. Arch. Sade. Unpublished letter.

30. Arch. Sade. Unpublished letter.

31. Draft. Arch. Sade. Unpublished document.

32. Arch. Sade. Unpublished letter.

33. From Mme de Sade to her husband, January 1, 1779, in Lely, *Vie*, vol. 2, p. 26.

34. From Mme de Sade to her husband, July 11, 1781, in *L.M.L.*, vol. 2, p. 285.

35. Letter to M. de Sade, September 30, 1783, in *L.M.L.*, vol. 2, p. 340.

36. Letter to M. de Sade, November 23, 1783, in *L.M.L.*, vol. 2, p. 344.

37. Letter to M. de Sade, December 13, 1783, in *L.M.L.*, vol. 2, p. 346.

38. To Mme de Sade, early March 1783, in *L.M.L.*, vol. 3, p. 131 and note 57, p. 222.

39. *L.M.L.*, vol. 2, p. 283 and note 17.

40. This strange inventory can be studied in *L.M.L.*, vol. 1, pp. 275–94.

41. *L.M.L.*, vol. 1, p. 279.

42. Letters to his wife, December 14 and December 30, 1780, in *O.C.*, vol. 12, pp. 254–62.

43. To Mme de Sade, December 15, 1781, in *L.M.L.*, vol. 3, p. 104.

44. Letter to Mme de Sade, July 3, 1783, in *L.M.L.*, vol. 3, p. 152.

45. To Mme de Sade, November 23–24, 1783, in *O.C.*, vol. 12, pp. 412–17.

46. From Mme de Sade to Mlle de Rousset, July 27, 1781, in Bourdin, op. cit., pp. 172–73.

47. From the marquis to Mme de Sade, approx. July 15, 1781, in *L.M.L.*, vol. 3, p. 94.

48. From Mme de Sade to her husband, July 21, 1781, in *L.M.L.*, vol. 2, pp. 288–89.

49. From Mme de Sade to her husband, July 24, 1781, in *L.M.L.*, vol. 2, p. 293.

50. The nun who held the lodgers' money, records, and titles.

51. From Mme de Sade to the marquis, September 10, 1781, in *L.M.L.*, vol. 2, pp. 298–99.

52. From Mme de Sade to Gaufridy, September 12, 1784, in Bourdin, op. cit., p. 206.

53. From Mlle de Rousset to the marquis de Sade, December 26, 1778, in *L.M.L.*, vol. 1, p. 320.

54. Ibid., p. 321.

55. Ibid., p. 63.

56. Ibid., p. 329.

57. Ibid., p. 324.

58. Ibid., p. 322.

59. Ibid., p. 329.

60. *O.C.*, vol. 12, p. 389.

61. *L.M.L.*, vol. 1, p. 323.

62. Ibid., p. 322.

63. To Mlle de Rousset, May 1779, in *O.C.*, vol. 12, pp. 212–18.

64. From Mlle de Rousset to Gaufridy, May 29, 1779, in Bourdin, op. cit., p. 143.

65. From Mlle de Rousset to M. de Sade, May 11, 1779, in *L.M.L.*, vol. 1, p. 355.

66. From Mlle de Rousset to Gaufridy, November 9, 1779, in Bourdin, op. cit., pp. 148–49.

67. *O.C.*, vol. 12, p. 349.

68. Bourdin, op. cit., p. 157.

69. From Mlle de Rousset to Gaufridy, October 23, 1780, in Bourdin, op. cit., p. 157.

70. Lely, *Vie*, vol. 2, p. 91.

71. Bourdin, op. cit., p. 194.

72. Letter to his wife, February 3, 1784, in *L.M.L.*, vol. 3, p. 178.

73. Letter to Mlle de Rousset, undated, in Bourdin, op. cit., p. 176.

74. Letter to Mlle de Rousset, April 17, 1782, in *O.C.*, vol. 12, pp. 350–51.

75. From Mme de Sade to her husband, April 18, 1787, in *L.M.L.*, vol. 2, p. 371.

76. From Mme de Sade to Gaufridy, May 24, 1785, in Bourdin, op. cit., p. 212.

77. From Mme de Sade to Gaufridy, June 2, 1777, in Bourdin, op. cit., p. 85.

78. To Mme de Sade, approx. June 15, 1777, in *L.M.L.*, vol. 1, p. 59.

79. From Mme de Sade to her husband, October 30, 1780, in *L.M.L.*, vol. 2, pp. 253–54.

80. From Mme de Sade to her husband, October 16, 1778, ibid., p. 150.

81. To Mme de Sade, January 1784, in *L.M.L.*, vol. 3, p. 174.

82. To Mme de Sade, March 22, 1779, in *O.C.*, vol. 12, p. 196.

83. See Funck-Brentano, *Revue historique*, March 1890, pp. 289–90.

84. See Philippe Roger, "Rousseau selon Sade ou Jean-Jacques travesti," *Dix-huitième siècle*, no. 23, 1991, pp. 381–403.

85. Letter to his wife, June 15, 1783, in *L.M.L.*, vol. 3, p. 147.

86. From Mme de Sade to her husband, July 28, 1783, ibid., vol. 3, p. 147.

87. Letter to his wife, July 1783, in *O.C.*, vol. 12, p. 395.

88. Ibid., pp. 396–97.

89. Roger, "Rousseau selon Sade," p. 391.

90. To Mme de Sade, September 15, 1783, in *L.M.L.*, vol. 3, p. 159.

91. To M. de Sade, August 6, 1782, in Lely, *Vie*, vol. 2, p. 122.

92. To Mme de Sade, September 20, 1780, in *L.M.L.*, vol. 3, p. 57.

93. Ibid.

94. To Mme de Sade, July 27, 1780, in *O.C.*, vol. 12, p. 250.

95. To Mme de Sade, approx. March 28, 1781, in *O.C.*, vol. 12, pp. 282–83.

96. To Mme de Sade, November 23, 1783, in *O.C.*, vol. 12, p. 416.

97. Maurice Blanchot, *L'Inconvenance majeure* (Paris: J.-J. Pauvert, 1965), pp. 19–20.

98. Barthes, *Sade, Fourier, Loyola*, p. 186.

99. From Mme de Sade, May 18, 1781, *L.M.L.*, vol. 2, pp. 278–79.

100. From Mme de Sade, July 6, 1782, in *L.M.L.*, vol. 2, p. 321.

101. *L.M.L.*, vol. 3, pp. 140–41.

102. To Mme de Sade, February 3, 1784, in *L.M.L.*, vol. 3, p. 178.

103. To M. de Sade, October 30, 1780, in *L.M.L.*, vol. 2, p. 255.

104. To Mme de Sade, March 8, 1784, in Lely, *Vie*, vol. 2, pp. 159–63.

105. Letter to M. Le Noir, March 21, 1784, in *L.M.L.*, vol. 1, p. 77.

106. To Mme de Sade, March or April 1784, in *L.M.L.*, vol. 1, p. 80.

107. To Mme de Sade, September 1784, in *L.M.L.*, vol. 3, pp. 192–93.

108. Letter to Major de Losme, late September or early October 1787, in *L.M.L.*, vol. 1, p. 117.

109. Arch. Sade. Unpublished document.

110. Arch. Sade. Unpublished letter.

111. Sade, *Œuvres* (Paris: Gallimard, 1990).

112. "Kant avec Sade," *Critique*, April 1963.

113. *O.C.*, vol. 13, p. xxiii.

114. Ibid., p. lxxxv.

115. *L.M.L.*, vol. 1, p. 126.

116. Lely, *Vie*, vol. 2, p. 186.

117. Lely, *Vie*, vol. 2, pp. 263–72.

118. A.N., F⁷ 4954³, document 9.

119. *Tableau de Paris*, 1788, vol. 12, pp. 35–40.

120. Arch. Sade. Fonds Bégis. Unpublished document.

121. B.M. Orléans, ms. 1423, cited by Robert Darnton, "Les papiers du marquis de Sade et la prise de la Bastille," *Annales historiques de la Révolution française*, no. 202, October–December 1970, p. 666.

122. Desbordes, op. cit., pp. 244–45.

123. *Moniteur*, March 15 and 18, 1790; L. I. 709; B. 2, 200.

124. Lely, *Vie*, vol. 2, p. 282.

125. Mme de Montreuil to Gaufridy, March 23, 1791, in Bourdin, op. cit., p. 262.

17. Free! . . .

1. This, at any rate, was the story he told later. In fact he knew full well where to stay, because on the day he left Charenton, his wife gave Gaufridy M. de Milly's address. Letter of April 2 [*sic* for April 3], 1790, in Bourdin, op. cit., p. 262.

2. Bourdin, op. cit., p. 263.

3. Edouard-Ferdinand, vicomte de Beaumont-Vassy, *Mémoires secrets du XIXe siècle* (Paris, 1874), pp. 136–37.

4. It is interesting to compare this desperate remark with what his father wrote thirty years earlier. Both men were tempted by the void: "I plan to retire to some corner of the world, to think only of my end, and to live ignored by the entire world. I shall bid you an eternal farewell, begging your pardon for all the wrongs I've done and all the sorrow I've caused you." Letter from the comte de Sade to his sister Gabrielle-Laure, July 30, 1762. B.N. Ms. N.a.fr. 24384, fº 319.

5. Bourdin, op. cit., p. 272.

6. Bourdin, op. cit., p. 269.

7. See the excellent book by Pierre Fayot and Camille Tiran, *Mazan. Histoire et vie quotidienne d'un village comtadin à travers les siècles* (Carpentras: Le Nombre d'Or, 1978), pp. 346ff.

8. See Michel Vovelle, *De la cave au grenier*, II.2, pp. 187–208.

9. The revolutionary municipal government would seize the revenue from this seigneurial tax in September 1791.

10. Archives of Haute-Provence. Lacoste B.2180.

11. Letter to Reinaud, May 19, 1790. Bourdin, op. cit., p. 267.

12. Bourdin, op. cit., p. 271.

13. Letter of February 6, 1792. Bourdin, op. cit., p. 310.

18. A Playwright's Tribulations

1. Lely, *Vie*, vol. 2, p. 406 and n. 2.

2. On all the foregoing, see the excellent introduction by Jean-Jacques Brochier to Sade, *Théâtre* (Paris: Pauvert, 1970), vol. 1, pp. 11–33.

3. Letter published by Lely in his preface to *Monsieur le 6*, p. 46.

4. Arch. Sade. Handwritten note, undated, unsigned. Published in *Théâtre* (Pauvert edition), vol. 4, pp. 10–11.

5. Arch. Sade. August 21, 1791. Unpublished letter.

6. Arch. Comédie-Française. Letter of September 20, 1791. Unpublished.

7. Arch. Sade. October 20, 1791. Unpublished letter.

8. Bourdin, op. cit., p. 298.

9. Arch. Sade. Fonds Bégis, reproduced in Lely, *Vie*, vol. 2, p. 322.

10. Bourdin, op. cit., p. 313.

11. *Histoire de Juliette*, in *O.C.*, vol. 8, p. 443.

12. On this point and many others I am in agreement with Jean-Jacques Brochier in his preface to Sade, *Théâtre*.

13. Price indicated in *Feuille de correspondance du libraire* for 1791.

14. *Feuille de correspondance du libraire* (Paris: Aubry, 1791), no. 1968, p. 406.

15. *Affiches, annonces et avis divers, ou Journal général de France*, September 27, 1792, Supplement, pp. 4095–96.

16. Roland Barthes, *Sade, Fourier, Loyola* (Paris: Seuil, 1971), p. 140.

17. *Le Tribunal d'Apollon*, vol. 2, p. 12.

18. Maurice Heine, *Le Marquis de Sade*, p. 229.

19. Barthes, *Sade, Fourier, Loyola*, p. 130.

20. *Le Tribunal d'Apollon* (Paris, Year VIII), vol. 2, p. 192. Italics added.

21. Arch. Sade.

19. The Hermit of the Chausée d'Antin

1. Sade used the spelling *Reinelle.* According to her death certificate, Marie-Constance Quesnet was seventy-five when she died in 1832, which would make 1757 the year of her birth. (A. D. Val-de-Marne. Decennial Tables. Charenton deaths, 1792–1859: SE 19.)

2. He would remember her in his will, drawn up at Charenton on January 30, 1806: "Wishing to make this lady aware, so far as my feeble powers permit, of my extreme gratitude for the care and sincere friendship with which she has provided me from August 25, 1790, to the day of my death . . . "

3. Arch. Sade. Unpublished document, published as an appendix to the French edition of this work.

4. "Florville et Courval," in *Les Crimes de l'amour, O.C.*, vol. 10, p. 221, note.

5. Letter of June 12, 1791. Bourdin, op. cit., p. 289.

6. Undated letter [1803], in *O.C.*, vol. 12, pp. 598–99.

7. Klossowski, *Sade, mon prochain*, p. 192.

8. To Gaufridy, August 18, 1790. Lely, *Vie*, vol. 2, p. 298.

9. Private collection. Unpublished letter.

10. Gaufridy to Reinaud, February 4, 1792. Arch. Sade. Unpublished letter.

11. Mme de Montreuil to Gaufridy, March 23, 1790. Private collection. Unpublished letter.

12. *O.C.*, vol. 8, p. 173.

20. The Grand Illusion

1. Jules Janin, "Le marquis de Sade," *Revue de Paris* (November 1834), pp. 321–22.

2. *Biographie Michaud*, vol. 39, 1825, p. 476.

3. Taine borrowed the expression: see his *Origines de la France contemporaine* (Paris: Hachette, 1885), vol. 3, pp. 307–8. Oddly enough, Camus also characterized Sade as a "professor of torture" in *L'Homme révolté* (Paris: Gallimard, 1985), p. 59.

4. *Histoire de la Révolution française* (Paris: Laffont, 1990), vol. 2, pp. 784–85.

5. In *La Révolution surréaliste*, no. 8, December 1, 1926, pp. 8–9.

6. "L'Intelligence révolutionnaire. Le Marquis de Sade (1740–1814)," in *Clarté*, no. 6, February 15, 1927, p. 138.

7. See Françoise Laugaa-Traut, *Lectures de Sade* (Paris: Armand Colin, 1973), pp. 182ff.

8. *Le Surréalisme au service de la Révolution*, no. 3, p. 32.

9. André Breton, *Manifestes du surréalisme* (Paris: Jean-Jacques Pauvert, 1962).

10. *Bâtons, chiffres et lettres* (Paris: Gallimard, 1965), p. 216.

11. Nos. 74 and 75, December 1951 and January 1952; reprinted in *Privilèges* (Paris: Gallimard, 1955).

12. Op. cit., p. 70.

13. *Le Nouvel Observateur*, no. 68, March 2–8, 1966; no. 69, March 9–15; no. 70, March 16–22.

14. *Esprit*, vol. 40, February 1972, pp. 184–92.

15. Philippe Roger, "Sade et la Révolution," in J. Sgard, ed., *L'Ecrivain devant la Révolution. 1789–1820* (Grenoble: Presses de l'Université de Grenoble, 1990).

16. Program broadcast on Antenne 2, August 4, 1989.

17. Letter of December 5, 1791. Bourdin, op. cit., p. 301.

18. *La Châtelaine de Longeville*, in *O.C.*, vol. 14, p. 267.

19. On these questions see the excellent overview by Jean-Louis Harouel, "De l'Ancien Régime à la Révolution," *Histoire des institutions, de l'époque franque à la Révolution* (Paris: Presses Universitaires de France, 1987), pp. 509–55.

20. *O.C.*, vol. 12, pp. 392–93.

21. Ibid., p. 229.

22. Ars. Ms. 12456, f°s 700–701.

23. Bourdin, op. cit., pp. 67–68.

24. François Furet and Denis Richet, *La Révolution française* (Paris: Fayard, 1973), p. 33.

25. To Mme de Sade, early January 1784, *O.C.*, vol. 12, p. 420.

26. To Mme de Sade, April 30, 1781, *O.C.*, vol. 12, p. 422.

27. *Aline et Valcour*, in Sade, *Œuvres*, vol. 1, p. 388.

28. See Jean-Marie Goulemot, "Lecture politique *d'Aline et Valcour*. Remarques sur la signification politique des structures romanesques et des personnages," in *Le Marquis de Sade*, proceedings of a colloquium organized by the Centre aixois d'Etudes et de recherches sur le XVIIIe siècle (Paris: Armand Colin, 1968), pp. 115ff.

29. Sade, *Œuvres*, vol. 1, p. 447.

30. Ibid., pp. 640, 701, 541.

31. Bourdin, op. cit., p. 267.

32. Ran Halévi, "Monarchiens," in François Furet and Mona Ozouf, *Dictionnaire critique de la révolution française* (Paris: Flammarion, 1988), p. 398.

33. B.H.V.P., Ms. 773, f°s 215–16. Letter partially published by Bourdin, op. cit., pp. 272–73.

34. Lely, *Vie*, vol. 2, p. 316, note 1.

35. Excerpt from the minutes of the deliberations of the general assembly of the place Vendôme, January 24, 1791. Imp. Ve Desaint. (B.N. Lb40 2061).

36. The principal and incontestable source of the Swedish episode in *L'Histoire de Juliette* is a pamphlet by Cadet-Gassicourt, *Le Tombeau de Jacques Molay ou le Secret des conspirateurs* (Paris, 1795).

37. Bourdin, op. cit., p. 286.

38. Paris, June 1791, printed by Girouard, 8 pages. *O.C.*, vol. 11, pp. 69–74.

39. *O.C.*, vol. 11, p. 72.

40. Ibid., p. 69.

41. Ibid., pp. 70–71.

42. *O.C.*, vol. 11, pp. 73–74.

43. Reinaud to Sade, August 29, 1791. Arch. Sade. Unpublished letter.

44. Bourdin, op. cit., pp. 301–2.

21. In Torment

1. Letter of May 19, 1790. Bourdin, op. cit., p. 267.

2. Letter of July 9, 1791. Bourdin, op. cit., pp. 291–92.

3. See F. Foiret, *Une Corporation parisienne pendant le Révolution: les notaires* (Paris: Champion, 1912), pp. 281–85.

4. Ibid., pp. 288–90.

5. Document signed on March 1, 1793. A.N. Minutier central: Et. XVI (Dufouleur), 900.

6. Jacques Godechot, *La Contre-Révolution* (Paris: Presses Universitaires de France, 1984), pp. 151ff.

7. Maurice Blanchot, "L'Inconvenance majeure," preface to Sade, *Français, encore un effort* (Paris: Jean-Jacques Pauvert, 1965), p. 25.

8. A.N. F^7 4954^3, documents 161 and 106.

9. Letter of March 26, 1792. Bourdin, op. cit., p. 312.

10. Letter of April 7, 1792. Bourdin, op. cit., p. 313.

11. Letter of April 19, 1792. Bourdin, op. cit., pp. 314–15.

12. See the Prologue of this volume.

13. Letter to Gaufridy. Bourdin, op. cit., p. 317.

14. Letters of June 18 and 19, 1792. B.N. Ms. N.a.fr. 24384, f° 16.

15. A.N. F^7 4775^9, document 22.

16. Letter of August 25, 1792. Bourdin, op. cit., p. 322.

17. *Notes littéraires*, *O.C.*, vol. 15, p. 16.

18. A.N. F^7 4775^9, document 17 (copy dated 24 thermidor, Year II).

19. G. Lenôtre, *La Captivité et la mort de Marie-Antoinette* (Paris: Perrin, 1902), p. 69.

20. Letter of September 6, 1792. Bourdin, op. cit., p. 323.

21. Letter of September 13, 1792. Bourdin, op. cit., pp. 323–24.

22. Arch. Sade. Unpublished letter.

23. Arch. André Bouër, quoted in Henri Fauville, *La Coste. Sade en Provence* (Edisud, 1984), p. 177.

24. Reinaud to Mme de Montreuil, November 1792. Arch. Sade. Unpublished letter.

25. Bourdin, op. cit., p. 335.

26. Reinaud to Mme de Montreuil, November 1792. Arch. Sade. Unpublished letter.

27. Bourdin, op. cit., pp. 331–33.

22. *The Patriotic Farce*

1. Ernest Millié, *Les Sections de Paris pendant la Révolution française* (Paris: Société de l'Histoire de la Révolution Française, 1898), pp. 24–25.

2. Quoted by Patrice Higonnet, "Sans-culottes," in Furet and Ozouf, *Dictionnaire critique*, p. 420 (English translation, p. 395).

3. *Histoire de Juliette*. *O.C.*, vol. 9, p. 137.

4. Ibid., p. 138.

5. Ibid., p. 135.

6. *Observations présentées à l'Assemblée administrative des hôpitaux*. No copy of the published text has survived. Lély published a version based on the proofs corrected in Sade's hand and preserved at the Archives Nationales (*Vie*, vol. 2, p. 353, n 1, and *O.C.*, vol. II, pp. 77–79).

7. *Section des Piques. Idée sur le mode de la sanction des lois, par un citoyen de*

cette section. De l'Imprimerie de la rue Saint-Fiacre, no. 2. Undated [November 2, 1792]. B.N. Lb⁴⁰487.

8. Sade sent a copy of his speech to his attorney, Reinaud, who had this comment: "I have read your address to the Section des Piques. Although well done, I will not hide the fact that other woirks of yours seem to me more finely wrought. When you allow your feelings to speak, you are infinitely more energetic." Arch. Sade. Unpublished letter.

9. Probably the "Idea on the Law's Mode of Sanction."

10. To Gaufridy, October 30, 1792. Bourdin, op. cit., p. 334.

11. See Eugène Vaillé, *Le Cabinet noir* (Paris: Presses Universitaires de France, 1950), p. 250.

12. Reinaud to Mme de Montreuil, November 1792. Arch. Sade. Unpublished letter.

13. See Philippe Roger, "Les Bastilles de Sade," in *Le Monde de la Révolution française*, no. 7, July 1989, p. 16.

14. To Gaufridy, April 13, 1793. Bourdin, op. cit., p. 340.

15. BN Lb 40 490 and *O.C.*, vol. 9, pp. 99–103.

16. To Gaufridy, October 30, 1792. Bourdin, op. cit., pp. 333–34.

17. To Gaufridy, April 6, 1793. Bourdin, op. cit., p. 339.

18. Italics added. Arch. Sade. Unpublished letter.

19. To Gaufridy, August 3, 1793. Bourdin, op. cit., p. 342. The fact that he uses certain terms in this letter associated with the Masons has contributed to the myth of his membership in the order.

20. Bourdin, op. cit., p. 365.

21. Jean Paulhan, *Le Marquis de Sade et sa complice* (Brussels: Complexe, 1987), p. 71.

22. To Gaufridy, August 3, 1793. Bourdin, op. cit., p. 342.

23. *Description de la pompe funèbre décernée par la section des Piques aux mânes de Marat el Le Peletier*, . . . , Bibl. de la ville de Lyon. Collection of Pr. Lacassagne.

24. *O.C.*, vol. 11, p. 121.

25. *O.C.*, vol. 15, p. 15.

26. B.N. Lb 40 2054.

27. *O.C.*, vol. 11, p. 129.

28. Sade, *Œuvres*, vol. 1, p. 590, note ***.

29. *O.C.*, vol. 11, p. 130.

30. *Recueil des actes*, vol. 8, p. 59.

31. Compare A.N. F16 105.

32. Bourdin, op. cit., p. 348.

33. Bourdin, op. cit., pp. 348–49.

23. The Prisons of Liberty

1. Based on the affidavit published by Lely, *Vie*, vol. 2, pp. 390–93.

2. A.N. F⁷ 4775⁹, document 35, ibid., p. 393.

3. A.N. F⁷ 4775⁹, document 34, ibid., pp. 393–94.

4. A.N. F⁷ 4778⁹, document 31, unpublished document.

5. To Gaufridy, November 19, 1794, in Bourdin, op. cit., p. 360.

6. Sade's name does not appear on the list of those who asked to serve in the royal guard in 1791. A.N. O¹ 3696, dossier 1.

7. Dulaure, *Collection de la liste des ci-devant ducs, marquis, comtes, barons, etc.* (Paris: Imprimerie des Ci-devant Nobles, Year II of Liberty, 1790), no. 31, pp. 5–8, and no. 32, pp. 1–4.

8. Lely, *Vie*, vol. 2, p. 402.

9. Private collection. Unpublished letter.

10. Dulaure, op. cit.

11. Olivier Blanc, *La Dernière Lettre* (Paris: Pluriel, 1986), p. 46.

12. The parliamentary archives refer to "les Picpus" as early as January 8, 1793, which invalidates the opening date of March 1794 given by Lely, *Vie*, vol. 2, p. 409.

13. Arch. de la préfecture de police, Aa 28.

14. See *O.C.*, vol. 10, p. 221, note.

15. A.N. F⁷ 4775⁹, document 3.

16. A.N. Series W, cart. 434, dossier 474, II, 87, reproduced by Hector Fleishmann, *Réquisitoires de Fouquier-Tinville* (Paris, 1911), pp. 144–57.

17. November 12, 1794. Bourdin, op. cit., pp. 359–60.

18. To Gaufridy, November 30, 1794. Bourdin, op. cit., p. 362.

19. November 12, 1794. Bourdin, op. cit., pp. 359–60.

20. A.N. F⁷ 4775⁹, document 13.

21. Bourdin, op. cit., p. 359.

22. To Gaufridy, November 19, 1794. Bourdin, op. cit., p. 361.

24. At Bay

1. To Quinquin, July 4, 1794. B.N. Ms. N.a.fr. 18312, f⁰ˢ 26–27 (Mf. 3090).

2. To Gaufridy, January 12, 1795. Private collection. Unpublished letter.

3. Compare B.N. Ms. N.a.fr. 18313, f⁰ 30.

4. Quoted in A. Soboul, *Précis d'histoire de la Révolution française* (Paris: Editions Sociales, 1975), pp. 379–80.

5. Furet and Richet, op. cit., chap. 8.

6. Roux to Sade, March 16, 1795. Arch. Sade. Unpublished letter.

7. To Gaufridy, January 6, 1795. Bourdin, op. cit., p. 363.

8. To Gaufridy, January 21, 1795, ibid., p. 365.

9. B.N. Ms. N.a.fr. 24390, f⁰ 409.

10. Published in Henri d'Alméras, *Le Marquis de Sade: l'homme et l'écrivain* (Paris: Albin Michel, 1906), pp. 283–84.

11. Bourdin, op. cit., p. 377.

12. B.N. Ms. N.a.fr. 24390, f⁰ 409.

13. See *O.C.*, vol. 16, pp. 31–32, note 28.

14. *O.C.*, vol. 3, pp. 483–84.

15. Ibid., p. 494.

16. To Gaufridy, August 5, 1795. Bourdin, op. cit., p. 375.

17. To Gaufridy, January 31, 1795, ibid., p. 365.

18. Ibid., p. 367.

19. Ibid., p. 373.

20. Her full name has not survived, but her correspondence, preserved in the Sade archives, leaves no doubt about her relations with both Donatien and Louis-Marie.

21. To Gaufridy, April 19, 1796, in Bourdin, op. cit., p. 388.

22. To Archias, ibid., pp. 369–70.

23. To Gaufridy, May 1, 1795. Bourdin, op. cit., p. 370.

24. To Gaufridy, August 5, 1795, ibid., p. 376.

25. Ibid., p. 393.

26. On the details of this affair, see Bourdin, op. cit., pp. 404–8, and Henri Fauville, op. cit., pp. 211–12.

27. To Gaufridy, January 10, 1798, in Bourdin, op. cit., p. 418.

25. Sade's Misfortunes

1. Bonnefoy to Gaufridy, October 27, 1797. Bourdin, op. cit., p. 416.

2. Sade to Gaufridy, October 27, 1797. Arch. Sade. Unpublished letter.

3. Ibid.

4. All these documents can be found in A.N. F^7 4954³ (document 34).

5. To Gaufridy, January 16, 1798. Bourdin, op. cit., pp. 418–19.

6. Barras, *Mémoires*, ed. Georges Duruy (Paris: Hachette, 1895), pp. 56–57.

7. Sade to M. de Bonnières, late December 1797. Arch. Sade. Unpublished letter.

8. Sade to his wife, early January 1798. Arch. Sade. Unpublished letter.

9. Letter of July 5, 1797, quoted in Furet and Richet, op. cit., p. 463.

10. Quoted in Tulard, Fayard, and Fierro, op. cit., p. 238.

11. B.N. Ms. N.a.fr. 3533, fᵒˢ 351–52. Quoted in Lever, *Les Bûchers de Sodome* (Paris: Fayard, 1985), pp. 398–99.

12. Accursed desire for riches, where will you not lead the hearts of mortals?

13. C.-J. Colnet du Ravel, *Les Etrennes de l'Institut national ou la Revue littéraire de l'an VII* (Paris: Chez les Marchands de Nouveautés, Year VII), pp. 79–80.

14. Arch. Sade. Unsigned draft of letter.

15. To Gaufridy, January 24, 1799. Bourdin, op. cit., p. 429.

16. To François Gaufridy, February 13, 1799. Bourdin, op. cit., p. 430.

17. "Excerpt from registers of decrees on petitions concerning émigrés from the former central administration of the Vaucluse." Arch. Sade.

18. Compare A.N. F^7 4954³, document 18.

19. To Gaufridy, August 2, 1799. Bourdin, op. cit., p. 433.

20. From Mme Quesnet to Gaufridy, August 4, 1799. Bourdin, op. cit., p. 435.

21. To Gaufridy, September 5, 1799. Ibid., p. 435.

22. *L'Ami des Lois*, 12 fructidor, Year VII (August 29, 1799), no. 1462, p. 3.

23. Arch. Sade. Quoted in Lely, *Vie*, vol. 2, p. 464.

24. *Le Tribunal d'Apollon* (Paris: Marchand, Year VIII), vol. 2, pp. 193–97.

25. *L'Ami des Lois*, 2 vendémiaire, Year VIII (September 24, 1799).

26. Compare Henry Lumière, *Théâtre français pendant la Révolution* (Paris: Dentu, 1894), pp. 358–60.

27. To Goupilleau, October 30, 1799, in Apollinaire, op. cit., p. 48.

28. To Gaufridy, October 27, 1799. Bourdin, op. cit., p. 440.

29. The records of the Versailles hospital, now in the archives of Yvelines, contain no trace of Sade's stay in this establishment, probably because he was classified as an "indigent" rather than a patient.

30. To Charles Gaufridy, February 1, 1800. Bourdin, op. cit., p. 442.

31. To Charles Gaufridy, May 2, 1800. Bourdin, op. cit., p. 444.

32. Gaufridy to Sade, May 17, 1800. Arch. Sade. Unpublished letter.

33. To Gaufridy, October 27, 1799. Bourdin, op. cit., p. 440.

34. See, in particular, Pierre Klossowski's introduction to the *Oeuvres complètes* (Paris: Cercle du livre précieux, 1966–67), vol. 10, pp. xxxvii–lvii, and Michel Delon's excellent preface to the recent edition of *Les Crimes de l'amour* (Paris: Gallimard, 1990), pp. 7–27.

35. Klossowski, *Sade, mon prochain*, p. 115.

36. *Journal des Arts, des Sciences et de la Littérature*, October 22, 1800, no. 90, pp. 281–84. Alexandre-Louis de Villeterque lived from 1759 to 1811.

37. Published in Paris by Massé.

26. Charenton

1. Sade also designated Laloubie using the initials E. L. in his account of the arrest. A facsimile of the police report of the search can be found in Jean Desbordes, *Le Vrai Visage du marquis de Sade*, pl. xxxviii–xxxix and p. 296.

2. Which is why Massé's name figures in the depot's daily log though Sade's does not: see A.N. F^{16} 112.

3. See Lely, *Vie*, vol. 2, pp. 544–46.

4. See A.N. F^7 6294, document 3.

5. *Zoloé et ses deux acolytes ou Quelques décades de la vie de trois jolies femmes. Histoire véritable du siècle dernier, par un contemporain* (Turin: Printed by the author, Messidor, Year VIII).

6. See above, note 3.

7. *La Revue rétrospective*, 1833, vol. 1, p. 256.

8. Hurard Saint-Désiré, *Mes Amusements dans la prison de Sainte-Pélagie* (Paris: De l'Imprimerie d'Everat, Year X—1801), p. 6. B.N. Ye 10350.

9. A.N. F^7 6294, document 8 and F^7 3119.

10. C.-F. S. Giraudy, *Mémoire sur la Maison nationale de Charenton* . . . (Paris, Year XII—1804). Quoted by Pierre Pinon, *L'Hospice de Charenton, temple de la raison ou folie de l'archéologie* (Liège: Mardaga, 1989), pp. 7–8.

11. Hippolyte de Colins, *Notice sur l'hospice de Charenton*, first published by Georges Daumas as an appendix to the *Journal inédit* of the marquis de Sade (Paris: Gallimard, 1970), pp. 123–24.

12. Ibid., p. 152.

13. *Mémoire historique et statistique sur la Maison royale de Charenton* (Paris: Paul Renouard, 1835), 192 pp.

14. L.-J. Ramon, *Notes sur Monsieur de Sade*, in marquis de Sade, *Cahiers personnels*, ed. Gilbert Lely (Paris: Corréa, 1953), p. 118.

15. Ibid., pp. 118–21.

16. See Daumas, op. cit., p. 21.

17. Letter from M. de Coulmier to Claude-Armand de Sade, August 20, 1804. Arch. Sade. Unpublished letter.

18. Prefecture of police to M. de Coulmier, May 1, 1804. B.M. Avignon, collection Requien.

19. Archives de la Maison nationale de Charenton. Published by Dr. Cabanès in *Le Cabinet secret de l'Histoire*, third series, p. 474, n. 1.

20. A.N. F^7 3126.

21. A.N. F⁷ 3126.

22. All that remains is a notebook in the author's hand.

23. A.N. F⁷ 3126.

24. A.N. F⁷ 3123.

25. Letter of July 20, 1803.

26. A.D. Val-de-Marne. AJ² 100.

27. According to a letter from Sade to his cousin Mme de Bimard dated May 4, 1811.

28. Michel Gourevitch, "Le Théâtre des fous: avec Sade, sans sadisme," in *Petits et grands théâtres du marquis de Sade* (Paris Art Center, 1989), p. 97.

29. Auguste Labouisse-Rochefort, *Voyage à Saint-Léger, suivi du voyage à Charenton* (Paris: C.-J. Trouvé, 1827), pp. 149–70.

30. Mlle Flore was mistaken: seventy-four was his age when he died, and he was no longer running the Charenton theater. The account is taken from *Mémoires de Mlle Flore, artiste du théâtre des Variétés* (Paris: Comptoir des Imprimeurs-unis, 1845), vol. 2, pp. 172–84.

31. Armand de Rochefort, *Mémoires d'un vaudevilliste* (Paris: Charlieu and Huillery, 1863), pp. 238–41.

27. Twilight

1. From Royer-Collard to M. de Coulmier, January 29, 1807. A.D. Val-de-Marne: A J² 100.

2. Coulmier to Royer-Collard, January 31, 1807. A.D. Val-de-Marne: A J² 100.

3. Arch. Sade, fonds Bégis, and Dr. Cabanès, "La Prétendue folie du marquis de Sade," in *Le Cabinet secret de l'histoire* (Paris: A. Maloine, 1900), p. 304.

4. Minister of the interior, August 1, 1807. A.N. F¹⁵ 2607.

5. Sade, *Journal*, ed. G. Daumas, op. cit., p. 62.

6. Arch. Sade. The handwriting is Claude-Armand's, but at the bottom of the page, in the marquis's hand, are the words: "Approved the above text. At Charenton, June 1, 1808. Sade."

7. This account follows that given by Sade in his *Journal*, pp. 70–72.

8. Arch. Sade. Unpublished letter.

9. Alexandre Cabanis to Louis-Marie de Sade, September 16, 1808. Arch. Sade. Unpublished letter.

10. Mme de Bimard to Claude-Armand de Sade, May 28, 1808. Arch. Sade. Unpublished letter.

11. Ministry of Justice. Civil Division, no. 2123. B. 8. Marriage. Arch. Sade. Unpublished document.

12. Note in Mme de Bimard's hand. Arch. Sade. Unpublished letter.

13. Arch. Sade.

14. Arch. Sade. Unpublished document.

15. A.N. F⁷ 3129.

16. Built in the fifteenth century, the château at Ham had served as a state prison since the eighteenth century.

17. A.N. F⁷ 3129.

18. Arch. Sade. Unpublished letter.

19. Arch. Sade. Unpublished document.

20. Arch. Sade. Unpublished document.

21. A.N. F⁷ 6294, documents 10–11, and *Revue rétrospective*, 1833, vol. 1.

22. Arch. Sade. Unpublished letter.

23. A.N. F⁷ 3130 and 6294, document 9.

24. From Sade to Claude-Armand, December 5, 1809. Arch. Sade. Unpublished letter.

25. Lely, *Vie*, vol. 2, p. 567.

26. A.N. AF IV 1236, document 33, fᵒˢ 4–5.

27. Instructions of M. de Montalivet, minister of the interior, to M. de Coulmier, October 18, 1810. B.M. Avignon. Collection Requien.

28. Heine, op. cit., 357–58.

29. *Mémorial de Sainte-Hélène* (Paris: Flammarion, undated), vol. 2, p. 598.

30. *Journal inédit*, p. 68.

31. Arch. Sade. Fonds Bégis.

32. *La Marquise de Gange* (Paris: Béchet, 1813).

33. Claude-Armand to his father, November 17, 1814. Arch. Sade. Unpublished letter.

34. Arch. Sade. Unpublished letter.

35. Arch. Sade. Unpublished letter.

36. Literary notes, 22, in *O.C.*, vol. 15, p. 28.

37. Arch. Sade. Unpublished document.

38. Marquis to Claude-Armand, May 18, 1810. Arch. Sade. Unpublished letter.

39. Claude-Armand to M. Corbin, August 23, 1810. Arch. Sade. Unpublished letter.

40. Desbordes, op. cit., pp. 326–27.

41. To Gaufridy, undated. Bourdin, op. cit., pp. 446–50.

42. *Revue anecdotique*. New series, vol. 1, 1860, pp. 104–6.

43. Esquirol, op. cit.

44. Arch. Sade. Unpublished letter.

45. A.N. F¹⁵ 2608. Dossier 4.

46. A.D. Val-de-marne: A J² 100.

47. A.N. F¹⁵ 1946.

48. Ibid.

49. Heine, op. cit., pp. 359–64.

50. Ibid., pp. 364–65.

51. Arch. Sade. Unpublished document.

52. See L.-J. Ramon, "Notes sur M. de Sade," in *O.C.*, vol. 15, p. 42.

53. B.N. Ms. N.a.fr. 24384, fᵒˢ 599–602.

54. B.N. Ms. N.a.fr. 24390, fᵒˢ 428–30.

55. *Journal inédit*, pp. 110–11.

Epilogue

1. L.-J. Ramon, "Notes sur M. de Sade," in *O.C.*, vol. 15, p. 42.

2. Arch. Sade.

3. *O.C.*, vol. 15, p. 42.

4. Ibid., p. 42.

5. A wholly fabricated but far more amusing version of the exhumation can be

found in a letter from Victorien Sardou to Dr. Cabanès. See the latter's *Le Cabinet secret de l'Histoire*, 1900, vol. 3, p. 366.

6. Ramon, "Notes," p. 43.

7. Text first published in my article "Richelieu, Voltaire, Sade . . . Pas de repos pour les dépouilles illustres!" *L'Histoire*, no. 109, March 1988.

8. *Notes littéraires*. Arch. Sade. The version given here is based on the manuscript, not on Lely's transcription, which for some reason combines earlier and later drafts.

Bibliography

N O T E: The author made use of extensive manuscript sources, a complete list of which is included in the bibliography for the French edition.—*Trans.*

I. Printed Sources

Affiches, Annonces et avis divers ou Journal général de France.

Almanach royal.

Argenson, marquis d'. *Mémoires et journal inédit.* 5 vols. Paris: Jannet, "Bibliothèque elzévirienne," 1857–58; also, in 9 vols. Paris: E.-J.-B. Rathery, 1859–67.

Aunillon, abbé. *Mémoires de la vie galante, politique et littéraire de l'abbé Aunillon Delaunay du Gué, ambassadeur de Louis XV près le prince électeur de Cologne.* 2 vols. Paris, 1808.

Bachaumont. *Mémoires secrets pour servir à l'histoire de la République des lettres en France, depuis 1762 jusqu'à nos jours ou Journal d'un observateur.* 36 vols. London, 1777–87.

Barbier, Edmond Jean François. *Chronique de la régence et du regne de Louis XV (1718–1763).* 8 vols. Paris: Charpentier, 1885.

Barras, Paul François Jean Nicolas, vicomte de. *Mémoires.* Edited by George Duruy. Paris: Hachette, 1895.

Casanova, Giacomo. *Mémoires.* Edited by R. Abirached and E. Zorzi. 3 vols. Paris: Gallimard, "Pléiade."

Choiseul, Etienne François, duc de. *Mémoires.* Paris: Mercure de France, 1983.

Clairambault-Maurepas. *Chansonnier historique du XVIIIᵉ siècle.* Edited by E. Raunié. 10 vols. Paris: Quantin, 1879–84.

Correspondance littéraire, philosophique et critique by Grimm, Diderot, Raynal, Meister, etc. Edited by M. Tourneux. 16 vols. Paris: Fayard, 1877–82.

Enfer de la Bibliothèque nationale, L'. 7 vols. to date. Paris: Fayard, 1984–88.

Flore, Mlle. *Mémoires de Mlle Flore, artiste du théâtre des Variétés.* 3 vols. Paris: Comptoir des Imprimeurs-unis, 1845. Republished in 1903 in one volume.

Gazette de France.

Hurard Saint-Désiré. *Mes Amusements dans la prison De Sainte-Pélagie.* Paris: De l'Imprimerie d'Éverat, Year X–1801.

Labouissse-Rochefort, Auguste. *Voyage à Saint-Léger, campagne de M. le chevalier de Boufflers, suivi du voyage à Charenton et des notes contenant des particularités sur toute la famille Boufflers . . .* , pp. 149–70. Paris: C.-J. Trouvé, 1827.

Luynes, duc de. *Mémoires sur la cour de Louis XV (1735–1758).* 17 vols. Paris: Didot, 1860–65.

Marais, Mathieu. *Journal et Mémoires.* 4 vols. Paris: M. de Lescure, 1863–68.

Marion, Marcel. *Dictionnaire des institutions de la France aux XVIIe et XVIIIe siècles.* Paris: A. Picard, 1923.

Mercier, Louis-Sébastien. *Tableau de Paris.* 12 vols. Amsterdam, 1782–88.

———. *Le Nouveau Paris.* 6 vols. Paris: Fuchs, Pougens, Cramer, [1798]. *Mercure de France.*

Mirabeau, Honoré Gabriel Riquetti, comte de. *Des Lettres de cachet et des prisons d'État. Ouvrage posthume composé en 1778.* 2 vols. Hamburg [Paris], 1782.

———. *Lettres originales de Mirabeau, écrites du donjon de Vincennes pendant les années 1777 à 1780 et contenant tous les détails de sa vie privée, ses malheurs et ses amours avec Sophie de Monnier, recueillies par P. Manuel, citoyen français.* 4 vols. Paris: Garnery, 1792.

Nodier, Charles. *Souvenirs, Épisodes et Portraits de la Restauration et de l'Empire.* 2 vols. Paris, 1831.

Pidansat de Mairobert, Mathieu François. *L'Observateur anglais ou Correspondance secrète entre Milord All'Eye et Milord All'Ear.* 4 vols. London, 1777–78.

Recueil des Instructions aux ambassadeurs et ministres de France. Paris: Ed. du C.N.R.S.

Richelieu, maréchal de. *Mémoires.* Edited by F. Barrière. 2 vols. Paris: Firmin–Didot, 1889.

Rochefort, Armand de. *Mémoires d'un vaudevilliste.* Paris: Charlieu et Huillery, 1863.

Sade, Jacques François Paul Aldonse, abbé de. *Mémoires pour la vie de François Pétrarque.* 3 vols. Amsterdam: Arskée et Mercus [Avignon], 1764–67.

Saint-Simon, duc de. *Mémoires.* 43 vols. Paris: A. de Boislisle et L. Lecestre, 1879–1930.

Voltaire (François-Marie Arouet). *Correspondance.* Edited by Théodore Besterman. 12 vols. to date. Paris: Gallimard, "Pléiade."

II. Bibliographies

Chanover, E. Pierre. *The Marquis de Sade. Bibliography.* Metuchen, N.J.: The Scarecrow Press, 1973.

Cioranescu, Alexandre. *Bibliographie de la littérature française du dix-huitième siècle.* 3 vols. Paris: Ed. du C.N.R.S., 1969.

Festa, Georges. *Les Etudes sur le marquis de Sade. Contribution à une bibliographie analytique.* Thesis, 3rd cycle, Université de Clermont-II, 1981. Typescript.

Martin, A., V.-G. Mylne, and R. Frautschi. *Bibliographie du genre romanesque français, 1751–1800.* London–Paris, 1977.

Verger-Michael, Colette. *The Marquis de Sade, the Man, His Works and His Critics: An Annotated Bibliography.* New York: Garland, 1986.

III. Works by the Marquis de Sade (Editions Utilized)

Bourdin, Paul. *Correspondance inédite du marquis de Sade, de ses proches et de ses familiers.* Paris: Librairie de France, 1929.

Sade, Donatien Alphonse François, marquis de. *L'Aigle, Mademoiselle . . .* Letters taken from autograph manuscripts and published for the first time, with a preface and commentary by Gilbert Lely. Paris: Georges Artigues, 1949.

———. *Cahiers personnels (1803–1804).* Newly published texts established, with a preface and notes, by Gilbert Lely. Paris: Corréa, 1953.

———. *Journal inédit. Deux cahiers retrouvés du Journal inédit du marquis de Sade (1807, 1808, 1814), suivis en appendice d'une notice sur l'hospice de Charenton par Hippolyte de Colins.* Taken from autograph manuscripts and published for the first time, with a preface by Georges Daumas. Paris: Gallimard, coll. "Idées," 1970.

———. *Lettre au commissaire Chenon, 19 juillet 1789.* Presented by Jean-Louis Debauve. Editions "A l'Ecart," 1985.

———. *Lettres et mélanges littéraires.* 3 vols. in 1. Paris: Broderie, 1980.

———. *Lettres inédites et documents retrouvés.* Edited by Jean-Louis Debauve. Paris: Ramsay–Jean-Jacques Pauvert, 1990.

———. *Mon Arrestation du 26 août. Lettre inédite suivie des Etrennes philosophiques.* Paris: Jean Hugues, 1959.

———. *Monsieur le 6.* Newly published letters, annotated by Georges Daumas. Paris: Julliard, 1954.

———. *Œuvres,* vol. 1. Text established by Michel Delon. Paris: Gallimard, "Pléiade," 1990. Contains the *Dialogue entre un prètre et un moribond, Les Cent Vingt Journées de Sodome, Aline et Valcour.*

———. *Œuvres complètes.* 16 vols. in 8. Paris: Cercle du livre précieux, 1966–67.

———. *Le Portefeuille du marquis de Sade.* Scarce and valuable texts presented by Gilbert Lely. Paris: Editions de la Différence, 1977.

———. *Théâtre.* Edited by Jean-Jacques Brochier. 4 vols. (Vols. 32 to 35 of the *O.C.*) Paris: Jean-Jacques Pauvert, 1970.

———. *La Vanille et la Manille, lettre inédite à Madame de Sade écrite au donjon de Vincennes en 1783* [actually, late 1784]. With five original watercolors by Jacques Hérold. [Paris]: Collection Drosera, 1950.

IN ENGLISH

———. *The Complete Justine, Philosophy in the Bedroom, and Other Writings.* Compiled and translated by Richard Seaver and Austryn Wainhouse. New York: Grove Press, 1965.

———. *The Gothic Tales / Marquis de Sade,* trans. Margaret Crosland. London: Peter Owen, 1990.

———. *The Marquis de Sade: The 120 Days of Sodom, and Other Writings.* Compiled and translated by Austryn Wainhouse and Richard Seaver. New York: Grove Press, 1966.

———. *The Passionate Philosopher: A Marquis de Sade Reader,* trans. Margaret Crosland. London: Peter Owen, 1991.

IV. General Bibliography

Alméras, Henri d'. *Le Marquis de Sade: l'homme et l'écrivain, d'après des documents inédits, avec une bibliographie de ses œuvres.* Paris: Albin Michel, 1906.

Amargier, Jean-Pierre. *Sade et la Révolution française.* Master's thesis, 1969. Typescript.

Antoine, Michel. *Le Gouvernement et l'administration sous Louis XV. Dictionnaire biographique.* Paris: Editions du C.N.R.S., 1978.

Apollinaire, Guillaume. *L'Œuvre du marquis de Sade.* Paris: Collection des classiques galants, "Les maîtres de l'amour," 1909.

Artarit, Dr. Jean. "Sade et la Vendée." In *Annuaire de la Société d'émulation de la Vendée* (1985): 111–21.

Baratier, Edouard, et al. *Histoire de la Provence.* Toulouse: privately published, 1987.

Barthes, Roland. *Sade, Fourier, Loyola.* Paris: Seuil, 1971; trans. Richard Miller: *Sade, Fourier, Loyola.* New York: Hill and Wang, 1976.

Bataille, Georges. *La Littérature et le mal.* Paris: Gallimard, 1957; trans. Alastair Hamilton: *Literature and Evil.* New York: Boyars, 1985.

Beaumont-Vassy, Edouard Ferdinand, vicomte de. *Mémoires secrets du XIXᵉ siècle.* Paris, 1874.

Beauvoir, Simone de. *Faut-il brûler Sade?* Paris: Gallimard, coll. "Idées," 1972. (First published in 1955 with the title *Privilèges,* in the "Les Essais" series.) Translated as *The Marquis de Sade: An Essay.* New York: Grove Press, 1953.

Béliard, Dr. Octave. *Marquis de Sade.* Paris: Ed. du Laurier, [1928].

Benabou, Erica-Marie. *La Prostitution et la police des mœurs au XVIIIᵉ siècle.* Paris: Perrin, 1987.

Berman, Lora. *The Thought and Themes of the Marquis de Sade.* Toronto: U. of Toronto, 1971.

Bidet, Dr. Charles. *D'Ebreuil à Châteauneuf: la vallée de la Sioule: Ebreuil et son abbaye.* Clermont-Ferrand: G. de Bussac, 1973.

Biographie universelle ancienne et moderne (biographie Michaud). Vol. 39 (1825), 472–80. New edition, vol. 37 (1863), 219–24.

Biver, Paul and Marie-Louise. *Abbayes, monastères, couvents de femmes à Paris, des origines à la fin du XVIIIᵉ siècle.* Paris: Presses Universitaires de France, 1975.

Blanchot, Maurice. *L'inconvenance majeure,* preface to *Sade, Français, encore un effort* . . . Paris: Jean-Jacques Pauvert, coll. "Libertés," 1965.

———. "L'insurrection, la folie d'écrire." Paris: Gallimard, 1969. Reprinted in *Sade et Restif de La Bretonne.* Brussels: Complexe, 1986.

———. "La Raison de Sade." In *Lautréamont et Sade.* Paris: Editions de Minuit, 1963. Reprinted in *Sade et Restif de La Bretonne.* Brussels: Complexe, 1986.

Bonnet, Jean-Claude, et al. *La Carmagnole des muses. L'homme de lettres et l'artiste dans la Révolution.* Paris: A. Colin, 1988.

Bournon, Fernand. *La Bastille.* Paris: Imprimerie Nationale, 1893.

Boysse, Ernest. *Le Théâtre des Jésuites.* Paris: Henri Vaton, 1880.

Breton, André. *Manifestes du surréalisme.* Paris: Jean-Jacques Pauvert, 1962.

Brochier, Jean-Jacques. *Le Marquis de Sade et la conquête de l'unique.* Paris: Losfeld, "Le Terrain vague," 1966.

———. *Sade.* Classiques du XXᵉ siècle. Ed. Universitaires, 1966.

Cabanès, Dr. *Cabinet secret de l'histoire,* fourth series. Paris: A. Maloine, 1900.

[Cabanès, Dr.]. *Le Marquis de Sade et son œuvre devant la science médicale et la littérature moderne, par le Dr. Jacobus X . . .* Paris: Carrington, 1901.

Campion, Léo. *Sade franc-maçon.* Paris: Cercle des amis de la Bibliothèque initiatique, 1972.

Camus, Albert. *L'Homme révolté.* Paris: Gallimard, 1951: in English, *The Rebel.*

Camus, Michel, et al. *Obliques* 12–13, "Sade."

Carter, Angela. *The Sadeian Woman.* London: Virago, 1979. French translation by Françoise Carrano: *La Femme sadienne.* Paris: Henri Veyrier, 1979.

Chérasse, Jean A., and Geneviève Guicheney. *Sade, j'écris ton nom Liberté.* Paris: Pygmalion, 1976.

Cleugh, James. *The Marquis and the Chevalier.* London: Andrew Melrose, Ltd., 1951.

Cormann, Enzo. *Sade, concert d'enfers.* Paris: Editions de Minuit, 1989.

Darnton, Robert. "Les papiers du marquis de Sade et la prise de la Bastille." *Annales historiques de la Révolution française* 202 (October–December 1970): 666.

Delpech, Jeanine. *La Passion de la marquise de Sade.* Paris: Ed. Planète, 1970.

Desbordes, Jean. *Le Vrai Visage du marquis de Sade.* Paris: Editions de la Nouvelle Revue Critique, 1939.

Didier, Béatrice. *Sade: une écriture du désir.* Paris: Denoël/Gonthier, 1976.

Du Bus, Charles. *Stanislas de Clermont-Tonnerre et l'échec de la Révolution monarchique (1757–1792).* Paris: F. Alcan, 1931.

Duchesne, Gaston. *Mademoiselle de Charolais.* Paris: H. Daragon, 1909.

Duehren, Eugène (pseud. of Dr. Iwan Bloch). *Le Marquis de Sade et son temps.* Translated from the German by Dr. A. Weber-Riga. Preface by Octave Uzanne. Berlin: Barsdorf–Paris: Michalon, 1901.

Dufour, Auguste, and François Rabut. *Miolans, prison d'Etat.* Chambéry: Société savoisienne d'Histoire et d'Archéologie, Botters, vol. 18 (1879).

Esquirol, Jean Etienne Dominique. *Mémoire historique et statistique sur la maison royale de Charenton.* Paris, 1835.

Fauskevag, Svein-Eirik. *Sade dans le surréalisme.* Solum Forlag A/S Norvège–Privat France, [1982].

Fauville, Henri. *La Coste. Sade en Provence.* Aix-en-Provence: Edisud, 1984.

Favre, Pierre. *Sade utopiste. Sexualité, Pouvoir et Etat dans le roman* Aline et Valcour. Paris: Presses Universitaires de France, 1967.

Fayot, Pierre, and Camille Tiran. *Mazan. Histoire et vie quotidienne d'un village contadin à travers les siècles.* Carpentras: Le Nombre d'Or, 1978.

Felkay, Nicole. "Quelques documents sur le marquis de Sade aux Archives de Paris." *Annales d'Histoire de la Révolution française* (January–March 1971): 130–43.

Fin de l'Ancien Régime, La. Manuscrits de la Révolution: Sade, Rétif, Beaumarchais, Laclos. (Papers by Annie Agremy, Michel Delon, Georges Festa, Maurice Lever, Jean-Jacques Pauvert, Philippe Roger). Presses Universitaires de Vincennes, 1991.

Flake, Otto. *Le Marquis de Sade.* Translated from the German by Pierre Klossowski. Paris: Grasset, 1933.

Fould, Paul. *Un Diplomate au dix-huitième siècle: Louis-Augustin Blondel.* Paris: Plon, 1914.

Funck-Brentano, Frantz. *Les Lettres de cachet à Paris. Etude suivie d'une liste des prisonniers de la Bastille (1659–1789).* Paris: Imprimerie Nationale, 1903.

Furet, François, and Denis Richet. *La Révolution française.* Paris: Fayard, coll. "L'Histoire sans frontières," 1973.

Furet, François, and Mona Ozouf. *Dictionnaire critique de la Révolution française*. Paris: Flammarion, 1988; trans. Arthur Goldhammer: *A Critical Dictionary of the French Revolution*. Cambridge: Harvard, 1989.

Garçon, Maurice. *L'Affaire Sade*. Paris: J.-J. Pauvert, 1957.

Gear, Norman. *Sade, le divin démon*. Paris: Buchet-Chastel, 1964.

Ginisty, Paul. *La Marquise de Sade*. Paris: Charpentier, 1901.

Girard, Joseph. *Evocation du vieil Avignon*. Paris: Editions de Minuit, 1958.

Giraudy, Ch.-Fr. S. *Mémoire sur la maison nationale de Charenton, exclusivement destinée au traitement des aliénés*. Paris, Year XII [1804].

Giudici, Enzo. "Bilancio di una annosa questione: 'Maurice Scève e la scoperta della tomba di Laura.'" *Quaderni di filologia e lingue romanze. Ricerche svolte dall'Universitá di Macerata*, vol. 2: 3–70. Edizioni dell'Ateneo, 1980.

Godechot, Jacques. *La Contre-Révolution (1789–1794)*. Paris: Presses Universitaires de France, coll. "Quadrige," 1984.

Gorer, Geoffrey. *The Revolutionary Ideas of the Marquis de Sade*. London: Wishart & Co., 1934.

Harouel, Jean-Louis. "De l'Ancien Régime à la Révolution." In *Histoire des institutions, de l'époque franque à la Révolution*. Paris, Presses Universitaires de France, 1987.

Heine, Maurice. *Le Marquis de Sade*. Text established, with a preface, by G. Lely. Paris: Gallimard, 1950.

Henaff, Marcel. *Sade. L'Invention du corps libertin*. Paris: Presses Universitaires de France, 1978.

Janin, Jules. "Le Marquis de Sade." In *Revue de Paris* 11 (November 1834): 321–60.

Jean, Raymond. *Un Portrait de Sade*. Actes-Sud, 1989.

Klossowski, Pierre. *Sade, mon prochain*. Paris: Seuil, 1947; trans. Alphonso Lingis: *Sade, My Neighbor*. Evanston, Ill.: Northwestern, 1991.

Krafft-Ebing, Dr. R. von. *Psychopathia sexualis*. French translation by René Lobstein. Paris: Payot, "Bibliothèque scientifique," 1950.

Laborde, Alice. *Sade romancier*. Neuchâtel: A la Baconnière, 1974.

Laborde, Alice M. *Le Mariage du marquis de Sade*. Paris–Geneva: Champion–Slatkine, 1988.

———. *Les Infortunes du marquis de Sade*. Paris: Champion, 1990.

Lacan, Jacques. *Ecrits II*. Paris: Seuil, 1971.

Lacombe, Roger G. *Sade et ses masques*. Paris: Payot, 1974.

Lacroix, Paul. *Curiosités de l'histoire de France*, second series: "Procès célèbres." Paris: Adolphe Delahaye, 1858.

Lambergeon, Solange. *Un Amour de Sade: la Provence*. Avignon: A. Barthélemy, 1990.

Laugaa-Traut, Françoise. *Lectures de Sade*. Paris: A. Colin, 1973.

Laval, Dr. Victorin. *Lettres inédites de J.-S. Rovère à son frère Simon-Stylite*. Paris: Champion, 1908.

Le Brun, Annie. *Les Châteaux de la subversion*. Paris: J.-J. Pauvert, 1982.

———. *Sade, aller et détours*. Paris: Plon, 1989.

———. *Soudain un bloc de l'abîme, Sade*. Paris: J.-J. Pauvert, 1986.

Lely, Gilbert. *D.-A.-F. de Sade*. Paris: Seghers, 1948.

———. *Etude sur sa vie et sur son œuvre*. Paris: Gallimard, coll. "Idées," 1967.

———. *Vie du marquis de Sade, avec un examen de ses ouvrages*. Paris: Gallimard, 1952–57. Republished in *Œuvres complètes*, vols. 1–2. Paris: Cercle du Livre Précieux, 1962, 1966, 1982 (J.-J. Pauvert, Ed. Suger); republished, Mercure de France, 1989.

Lever, Maurice. "Ange Goudard: quatre lettres inédites au marquis de Sade." *Dix-huitième siècle* 23 (1991).

———. "Le Marquis de Sade à Charenton." *Psychiatrie française* 1/89 (1989).

———. "Sade, le marquis 'sans-culotte' (1789–1795)." *L'Histoire* 113 (July–August 1988).

———. *Les Bûchers de Sodome*. Paris: Fayard, 1985.

Lizé, Emile. "A travers les chiffons d'Alexis Rousset." *Revue d'Histoire littéraire de la France* 3 (1978): 439–40.

Lumière, Henry. *Le Théâtre français pendant la Révolution*. Paris: Dentu, [1894].

Macchia, Giovanni. *Paris en ruines*. Paris: Flammarion, 1988.

Manuel, Pierre. *La Police de Paris dévoilée*. 2 vols. Paris: Garnery, Year II [1793].

Marciat, Dr. *Le Marquis de Sade et le sadisme*. Lyon: Storck & Cie., 1899.

Marmottan, Noël. *Le Pont d'Avignon, le petit pâtre Bénézet*. Cavaillon: Imprimerie Mistral, 1964.

Marquis de Sade, Le. Centre Aixois d'Etude et de Recherches sur le XVIIIᵉ siècle. Paris: A. Colin, 1968.

Mars, Francis-L. *Ange Goudard, cet inconnu (1708–1791). Essai bio-bibliographique sur un aventurier polygraphe du XVIIIᵉ siècle*. Extract from *Casanova Gleanings. Revue internationale d'Etudes casanoviennes et dix-huitiémistes* 9. Nice, 1966.

Mellie, Ernest. *Les Sections de Paris pendant la Révolution française*. Paris: Société de l'Histoire de la Révolution française, 1898.

Mendel, Gérard. "Sade et le sadisme." In *La Révolte contre le père*. 4th ed., ch. 7. Paris: Petite Bibliothèque Payot, 1974.

Michelet, Jules. *Histoire de la Révolution française*. 2 vols. Paris: Laffont, coll. "Bouquins."

Mishima, Yukio. *Madame de Sade*. French version by André Pieyre de Mandiargues. Paris: Gallimard, 1976.

Moulinas, R. *Histoire de la Révolution d'Avignon*. Aubanel, 1986.

Moureau, François. "Sade avant Sade." In *Cahiers de l'UER Froissart* 4 (Winter 1980). Université de Valenciennes.

Nadeau, Maurice. "Exploration de Sade." In Sade, Marquis de, *Œuvres*, 9–58. Paris: La Jeune Parque, coll. "Le Cheval parlant," 1947.

Neboit-Mombet, Dr. Janine. *Qui était le marquis de Sade?* Paris: Le Pavillon, 1972.

Paulhan, Jean. *Le Marquis de Sade et sa complice ou Les Revanches de la pudeur*. Brussels: Complexe, "Le Regard littéraire," 1987.

Pauvert, Jean-Jacques. *Sade vivant*. Vol. 1: "Une innocence sauvage 1740–1777"; vol. 2: "Tout ce qu'on peut concevoir dans se genre-là . . . "; vol. 3: "Cet écrivain à jamais célèbre . . . " Paris: Robert Laffont, 1986–90.

Peise, L. "Rovère et le marquis de Sade." *Revue historique de la Révolution française*, 1914.

Pensée de Sade, La. Tel Quel 28 (Winter 1967). (Articles by P. Klossowski, R. Barthes, Ph. Sollers, H. Damisch, M. Tort).

Perraudeau, Henri. *Saint-Ouen pendant la Révolution*. Paris, 1912.

Petits et grands théâtres du marquis de Sade. Paris Art Center, 1989.

Peuchet, Jacques. *Mémoires tirés des archives de la police de Paris*. 3 vols. Paris, 1838.

Pinon, Pierre. *L'Hospice de Charenton, temple de la raison ou folie de l'archéologie.* Liège: Mardaga, 1989.

Pithon-Curt, abbé Jean-Antoine de. *Histoire de la noblesse du Comtat Venaissin, d'Avignon et de la principauté d'Orange, dressée sur les preuves.* 3 vols. Paris: Veuve de Lourmel et fils, 1750.

Piton, Camille. *Paris sous Louis XV.* 5 vols. Paris: Mercure de France, 1911–14.

Pitou, Louis-Ange. *Analyse de mes malheurs et de mes persécutions depuis vingt-six ans.* Paris: Chez L.-A. Pitou, Pelicier-Delaunay, 1816.

Poisson, Georges. *Choderlos de Laclos ou l'obstination.* Paris: Grasset, 1985.

Porquet, Charles. "Le Château de Béthune." *Revue d'Histoire de Versailles* (1909).

Queneau, Raymond. "Lectures pour un front (September 23, 1944–November 12, 1945)." In *Bâtons, chiffres et lettres.* Paris: Gallimard, 1950.

Roger, Philippe. "Rousseau selon Sade ou Jean-Jacques travesti." *Dix-huitième siècle* 23 (1991): 381–403.

———. *Sade: la philosophie dans le pressoir.* Paris: Grasset, 1976.

———. "Sade et la Révolution." In *L'Ecrivain devant la Révolution. 1789–1820.* Edited by J. Sgard. Grenoble: Presses de l'Université de Grenoble, 1990.

Sade. Revue Europe (October 1972).

Sade: Ecrire la crise. Centre culturel international de Cerisy-la-Salle (direction: Michel Camus and Philippe Roger). Paris: Belfond, 1983.

Sade, Thibault de. *Lecture politique de l'idéologie du marquis de Sade, ou des systèmes politiques raisonnées.* Thesis for the DEA d'Etudes politiques, 1982. Typescript.

Sérieux, Dr. Paul. "L'Internement du marquis de Sade au fort de Miolans." *Hippocrate* (September–October 1937): 385–401 and 465–82.

Soboul, Albert. *Mouvement populaire et gouvernement révolutionnaire en l'an II (1793–1794).* Paris: Flammarion, 1973.

———. *Précis d'histoire de la Révolution française.* Paris: Editions sociales, 1975; trans. Geoffrey Symcox: *A Short History of the French Revolution.* Berkeley: University of California Press, 1977.

Sollers, Philippe. *L'Ecriture et l'experience des limites.* Paris: Seuil, coll. "Points," 1971.

Thomas, Chantal. *Sade, l'œil de la lettre.* Paris: Payot, 1978.

Thomas, Donald. *The Marquis de Sade.* London: Weidenfeld & Nicolson, 1976. French translation by A.-M. Garnier and G.-G. Lemaire. Paris: Seghers, 1977.

Tulard, J., J.-F. Fayard, and A. Fierro. *Histoire et dictionnaire de la Révolution française 1789–1799.* Paris: Laffont, 1987.

Vaille, Eugène. *Le Cabinet noir.* Paris: Presses Universitaires de France, 1950.

Vovelle, Michel. *De la cave au grenier.* Québec: S. Fleury, 1980.

Weiss, Peter. *La Persécution et l'assassinat de Jean-Paul Marat représentés par le groupe théâtral de l'hospice de Charenton sous la direction de Monsieur de Sade.* Translated from the German by Jean Baudrillard. Paris: Seuil, 1965.

Index